EZRA POUND : POET

BY THE SAME AUTHOR

Virginia Woolf (Oliver & Boyd), 1963

Shakespeare: The Merchant of Venice (Edward Arnold), 1964

'The Waste Land' in Different Voices, ed. (Edward Arnold), 1974

Thomas Stearns Eliot: Poet (Cambridge University Press), 1979, 1994

At the Antipodes: Homage to Paul Valéry (Bedlam Press), 1982

News Odes: The El Salvador Sequence (Bedlam Press), 1984

The Cambridge Companion to T. S. Eliot, ed. (Cambridge University Press), 1994

Tracing T. S. Eliot's Spirit. Essays on his Poetry and Thought (Cambridge University Press), 1996

Ezra Pound: Poet. A Portrait of the Man and his Work. Vol. I: The Young Genius 1885–1920 (Oxford University Press), 2007

Ezra Pound to his Parents: Letters 1895–1929, ed. with Mary de Rachewiltz and Joanna Moody (Oxford University Press), 2010

Ezra Pound: Poet. A Portrait of the Man and his Work. Vol. II: The Epic Years 1921–1939 (Oxford University Press), 2014

EZRA POUND : POET

A Portrait of the Man and his Work

III : THE TRAGIC YEARS

1939–1972

A. DAVID MOODY

'I do not think that he intended to hurt the U.S.A. But I do think that he operated in a different world from most of us.'
—Henry A. Wallace, US Vice-President 1941–5

OXFORD
UNIVERSITY PRESS

OXFORD
UNIVERSITY PRESS

Great Clarendon Street, Oxford, OX2 6DP,
United Kingdom

Oxford University Press is a department of the University of Oxford. It furthers the University's objective of excellence in research, scholarship, and education by publishing worldwide. Oxford is a registered trade mark of Oxford University Press in the UK and in certain other countries

First Edition published in 2015

Impression: 1

Published in the United States of America by Oxford University Press
198 Madison Avenue, New York, NY 10016, United States of America

British Library Cataloguing in Publication Data
Data available

Library of Congress Control Number: 2014957588

ISBN 978–0–19–870436–2

Printed in Italy by
L.E.G.O. S.p.A.

FOR MARY DE RACHEWILTZ

Lux enim—

versus this tempest

CONTENTS

ILLUSTRATIONS

TEXT ILLUSTRATIONS

PREFACE

Bracton:
Uncivil to judge a part in ignorance of the totality
nemo omnia novit

This volume presents the five act tragedy of a flawed idealist and a great poet who, in a time of war, carried to excess his exercise of the rights and freedoms of a United States citizen, and who, in consequence, suffered the loss of both his freedom and his civil rights. Yet out of that personal tragedy in a tragic time there came his finest poetry, a poetry that deliberately rose above tragedy and cultivated instead a mind intent on what humanity had achieved, and might yet hope to achieve, in the way of a well-ordered society at home in its universe.

It was a three-ring, even a four-ring tragedy. There was the war, the destructive element in which his whole world was immersed, and he with it. There was the hubris of his personal involvement in that war on the side of Fascism. That led inevitably to his being perceived as a traitor and a Fascist, when in truth he was neither. Beyond that, as the deeper injustice, there was the accident that it was those whom he trusted to support and aid him who were responsible for his being incarcerated for twelve years and more among the insane, and also for his being made a non-person in law, and kept in that condition for the rest of his life. Behind all, and not subject to the law, even allowed by the law, was his moral offence, the anti-Semitism of which he was guilty, and for which he was made to pay, unlawfully yet in rough natural justice, by the loss of his freedom and his legal rights.

The law, if it had taken its course, should have found him not guilty as charged; and the law should have been allowed to take its course because he was not in fact insane—the judicial finding that he was not competent to stand trial being a travesty of psychiatry and of justice. There would have remained the extra-judicial guilt of his anti-Semitism, and for this he has been justly condemned, and unjustly made a scapegoat for the Nazi Holocaust of the Jews, and for the anti-Semitism endemic in his society. That is the crime at the root of his tragedy, the crime that roused the Furies his friends thought to fend off by having him declared insane. The Furies were not appeased then, and hound him still, seeking not justice but endless prosecution.

Justice requires that the whole truth be told, 'the truth, the whole truth, and nothing but the truth'. The 'whole truth' is of course an unattainable ideal—'nemo omnia novit', as the jurist Coke acknowledged, no one knows it all. But at least we can know more than is told by the prosecuting labels automatically stuck onto Pound, reiterating that he was 'mad', 'a traitor', 'a fascist', 'a money crank', 'an anti-Semite'. The evidence, when one examines it, indicates that he was neither mad nor a traitor. His involvement with Fascism, especially through the course of the 1939–45 war, is a more complicated matter, too complicated for any simple judgment, having been more an endorsement of its economic and social arrangements than of its politics, and having included, along with a degree of blindness to its operations, an endeavour to reform it with an injection of Confucianism. Indeed, if one must use labels, 'Confucian' would be nearer the truth than 'Fascist'. (As for 'fascist', that is no longer fit for any responsible use.) But before and above all Pound's primal commitment was always to the principles of the American Constitution. He never once suggested that his country should adopt Fascism, and consistently urged it to be true to its own democratic principles. One of those principles was that the people's government should control the money supply in the interests of the whole people, with the corollary that the government should not allow the common wealth to be controlled by private banks in their own interest. Only those ignorant of what he actually wrote and stood for, and with a mind closed to the current financial crisis, would regard that as 'cranky'. In the end just one accusation sticks, indelibly, the charge of anti-Semitism, though that, it has to be borne in mind, is not at all the whole truth.

Can we go wrong without losing rightness? Can a man capable at times of speaking evil of the Jews yet be capable of speaking truth about human affairs, and be capable of composing good poetry? Some say not, implacably, blotting out Pound's motivating commitment to economic and social justice, and blotting out the enlightened vision and the mastery of his poetry, thus righteously extinguishing a light in our darkness. But it is possible for a mind subject to a paranoid complex, such as Pound's anti-Semitism became, to be otherwise sane and creative. In Louis Zukofsky's judgment in 1946, 'His profound and intimate knowledge and practice [of literature and music] still leave that part of his mind entire.' The human truth and the creative vision remain for those who, in the words of Robert Creeley, 'go to that work to get what seems to me of *use*, and the rest I toss out, condemning it just by that act'.

It is Pound's poetry that is of enduring utility. He is of concern to us still just because of it, and we cannot do full justice to him without engaging with the poetry and doing justice to it. In one aspect his *Cantos* are inseparable from his crusade for social justice and good government; and in another they are distinct from that crusade, being committed not to immediate reform but to contemplating the causes and consequences of political and economic behaviour, and to defining the governing principles of a good society. They are political, as Pound said, but political in the way that Dante's *Divine Comedy* and Shakespeare's history plays are political. In a time when monetary and market values are dominant in our politics we need, in Robert Duncan's phrase, an 'answering intensity of the imagination to hold its own values'.

While held as a prisoner by the American army in the summer of 1945 Pound composed his *Pisan Cantos*. Incarcerated for a dozen years in a Washington institution for the insane, he translated the Confucian *Book of Odes* and two Greek tragedies, then composed a sequence of twenty-five new cantos, *Rock-Drill* and *Thrones*. Although confined, and under conditions most would find soul-destroying, he kept working at his epic subject, the struggle for individual rights and responsibilities and for civic justice. He was still, even in his personal hell and purgatory, doing what he could to envision a possible *paradiso terrestre*.

He was freed from St Elizabeths when the charges against him were dropped, but he was never freed from the custody of his devoted and unrelenting wife. Through the remaining fourteen years of his life he was denied even the simple rights of the free citizen, the right to his own money, to control of his own property, the right to make a will. And this injustice, like that of his confinement in St Elizabeths, he accepted as his fate, with dignity and without protest. It was a tragic fate, but he would not be crushed by it. Marianne Moore was struck by his resilience in his St Elizabeths years. And for Robert Lowell a visit to Pound in his last years 'was awesome and rather shattering, like meeting Oedipus'. There was 'a nobility I've never seen before', he wrote afterwards, 'the nobility of someone, not a sinner, but who has gone far astray and learned at last too much. . . . No self-pity, but more knowledge of his fate than any man should have.' Words of Geoffrey Hill might be adapted to fit both his life and his work—

> Partial, impartial, unassailable
> though many times assailed, like poetry—
> —*The Pisan Cantos, The Confucian Odes*

CHRONOLOGY

1939 28 Jan., death of W. B. Yeats at Cap Martin on the French Riviera.
Mar., Hitler invades and occupies the remainder of Czechoslovakia.
April, Italy annexes Albania.
Apr., EP's *What Is Money For* published by Greater Britain Publications.
Apr.–June, EP goes to America in hope of persuading President Roosevelt to keep USA out of the looming European war. Awarded honorary doctorate by Hamilton College.
26 June, death of Ford Madox Ford at Deauville, France.
Aug., EP contributing to *Meridiano di Roma.*
1 Sept., Germany invades Poland, thus setting off the Second World War.
Nov., EP declares 'my economic work is done', prepares to write his *paradiso.*

1940 Jan., *Cantos LII–LXXI* ['China'—'John Adams'] published by Faber.
Feb., EP made life member of American Academy of Political and Social Sciences.
Apr.–May, Germany invades Denmark and Norway, then Belgium, Holland, and France.
June, fall of France; Italy enters war.
Sept., EP attempts to return to USA, but no clipper passage available.
Oct., Italy invades Greece.

1941 Jan., EP begins broadcasts over Rome Radio. Death of James Joyce in Zurich.
Apr., Germany invades Yugoslavia and Greece.
June, Germany invades Russia.
July, US State Dept. limits EP's passport to six months and for return to USA only.
Sept., EP translating *Ta Hio* into Italian.
Oct., EP tries to arrange visit to USA but feels rebuffed by US Chargé d'Affaires in Rome. US Federal Communications Commisssion (FCC) begins monitoring EP's broadcasts.
7 Dec., Japan attacks US naval base at Pearl Harbor, Hawaii; 8 Dec., USA declares war on Japan; 11 Dec., Germany and Italy declare war on USA.
Dec., EP suspends broadcasts, but tells Reynolds Packard that he intends to stay on in Italy.

1942 29 Jan., EP resumes broadcasts. Granted official permission to remain in Italy.
Feb., death in Rapallo of Homer Pound, EP's father.

June, report in US newspaper that EP had been prevented by the US Chargé d'Affaires from leaving Italy with other Americans on the last diplomatic train. However, there is no other evidence that he sought repatriation at that time; and in 1960 he could not recall having been directly refused permission to leave Italy in that year.

Oct., second battle of El Alamein begins defeat of Axis forces in North Africa.

Dec., EP's *Carta da visita* published in Rome.

1943 *Jan.–Feb., battle of Stalingrad and defeat of German army there, followed by retreat from Russia.*

July, EP indicted with others *in absentia* for treason against the USA.

July, Mussolini dismissed by king, arrested, and imprisoned. Allies bomb Rome.

Sept., Italy surrenders; German forces now occupy Italy; Allied forces land in southern Italy; Mussolini rescued from captivity by German troops and under German direction sets up Repubblica Sociale Italiana (RSI) from Salò on Lake Garda.

Nov., EP begins writing his own propaganda for Salò government.

1944 Jan., US authorities order eventual arrest and interrogation of EP.

Feb., EP's *L'America, Roosevelt e le cause della guerra presente* published in Venice by RSI press.

Apr., EP's *Oro e lavoro* published in Rapallo.

May, German authorities order evacuation of Rapallo seafront—EP and DP move in with OR at Sant'Ambrogio.

June, EP's *Introduzione alla natura economica degli S.U.A.* published in Venice by RSI press.

June, Rome falls to Allies; Allied landings in Normandy.

July, *Testamento di Confucio*, 'Versione italiana di Ezra Pound e di Alberto Luchini', published in Venice by RSI press.

15 Aug., Allied forces take Florence; 25 Aug., liberation of Paris.

Sept., *Orientamenti*, a collection of EP's contributions to *Meridiano di Roma*, published in Venice by RSI press.

Dec., *Jefferson e Mussolini*, EP's Italian version of *J/M*, published in Venice by RSI press.

1945 Feb., *Chiung Iung/L'asse che non vacilla*, EP's Italian version of *Confucius: The Unwobbling Pivot*, published in Venice by RSI press.

28 Apr., Mussolini caught and killed by Italian Communist partisans; 30 Apr., Hitler commits suicide in Berlin bunker.

2 May, German forces in Italy surrender; 7 May, all German forces in Europe surrender to Allies. The war in the Pacific continues until Japan surrenders 14 Aug. after USA drops atomic bombs on Hiroshima and Nagasaki.

3 May, EP taken prisoner by two ex-Fascist petty criminals now acting as partisans and driven to partisan command in Zoagli, where he asks to be

taken to the US command in Chiavari; taken instead to partisan command in Chiavari, where EP again asks to be taken to the Americans. The partisan in charge tells him he is free to go home if he wishes, but then at EP's insistence has him driven to the American command in Lavagna. From there he is driven to Genoa for arrest and interrogation at the US Counter Intelligence Center there.

24 May, EP transferred to 6677th Disciplinary Training Center (DTC) north of Pisa and there confined in a steel-reinforced cage in the maximum security area until 18 June, when he is provided with a tent in the medical compound and allowed some freedom of movement.

Between the end of June and mid-October composes *The Pisan Cantos*; and between 5 Oct. and 5 Nov. types up his English version of *Confucius: The Unwobbling Pivot & The Great Digest.*

17–18 Nov., EP flown from Rome to Washington DC to answer treason charges, delivered to District of Columbia jail.

19 Nov., preliminary arraignment before Chief Justice Bolitha J. Laws.

27 Nov., formal arraignment with a freshly drawn up indictment; Cornell, appearing as EP's attorney, says EP is unfit to plead on grounds of insanity, and he is remanded to Washington Asylum and Jail.

4 Dec., transferred to psychiatric ward of Gallinger Hospital for examination and observation by four psychiatrists.

21 Dec., the psychiatrists report to Court that EP 'is insane and mentally unfit for trial', and EP is ordered to be transferred to St Elizabeths Hospital for the insane; Justice Department calls for a statutory insanity hearing to test whether EP is feigning insanity. The psychiatrists at St Elizabeths, apart from their director, do not find him insane.

1946 13 Feb., at the hearing the four psychiatrists again all testify that he is unfit to plead or to stand trial, and he is committed to be confined indefinitely in St Elizabeths where he will be held in Howard Hall with the criminally insane until Feb. 1947. While there he will draft translations of the 305 Confucian odes.

July, DP arrives Washington DC, and will visit EP on nearly all visiting days for the following twelve years.

30 Oct., Cornell has Court appoint DP 'Committee' in charge of the person and property of Ezra Pound.

1947 3 Feb., EP transferred from Howard Hall to Cedar Ward in Center Building.

March, EP's translation, *Confucius. The Unwobbling Pivot & The Great Digest,* published by New Directions.

1948 Jan., OR has six of EP's Rome Radio broadcasts privately printed in Siena and distributed gratis as '*If This Be Treason . . .*'.

Feb., EP transferred to Chestnut Ward in Center Building, where he will remain until released in 1958.
9 Feb., death of Isabel Weston Pound, EP's mother, at his daughter's castle in the Italian Tyrol.
July, *The Pisan Cantos*, and *The Cantos of Ezra Pound* [I–LXXXIV], published by New Directions.
Sept., Mary and Boris de Rachewiltz acquire Schloss Brunnenburg at Dorf Tirol above Merano in the Adige valley.

1949 Feb., EP controversially awarded the Bollingen Prize for Poetry.
EP working on the sound of the Confucian odes, and on a version of Sophocles' *Elektra*.

1950 EP's translation of *Confucian Analects* published in *Hudson Review*.
The Letters of Ezra Pound 1907–1941, ed. D. D. Paige, published by Harcourt, Brace in New York.

1951 John Kasper begins publishing Square $ series of EP's required reading.
Dec., EP's version of *Confucius. The Great Digest & The Unwobbling Pivot* with facing Chinese text from the original 'Stone Text' published by New Directions.

1952 Jan., Sheri Martinelli, his beloved muse in *Rock-Drill*, begins visiting EP.
Apr., OR visits EP for the first time.

1953 Mar., EP resumes drafting cantos.
Mar.–May, MdR in Washington DC visiting EP.
July, *The Translations of Ezra Pound* published by Faber.
Nov., EP's version of Sophokles' *Women of Trachis* published in *Hudson Review*.

1954 Jan., *Literary Essays of Ezra Pound*, ed. T. S. Eliot, published by Faber.
Sept., EP's *The Classic Anthology Defined by Confucius* published by Harvard University Press.

1955 June, OR's second visit to EP in St Elizabeths.
Sept., *Section: Rock-Drill/ 85–95 de los cantares* published in Milan by Vanni Scheiwiller.

1956 Apr., canto 96, the first of *Thrones*, published in *Hudson Review*; canto 97 published there in October.
Sept., Marcella Spann, who will be the muse of his last cantos, first visits EP.
Nov., EP's version of Sophokles' *Women of Trachis* published by Neville Spearman in London.

1957 Oct.–Dec., EP drafting the 'Coke cantos', 107–9, which conclude *Thrones*.

1958 The efforts of Archibald MacLeish, assisted by Robert Frost, and supported by Dag Hammarskjöld, finally persuade the President, the State

Department, and the Justice Department to agree to drop the treason charge against EP.
18 Apr., Judge Bolitha J. Laws orders that the indictment be dismissed—EP is freed from St Elizabeths, but is still in the care of his Committee.
30 June, EP, DP, and Marcella Spann (MS), sail from New York for Genoa, arriving 10 July, and going on to be welcomed by Mary and Boris de Rachewiltz at Brunnenburg.
19–21 Sept., and again 10–13 Nov., EP and MS visit Venice; in Dec. EP sketches opening lines of canto 110 with reference to Torcello.

1959 11–15 Jan., EP, DP, and MS visit around Lake Garda—EP drafting 110. The rest of *Drafts & Fragments* drafted in notebooks in following months through to Aug.
27 Feb., EP, DP, and MS leave Brunnenburg for an apartment in Rapallo.
Apr., EP interviewed by Bridson for BBC.
28 Sept., MS returns to America.
4 Oct., EP and DP move back to Brunnenburg; EP, seriously depressed, is in a state of collapse.
Dec., *Thrones/96–109 de los cantares* published in Milan by Vanni Scheiwiller. Last fragments of drafts in poetry notebooks.

1960 10 Jan., EP goes down to Rome, staying with Dadone, an old friend; DP goes to Rapallo.
Feb.–Mar., EP interviewed by Donald Hall for *Paris Review*.
June, EP leaves Rome for Rapallo.
15 July, EP and DP go up to Brunnenburg, and EP, physically in a bad state and not eating, goes into clinic in Merano for two weeks. Afterwards depression deepens.

1961 3 Jan., EP writes to OR, 'Why o couldn't I have come to you?'
Mar., EP goes down to Rome again to stay with Dadone.
May, MdR, summoned by Dadone, puts EP into a Casa di Cura in Rome for a month; OR visits him there.
15 June, MdR and OR take EP to Merano and place him in the Martinsbrunn Casa di Cura—he will remain there until Apr. 1962.
Sept., death of HD.

1962 26 Apr., MdR takes EP to Rapallo where OR is to care for him. Diagnosed as having been suffering from enlarged prostate causing retention of urine and serious uremic blood poisoning requiring urgent treatment in Dr Bacigalupo's Villa Chiara. Will live henceforth with OR in Sant'Ambrogio and Venice. Increasingly silent with those to whom he has nothing to say.
June, BBC broadcasts new production of EP's *Le Testament*.

Nov., *Poetry* (Chicago) awards its 50th Anniversary Harriet Monroe Memorial Prize to EP.

1963 Feb., EP interviewed by Grazia Livi for *Epoca*.
4 Mar., death of William Carlos Williams.
Aug., awarded Academy of American Poets Fellowship for 1963.
Nov., successful disintoxification treatment at Clinique La Prairie near Montreux in Switzerland.

1964 *Confucius to Cummings/An Anthology of Poetry*, edited by Ezra Pound & Marcella Spann, published by New Directions.

1965 4 Jan., death of T. S. Eliot in London. EP attends memorial service in Westminster Abbey on 4 Feb.; then goes on to Dublin to see Yeats's widow.
July, EP is Gian-Carlo Menotti's guest of honour at his Spoleto Two Worlds Festival, where *Le Testament* is being performed as a ballet; he reads works by Marianne Moore and Robert Lowell, and, in the piazza, from his own *Cantos.* EP a presence at Spoleto Festival each year to 1971. 21 Oct.–3 Nov., guest of Dominique de Roux in Paris for his 80th birthday on the 30th.
4–11 Nov., visit with OR to Greece, a birthday gift from Natalie Barney.

1966 Proposal for establishing in Beinecke Library of Yale University a Center for the Study of Ezra Pound and his Contemporaries, upon the acquisition of the Pound Archive.

1967 Jan., EP visits Joyce's grave in Zurich, and gives directions for his own to be in Hailey, Idaho.
June, on visit to Paris attends Beckett's *Fin de partie* and is called on by Beckett.
Oct., Allen Ginsberg conversations with EP in Venice.
Dec., EP's selection, *Selected Cantos*, published by Faber.

1968 Jan., interview for RAI, partly with Pier Paolo Pasolini.

1969 April, *Drafts & Fragments of Cantos CX–CXVII* published by New Directions.
June, EP and OR fly to New York for the opening of an exhibition of the original drafts of *The Waste Land* with EP's annotations, and to attend a meeting of the Academy of American Poets. Since Laughlin is about to be awarded an honorary degree at Hamilton College they accompany him, and Pound is accorded a standing ovation.

1970 Oct., EP attends Buckminster Fuller's lectures in Venice, and they talk.

1971 July, EP nominated by the selecting panel to be awarded the prestigious Emerson-Thoreau medal of the American Academy of Arts and Sciences, but the nomination is overruled by the Council of the Academy.

1972 5 Feb., death of Marianne Moore—EP organizes memorial service in Venice and reads her poem 'What Are Years?'

26 Oct., DP applies to Washington Court to be replaced as Committee by her attorney.

1 Nov., death in Venice of EP.

3 Nov., funeral service in San Giorgio Maggiore, followed by burial on the cemetery island San Michele.

1973 8 Dec., death of DP near Cambridge, England.

1996 15 Mar., death of OR at Brunnenburg, buried beside EP in Venice.

PART ONE : 1939–1945

Congress shall make no law . . . abridging the freedom of speech

—US Constitution, 1st Amendment (1791)

Thy tongue give not too much libertie lest it
Take thee prisoner

—from copperplate MS leaf tipped into EP's copy of Coke's *The Third Part of the Institutes of the Laws of England: concerning high treason . . .* (London, 1648)

1 : Between Paradise & Propaganda, 1939–40

Pound left New York for Genoa on 17 June 1939, first class on the '*Conte di Savoia*', and by the 25th he was back in Rapallo. Finding that Olga Rudge had gone from Sant'Ambrogio to Siena, he protested, 'He come bak to see her, dambit and she ain't here'. Olga told him why, in a long, exasperated letter:

> He has put her off every time she tries to get Him to consider subject of present triangle—I see no reason for a 'marital front' or façade—kept up (as I was told in 1924) out of respect for feelings of D's parents, to be kept up now in same way when circumstances have changed... I dont know how a Confucian would view a woman who had not wanted children by her husband, & who then introduced another man's child into the family as her husband's, being given all the consideration owing to a wife—while the true child had not even legal status, & any privileges given it, or planned for it, were at the expense of its mother—i.e. an adoption that would make it over to you and implicitly to D. while I would loose every right...

Pound had in fact looked into the possibility of legally adopting his own daughter while in the United States—the attorney had sent him a copy of the Pennsylvania Statute on Adoption—and it would appear that he had done this without first discussing it with her mother, who closed her letter thus, 'Am fed up with you & D. deciding la mia sorte between you—and then presenting me with faits accomplis.' Before that she had asked that 'before D. leaves [to be with Omar in August]—[He] consider the situation with her'. When Pound went down to Siena about 8 July he found Olga's door locked against him, but they made up and he stayed with her for a fortnight. He was back in Siena for the *Settimana musicale*, 16–21 September, in which the entire week's programme that year was devoted to the music of Vivaldi—a high point in their Vivaldi revival. Then they went on together to Venice for a month or so, and Mary joined them there. Pound mentioned to Dorothy that he was playing tennis with Mary on the Lido.

Possibly as a consequence of Olga's being so fed up Ezra and Dorothy each wrote to Pound's parents towards the end of July telling them that the supposed grandson whom they cherished was not in fact Ezra's child. Homer wrote to Ezra, 'A clap of Thunder out of a clear sky could not have been more startling than yours and D's letters. For over 10 years we have been here. D. has been giving us Omar's photos o k and it is hard to realize the truth.' Isabel wrote, 'Dear Son | The situation is to me amazing—one disloyalty provokes another is understandable but why continue the deception so many years one can not transfer affections.' And Homer spoke for both, 'there is no pleasure in our continuing here. We shall arrange to depart.' The sharpness of the rift is reflected in Pound's note, 'Dear Dad, I hope you will at any rate keep up correspondence on matters of general interest.'

As things turned out the elder Pounds did not leave Rapallo. The war made it difficult, then impossible. Homer would die there early in 1942. Isabel would live on through the war into 1948, and be cared for in her last months by the granddaughter she had been denied knowledge of. Mary had been in Rapallo in April when her father was about to leave for America, sharing in the excitement, but on the day he went to board the boat in Genoa her grandparents had accompanied him, and she had gone separately with her mother to see the boat pull out 'from some place high up where one could see the harbour'. It seemed strange to her that she could not see her grandfather whom she knew was in Rapallo, nor meet her grandmother. She had never heard of Dorothy, nor of Omar, and would learn of their existence only well on in the war. The problematic triangle with its deceptions and its complications was not resolved in 1939, and would remain a source of complications and deceptions to the end of Pound's life, and beyond.

During Pound's absence in America, in April, Italy had invaded and annexed Albania. Mussolini was emulating Hitler's annexations, but he was also intent on blocking his expansion into the Balkans. Then in May Mussolini entered into an agreement with Hitler that if either country went to war the other would support it 'with all military force'. This 'Pact of Steel' was made in spite of Italy's military being ill prepared for war—it would not be ready before 1943 in Mussolini's own estimate—and in spite also of his determination not to be drawn into the European war which he foresaw as inevitable. He was simply hoping, as Britain's ambassador to Italy explained to prime minister Chamberlain, that the pact would put him 'in a stronger position to restrain Hitler from moves which would involve Italy in an unwelcome and unpopular war'. But while Mussolini might have hoped the pact would make for peace, Hitler, on the day after it was sealed, was secretly briefing his generals to be ready for total war against Poland at the earliest opportunity.

By the end of June Germany's plans to mobilize all of its now very large armed forces were ready for execution. This time the excuse for the invasion of an independent country was to be Danzig with its large German population. Danzig, now Gdansk, had been taken from Germany under the treaty of Versailles and made a free city in order to give otherwise landlocked Poland a port on the Baltic. Hitler was demanding with increasing belligerence a revision of its status, but that was just the cover for his determination to invade Poland and subject it in every way to the German Reich.

Pound was refusing to believe that anyone would go to war over Danzig. Even so late as 25 August, when Chamberlain had spoken of defending Poland, he told Dorothy that he thought London was creating a crisis unnecessarily since no one was actually attacking that country. The next day he admitted that he had 'Mebbe been a bit callous as haven't believed anyone wd/be ass enough to die over Danzig'. He still considered that the threat of a railway strike in Britain that evening looked 'more like something with a meaning'. Both his letters were returned to sender because Dorothy, who had been with Omar in Annecy—'sacrificing for one's offspring', as she put it—had sensibly responded to the rumours of war and to the mounting anxiety in France by packing Omar off to England and getting herself back to the relative calm of Rapallo.

Pound's mind was on his cantos' *paradiso* that summer. But first he thought he should clear up once and for all the matter of money. He had no doubt that if there were to be war then money, loan capital, would be at the bottom of it. In July he went through a copy of his *ABC of Economics* carefully revising it for a new edition to be published by Laughlin in America. He refined a number of his 1933 Douglasite formulations in the light of his later discovery of Gesell, and generally pruned and clarified the prose. Then on the endpaper he drafted a hopeful note dated 'July 1939':

> Since its writing ... and publication in 1933, many of the ideas here set forth have gone into action, others have been announced in state programs, not, gentle reader, because of my having written them, but because they are in the current of living thought daily more apparent to more and more people.

In the event, rather than print a new edition Laughlin imported 300 sets of sheets of Faber's first edition and reissued that, without Pound's note or revisions. Having revised his *ABC*, in intention at least, Pound plotted a definitive study. At the beginning of August he told Ronald Duncan that he was too busy to write anything for his *Townsman* because he had '29 Cantos AND that treatise on money to DO'—he wanted to make it 'THE book on Money', as thorough as his edition of Cavalcanti. Near the end of the month he mentioned to Dorothy that he was 'trying to pull that book on money together'. And that is the last we hear of it. In early November, in the course of discussing a possible collaboration with a proposed new magazine, he told Douglas McPherson, the young would-be editor, 'My economic work is done (in the main)'. It would still have to be 'diffused, distributed, put into popular education, etc.', but that job, he implied, could be left to Overholser whose *History of Money in the United States* was 'the *only* American book that *needs* reading'. He had re-read Willis Overholser's little book in late August, been struck by it afresh as 'the most lucid on money I have ever seen', and had concluded apparently that because it existed there was no call for him to go on with his own would-have-been definitive treatise.

'My economic work is done', he thought—if only! If only there had been no war, and he really had been able to leave the economic war to others to carry on, how different the rest of his life would have been. The war in fact had already begun when Pound made that declaration in November 1939. Hitler had begun his conquest of Poland on 1 September and completed it by the 27th, with Russia also invading at Hitler's invitation and seizing a large slice in the east; and Great Britain and France had been formally at war with Germany since 3 September. Italy and the United States were not yet involved, and Pound was strongly of the opinion that they should not get involved. He was wanting to turn his mind away from warring. Thinking of his own decade-long offensive against economic ignorance and error in what for him was the only real and necessary war, he told McPherson that he had done his bit, that now 'the younger generation ought to do the killing and carrying away of corpses'. 'I've got my time cut out now for positive statements', he wrote, 'am now definitely onto questions of BELIEF.'

'Belief' was to be the great subject of the cantos still to be written. 'There shd. be about 100 cantos in all', he informed Eliot at the end of September, 'The latter 29 will move slow, as it is roughly the paradise. Having wiped up history I shall move on to philosophy and outline the kind of religion a healthy man can BELIEVE.' To Laughlin he wrote, 'From 72 on we will enter the empyrean.' In Dante's *Paradiso* the empyrean is the ultimate heaven whence emanates the pure light of animating intelligence, the light that informs and shapes the natures of all things in the universe. In *The Spirit of Romance* Pound had described the *Divine Comedy* as 'a symbol of mankind's struggle upward out of ignorance into the clear light of philosophy', and had implied that in that clear light 'the laws of eternal justice' would be revealed to the contemplative mind. He was reaching now for that paradisal vision in which the laws governing the just and good society would be so clear and compelling that they would enter into the mind as convictions, active beliefs, forming and directing the way people lived together.

In December 1939 he sought the help of the American philosopher long resident in Italy, George Santayana, whose clarity and integrity of mind he admired. Arranging to call on him at the Hotel Danieli while he was in Venice over Christmas, he explained that having got to the end of 'money in history' he had next to 'tackle philosophy or my "paradiso"', and that he was hoping for 'sidelights' on his 'notes to Cavalcanti and one or two Chinese texts'. 'Might tear up the carpet, perhaps along the line: We believe nothing that is not European,' he added. It is likely that when they met Pound used Santayana as a sounding board for his rather scattered ideas about philosophy and religion and 'European' belief, touching upon Confucius and Mencius and Aristotle and Aquinas and John Scotus Erigena and Cavalcanti, upon the decline and failure of Christian belief, and upon his commitment to recovering a paradise of the mind in his cantos. Santayana, perhaps grasping at something definite to hold on to, sought enlightenment concerning the Chinese ideogram, but failed 'to *see* the connection' with Cavalcanti and the rest. Possibly feeling rather talked at as by an over-excited teacher he told Pound an anecdote about how Henry Adams, author of *The Education of Henry Adams*, had remarked, 'Teach? at Harvard? | Teach? It cannot be done.' It wasn't though that Pound was trying to teach Santayana, it was just that when his mind was in a ferment he needed to communicate with someone who could help him sort out his ideas. To Mary, who was with Ezra and Olga in Venice, he said, '"A relief to talk philosophy with someone completely honest – a nice mind."' She had seldom seen him 'so eager and yet so contented'.

She recalled in her memoir how they had gone one evening to see a Ginger Rogers–Fred Astaire film, and 'All the way home from the cinema Babbo tapped and leaped and encouraged me to do likewise and "get nimble".' Back in the Pensione Seguso he threw off his coat and jacket and 'leapt and tap-danced more freely', until Olga reproved him, '"*Caro!* I refrain from practising for fear of disturbing the other guests and you bring the house down in the middle of the night".' 'Babbo was mortified,' Mary observed, but 'it was hard for him to keep still before having fully danced out the rhythm he had absorbed'.

In the latter part of 1939 and into 1940 Pound was trying to keep his mind focused upon constructive beliefs. He read through an old *Handbook of the History of Philosophy* which had belonged to Dorothy's father, and particularly marked passages affirming that mind shapes matter, that ideas animate, that an efficient intelligence creates its world. From Aristotle he had picked up the term *teXne*, meaning sound technique or skill in making, and he was using it to emphasize his old axiom that fine ideas were true only so far as they were made to work in the real world. The ideas he was after would be ideas-in-action. When he looked into the writings of Scotus Erigena, whose assertion that 'authority comes from right reason' had been a *mantram* for him in canto 36 and *Guide to Kulchur*, he was excited to find him saying 'a lot about light that hooks up with Guido['s] Donna mi prega'; and he would put into the *Pisan Cantos* Erigena's 'omnia, quae sunt, lumina sunt'—'all things that are are lights'—meaning that every thing that exists is made by and composed of the universal Light. That axiom too committed him to seeking his illuminating ideas in their real-life, practical, manifestations. It meant that his 'serene heaven of philosophy' must exist, if at all, as a *paradiso terrestre*.

His interest, he told Eliot, was in 'civilizations at their MOST'. More precisely, his interest was in what gives rise to and sustains civilizations, that is, their roots rather than their flowerings; and this, he was convinced, had to be a religion of powerfully animating and guiding beliefs. That was not a new conviction, of course. It was present in embryo in Pound's *Imagisme*, with its call for poems to be seed-*gestalts* formed in minds 'ever at the interpretation of this vital universe'; it was present in a more developed form in his turn to the Confucian *paideuma* to reform a failing Occident; then in his thinking about the intelligence of love in relation to Cavalcanti; and present again in *Jefferson and/or Mussolini*, in his affirmation of the civilizing force of germinal intelligence. His references now to the religious beliefs he thought viable in the mid-twentieth century tended to be brief and allusive, as in 'Statues of Gods', a note in *Townsman* in August 1939:

What we really believe is the pre-Christian element which Christianity has not stamped out. The only Christian festivals having any vitality are welded to sun festivals, the spring solstice, the Corpus and St. John's eve, registering the turn of the sun, the crying of 'Ligo' in Lithuania, the people rushing down to the sea on Easter morning, the gardens of Adonis carried to Church on the Thursday.

The truly believed cults, he insisted, were those of Aphrodite and Helios—sex and the sun, in current vernacular. In a later note, under the heading 'Religio', he said simply,

Paganism included a certain attitude toward; a certain understanding of, coitus, which is the mysterium.

The other rites are the festivals of fecundity of the grain and the sun festivals, without revival of which religion can not return to the hearts of the people.

'The religious man communes every time his teeth sink into a bread crust', he declared in another note, with this further charged thought, 'The essence of religion is the *present* tense.'

There was a dark underside to these positive statements. Pound was now blaming the weakening of Christian belief on 'semitic infections', and calling for 'a European religion' purged of Old Testament myths and metaphors, and purged of tolerance of 'usury and mercantilism'. In the summer of 1939 he had drafted an article with the heading 'European Paideuma' which he hoped would be translated and published in Germany by Douglas Fox of Frobenius' Institute for 'Kulturmorphologie' in Frankfurt. 'What we believe is EUROPEAN', he began, and went on to indicate what he regarded as the 'roots' and 'valid elements' in European culture—the festivals of 'the sun, the grain, the harvest and Aphrodite', and again 'feasts of planting and harvest and feasts of the turn of the sun'. But against these he saw ranged the 'semitiz[ing] forces' of usury and a revival of the Old Testament. And only in Germany, he wrote, 'is there enough force toward a purgation'—towards ridding European culture of its 'semitic microbes'. The article ranged over other points in his thinking—Ovid, Erigena, amour courtois; it remarked, 'Sound ethic we have from Confucius via Mencius'; it also allowed that Aristotle and Aquinas, by intellectualizing too far in their philosophy, 'were largely destructive' of belief. But there is no getting past that assigning to Germany, in 1939, the function of purging Europe of its 'semitic microbes'. That was typical Nazi double-speak, and though Pound's immediate context concerned impersonal cultural elements he was nonetheless using the arguments and the language of Nazi anti-Semitic propaganda, and would almost certainly have been understood in Germany to be endorsing the Nazi measures to rid Germany of its Jews in the pursuit of 'racial purity'. His habit of identifying and confusing the practice of usury with Jews and Judaism for rhetorical effect had become so ingrained that he could at times lose all sense of the error of doing so; and now the error was bringing him near to evil. In this draft article, and in some of his correspondence around this time, his call for 'European' culture to be purged of 'non-European' 'semitic elements' is fearfully near to Hitler's lethal myth of an 'Aryan' culture needing to be purged of Europe's Jews. Along with that, the Nazi appropriation of sun-seeking and fertility for their own perverse ends could render suspect at that time even Pound's longstanding and profoundly sane enthusiasm for Helios and Adonis and Aphrodite.

There is evidence of Pound's struggling to correct himself. He wrote to Eliot on 1 February 1940, 'I don't think I am ready for an analysis of Christianity into its various racial components, European and non-

European.' In spite of that he did write to the Revd Henry Swabey in early March, 'Re European belief: Neither mass nor communion are of Jew origin . . . and are basis of Xtn relig.' But then in a letter to Ronald Duncan he referred to that statement, and pulled himself up: 'what's use my saying THAT especially as I have NOT studied the Mass.' The rest of that letter is like a contest between two sides of Pound's mind, one insisting 'Christianity is (or was when real) antisemitism', and the other retorting 'what is the use of arguing (my arguing) with undefined terms'. He asserts, 'Protestantism a usury politic', but then thinks 'No use MY going off half-cocked on large subjects whereon I have not yet arrived at conclusion'; again he asserts, 'I doubt if ANY single ethical idea now honoured comes from JEWRY', and then reflects, 'BUT . . . I only finished my historic econ/ section a year ago, and dont want to make wild statements.' The resolution of the contest between the closed and the open mind comes with the realization, 'Need ALL the circumjacent intelligence for immediate things,' meaning that it was not the time for speculation about matters he had not got to the bottom of. 'Tempus tacendi', he concluded wisely, time to shut up. But then he added, as if aware of how unfixed his mind was, 'I dont know how long it will last.'

It was not in Pound's nature to remain silent for long. He valued stillness and silence in his contemplative moments; but his mind was more often hyperactive, and eager to converse, to communicate, to teach. When in Rome, as he often was in these years, he would look up all sorts of contacts in the search for information and conversation, not always successfully. In a wry passage in a letter to Katue Kitasono in August 1940 he described a recent visit to Japan's 'cultural relations bureau'—he had been hoping for a meeting of minds:

> After half an hour one of 'em vaguely thought I must be someone he had heard of; Fenollosa meant nothing to 'em. They thought I ought to get wise to MODERN Japan and not bother with Noh.
>
> Well, they gave me a damn good cup of COFFEE. So I kidded 'em about disappearance of tea ceremony.
>
> And they hoped to see me again
> BUT Americans are suspect. Naturally.

Pound fared rather better on his regular visits to the Italian Institute for the Middle and Far East to look up Chinese materials. There he met a young Chinese instructor, Fengchi Yang, and tried to convert him to his view that China's real enemy was not Japan but international usury. Yang, with his more intimate acquaintance with Japan's invasion of China, was unimpressed, but did assist Pound with his Chinese studies, and later with his translation into Italian of two of the Confucian Four Books.

His desire to teach America was still strong, in spite of America's not wanting to be taught by him. Just after his return he had written to Ibbotson about visiting Hamilton again to lecture to 'the student body' in the spring of 1940, perhaps annually. Nothing came of that notion. Then he had been proposing for some time to edit a 'Founders series' for Laughlin's New Directions in order to put into circulation at a dollar a copy the gists of Jefferson and Adams and Van Buren. But at the end of November 1939 Laughlin had to tell him that such a series 'would be a dead loss' since 'nobody would touch it because of your association with it'. Laughlin had been touring the country selling New Directions books to the stores and had found 'that you are in great disfavour with your compatriots'. Most stores would not take his books, saying it was 'because you are a Fascist', or saying 'youth has lost interest in you and they can't sell them'. Laughlin could foresee that 'These next years are going to be bleak for you because of your views and the sentiment against you.'

Laughlin still had faith in Pound's poetry, and firmly intended New Directions to become its publisher in the United States. He wanted to take over and reprint the 1926 *Personae* at a dollar as 'the best move at the moment to save your reputation'. And he did manage to take over the contract for publishing the *Cantos*, believing that 'when monetary sanity does return to this earth the Cantos will be recognized as an epic of money, of the greatest world importance, in fact a sort of prophetic monument to the new age'.

But as for Pound's idea that he should edit and Laughlin publish a weekly newsletter or monthly review in order to further communications between Europe and America, Laughlin declared with some force that 'There could be no connection with New Directions and no hint that you were connected with it—if anybody smelt you in it, or your Italian hand, they would simply discount the whole thing as lies.' Further, 'I will not run an anti-semitic sheet or be in any way connected with one.' He had already told Pound that he would not 'print anything that can fairly be construed as an attack on the Jews', and that he would have that stated in the contract for *Cantos LII–LXXI*. Now he went on,

I cannot tell you how it grieves me to see you taking up with [anti-semitism]. It is vicious and mean. I do not for one minute believe that it is solely the Jews who are responsible for the maintenance of the unjust money systems. They may have their part in it, but it is just as much, and more, the work of Anglo-Saxons and celts and goths and what have you.

Undaunted, Pound kept on at Laughlin about the need for intercommunications. After Italy entered the war in June 1940 he felt this all the more. He wanted news from abroad, he told Laughlin, 'fer preventin me from falling into ERROR'; even more he wanted to be communicating his own news sense. In November 1940 he wrote, 'Until the war started I had ten thousand circ[ulation] via Action, and was educatin a LOT of live Britons . . . men writing, and blokes speaking to large audiences', and now that 'English papers [were] closed for the duration' the 'U.S. should take advantage' and publish him more. Laughlin had to remind him, 'Yr hon [our's] name is absolute mud wherever mentioned because of yr present whereabouts and known affinities.'

His 'present whereabouts and known affinities' were indeed problematical. From America he was perceived as un-American, even anti-American, and certainly Fascist. In Italy he was perceived as altogether American, though sympathetic to Fascism. To himself he was all-American and unwaveringly loyal to the Constitution of the United States; and as for Fascism, he saw that as right for Italy at that time, but not for a moment did he think it should supplant the democratic ideal in America. As an American in America he took his stand unequivocally with Jefferson and John Adams. But he was not in America, he was in Italy, and for the most part his devotion to America came out in the negative—in disappointed and angry criticism of it for not living up to its ideal. And it didn't help when he invited America, in an Italian journal, to look to Fascist Italy as the effective heir to the American Revolution. In May 1939, while he was in the United States, an article over his name appeared in *Meridiano di Roma*, a serious journal of ideas, lamenting, first, Americans' ignorance of their own history and Constitution, and then their ignorance about Fascist Italy. If only they would understand and uphold their own Constitution, he suggested, then 95 per cent of their prejudice against the totalitarian states would be removed. In January 1940 in another article in *Meridiano di Roma* he put it more strongly, declaring that American hostility to Fascism was based not just on errors about it but upon a deep-festering ignorance of American history. In April he affirmed that *his* revolution was the American one of 1776, and then went on to salute the Fascist revolution as its continuation, in that the Fascist state was opposed to mercantilism and usurocracy. In June 1940 he candidly suggested that the United States might learn from the *l'idea statale* how to be true to its own ideal. To Pound these were self-evident truths, not even paradoxes. But to others, and to his fellow Americans in particular, the contradictions were simply insupportable.

With England closed to him by the war, and America closed to him by a general prejudice against him, the only outlets Pound could find for his communications were in Japan and Italy—in Japan until September 1940, and after that only in Italy. His Japanese friend Kitasono had introduced him, in May 1939, to the editor of *The Japan Times and Mail*, 'the first and oldest English language newspaper edited by Japanese in Japan', and over sixteen months he contributed a dozen 'Letters from Rapallo', hoping to act as a sage medium between East and West. The editor had asked him to send 'cultural news'—'art, poetry, music'—and made it clear that he 'naturally would prefer nothing which will provoke Americans in political issues—kindly stick to literary subjects'. The editor was of course aware that his paper would be scanned in the press office of the American Embassy in Tokyo for interesting items to be clipped and forwarded by diplomatic bag to the State Department in Washington. There is no evidence that Pound made any allowance for that. For him, of course, 'literary subjects' embraced economics and politics. So, in his second contribution to *The Japan Times*, after touching on a number of 'literary subjects'—the recent deaths of Frobenius and Yeats, new poetic drama in Europe, books worth reading by 'Orientals wanting a clear view of the west'—he declared that what most interested him, and should concern all serious writers, was the political question of 'how people can live together in an organized or organic social system', the great problem being economic and monetary pressures militating against the freedom of 'the individual in the state'. Then in October 1939, with the war under way in Europe, he told the editor that he would 'prefer to write about history for the moment, including current history', since 'We are having a LOAN-capital war', a usurers' war, or as 'Some say a jew war against the aryan population of Europe', 'and all this is subject matter for literature', he insisted. In spite of that his contributions were restricted for some months to cultural intercommunications, such as the value to the West of Fenollosa and the Noh, and of Confucius and Mencius, and the value to the East of early Greek thought. It was not until April 1940 that he entered directly upon 'current history', by recommending Basil Bunting as a poet conscious of 'the age-old infamy of the money monopoly... of attempts to starve mankind in general, by the trick of trapping and withholding the power to buy'.

Through the following months he wrote almost exclusively about the war and its economic causes. His July 'Letter from Rapallo' began, 'With the Hitler interview of June 14, the continental war aims are once more made clear in their essential fairness and, for a victorious army, their mildness.' 14 June was the day Paris fell to the German army. Mussolini had brought Italy into the war on 10 June, attempting without much success to invade

France through the Alps and along the Riviera. Before that, in April and May, Hitler's forces had occupied Denmark, invaded and defeated Norway, Holland, and Belgium, in each case, according to Hitler, to save and protect those countries from the Anglo-French alliance. Now France had fallen to the Reich. And Pound was somehow persuaded that responsibility for 'the million dead in Poland, Flanders, Norway, etc.' lay with the monopolists of money with their Jewish names and connections who 'make wars for the sake of creating debts and for the sake of monopoly'. Hitler's essentially 'fair' and 'mild' war aims, he seems to have been implying, were to defeat those warmongering financial interests and to prevent them from destroying Paris. In his next 'Letter' he referred to the war simply as 'the present Anglo-Jewish war on Europe'.

Laughlin would have dismissed all that as 'German propaganda stuff'. The likelihood is though that Pound was sincerely deluded and really believed his incredible interpretation of Hitler's long-plotted, ruthless, and brutal conquest of Europe. He must have been blanking out the manifest realities of the war by thinking only of a sentence he had isolated from *Mein Kampf*, 'The struggle against international finance and loan capital has become the most important point in the National Socialist programme: the struggle of the German nation for its independence and freedom.' His holding on to that old claim in the face of all that Hitler had done and was doing can only mean that his usury complex was now so developed and so dominant that he was no longer capable, when considering the unwelcome war, of seeing it as it was but only as he was convinced it must be. Many years later he would reflect, 'Telescope is totally blind to everything save the spot it is focussed on', and would take that as illustrating his own 'total blindness | AT moments'.

His contributions to Italian papers, mostly to *Meridiano di Roma*, were along the same lines as his articles for *The Japan Times*. The actual war, he would insist, was an Anglo-Jewish war on Europe, to make the world safe for usury; with the implication that the Axis powers had gone forth to conquer the forces of usury. That was in accord with what he had written to Odon Por while Poland was being overrun, 'Germany is about 90% right in this shindy','and Eng/stinking/land I.E. the yitts that run her, 100% wrong'. There were a few more or less lucid moments. In March 1940 in an article in *Meridiano di Roma* under the heading 'Gli Ebrei e questa guerra'—the Jews and this war—he confessed that his thinking was falling short of Latin clarity and simplicity, that he was lumping together Jews considered as a race and Jews as individuals. He was still blaming the race for the fact that Britain and France and the United States were effectively governed by financial interests against the true interests of their people. At the same time he recognized that it was not only the Rothschilds and Sassoons and Monds who were immediately responsible; there were plenty of Aryan bankers and capitalists in it too, and both those Jews and those Aryans should be condemned equally. The evil was not 'semitism', he could see, it was 'mercantilism'. That correction did nothing to alter the conviction that it was a usurers' war and a war against usury. In July 1940, after the fall of France and the evacuation of the British Expeditionary Force from Dunkirk, he wrote, 'the hecatomb of English soldiers will be the last tribute paid to the bestial superstition, the respect for gold', and he prophesied that 'every nation which tolerates a state of usury behind the official state will fall', as France had fallen, and as England he was sure would soon deservedly fall.[1]

Pound was drifting rather rapidly towards engaging in propaganda that could serve the Fascist interest. In early September 1939 Odon Por told Pound that he had been approached 're giving a more efficient turn to our propaganda', and that 'If you have some suggestions to make re. OUR popularity in Am. (And not Adolf's) we are ready to listen.' Pound declared himself ready 'to popularize Italy and NOT Adolph', provided Por would learn to 'USE American history', and would understand that he, Pound, was 'FOR monetary reform' as the necessary condition of world peace. He drafted a relatively mild open letter to the English, and another to Americans condemning England and telling them 'America's place is OUT of this damn war'. Por used neither letter, but went on discussing possible projects with Pound.

Pound was being caught up in and also himself deliberately weaving a web of connections with the propaganda services. He sought clearance from them in April or May 1940 for at least one of his articles for the *Japan Times*—the one published on 13 June presenting his economic interpretation of the war in Europe—and he did this although Italy was not yet at war and his communications with Japan were not subject to censorship. He seems to have been bringing himself to the notice of the Italian authorities as a potential collaborator. The clearance was given without any indication that he was regarded in that light by the officials concerned.

[1] There was no 'hecatomb of English soldiers': virtually the entire BEF had been successfully evacuated from the beaches of Dunkirk between 26 May and 4 June. Pound's misinformation would have come from German reports relayed in the Italian press and radio on which he was dependent for news throughout the war. Redman notes that 'Pound was an avid reader of Italian newspapers, reading daily *Popolo d'Italia*, *Giornale di Genova*, *Regime Fascista*, *Gazetta Popolare*, *Corriere Mercantile*, and *Corriere della Sera*' (197–8).

His Rapallo friend Ubaldo degli Uberti, a retired naval officer with literary interests and press contacts, had introduced him in the autumn of 1938 to Cornelio Di Marzio, the director of *Meridiano di Roma* who would serve during the war as secretary-general of the Fascist Confederation of Professionals and Artists. Pound began corresponding with Di Marzio, 'offering advice', according to Redman, on 'the effective presentation of Italian economic ideas... in foreign propaganda'; and in February 1939 Di Marzio invited him to become a regular contributor to *Meridiano di Roma*.

In November of that year Pound put to Di Marzio his idea for an English language review which he would edit with the aim of promoting a better appreciation of Fascism in America. It would deal in part with Italian literature, art, and music, and in part with political and economic life in Italy compared with life in America. Di Marzio suggested he approach Luciano De Feo, director of the Institute for Foreign Cultural Relations, and when Pound did that his letter was sent on to the Ministry of Popular Culture, where it was considered by Luigi Villari whose field was cultural relations with the United States. Villari reported to the propaganda directorate that Pound had put forward three projects: a series of studies of America's great early leaders whose ideas in some way bore comparison with Fascist theory, ideas which America's current leaders were failing to honour; secondly, the English language review; and a third project, a weekly column of items selected by Pound from Italian daily papers. All three projects would bear the stamp of propaganda, Villari noted, and that would diminish their value. Moreover, for Italy to publish tendentious historical studies of the kind proposed could appear a rather inopportune intervention in America's internal affairs. Villari entered further weighty reservations concerning Pound himself:

> Signor Pound is an American poet resident in Rapallo, with a love of Italy and a strong sympathy with Fascism... He is a man of real talent and culture and is moved by the finest feelings towards us, but he has a disorderly mind and tries to take on economic and financial questions about which he has some rather fantastic notions.
>
> In the United States Pound is well thought of as a poet but his writings on politics and economics are not taken seriously. Any initiative coming from him would not carry much weight.

Villari's advice that Pound's projects should not be taken up was communicated by the director general of propaganda services, Armando Koch, to Alessandro Pavolini, the minister for Popular Culture, and the poet's proposals were dropped.

Pound did not give up. On 25 April 1940 he presented himself at the Ministry for Popular Culture in Rome asking to see Armando Koch, and was told he was away. The official who did talk to him made a note for the director general of what Pound had had to say. He had brought a proposal for the twenty-five articles he had written for the *British-Italian Bulletin* at the time of the Ethiopian war to be republished. He had expressed concern that because of the overwhelming domination by Jews of the north American press and publishing houses 'our' voice was not being heard in the United States. Evidently Pound was still wanting to promote his idea of a review, and when the official objected that it would be expensive to keep one going in America Pound had replied, 'It wouldn't take a lot of dimes but a lot of intelligence.' Nothing came of this visit to the Ministry, and nothing came of a direct approach by Pound to Alessandro Pavolini in November 1940. But by then he was finding the propaganda section of Rome Radio more receptive to his offers of collaboration.

There was pressure to return to the United States. In November 1939 there had been a general notice from the Consular Service in Genoa that by order of the Department of State all US passports had to be validated by an American consular office prior to 1 January 1940. Then in May Secretary of State Cordell Hull sent a telegram to the US ambassador in Rome agreeing, even though neither Italy nor America were as yet involved in the war, 'that in the light of your conversation with Ciano today the time has come when you should strongly urge all Americans to leave Italy at the earliest possible opportunity'. The Embassy gave out that advice and offered assistance to US citizens unable to arrange or to pay for their passage back to America. There is some evidence that Pound considered leaving then, but nothing came of it.

When Italy entered the war on 10 June 1940, Pound decided that it was time to make his will, and did so a week later, declaring Mary Rudge to be his daughter, leaving everything to her, and providing for her to be his literary executor when she reached the age of 18 years.

Then the war began to have its effect. He was warned by Odon Por and by Olga Rudge that his letters were being opened by the censor. His bank account was frozen, and his sources of income were drying up along with his sources of information. (In October he was telling Kitasono, '*J.T.* my last remaining source of information re/ the U/S. I don't even know whether Jas/ has got out the Am/ edtn/ 52/71 Cantos.') Payments from England had been stopped, so that he was receiving nothing for his writings from there, and Dorothy's income was withheld. Then the banks started refusing to cash dollar cheques. His only source of income from abroad was

WILL of Ezra Pound , of via Marsala I2/5 Rapallo
drawn this the I7th day of June, a.d. I940.

I, Ezra POUND, being sound of mind and body, hereby bequeathe all that I possess to Mary Rudge, daughter of Olga Rudge of 252 Calle Querini, S. Gregorio, Venice. The said Mary I declare to be my daughter.

Among the possessions to pass to the said Mary Rudge are counted all my manuscripts, all author's rights in my writings, both published and unpublished, all money in various bank accounts whether in Italy or elsewhere, all securities in safe deposit, wheresoever.

My personal effects, books, works of art (chiefly by Gaudier Brzeska) now at I2/5 via Marsala , Rapallo are to remain in possession of my wife, Dorothy, for her lifetime. My wife is aware of the nature of this will and has approved it. The will is in no sense to be taken as injurious to her as she and her son are otherwise provided for, by trust fund etc; and the money hereinbefore mentioned is a small amount in comparison with what she holds.

The aforesaid Mary Rudge is to act as my literary executor after she shall have attained the age of 18 years. If she be minor at the time of my death, her mother is to act as her trustee and guardian.

Given this the I7th day of June, a.d. ~~140~~ 1940, Era Fascista XVIII
in Rapallo

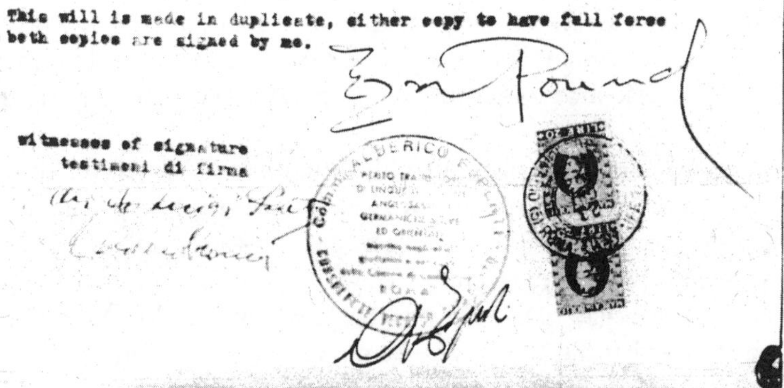

This will is made in duplicate, either copy to have full force both copies are signed by me.

Ezra Pound

witnesses of signature
testimoni di firma

WILL of Ezra Pound, of via Marsala 12/5 Rapallo drawn this the 17th day of June a.d. 1940.

the 'thin line of supplies' from his articles in *The Japan Times*, and with that there were frustrating complications. One payment of ¥97 should have yielded Ł450, equivalent to $20, but because of some slip yielded only Ł45 and had to be sent back for correction. Pound's total earnings from his dozen contributions probably brought in less than Ł1000. Worth more to him were the privileges that came with being made an accredited correspondent of *The Japan Times*, the journalist's card entitling him to reduced rail fares and membership of the press association.

The need to earn cash to support himself and Dorothy and Mary, and to help his parents when Homer's pension cheques from America became casualties of the war, must have been an urgent reason behind his proposals to the Ministry of Popular Culture and to Rome Radio. He was down in Rome in early August 1940 looking for work and when a chance turned up he jumped at it eagerly. 'De F/ asked me who cd/ translate yr/ Pol/ Econ/ Soc/', he wrote to Odon Por, meaning that De Feo, director of the Institute for Foreign Cultural Relations, was looking for someone to translate Por's recently published *Politica economia-sociale in Italia anno XVII–XVIII*, and Pound had said at once, 'EZ can'. A couple of weeks later he was in Rome again and wrote back to Olga Rudge in Siena, 'Waaal, mebbe papa bring home the bacon | not official but sum under consideration dieci mille'—10,000 lire that would have been. However Redman records that he received only 2,500 lire for the 200-page book, *Italy's Policy of Social Economics 1939/40 by Odon Por*, when it was published in Bergamo a year later.

There was no Palio in Siena that August due to the war, but there was an expectation that the war would be over in September, and then there would be a Victory Palio. Pound was encouraging Olga to think that Hitler 'will be in London by September 15th, after which 'spose the war will die down a bit'. The battle of Britain was at its height when he wrote that on 28 August, with the Luftwaffe attempting to wipe out the Royal Air Force as a prelude to the expected invasion of England. 'Londres delenda est', Dorothy Pound had written in her diary on the 17th, a few days after the air battle began, adapting ancient Rome's fulmination against Carthage—it was the Bank of England and the government that she particularly wished blasted out of existence. The German attack was indeed turned upon London from 7 September in bombing raids which continued daily through to 2 November. Dorothy, in Rapallo—Olga had made it clear that she would not be pleased if 'His legitime' were to be in Siena for the Scarlatti *settimana musicale*—was getting news of the Blitz from the radio and from Italian papers. She noted a report that the John Lewis department store in Oxford Street was in ruins, and could not imagine 'how Churchill & co. can continue'. There was also news of Italian bombing raids in Egypt and Libya, where the Italian forces were driving back the English, and this news she supposed was good, though she felt that even worse than the Blitz would be a telegram from Alexandria—presumably she was fearing for the safety of Omar's father. On 28 September, having heard the news of Japan's joining the Axis in a transmission from Berlin in German, Italian, and Japanese, she exclaimed 'Banzai!', and reflected, 'Japan will be the only other place to go to, or to take the children to'.

Pound meanwhile was in Siena with Olga, and Mary was with them there this year for the first time. Her mother had inspected her in Florence at the end of August after she had, to Olga's sense, gone 'back to the soil' in the Tyrol for the summer, and had decided that after all she was 'shaping nicely' and was now sufficiently 'pretty, well groomed, and graceful' to be seen in Siena's suave society. She was taken to the concerts and met the composers and musicians, and the distinguished Count Chigi, the founder and patron of the Academy of which her mother was the busy social secretary. The mornings were for study, Pound at his typewriter or reading Confucius in the original—'seem to remember a bit more each time'—and Mary working at Greek and Latin. In the afternoon they played tennis, Pound teaching Mary 'the correct basic movements with great perseverance'. 'When it was not tennis, it was history or art,' she recalled, 'He showed me Siena stone by stone, as he had done Venice.' And, 'As usual, he would make me describe in writing what we had seen.' In her memory the month was unshadowed by the war, with new things to learn and do, '*Apfelstrudel*... our great weakness', and the highlight Scarlatti's comic opera *Il trionfo dell'onore*.

Mary seems not to have registered at the time how shaken Pound was by the Three Power Pact signed in Berlin at the end of August. Japan was entering into a military alliance with Germany and Italy, and the three powers were promising to assist each other in the event of an attack by the United States. Intended to warn America to maintain its neutrality, the pact nevertheless reinforced the perception that that country was against the Axis and allied with its enemies. Evidently disturbed by this Pound returned at once to Rapallo and engaged in a flurry of arrangements to leave for America. His books and their most valued possessions—the Gaudier-Brzeska and Brancusi sculptures, the Wyndham Lewis drawings and paintings, the Dolmetsch clavichord—were to be taken care of by the degli Uberti family 'for as long as you are gone'. Before the end of the month Ubaldo degli Uberti wrote that the books were in his son's study in Genoa, and the rest of the property was 'in Rome: via Chelini 16'. About 4 October Pound went from Rapallo to join Olga and Mary in Venice—'Our last holiday in Venice', Mary recalled. It was cold, there was an air of gloom and impending austerity, the foreigners to whom Olga usually leased her small house had all left, and 'Babbo did not stay very long'. He went on to Rome to make the travel arrangements—it would have to be by flying-boat since surface sailings to the United States had ceased. He obtained a letter dated 'October 9, 1940' from the American Consul General to the Consul of Spain in Rome:

Sir and dear Colleague:

Mr. Ezra Pound, bearer of American passport No. 121, issued by the American Consulate General at Genoa, Italy, on December 9, 1937, and his wife, Mrs. Dorothy Pound, bearer of American passport No. 963, issued by the American Consulate General at Genoa, Italy, on February 17, 1937, desire to return to the United States, traveling via Spain and Lisbon.

Mr. and Mrs. Pound have made arrangements to leave Lisbon on the 'Yankee Clipper', on the first available date.

Any courtesy you may be able to extend to Mr. and Mrs. Pound in expediting the granting of a transit visa for Spain will be appreciated.

The fact that the original letter, with its file reference, '811.1—Pound, Ezra and Dorothy', and the signature of Graham H. Kemper, American Consul General, was still among Pound's papers after the war, must mean that it was never presented at the Spanish Consulate in Rome. There were no seats to be had on the Clippers flying from Lisbon, so Pound was told at the American Express office, or none just then. He dashed off a note to his father on Friday 11 October, 'all vurry interestin' = but also wearing to nerves./nothing very clear yet & several people wanting clipper passages.' He wrote the same day to Olga, 'I don't think I can get you a clipper reservation until Am. Ex. has yr. passport. The Portagoos visa waits till transport from Portugal is arranged.' To that he added, 'He don't want 'em to be on two sides of a blinkin ocean fer indefinite.' Presumably he had obtained a letter from the American Consulate on behalf of Olga Rudge and her daughter Mary Rudge, and another on behalf of his parents. There had been some difficulty or delay over Mary's passport application, and Pound had said to her that her 'legal status and citizenship would be set right as soon as we were able to get to America', but he did not mention that as a problem now. On the Saturday he wrote to Olga, 'niente sino al 14 novembre', nothing before 14 November. On the Monday, 14 October, he bought American Express dollar travellers cheques to the value of $1,390, having raised the money by selling an investment bond into which he had put his *Dial* award in 1928. But then on the same day he sent a telegram, 'Non vado in America—tornerò a Rapallo', not going America—returning Rapallo. He followed that up with a letter: 'Thank gawd thazz over . . . the clippah don't take nobody more till Decembah-middle, cause it's behind with the mail... He ain't been so glad about anything for a long while.' Olga too was glad, since she had not wanted to go by the expensive Clipper 'unless necessary', and it still did not 'feel like a war here'. At the end of the month he told Kitasono about the 'great excitements', 'but Clipper won't take anything except mails until Dec. 15, so am back here at the old stand/ Thank god I didn't get as far as Portugal and get STUCK there.'

Being back at the old stand meant applying again to the Ministry, this time to its Radio Department. He sent in a sample script on 9 November, offering to go down to Rome 'at once if you telegraph, and carry on for at least six brief talks of this sort, or register 'em on discs'. In the script he dramatized his situation in a folksy idiom which he believed would get his talk over to ordinary Americans. He had been driven to the radio, he implied,

having tried at the last moment in the flurry subsequent to the three Power Pact to get 'home' by Clipper, and found it, i.e. Clipper, entirely full of escaping diamond merchants, secret (more or less) agents, delayed mail etc. to such degree that no simple and private Americans could find place....

Of course this isn't the first time I have approached (approached is the right word) the microphone. Shortly after they started short wave to America, that is several years ago, I came down here and said a few words about Major Douglas Social Credit Scheme: forget whether Bible Bill had bruk loose in Alberta. BUT the boys here didn't tell my friends I was going to speak, so I think my audience consisted of one young lady on Broadway. Then again I came down here again last year and suggested that as it cost 30 cents per letter, it would convenience me to use the air in communicating with several etc. Well the Ministro looked at me careful and said in perlite words to the effect that: Ez, or probably he said 'Mio Caro Signore' if you think you can use OUR air to monkey in America's INTERNAL politics you got another one comin'. Then by the end of SeptemBAH this year 1940 I knew so little about America that even I, with my perennial urge to utter, didn't know what I wanted to tell brother Mencken, and the distinguished H. Fish, let alone the effete licherati. I then said NO, lemme git onto that Clipper and SEE what is doin and bigod somebody went and sold the rock of ages (i.e., Ligget and Meyer's bond) so I could pay fer a clipper passage, which WAS NOT, and ain't yet, at least not unless the American Express Co. is a liar. They said—and charged me telegraph costs to Lisbon—'Nuts, not till Dec. 15', which is, or was, no use to Ezry.

The Ministry considered the script and replied in polite form that it was not able at present to make use of his writing on their American Programs. Pound would persist, feeling the need to talk to America and needing money, and the Ministry would change its mind and grant him his ill-fated wish.

2 : A Dutifully Dissident Exile, 1941

Interviewer: What did you write during those years?
Pound: Arguments, arguments and arguments. Oh, I did some of the Confucius translation.
—*Paris Review* interview (1962)

'I will BUST i.e. EXPLODE if some use isn't made of me', Pound exclaimed in early January 1941 to Camillo Pellizi. He wanted to be a 'Megaphone to shout out this or that to deaf americans'. Pellizi had had a hand in Pound's writing for the *British-Italian Bulletin* at the time of the Italian invasion of Abyssinia, being then professor of Italian at University College, London, and 'the boss' of the Italian Fascists there. He had remained on friendly terms with Pound, and now at once phoned Adriano Ungaro and Gabriele Paresce, the men in charge of foreign broadcasts, to assure them that they could safely take him on. An offer followed from the Ministry of Popular Culture on 18 January inviting Pound to collaborate in transmissions to North America and Great Britain, and by the 21st he was down in Rome recording talks to be broadcast on short wave to America and medium wave to Britain. A couple of days later he told Olga, 'made 2 discs yesterday . . . 9 discorsi in a fortnight'.

He was doing his duty, as he saw it, his duty as an individual, as a poet, and as an American citizen. He had been told by Senator Wheeler when he was in Washington 'trying to see if there was any way of staving off the war', that even Senators were powerless to prevent breaches of the Constitution by the President, and he had concluded that 'when the Senator cannot function, the duty . . . falls back onto the individual citizen'. That was why, he declared in a formal statement in 1958, 'when I got hold of a microphone in Rome, I used it'. At the time, as he was campaigning to get hold of it, he said in a letter to *Meridiano di Roma* that poets too had a part to play in the war. 'Whoever is unwilling to fight at this moment is no poet,' he trumpeted—'*Chi non vuol combattere in questo momento non è poeta.*' The radio would be his weapon. As for what he was fighting for, he would say that it was for the rights and liberty of the individual person. And since, as he saw it, 'the only defence against... tyranny lies in the education and discrimination of the individual', he would use the Fascist radio to combat his fellow Americans' ignorance of their own history, to confirm the widespread feeling that they should keep clear of Europe's war, and to empower them to stand up for themselves against the violations of their Constitution.

The Italian authorities were naturally puzzled and suspicious, and nevertheless remarkably tolerant of Pound's highly idiosyncratic broadcasting. Enquiries into his acceptability had been made when he first directly approached them about radio work in November 1940. The Washington Embassy had been telegraphed for information about the 'well-known American writer, presently residing in San Remo' (*sic*), and similar telegrams had been sent to the Ministries of Foreign Affairs, of the Interior, and of War. The replies came back only after the first set of Pound's talks had been transmitted, those beginning on 23 January. The Ministry of the Interior had no reservations concerning Pound's attitudes and intentions. The Embassy reported at the end of February that during his 1939 visit to America Pound had 'displayed his friendly feelings for Fascism and granted courageous interviews'; moreover, his 'recent broadcasts from Italy were [the] subject of vital interest and considered to be very efficacious'. They had been asked specifically about his 'racial background', and gave the assurance that 'notwithstanding his Biblical name, he is of Aryan race'. A week or so after receiving that report the Inspector for Broadcasting and Television informed the Chief of Cabinet of the Ministry of Popular Culture, Celso Luciano, that he intended to 'entrust Ezra Pound with the wording of at least five conferences per month besides the drawing up of two political notes each week'—these latter would have been for others to use. He was thinking of paying him a monthly sum because in that way 'a greater number of conversations and political notes would be had and his useful suggestions could be used to the advantage of a greater efficiency of our propaganda for North America'. However the Ministry of War warned at the end of March that Pound might have ulterior motives—it was known that he was associated with the American Consulate in Genoa in buying English books to be sent to British subjects interned in Italy, and during a recent trip to Rome he had had 'a long interview with the American ambassador'. On those grounds the Ministry of War judged that Pound's offer of collaboration should be rejected, and Luciano in his turn urgently advised that no further use should be made of Pound. In spite of that, after a brief break, he was back on the air. From time to time after that 'some high-ranking personality' would ask, 'What does this man want? Can we be absolutely sure that he is not using a code system in his talks? That he is not a spy?', and Pellizi would give the assurance that so far as he could tell Pound was no spy.

The simple answer to 'What does this man want?' would have been, to communicate with America. His isolation irked him. In November 1940 he had sounded off about it to Ibbotson—

> Is it conceivable that in any other damnd country on earth a man cd/ get thru the work I am KNOWN to have got thru and find himself at my time of life (54 not being infancy) with no means of communicatin' wiff his com/damn/patriots save by private letter.

After his first eight talks had aired Pound wrote to Villari that he hoped they would be continued, since 'This is my only way of communicating with my friends in the U.S. without loss of five or eight weeks'. He drafted a note to be sent from the Ministry to his friends and correspondents in America giving details of the frequencies and times of the broadcasts; but it was not his friends that he was wanting to speak to so much as the mass audience radio could reach. In *Guide to Kulchur* he had noted that in the radio age government could be, even must be, by radio: 'Lenin won by Radio, Roosevelt used it, Coughlin used it as a minority weapon.' And Mussolini and Hitler, he might well have added, used it to powerful effect. Very likely he regarded radio simply as a medium for speaking to the masses. He had never owned a personal radio until he noticed a small medium wave portable Natalie Barney had with her when she stopped over in Rapallo in March 1940, and he was so appalled, and then so taken with it, that she presented him with one. He was appalled by it as a hellish invention likely to disperse and destroy the inner life of the individual—those 'personae now poked into every bleedin' 'ome... smearing the mind of the peapull' and reducing them still further into a 'state of passivity'. It was only because he was 'the last survivin' monolith who did not have a radio in the 'ome' that he had been able 'to do 52/71'. And there was that 'double sense of the blessedness of silence when the damn thing is turned off'. Yet 'the devil box' that was a menace to his own meditations could allow him to get at the minds of others, of a whole mass of others, and to make them think. He would use it 'to induce [the auditor] to listen to historic information in order to understand Fascism and how to beat the financiers'.

Viewing radio as a dramatic medium—'what drammer or teeyater *wuz*, radio is', he remarked to his dramatist friend Ronald Duncan—Pound set out to assume a dramatic, even histrionic, persona. 'Nothing solemn or formal will hold the American auditor', he explained to Paresce, 'If I don't sound a bit cracked and disjointed, they will merely twirl the button and listen to the next comic song, dance or ballyhoolah "Soapopry". Hence the indications of American dialects etc. in the spelling.' After his first broadcasts he asked Ungaro, should he 'compose scripts with calm and detail | or let the anger boil?' He had been drafting 'a half-dozen little speeches' back in Rapallo, and 'right now I "boiled" | in short such a rage as to be almost indecipherable'. Anger and rage would be one staple of his radio persona, as it had always been of his agitprop prose, but he would learn that he could not afford to let it be 'indecipherable' over the airwaves. In May 1941 Dorothy advised him from Rapallo (in a letter stamped by the Commissione di Censura in Rome): 'Yr. discorso came over last night quite clear. Slowness v.g. as you have lots of matter. I think it would be better a little *less* loud: (not necessarily less vehement). The loudness reverberates sometimes.... I only hope some of the s. of b.'s heard it. The violence quite apparent.' 'I don't so much write as I roar,' he told Laughlin, but 'I reckon I was a little too loud last night . makes the diaphram, diaphragm how the hell is it spelt, rattle'—that would have been the diaphragm in his microphone. Seeking guidance as from a fellow Axis propagandist he wrote to William Joyce, an Irishman broadcasting to Britain from Berlin—he became known as 'Lord Haw-Haw' in mockery of his forced English accent—saying he had been hearing his transmissions daily and 'shd be glad to profit by experienced criticism'. Joyce, however, would not presume to criticize: 'Your methods are unique,' he told Pound, 'nobody could imitate them successfully'. Well, said Pound, though it was a 'New technique for Unkle Ez', quite different from a poem since the talk 'has to take effect NOW or never', still 'I think I have got my voice right at last'. The next day he confessed to Olga, the concert performer, 'am developing prima-donnitis'. And in October Dorothy, after hearing a broadcast of his 'This War on Youth', told him that the word 'youth' had not carried well, but the talk 'Otherwise came very clearly', and it had been 'a good plan to change your method every little while—gentle, suave; vituperative, desperate'. At times Pound was content to cast himself as what Gertrude Stein had called him,'an explainer'—a 'village explainer' had been her actual barb.

His talks were not, are not, easy listening. In the recordings made of them by the United States Federal Communications Commission the voice is often harsh and over-insistent, and that effect is sometimes compounded by static and distortion. The voice can be made to screech or blur, and words, even whole phrases or sentences, can be lost. There is also the sense that Pound felt he must project his voice through the crackling aether and across oceans and continents to reach an unknowable audience. There is no intimacy, as if he imagined his voice issuing from loudspeakers in public places, and not from radios in families' kitchens and living rooms. At times what is being said is nearly unintelligible and only the sustaining rhythm comes through, reminding that this was after all a poet speaking. It makes for painful listening, and the talks could never have been seductive or persuasive even at their clearest.

Pound's most devoted listeners, possibly his only regular listeners, were the FCC monitors charged with recording and transcribing the talks, and the errors in their transcriptions—such as 'Céline' being heard as 'Stalin', 'Lenin' as 'seven', 'to debauch its currency' as 'to divorce its currency'—are one indication of how such listeners as there were might have been baffled as to what Pound was on about. In mid-1941 a bank teller in Rutherford did make out '"Something about ol' Doc Williams of Rutherford",' and when Williams heard about it he wanted to know '"What the hell right has he to drag me into his dirty messes?".' In his fury Williams 'lashed out at' Pound, venting all his old antipathies in an article headed 'Ezra Pound: Lord Ga-Ga!' He was even more infuriated when some time later the FBI called on him with questions about his association with Pound, and was he a loyal American citizen, and was he prepared to testify that the voice on their recordings was Pound's?

The fact that Pound was talking on the radio was being noticed in America, mostly negatively. As early as April 1941 Pound was telling Ungaro, 'I see by a Chicago rag that I am "charged with fascism" and that critics have been trying to defend me, but that the label must stick.' At the same time Laughlin was telling Pound, 'Yr politics have cooked yr revered goose to a point you wd. not believe.' Later in the year he was more specific, 'You are pretty much disliked for your orations. Yr name in general might be said to aspire but not attain to the dignity of mud.'

His name was mud with the State Department. In April all United States passports were withdrawn and had to be replaced. 'New passports are free & time rather short to get 'em', Pound wrote from Rome to Dorothy, 'I think you better go to Genova and get yours. I will try to get mine in Venezia.' Passport No. 3154 was issued to him there on 4 April 1941, valid for six months to 4 October 1941. Then on 4 June Henry H. Balch, the American Consul General in Genoa, wrote to the State Department concerning 'Political Activities of Ezra POUND', and suggested that 'it may be desired to use the discretionary power of the Secretary of State to refuse Mr. Pound further passport facilities for continued residence abroad'. Someone in the State Department noted 'Yes' alongside that suggestion, and on 12 July a telegram was sent from the Department to the Embassy in Rome to the effect that Pound's 'Passport should be limited for immediate return to the United States'. This appears to have been in reaction to his broadcasts, and it meant that he was expected to 'go home' by early October and to remain there. It is not clear when Pound learnt about this instruction—'Jus italicum', an article in *Meridiano di Roma* in August, may have been a response to it. Then at the end of September he went down to Rome from Siena rather suddenly with the intention, his daughter gathered, of arranging to visit America. But there was to be no visit to America, 'Things were too complicated', she was told, 'The officials at the American Consulate had been very nasty.' And indeed a State Department memorandum dated 11 October 1941 by J. Wesley Jones, an official just back from Rome, reported that Pound was 'still in Italy broadcasting his views', and suggested that his name might be added to the 'list of pseudo Americans living in Italy'. That may have been simply because he would not 'go home' on the State Department's terms. It is likely though that Pound had attempted to make George Wadsworth, the Chargé d'Affaires, understand that his relation to his homeland was not as simple as the official mind would have it, and that the exchange of irreconcilable views had become heated.

In his 'Jus italicum' article Pound had made a serious attempt to square his US citizenship with his commitment to Fascist Italy. He thought it neither permissible nor possible to change nationality—for better and for worse he was and must remain an American citizen. To renounce his citizenship would be 'il gran rifiuto', the ultimate cowardice of denying the possibility of his country's rebirth. However, 'when I swear loyalty to the American constitution, as I do every time I renew my passport (even if the Consul forgets to require it), I swear fidelity to a government which does not exist'—to a *Constitutional* United States existing for now in the mind only. And because his own country was in such disorder he was not able to live there, and was instead self-exiled in Italy. In Italy, being alien-born, he could not claim citizenship. All that he sought was the civil status accorded in imperial Rome to aliens who came to it with a will to make themselves in some way useful. For example, he might facilitate relations between his country of origin and the one in which he was resident. In any case, he should give some positive and active proof of willingness to contribute; and in return he should be granted an exile's right of residence and the right and possibility of doing useful and honest work. So far Pound might have been seeking no more than work and residence permits. The fact that Italy was at war, however, if not yet with the United States, put his willingness to be of use in a very different light, and Pound did indicate a readiness to join in on its side. But that did not mean 'a divided allegiance', he insisted, because what Italy was fighting for, in his special view of the war, was the same thing as an American loyal to the Constitution should fight for—their common enemy was the financial system which had undone the American republic and had undone the European democracies. To further justify his position Pound cited Lincoln's saying to Congress during the Civil War, 'I have two great enemies, the army of the South before me, and the financial set-up behind—and the latter is the worse enemy.' That was the perennial enemy against whom he was prepared to fight alongside Fascism, as a true American and for a reformed United States.

The Chargé d'Affaires and his officials, if invited to view Pound's case in this very special, very individual light, might well have lost patience and dismissed the argumentative patriot as a 'pseudo American'. In his own mind, though, Pound was being true to his oath of loyalty in the only way he knew how in the situation he found himself in.

While he could not persuade the American authorities to see things in his way he was to be granted more or less all he asked for from the Italian authorities. In September 1941 Dorothy was warned by the Carabinieri in Rapallo that foreigners must not leave their residence without first notifying them and obtaining a travel permit. Pound, then in Siena, was anxious about having failed to do the right thing, and had to be calmed by Dorothy, and told 'just apply next time you go away'. In January 1942, with the United States now at war with the Axis, he applied for permission for himself and his family to remain in Italy for the duration of the war, and this was formally granted by the Italian Supreme Command on 26 January. He applied at the same time through the Ministry of Foreign Affairs to the Finance Ministry for exemption from the financial restrictions applied to foreigners—the family's bank accounts and safe-deposit boxes were blocked just after America's entry into the war in December 1941. In this matter the authorities at first granted only partial relief: the accounts were blocked again in April 1942; in September he was allowed to withdraw just 1,000 lire per month for living expenses; and the restrictions were finally lifted only in January 1943. His right to work for Rome Radio, however, appears not to have been in question.

From January through to December of 1941 Pound went down to Rome for several days each month to record his scripts and to contribute in other ways to the propaganda activities of Ente Italiano Audizione Radiofoniche (EIAR), staying always at Albergo d'Italia in Via Quattro Fontane. He was officially employed as a script writer and political and cultural commentator; in addition he freely offered suggestions and advice for broadcasts by others. 'I got up from bed to send you two ideas,' begins one letter to Ungaro written at 5 a.m. on an April morning. Redman, who cites that letter, concludes from his survey of the correspondence that at this time 'Coming up with ideas and approaches for Italian propaganda dominated his thinking.' He would take his typewriter with him to Rome so that he could work on scripts there as well as in Rapallo. In May he was turning out talks under pressure and told Dorothy, 'Looks like he wuz to emit twice weekly'. By his own account he gave 'between 70 and 100 talks on the radio' in that year. His letters to Dorothy through the summer convey the excitement of being kept very busy with his talks, as well as with writing articles for Italian journals, and with being translated into Italian—Signora Olivia Rossetti Agresti's translation of *What is Money For?* appeared in *Meridiano di Roma* in July. Part of the excitement was the feeling of being highly useful and of getting his own ideas across.

The pay, according to the files of the Ministry of Popular Culture, was 150 lire for writing each script, and a further 200 lire for recording it (350 lire would have been worth about 17 US dollars at that time). The money would come through to him, after a complicated and often retarded bureaucratic process, at the Rapallo Tax Office, but would not have to go through his recurrently frozen bank account. He reckoned that up to 1 December 1941 he had earned 16,400 lire, equal to nearly $1,000. That was evidently sufficient to support himself and Dorothy and Mary, and to help out Olga Rudge and his parents.

He was collaborating with a motley group of people at Rome Radio, many of them, according to someone who worked there, eccentrics, 'so that Pound did not stand out'. The editor of 'The American Hour' was George ('Giorgio') Nelson Page who had renounced his American for Italian citizenship. Another contributor was an Englishman, James ('Giacomo') Strachey Barnes, who described himself as 'chronicler and prophet of the Fascist Revolution'. The Princess Troubetzkoi, born Amélie Rives in Virginia and Russian by marriage, was a novelist and playwright—'her special kind of propaganda consisted in making up optimistic sketches of life in Italy which she transmitted to Russia and to England'. Signora Agresti, born in England to the son of an Italian émigré and herself Italian by marriage, was an altogether more serious character than the rest, and a close friend of Pound's. He was always conscious that Dante Gabriel Rossetti was her uncle and Ford Madox Ford her cousin, but she was distinguished in her own right as an economically literate intellectual who had helped set up the International Institute for Agriculture which later became the FAO. She was a committed supporter of Mussolini's economic programme. Then there were the Fascist officials, several of whom Pound would see socially while in Rome, among them his friends Camillo Pellizi and Luigi Villari.

In the autumn and winter of 1941–2 Pound also frequented a very different circle of Fascists, one made up of idealistic younger writers and intellectuals who dreamed of a Fascism that would be true to Mussolini's founding vision, much as Pound himself dreamed of an American democracy that would be true to its founders' vision. He was introduced to these 'Fascists in crisis' or 'dissident Fascists', as they regarded themselves, by his friend Odon Por who must have been in sympathy with them. They met at the home of Felice Chilanti, the editor of their journal *Domani* which had just been suppressed by Pavolini '"on orders from the Duce"'. Chilanti had written an article demanding to know the reasons for the war, and extracting from Mussolini's own writings and speeches 'the ideology of a war for social revolution, for the overthrow of the capitalist system and the creation of a new order free from plutocrats and usurers'. Another of the group 'had put our heated discussions of the treason of Italy's great capitalists into an editorial protesting their enrichment at the expense of our dying soldiers at the front'. They had blamed the plutocrats, 'the industrialists who sell the state cardboard shoes and tinfoil tanks', for having wanted war, and for the inevitable defeat brought upon Italy 'by the sordid souls of usurers and profiteers'. And Pavolini had said to Chilanti, '"We can't understand what it is you people want".' What they wanted, they explained to Pound, was 'an Italian society made up of equals'; and, in practical affairs, 'the capacity to produce good shoes, good cloth, blankets that keep you warm, airplanes that are swift and well-made; capacity to produce merchandise without the yoke of capitalist exploitation'. And all of this was to be achieved by re-establishing Mussolini 'in that proud ideology which he himself called "a civilization of labor"'.

Pound read their suppressed magazine, and listened, 'attentive and friendly', to the lively debates, occasionally saying 'sí, sí', 'yes, yes' to thoughts that were so close to his own. Once he suggested they read Confucius, and another evening he talked of Jefferson. To Chilanti, 'The very fact that he would visit us, join us, meant that he did not like the *Fascist Fascists*, the real Fascists'; it meant that 'he shared our disgust for the party hierarchs' stupidity and criminal activities'. Then in April 1942 Chilanti and his friends were all arrested, and he was sentenced to five years *confino*. Pound was shocked to be told they were all in prison when he next went to visit the group, and turned back down the stairs 'with the air of a fugitive', or so it seemed to Signora Chilanti. He had said to her, 'How can I bring myself to talk on the radio tomorrow night? What can I say, tomorrow?' In spite of that his habitual haranguing of America and England did continue, but after the war Chilanti found an echo in the *Pisan Cantos* of the dissident conversations Pound had listened to in his apartment—

> 'I would do it' (finish off Ciano) 'with a pinch of
> insecticide'
> said Chilanti's 12 year old daughter

Chilanti also associated with these conversations Pound's judgment upon the Fascist regime—

> and the dog-damn wop is not, save by exception,
> honest in administration any more than the briton is truthful
> Jactancy, vanity, peculation to the ruin of 20 years' labour

If Pound was forming that judgment already in 1941 and 1942 he did not share it then with his American and British listeners. Nor did he follow the example of his young Italian friends and declare himself explicitly a dissident American democrat, as he well might have done.

He did say, emphatically, in reaction to a New York critic's saying he had 'given himself to fascism', that he had NOT so *given* himself. He had simply insisted on 'the constructive elements in Fascism, and particular facts of the corporate state which deserved comparison with the best efforts of the Founders of the North American system'. He maintained that he was as a matter of fact defending the 'United States heritage' in his radio talks, that is, 'the beliefs of Washington, John Adams, Jefferson, Jackson, Van Buren and Lincoln', and those could not be 'laughed off as mere Fascist propaganda'. He was defending the Constitution as the basis of social justice and equity—of the state's 'capacity to give every man a square deal'. But he was against those who want war and who bring on war—by which he meant the loan sharks, the speculators in war material, the scarcity makers, the monopolists, and all such. He was especially against 'Churchill and company' as representing 'usury ... tyranny, oppression, greed, unrestricted exploitation of humanity'. And he was against Roosevelt taking the United States into Churchill's war against Germany, that being, he still maintained, a war against an honest concept of money.

There was not much that was new in these broadcasts. In his letter to William Joyce he mentioned that he had read 'What is Money For' over three evenings—though Dorothy was sure 'they did the third disc twice and omitted the first or else used it at a different hour'. Other previous writings he was drawing on included the article he had written for the Washington *Capitol Daily* during his 1939 visit, articles in issues of *Meridiano di Roma* which had been suppressed in the USA, and the 'Mensdorff letter' of 1928. And he kept 'hammering on parallels between our U.S. revolution of 1776 and the Axis fight against international Leihkapital etc.' What he was putting over was his own familiar propaganda, and his own fixed idea of the war. There is no evidence of his being subject to the dictation of the Fascist authorities. At the same time his talks were deeply coloured by what he was reading in the Axis press and hearing on the Axis radio. Moreover, in 'hammering on the Axis fight against international Leihkapital', and in constantly asserting that it was Jewish financiers behind Churchill and Roosevelt who were responsible for the war, Pound's propaganda was fully in accord with a major theme of Nazi propaganda.

It becomes remarkable that Pound hardly mentions the actual events of the ongoing war. In 1941 the Italian armies in North Africa were driven back by the British and the Australians and New Zealanders, and later reinforced by the German Afrika Corps which would prolong the desert war into 1943; German armies took Yugoslavia and Greece, after the Greeks had defeated the Italian 9th army; in June Hitler launched 'Operation Barbarossa' against Russia and by the end of the year his armies were besieging Leningrad and attacking Moscow. These were major developments in the most devastating war Europe had ever experienced, but for Pound the real war remained the perennial economic war, the war behind the war. And his real enemy was as ever the capitalists and their financial system, characterized as ever as Semitic. In one talk he might say, 'I propose to use the word KIKE regardless of race', but the word is inescapably racist and the prejudice infects most if not quite all the talks.

There are odd brighter moments: 'the idea that a man can own all that he can *use*' and 'may not own what he can't use'; the perfectly serious and wonderfully idealistic proposal that to secure peace in the Pacific the USA should give Japan the island of Guam in exchange for 'one set of color and sound films of the 300 best Noh dramas', these being of greater potential value to American civilization than any material wealth; the conviction that Siena's keeping on with its music week in 1941 regardless of the war was evidence 'that Italy is carrying ON. *La rivoluzione continua.*' Some talks were clear and cogent, such as the formal obituary for James Joyce in 1941, or the one with the title 'Consolidation' cited in a previous paragraph. In others the listeners would likely have been put off if not wholly alienated by the predominance of a hectoring or vituperative tone, of twisty language and out of focus perceptions, of half truths and ill-founded generalizations.

But the main effect of reading through the dozen broadcasts from 1941 included in Doob's selection—that is, just reading them on the page, not having them grate harshly on the ear—is a dispiriting sense of the futility of the effort and the awful waste of Pound's gifts. His profound idealism, his utopian intentions, his unshakeable vision of what makes for a good life and his uncompromising critique of what does not, his refusal to let the pressing actuality displace the deeper reality, all of this virtue is marred and undone by his blindness to the evil of Hitler's Nazism and to the necessity of opposing it, and by his inability to recognize that Mussolini's Fascist experiment had gone terminally wrong. And in the end, whatever he might say, the medium, the Fascist radio, was going to be *the* message for anyone who heard him.

Pound had not entirely lost touch with the wholly different mindset of his cantos and their striving toward a natural paradise. In a letter to Kitasono in February 1941, having mentioned that because of the war there would be no concerts that year in Rapallo—'the foreign subscribers are gone... no pianist / no public'—he gave him this image of music persisting in a private world:

> Stage, a room on the hill among the olive trees
> the violinist playing the air of Mozart's 16th violin sonata /
> then a finch or some bird that escapes my ornithology tried to
> counterpoint. all through in key

Of such marvellous moments Pound would build his paradise. He added, as if by way of putting ground under it, 'this is the season when the olives fall, partly with wind or rain / hail for a few minutes today | The impatient peasant rattles a bamboo in the olive twigs to get the olives down, but this is now against the regulations as they, the olives, are supposed to give more oil if they fall by themselves.'

Two or three weeks later Pound enclosed in a letter to Kitasono these more extensive 'Lines to go into Canto 72 or somewhere', just to show 'that I am not wholly absorbed in saving Europe by economics':

> Now sun rises in Ram sign.
> With clack of bamboos against olive stock
> We have heard the birds praising Janequin
> And the black cat's tail is exalted.
> The sexton of San Pantaleo plays '*è mobile*' on his carillon
> '*Un' e duo... che la donna è mobile*'
> In the hill tower (videt et urbes)
> And a black head under white cherry boughs
> Precedes us down the *salità*.
> The water-bug's mittens show on the bright rock below him.

The first line recalls how the ancient Chinese observed the seasons, as rendered from *Li Ki* in canto 52; while the rest is from Pound's own immediately present world of Sant'Ambrogio. In a note sketching a possible outline for this decad he had written, 'LXXII Erigena | 73–80 =

paralleli 52–61 | [81 Usura?]', indicating an intention to make the initial theme 'omnia quae sunt Lumina sunt', and to have the following cantos correspond in some way to the China cantos. The nearest correspondence would be his taking up again the leading theme of those cantos, 'the abundance of nature | with the whole folk behind it', only transposing it now into the terms of his own known world. That would be the implication of the Latin aside, '(videt et urbes)', a phrase from the opening lines of the *Odyssey* where Odysseus is introduced as a wandering exile who has seen the cities and learnt the minds of men, and whose story will tell of his world as he himself has experienced it. 'The clack of bamboos' is the sound of the olive harvest in the groves on the hillside terraces of Sant'Ambrogio; 'the birds praising Janequin' would be responding to Olga Rudge's playing his 'Song of the birds' on her violin there; the popular song from *Rigoletto* played by the sexton on his church bells would be sounding from the square tower of San Pantaleo visible half a kilometre away across the hillside; the *salita* is the hill path leading down to Rapallo which Pound must have walked nearly every other day; and the water-bug, seen with such clarity, could be on the stream the path crosses at its foot. These sounds and sights combine to evoke, responsively and with good humour, a local peace and abundance, such as China's farmers celebrated in canto 53 as they sang '"Peace and abundance bring virtue."'

A handful of other jottings of lines for cantos from this time try out combinations of ancient and contemporary notations of natural abundance and wisdom. One of the longer fragments invokes the Greek and Roman 'field gods' after Ovid's *Fasti*, a calendar of country festivals and their rites:

First Jove and the earth our mother
          second the sun and moon
...
that are the measure of time
Jove and our mother, that are the fountain of all things
Ceres and Liber third
Flora et Regibus
          Flora ac Regibus   Robigalia
               lest blight come lest flower come not
Athene, and Cythera, of the olive, of gardens
               to Jove   the Vinalia
     to these the wine feasts.
Lympham ac bonum eventum
                    without him frustrata est   non cultura
and without water all things are dry   these are the field gods

In another fragment the thud of the mill on the ground floor under Olga Rudge's apartment as it crushes the olive stones is connected with Persephone, with her Tiresias 'who even dead yet hath his mind entire', and then with her spring blossoming. Another note—marked as a possible opening for a canto—is still more explicit about the vital function of mind in the process: sun's 'Fire causeth not beauty, nor the earth, but NOUS | knowing the handiwork'. That would be the knowing of a Tiresian mind fully conscious of the sustaining processes of the living world. There are also stillness of mind 'here in Tigullio', and 'April birds thru the stillness'.

Stillness against his unstillness: a stillness entering the mind as it contemplates its immediate world, against its unstillness when grinding out wordy propaganda. There was a middle ground in translation. In the summer of 1941 Pound translated a novella called *Moscardino* written by Enrico Pea and first published in 1921. He did this, he told Laughlin, 'fer the sake of bein' literary amidst mundane excitements'; but he also saw it, or so he told Dorothy, as having 'propagandist scope'. This is how Pea's story of rural life in a region of Italy in the nineteenth century begins in Pound's translation:

> The Signora Pellegrina went into mourning at once, she put on black silk, put a black hem on her nightgowns, lowered the blinds, and lit a lamp on the wide linen-cupboard.
>
> She was of high lineage and had come in for the shares of two sisters who had gone into convents and passed away early, but her husband had been a poor hand at guiding the domestic economy and had left little either of her good heritage or of his own. He had been honorary physician to the Confraternity of the Misericordia, and High Chamberlain of the Church of San Lorenzo; he had had, therefore, a magnificent funeral.
>
> The Signora Pellegrina showed no sign of grief at his passing. She said: Well out of it; you are.

She then tells her three sons to divide the remnant of the estate, shuts herself in her room and turns mute. One son, being sickly and retarded, had been intended for the priesthood, to secure a stipend, but was thrown out of the seminary. A second son was ugly and ape-like. And the third, who in his youth had run away and gone venturing, and who 'had planted the liberty tree in the town square', couldn't stand either of them and had fits of terrifying rage. All three hang about the house doing nothing. The third son seduces the servant girl from the mountains, marries her, and then, she being a truly beautiful woman, goes mad with jealousy, and is carried off in a strait-jacket to the asylum. At that Signora Pellegrina throws herself out of her window, a suicide, barred from the last rites. The beautiful servant will die slowly of consumption. And so the tale goes on, with a naturalism to outdo Zola; yet there is so much sympathetic imagination, and such freedom and invention in the telling that the grim events appear at times surreal, at times dreamlike or lyrical. The writing does merit Pound's high regard.

All the same, what propaganda value could he have seen in this unedifying image of country life where the only rites and customs have to do with property and death? It is so far removed from his own paradise of natural abundance as to be hellish—and that must have been its value to his mind. *Moscardino* can be read as a ruthlessly clear-eyed picture of how life was in rural Italy before Mussolini, with the last inheritors of the land-owning class impoverished and degenerate, their natural impulses weak and thwarted, dragging out their feeble unproductive existences while sucking the life-blood from their peasant servants, under a moribund church and with death the dominant note. It was an Italy, one might well argue, much in need of the Fascist revolution. But the book, and the translation, do not argue, do not go in for propaganda. They operate as literature must, showing how things were, beyond argument, and allowing the reader to contemplate them in imagination, beyond argument. Translating *Moscardino* must have been restful for Pound's over-excited mind.

After *Moscardino* he turned to translating Confucius into Italian with the assistance of Alberto Luchini, the latter putting Pound's Italian draft into 'real Italian'. The first chapter of the *Ta Hio* (which he had learnt to call *Ta S'eu*), the part supposed to be Confucius' own text, appeared in *Meridiano di Roma* as 'Studio integrale' at the end of October. He told Cummings that he had 'propsed a nedition on a Monday, and got it approved on A Tuesday, and had the first chapter of chink in the zincogaphers on Wednesday', and thence it had gone straight into print—'though the accompanying traduction contains one bad error | mine | one oversight also mine | and one gawdawful emendation of me colleague . me unbeknownst'. There was a still worse error. Confucius' text was copied onto the zinc plates from Legge's edition of *The Great Learning* in four blocks of ideograms just as they appeared on his pages, and these blocks were then distributed at random and in the wrong order through the two pages of Pound's article, thus making a nonsense of the 'bilingual edtn' he intended.

Pound had for some time been seeking to introduce the doctrine of Confucius into Fascism as he understood it. He declared in *Meridiano di Roma* in May 1941 that the *Ta S'eu*, as the Confucian 'digest par excellence of statal philosophy', should naturally form part of 'the educative program of Fascism'. 'Fascism needs such masterworks,' he added. Evidently his translation was intended as a constructive offering, but also as a warning.

'Studio Integrale was done as a warning to Muss/', he would tell Mary, 'allusion so clear that Monotti joked: you for the confino'. And indeed the terms in which he was recommending Confucius' doctrine were quite un-Fascistic, even anti-Fascist. The basic principle, in his account in *Meridiano di Roma*, was the self-responsibility of the individual: the proper running of the state depended upon the individual, the responsible individual, necessarily, but still the individual; and while the whole nation of individuals should act responsibly, still the health and welfare of the nation had to follow from the good behaviour of its individual members. This was the Confucian idea, as Pound had affirmed it when he first translated the *Ta Hio* in 1927, but it was rather far from the Fascist idea. For Fascism the collective, the corporate state under its leader, came first, and the individual should exist and act only in accord with the state. Putting the individual first was condemned as bourgeois heresy; the more so that the truly self-responsible individual, following his own imperatives, might well question the state's claim to be always right—and then have to be suppressed in the interests of the state, like Chilanti's group of dissident Fascists. It was a quixotic delusion of Pound's, a projection onto Fascism of his own highly developed sense of individual responsibility, to imagine that Fascism valued, or could be brought to value, the individual consciousness of how things should be.

Yet, as with Quixote, the delusion did not altogether invalidate the effort. To affirm the importance of the individual person in Fascist Italy, however ineffectually, must have been worth something. And Pound had other motivations. He was concerned to foster the habit of accurate perception necessary for the right conduct of the individual and thence of the state. As he recommended the Confucian ethic he recommended also, as the cure for the disastrous human tendency to lose sight of the particular in the general case by relying on statistics and abstract categories, the ideogrammic method with its discipline of concentrating upon concrete phenomena and the precise workings of things. Beyond that, because 'the life and thought of Confucius unfold in a world of light and flowing water', Pound felt the Confucian universe to be in sympathy with that of Scotus Erigena, and to be a universe of light such as Cavalcanti immersed himself in before writing 'Donna mi prega'. In 1941 he must have believed, or wanted to believe, that such enlightenment was still possible and could have effect in Mussolini's Italy.

For Pound's daughter Mary that year from July to December became a mostly idyllic time as she looked back on it in her memoir. Because of the war she would not be returning to the convent in Florence, and in high summer, just turned 16, she was with her foster family in the high Tyrol delighting in 'Freedom, joyfulness and common sense after a lot of restrictions, mannerisms and artificialities'. 'Working in the fields once more was fun,' and 'Young people flocked to our house and there was much singing and music and I loved dancing with the young men in their Tyrolean costumes or *Alpenjäger*.' It seemed unimportant that the young men were being called up and were singing 'Deutschland über Alles', the Tyrol having opted for Germany.

In September she joined her mother in Siena for the music festival. She remembered their being invited often to lunch or dinner with Count Chigi, who 'still had supplies of wine, oil, wheat and vegetables' from his estate, and how 'on our leaving the palazzo the butler would hand us a neatly wrapped... loaf of homemade bread'. 'A threatening feeling of hunger seemed to be hanging over us,' she recalled. When Pound was with them he would spend most of the day banging the typewriter. The highlight of the festival that year was Vivaldi's oratorio *Juditha Triumphans*, described by Pound in one of his radio talks as 'a musical whoop in two parts, to celebrate the retaking of Corfu from the Turks in 1715'. He heard it twice, 'once from the top centre, and once in a box hangin' over the orchestry, once for the whole and once for the details'. That was to be their last music festival in Siena. Her mother's position as secretary of the Academy was in doubt, because she was an American, and the Count's 'world was being dispersed' by the war.

After the uncertainty in October about Pound's going to America, and about whether she and her mother were to go with him, Mary settled into her mother's Casa 60 at Sant'Ambrogio. At first it was not easy. 'I will have to pass you off as my cousin,' her mother said. 'It will be easier for you to get along on the Italian identity card'. She was anxious about being a foreigner, fearing 'reports to the police' and having their ration cards taken away. Then there was her strict regime for them both: alarm at 6.00 a.m., exercises, wash in cold water drawn from the deep well—and Mary 'hated pulling up that endless rope with the bucket jerking against the walls and spilling'. 'But soon I came to see the logic and the beauty of my new life: strict discipline and routine left more freedom for one's thoughts.'

The house inside, to Mary's sense, was white and empty, furnished with light; its four rooms had polished red brick-tile floors, and windows that looked over olive and cherry trees to the sea and the bay of Rapallo. A table and chairs, a desk, a bookcase, were of Pound's making. In the kitchen there was an iron funnel over charcoal, though her mother preferred cooking with pine-cones, and there was a row of dark brown clay pots on the broad mantelpiece. Nowhere any junk or clutter. As Stella Bowen had observed,

Olga 'had almost no material possessions, but her well-proportioned rooms furnished with big rectangles of sunshine had a monastic air which was highly conducive to the making of music'. 'In a sense', Mary would reflect, 'our life too had become a work of art: nothing superfluous, nothing wasted, nothing sloppy.'

Her mother would practise the violin all morning, while Mary continued her studies. She was having lessons twice a week in Latin and French from Father Desmond Chute, a learned and reclusive aesthete; improving her English by reading Jane Austen and Hardy and Henry James with her mother; and Pound had set her to translate Hardy's *Under the Greenwood Tree* into Italian, and to learn to recite and translate the *Odyssey* a few lines at a time. Her life centred around her father's visits, 'for he brought with him a dimension of—no, not stillness, but magnitude, momentum'. He made her feel 'that work, learning, was worthwhile, exciting'.

Pound walked up to Sant'Ambrogio every other day, sometimes for lunch, sometimes staying for dinner, and Mary would have two to three hours instruction from him. He would read them his radio speeches, and then read the five new lines of her next assignment from the *Odyssey*. And it seemed to Mary that 'he possessed two voices: one angry, sardonic, sometimes shrill and violent for the radio speeches; one calm, harmonious, heroic for Homer, as though he were taking a deep refreshing plunge into the wine-coloured sea after a scorching battle'. There would be a moment for tea, camomile or mint, whatever one could get; and after the *tisane* always some Mozart or Bach or Vivaldi. Then she would walk down the hill path with her father, a time for discussion. In retrospect Mary would regret that 'The humility and the gentleness, the fun and efficiency of Pound's behaviour in his family circle is too often overshadowed by his public imperatives.'

One of Pound's more enlightened public imperatives at this time was a campaign to alleviate the food shortages by increasing the cultivation of peanuts and soya beans. He began in August 1941 by obtaining some seeds in Rome and instructing Dorothy to plant them in pots of sandy earth on their rooftop terrace to see how they would do—he hoped to encourage the local peasants to grow them. Dorothy noted in her diary on 15 September that she had 'planted peanut and soya—planted finger deep', but there is no record of their germination. (She did note, on 11 November, 'HLP broke hip.')

Pound wrote an article which appeared in *Meridiano di Roma* on 5 October arguing with facts and figures that Italy needed *arachidi* to become self-sufficient in essential vegetable fats. He explained that from peanuts a butter was made different from that from cows' milk, a butter which could be carried in a submarine for six months without going off, and which was highly nutritious—three peanut butter sandwiches made a simple meal full of proteins. Against those who said groundnuts could not be grown in Italy he set the replies to his own soundings among peasants in Viareggio and Modena and Rapallo, all of them saying positively that, yes, they did grow well there. He mentioned that in America an old Negro born in slavery, George Washington Carver, had brought wealth to three states by demonstrating the many uses to which the peanut could be put. He cited an Italian authority and a how to do it book; and he concluded by calling for the increased production of *arachidi* as a major contribution to the war effort.

Felice Chilanti gave an account of how Pound had tried to persuade him to grow peanuts on his terrace in Rome. On one of his last visits—this was in March 1942—Pound had noticed the pale face of Chilanti's young daughter Tati, and had said, 'You ought to eat a lot of butter', and he had been told, 'But you can't get any butter. Italy is out of oil and butter. They are used up by the war industry.' The next day he came back in the late afternoon, 'handed Tati a small jar of peanut butter' and had her taste it right away—'Tati liked it'. Chilanti continued:

> Then we went up to the terrace of my home, a large terrace *alla romana*. Up there, at that hour just before evening, Ezra Pound suggested we plant peanuts on the terrace, and that we convince everyone living in the centre of Rome to transform their terraces into peanut plantations. He said: 'To get the butter, just smash the nut'....
>
> He pointed to the terraces all round, from the Pincio to the Tiber. He moved his arm as if he were spreading seeds. We were a little surprised to take part in that strange, imaginary sowing. But planting peanuts on the terraces was, after all, one subject in the larger program to give the world a government of poetry, and ransom men from need and from the tyranny of usury.

Enrico Pea, the author of *Moscardino*, gave a contrasting image of Pound in late 1941. He lived in Viareggio which is on the line between Rapallo and Rome, and Pound would frequently stop off between trains to get help with translating dialect words and for conversation with a real writer who, 'Like Confucius, [had] knocked 'round and done all sorts of jobs' and who wrote 'like a man who could make a good piece of mahogany furniture'. Pea kept 'a vivid memory of what proved to be [Pound's] last departure':

> I went along with him to the station. We found the barrier already closed, and the train beginning to move off. Pound lost no time in farewells. Taking a firm grip on the handle of his typewriter with his left hand, he took a flying leap over the barrier

and jumped onto the moving train with all the ability of an American cowboy who vaults onto the back of a fleeing horse.

It is an image out of a Hollywood Western, with the Idaho Kid's typewriter in place of the gunfighter's Colt .45.

Among the scripts Pound was bashing out on his typewriter in the autumn of 1941 were some to be read out by one of his superiors, Prince Ranieri di San Faustino, who happened also to be a Rapallo friend. Dorothy commented on one, 'Your talk via Ranieri yesty. p.m. v.g.—the one on Elders of Zion'. She had wanted to lend *The Protocols of the Elders of Zion* to 'poor Kate who has nothing to read', and regretted that 'we have no spare copy'. Ezra wrote of a later talk, 'It was my material as you divined, and Ranieri tryin' his new american voice.' He himself had recorded six discs the previous day. At the end of November he mentioned that 'a lot of old discs have been used 4 times—double to America & then London', and that he was going to record cantos 45 and 46. Ranieri was then 'in Parigi', that was Nazi occupied Paris; he went on to Berlin, and came back, so Ezra reported to Dorothy, 'completely converted or bewitched or whatever' by 'life in Berlin / etc/', and saying 'our labours are appreciated'.

Pound's labours were not being appreciated however by Dorothy's Omar, now 15 and at boarding school in England. In October 1941 British 'Imperial Censorship' in Bermuda intercepted a letter sent to her via a friend in New York by her London legal adviser, Arthur Moore of Shakespear and Parkyn. The Censor's report, headed 'Son of American Anti-British author at Charterhouse', copied these sentences:

'... Omar has developed a total dislike to CHARTERHOUSE, and I feel that if he remains his health will be impaired. The trouble has I believe arisen owing to reports received of his Father's activities.... He natirally (*sic*) defends his parents and in doing so gives offence to other boys whose parents are no doubt engaged in the common war effort.'

'... He has reached the age when by pondering over your early letters he has begun to think for himself, and on the extreme views on the War which were sent to him by you (anti-British, anti-America, and pro-Fascist).'

Dorothy received the letter towards the end of November and told Ezra that Omar was suffering from 'nervous unhappiness at school', having no friends 'owing to politics and your activities'. Ezra advised withdrawing Omar from the school and having him tutored privately. Dorothy thought of sending him to Ronald Duncan who was experimenting in rural economy on a farm in deepest Devon. In the event Omar remained at Charterhouse until 1943.

Dorothy listened to broadcasts from Berlin, and from time to time would copy anti-Semitic propaganda to Pound. She had noted in May that a research institute in Frankfurt-am-Main was doing 'Work on the Jewish Question' with reference to 'the poisonous propensities of Jewish blood'. The question was, 'Where and how we will dispose of the Jews', and should it be 'in the form of a Jewish Reserve'—Dorothy underlined 'Reserve' as 'a rather quaint word?' They should have guessed even if they did not know for certain that the Nazi 'Reserve' was likely to be, what it already was for the two and a quarter million Jews in Poland, a closed ghetto or a concentration camp. They could not have known yet of Hitler's Einsatzgruppen whose special task was to exterminate all Jews in the wake of his conquering armies—over 33,000 were massacred at Kiev in September. And no one was allowed to know that the Final Solution of the Jewish Question, the total annihilation of Europe's Jews, which Hitler had prophesied in 1939 as a concomitant of war, had been decreed at the same time as his orders for the invasion of Russia. It only remained in 1941 to find a method more efficient and less upsetting for German soldiers than shooting Jews one by one, and in September the first trials of gas chambers were carried out at Auschwitz. Pound would have known nothing about that. But he could well have heard from Gerhart Münch whom he saw in Rome at the beginning of December, 'looking stern and teutonic', that Jews now had to be marked out by a yellow star.

Pound was well placed to pick up news of how the fighting war was going. The Italian forces in North Africa and in Yugoslavia and Greece had been less than conquering and German forces had brushed them aside in those theatres, easily overrunning the Balkans and Greece. On the Eastern front the invading German armies were no longer having it all their own way—Dorothy had believed that the 'Bolshies' were beaten when Kiev fell in September, but in November and December the Soviet forces were counterattacking and Moscow did not fall. Of direct significance for Pound were the moves by the United States against the Axis and in support of Britain: on the one hand freezing German and Italian assets in America and imposing an oil embargo, and on the other agreeing common democratic principles with Britain in the Atlantic Charter. There could be no doubt which side it would take if forced to choose.

On Sunday 7 December 1941 the FCC monitors recorded a talk in which Pound argued in his impassioned way that it would be misguided of America to get into the war in order to save a British Empire already rotted from inside by 'the Jews in London—whether they are born Jews, or have taken to Jewry by predilection'. America should rather be saving itself, starting with the problem of how it issued its money. The talk was of course pre-recorded. By the time it was broadcast by Rome Radio it was known that earlier that day Japanese carrier-borne aircraft had attacked the United States main Pacific naval base at Pearl Harbor in Hawaii, and had thus effectively settled the issue of America's involvement in the war. Formal declarations of war followed, by the United States and Britain against Japan, and by Germany and Italy against the United States. The war in Europe had gone global. Pound, as he put it in his next talk broadcast at the end of January 1942, 'retired from the capital of the old Roman Empire to Rapallo to seek wisdom from the ancients'.

Before he left on that Sunday he sought out the American journalist Reynolds Packard, director of the United Press bureau in Rome, whom he had known from his Paris days. Earlier in the year, in May, a 'huge lunch' with Packard had been the highlight of a day in Rome—they had talked of Packard's time in China, and of his bull-fighting. Now, according to Packard's account written when he was back in America the following year, Pound said to him that 'war between the United States and Italy was inevitable but that he intended to stay on', and Packard 'told him that he would be a traitor if he did so, and that now was the time for him to pipe down about the alleged glories of Fascism'. Pound apparently then said, 'But I believe in Fascism . . . and I want to defend it'—this accompanied by a Fascist salute, according to Packard—and then said, 'I tell you I want to save the American people.' Packard couldn't imagine how defending Fascism could be reconciled with saving the American people. 'There was no way to reason with him,' he concluded.

3 : In a Web of Contradictions, 1942–3

On 29 January 1942 the FCC monitors listening in to Rome Radio were taken by surprise when the station announcer read out a statement before Pound's voice came on the air and so failed to catch all of it on their recording equipment. With his next broadcast, on 3 February, they managed to record this announcement:

The Italian Radio acting in accordance with the Fascist policy of intellectual freedom and free expression of opinion by those who are qualified to hold it, following the tradition of Italian hospitality have offered Dr Ezra Pound the use of the microphone twice a week. It is understood that he will not be asked to say anything whatsoever that goes against his conscience or anything incompatible with his duties as a citizen of the United States of America.

One can imagine the fun the FCC personnel might have had with that combination of the words 'Fascist' and 'freedom', surely a glaring contradiction if ever there was one. Yet, in this case at least, there was no contradiction—Pound was to speak his own American mind quite freely in the broadcasts prefaced by that statement over the next eighteen months.

The more likely contradiction was in the second sentence, between 'his conscience' and 'his duties as a citizen of the United States of America'. His conscience was telling him that it was his citizen's duty to do everything in his power to save what was left of the true America from its misguided government. In December, while he was off the air following America's entry into the war, he had been insisting, to Ungaro and to Di Marzio among others, that 'my speeches on the radio must continue IN MY OWN NAME, and with *my* voice, and NOT anonymously'. It had evidently been suggested to him that he was putting himself in danger by so continuing, but he was adamant that so long as he said nothing 'that can in any way prejudice the results of American military or naval (or navel) action, the armed forces of the U.S.A. or the welfare of my native country', then it was his right and his duty to go on telling America what he was convinced it urgently needed to be told. He could not, or would not, see that the US government would naturally view his broadcasting criticism of it over an enemy's radio as hostile to American interests and incompatible with his oath of loyalty. He had sworn, in his own strict interpretation of that oath, to uphold the Constitution, but not to be loyal to an administration which was betraying it. He might have added that it was altogether in the spirit of the American Revolution to distinguish between 'acts against the *government* and acts against the *oppressions of the government*'. But Thomas Jefferson, who made that distinction, did so in the course of observing that it was one rarely respected, since 'most codes extend their definitions of treason to acts not really against one's country'. That was the jeopardy Pound was placing himself in.

He could have played it safe had he wanted to, he defiantly declared in that first broadcast in January 1942, he had 'a perfectly good alibi', 'a nice sizeable funk hole' to hide away in, having occupation enough for some years in his work translating the *Ta S'eu* and Mencius and the Confucian book of Odes. But there was 'the SITUATION' to be faced. The President of the United States had, to his mind, 'violated his oath of office . . . the oath of allegiance to the United States Constitution'—apparently by 'criminal acts' which had led to America's being now at war with the Axis. And in Mencius he read, 'the true sage seeks not repose'. So there he was at the microphone once more to inform Americans that 'someone in charge of American destiny' had blundered, and they were being asked to go out and die like the English for 'gold, usury, and monopoly'. 'That was what the war was about: gold, usury and monopoly,' as he had tried to tell them when he was last in America, and would keep right on telling them.

He had been warned often enough, especially by Laughlin, that he was not being listened to in America. Worse, so far as he was listened to it was by monitors whose job was to gather evidence that could be used against him. It seemed obvious to an Italian writer, Romano Bilenchi, who met Pound in Rapallo in early 1942 and heard about his broadcasting, that 'if he failed to escape after the war, the Americans would send him to the gas chamber'. Told this, Pound's outward reaction was only 'his usual gesture of shooing an insect away from his face'. Bilenchi—according to the account he gave a quarter of a century later—attempted to persuade Pound that his faith in Mussolini was misplaced, and that he was quite wrong about many aspects of Fascist Italy. When Pound spoke of enjoying 'intellectual freedom and free expression of opinion' Bilenchi retorted that in truth Italians 'were living in a state of complete tyranny that made it impossible to speak and act freely'. (The suppression of Chilanti's *Domani* would have been evidence of that.) Pound brought up the national corporations—the Fascist unions in which workers and employers, rather than serving each their own class interest, were to collaborate for the good of the state—and declared them 'the most important invention of the century; a fusion of nationalism and socialism'. To that Bilenchi replied that in practice the national corporations 'were void of any meaningful socialism'. Along with many other young people of his generation he had believed that Mussolini intended gradually to destroy the old power structures, but they had become disillusioned as instead he became 'the main buttress for those structures'. I was a Fascist once, Bilenchi said, but not any more—in fact he was about to join the Communist Party. Then there was the war—Pound 'was sure that the Italian people had wanted the war and wanted to win it'—but Bilenchi had to tell him 'that no war had ever been less popular in Italy, that we were drawing near to a terrible catastrophe'. He tried to tell Pound 'all the things I was seeing and hearing in the streets that proved the opposite of what he believed'. Right there in and around Rapallo people 'were not concealing their aversion to Fascism from anyone'. Even among the Fascists themselves the war was unpopular. Pound listened to Bilenchi's stories, was 'pensive for a moment', then 'rocked back in his chair and again made the motion of waving away a bothersome insect with his hand'. 'All of these complaints and lamentations... will stop after we've won the war,' was his answer; and then the things Bilenchi had hoped for from Fascism might come about. His own faith in Mussolini appeared unshakeable.

In *Carta da visita*, a 62-page booklet published in Rome in December 1942, Pound wrote out a carefully considered if rather cryptic statement of his thinking. 'LIBERTY A DUTY', declared the epigraph, an abbreviation of a phrase of Mussolini's which Pound was using on his letterhead, 'Liberty is not a right but a duty'. The first paragraph, headed 'FASCIO', likened 'the liberty of the individual in the ideal and fascist state' to 'a thousand candles together blaz[ing] with intense brightness—no-one's candle's light damages another's'. That could accord with the idea of liberty mentioned in the next paragraph, the idea defined by 'the revolutions of the [eighteenth] century... as the right to do anything that does not injure others'. However, he went on, 'with the decadence of the democratic—or republican—state this definition has been betrayed in the interests of usurers and speculators'. Hence, he implied, 'the following elucidatory statement' heard on Berlin radio in August 1942: 'the power of the state, whether it be Nazi, Fascist, or Democratic, is always the same, that is—absolute'. Rather than offering to explain how the absolute state was compatible with individual liberty, Pound then shifted from the political to the moral register. 'We find two forces in history', he wrote, 'one that divides, shatters, and kills, and one that contemplates the unity of the mystery.' The reader is left to deduce that the force which 'divides, shatters, and kills' is greed, the motive force of usurers and financial speculators; and that from contemplation of 'the unity of the mystery' with its 'tradition of the undivided light' comes the will to secure peace and abundance for all. Cavalcanti would be behind the latter formulation, along with Confucius and Mencius, and always the axiomatic 'abundance of nature and the responsibility of the whole people'. One glimpses a utopian dream of a perfect state from which private greed has been banished, and which is composed altogether of free individuals each blazing brightly and all of one mind and will. Perhaps a little closer to the real world was Pound's perception of Italians as a nation of such developed, indeed exaggerated, individualism that 'Nothing less than the Fascist system would keep these people together.' In an article in *Meridiano di Roma* he had approved 'The Fascist idea that the state should absorb all the energies of a man without crippling the man'. He meant that the enlightened individual should want and should freely choose to work with all his force to further the aims of the totalitarian state.

While he held his own country strictly to account and found it guilty of betraying its founding principles, Pound somehow persisted in his faith that Fascist Italy, and even Nazi Germany, were promising to secure their nations' credit for the benefit of all the people. 'I insist on the identity of our American Revolution of 1776 with your Fascist Revolution', he wrote in *Carta da visita*. Then he added this revealing gloss: 'Two chapters in the same war against the usurers, the same who crushed Napoleon.' We have constantly to remind ourselves that Pound's faith in Fascism, even in the midst of that war, was a hopeful faith in it as an economic system, and that he simply elided the political and military facts. Challenged by a note in the London *Sunday Times* which described his admiration of the Fascist regime as a notorious 'aberration', he devoted one of his radio talks in April 1942 to explaining why it was no aberration. His justifications listed the Fascist achievements of draining ancient malarial swamp lands and bringing them into healthy cultivation, increasing grain yields, creating new housing and water and electricity supplies, improving the nation's health—all the things he had written up a decade before in *Jefferson and/or Mussolini.* He made much of the Fascist version of representative government, whereby every worker should have a voice through his *sindicato* or professional corporation. He did also mention Italy's standing up to the bullying League of Nations as a reason for admiration, though without saying the words 'Abyssinia' and 'unprovoked aggression against'. And he said nothing of Italy's then current aggressions in Europe and North Africa, but if he had it would certainly have been along the lines of 'We are fighting for the liberty not to go into debt, i.e. the liberty not to be driven into debt.' That conviction was the rock upon which his faith in Mussolini's totalitarianism was founded.

In North Africa the Axis forces had the advantage over the Allies until August 1942, after which the battles went against them up to their surrender in May 1943. In July of that year the Allies would secure a foothold on Sicily and bomb Rome. On the Russian front the Germans had pushed as far as Stalingrad in the south by September 1942, but the Soviet counter-offensive forced a surrender at Stalingrad in February 1943 and continued to drive the Germans back throughout that year. In northern Europe the air forces of Germany and Britain were carrying out massive bombing raids on each others' cities. In France, in November 1942, the Germans and Italians moved into the formerly unoccupied Vichy zone. In the summer of 1942 it became known at least to some in England and the United States, that in the wake of their conquests in Eastern Europe the Nazis were systematically carrying out mass executions of Jews. The BBC mentioned gas chambers in December 1942.

Heedless of the grim battles and the heavy bombings, of the elusive victories and mounting defeats, and of the intensifying worldwide carnage, Pound steadfastly held to his special view of the war in his broadcasts and in his articles in *Meridiano di Roma*. In an article which appeared in mid-January 1942, just a month or so after the Japanese attack on Pearl Harbor had brought America into the war, he wrote that he did not feel himself to be above the conflict, but rather under it and overwhelmed by it. It could not be ignored, and had to be understood. To do that he viewed it in the light of the timeless laws of good government as condensed by Confucius, and it showed then as another phase in the war which had been ongoing in Europe and America since the founding of the Bank of England in 1694, the war of the greedy against the common good. In his radio talks during the year he would repeat tirelessly that the real enemy of civilized society was greed, avarice, usury; greed that monopolizes a nation's credit for private gain; greed that hogs nature's increase and breaks down the bonds and structures of social life. And in the perennial war, the real war of which this war of the moment was just a further phase, the Axis, in Pound's view, opposed the evil of usury, while the Allies, Britain and the United States, by opposing the Axis were siding with the enemy.

It followed that the Allies must be defeated in order to defeat the power of the usurers. 'If we don't snatch Malta from the English', he wrote in May 1942 when the strategically vital island was under Axis siege and bombardment, 'there will be no justice, no future, no Europe.' His implicit identification with the Axis war effort became explicit there, as it did again when he wrote in June 1942, 'Intellectual work—propaganda, providing data, correlation, and whatever else contributes to the prosecution of the war and to victory should be carried out.' He had closed his mind to the glaringly obvious fact that his war aims had nothing in common, or at least should have had nothing in common, with those of Hitler and Mussolini.

Pound would not say directly that America, his own country, was the enemy. The enemy was always the usurocracy, the conspiracy of international bankers and financiers, the 'Jewish' conspiracy which had Roosevelt under its thumb and which, through its control of the press and the media, kept Americans in the dark about its sinister operations. He would say repeatedly in his radio talks and in his Italian journalism that the Allied governments were the dirty agents of 'the Jews', and that it was 'the Jews' who had wanted the war and brought it on, for their own financial profit and to destroy Europe's civilization. He would rant that the 'Jews' were a minority highly organized to wage war on Europe, on humanity, on European religion; and he would urge America to organize against 'the Yidd'. So the enemy became 'the Jews'. But he would not advocate killing Jews. 'Don't start a pogrom,' he said in April 1942—to America not to Nazi Germany—'That is, not an old style killing of small Jews'—

> That system is no good whatsoever. Of course if some man had a stroke of genius and could start a pogrom UP AT THE TOP there might be something to say for it. But on the whole legal measures are preferable. The sixty Kikes who started this war might be sent to St. Helena as a measure of world prophylaxis. And some hyper-kike or non-Jewish kikes along with 'em.

All of this infected garbage had no better source than the so-called *Protocols of the Elders of Zion* and Hitler's *Mein Kampf*, both of which Pound was reading during the war and occasionally recommending as useful reading in his talks and articles.

In the course of these infernally twisted inventions and evasions Pound would insist on the need for precision in the use of words. 'The true definition of a single word always draws towards a better understanding of life and economics', he wrote, thus 'a false definition [of money] leads to the banks and usury', while 'the true idea leads to grain and groundnuts'. The enemy of accurate understanding, he laid it down, is 'abstraction' and the use of 'generic terminology'. And this was in an article with the title, 'L'Ebreo, patologia incarnata', with this as its first sentence: '[The Jew] is not only pathological, but is the pathology itself, constituting the pathology of the race he lives among'—which was as much as to say that 'The Jew' is 'a sum of morbid processes or conditions'. As a definition of the noun 'Jew' that would be likely to lead not just to misunderstandings but to genocide. 'All fanaticisms come from general (abstract) statements,' Pound would write in a letter to Santayana after the war. But while in the middle of the war he must have been so badly in need of an enemy he could attack unequivocally that he let himself be carried away from all consideration of truth and precise definition.

How far from right his mind was when it came to identifying his enemy shows in the way he dealt with the *Protocols of the Elders of Zion.*[1] Having long been 'put off by rumour that they were fake', he finally read *The Protocols* in April 1940, and found them 'DAMN dull, hideously written, but complete code, and absolute condensation of history of the U.S.A. for the past 50 years'. He wrote to Williams, 'their origin is not the point/ it is their diagnosis of what has (now) happened that makes 'em educative'. And to Swabey in England he wrote, 'You better, all of you, read the protocols, not as the emanation of any sect, but as a very brief and clear description of process.' That was to say in effect: attend to the planned action and forget about the alleged agent. If one can read the *Protocols* in that way, without prejudice and ignoring the prejudicial attribution of the plot to the 'Elders of Zion', then there are substantial parts where a nineteenth century Machiavelli might be cynically laying out the ways of gaining and holding power in the capitalist era:

In our day the power which has replaced that of the rulers who were liberal is the power of Gold. (1.7)

The political has nothing in common with the moral. (1.11)

Our right lies in force. (1.12)

Violence must be the principle, and cunning and make-believe the rule. (1.23)

Through the Press we have gained the power to influence while remaining ourselves in the shade. (2.5)

We shall create an intensified centralization of government in order to grip in our hands all the forces of the community. (5.1)

[1] The original source of this false document was a satirical fiction, *Dialogues in Hell between Machiavelli and Montesquieu*, published in France in 1864 by Maurice Joly, ostensibly revealing a hellish plot (not by Jews) against Napoleon III. In 1868 Hermann Goedsche plagiarized Joly's work in his novel *Biarritz*, his original contribution being to turn it into a revelation of a Jewish plot to take over the world. Thirty years later, OKRA, the Russian secret police, borrowed heavily from Goedsche's novel in fabricating the *Protocols*, a supposed record of the deliberations of a Jewish cabal plotting world domination. OKRA's intention had been to strengthen the hand of Tsar Nicholas II by turning Russia's anti-Semitism against its revolutionaries. Published in St Petersburg in 1902 and translated into many languages the *Protocols* then served anti-Semites everywhere as proof that 'the Jews are now a world menace'.

[Our] art of directing masses and individuals by means of cleverly manipulated theory and verbiage ... (5.4)

The intensification of armaments, the increase of police forces—are all essential for the completion of the aforementioned plans ... there should be in all the states of the world, besides ourselves, only the masses of the proletariat, a few millionaires devoted to our interests, police and soldiers. (7.1)

Anyone reading those *Protocols* in the 1940s without prejudice should surely have thought, here is a blueprint for Hitler and Stalin, those being the dictatorships then seeking world domination. No hidden hand was needed to account for what was by then open for all to see. Yet Pound seems not to have seen that at all. It was American history he thought the *Protocols* explained. He took some words about monopoly capital to be the key, and singled out for citation in a radio talk in April 1943 just one paragraph to the effect that

We shall surround our government with a whole world of economists ... Around us again will be a whole constellation of bankers, industrialists, capitalists and the main thing, millionaires, because in substance everything will be settled by the question of figures. (8.2)

That may be more or less where we are now, in the capitalist democracies; but to focus on that paragraph in Europe in 1943 must have required the narrowest possible tunnel vision.

But by then he was taking the anti-Semitic line and twisting away from clear sense and justice. He began that radio talk by turning around the charge that the *Protocols* are a forgery: 'Certainly they are a forgery,' he said, 'and that is the one proof we have of their authenticity'—because, he went on, 'The Jews have worked with forged documents for the past 24 hundred years.' It is unimportant who actually concocted the *Protocols*, he then said, their interest being, now that 'the program contained in them has so crushingly gone into effect', in 'the type of mind, or the state of mind of their author'. He might well have been paraphrasing a paragraph in Hitler's *Mein Kampf*:

To what extent the whole existence of this people is based on a continuous lie is shown incomparably by the *Protocols of the Wise Men of Zion*, so infinitely hated by the Jews. They are based on a forgery, the *Frankfurter Zeitung* moans and screams every week: the best proof that they are authentic .... It is completely indifferent from what Jewish brain these disclosures originate ... The best criticism applied to them is reality. Anyone who examines the historical development of the last hundred years from the standpoint of this book will at once understand the screaming of the Jewish press. For once this book has become the common property of a people, the Jewish menace may be considered as broken.

'Is it possible to arouse any interest in verbal precision?', Pound demanded of his microphone, and failed to question his own discourse. 'Was there a deliberate plot?', he wound up that talk, 'WAS there a plot? How long had it been in existence? Does it continue, with its Lehmans, Morgenthaus, Baruchs?... With Mr Willie Wiseman, late of the British secret service, ensconced in Kuhn, Loeb and Co., to direct and rule you?'

While Pound was broadcasting in that vein the Nazis were pursuing their policy of rounding up and massacring or deporting to concentration camps every Jew they could find wherever their writ ran. Only in Italy and in zones under Italian control was that not the case. Mussolini, now cowed by Hitler, paid lip-service to German demands for Jews to be deported, but covertly countermanded the orders and encouraged resistance to the Nazi policy. For one instance, noted by Nicholas Farrell, 'On 21 March 1943, the Italian Supreme Command in Rome issued orders to its generals in the Italian-occupied south-east of France which said: "As regards the measure proposed by *Il Duce* in reference to the Jews: no. 1 priority is to save Jews living in French territory occupied by our troops whatever their nationality".' Farrell mentions a range of particular acts by the Italian authorities in Italy, France, Yugoslavia, and Greece: refusing to deport Jews from Italy; blocking the arrest by Vichy police of 7,000 foreign Jews in Megève; refusing to deport Jews in Yugoslavia; guarding the synagogue in Athens to protect Jews from Nazi-supporting Greek students. 'Everywhere', Farrell wrote, 'Italian government officials and senior army officers saved Jews from the Germans and others.' Pound should have known that Europe's Jews were powerless and in mortal peril, and that Fascist Italy was protecting them from the Nazi holocaust where it could, and still he persisted in broadcasting to the Allies that it was 'the Jews' who were the real threat they should be confronting. This was his worst error, not the treason that was not really treason, but this failure of intelligence, of judgment, and of humanity. 'All fanaticisms come from'—or have as their *modus operandi*—'general (abstract) statements'.

Pound was another person when his affections were engaged. In mid-December 1941 he wrote in a letter to di Marzio,

> I am now responsible for my 83-year-old father, who a month ago broke his hip; at his age I don't believe it will heal (and with him my 82-year-old mother). The old man has not left the house for two years; he therefore cannot leave Rapallo.
>
> Olga has a small house in Venice, and she gets 300 a month in rent. But you already know her situation. Besides I must also provide for a ward.

The family doctor and friend who was attending to Homer, Guiseppe Bacigalupo, observed how Ezra was a most affectionate and attentive son, visiting his bedridden father every day and gladly doing for him whatever little he could. One thing was to 'read him a few pages of Aristotle in the Loeb Classical Library, English version, to take his mind off' the pain of his broken hip. When Homer died near the end of February 1942 Pound, 'with red eyes', hugged Mary up at Casa 60 and told her, 'Il tuo nonno è morto.' Then Olga spoke of her grandmother for the first time, '"The old lady has been admirable, for weeks she has nursed him all on her own."' Homer was buried in the Protestant section of Rapallo's cemetery, and Pound, following a Confucian rite, placed on the body an archaic jade ring which had been given to him in his London days by Edgar Jepson. It may have been about this time that he drafted these Confucian lines:

> To attract the spirits by the beauty of jade
> that the music be an announcement to the air between earth and heaven
> and thrice go up to the roof corner to call the departed spirit

Mary remembered how 'For a few visits' her father 'just threw himself on the couch and wanted to be left in peace and listen to music.' 'Then he went to Rome again.' But before doing that he called on Dr Bacigalupo to present him with a fine oil painting by Max Ernst, saying 'You did all you could for my old father and I want this to be a keepsake from him and from me.'

In mid-March of 1942 Dorothy mentioned to Pound who was in Rome that 'There is a rumour of a boat leaving for USA carrying some citizens aboard.' Pound showed no interest in this rumour. Indeed, just a few days later he wrote to Uberti about recovering his personal library. Nor, it would appear, did he respond to circulars and questionnaires from American officials operating out of the Swiss Legation which was now representing American interests in Italy and who were preparing lists of US citizens interested in being repatriated. These lists were sent to the US State Department in May 1942, and in none of them is there any mention of the Pounds and the Rudges. Yet this is strange, since it is known that the Pounds received mailings concerning repatriation, and since there were lists not only of those who did wish to be repatriated, but also of those who had not replied by 2 April 1942, and even of 'American citizens, not of Italian parentage, who were in possession of valid passports or registered on December 11, 1941'. The explanation may lie in a memorandum dated 18 June 1942, from the State Department's Division of Foreign Activities:

On July 12, 1941 this Department instructed the American Embassy at Rome to limit Pound's passport for immediate return to U.S. However, he refused to return home and to best of our knowledge is still residing in Italy.

...Mr. Pound should never again be granted passport facilities by this government.

Evidently if Pound had attempted to return to the USA in 1942 the State Department would have made it difficult if not impossible for him to do so. But was his name deliberately left off those lists? Dorothy Pound told A. V. Moore many years after the war, in 1955, that 'a (reliable) friend' had seen, 'by accident, a list on the table of names (to go home?) & at the bottom of the page in pencil four names to be discriminated against'. She does not say whose were the four names, nor when the list was seen, and she is uncertain of the purpose of the list; but she did say that it had to do with 'The question of the Consulate refusing us permission to go back to the USA'. She also said that the story that the Consulate had refused permission was 'not susceptible of proof'—it was, as Pound would say, only 'hearsay'.

That story spread in America in June 1942. Williams 'Had a call from *Time*... asking for news of dear Ezra. The rumour has got about that he is trying to return to U.S. and that he is being refused entry. They say he's starving, more or less.' The rumour had been started by a report from Associated Press picked up by a Philadelphia paper and by others on 5 June:

Nancy Horton, American woman who returned Monday from Italy... says Ezra Pound... was refused permission to leave Italy aboard a diplomatic train carrying other Americans. Miss Horton said Pound told her that George Wadsworth, U.S. Chargé d'Affaires in Rome, had informed him that he could not return to the United States.

That was all Miss Horton had to say on the matter, or all that is on the record. There is no indication of when Pound had told her this, nor of when Wadsworth informed Pound that he could not return to the United States. One can imagine a dramatic scenario: Pound on the railway platform with the other departing Americans, Miss Horton among them, and Wadsworth telling him that he was not on the list of those authorized to get on the train, and Pound explaining to Miss Horton as she boarded why he was being left behind.

It is a fact that Wadsworth was responsible for drawing up the list of American citizens permitted to leave Italy for the USA in May 1942 on the last diplomatic train to Lisbon where a ship would take them on to America, and so he was in a position to exclude Pound. However, when Donald Hall asked Pound himself what were the circumstances of his being prevented from returning to America in 1942—this was in 1960 for his *Paris Review* interview—Pound replied, 'Those circumstances were by hearsay,' and he could not recall being directly refused permission to leave Italy in that year. Moreover, apart only from the Associated Press report, there appears to be no evidence of any sort that he did seek repatriation in 1942, and what is known indicates that he was then dug in with his extended family for the duration. A note in the Justice Department files dated 14 October 1942 states that 'Pound refused to return home at the time the American Embassy, Consular officials and their staffs were repatriated'—this was apparently on the basis of information received from the State Department. As for the Nancy Horton report, it seems likely that Pound had been referring to his trouble with Wadsworth the previous year. That was when his passport had not been renewed, and when he had been left in no doubt that, as 'a pseudo American' who had apparently refused to go home when he had been directed to do so, he would be refused consular assistance and effectively prevented from returning to America.

By the end of 1942 Mary had nearly completed her translation of Hardy's *Under the Greenwood Tree* and Pound encouraged her by talking of finding a publisher for it. He suggested she next try translating his cantos. She had the sound of his reading them in Venice in her mind's ear, but then she had understood not a word. Now, with her limited English, she had to struggle to make out their sense and to find how it might be said in Italian. She would produce a neatly typed page and 'invariably he set out to tear it to pieces'. In time she realized that he was wanting to find out how he would 'express himself were he writing at this time in Italian'; and moreover, since he 'was of the opinion that Italian poetry had steadily gone downhill since Cavalcanti and Dante', that he was preferring 'their voice and modes rather than the contemporary language'. If she 'ventured: "*Non si dice*", he would say: "Time they did."' Questions such as 'who were Lir, Schoeney, Picasso?', were to be kept for the *salita*, the hill path, and then she might get the answer, '"It doesn't matter. Some bloomin' nymph",' or she might be told an anecdote about Picasso and Picabia in Paris. After some weeks on canto 2 she 'was told to try Canto 13 . . . a much easier one'; then it was 27, starting in the middle at '*tovarisch*' and only going back to the beginning 'when the second half got into the flowing stage'; later 'We switched to the Malatesta Cantos and Babbo turned up with books and documents; Yriarte's *History of Rimini* and his own notes.' And Mary was finding that 'The more I got absorbed in the Cantos the more eager I became for further knowledge.'

For Christmas 1942 her father gave her *The Complete Works of Alfred Tennyson*, a book which had belonged to his grandmother Mary Weston, and 1,000 lire. Asked what she would do with the money, her only thought was, '"I would like to go to Rome with you."' She was now a published translator, a piece from Frobenius on farming in Africa having appeared in *Meridiano di Roma*; and other translations there were being credited to 'M.R.' or to 'Mari' or 'Maria Rudge'. But her mother considered that more was needed for her to be considered fit to be seen with her father in Rome—dress, deportment, facial expression, table manners, grooming, all had to be polished. 'By April it seemed I had fulfilled Mamile's requisites and she gave me a lovely emerald ring to wear on my little finger.' In Rome Pound was very busy with his radio work, but they would meet for lunch, and in the evenings she would go with him to dine at a restaurant or with his many friends 'who all seemed eager to entertain and feed him', such friends as Signora Rossetti Agresti, Ubaldo degli Uberti, the San Faustinos, the Monottis. Pound reported to Olga that the 'Sprig looked very well in black at a dinner' at the Monottis.

Princess Troubetzkoi, her chaperone when Pound returned to Rapallo, arranged a picnic for her in an idyllic landscape outside Rome, and made up a story about it for one of her broadcasts. On the peaceful, clear spring day, by a temple to Juno, the members of the little picnic are a local farmer who had appeared as if from nowhere; a boy, Boris, with an Italian father and a Russian mother whom Mary had just met and found, when she gave him a chance, 'an enticing and brilliant talker'; and Mary herself, a girl with American parents brought up in Italy. And with all of them 'understanding and liking each other', the Princess marvelled, 'Why wars?' The *contadino* agreed, and thought 'that Mussolini would have preferred to let his people work in peace conducting only *la battaglia del grano*'. In Rome that evening the sirens were sounding, and during the night Allied planes dropped propaganda leaflets urging surrender.

Mary would have liked to stay on, but her mother warned her to be back in Rapallo by 20 May to have her ration card stamped. Now 'there were soldiers stationed along the railroad close by' when they went down from Sant'Ambrogio to the sea to swim; and there were Allied air raids on Genoa up the coast, and occasional air-raid alarms in Rapallo itself. In one of the raids on Genoa Riccardo Degli Uberti's studio was hit, and Pound's Gaudier-Brzeska charcoal drawings stored there in a suitcase were nearly lost in the fire. In July Olga decided that Mary, after her 18th birthday on the 9th, 'should go back to Gais for a month or so'. She would be safer there, and since at the alpine farm there would be more to eat she could leave behind her ration card. Olga was concerned that Ezra, driven as he was, was undernourished. His weight had already come down to 80 kilos the previous May.

Dorothy was keeping an ironic and bitter record of his afternoons with Olga and Mary up at Sant'Ambrogio: 'EP out to lunch', she would write in her diary on two or three days most weeks throughout 1942 and into 1943. Then another story takes over in the brief entries through two dramatic weeks in the summer of 1943: '*July 19* Rome bombed—*July 25/26* Mussolini demissioned—*July 27* EP started for Rome 7.30—*July 28* Fascist Party dissolved—*August 3* EP back 7.30'. 'Is it still era fascista?', she wondered in a note to Pound on the 28th, 'Somebody has chalked up opposite our front door *abasso M. porco*'. 'I wept', she told him. Mussolini had been deposed by a *coup d'état* headed by the king, partly because he could not persuade Hitler to let him make a separate peace, and all Italy wanted out of the war.

Pound had been in Rapallo on the evening of 25 July, and had just listened to what would prove to be the last broadcast in his own voice over Rome Radio, 'when there came over the radio the announcement that Mussolini had been overthrown and Marshall Badoglio had taken over the Italian government'. That was the first shock. The following evening he was listening to the news on the BBC and heard that Ezra Pound had been indicted for treason by a Grand Jury in Washington DC. He went down to Rome to see if he could learn more from the Swiss Legation, but they could tell him nothing. A third shock was to be told while he was in Rome that he was being 'kicked out' of broadcasting by the Badoglio government—that would have been because the new government was anxious to make its peace with America. He was quite unprepared for this triple catastrophe—Mussolini's sudden downfall, with its immediate consequences for himself, and on top of that his own indictment as a traitor.

Just two months before, around 10 May, his hopes for Mussolini and the Axis had still been strong in spite of the 'bad news' coming in of the defeat and surrender of the German and Italian forces in North Africa, and in spite too of the increasingly damaging bombing raids on Italy. Dorothy was 'Afraid that raiding is nearing Rome, with Civ[ita] Vech[ia] last night'. 'She not be downcast,' was Pound's response. He was in fact rather stimulated by the need 'to chuck most of the discorsi not yet registered & do a new set' of talks that would be better adapted to the changed situation. The next day, the 10th, he 'Did 5 more discorsi' between 8.30 and 12.30.

In the same letter he assured Dorothy that 'oh yes | the Boss rec'd | his copies of Carta da visita | & Confucio – a month ago | but communicated | via the burocracy.' Also on the 10th he addressed a lengthy letter to Mussolini personally, 'Eccellenza e DUCE', all about 'moneta prescrittibile', Gesell's stamp scrip. That Pound should write to Mussolini on that subject at that moment of military crisis is sufficiently surreal; even more surreal is that his letter was taken seriously. It was sent in to Mussolini with a clarifying note from his secretariat: 'He is an American presenting his idea to the DUCE... a project for monetary reform... to defend the lira and the country... and make the Nation 17% better off.' Mussolini read the letter and directed his private secretary, Nicolò De Cesare, to look into this 'moneta prescrittibile', and to invite Pound to come and explain it to him. The invitation went to Pound at his Rome hotel, but could not be delivered because he had just returned to Rapallo. De Cesare did not pursue Pound, but he did summarize *Carta da visita* for Mussolini, who then directed that the Finance Ministry should be asked to think about Pound's idea.

That was the form in which Pound was manifesting his continuing devotion to Mussolini and to Fascism in May 1943 as things were going from bad to worse for the regime and for the country. At the same time he was manifesting his continuing concern for the United States in his broadcasts, now telling his compatriots 'that the American troops in N. Africa, all of 'em ought to go back to America: IF they can get there'; and that 'America ought not to be makin' war on Europe'; and that 'Italy was and IS the United States' natural ally'—meaning Jeffersonian America 'was and IS'. 'Ezra Pound speaks from Rome', he concluded the broadcast recorded on 24 May, 'in a regime under which liberty is considered a duty; and where one knows that economic freedom carries with it the freedom from falling into debts.' But against that, as he declared in the set of five talks broadcast between 11 and 25 May, there was 'economic aggression' and 'economic oppression', as had been waged against Italy, and was being waged at that moment against 'Europe' by the 'three outstanding aggressors', i.e. 'England, Russia, America'. He was very down on the alliance of convenience between those three powers.

Meanwhile in the United States the FBI was interviewing Pound's known associates and asking if they were prepared to testify against him. The investigation had been set going in October 1942 following a note from the President to the Attorney General, Francis Biddle—

> There are a number of Americans in Europe who are aiding Hitler et al on the radio. Why should we not indict them for Treason even though we might not be able to try them until after the war? I understand Ezra Pound, Best, Anderson and a few others are broadcasting over Axis microphones. F. D. R.

The Attorney General's office at once asked the FBI to obtain transcripts of Pound's broadcasts and a draft indictment was prepared. In February 1943 the Secretary of War, Henry L. Stimson, wrote to Biddle, noting that there had been numerous stories in newspapers and magazines through the previous twelve months concerning persons 'treasonably broadcasting from Berlin or Rome', and that Representative Celler of New York was proposing that the Articles of War be changed to permit the trial 'in absentia' of six such persons. That would have been, as Carpenter points out, 'a travesty of justice'. What should rather be done, Stimson and Biddle agreed, was simply to indict the traitors 'in absentia', 'leaving their trial and conviction until the successful conclusion of the war'; but at the same time, to leave no doubt that they were determined to punish the traitors, they should hit the headlines by indicting a large number of them simultaneously and by releasing for publication 'a story which thoroughly discredits them before loyal citizens'.

The FBI had no difficulty finding old friends, old enemies, and old acquaintance willing to speak to Pound's discredit. A tone had been set some time before by Eunice Tietjens who had been a contributor to *Poetry* in its early years when Pound was Harriet Monroe's Foreign Correspondent, and whose scars from certain disagreements and quarrels with him in those years were evidently still raw. In *Poetry* in April 1942 she had written that, because of his 'deliberate attempts to undermine the country of his birth through enemy propaganda'—this coming on top of his general disagreeableness—'The time has come to put an end to the countenancing of Ezra Pound'. In the report the FBI put together in May 1943 there is much of that sort of disavowing and denouncing of Pound in the statements the agents had gathered from their interviewees, though little that would have been relevant or admissable as evidence in a treason trial.

Williams had told the agents that 'in his opinion Dr Pound had gone completely insane as far as any sense of reason and judgment was concerned'. Many, including Laughlin, were more or less of that opinion. At the same time Williams couldn't help letting out some of his perennial grievances and resentments against Pound. Antheil, now in Hollywood doing background music for films, was another burning to settle old scores and get his own back for wounds to his self-esteem. The wife of Professor Edward Root told the FBI about Pound's having only one shirt with him when he stayed with them at Hamilton in 1939, and his wanting it laundered and ironed each day after his tennis—she couldn't forgive him for treating her like a servant and was ready to testify against him for that. More seriously, 'James Laughlin', according to the report, 'advised that when Pound came to the United States in 1939 ... Pound had had his fare to the United States paid by the Italian government.' Asked whether 'Pound had definitely told him' this, he could not recall that he had, 'but stated that he knew that Pound had no money and therefore it was impossible for Pound to come to the United States in any other manner'. The statement was as gratuitous as it was false. There were journalists and others just as ready to assert supposition as fact, and not just that his fare in

1939 had been paid by the Fascists, but that he was now willingly saying over the radio what the Fascists wanted him to say. Given that what was at issue was a capital charge, the report reveals a frightening willingness on the part of a good many loyal Americans, when under the pressure of FBI questioning, to speak of what they did not know, and to give free rein to self-serving and often petty motives. Very few were prepared to speak up for Pound's poetry or to engage with what he had actually said in his broadcasts. Young James Jesus Angleton, recently graduated from Yale, was one of these few, though he too was prepared to testify for the prosecution.

The Grand Jury Indictment of 26 July 1943 was written in a legalese designed to allow for every possible line of investigation and prosecution:

That Ezra Pound, the defendant herein, at Rome, Italy, and other places within the Kingdom of Italy, and, as hereinafter described, in the District of Columbia, within the jurisdiction of this court, and at other places throughout the United States and elsewhere, continuously, and at all times beginning on the 11th day of December, 1941, and continuing thereafter to and including the date of the presentment and filing of this indictment, under the circumstances and conditions and in the manner and by the means hereinafter set forth, then and there being a citizen of the United States, and a person owing allegiance to the United States, in violation of his said duty of allegiance, knowingly, intentionally, wilfully, unlawfully, feloniously, traitorously, and treasonably did adhere to the enemies of the United States, to wit, the Kingdom of Italy, its counsellors, armies, navies, secret agents, representatives, and subjects, and the military allies of the said Kingdom of Italy, including the government of the German Reich and the Imperial Government of Japan, with which the United States at all times since December 11, 1941, have been at war, giving to the said enemies of the United States aid and comfort within the United States and elsewhere.

It was further specified that 'The said defendant asserted, among other things, in substance, that citizens of the United States should not support the United States in the conduct of the said war.' Lawyers could argue on both sides of that particular charge, but nothing in the indictment could have been brought to proof at that time. What counted was that the indictment stood as a statement of intent to prosecute.

Francis Biddle, speaking to the press as Attorney General, put the case against Pound and the seven others indicted with him in clear language:

It should be clearly understood that these indictments are based not only on the content of the propaganda statements—the lies and falsifications which were uttered—but also on the simple fact that these people have freely elected, at a time when their country is at war, to devote their services to the cause of the enemies of the United States. They have betrayed the first and foremost sacred obligation of American citizenship.

The BBC news report heard by Pound would have been based on Biddle's statement rather than on the formal indictment.

When he was unable to learn anything more from the Swiss Legation in Rome Pound went back to Rapallo and wrote out a full statement of his situation as he understood it, addressing the letter to Francis Biddle:

I understand that I am under indictment for treason. I have done my best to get an authentic report of your statement to this effect. And I wish to place the following facts before you.

I do not believe that the simple fact of speaking over the radio, wherever placed, can in itself constitute treason. I think that must depend on what is said, and on the motives for speaking.

I obtained the concession to speak over Rome radio with the following proviso. Namely that nothing should be asked of me contrary to my conscience or contrary to my duties as an American citizen. I obtained a declaration on their part of a belief in 'the free expression of opinion by those qualified to have an opinion'.

There was more to the effect that 'Free speech under modern conditions becomes a mockery if it does not include the right of free speech over the radio.' He wrote of his duty as a citizen in a democratic society to make known to the people the things that he knew and they needed to know. He declared explicitly,

I have not spoken with regard to *this* war, but in protest against a system which creates one war after another, in series and in system. I have not spoken to the troops, and have not suggested that the troops should mutiny or revolt.

He briefly outlined what he had tried to make better known:

The course of events following the foundation of the Bank of England should be known, and considered in sequence: the suppression of colonial paper money, especially in Pennsylvania. The similar curves following the Napoleonic wars, and our Civil War, and Versailles need more attention.

'In fact', he asserted, 'all the matters on which my talks have been based [are] of importance to the American citizen; whom neither you nor I should betray either in time of war *or* peace.' A final paragraph summed up his defence:

At any rate a man's duties increase with his knowledge. A war between the U.S. and Italy is monstrous and should not have occurred. And a peace without justice is no peace but merely a prelude to future wars. Someone must take count of these things. And having taken count must act on his knowledge; admitting that his knowledge is partial and his judgment subject to error.

It was an astute defence so far as it hinged upon what was said, and more especially on his motives for speaking, since before he could be convicted of treason a deliberate intent to strengthen America's enemies in the war, or to weaken America's power to resist those enemies, would have to be proved. The offensive fact of his having spoken at all over Rome Radio, and the further fact that some American troops did hear at least some of his broadcasts, might be enough to make the case in the popular view; but in court it would not be so easy to establish, what Eunice Tietjens had confidently asserted, that he had deliberately attempted to undermine the country of his birth.

Pound took his letter, dated 4 August, down to the Swiss Legation in Rome and it was forwarded to the US State Department on 25 August. There was of course no reply. At the same time the Swiss Legation returned to the State Department 'Passport No. 3154, Ezra Loomis Pound, date April 4, 1941', with a note, 'left behind . . . and has expired'. Pound would later explain that after handing his passport to an official he had been kept waiting, and after half an hour he began to fear he would be arrested and had left the building. The passport, he would say, was never returned.

4 : 'To Dream the Republic', 1943–4

In September of 1943 Pound walked into his dream of a Utopian way of life in the countryside somewhere north of Rome, or so he said by way of introducing one of his economic pamphlets the following spring:

On the 10th of September last, I walked down the Via Salaria and into the Republic of Utopia, a quiet country lying eighty years east of Fara Sabina. Noticing the cheerful disposition of the inhabitants, I enquired the cause of their contentment, and I was told it was due both to their laws and to the teaching they received from their earliest school days.

They maintain (and in this they are in agreement with Aristotle and other ancient sages of East and West) that our knowledge of universals derives from our knowledge of particulars, and that thought hinges on the definitions of words.

. . . I was also informed that by learning how to define words these people have succeeded in defining their economic terms, with the result that various iniquities of the stock market and financial world have entirely disappeared from their country, for no one allows himself to be fooled any longer.

And they attribute their prosperity to a simple method they have of collecting taxes or, rather, their one tax, which falls on the currency itself. For on every note of 100 monetary units they are obliged, on the first of every month, to affix a stamp worth one unit. And as the government pays its expenses by the issue of new currency, it never needs to impose other taxes. And no one can hoard this currency because after 100 months it would have lost all its value. And this solves the problem of circulation.

And so the dream went on: 'they are not compelled to make wars to please the usurers. In fact, this profession—or criminal activity—is extinct in the country of Utopia.' There, 'no one is obliged to work more than five hours a day', 'Trade has few restraints', and 'They attach the importance to skill in agricultural tasks that I attached in my youth to skill at tennis or football.' After hearing 'these very simple explanations of the happiness of these people', the dreamer fell asleep under the Sabine stars, 'marvelling at the great distance separating the twentieth-century world from the world of contentment'.

In truth, the distance could hardly have been greater. Pound did walk out of Rome on 10 September, heading north through the Sabine hills, but with all Italy in chaos and being drawn ever deeper into the fatalities of war. In the six weeks or so since the dismissal and arrest of Mussolini, Marshall Badoglio, as head of the Italian Government, had been playing a double game, assuring the Germans that Italy would fight on with them while secretly negotiating surrender terms with the Allies. An unconditional surrender was signed in secret on 3 September, the day of the first Allied landings in the south of Italy, in Calabria. The armistice was not declared until the evening of the 8th, a few hours before the main Allied invasion at Salerno. Hitler, anticipating Badoglio's surrender and viewing it as a betrayal, had already ordered his commanders to seize control of Rome immediately the surrender was declared, and to occupy and hold as much of the country as they could. Most of Italy's armed forces, given no clear orders, would be disarmed by the Germans, in effect being compelled to surrender to them and not to the Americans and the British. Italy had become overnight a country defeated by both its former enemies and its former allies, a country out of the war yet now a theatre of war, invaded, occupied, and fought over by two desperate foreign armies, neither of which would protect its people, or their homes, their cities, or their heritage, from the fury of total war. Furthermore, within the major conflict there would develop a complicated civil war, with Italian troops engaged on both sides, and also with anti-Fascist partisans hunting down Fascist loyalists and former Fascists. That was to be the actual state of the country in the twenty months between the surrender by Badoglio in September 1943 and the surrender of the German forces in May 1945.

Pound had gone down by rail from Rapallo to Rome on 5 September, being 'only slightly delayed on the way' by the results of Allied bombing. Apparently he was hoping to be allowed to resume broadcasting, 'as an American etc.', under the new regime. During August he had sent in four or five talks, as usual attacking Roosevelt and the international financiers, and these had been broadcast as by 'Piero Mazda' and paid for at 300 lire per talk. On the 7th he wrote to Dorothy, 'They seem to be . . . about to make statement re my position.' 'She not give way to despair,' he urged, and added in a postscript, 'The war can't last forever.' Then came the announcement of the armistice, followed by the flight of the king and Badoglio to Brindisi in the south, and the desertion of Rome by the heads of the armed forces, along with all the senior members of the Government and the high officials of the ministries. There was no one giving orders, and a fearful uncertainty reigned in the city. Whose side was Italy now on? Would the Allies come in to take Rome and drive out the Germans? Would the Germans resist? The Allies did not seize the moment, and on the 10th German troops were rushed into Rome.

That morning Pound settled his account at the Albergo d'Italia and left with the clerk his elegant malacca cane and borsalino hat. He called on Admiral Ubaldo degli Uberti and his wife and borrowed their son's heavy ski boots, a walking stick, a rucksack, and a detailed road map. They offered to shelter him but he would not stay. He went to the EIAR office and saw 'Giacomo' Barnes about 'papers' of some sort, but there was no one in charge, everything was in confusion. About midday he called on Naldo and Nora Naldi, seeking directions on the best way out of the city on foot. He would walk in order 'to avoid German control, to keep free'. He told them he wanted to get up to Gais to see Mary, though that was a difficult 450 miles distant. They gave him something to eat—two black market eggs, tea, and bread—and put into his knapsack a third hard-boiled egg, a tea-bag, and the remainder of the loaf. Naldi marked his map and went with him to the corner of their street to put him on the right way. They shook hands wordlessly, and Naldi later reflected, 'It is difficult to find the right words when things are so enormously complex.' He watched Pound 'go off, his stick striking the footpath regularly'.

The Via Salaria, the old salt road, goes to Rieti, about fifty miles north of Rome. That first day Pound passed an aerodrome where two soldiers told him they had no officers and were asking 'what ought we to do?' At Sette Bagni a group of peasants, when he said he was heading for Rieti, invited him to spend the night there with them, even though 'there is only one room for the lot of us'. They shared with him their good bread and thick soup and heavy wine, saying '"money is nothing" | "no, there is nothing to pay for that bread" | "nor for the minestra"'. The next day his road passed within a couple of miles of Fara Sabina, but there were few villages on the road itself, and it may have been this night that he slept 'under the stars'. The following night he spent 'on a bench at Rieti'. From there he managed to get on a train going north. The trains were crowded with soldiers of the abandoned Italian army, and Pound noted how 'the first day they kept their packs | and the second got rid of all military impedimenta', so anxious were they to escape the German military. This collapse, 'Lo sfacelo', put him in mind of Hemingway's account in *A Farewell to Arms* of the demoralized retreat of the Italian army in 1917, after the breakthrough of the Germans and Austrians at Caporetto, and he understood 'why Hem had written, | that is, his values'.

He probably had to get off and on more than one train, and may have had to do more walking, hitching lifts where he could, before he reached Bologna. There he slept on a camp bed in an air-raid shelter, and passed the next night, 'after food at the cab-driver's friend's trattoria', on the railway station platform in order to get on a train to Verona. Here in the north there was some order, the Germans being now in control, and it was in Verona that the peril and absurdity of his situation came home to him. Because his map was a military map and covered with his markings and comments, he was in some danger, while being wanted for treason by the Americans, of being taken for an American spy by the Germans. He debated whether to take the next train to Milan from where he should be able to get back to Rapallo, but held firm to his original intent. On his mind was something he had to tell Mary while he still could. A train took him up the Adige valley, though he had to walk again at the end so that he arrived at Gais 'covered in dust like a beggar' and with swollen ankles and blistered feet.

Now Mary 'learned that in Rapallo there was also a wife . . . with a son in England', not his son. '"Things would be set right,"' her father promised, '"If this war ever ends."' When he had finished unburdening himself, at three in the morning, she 'felt no resentment, only a vague sense of pity'.

Later she would sense the inherent tragedy of their predicament, and assent to his '*it all coheres*'. That night she learnt also that her mother 'had wanted a son. A torchbearer', and understood why she had always felt uneasy with her, understood '"The impossibility of winning the mother's affection."' That confirmed the commitment, implanted during her two years in her mother's house at Sant'Ambrogio, to her father's inner order and values: she would prove herself indeed his torchbearer, participating in his work through translation, and through study of his ideas and theories. And 'This meant more to me than being legitimate or illegitimate,' Mary would write, though 'Records would have to be set straight, eventually,' since history should not be falsified.

The next day Mary went into Bruneck to send Olga a telegram, letting her know where Pound was, and asking her to send Papiers Fayard for his blisters. The presence of the stranger out of hated Italy had been noticed by the local Nazi authorities, and Herr Bernardi, the butcher, and Herr Bacher, the woodcarver, old friends of the Marchers, appeared at their house bearing rifles and demanding to know, formally, 'Who is this man out of Italy who says he is an American?' It didn't help that Pound, to establish his identity, presented his Italian journalist's card. But what were they to make 'of a man who was clearly not Italian, not a spy, not a Fascist, not a Jew?' They all began to discuss politics, then economics, and Herr

Bernardi became interested in what Pound was saying about the Wörgl experiment, and in what he had said in his broadcasts to America, while the sculptor in Herr Bacher became interested in the shape of Pound's head, and thus the formal investigation was forgotten. For a few days Pound rested and looked for things to mend around the house. He repaired a staircase that had needed something doing to it for years. He visited Bacher's studio, admired his traditional madonnas, and wondered if he should take up woodcarving, or should he offer to work in the sawmill. But Mary's telegram had got through to Olga who sent the onionskins for the blisters, and wrote that things were calm in Rapallo, so Pound went down to Bruneck to obtain the permit he now needed to leave Gais.

The *Ortskomandant*, Herr Bernardi's brother, was reluctant to allow Pound to leave. Or he should go to Berlin, 'That was the place for such a brain, the German Rundfunk!' To that Pound 'merely blinked in friendly fashion', according to Mary who was with him. They had to go on to Bozen, to apply to the provincial Gauleiter. Pound 'was depressed and bewildered by the arrogant militaristic atmosphere' of the occupied city, so Mary did the talking, relying on the prestige in that place of someone's having to catch a train, and 'By early afternoon Babbo had his permit to leave the province.' His train had just one third-class carriage for passengers tacked on to an endless clanking chain of open freight cars carrying field guns from Germany south to the front. There were also horses on it, Mary later recalled.

Pound now entered the Socialist Republic of Italy, as northern Italy had been designated by Mussolini on 18 September, a republic of which the restored Duce was nominally head of state and head of Government, while the state and the Government were in fact totally subject to the occupying German forces. His then was a puppet regime; yet it might more exactly be regarded as a virtual regime, since he was free to dream up the ideal socialistic republic he had no power to legislate into existence. That was a republic Pound could work for.

On 12 September Mussolini had been snatched by German commandos from the mountain-top hotel in the Abruzzi where he was being held prisoner, and flown to Hitler in his East Prussia headquarters. There he was made to understand that unless he agreed to head up a government of northern Italy in alliance with Germany, then Italy, for having betrayed its ally, would suffer an even worse fate than Poland. In the hope, as he expressed it, of creating 'a buffer between the vendetta of the betrayed Germans and the Italian population', Mussolini bowed to the will of Hitler, who repaid him with the reflection that his weak associate was too bound to his own Italian people to be a thorough revolutionary like himself. To cancel out that bond Hitler would not allow Mussolini to set himself up in Rome or Milan, or in any major city. Forced to go into exile in his own country Mussolini, as Farrell puts it, 'chose Salò on Lake Garda near Gardone where d'Annunzio, the poet-warrior and spiritual father of Fascism, had lived and was buried'. Mussolini did have his own way at least in the naming of his regime. Hitler wanted it to be called 'Repubblica *Fascista* Italiana', but it was officially declared to be the 'Repubblica *Sociale* Italiana' (RSI). Mussolini, by his own account, 'did not believe in a possible resurrection of Fascism'.

He believed instead that by his fall he had been set free to return Fascism to its socialist roots, and in the process to disentangle it from Hitler's National Socialism. He had no illusions about his situation, that he was the powerless prisoner of his SS minders who took their instructions from Hitler, and that his Italy was 'an occupied territory and a subject people like all the others'. He wished he could put an end to the farce of the Germans pretending they were allies, but he didn't dare. What he could still do was to think and to write how Italy might rise again; how it would be purged of the errors that had undone Fascism, especially those due to its tolerance of the monarchy, and then those due to its disastrous alliance with Nazi Germany; and how it could be recreated upon the principles of social justice as he had first meant it should be.

The notional constitution of the new republic was agreed in Verona on 14 November by the first congress of the reconstituted Fascist Party. Mussolini was not present, but he was behind what came to be known as the Verona manifesto or charter. This would commit Italy to a revolutionary struggle against capitalism and Anglo-American imperialism, and equally against Communism and Soviet imperialism. The Socialist republic would be founded upon the value of work, not the value of capital. There would be a right *to* private property, as the product of work; but no rights deriving from the ownership *of* property, and specifically no right to exploit the labour of others for private profit. Labour and capital should be equally represented on the boards of large private companies, and public services should be nationalized. The Manifesto was intended to rally the party and to win the support of urban workers; but the party was divided, its remaining members 'more interested in recrimination and revenge than reconstruction'; and the workers no longer had faith in Mussolini. He had altogether lost the support of his people.

Pound's faith, however, was re-invigorated by the Verona programme. He responded enthusiastically to the principle of the right *to* but not *of* property. He also proposed that a few further important principles should be included in the programme: 'Freedom of discussion . . . Habeas corpus . . . the doctrine that money is subject to state control.' He was eager to renew his support for Mussolini, though not as a follower, rather as a counsellor. He evidently believed that Mussolini had a renewed will to achieve a just social order, and that he could help him do it. Very likely, as his journalist friend Francesco Monotti pertinently remarked, 'He believed in us more than we believed in ourselves.' His conviction that he might influence the German-controlled Salò regime and re-educate its people was beyond belief.

Pound had got back to Rapallo on 23 September, and was soon writing to senior members of the regime. In one of several 'Service Notes'—this one marked for the attention of Il Duce personally—he suggested that it would be good propaganda to make an official announcement 'that a reform, a real monetary reform, will be put into effect for the benefit of the Italian people'. This, he urged, 'would enhance the prestige of the Republic' among monetary reformers everywhere, 'In New Zealand, in Texas, etc.' Another note, this one to be referred to 'Offices of Communications and Interior', was more practical. 'Liguria is now completely cut off from all means of communication', he wrote, meaning evidently that it was impossible for him to get directly from Rapallo to Salò. This would have been because of the Allied bombing of the railway tracks and marshalling yards. Even 'to reach Milan from Rapallo' it was now necessary to spend a night in Genoa. He proposed therefore that there should be 'an autobus from Spezia to Salò via Genoa, Tortona, Piacenza, and Cremona', in order 'to give the Republic a new backbone'.

Alessandro Pavolini, now at Salò as Secretary of the Fascist Party, invited Pound 'to come north if [he] could get there'. He passed on to Giacomo Barnes the news that Pound was 'safe and sound in Rapallo', and Barnes, who was involved in setting up an English language propaganda service to broadcast from Milan under close German supervision, wrote from Salò on 4 November to invite Pound to 'come here for a few days toward the end of the month to help me galvanize the situation'. On the 9th Pound wrote to Pavolini that he had heard from Barnes about the reconstruction, and that if there was need for him to go up to the Lake then a place in a German truck would be preferable to one on a train. He took the opportunity of bringing to Pavolini's notice the fact that he had been received by Mussolini in 'anno XI', and that since then 'il Capo del Governo' had not received the information—implicitly information Pound had tried to communicate—which might have been of service. He didn't know, Pound probed, whether he, 'il Capo', was yet ready to listen or to receive advice which didn't come 'from Volpe et cie'. In a postscript Pound added that he had heard that only two of the ministry's forty-five employees had chosen to leave Rome for Salò, and that at need he could suggest a typist and translator, one brought up in the Fascist faith, a 'capo squadra', who, besides Italian, had known the Pustertal dialect from infancy, wrote German well enough for office work, both wrote and spoke English, spoke French with a fine accent, was of a serious character, and more intelligent than the employees he had been used to seeing. Pavolini cordially thanked Pound for this useful information, which he had received with great pleasure, and had passed on to the Ministry of Popular Culture to whom it would also be of interest. As to his being received by 'il Duce', however, a communication was sent from the Ministry of Popular Culture on 22 November to inform him that 'at this particular moment that is an impossibility'. Added by hand was a note from the head of the ministry, Fernando Mezzasoma, saying that if Pound would like to confer with him he would be glad to see him.

Pound got himself to Salò by the 23rd, when he told Dorothy that he had 'already begun discussions'. Dorothy had to tell him about the 'letter from Cul. Pop. postmarked Brescia saying the boss can't possibly see you'. He was also unable to see Pavolini, but did receive a message from him, acknowledging Pound's telegram and saluting his 'unaltered and fervent fascist faith'. It was with Mezzasoma that Pound talked, and what he told him, according to the account he gave the FBI in 1945, was 'that even if Italy fell I must go on with my own economic propaganda, that is, my observance of the money clause in the United States Constitution'.

He prompted Dorothy on the 26th, writing as from 'Ministero della Cultura Popolare', to 'ask Andermacher and Nassano' if it was possible for Olga to be lent one of the radios confiscated from the Jews so that she could help him in his work. The letter was in Italian, 'uno delle radio sequestrati dagli ebrei ecc. "per aiutarmi nel mio lavoro"'. All their letters would have to be in Italian from now on, he explained, so as not to have them held up by the censor. He asked for six copies of his Italian version of Confucius, the *Studio Integrale*, to be sent to 'Dott. M. Politi, qui al ministro', here at the ministry; and he ended the letter with, 'Tell everyone that the new government is alive.'

'I had a very pleasant visit from Schwartz yesterday', Dorothy had written on the 24th, 'He works with Wm. Joyce on Calais-Bremen and may be up your way quite shortly.' Pound wrote back on the 27th, 'Schwartz arrived yesterday—recorded 3 this morning, one in German—to begin from Milan in a week on medium wave, later on short wave.' In the German talk he declared, echoing his Rome Radio statement that he would say nothing incompatible with his duties as an American citizen, 'Nein, ich spreche nicht gegen mein Vaterland,' and he advised the Germans, rather daringly under the circumstances, to read the second part of *Faust* where Goethe touches upon gold and the Mephistophelian invention of paper money.

His letter of the 27th was on paper from the Office of the Prefettura. Giacchino Nicoletti, who was about to be made Prefect and who had been a journalist, had shown him the proofs of a new journal, *Volontà Repubblicana*, which seemed to Pound to offer 'at last the chance of a true or real review'. Later, in three of the *Pisan Cantos*, Pound would recall an exceptional moment of stillness and silence with him beside the lake at Gardone, with the water 'silent as never at Sirmio' on the other side, and a cat walking the guard rail, and in the silence Nicoletti saying, 'this wind out of Carrara | is soft as *un terzo cielo*', and again,

> in the stillness outlasting all wars
> 'La Donna' said Nicoletti
> 'la donna,'
> 'la donna!'

—thus consecrating the moment by reciting a sonnet he had written when young.

There was another singular moment early in December. Pound had in his hand a volume of the Confucian Odes, one of the handsome set Kitasono had given him in 1937, when he came upon three Japanese, envoys from their Embassy, and the Odes, as he told Dorothy, served as introduction. A 'genial discussion' followed, or, as he expressed it in a letter to Olga, 'lunge e cordiale colloq'. In May 1945, under arrest but wishing he 'could bring the slaughter in the Pacific to a sane and speedy end', he would tell his interrogators that the experience yielded 'the perception of a diplomacy based on humanity', one which might seek peace rather than make war:

> When I without credentials can meet Japanese envoys in the middle of chaos, and talk man to man because I happen to be carrying the third volume of the Confucian anthology, there is an avenue of approach NOT closed by the horrors of jungle warfare.

One must wonder though, remembering the unresponsiveness of the Japanese officials he had called on in Rome in 1940, whether Pound's talking 'man to man' about the Confucian ethic would have had much effect.

A striking feature of the incident, as of much else in Pound's behaviours at this time, is his capacity for taking no notice of the blindingly obvious. Or if that is too strong, there is at least a disconnection between the obvious reality and what is urgently real to him. It was a fine thing for him to feel that 'If I had not handed them a copy of my *Studio Integrale* (*Ta S'eu*) I might not believe in my capacity to talk to them as a gun merchant could not.' But Confucius is not much honoured in Japan's traditions; and these envoys were representing a nation hell-bent on conquering China and much of South-East Asia and the Pacific. How could the *Ta S'eu* mean to them in their frame of mind what it meant to Pound in his? It was like his passionately advocating monetary reform while Italy was being fought over and blown up and torn apart; or his talking of Goethe on money to Hitler's Germany. To take a different case, how could he coolly ask his wife to try to obtain a radio for the other woman, so that she could assist him in his work, when he knew how the wife resented and hated her? Then there is the seriously missing connection between the radio and its former owners, the one 'sequestrated' and wanted, the others given no thought.

It is likely that he would have heard in the days before it was announced over the radio on 1 December that Buffarini, Salò's Minister of the Interior, was about to order the arrest and internment of all Jews resident in the Republic, along with 'the immediate confiscation of their property'. He would certainly have known that in the Verona manifesto Italy's Jews had been redefined as '"aliens", to be regarded as "enemy nationals" for the duration of the war'. But he could also have heard in Salò that these anti-Jewish decrees were made to satisfy the SS, and that the Salò regime would resist implementing them where it could. Indeed, Meir Michaelis concluded, in his study of 'German–Italian Relations and the Jewish Question in Italy, 1922–1945', that 'If the "Jew-lovers" of Salò'—as they seemed to the Nazis—'had been masters in their own house, no Italian Jew would have perished in the Holocaust.' Yet the brute reality was that from the first days of the Salò regime the Nazis had been implementing their Final Solution in the occupied Republic, rounding up all the Jews they could find and deporting them by the trainload to Auschwitz. Twenty-five Jews were caught in a raid in Merano between 16 and 18 September and deported to Auschwitz; in October there were raids in Trieste and Rome; in November in Genoa and Milan; by the end of 1943 10,000 Jews had been captured for deportation. There is no knowing what exactly the people Pound talked to at Salò in November and December of 1943 knew or suspected of their fate, and no knowing how much he knew or suspected. But enough was known in January to cause Buffarini to protest to the Germans 'against the "illegal" deportation of Italian Jews to the East'. That protest, like all of Salò's protests, was ineffectual, but at least it was some response to what was being done to the Jews. In Pound's unfeeling 'uno delle radio sequestrati dagli ebrei ecc.' there is just no connection with the Jewish victims.

Pound's detachment was deliberate. Compassion would do them no good, he thought, and besides, it could be demoralizing. What was needed was understanding. On 2 December he wrote to Pavolini seeking his support for a proposal he had made a few days earlier, 'possibly his best proposal ever', that there should be a positive law requiring every bookshop to display for three months, or permanently, certain books necessary for the development of the sense of civic responsibility. Among the more important, especially at that moment, he would place—

I Protocolli di Sion
I Doveri dell'Uomo, di Mazzini
La Politica di Aristotele
Il Testamento di Confucio

The *Protocols* were needed just then, he explained, because the arrest of Jews would create a wave of useless pity, 'un'ondata di misericordia inservibile', and intellectuals would keep on feeling that way until they understood the reasons, 'le ragioni', for what was being done. So he reasoned away the brutal reality of what was being done to the Jews, reasoning against pity, and against his own better knowledge.

Pound was 'ordered to Milan tomorrow or a.s.a.p.' on 3 December, and got there, by standing for three hours in a railway cattle truck, by 6 December. That was no way, he complained to Gilberto Bernabei, for a propaganda office to look after its human instruments. He had a letter of introduction from his friend Nino Sammartano, then Inspector of Radio, to the general manager of the new Republic of Salò radio station, Signor Daquanno. Pound was as ever eager to get to the microphone, but Daquanno took the view that the best thing would be for him to broadcast for the German network from Berlin or Paris. Pound was unwilling to do that, being committed to the Socialist Republic of Italy and to his own propaganda, and things were awkward at first. He was not provided with accommodation, whereas at Salò and Gardone he had probably been put up in 'foresteria', the regime's own guest-houses. Here in cold, foggy, bomb-damaged Milan, he had to sleep 'in a kind of corridor' in the Prefettura for two nights at least, and was overjoyed to at last find a room with heating. Then there was a difficulty over expenses: 'I see you refuse to pay my hotel bill,' he wrote crossly to Sammartano, who later apologised for a bureaucratic mixup.

There was civil war in Milan. 'Milano Caina', he wrote in a draft which would find a place in canto 78, associating the city with the kin-killers at the bottom of Dante's inferno—

Milano Caina / the four popes ferocious in silver | resisting.
    in the fury of candles / amid the thick tempest of incense
amid ruin, destruction / maintaining.
                                        and that week they
assassinated the federale Reseda aldo fascista.

The 'four popes ferocious in silver | resisting' were silver reliquaries which Pound saw on the altar of the bomb-damaged church of San Sepolcro when he looked in on 8 December. He would have known that the Fasci di combattimenti had held their first meeting in the Piazza S. Sepolcro, and were known thereafter as 'sansepolcristi'.

Now what remained of the regime was powerless and dysfunctional. Pound was kept waiting on decisions by people in a ministry who couldn't, as he raged to Dorothy on the 11th, 'decide whether to decide or to undecide decisions that had already been decided'. Trying to be patient was driving him crazy, he wrote, 'paz i en ZA dev'esser in parentela pazzIA'. At the same time he was bothered by the way the Germans were censoring everything. He reported to Sammartano that 'the E.I.A.R. tells me that the short waves won't be in service for 'several months'/therefore the only possibility for transmission to the U. S. A. will be with the strictest German collaboration'. He clearly was not happy about that. As it happens a talk of his was broadcast on 10 December, but it was most probably one of the three he had recorded for Schwartz at Salò. This talk, denouncing Badoglio, Ciano, and the rest of the Italians who, in the eyes of Mussolini and of the Germans, had betrayed first the Duce and then the Axis cause, was beamed rather bizarrely to American troops in Europe and North Africa. Pound declared in 1945, 'At Milan I refused to broadcast to American troops and no pressure was put on me.' But he did still want to talk freely to America and was frustrated by being left hanging about doing nothing.

On Monday 13th he managed to see the man in charge of the broadcasts to American troops, Carl Goedel, and he had lunch with him the following day. Goedel was a 50-year-old German, who had been raised in Philadelphia, had served as a translator with the German army in 1914–18, and had been working since 1940 with EIAR in Rome, and now in Milan. He was close to the German authorities, yet Pound would develop a working relationship with him in 1944, the more readily perhaps because Goedel did not try to tell him what he should say or do. Instead Goedel saved him out of the immediate chaos of things in Milan by having one of his officials give him 3,000 lire, equal then to about thirty dollars, towards his expenses.

That did not ease Pound's frustration. On the Sunday he had told Olga that he would be back for Christmas if not within the week; on the

Wednesday he told Dorothy that he was wasting his time in Milan, getting nothing done; and on Saturday 18 December, as Dorothy recorded in her diary, he was back in via Marsala at 5.30. He was so discouraged by the disorder in Salò's propaganda operation that he decided that Mary would be better off staying on in the Tyrol rather than taking up an offer from Sammartano to employ her in Salò as an interpreter. Possibly the only satisfying event in his ten days in Milan was managing to arrange a half-hour interview with Pellegrini, the Minister of Finance, and being able to present to him 'my stamp scrip plan for financing the new Government'.

Pound was being listened to, even taken seriously, by some of Salò's leading men. Perhaps the American's earnest efforts to advise and to direct their operations as if they were quite real allowed them to feel that they might have some authority after all. Virtual worlds depend upon illusion. Mezzasoma, head of the Ministry of Popular Culture, recommended Pound's proposal for a bus service between Spezia and Salò to the consideration of the Minister of Communications, and endorsed it as coming from 'The collaborator Ezra Pound, American writer, old and proven friend of Italy to whose service he has devoted his intelligence'. In Italian, as in English, *collaboratore* can mean 'a colleague, a co-worker', as well as 'one who works with the enemy', and there must have been an ambiguity, a sense of Pound's compromised situation, in the Salò officials' way of referring to him, when circulating his missives around their ministries, as 'the collaborator Ezra Pound'. All the same, the reality of his devotion to Mussolini's illusory republic appears to have led them to regard him as virtually one of themselves. He was able to put his proposals and exhortations to Mussolini's private secretary, Giovanni Dolfin, to the Chief of Staff of the Army of the Salò Republic, to the Ministers of Finance and Labour, to the Commissioners of the Confederation of Professional Men and Artists and of the National Institute of Fascist Culture, to the Mayor of Milan, and so on through the full directory of ministers and heads of department and senior officials of the phantom government.

In the mind of the American authorities, however, there was no ambiguity: quite simply, the collaborator Ezra Pound was wanted on a charge of treason and when captured was to be 'thoroughly interrogated concerning his radio broadcasting and other activities on behalf of the Italian Government'. On 24 January 1944 the US Attorney General wrote to the Secretary of War to that effect, and the order was duly passed to the command of the US Fifth Army in Italy, together with a photograph and a passport description of the wanted 'Dr Pound'.

That neat and simple view missed the complication that Pound, while working with the Salò government, was not working for it nor on its behalf in the sense of the indictment; but was rather working through it, and upon it, on behalf of his own agenda. He was not speaking for the new republic, he was speaking to it. His mission, as he conceived it, was to educate its people, to overcome their ignorance and to foster their intelligence, and so to bring about enlightened government. To Giovanni Gentile, president of the newly established Academy, he sent a proposal for a national education programme, with a syllabus listing Homer, Catullus, Ovid, Dante, Chaucer etc., along with some 'readable' historians and economists. Gentile forwarded the proposal to Il Duce, who added Plato's *Republic* to the list. Encouraged by a decree issued by the Council of Ministers on 13 January 1944 which promised some of the economic reforms he had been calling for, together with a right of *habeas corpus* and a right of free speech, Pound sent Mezzasoma 'a brief summary of EDUCATIONAL MATERIAL', on this occasion listing

BROOKS ADAMS: The Law of Civilization and Decay; The New Empire
KITSON: The Bankers' Conspiracy
OVERHOLSER: History of Money in the U.S.A.

These, Pound advised, were 'The most useful books with which to combat the expressed opinions of the Anglo-Saxon-Jewish-Yankee press', and to counter the opposition to economic reform bound to come 'from the mercantile industrialists, usurers, etc.' He also suggested, following a 13 January decree developing the eighteen points of the Verona programme, that a translation of his own *Jefferson and/or Mussolini* 'might find readers in Italy'. In fact all the books on his list would have to be translated and published in Italian, if ever the printing presses were running again. He emphasized that point: 'Without a printing press and a microphone it is difficult to educate these people.' The education he intended was clearly one which should make them economically literate and armed against usury, no matter that usurious banking was not among the Italian republic's more pressing concerns. Yet Mezzasoma's staff quite promptly forwarded Pound's suggestions to Nino Sammartano, now in Venice as director general of the Cultural Exchange Division of the Ministry of Popular Culture, to the director general of Foreign Press and Radio, and to the Ministry of Propaganda.

Pound felt at liberty to criticize Mezzasoma's ministry quite severely. 'You people refuse to learn,' he told him, 'I am fed up . . . Perhaps I am wasting my time, but I am anxious to help.' What had set him off on that day, 16 January, was an ignorant propaganda 'note on this morning's

"Radio Journal"', ignorant, that is, of how the Anglo-American mind would inevitably react to the socializing 'provisions of the 13th'. 'We are wasting time', he went on, 'In twenty years the Ministry has never really controlled its own printing press', and 'ignorance has been created, fomented and spread by the putrid Italian-Jewified plutocratic press'. Ignorance was the basic problem, from the ignorance of the uninformed young to 'the ignorance of newspaper publishers and government officials', all of them 'not even aware that a monetary problem exists in Italy'. A week later he was complaining that his efforts to remedy that ignorance were being held up. 'The material left with Nicoletti has not been printed yet'—'Nothing will get done until I or Nicoletti or someone who understands the meaning of this war has been granted the use of a printing press.' In a paranoid moment he hesitated to say where an article of his on money had recently appeared, 'because one of those mysterious counter-orders to which we have become accustomed, might prevent publication of a second article'. At the end of March, writing at 4.00 a.m. after listening to London's BBC flooding the night air, he advised transmitting to America in the small hours short speeches on the theme, 'London lies'. 'My own voice should probably be used for this project', he proposed. In the same letter he accused EIAR of 'being full of treachery', because 'Some of the music played over the air these days . . . is enough to make one sick. If this isn't deliberate sabotage, then what is it?' Mezzasoma may not have felt behind that last complaint the authority of Mencius' Confucius, who 'Through the rites of a state could see its government; through its music, the moral quality of its ruler'.

Pound's own voice would not be used again by EIAR, nor would he have his scripts read by others. Instead he would provide odd items for others to work into their programmes if and where suitable. On 23 February, Tamburini, the Director General of the Milan radio, sent a memo to the Head of Foreign Press and Radio to the effect that

> Radio Division IV in Milan has recently invited the collaborators Ezra Pound and Giacomo Barnes to join them. They will each send two or three messages per week to Milan; these messages will be of polemic nature suitable for insertion into news reports in foreign languages.

At the end of the war Tamburini told the FBI that Pound's messages consisted of 'comments and short news items', and that 'sometimes he would create slogans such as "America is running herself into debt."' He also said that 'the material he furnished us with was often anti-Semitic in nature'. Parts of what Pound sent in would be used 'in the scripts for *Jerry's Front Calling*', a programme of German-directed propaganda run by Carl

Goedel and beamed at American troops in the Mediterranean theatre. Pound told his interrogators in 1945 that from September of 1944—this was following the radio station's move from Milan to Fino Mornasco on Lake Como—he would send Goedel two copies of his material, one of them addressed to him at the German Consulate in Milan, and he supposed that was 'for record and censorship'. Goedel, he had been told, 'uses your stuff in his own way'.

Pound wanted it to be understood that while he worked with him, he 'did not work for Goedel, but for the Republican Fascist Ministry of Popular Culture'; he insisted, moreover, that he was not paid by the Germans but by the Italians. Tamburini also made a point of saying that the 'German authorities in Italy never paid Pound any money because he was receiving a regular monthly check from the Italian Ministry of Popular Culture'. It was as if he was not really contributing to German propaganda, even though his material was being used by Goedel in *Jerry's Front*, so long as he was not being paid by the Germans. There was another and rather more convincing distinction which Pound maintained, this one in relation to the RSI. He would not fill out an employment application sent to him by the Ministry of Popular Culture, and he would regularly cross out the words 'enclosed is your salary for the month' and insert instead, 'for services rendered'. This was to maintain the status of a free agent and not a salaried employee, and to make it clear that he was doing his own thing, not following orders. But then, 'I always accepted the checks', he said. At first he received 'eight thousand lire about $80 per month', paid by checks drawn on the Banco di Lavoro in Venice and cashable in his Rapallo bank; then a bonus raised his 'monthly pay check to about eleven thousand lire'; but in early 1945 a general salary cut reduced it again by 10 per cent.

In Pound's own account his main work in 1944 and 1945, the work for which he was being paid, was advising and writing for the Cultural Exchange Division of the Ministry of Popular Culture, and particularly for its publishing press, Casa Editrice delle Edizioni Popolari. Sammartano, upon being transferred to Venice to take charge of the office of Cultural Exchange, had sought Pound's collaboration—the former Professor of Education at Rome University was evidently impressed by Pound's determination to 'educate these people'—and Pound had seized upon the chance of having at his disposal a printing press and a well-disposed director. It was agreed between them in January 1944 that Pound would write a series of books or pamphlets, and these six were printed over the following twelve months:

L'America, Roosevelt, e le cause della guerra presente (about March 1944)

Introduzione alla natura economica degli S. U. A. (June 1944)

Testamento di Confucio (reprint of the Italian translation of the *Ta S'eu*, July 1944)

Orientamenti (a collection of Pound's *Meridiano di Roma* articles, September 1944)

Jefferson e Mussolini (*J/M* revised, adapted and translated by EP for Italian readers, December 1944)

Chiung Iung. L'Asse che non vacilla. Secondo dei libri Confuciani (Pound's new Italian version of 'The Unwobbling Pivot', February 1945)

Pound also secured publication in May 1944 of a pamphlet, in Olga Rudge's Italian, based on Kitson's *The Bankers' Conspiracy* (1933) and *Industrial Depression* (1905), with the title *La storia di un reato* (The history of a crime), the crime being of course that of the bankers whose usurpation of credit for their private profit was the perennial cause of wars.

Those were more or less the terms in which Pound's first and second pamphlets presented yet again his economic interpretation of American history. 'The reason for this publication, at this moment', he wrote at the end of *L'America, Roosevelt, e le cause della guerra presente*, 'is to show how the present war has its place in a series of wars provoked by the same agency: the world-wide usurocracy, or web of high finance.' A brief prefatory note indicated that the little book would be principally concerned with the enlightened Revolution of 1776, and with the subsequent fall of America during its Civil War into the grasp of the international usurocracy. Roosevelt is mentioned, and cursed, only at the very end; and the reader is challenged to consider the bearing of this American history upon the current war.

The argument was spelt out again in *Introduzione alla natura economica degli S. U. A.* Sammartano, evidently approving of his first pamphlet, had asked him to do another on the economic history of the United States. Pound obliged at once, sent in his *Introduzione* about the end of May, and was informed by Sammartano on 5 June that the Minister had passed it for publication. It was as good an account as he had given in prose of his understanding of history, with the argument developed coolly and clearly through detailed illustration, without rage, and without anti-Semitism. It is genuinely a history lesson, and not a prosecuting polemic; nor was it propaganda in any simple sense, least of all Axis propaganda. Pound declared his personal interest at the start:

> For forty years I have schooled myself, not to write an economic history of the U.S. or any other country, but to write an epic poem which begins 'In the Dark

Forest', crosses the Purgatory of human error, and ends in the light, and 'fra i maestri di color che sanno'. For this reason I have had to understand the NATURE of error.

The investigation led to his usual findings—findings which were still news sixty-four years on:

The trap of the banking system has always worked in the same way. Some case of abundance is used to create optimism. This optimism is exaggerated, usually with the help of propaganda. Sales increase; prices of land, or of shares, rise beyond the possibility of material revenue. The banks having favoured exaggerated loans in order to manoeuvre the increase, restrict, recall their loans, and presently panic overtakes the people.

The consequent ruin, he wrote, as it has been written again in our time, 'has its roots in the greed for lucre, a greed which abandons all common sense and every sense of proportion, and blindly creates its own undoing'. But the lesson that history teaches is never learnt, Pound noted as he repeated it, the lesson that '*It is idiotic to leave the pocket-book of the nation in the hands of private and, perhaps foreign, irresponsible individuals*'—the lesson that in any democracy money should be democratized, socialized, and regulated for the public good, as against private profit.

There are two remarkable things about these two pamphlets, and indeed about all Pound's Salò publications. The first is that they show him pursuing as always his own agenda even while being paid and published by the regime. More remarkable is that they show him earnestly putting his educational material into his odd Italian for the benefit of a shrinking republic whose inhabitants, one can be fairly certain, were otherwise occupied, as with surviving the severe shortages of food and of all other necessities, surviving the bombing of their towns and cities, surviving the strain of being under German occupation, and the further strain of their own internal divisions, not to mention the worry of the slow grinding advance of the Allied forces. Pound's sublime disregard for all that must have been the correlative of his being totally possessed and driven by his imperative conviction that he alone understood the true nature of the war. He would not be distracted from the perennial war by this war of the moment. Nor would he give up on his mission to reform the Republic.

But then, after the taking of Rome by the Allies in June and of Florence in August, the Republic would give up on Pound. Very nearly the entire edition of *Orientamenti* would be destroyed in October or November, 'because of its political and economic nature'; for the same reason the entire edition of *Jefferson e Mussolini* would be destroyed as soon as it was printed; and finally the bulk of the edition of the *Chiung Iung* would be 'burned immediately after the Liberation because ("asse" being the Italian word for "axis") the text was condemned, unread, as propaganda in favour of the Berlin–Rome–Tokyo Axis'. Thus two of his six works would be made phantom publications on account of the anxieties of Sammartano and the Salò authorities, fearful of what the oncoming Allies might make of them; and a third would be destroyed because it was taken by someone unknown to be precisely what it was not.

There were other projects and proposals which came to nothing. At the end of January 1944 Pound suggested to Mezzasoma that there should be a daily or weekly newspaper printed in Rapallo, only to be told that the paper shortage made that quite impossible. In February he wrote to Sammartano about the need for suitable propaganda material in English to be given to British and American prisoners of war, and in April he sent in his list of recommendations. There were the usual books on money and the bankers' conspiracy—Brooks Adams, Kitson, Overholser—there were books on American history, and his own *Cantos* 'because they contain history in a much more condensed form than prose, especially cantos LII/LXXI, the economic history of China [and] the Life of John Adams'; there was his *Jefferson and/or Mussolini*; and, less obviously, there were Wyndham Lewis's *The Apes of God*, a merciless mirror held up to literary London, and Cummings's *Eimi*, an idiosyncratic mirroring of Soviet Russia. It was, as Redman remarks, 'Pound's ideal list', but hopelessly unrealistic. Sammartano simply told him, 'for the moment the publication of volumes in a language other than Italian cannot be foreseen'. Later in the year Pound mentioned that he was translating an economic work by J. P. Angold, to be called *Il ruolo del finanziere* (The Role of the Financier), but this appears to have become an unfinished or lost work. In October he wondered if a monumental microphotographic edition of Vivaldi might be possible, or a more modest edition, or, if not that, still, he suggested, there would be publicity value in announcing that the work of preserving important literary and musical materials from wartime damage was continuing. The diminuendo suggests that he knew Salò would not be doing any kind of edition of Vivaldi.

Pound's most ambitious unrealized project was for a series, to be published in Italian by Edizioni Popolari, of the essential classic Chinese texts. He outlined the plan in a letter to Mezzasoma dated 15 March 1944:

1. My bilingual edition of STUDIO INTEGRALE of CONFUCIUS…
2. *L'Asse che non vacilla* (Invariabilité dans le Milieu) to be translated from the French of Pauthier by Soldato. Work already begun yesterday.

3. Speeches by Confucius [i.e. *Analects*]. Soldato will continue with this and with the
4. Book of Mencius (from Pauthier's translations).
5. *Shu King* 2235–719 BC That is, documents collected by Confucius, translated by Gorn Old. Necessary in order to understand on what Confucius based his deductions.
6. *Odes*, Anthology of ancient poetry collected by Confucius with the Latin translation of Lacharme, notes of J. Mohl 1752; published in 1830.

Pound was also 'looking for an edition of "Spring and Autumn"'; and proposing 'An IDEOGRAMMIC CHINESE–ITALIAN DICTIONARY to be based on what exists, but certainly to include Morrison with additions and notes by Karlgren'. He was clearly impatient to get done what could be done at once; but he was also projecting major undertakings which would have taken experts years to accomplish. Evidently he had set Giuseppe Soldato, a Rapallese writer and friend, the task of translating three of the classics from Pauthier's French versions so as not to lose time by beginning afresh from the originals. In the event, though, *L'asse che non vacilla* was published in Pound's own translation, and the other works Soldato was to translate did not materialize; nor did an Italian *Shu King*. Mezzasoma gave his approval for an edition of the *Odes*, but, hardly surprisingly, that did not materialize either. As for the dictionary, the scale of that undertaking, and the expertise required, can be measured by its having to include the seven folio volumes of Morrison, plus 'additions and notes by Karlgren'. In the prevailing circumstances that was crying for the moon.

But then Pound intended the Confucian classics to be his founding contribution to the Republic. 'I am absolutely convinced', he would tell Mezzasoma in January 1945,

> that in bringing to Italy a greater knowledge of the heroic doctrine of Confucius, I will bring you a gift of greater service than the Platonism that Gemisto brought you in the 14th century, which rendered you so great a service in stimulating the Renaissance.

'The importance of the Confucian culture', he had previously told Sammartano, was in its maintaining 'the civic sense for the construction of an empire'. And when he sent his translation of *L'asse che non vacilla* to Sammartano he described the work as '26 chapters adapted to the moment', implying an immediate need of the Confucian civic sense in Mussolini's republic. In May 1945 he would declare that the Republic had flopped because it had not followed Confucian principles thoroughly enough.

Pound could be philosophical about the end of Mussolini and his Fascism because that had been his attitude for some time, if not all along. His attachment had not been simply to the man and the party, but had been rooted in the idea of social justice which he credited them with attempting to realize. That is the key to making sense of his relations with Fascism in general, and with the Salò regime in particular. In February 1944 he had declared, in a manifesto signed with four other 'Tigullian writers' (Giuseppe Soldato being one of them), 'No individual will succeed Mussolini, his successor will be THE REPUBLICAN IDEA.' Confucius had given 'l'IDEA REPUBBLICANA' a form which had sustained dynasties, a universal form or *paideuma* persisting beyond and above its particular manifestations. Pound had taken, or mistaken, Mussolini's Fascism to be one such manifestation; but as the IDEA of a just republic would outlast his end, so Pound's faith in that idea would endure. It had not been a faith in what is labelled 'Fascism', but a commitment to what he had taken, rightly and wrongly, to be the idea behind it. It was a commitment to what he was now calling a philosophy, specifically the Confucian philosophy, but with the rider that a man's philosophy reveals itself more in his deeds than in his words.

Pound's words were his deeds. But how could he have hoped to inculcate, all by himself, a Confucian ethic within, and via the media of, a Fascist-Socialist regime subject to Hitler's Nazism? The simple answer, that he was mad, is altogether too simple. He was absolutely in his right mind, and he was well aware of what was happening around him. Nor was he immune to the stresses and dangers of the time. But his response to them was to hold on to and to assert all the more vehemently his visionary idea of a better state of the world. He went on believing in the impossible.

5 : For the Resurrection of Italy, 1944–5

At a critical moment in May 1944 the German military authorities in Rapallo ordered the evacuation within twenty-four hours of all seafront apartments. They were taking measures against feared Allied landings. The Allies' advance, which had been stalled for months at Monte Cassino and Anzio, was moving again; Rome would fall to them on 4 June, and Florence in August. Through April and May the Allies intensified their aerial bombardment of Italian cities, causing 'huge destruction and loss of life'. Yet the Germans were determined to hold them back, and by desperate fighting in the mountainous country between Florence and Bologna would drag the war out through the winter and into the spring of 1945.

Ezra and Dorothy Pound, when they had to leave their seafront flat, were invited by Olga Rudge to share her six rooms in Casa 60, Sant'Ambrogio. They would retain the lease of the Rapallo flat, and leave some of their things there, notably the Gaudier Hieratic Head on the rooftop terrace. But much of the twenty-year accumulation of books and papers, and some furniture and other household goods, were carried down the long descent of stairs to be stored elsewhere. Some went to the house of Pound's good friend Dr Bacigalupo; some, with the assistance of their peasant friend Baccin, to his mother's apartment in the Villa Raggio in Cerisola, the hilly suburb behind the town; the journals and periodicals were taken by Ezra and Olga to rest on the empty shelves of the Casa del Fascio library; and the more treasured books and papers, as Mary understood from her mother, were carried by her parents, 'in briefcases and knapsacks', up the long *salita* to Sant'Ambrogio. And 'Somewhere they found a cart with two horses', Dorothy recalled for Hugh Kenner in 1965, 'to haul the books and heavy things up the hill'. Dorothy would have Mary's room, Ezra another.

Olga Rudge, in a 1977 notebook, recalled their first evening together:

To help tide over the awkwardness—the three of us forced to converse at the end of a tiring day, I thought EP & D. would like me to show that I was minding my own business—I went to my room and played the Mozart Concerto in A major, as well as I have ever done. The next morning E. told me that D. remarked, '*I* couldn't have done that'. (D. said nothing to me, good or bad or indifferent... pointedly spoke to me as she might have to a housekeeper.) I never played—or was asked to play—again. It was the last time EP had music at Sant'Ambrogio.

Olga Rudge added, 'After the first night DP and EP sat listening in the dark to the BBC broadcasts.'

Olga was teaching English three days a week at a school down in Rapallo, and would bring back their meagre rations, bread, 'meat once a week, occasional fish'. Dorothy told Kenner that sometimes she had had to cook, though she had never cooked before, on principle. From her diary one gathers that so far as possible she cooked and ate and did things with Ezra alone; and that when Ezra and Olga were doing something she kept to her room. Though she was living in Olga's house, she maintained only the most distant and frigid relations with her. And Olga seethed with resentment. 'One solid year, Dorothy made use of me to the fullest,' she wrote when the year was over, while 'I worked like a slave—cooking, cleaning, finding food—which I only undertook owing to her incapacity, so that E. should not suffer.' It seemed to her that Dorothy had behaved with 'incredible meanness... in terror lest I have some advantage over her'. And Dorothy, when she had left Olga's house and was with Isabel Pound, noted that her life then was 'a mild purgatorio compared to the HELL of No. 60'.

That inferno of freezing hatred and burning resentment was covered up according to the code of behaviour they had in common, a code which held that social relations required the suppression of personal feelings. 'We were all civilized people,' Olga Rudge told Humphrey Carpenter in 1983. And Ezra, as the lofty apex of the two-sided triangle, with his principle of taking no account of personal feelings, would have affected to be merely diverted by their 'asperities'. But when Olga came to read the lamenting cry 'AOI' in the draft of canto 81 he sent out from the Pisan prison camp, she wept unrestrainedly before her daughter, hearing in it the stress of the year when he been 'pent up with two women who loved him, whom he loved, and who coldly hated each other'.

Life was difficult enough without all that. After the war Dorothy recalled how there had been 'no water at Olga's' in the dry season; and in the cold no heating, and a 'perpetual struggle about wood and/or charcoal' for cooking. There had been bombers overhead most nights—'we used to see and hear over the mountains Genoa being destroyed week after week'. Some bombs were dropped on Rapallo—the main church and a railroad bridge were badly damaged—and one morning the church of S. Giorgio at Portofino across the bay was gone from the skyline. On 14 September 1944, Pound wrote to Mezzasoma about a local treasure under threat:

In Rapallo the main plaza has been devastated by bombs, although several of the arches dating back to the fourteenth century were undamaged. It now seems that Genoa's civil engineer has ordered them torn down, probably with good intentions, but...

The Riviera has already lost much and we do not want the plaza at Rapallo to be among the treasures lost. These old arches resisted the bombing raid and several of them are works of art...

Perhaps you can put this letter in the hands of someone who can halt the destruction. The city is so completely abandoned that I don't know who recognizes me these days.

That feeling plea was followed by a down to earth recommendation that the same 'someone'

...would do well also to bring a little cement and calcimine to help the people in these mountains make cisterns so that they can go on a bit longer. The main problem in these hills is the lack of water; the evacuees (myself included) drink up what little there is left.

Pound had been under pressure for some time to move to Milan in order to be on call for more radio work. In mid-May he wrote to Giorgio Almirante of the Ministry of Popular Culture, saying that he was already writing 'every day for the radio', but that he would 'find the means – or at least... attempt to find the means—to get there', that is, to Milan, 'the minute I am convinced that my voice should be heard over the radio'. He would like to be able to go 'occasionally by camion for two or three weeks at a time', as he had formerly gone down to Rome, in order to record a batch of radio speeches for broadcasting. But he would need, he warned, 'some sort of porter service', since 'my physical strength is not what it used to be... I can no longer lift or move heavy suitcases.' No doubt his ability to carry heavy suitcases had just been exhausted; but what the letter really meant was that he did not want to go to Milan at all unless it was to resume broadcasting in his own voice to America. Otherwise, from his isolation in Sant'Ambrogio, he would keep on doing what he thought the world situation called for.

'Isolation is very instructive', he told Mezzasoma near the end of September, in a letter implying that Confucius was his consolation; but 'not everyone', he added, 'can grasp a millennial text to reinforce their morale'. He was immersing himself again in the constructive element of the Confucian texts, and trying to get them published in Italian for those who might grasp them whole. For the rest, among the people of Rapallo, for example, he was trying to spread at least some key thoughts and sayings to keep up their morale. The broadsheet manifesto signed by Pound with other 'Tigullian' writers had contained the first of these Confucian principles: 'Il tesoro di una nazione è la sua honestà,' 'a nation's treasure is its honesty,' or 'Equity is the treasure of states.' Then he had posters printed, half a metre long, to be pasted up on walls:

COSI' VIVERE CHE I TUOI FIGLI E I LORO DISCENDENTI TI RINGRAZINO
[*So live that your children and their descendants will be grateful to you*]
LUCRO privato NON costituisce la prosperità
[*Private PROFIT does NOT create prosperity*]
L'ARCERE che manca il centro del bersaglio cerce la causa dell'errore
dentro sè stesso
[*The Archer who misses the bulls-eye seeks the source of the error within himself*]
La Purezza Funge Senza Termine, in tempo e in spazio senza termine
[*The Light of Heaven Acts Without Limit, in time and in space without limit*]

Another poster, bearing Pound's own Blakeian slogan, was much larger, 33 cm. × 69 cm.:

Una nazione che non vuole indebitarsi fa rabbia agli usurai!
[*A nation that will not go into debt puts the usurers in a rage!*]

Some of these may have been posted on *La voce della verità*, a wall used for information and propaganda in Alessandria; and Pound urged Mezzasoma to have the radio use these and other such slogans. He regarded them as seeds of enlightenment which, if they took root in people's minds, would clarify their understanding and direct their will. 'Propaganda', he told Mezzasoma, 'should aim for the creation of a state of mind which is conducive to action.' What he did not spell out in so many words was that his propaganda was ethical, not political nor military, and that it was designed to instigate a socially responsible reconstruction of Italy.

The only regular outlet for his propaganda through 1944 and into 1945 was an RSI newspaper published by the Federazione dei Fasci Repubblicani di Combattimento in Alessandria, an undistinguished provincial capital situated on the plain north from Genoa and south from Turin and Milan. *Il Popolo di Alessandria*, in its first year a single sheet printed on both sides, came out twice a week and had a circulation of around 135,000. Pound had aspired to write for the older and more prestigious newspapers, Turin's *La Stampa* and Milan's *Corriere della sera*, and had been recommended to the latter by Mezzasoma, but its editor deemed Pound's Italian 'incomprehensible' and wouldn't print him. Pound riposted that being able to write good Italian did not guarantee good sense. To the editor of *Il Popolo di*

Alessandria, however, he admitted that his style was rough, and that the editor, Gaetano Cabella, might want to correct it. Cabella invited him, in January 1944, to send in 'brief articles, both lively and polemical, on the subjects in which we have seen you to be so well versed'. Between February and August Pound contributed something to nearly every issue of the paper, forty-four items in all, and then a further sixteen between November and April 1945. A lot of these were very brief, as Cabella had stipulated, just a slogan or few column inches at a time, though he was allowed up to a full column after the paper doubled in size in September 1944.

One can read through Pound's articles and notice only the expected subjects: economic matters—the nation's money—the malign power of the usurers and their perennial war—the deficiencies of the intelligentsia and the consequent ignorance of the populace—the immediate need of Confucius—the need for informed action, especially on the part of writers. Thus one reads again, 'This war did not begin in 1939. It is a phase of the thousand-year war between the usurer and whoever does an honest day's work.' Then, 'Against this infamy Italy rose up, then Germany rose up, with the result'—and here there is a shocking cut to the present—'with the result that the slaves of Judah are destroying the masterworks of Siena, Pisa, and Rome'. The following adjustment of focus is no less injurious, 'No use being anti-Semitic while leaving their monetary system in place.' One reads again, and wishes again that he would apply it to his own propaganda, that the professors have forgotten 'Aristotle's precept, that knowledge of universals comes from knowing particulars'. But then there is a concerned paragraph that does draw on his local knowledge, about sabotage of the 'Amassi', the system for paying the peasants a fair price for their grain and olive oil and for ensuring a fair distribution of the produce. In the end, though, one's expectations are pretty well confirmed, and it seems just right that the last words of his final article, a citation of Gesell published on 23 April 1945, should be 'la moneta', money.

However, when one pays attention to a few articles that stand rather apart from those invariables of Pound's prose, and to his correspondence with Mezzasoma, one finds a remarkable (but unremarked) change taking place in his attitude to the 'Rivoluzione Fascista'. In February 1944, in the first of his regular contributions to *Il Popolo di Alessandria*, he was implicitly blaming the downfall of Fascism, not on Ciano and the others who had just been shot for having supposedly conspired to overthrow Mussolini at the time of his dismissal by the king, but on 'I GRANDI AVVELENATORI', the 'great poisoners', who had first made the Revolution necessary and had ever since undermined it. Then in March he was concerned about those who through ignorance had no faith in Fascism, and about those who had lost their faith in it. Short-sighted liberals, profiteers, and all sorts of Italians, were anti-Fascist, he suggested, simply because, not knowing how agriculture had been ruined under imperial Rome by the importation of cheap wheat from Egypt, they did not appreciate the importance of making Italy self-sufficient. 'Italy is full of people who do not know what Fascism means,' he told Mezzasoma, 'They see only the riots and the strict regimentation of the system.' He concluded, 'The Fascist regime is only as good as its propaganda,' meaning, presumably, that people would not support what they did not understand and could not believe in.

Then there were those who had once believed and who had become disgusted with 'the many betrayals'. In an article which appeared near the end of May Pound wrote that he was sorry but he had to write about someone who had become so embittered by the disparity between the regime's programme and its practice that he had reached the point of no longer believing in the efficacity of any idea, not just of the Fascist idea. There was someone else, someone who had been there for the March on Rome and the war in Spain, but who now would only curse the bad faith of those in high places whom everyone now knew to have been in bad faith. And it grieved Pound that these people would not join in the task which seemed to him to be the image of their desire. What exactly that task was he did not say just then. But a fortnight later, on 8 June, he introduced a 'document' apparently sent to him as a response to that article by an Italian whose credentials were that he had resisted both the dismissal of Mussolini and Badoglio's surrender. This 'document' implicitly accepted the truth of what Pound had reported, and set out what the new Italian should be doing to recover his good name and prestige, beginning with this elementary requirement: 'It is time for schools in the Repubblica Sociale Italiana to teach the young... respect for the given word, fidelity to a pact freely entered into, and a love for truth and justice.' Pound endorsed this, associated it with the Confucian doctrine that civic order is from ethical order, and concluded with this striking statement, 'The Italian Risorgimento was a light in the world—that light will rise again.' The previous week he had written that whoever had not the Fascist faith, 'una fede fascista', was in a death-like state; but here, with the RSI's teaching and practice in question, it was instead the *Risorgimento*, the nineteenth-century resurgence of Italy, that he invoked. One senses a cooling toward the Salò regime, as in that voicing of disaffection, and in the implication that the regime was failing through lack of integrity. Yet there is still an unshaken commitment to recovering the desired and prerequisite ethical order.

By November of 1944 Pound was insisting to Mezzasoma that the recovery had to be brought about, not by state propaganda, but rather by individuals studying and teaching, and that this was the task in which all who desired the renewal of Italy should join. He wanted the Ministry to launch an appeal through the press and the radio along these lines:

all men of goodwill who have a small degree of culture and those who formerly opposed the errors of the regime... those who opposed the hidden treachery and the sabotage that was carried on even before the year XXI (for example, censorship not decreed by the government but that masqueraded and pretended to be official), those who have learned something of this treachery and of the chaos that followed it, are invited to bridge the gaps of their political culture.

They were to do this by learning the facts of economics, through the study of Pound's favoured authors; and further, by reconnecting with their cultural roots:

All scholars isolated in invaded territory as well as in the Republic are invited to reread the Greek and Latin classics so as to find therein the reason the enemy wants to suppress or diminish the studies of the sources of our culture and our political wisdom, which is our most precious heritage.

In another letter to Mezzasoma about the same time Pound added another element to the appeal to be addressed 'to all those who could do something useful for the future of Italy'—

Study, inform yourselves, publish as much as you can and prepare in silence if you are in invaded territory, even if you are in danger; study the truth which we want to see disseminated and which the enemy fears...

We want facts; we want truth. We are against usurers and monopolists. Only an autonomous nation can resist the infamy of universal usury. Anyone who has texts useful for the enrichment of our invaded territory should study them, publish them, distribute them.

Pound was already doing his own bit for this programme, with the economic pamphlets and translations of Confucius published by Sammartano, and with a selection of the sayings of Confucius soon to appear in *Il Popolo di Alessandria*.

The programme was of course altogether his own, and in these and other letters he was encouraging Mezzasoma to popularize it as if it were what the regime itself stood for. In effect Pound was seeking to convert the RSI's propaganda effort to his own ends. Still more subversively, he was calling for the reconstruction of Italy to be the work, not of the discredited Fascist Party, but of individuals of good will and active intelligence. He was looking beyond Fascism, and beyond Mussolini, to a return to the permanent ground of a good society, and to the democratic principle that 'our cherished rights of liberty and equality depend on the active participation of an awakened electorate'. His faith in Fascism, which had been mostly a faith in Mussolini, had failed with the failure of Fascism's revolution. But he had not lost faith and hope in the fundamental republican idea. Back in February 1944 he had stated that idea quite bluntly to Mezzasoma, 'Enforcement of the law comes from the consent of the people.' That, as Redman remarked, 'is not exactly a fascist slogan'. It is rather a principle that would restore power to the people, as it had done as the basis of America's revolution of 1776.

On 16 December 1944 a dejected Mussolini—'cajoled', Farrell writes, 'by diehard Fascists such as Pavolini'—travelled from Lake Garda down to Milan to give what would prove to be his last public speech. He spoke of his vision of a socialist concord, and of those who had betrayed it. The speech had been signalled on the radio as an event of 'exceptional importance'; the Teatro Lirico had been packed; the applause had been 'spontaneous and deafening'; and afterwards 'enormous crowds [had given] him a hero's welcome'. Yet Pound made no overt reference in *Il Popolo di Alessandria* to this reappearance of Il Duce.[1] However he did begin an article, on 23 January, with what may well have been an indirect allusion to what Mussolini had said. 'It is the common fate of all revolutions to be betrayed,' he wrote, instancing the way the American revolution had ended in a victory for the usurocracy. Then he went on, now alluding fairly directly to Mussolini's RSI programme, 'To establish social justice, a new order based on work. Very good!' But he evidently expected that this new phase of the Fascist revolution, if it were achieved, would be betrayed in its turn, by allowing the plutocrats back in—unless the issue of money were studied, and unless the classics were studied. He was relying on those studies, and no longer on Mussolini, to save and to continue the revolution.

In mid-November 1944 Pound had enclosed some 'cantos' in a letter to Mezzasoma, evidently hoping they might be 'useful' in some way, while fearing that they would prove 'too crude for the refined and too complex for the simple-minded'. These cantos would have been in Italian, and it has been assumed that they were the cantos 72 and 73 notoriously not included in collected editions of *The Cantos* in Pound's lifetime. However, those two cantos, we can be fairly certain, were not written, or at any rate not completed, before the end of December 1944. That makes it probable that the cantos Pound offered Mezzasoma in November were translations

[1] It is true that on the 14th he had complained to Nicoletti, '*Popolo di Alessandria* in confusion. I don't have an outlet. Presses stopped.'—but then his articles did go on appearing there occasionally from the end of December into April 1945.

of previously published cantos, possibly ones he had set Mary to translating in 1942, the Malatesta sequence, or cantos 13 ('Kung') or 27 ('tovarisch'). Any of those could have come within Pound's idea of what would be useful at that moment. But whatever it was Pound sent remained unused.

Mary had concluded, when her father tore into her neatly typed translations, that he was really trying to find out how to compose cantos in 'the voices and modes' of Cavalcanti and Dante, and that is precisely what he was attempting in his two 'Italian cantos'. Canto 72 is in the mode of a canto of Dante's *Inferno*, and canto 73 is mostly in the mode of Cavalcanti's 'Ballata IX'. Pound sent both cantos to Mary, then working as a secretary in a hospital for German soldiers in Cortina, as a gift for Epiphany, 6 January 1945. But to Mezzasoma he sent only the prologue of 72, on 26 December, and a 26-line extract from that opening was the only portion of the canto published by Pound then or later. The whole of canto 73 was sent to Mezzasoma, and also to Cabella the editor of *Il Popolo di Alessandria*, on 9 January; and it appeared entire in *La marina repubblicana* on 1 February.

The fragment of 72, perhaps significantly described as its 'conclusion', appeared in *La marina repubblicana* on 15 January, headed 'Presenza di F. T. Marinetti | di Ezra Pound'. It was prefaced by a fulsome eulogy of Pound by his friend the retired admiral Ubaldo degli Uberti who had just taken over the editorship. 'Ezra Pound', he wrote, 'an American, but a friend of Fascist Italy in the highest and purest sense of the word', and a profound poet, has raised up from the dead the spirit of his recently deceased friend Marinetti, so that the patriotic hero might encourage the living, 'who must still fight on in the mud and destruction, to hold our heads high and not be overwhelmed'. '*Presenza*' would indicate that Marinetti though dead is a real presence; further, when in the final line of the extract his spirit shouts 'PRESENTE', it is as if he were answering a military roll-call; and beyond that he might be participating in 'the simple rite' observed in Fascist meetings where the names of fallen comrades were called one by one and all together shouted '*Presente!*', so as to give the dead a forceful presence among them. Mussolini's idea was that dedicated Fascists should be made ready to follow the lead of their 'martyrs'.

In the dialogue with Marinetti Pound, while allowing him a heroic and exemplary presence, explicitly declines to follow his lead. 'Go make yourself a hero again', he tells him, go on fighting Italy's enemies if you want to; but his own chosen part will be to 'sing of the eternal war | between light and mud'. He does promise to give Marinetti a place and a voice in his canto beyond that 'PRESENTE'. What he has him say though, in the then unpublished lines that follow, is an inwardly reflective judging of himself and of the poet:

'I followed vain emptiness in many ways,
                    show more than wisdom,
and knew not the ancient sages
                nor read Confucius & Mencius
I sang war, and you wanted peace.
Both of us blind, me to the inner things
                            you the things of today.'

A little further on the poet passes his own judgment on Marinetti, saying that he had wanted the future too much, and

Too much eagerness shoots past the mark
He wanted to clear away too much
and now we see more destruction than he wanted.

The end of that encounter is the poet's hearing Marinetti's voice joining in the fierce singing from 'a white skull on the white sand' of Macalé in former Abyssinia and of El Alamein in Egypt, a song insisting '"we will return | *We* w i l l r e t u r n"', to fight again in those places where Italian forces had endured decisive defeats. 'I believe you', the poet says, to pacify him.

The rest of the canto is dominated by the savage voice of Ezzelino da Romano, a bloody tyrant speaking as if from the hell where Dante placed him, or as if rising from the pages of Mussato's Senecan tragedy in which he figures as a monster-begotten Terror of Italy. The voice thunders that he has risen from the earth 'to drive out the foreigners' who have destroyed Forlì, burned Rimini and the Tempio—'"divine Ixotta's" resting place'—who have brought 'Rape and fire as far as Bagnacavallo', and whose 'dung flow has got to Bologna'. He goes on to honour Fascist heroes, Farinacci—a proponent of violence and of the alliance with Hitler, mistrusted by Mussolini—and a dozen generals who had fallen in the Abyssinian and Egyptian campaigns. 'Blazing phrases without sense' follow, until other voices break in, 'Confusion of voices as from several transmitters', and the poet makes out

Many birds singing in counterpoint
In the summer morning
        and through their twitterings
a suave tone:
        'I was Placidia and slept beneath the gold'.
[It sounded like a note from a well tuned string.]
        'Woman's melancholy and gentleness,'...
                        I began to say

But what the poet would say in response to her musical voice is prevented by Ezzelino seizing him in an iron grip and forcing him to listen only to his own fierce voice, before he turns 'back into the night | Where the skull sings: | The regiments and the banners will return.'

This conclusion to the canto dramatizes the predicament of the poet gripped in an infernal nightmare where the voices of violence and war drown out the gentler, peaceful sounds of birdsong and Placidia. Taken as a whole, the canto represents those who would make war as being in an infernal state of mind, which the poet would escape if he could. Hastily read, it could seem to endorse Marinetti's and Ezzelino's singing along with the Fascist death's head. But once register how all three are placed in the violent darkness of a Dantescan hell and the judgment goes against them. Small wonder if Pound did not send the entire canto to Mezzasoma.

The wonder then is that canto 73 should altogether lack that saving irony. After his nightmare the poet sleeps, and wakes to see and hear Dante's heretical friend Guido Cavalcanti denouncing, in terms near to a recent speech of Mussolini's, Roosevelt, Churchill, Eden, and their usurers' war and ways. He is looking for the morning star or dawn of the *riscossa*, a word much in the mouths of Mussolini and his propagandists, and open to interpretation. It could mean the recovery, as from defeat; or liberation, as from enemy occupation; or repayment, as by revenge; or it could mean redemption, as from guilt or dishonour. In the canto Cavalcanti finds promise of *riscossa* in the action of a peasant girl of Rimini. She had been raped by Canadian soldiers when Rimini fell to them. When another group of Canadians, with German prisoners, ask the way to the Via Emilia she leads them into a minefield and is blown up with them—the Germans are saved. Cavalcanti, a spirit from Dante's *terzo cielo*, the sphere of love, comes upon her spirit singing joyfully of love, with a German on each arm, and he celebrates her joy in dying gloriously for her country, or (in Mussolini's phrase), *nella riscossa della Patria.* So Pound's Cavalcanti, the poet of the intelligence of love, is presented perceiving a sort of suicide bomber as a redeemer of the Romagna's and of Italy's honour, and as a heroine leading the recovery of its Fascist spirit. 'In the [Fascist] North the fatherland is reborn,' he ends, making her now representative of the young who 'wear the black' of Pavolini's notoriously violent *Brigate Nere*, Salò's 'volunteer force similar to the Fascist *squadre* of old'.

The story as a matter of fact was straight from current propaganda. Rimini had been bombarded more than any other city in Italy, from air, land, and sea—Sigismondo Malatesta's Tempio had been seriously damaged, to Pound's great grief—and the final battle for it in August and September 1944 was one of the most notable of the war. Rimini fell to

Greek and Canadian troops on 21 September, and the battle around it ended on the 29th. The story of 'the heroine of Rimini' was broadcast on Milan radio that day, taken up on 1 October by *Corriere della sera* and other newspapers, then retold over and over again in magazines and books through the following months. It was almost certainly a fabrication. The heroine was never identified, the supposed facts were never substantiated; but that meant that the story served all the better as allegory and myth. The heroine who revenges her dishonour and thus symbolically regains her honour stands for Italy raped and dishonoured by the enemies of its revolution, and in symbol meets its need for redemption.

Pound sought to transform the propaganda into poetry by making Cavalcanti its celebrant, and by imitating the taut phrasing and rich rhyming of his *canzone* and *ballate*. The result is a powerful and effective rhetorical composition, but one in which the art serves the propaganda without bringing a properly poetic and critical intelligence to bear on it. One might well conclude that in this canto at least Pound had finally given up his voice to Fascism.

Yet there is more to the canto than that, something more deeply and more significantly challenging. Pound's introducing Cavalcanti as the perceiver of the story manifests his own will to perceive the violent acting out of a just anger as an action of heavenly love—a will to identify *Ira*, the anger that destroys what it hates, with *Amor*, the love that animates and sustains the right ordering of things. What Pound apparently wanted, over and beyond any propagandist intent, was to have the heroine's violence understood as the negative aspect of a positive desire for justice, and as being not against, but essentially in accord with natural law.

A will to identify the 'Charybdis of action' with the paradise of love lies behind a group of drafts in Italian, for a canto or cantos to follow 73, which Pound was working on in January and February 1945. The drafts were abandoned before reaching a final form, probably because of the strains and distractions of the last months of the war in Italy and in Europe, though some of the leading elements would resurface in *The Pisan Cantos.*

The concern evident in them was not new. An earlier fragment (headed 'LXX...') had declared Pound's own action in writing radio scripts to be from love of right order. 'Est deus in nobis', there is a god in us, he wrote, and named the god 'Amor': 'Know Mithra est Amor... | est Amor Mazda.' Mithra was the god of the Roman legions, and 'Piero Mazda' a pseudonym under which Pound had written some scripts for Ranieri to broadcast immediately after the fall of Mussolini. The fragment goes on to associate his 'putting his ideas in order', in his propaganda, with Venus and Adonis and the rites of abundance, and then with the divine intelligence, 'nous-amor'. That gives a stark indication of the state of mind and the preoccupation which he was attempting to work out in the drafts of January and February 1945.

One immediately striking feature, especially when one comes to them after reading 72 and 73, is how distanced the infernal war is now, and how indirectly it is noticed. Instead there are glimpses and intimations of a *paradiso terrestre* such as Dante enters at the summit of his *Purgatorio*. The actual scene is Pound's own Sant'Ambrogio, with its hillside of olive groves, its birdsong, its *salita* and trace of the old Roman Aurelian Way, and with the Tyrrhenian sea below. In the fresh spring sunlight numinous presences appear, both human and divine.

An alba-like passage has the birds start up again the sweet singing that had accompanied Galla Placidia's interrupted words in 73. With her now comes Cunizza da Romano, Ezzelino's sister and Sordello's lover, whom Dante placed in his *terzo cielo*; and with Cunizza are troubadours singing in her honour of the love which moves the gentle heart—Arnaut's rendering of birds in spring, 'Douz brais e criz', and Bernart de Ventadorn's 'no other sight can match her image in my mind'. 'Love overcame me,' Cunizza says, as in Dante, and becomes a ray of light which draws the poet's sight upward, until he sees on their thrones Gautama Buddha and Confucius, the former in an eternal dream of beauty, and Confucius 'who gave the eternal law... and rules a lasting dynasty'. The poet comments, 'fine thought | and fine action are two in this aspect'; and yet he would see them as connected if he could. The voice of Erigena (for whom all that exists is formed of Light) assures him that they are indeed linked, while adding that the poet is not yet in a position to see them directly.

Next to appear is Caterina Sforza, a martial woman one would not expect to meet in this celestial company. Machiavelli had diplomatic dealings with her and was deeply impressed by 'her beauty, her greatness of soul, and the strength of her castle'. Pound has her come demanding, 'Why do you not bear arms', and highlights one incident in her remarkable career. When her enemies had her under siege in her castle and were threatening to hang her children from the walls if she did not surrender, Caterina defied them from the battlements, lifting her skirt and calling 'Ne ho ancora lo stampa,' 'I still have the mould.' Also recalled is her shooting those on her own side who refused to fight for her, two out of every ten. Basinio, court poet to Sigismundo Malatesta, greets her as 'hawk-eyed lady', and declares that in her 'beyond love there shines forth courage'. 'One does not live by reason | without *ira* and without substance', he further comments, and concludes, 'you are because you loved'. She changes in his sight then, much as Cunizza had changed, appearing as 'a spark | colour of Mars . . . from hammered iron on the anvil'. She too, we gather, is to be seen as an illuminated spirit in the paradise of love, along with Cunizza, though in counterpoint to her.

The third major presence first appears on the *salita* as a barefoot girl saying 'I am the evacuee. I am la luna | . . . | where I lived has just been destroyed | la sofia of the cliffs | my chapel.' In another more developed draft she appears on the *salita* after the dawn vision of Cunizza and Gautama and Confucius, and, as the poet wonders that she is neither known to him nor unknown, she says, 'my house is broken | Della Grazie is tumbled down into the sea | by the bombers | I go to Pantaleo to find rest.'[2] Yet another draft recognizes her as the compassionate Madonna of Montallegro on Monte Rosa, where she is honoured as the help of sailors in shipwreck; it then associates her with Kuanon, the Chinese spirit of compassion, and with Lucina, the Roman goddess of childbirth. She protests that she is not 'Sophia . . . hieratic/mosaic'd'; rather she is 'the driven out one', known also as 'Pietà' with her crucified son in her arms. 'Io son l'assunta', are her last words, I am she who has been taken up into heaven.

There is no clear indication of the relation of this composite figure of divine compassion to Cunizza and to Caterina. Pound has them meet at 'il triedro', which he once likened to 'the inside corner of a cube-shape', thus suggesting the joining together of three distinct planes or dimensions. Evidently the three are meant to form a trinity of the powers which made up Pound's vision of paradise in the early months of 1945: refining love, active courage, and compassion. The love and the courage are both of them perceived as perfections of human nature, while the compassion, it would appear, is something driven out and still to be hoped and prayed for.

'I thank god that soon this war will be over,' Pound wrote to Mary on 6 March 1945. He was 'living, per forza, poeticamente | go down to Rapallo once a week'. But 'i forti sono partiti', those who might stand firm were all gone, and it was a job 'to find 3 persons to agree'—to agree, that would have been, on the second manifesto which he was then composing. Still, that was a day on which he had worked well, he told her, being 'in the middle of a new opusculus, "Lavori e privileggi"—Angold; Gesell; etc.'

A week later he was gathering material for new cantos, and had spent a whole day 'looking for a bit of Frobenius to attach to another from Herodotus . . . but cdn't find it in *Erlebte Erdteile*.' He was looking for the

[2] The shrine of the Madonna of Monte Allegro (also known as Monte Rosa) is above Rapallo; San Pantaleo is a little church on the hillside of Sant'Ambrogio, some way along from the top of the *salita*; the sanctuary of the Madonna della Grazie is on the cliffs down the coast from Rapallo.

Soninke legend of 'Gassir's Lute', which tells how the city called Wagadu fell and was rebuilt four times, falling through vanity, then through falsehood, the third time through greed, and finally through dissension; and each time it was rebuilt from the image of it in the mind and the longing for it of her children. Pound had the idea of connecting the cry for its rebuilding with the evocation in Herodotus of the wondrously planned city built by Deïoces the just ruler of Ecbatan, a city ringed by seven strong walls rising one above the other and each of a different colour.

His mind was running on images of construction and reconstruction, but not on any rebuilding of Fascism. 'Caro Ub, non si costruisce sulla merda', he wrote on a postcard to Degli Uberti, one doesn't build on shit. His conviction was that one must build rather, as it is written in the *Ta S'eu*, with 'the light which comes from looking straight into the heart and then acting'. Back in January he had been reading Dante's *Paradiso*, and one can see in one of his copies of the poem an ideogram from the *Ta S'eu* set in the margin against some lines in the final canto. There Dante is declaring how his will was informed by a vision of 'the Love that moves the sun and other stars', and against that stands the ideogram for 'the action resultant from the straight gaze into the heart'. It is as if Pound's response to Dante's ecstatic vision was to recall the Confucian principle that the empowering light is to be looked for in the individual heart.

That principle lies behind the *Secondo Manifesto del Tigullio*, a broadsheet dated '23 Marzo anno XXIII'. Pound had after all found his three other signatories in Rapallo. Their opening statement was along the lines of what Pound had been putting to Mezzasoma in the previous year, that the real enemy of the Republic was ignorance, ignorance of economics and of the classics. Then come some constructive memoranda, and it is here that one finds the Republic projected in Confucian rather than in Fascist terms. First it is asserted that the function of the system of *amassi* should be, as it was at the start, to guarantee a just return to the producer, and further, to pay him to cultivate his land to the utmost. Then, in parallel, it is asserted that cultivated Italians should be enabled and encouraged to increase their useful knowledge and to make it available to the collectivity. In each case what is desirable and necessary for the common good originates with the productive individual, and the function of the state is ancillary.

But all of that was of no account in these last days of the war in Europe. The end, when at last it came, came very quickly. On 18 April German forces in western Germany surrendered, and on the 21st, the Russians entered Berlin. In Italy, the Allies entered Bologna on the 21st, with the Germans retreating in disorder along the Po. During the night of the 23rd/24th the RSI's military left Genoa heading north, leaving the city to be viciously contested for the moment by Germans, local Fascists, and partisans.

In Rapallo, 'partigiani took over', Dorothy noted on the 24th, and on the 26th, 'occupation by USA'. The 'Buffalo' division of the US Army—enlisted black soldiers with white officers—was moving through. On the 27th, Olga Rudge's students were let out to celebrate the liberation, and she tried to report herself to the US Army Command set up in a hotel on the waterfront, but the officers there had no time for a stray expatriate American, so she went back up to Sant'Ambrogio. The next day, a Saturday, Pound went down himself, 'not in a spirit of surrender' but meaning to put his expert knowledge of Italy at the disposal of the Americans, only to find they had moved on to Genoa, now abandoned by the Germans. He came across a lone black soldier 'lookin' fo' his comman'', who offered to sell him a bicycle. He walked home up the *salita* and went on with his translation of Mencius.

In the afternoon of that day, the 28th, Mussolini was shot near Lake Como by the Communist partisans into whose hands he had fallen, and his body, along with those of his mistress, Clara Petacci, and of sixteen other leading Fascists who had been captured with him and executed by firing squad, were taken to Milan and dumped in Piazzale Loreto in the middle of the night. On the Sunday the corpses of Mussolini, Petacci, and five others were abused by the crowd then hung upside down from the girders of a nearby petrol station. Dorothy wrote in her diary, 'giustizati', put to death, 'Mussolini Benito | Pavolini Alessandro | Mezzasoma...'

The next day Olga, evidently fearing that any violence was now possible, wrote to Mary as if for the last time, 'in case anything should happen to me', giving her the addresses of family and friends and details of important papers and possessions. Her 'last words' were, 'Take care of yourself, and try to forget the war and be happy...read EP's works and study them well...You have always been a joy and consolation to me.'

On Monday the 30th Hitler put an end to his own life in his Berlin bunker. The German forces still in Italy surrendered on 2 May—the unconditional surrender of all German forces in Europe would follow on the 7th. By then Pound was in American custody.

On Thursday 3 May he was alone in the house at Sant'Ambrogio. Dorothy had gone down at 9.00 to the flat in via Marsala, and then to visit Isabel Pound for lunch. It was 'very cold', she noted. Olga was also down in Rapallo seeking information, having heard that the Americans were back. She waited an hour to see the officer in charge, but he 'was busy with the local authorities and refused to see her'. During the morning Pound was working on his Mencius translation when there was a hammering on the door. He opened it—some say it was kicked open—and he was confronted by two men, one pointing a tommy-gun. 'Seguici, traditore', he was ordered, 'traitor, come with us.' That they should call him 'traitor' rather than 'Fascist' was interesting. Evidently they were 'partigiani', but the swelling numbers of partisans were mostly engaged in the *caccia al fascista*, the hunting down of Fascists. This pair—later denounced as ex-Fascist petty criminals, one of whom would be executed for murder and the other jailed for theft—apparently knew that Pound had been charged with treason and supposed that the Americans would be offering a reward for turning him in. Pound pocketed two of the books he had open on the table—a one-volume edition of the Confucian *Four Books*, and a small Chinese–English dictionary—locked the door, and handed the key to the neighbour who lived on the ground floor. She asked where they were taking him, and was told, 'the command in Zoagli'. He was led down the *salita* towards Rapallo, on the way picking up a dried seed from a eucalyptus tree beside the path, and at the foot of the *salita* was put into a car and driven the two or three miles round the coast to Zoagli. When Olga found the door locked, and learnt where he had been taken, she immediately set out for Zoagli by the *salita* which goes directly down to it from the chapel of San Pantaleo along the hillside. Dorothy returned to the house about 6 in the evening to find both Ezra and Olga gone—'EP gone away | Olg followed', she wrote in her diary. She would leave Casa 60 when Olga returned without Pound some days later, packing all her things and arranging for them to be carried back down to via Marsala. She would move in with Isabel Pound who lived in the Villa Raggio in the Cerisola part of town.

In Zoagli Olga found Pound being guarded by armed men while a civilian, apparently the new mayor, interrogated a Fascist prisoner. When it was Pound's turn he asked to be taken to the American command further down the coast in Chiavari. It was now one o'clock and Olga went out and begged some food from English troops stationed in the town—'DEElicious ham sandwich', according to Pound, and canned beer. At four o'clock he was taken to Chiavari, Olga insisting on going with him. The driver could not find the American command and instead took them to the partisan prison. There 'the courtyard... had obviously been used for executions', Pound later recalled. According to Olga, 'They had been paying off old scores' and the walls were covered in blood. Again he asked to be taken to the American command, which was in fact across the river in Lavagna. The partisan in charge, a respected member of the Resistance, said that Pound was perfectly free so far as he was concerned, and he was damned if he would give him up to the Americans, unless that was what he wanted.

Pound said that was precisely what he wanted, and was then driven in an army jeep to the Allied Military Post. There a Colonel Webber had heard of Ezra Pound. He asked if they were hungry, had 'K-ration box lunches' given to them, and gave an order for them to be driven up to Genoa and to be delivered to the US Counter Intelligence Center there. They set out about five o'clock and arrived at the CIC about seven.

Pound was now a prisoner, and would never again be completely free.

PART TWO : 1945

6 : Talking To The FBI

Pound was resolute that he had done no wrong. He was eager to explain himself, confident that when they had heard him out the American authorities would see reason. And he wanted to make himself useful, to show them that he was a responsible citizen. At the first opportunity he asked that a cable be sent on his behalf to President Truman, begging to be allowed to negotiate peace terms with Japan via its embassy at Salò. 'FENOLLOSA'S EXECUTOR AND TRANSLATOR OF CONFUCIUS CAN WHAT VIOLENCE CANNOT', he dictated, meaning that 'he would appeal not to the Japanese militarists, but to the ancient culture of Japan'. At the same time he drafted an 'exclusive' for Reynolds Packard of Associated Press, 'Man I most want to talk to is Kumrad Koba (Stalin) hope to meet him in Georgia'—'(Caucasus Georgia)', he added, to avoid misapprehension. He was thinking of setting Russia's absolute ruler right about the 'one point' Communism had got wrong, that 'you need not . . . take over the means of production'. But of course there wasn't a hope of his meeting Stalin, any more than there was of his negotiating a peace with Japan, and at some level he must have been perfectly aware of that.

Objectively considered, those were crazed fantasies; subjectively, however, they were play-acting with a purpose. Pound was trying to take control of his situation, and to determine how he should be perceived—not as a traitor, but as someone who could advise the world's leaders. For over a decade he had done his best to advise Mussolini; in 1939 he had attempted to advise Roosevelt; so now he would naturally seek to address Truman and Stalin. Of course his professed faith in the efficacy of speaking simple truths to the powerful was absurdly out of touch with the realities of power. But in his immediate predicament it made sense to appear in his self-appointed role of mentor to the mighty.

He could not gauge, however, the depth of routine prejudice with which he was eyed by the intelligence services of the United States and of Great Britain. To them he was clearly and simply an indicted traitor who had gone over to the Fascist enemy.

In Britain MI5 had been interested in 'P[olice] F[ile] 34319. POUND' for some time. In 1943 they had added to his file an 'Extract from article in "News Review" dated 5.8.43', concerning the indictment in America of 'eight Haw-Haws for treason':

For weeks the criminal division of the U.S. Department of Justice, Federal Bureau of Investigation and Special War Policies Unit had listened patiently to regular broadcasts by these Fascist stooges over the Axis radio.

Declared Attorney-General Francis Biddle: each of the octet will be tried by a jury of fellow citizens, if and when apprehended. The punishment for treason is death.

Only one of the eight is believed to be in Italy and consequently in immediate danger of apprehension: bearded, foppish, egocentric poet Ezra POUND (57) an expatriate from America since 1911 . . .

Well before this MI5 had been noting Pound's connections with the *British-Italian Bulletin* and with the British Union of Fascists, and had been intercepting his letters to suspect persons and organizations.

One letter intercepted in January 1940 and photocopied for the file was to Dorothy Pound's solicitor, A. V. Moore. In it Pound advised Moore 'to look into English constitutional law' on the subject of 'ex post facto laws'. MI5 read this with prejudice:

As shown by previous record (P.M.S. 0113) the writer corresponds with Fascists in England. Here he is encouraging addressee to take action in connection with some alleged breach of the constitution.

No matter that Moore, Blimpishly patriotic, would have had nothing to do with Fascists of any colour; and no matter that Pound's concern for constitutional law had nothing to with Fascism. A letter of March 1940 to Raven Thomson, editor of the British Union of Fascists' magazine *Action*, was copied for the file even though it consisted mainly of 'clauses from the preamble of Bill H.R.8080, introduced by Mr Voorhis of California, in the American "House of Representatives" on January 23 of this year'. Voorhis was challenging 'the custom of the sovereign Government borrowing from the banking system for the purpose of waging a war, thus increasing the public indebtedness', the basis of his challenge being that 'the financial credit thus lent to the Government is in reality based upon the real credit of the people, which belongs to them and not to the private banking system'. Very likely that still neglected truism had no intelligence value for MI5, the significance of the letter being just that it connected Pound with 'P.F. 46785 Raven Thomson', who was about to be interned as a British Fascist. In the same way their interest in a letter to the BUF leader Sir

Oswald Mosley, intercepted and filed in May 1940, would have been simply that it was addressed by 'P. F. 34319' to 'P. F. 48909 MOSLEY'. It was of no account that Pound was enthusiastically recommending Brooks Adams's *Law of Civilization and Decay*, and telling Mosley 'we must educate, and keep on educating'. To MI5 whatever Pound might write for Fascist publications, or even for the Social Credit Party, was simply 'Fascist' regardless of what he was trying to get across.

For the American investigators too the medium of his broadcasts was the only message: that he had broadcast on Rome Radio was enough to condemn him as anti-American. An order sent to the commanders of the US Fifth and Seventh Armies in Italy on 19 September 1943 had left small room for doubt about his guilt:

> Cable received from AGWAR as follows. 'Indictment against Doctor EZRA POUND was returned by Federal Grand Jury at WASHINGTON, DC, on 26 July 1943. Charging treason, based on his vicious anti-American broadcasts from ROME which began in 1940 [*sic*]...The Department of Justice is being requested to indicate what action it wishes taken in the event that POUND should be taken into custody.' This headquarters will be notified at once should POUND be taken into custody.

There followed a request in January 1944 from Attorney General Biddle to the Secretary of State for War:

> In the event that Dr. Pound is taken into custody by the military authorities, it is requested that he be thoroughly interrogated concerning his radio broadcasts and other activities on behalf of the Italian Government. It is also desired that an effort be made to locate and interview persons, particularly American citizens, having information regarding his acts of treason who might be utilized as witnesses in the event of prosecution...

An FBI special agent, Frank Amprim, had in fact been on Pound's case since August 1943. In June 1944 he was going through the files of EIAR in Rome and interviewing its employees; in November he was digging out the copies of Pound's scripts from the files in the Ministry of Popular Culture. Long before Pound turned up in Genoa Amprim had prepared himself to interrogate him 'regarding his acts of treason'. There would be no presumption of innocence.

The US 92nd Infantry Division Counter Intelligence Corps Detachment, briefed that Pound was 'an FBI target' whom they should 'apprehend and hold', had been 'on the lookout for him' for some time. They passed through Rapallo on their way to Genoa at the end of April, aware that

Pound had been living there, but in too much of a hurry to stop to search for him. In any case they thought he would have fled to northern Italy. A Special Agent did go down to Rapallo on 2 May, 'to arrest or check on Subject', but, misled by information that he was at Portofino, only got to Rapallo on the morning of the 3rd and so missed him. But then late that afternoon Ramon Arrizabalaga, the Special Agent in Charge of CIC in Genoa (whose 1956 'Memoir' is the source of this account), learnt that 'a Regimental Commander had in his protective custody an American Citizen, whom he was protecting from the Italian Partisans'. It was arranged that Pound should be delivered at once to the CIC office in Genoa, where he would be held according to orders at the disposition of the FBI. A couple of days later Fifth Army Headquarters in Rome announced to the press that 'The American writer and poet Ezra Pound has been captured in Northern Italy.' *Stars and Stripes*, the US Army paper, was not so careful—'Traitor Pound Reported Captured Near Genoa' was its headline.

Pound was apparently left under the illusion that he was being taken to the American command in Genoa at his own request, and had no suspicion when he was led up to the CIC offices on the sixth floor of 6 Via Fieschi that he was expected there. Olga Rudge used to tell how they were shown into a large waiting hall with hard shiny chairs. There were guards, Italian *carabinieri*, serving the Americans. People came and went, fewer and fewer as the evening wore on, and no one spoke to them. It was cold, they had nothing to eat or drink, and they had to endure the torture of the hard chairs. This went on until late in the afternoon of the next day when Pound was finally taken into an office where Frank Amprim introduced himself as an FBI Special Agent. Pound had evidently been kept waiting while the Agent on his case was notified of his capture and travelled up from FBI headquarters in Rome.

Amprim spent that first two-and-a-half hour interview getting the measure of Pound and gaining his trust. To John Drummond, whom he contacted in Rome in July in the course of his investigation, Amprim 'seemed a very decent and fair-minded person'. He wanted Drummond to confirm that the manuscripts and talks he had collected were by Pound, and Drummond, a good friend of Pound's, was happy to do that for him, simply on the 'internal evidence', being assured that Amprim was fair-minded and not looking just for 'what would help the prosecution'. 'He got on well with Ezra', Drummond reported to Ronald Duncan, 'liked him, and appeared quite convinced of his integrity, disinterestedness, and appreciates his genius'. The agent was evidently very good at his job. He could also assert his authority quite coolly. When Pound's first words were that a cable he would dictate must be sent at once to President Truman, Amprim took down the cable before telling him that 'he could not dispatch such a cable for him'. Pound 'became very indignant', Amprim reported later to his Director, J. Edgar Hoover. Pound then produced a radio script with the heading 'Ashes of Europe Calling', asking for the peace to be based on justice, and again Amprim told him 'that he could not arrange for him to make any such broadcast'. Once it was clear who was in charge Pound began to talk about his activities and ideas, all the more freely as he found in Amprim an encouraging listener. There was coffee, and some was sent out to Olga. At the end of that session Amprim arranged for them both to be put in a room with a couch and easy chairs—Olga would sleep on the couch, and Ezra on the two chairs pushed together—and made sure they were provided with 'Army K-rations, coffee and milk, and a means of heating food'. Pound was quite won over. He would say later that Amprim 'expressed himself as convinced that I was telling him the absolute truth', and that for himself he had no reason to doubt the agent's 'good faith'.

Amprim's formal interrogation of Pound went on over three days, 5, 6, and 7 May, with Arrizabalaga assisting at times. They made careful notes of what Pound said, put questions to him, then prepared a draft of the 'sworn statement' Amprim was after—a statement which, Pound acknowledged in the opening paragraph, 'can be used against me in a court of law', and which would declare, 'I am willing to return to the United States to stand trial on the charge of treason against the United States'. Pound had no legal counsel to advise him. He did insist, however, on his right to make changes and corrections to the first two or three drafts he was asked to sign. One sentence in an early draft read, 'I never was a member of the Fascist Party, but used to give the Fascist salute at all times'. Pound crossed out 'at all times' and wrote in 'occasionally'. Another sentence read, 'I was told my radio talks were giving comfort and aid to the enemies of the United States'—a sentence which could be represented as an admission that he had knowingly and deliberately committed treason. Pound wrote in the margin, 'I think my talks were giving pain to the worst enemies of the U.S.A.', and had that sentence removed. After five hours of questioning on the first of the three days Amprim could cable to the Bureau in Washington nothing more incriminating than 'ADMITS VOLUNTARY BROADCASTS FOR PAY'.

Pound wanted to explain his motives in broadcasting and the nature of his propaganda, but Amprim wanted the material facts—how did he get into broadcasting for Italian radio, who were his contacts in EIAR, how often did he broadcast, how was he paid and how much, what other related radio work had he done, and so forth. Pound evidently gave him a full and detailed account of all of that up to the moment when he walked north out of Rome in September 1943. The statement goes on to describe his work for the Salò regime, and here Pound put into the record how he had said to Mezzasoma

> that even if Italy fell I must go on with my own economic propaganda, that is my [fight for] observance of the money clause in the United States Constitution which my grandfather had fought for in 1878, saying the same things I was saying.

Instead of elaborating on his 'economic propaganda' the statement returns to Pound's dealings with the Republican Fascist Radio in Milan and with Carl Goedel in particular, again going into detail about payments. One defensive sentence stands out, 'At Milan I refused to broadcast to American troops'. Another sentence goes off at a tangent:

> However my main work from this time on [i.e. May to September of 1944] was writing and advising the CASA EDITRICE EDIZIONE POPOLARE of Venice, which publishing firm printed my version of the CHUNG YUNG of CONFUCIUS and my pamphlets on economic history. I also wrote articles on economics for 'rebel papers in smaller towns' which articles were excluded from the larger press.

Amprim appears to have shown no interest in this 'main work'. Elsewhere one detects traces of his leading questions, as in a few sentences beginning 'I admit', for example, 'I admit that during my broadcasts in 1942 and 1943 over EIAR I charged that the International Financiers of New York and elsewhere plotted to "drag" the United States into the present war'; and again, 'I admit that after December 8, 1941 [the date on which the USA declared war on Japan], I suggested in my radio talks that PRESIDENT ROOSEVELT be looked at by a psychiatrist because he seemed to be struggling against some more or less hypnotic influences.' But Pound evidently felt that what he really wanted to put into the record was being left out, and he could only say, 'This statement should not be considered separate from a statement which I will write out by myself as to the "main foundations" of my beliefs and the objects of my thirty years of writing.'

Amprim was content to leave Pound to get on with his supplementary statement on his own. Once his sworn statement was duly signed on 7 May, with the signature witnessed by both interrogators, Amprim had him address to Dorothy Pound an authorization to 'give bearer' various books and papers:

> my New York scrap book clippings—interviews 1939 (box foot of my bed)
> Mandati of receipts (radio)—sack in wardrobe etc.
> MSS of Radio Discorsi = separate package = not in files.
> Orientamenti
> ConfucioTa Seu—bilingual.

Asse che non Vacilla.
Jeff./Muss.
ABC of Economics.
Last [?] letter files
Storia d'un Reato
Introd all[a Natura Economica degli S.U.A]
Roosevelt & Cause della Guerra
my Trans. Odon's Italys Econ. Policy

A separate sheet gave directions for finding a number of items, and asked for two or more copies of each, at least one for Amprim and one for himself. He also wanted copies of 'BOTH the Tigullio manifestos', *Oro e lavoro*, *What is money for?*, *Introductory Text book* / 'the one leaf affair'. Clearly he was hoping to engage Amprim in an extensive discussion of his economic writings and Confucian translations.

Armed with the authorization, Amprim and Arrizabalaga drove down that afternoon to Rapallo, taking Olga Rudge with them. (Olga, who was not to see Pound again until 1952, would say that the days she had spent shut up with Ezra in a room in the CIC had been 'among *the happiest of my life*'.) They reached Casa 60 at Sant'Ambrogio about 6.30, and found Dorothy all prepared to leave the next morning. Amprim handed her the authorization, and afterwards, in his memo to the FBI Director, he noted that she 'was very cooperative in finding incriminating evidence against her husband and did not seem to be in the least disturbed when I searched the premises'. The '2 USAs' (as Dorothy identified them in her diary) initialled and dated the books and pamphlets as they gathered them up.

The next day, 8 May—which happened to be the day on which Germany's unconditional surrender was announced—Pound made a further statement to Amprim of two typed pages 'complementing previous signed statements', and this was formally witnessed by Amprim. 'This partial statement', it declared, 'is not to be considered separate from my outline of my position', an 'Outline' consisting of a further seven typed pages and bearing the same date, '8 May 1945', but neither signed nor witnessed.

The 'partial' signed statement reads very differently from the first. That was a narrative testimony drafted by Amprim and Arrizabalaga on the basis of their interrogation, while this appears to be a more direct report of what Pound wanted them to know. He told them that he had had 'no intention of getting or of seeming to get under any foreign control', and that he had solicited and been granted the freedom of Italian radio, '"According to the Fascist principle of free expression of opinion on the part of those competent to have an opinion"'. (In his first statement he had said that this was 'a rather forced definition of Fascism', and an instance of his 'defining Fascism in a way to make it fit my own views'.) 'My fight has been against censorship', he declared, and followed that with this justification of his broadcasts—

> Even during time of war one has the right to criticise the fundamental causes of the series of wars into which humanity has been and still may be plunged. Naturally, none has the right to supply information of a military nature to the enemy. For example, after the United States entered the present war, I criticized President Roosevelt because I thought he had received imperfect and incomplete information and was influenced wrongly.

That 'example' doesn't obviously go with 'the right to criticise the fundamental causes of the series of wars', and this next statement seems even more disconnected—

> I am not anti-Semitic, and I distinguish between the Jewish usurer and the Jew who does an honest day's work for a living.

But of course, in Pound's mind, it is usury that is the fundamental cause of wars, and the cause of Roosevelt's going wrong was the malign influence of Jewish financiers. That is the hidden link, and it gives a mind-bending logic to his saying next,

> Hitler and Mussolini were simple men from the country. I think that Hitler was a Saint, and wanted nothing for himself. I think he was fooled into anti-Semitism and it ruined him. That was his mistake. When you see the 'mess' that Italy gets into by 'bumping off' Mussolini, you will see why someone could believe in some of his efforts.

Leaving aside the altogether surreal vision of Hitler as a saint—'a Jeanne d'Arc', he would specify to an American reporter later that day—this gratuitous introduction of Hitler's anti-Semitism into his defence looks like a telling if oblique confession. It is striking that he should think it was anti-Semitism that had brought about Hitler's downfall—not many would have thought that at the time, and for Pound to do so suggests that he had it very much on his mind. If that had been Hitler's fatal mistake, then had Pound gone wrong in that way himself? He would not admit to it—'I am not anti-Semitic', he has just said, exculpating himself in advance—but he knew that he was widely perceived as anti-Semitic, and that Laughlin and others thought him ruined by it. And he had sought to justify Mussolini's race laws in 1938, and the treatment of Italy's Jews in 1944 and 1945. Was there then a self-saving impulse behind his wanting Hitler to be seen as somehow not responsible for his genocidal anti-Semitism, even as a victim of it? One can only speculate about this, about whether he felt personally implicated. But there was certainly some mental and moral derangement in his view of Hitler at that moment.

The other longer statement, the 'Outline' which he wrote out on his own and dated as of 8 May 1945, began confidently. First, there was an 'OUTLINE OF ECONOMIC BASES of historic process/'. This cited, as an instance of the 'distributive ~~nature~~ function of money', the Chinese emperor who in 1766 BC coined copper disks to enable the poor to buy grain; it took into account 'The Mediaeval doctrine of the just price'; came then to the founding of the Bank of England and the modern banking system, and thus to the 'iniquity' of 'A bank lending ten times as much as its deposits', i.e. 'lending a good it hasn't got'. To these familiar 'bases' Pound now added a more recent 'datum', Lenin's dictum that 'As long as capitalism is capitalism surplus capital will never be used to raise the standard of living of the people inside a country. BUT it will be sent abroad to "backward countries" to increase the profits of the capitalists.' Pound's 'SECONDLY', his counter to the inequity of capitalism, was a re-affirmation of 'the principles ascertained by Confucius' as a proven foundation of good government. 'Whenever a Chinese dynasty has lasted three centuries it has been founded on' those principles.... Dynasties not so founded have flopped'—and here he added, 'as have the systems of Mussolini and Hitler'. And he went on, asserting his efforts to introduce Confucian enlightenment into Mussolini's Fascism, 'Hence my translations of the Testament, the first, and of the Unwavering or Unwobbling axis, the second of the FOUR chinese classic confucian books'. That brought him to reiterate his desire for the Confucian heritage to be made the basis of peace with Japan.

The writing up to that point is clear and coherent, and if he had stopped there he would have quite effectively 'indicated one or two [of] the points I have been trying to make during the past 25 years, and which I rashly did NOT stop trying to make when caught off side, but in reach of a microphone.' However, there is a hesitation, 'I am trying to put things in simple words, and briefly,' then a listing of 'the sort of material I have been trying to force into Italy in an attempt to educate the italians in democracy and economics', and after that the statement loses its initial focus and an underlying anxiety and defensiveness show through. 'At any rate I hope the errors will be considered in relation to the main picture,' Pound wrote. His knowledge may have been fragmentary, he admitted, and 'No one sees everything.' All the same, 'the citizen possessed of odd bits of knowledge that might be useful has not only the right but the duty to try to communicate with the competent authorities, even at the risk of seeming excentric or making a fool of himself'. The fifth page of the statement tails off, 'I have also seen things in Italy knowledge of which might conceivably be of use at this time.'

Probably after a break, Pound typed two more pages of 'Further Points', and here he was at first very much on the defensive.

1. That in an age of radio, free speech that does not include freedom to transmit by radio is a hollow sham.

2. That the constitution was being violated, most notably in the money clause/ ... Only the citizen who had not consented in the violation was in position to raise the issue.

...

4. The question of ex post facto law ... At least so far as I am concerned, I do not YET know at what date the mere use of radio in foreign territory became a crime. I certainly had no news of its being illegal before the date, whenever it was, that I heard I was accused of treason.
And I do not believe I have betrayed anyone whomsoever ...

After that declaration the tone becomes more assertive and defiant:

It is one thing to tell troops to desert, another to try to build up political indignation to take effect AFTER the end of hostilities. After the last war ONLY those countries where the returned troops came to power managed to effect reforms.

The reforms to be hoped for were, one gathers, 'the improved distribution, diminution of unemployment etc. achieved by Mussolini and Hitler ... all of which can be separated from the militarism etc.' More exactly, 'The question is whether Germany has learnt NOT to try to effect by violence what can only be effected by understanding.' That was a good question, and a commendable principle, but what was Pound up to here? Recognizing that it took him 'out of the present case', he went on, 'One comes back to the fundamental question of free speech, VERITABLY free, and the need of assuring the diffusion of useful information.' It is as if he had introduced Mussolini and Hitler as exemplary reformers in order to assert, boldly and defiantly, that there should be no limit whatsoever to freedom of speech in a good cause. That was to be his main line of defence against the charge of treason, a dangerously absolutist line taking no account of the precise nature of the charge, nor of the passion, and the prejudice, behind it.

An American journalist, Edd Johnson of the *Philadelphia Record* and the *Chicago Sun,* was allowed an interview with Pound on 8 May, and reported that he had 'talked about Confucius and kindred subjects':

Among the many things he said today were these:
'Adolf Hitler was a Jeanne d'Arc, a saint. He was a martyr. Like many martyrs he held extreme views.

'There is no doubt which I preferred between Mussolini and Roosevelt. In my radio broadcasts I spoke in favour of the economic construction of Fascism. Mussolini was a very human, imperfect character who lost his head...

'I do not believe I will be shot for treason. I rely on the American sense of justice.'

The reporter was impressed by the depth of Pound's interest in Confucius, and commented that 'He is probably the only man ever to be interviewed while awaiting trial for treason who talked more of various interpretations of Oriental ideographs than he talked of his own impending trial.' 'Pound is definitely not senile,' Johnson concluded, 'And if he is off his rocker, it does not show in any of the usual manifestations of nuttiness.'

Amprim returned to Rome a day or two after that interview, and from there urgently requested a 'decision from WASHINGTON regarding disposal' of Pound. Arrizabalaga was also making 'requests to higher headquarters to be relieved of Ezra Pound'. But for ten days no decision was reached in Washington, and Pound contentedly went on 'doing Confucio e Mencio, for american reader, if any'. On the 16th a US Army photographer took a picture of him 'posing at the typewriter', with a copy of his *Confucio. Studio Integrale* open alongside it. 'He continues his work while in custody of 92nd Div., C.I.C', stated the official caption. Another picture was taken showing Arrizabalaga in a pressed uniform shirt and tie, and Pound bearded and in a casual open-necked shirt, sitting one beside the other on a leather sofa, with the prisoner making a point and the officer regarding him intently and expressionlessly, his pen poised over his open notebook. This photograph was probably not taken during an actual interview, but would have been set up for the official record. On 21 May word came through that Pound was to be held 'in a military stockade near Pisa' while the investigation of his case continued. Three days later, on 24 May, Pound typed hasty notes to Dorothy and to Olga, saying, 'Talk is that I may go to Rome oggi, in which case hope to see you en passant.' The note closed 'Non sto', got to go, without signature. In fact the order for his transfer, issued by the Commanding General, Mediterranean Theater of Operations, United States Army, had instructed:

Transfer without delay under guard to MTOUSA Disciplinary Training Center for confinement pending disposition instructions. Exercise utmost security measures to prevent escape or suicide. No press interviews authorized. Accord no preferential treatment.

That meant that 'American civilian Doctor EZRA LOOMIS POUND' was to be treated by the US Army as if he had already been convicted of a serious criminal offence.

Arrizabalaga recalled how that order was carried out on 24 May, a Thursday:

> 5th Army Provost Marshal sent several Jeep loads of MP's to Genova to take him away. It was actually rather a sorry sight to see the big six foot MP's commanded by a Captain relieve Subject of his shoestrings, belt, necktie [?] and clamp a huge pair of handcuffs to one of his wrists, the other end to an MP's wrist and take him away. We had treated him courteously and he couldn't understand it. He said to me, 'I don't understand it.' I said, 'Mr. Pound, you are no longer under my jurisdiction, and I can't help it.' He then said, 'Do they know who I am?' I answered, 'Yes they do.' They took him to Pisa.

A 'priority' message from Fifth Army reported 'Doctor EZRA POUND delivered to MTOUSA 1500 hours 24 May this year'.

7 : A Prisoner in the Eyes of Others

The 6677th Disciplinary Training Center was a vast stockade off the dusty main road about 3 miles north of Pisa—the leaning tower could be made out in the distance across the flat plain. A few miles to the east the hills rise up to an 800-metre mountain. The DTC was a concentration camp for the US Army's own criminals, but with the difference that its aim was to release its prisoners back into active service. The 'trainees', as they were called, three and a half thousand of them in 1945, insubordinates, deserters, gangsters, murderers, rapists, thieves, were put through a punishing regime of 14-hour days of drills and exercises, and those who could stand it for a year could be returned to duty and earn an honourable discharge. Those who could not might be shut up for a week or two in the solitary punishment cells, narrow, shallow, and windowless concrete boxes, in which a man could just stand or lie down; or if they were deemed incorrigible they would be penned in one of the row of wire cages before being shipped back to a federal penitentiary. A few who made a run for it were shot down by the guards in one of the towers before they reached the first barbed-wire. There were guard-towers at each corner of the half-mile square stockade, and a further two towers on each of its four sides.

A brutal military discipline prevailed, the whole idea of the military police in charge of the training being to make life hell for the deviant until they conformed and responded like automatons to even the harshest and most whimsical orders. It was no place for an intensely individual civilian not subject to the disciplines of war. Yet the order was to confine Pound there, according no preferential treatment, and exercising utmost security measures to prevent escape or suicide. To the major of the Corps of Engineers who was temporarily in command that meant caging him with the incorrigibles in the maximum security area within view of the provost marshals' office, and the camp gate and the road. On second thoughts it seemed best to the major to replace the heavy gauge wire mesh of the ordinary observation cages with lengths of the even stronger steel mats used to make landing strips—there had been an emergency landing field in that place. So for thirty-six hours engineers cut and welded the steel with blow torches to construct a special gorilla cage, as Pound would call it, for this odd prisoner, keeping him awake for that time while they did it. Then they cut away the original wire mesh, leaving just a few inches of it sticking up from the concrete floor, the exposed ends an invitation to suicide, or so the over-stressed prisoner began to suspect. A photograph of the row of ordinary cages shows just a corner of this special one. All have concrete slab floors, about six feet wide and six and a half long, simple timber frames, ¼″ wire netting walls, flat wood and tar-paper roofs, except that for Pound's the steel grille is about an inch deep with four-inch interstices. The cages were open to the elements, to the summer sun, to wind and rain, to the dust blown in from the road to Pisa or from the drill field on hot windy days; and open too to the constant observation of the guards posted to watch him night and day, and to the gaze of passing military police and prisoners on their way in or out of the camp. All night a bright 'reflector' light shone on the cage. For furniture he was at first given just a slop pail and six blankets, and slept on the concrete; after some heavy rain, a cot was put in, and took up half the space; then he was given a pup tent which could be arranged to provide shelter from sun and rain. There was a general order that he was not to be spoken with—anyone could stare at him in his cage, but no one was to have a word with him.

What some saw, or later recollected seeing, was an elderly man in army fatigues unbuttoned at the neck, the trousers hanging loose—no belt, no boot laces either—'red-bearded', or 'with a stubby graying growth of a beard', and 'a curly full head of hair'. They would see him pacing back and forth the short length of his cage, or playing what appeared to be ping pong or tennis, 'making graceful, looping forehands and backhands', or dancing 'nimbly about the cage, shadow boxing' and fencing, or just sitting for hours with his head in his Chinese book. One curious young soldier who sat staring at the poet—he knew who he was and would have liked to talk to him—was startled to find himself spoken to, 'a good voice' saying from the cage, 'Can you get me some boric acid? They won't let me have it... I use it with water for my eyes.' The young man did get him boric acid and watched him use it on his eyes which were inflamed by the glare and dust. In the DTC mugshot of 'Ezra Loomis Pound' dated 'May 26 1945'—was he not processed until that Saturday?—those eyes look fiercely back at the lens. The head of hair is tangled, uncombed, the thin beard straggly, the army shirt loose and open at the collar. The face is lean, fined down from its prewar heaviness and defined now more by bone structure than by flesh; the line of the mouth is taut, the lips shut tight; and there is a great tension in the expression, as of a mind concentrated under extreme pressure, challenged, fully alert, at bay.

In his cage, poetry, lines for cantos, kept forming in his mind—'The enormous tragedy of the dream in the peasant's bent shoulders . . .'. 'It's terrible to have it coming to you like that and not be able to put it down', he would recall. But at least the ten lines that would open *The Pisan Cantos* got written down in pencil on two sheets of toilet paper, then copied again onto the inside cover of his Chinese book.

The regular camp commander, Lieutenant Colonel John L. Steele, returned from compassionate home leave and resumed command on 13 June. The next day a psychiatrist, Captain R. W. Fenner, was assigned to examine Pound and form a view of his mental state. In his report he wrote:

> Placed in confinement here at the D.T.C. he had a 'spell' about a week ago. This occurred while he was sitting in the sun, and the patient describes it as a period of several minutes during which he had great difficulty in collecting his thoughts.

The 'patient' also spoke of recent 'difficulty in concentration', 'easy fatigue-ability', and 'worries a great deal that he'll forget some messages which he wishes eventually to tell others'. 'Patient talks a great deal', he observed, 'Wanders from the subject easily, and needs to be constantly reminded of a particular question to which [h]is complete answer is sought.' He detected 'No paranoia, delusions nor hallucinations'—'No evidence of emotional instability'—'no notable personality defect—Memory, 'good'—'Insight–good'—'Apparently very superior intelligence'. And Captain Fenner left it at that. A second opinion was given by another psychiatrist, Captain Walter H. Baer, on 15 June:

> 1. This 59½ year old 'prisoner' was referred for N-P work up because of recent spell of confusion and complaints of 'claustrophobia'. . . . His present complaints are temporary periods of confusion, anxiety, feelings of frustration, and excessive fatiguability. There is no evidence of psychosis, neurosis or psychopathy. He is of superior intelligence, is friendly affable and cooperative. He does, however, lack personality resilience, shows some anxiety, restlessness, tremulousness and has had an attack of confusion.
> 2. Due to his age and loss of personality resilience, prolonged exposure in present environment may precipitate a mental breakdown, of which premonitory symptoms are discernible. Early transfer to the United States or to an institution in this theatre with more adequate facilities for care is recommended.

The psychiatrists' distancing objectivity and euphemisms—'the patient' and 'care'—wonderfully elide the inhumanity of Pound's 'confinement' and 'present environment'; but at least Captain Baer suggested that something be done about that. Colonel Steele took the hint at once, and the prisoner was moved on 18 June, after twenty-five days in the cage, into the medical compound, and given one of the pyramidal tents set up there for officer prisoners.

The Catholic chaplain, Father Aloysius H. Vath, told Wendy Flory in 1981 that after a time some of the medical staff became concerned about the consequences of his having no one to talk to. They feared that if this important prisoner went crazy they would be blamed. So he was told he could choose someone to talk to, and he asked, 'Do you have an RC chaplain?', and said 'I'll talk to *him*'. Mostly he wanted to talk about the Catholic religion and how it might correlate with his own Confucianism. When the priest gave him a copy of the *Catholic Prayer Book for the Army and Navy* he copied ideograms in its margins from his Confucian *Four Books*, and noted that 'The confucian, qua Confucian, is *constantly* in the state of mind indicated in the "Directions for confession" (p.34)'. Father Vath remembered their talking as they walked around the prison compound, 'every day, morning and afternoon . . . for about an hour'.

The words 'mental breakdown' from Captain Baer's report got back to the FBI and the Department of Justice in Washington, and roused concern about Pound's 'mental competence', meaning his competence to stand trial. On 3 July a message went from the War Crimes Office urgently requesting further examinations and reports from those two psychiatrists, 'and from some other psychiatrist as well'. Fenner and Baer had already left the DTC, but a higher ranking psychiatrist, Major William Weisdorf, was available to examine Pound on 17 July, and reported at length on his condition. He noted that the prisoner, during his first weeks 'in rather close confinement', had developed symptoms 'of anxiety, fatiguability . . . difficulty in concentrating . . . momentary lapses of memory'; however,'When removed from strict confinement, and given more freedom of movement, and improved physical facilities, the above noted symptoms rapidly cleared up'. To Weisdorf 'He made few complaints regarding his physical health, stated that he had a good appetite, slept well, and no longer was physically fatigued.' The psychiatrist concluded:

> He shows no evidence of psychosis, or neurosis at the present time. It is the opinion of the examiner that he may be safely kept in confinement in his present surroundings for the time being. However, because of his advanced age, and already demonstrated limited resistance he should be protected from undue

physical stress or exposure. Some provision should be made for mental stimulation in the form of reading matter of such variety as may be decreed advisable and appropriate. The counter action of the boredom of confinment [*sic*] would be good mental hygiene.

Those appalling final sentences show how little insight the psychiatrist had into Pound's mind, and that he had not the least idea that what was really keeping him sane was his immersion in the Confucian texts and in the composition of new cantos.

Of course it is quite likely that Pound's mind had been elsewhere in that interview. At any rate Weisdorf concluded from his 'voluble' speech and 'prodigious flow of thought'—which sounded 'on the whole relevant and coherent'—that

Mental content is centered about theories relating to money and monopoly as the basis for the ills of world, with the firmly expressed conviction that in expounding these ideas, he had done his utmost to prevent war and uphold the American Constitution. He feels that he has invaluable knowledge and experience with foreign affairs, which the American government could use. He defends his radio broadcasts on the Italian radio as the right of free speech and contends that he was not treasonable. There is no evidence of hallucinations or delusions...

No evidence of delusion? Pound must have spoken very convincingly indeed, something worth noting since he was there rehearsing his defence, and doing so no doubt for the benefit of those to whom Weisdorf would be reporting. It seems not to have occurred to the psychiatrist that the apparently very intelligent object of his observation would have had his own sense of what was going on, and his own agenda, and that he might be using him to make his case to the FBI and the Justice Department.

Colonel Steele sent off the three psychiatrists' reports as requested by the War Crimes Office, with a note explaining that it was the common practice where there was risk of suicide or escape to place prisoners 'in a small open cell with walls of steel grating in order that [they] might be under constant observation'. Nonetheless, Pound had been moved on 18 June, and 'also provided with reading and writing materials'. He gave the assurance the FBI and the Justice Department were wanting, that Weisdorf's report 'indicates that Pound has made a satisfactory mental adjustment to his present situation and is mentally competent'.

Steele 'was walking on eggshells', someone who had been an officer in the camp reflected years later, 'It was a career situation: if anything goes wrong he's done for.' And Steele himself, also years later, indicated that he had had to worry about 'ensuring responsible care that was somehow short of the forbidden "preferential treatment".' Allowing the prisoner to write had seemed the acceptable 'defense against mental deterioration, which we certainly did not want to risk'. He was vague about what reading materials might have been provided, if any. '*The Bible* was the only reading material authorized any prisoner', as he remembered, though '*The Stars and Stripes* and *Yank* magazine were probably available', and the camp personnel would have had other magazines and a surprising assortment of pocket books. (Among these latter would have been the copy of *The Pocket Book of Verse* which someone left in the latrine, a lucky find for Pound.) But Steele frankly admitted that 'We had almost no resources to offer', beyond writing materials—(some US Army standard issue writing pads were found for him)—and allowing him 'to use a typewriter at the medical building during off-duty hours'. So he came back to their having done what they could for Pound by letting him write, having decided that that 'would be good therapy and good preventative medicine'. It was the happy solution to the problem of keeping the special prisoner both secure and 'competent'.

The prisoner could be heard at night typing furiously in the Medical Center dispensary. Robert Allen, who worked there, remembered 'The constant clanging and banging of the typewriter, which he punched angrily with his index fingers', and the 'high-pitched humming sound he made as the carriage raced the bell'—that would have been when he was composing cantos. He also typed up his English version of *Confucius: The Unwobbling Pivot & The Great Digest*, and dated it 'D.T.C., Pisa; 5 October–5 November, 1945'. Allen also recalled how 'He swore well and profusely over typing errors.'

No one was supposed to talk to him still, but he would talk freely to anyone who was near. According to Allen, after typing he would 'let down completely to rant and rave' to the Charge of Quarters in the dispensary, 'about the "dunghill usurers" and "usuring cutthroats"', about how 'wars could be avoided if the true nature of money were understood', or '"When", he would ask, "will the United States return to Constitutional government?"' To young Homer Somers he tried to explain Gesell. With the medical staff, if he went in for some treatment after the trainees' sick call, for eye drops or a foot bath, 'he seemed anxious to discuss the charges against him'. He would exchange banter through the barbed wire with trainees in the adjacent compound, and picked up and parsed the army vocabulary, all forty-eight words of it.

He was seen moving freely around his compound where his regular walk wore a circular path in its grass. Allen mentions that he found an old broom handle and used it as a stick 'which he swung out smartly to match his long stride'. The stick also became a tennis racquet, or a rapier, or a bat to hit small stones with. When the chaplain walked with him there was always a guard close behind; and guards would move him to the mess to collect his food in an army mess kit, or to the showers. There were usually two men to a tent, but Pound had his to himself. Allen remembered his having an army cot and a small packing crate, and later 'a second packing crate and a table'. That was where he would write during the day, or read. He read 'everything that was given to him', according to Allen, and 'The Mediterranean edition of *The Stars and Stripes* and the overseas editions of *Time* and *Newsweek* were his sources of news.'

For months, through June, July, August, no one outside the camp apart from Frank Amprim was permitted to see or to communicate with the prisoner, nor even to know where he was being held; and he was not permitted to communicate with anyone, not with his wife, nor with legal counsel. The American Consulate in Rome would only refer Dorothy Pound to the US Army authorities, who would defer to the FBI on this matter; and Amprim told John Drummond in July, when he interceded on Dorothy's behalf, that there could be 'no communication whatever' between Pound and his family.

All the while US Army Headquarters in Italy, following up the second psychiatrist's recommendation, were urging Washington to transfer Pound to the United States without delay. They wanted him off their hands. But the War Crimes Office wanted him held in Italy in case there was a need for 'reinterrogation in connection with any statements which may be made by prospective witnesses'. Amprim was still at work on the case. In June he had sent to the Director of the FBI in Washington a sampling of the material he had gathered, including 'summaries and short items which were announced on the Fascist Radio by various announcers employed there', and Hoover had written back on 4 July:

From an examination of the documentary evidence submitted in this case, it is noted that considerable handwriting and typewritten material evidently prepared by Pound is included. However, in order to have available adequate known specimen's of subjects handwriting and specimens from his typewriter for comparison purposes, it is desired that you reinterview Pound and secure the following: (1) Typewritten specimens properly identified by competent witnesses, that is, specimens identified by you and one other person who would be competent to testify regarding them. In this connection, it is suggested that [*name blacked out*] Counter intelligence Agent of the 92nd Division, U.S. Army, be utilized if possible inasmuch as he has previously identified a considerable portion of the documentary evidence in this case and in all probability will be called as a witness. The typewritten specimens should be secured from all typewriters available to Pound. There should be numerous specimens in similar wording to that in Pound's documents and if possible the documents should be prepared on paper similar to that used in Pound's original manuscripts. With regard to the taking of the specimens, you should use light, medium, and heavy touch and the specimens so taken should be properly designated as being light, medium, or heavy.

Amprim carried out this instruction to the letter. He confiscated Pound's Everest portable typewriter, Model 90, serial no. 27780, on which the 't' had become misaligned, and interviewed the salesman from whom Pound had bought it in February 1938, to have proof that he had owned that typewriter. He also confiscated an Olympia office typewriter found in the Ministry of Popular Culture in Rome and identified as one Pound had used. He selected specimens of the scripts, articles, and letters Pound himself had typed, and had him initial and date them to acknowledge them his. And he had specimen pages typed as directed, not only with light, medium, and heavy touch, but also in blue and in black ink. In August he had Pound certify that he was indeed the author of the books and pamphlets that named him as author. Through to November he kept on gathering more and more potential evidence, from Sant'Ambrogio, from the former Fascist Ministries in Rome and Salò and Milan, from Mussolini's files, from interviews. In the end he assembled thousands of pages, 'enough to fill up the better part of fourteen volumes of FBI files'.

All this was in order to establish doubly and triply and to unmanageable excess what Pound was altogether happy to confirm. Convinced that the more evidence there was the more it would prove that he had intended only good to America, Pound was comforted by Amprim's zeal, and delighted that he had 'collected far more proof... than I or any private lawyer could have got at'. He seems not to have internalized the fact that Amprim's mission was to gather evidence that could be used against him. 'My instinct all along has been to leave the whole matter to the U.S. Dept. of Justice,' he would write to Dorothy's lawyers in October, demonstrating, if nothing else, his certainty that he was not guilty of treason, and his simple faith that the Department of Justice wanted only to establish the truth.

But the Justice Department needed still more evidence. Amprim had been sternly instructed in June that there was an 'Absolute need for 2 witnesses to each overt act treason', and that the

information and documentary material you furnished shows only general data. Nowhere have 2 witnesses been developed to same overt act treason. Concentrate on development 2 witnesses to same overt act and discontinue all general investigation.

In mid-July he was told again, 'Department wishes to know that you have developed 2 witnesses to same overt act of treason by subject before final plans made for his return.' A further message the following week was more specific:

> Though people named could testify they handled POUND's manuscripts in normal course business, there is no evidence they have personal knowledge POUND prepared manuscripts. Thus these witnesses would not fulfill statutory requirement of 2 witnesses to same overt act.
>
> This requirement best solved by finding at least 2 people who personally saw POUND make specific recording on specific date. Develop as many overt acts this kind as possible to which these witnesses can testify. Also if possible develop other sets 2 or more witnesses to other similar overt acts treason.
>
> ARMADO GIOVAGFOMI and WALTER XAHETTI who recorded some POUND's talks are suggested witnesses.

Amprim reported that neither two technicians whom he had interviewed as potential witnesses, nor 'two other witnesses [who] had [also] jointly seen and heard Pound make recordings on at least ten different occasions', could recall the dates of those recordings, or 'identify the subject matter of the talks as they do not understand the English language'. On 21 August he was sent further instructions on exactly how to 'develop' potential witnesses:

> Reinterview jointly MAUCERI and BADOLOTTO plus BRUNI, DE LEONARDIS, and ZACHETTI making all out effort ascertain more specifically as many times as possible when they saw POUND make recordings. Try tie these occasions with known event as Allied landing at SALERNO or other event prominent in their memory. Interrogate all 5 exhaustively regarding possibility other persons who saw POUND make recordings.
>
> Examination "Report of Registration Form" for 14 January 1943 shows operator was LUSSI and Engineer of Service was MELODIA. More information on LUSSI in last paragraph page 2 of your letter 20 June 1944. Find and interview these 2 as possible witnesses and others listed in same letter.

The search for witnesses went on into October, but at the end of that month an internal FBI memo to J. Edgar Hoover recognized that even two witnesses who could testify had yet to be found, and a Washington paper reported that Justice officials had admitted that 'Without such witnesses it is "doubtful" conviction can be obtained.' Nevertheless, as Pound read in November's *Stars and Stripes*, six of these 'witnesses' were being flown to Washington to testify against him. In the Justice Department's revised indictment five witnesses would be named—Armando Giovagnoli, Giuseppi Bruni, Fernando de Leonardis, Walter Zanchetti, and Fernando Luzzi—all former EIAR radio technicians who had been 'developed' and found wanting as witnesses. None of them understood English, and none of them could testify to any specific 'overt act of treason'.

Dorothy Pound wrote again on 31 July to the Office of the Provost Marshall General—'an enquiry requesting news of welfare and whereabouts of Ezra Pound', as an internal memo described her letter as it was passed from one section to another of that Office. The section concerned sent back a note to the effect that it had 'no objection to providing Mrs POUND the requested information', nor would it 'interpose any objection to a personal visit to Ezra Pound by Mrs Pound', and that they had 'checked with the FBI who are in agreement'. Mrs Pound was then advised, in a letter from the Provost Marshall General dated 24 August 1945,

> that your husband is at present located at the MTOUSA Disciplinary Training Center, APO 782, c/- postmaster, New York City, N.Y., located near Pisa. He is enjoying a good state of health.
>
> If you desire a personal visit with your husband, suggest a letter be written to Provost Marshall, Peninsular Base Section, A.P.O. 782, U.S. Army.

Dorothy Pound wrote as suggested, and received this reply dated '18 September 1945' on 26 September:

> 1. This letter will constitute your authority to visit your husband, Ezra Pound, at the MTOUSA Disciplinary Training Center, north of Pisa, on Highway #1, subject to the normal rules governing visits to confinees at that installation.
> 2. Clothing which is the property of your husband may be brought to him.
> 3. Correspondence between yourself and husband is authorized subject to usual censorship in effect.
> 4. Arrangements for travel and lodging must be made through whatever channels are available to civilians.

At the DTC Lieutenant Colonel Steele informed Pound of these permissions in a formal memo dated 20 Sept. 1945, adding

> If Mrs. Pound arrives for a visit arrangements will be made for you to see her at Post Headquarters, outside the stockade. Our regulations require that an officer of the organization be present during such a visit and limit the time of each visit to approximately one-half hour.

Pound at once dashed off a note in pencil to Dorothy, and that evening typed a longer note to her, excited by the prospect of reconnecting with his former life.

He wrote that he was 'famished for news, personal gossip anything', and asked that people be told they could write to him now, though for the present he could write only to her. She was to tell Olga and Mary, and 'Jas, Possum, Duncan—Angold if alive'. He wanted Laughlin and Eliot to be readied to bring out his '"One day's reading, the Testament of Confucius"', and 'There wd/ be enough cantos for a volume'. In fact he had 'done a Decad 74/83 (about 80 pages this typescript)', and he began at once to send batches of typescripts to be sent 'up the hill' for Olga and Mary to make clean copies for passing on to Laughlin and Eliot. The first batch, five pages containing canto 81 and the opening of 82, took over a fortnight to reach Dorothy instead of the usual week or so, possibly because Colonel Steele, who was personally acting as censor of Pound's mail, had difficulty deciding whether they were allowable or not.

Dorothy, for her part, responded to Pound's instructions, fed him news of friends, was sardonic about his aged mother with whom she was living and for whom she had to cook, let him know that she was keeping clear of Olga, also of Mary about whose appearance she was disparaging, and managed to include in nearly every letter some positive news of Omar. She may have thought that an emphasis upon Omar's being a devoted son now in the US Army would count in Pound's favour with the camp authorities.

The most significant preoccupation of the correspondence emerges at the end of Dorothy's first letter, dated 'Sept. 25. 1945', a long newsy letter in which she mentions being 'in correspondence with Moore' and that Drummond was proving 'a true friend', and then concludes simply, 'Please have counsel, & don't try to defend yourself'. Evidently Pound had declared that he would conduct his own defence and Dorothy had been seeking advice and assistance from A. V. Moore, the senior law clerk of her father's old firm, Shakespear and Parkyn, who acted as her legal adviser in London though he was not a qualified solicitor, and from John Drummond who was with the Allied Headquarters in Rome and who was helping both Dorothy and Olga. Everyone was being adamant that Pound should be dissuaded from conducting his own defence, but they had yet to light on any likely defender.

Drummond, prompted by Olga Rudge, had asked Elihu Root, known to Pound both as a fellow graduate of Hamilton College and as a fellow recipient of an honorary degree there in 1939, if he would take on the case, and Root, a successful corporate lawyer, had replied that it was not his kind of case, and besides Pound was merely an acquaintance and 'not a very sympathetic one'. He did however suggest Lloyd Stryker, who had been a contemporary of Pound's at Hamilton and was now a well-known criminal lawyer. The suggestion was put to Pound who responded, 'I have very cordial recollections of Lloyd Stryker, [but] he is now I believe one of the best known big lawyers in the U.S. whose fees are far beyond anything I could pay.' Dorothy argued, 'We can manage the cash side, one way or another,' and felt 'sure you'd better let someone used to the job, defend you'.

Pound was inclined to think that no lawyer could have a sufficient knowledge of his case to represent him. When Arthur Moore, writing in the name of Shakespear and Parkyn, formally advised him that he should not address the Court but take Lloyd Stryker as his counsel, Pound explained his hesitations at length. First he questioned whether 'your advice is given in full knowledge of certain essential facts of my case', such facts, for example, as that 'I was not sending axis propaganda but my own'; and that he was never 'asked to say anything contrary to his conscience or contrary to his duties as an American citizen'. Beyond that, did Moore know what he actually said on air, or that the economic enlightenment he had been calling for in his broadcasts and long before was now being enacted all over the place? How could Stryker possibly know enough about his efforts to spread a 'better understanding of certain economic fundamentals'? After all, 'The agent of the Dept. of Justice started by saying that they proposed to consider my past 30 years work,' and unless Stryker were prepared to do the same 'I do not know how he could tell the Court what the case is about'. Pound modestly left it to Moore to see how this led to the conclusion that no one could be so well-qualified as Pound himself to tell the Court about his thirty years' work. But on another occasion, in response to Omar's asking 'What KIND of man will he be', he was more explicit, 'Tell Omar I favour a defender who has written a life of J. Adams and translated Confucius. Otherwise how CAN he know what it is about?'

One weak link in Pound's chain of argument was the belief that the Department of Justice was seriously considering his '30 years work'. In fact what held Amprim's interest about this time was 'a sheaf of documents found among Mussolini's files pertaining to Ezra Pound', documents which he expected to be 'of extreme importance ... and of great aid in the prosecution of the subject' and 'the securing of proof in the case'. Neither the John Adams cantos, nor the 'Testament of Confucius' which Pound sent to Moore 'as an integral part of my defence', were likely to enter into the Justice Department's idea of their case against him.

Pound's less delusive line of resistance to the advice that he should ask Stryker to defend him was to refuse to be rushed into doing anything until he had canvassed old friends, in particular Archibald MacLeish. He told Moore, 'I should much prefer to see Mr McLeish before deciding on so important a matter as NOT speaking on my own behalf.' Or if he could not see him, 'the simplest plan would be for him to write to me as my lawyer (if I am correct in supposing that he is a lawyer) at any rate he has known my work for 20 years and has some concept of what I have been driving at'. MacLeish, distinguished poet and playwright, Librarian of Congress from 1939, then an assistant secretary of state under Roosevelt in the last year of the war, was indeed in a position to give an opinion of Pound's work, but it would not have been what he was hoping for. In 1943 MacLeish had sent Pound's old friend Ernest Hemingway transcripts of some of the radio talks with the comment, 'Poor old Ezra! Treason is a little too serious and a little too dignified a crime for a man who has made such an ass of himself, and accomplished so little in the process.' Hemingway had written back, 'He is obviously crazy... It is impossible to believe that anyone in his right mind could utter the vile, absolutely idiotic drivel he has broadcast. His friends who knew him and who watched the warping and twisting and decay of his mind and his judgment should defend him and explain him on that basis. It will be a completely unpopular but an absolutely necessary thing to do.' It had to be done because, crazy as he had become, Pound had 'a long history of generosity and unselfish aid to other artists and he is one of the greatest of living poets'. MacLeish agreed that Pound should not be hanged for his broadcasts, but the most positive thing he would say about them was that the 'misinterpretation of the American people... could only be justified on the ground that Pound knows nothing about them'. Otherwise what he had heard seemed 'a toadying attempt to please the Fascist government by beastly personal attacks on President Roosevelt, [and] by a recurrent anti-Semitism'.

Jas. Laughlin warned Pound in early September, having just heard from Drummond where he was and that he could be written to, that the above was the kind of support he must now expect from his friends:

I should hardly say I suppose that I hope to see you soon, because I'm afraid that things are going to be kind of tough for you here, but rest assured that though you have many spiteful enemies, you also have a few friends left who will do their best to help you. No one takes your side, of course, in the political sense, but many feel that the bonds of friendship and the values of literature can transcend a great deal...

Laughlin had his own view of the complexity of Pound's predicament. On 4 November he wrote to Dorothy Pound about the anti-Semitism in the broadcasts:

That angle, of course, is the one which makes it all so difficult. You simply cannot say those things publicly. I have heard only a few of the broadcasts but there is nothing in there which is indefensible on political grounds—very little that was not said openly here and accepted as free speech.

But if those outbursts of intolerance are publicized I can see no way out of the mess. Public opinion will force a conviction on the court...

To be as helpful as he felt able, Laughlin put forward the name of Julien Cornell as a possible defence counsel, recommending him as a lawyer with 'a good record in civil liberties cases and those involving conscientious objectors'. He told Drummond, who passed on the information to Pound via Dorothy, that Cornell was 'A Quaker, a man of the highest refinement & character', and that he 'has known him for some three years & has every confidence in his integrity & good judgement'. 'Jas pathetically insists on the "refinement" of his candidate', Pound commented, and held off from definitely accepting him.

Eliot wrote to him, 'Ez, you are not good at explaining yourself to the simple-minded,' and told him that he must 'talk only when [your lawyer] wants you to talk'. But he agreed that 'It must be a lawyer who is prepared to read all your works and try to understand them.' Dorothy told him, 'I don't believe in yr. trying to defend yrself, yourself—You always have such a rush of ideas & go off so far to the edge—trying everybody's patience and exhausting them!' That seems to have been the reaction of one of the officers who accompanied him when he was flown to Washington. Pound evidently talked a lot, hoping to enlist the officer's assistance, but what the latter made of it was that 'Mr Pound... is an intellectual "crack pot" who could correct all the economic ills of the world and who resented the fact that ordinary mortals were not sufficiently intelligent to understand his aims and motives.' Pound's friends clearly feared that he would fare no better with a jury. Yet in his parallel universe he remained intent on conducting his own defence, right up to the moment when the judge told him the charge was too serious for that.

The last weeks of Pound's six months in the prison camp were strained and overshadowed by the uncertainties of his inevitably approaching trial. His mind had found its freedom during the summer months of July, August, and September in composing the new decad of cantos. Now, in October, to keep his mind under control, he occupied himself with finishing up his English version of *Confucius. The Unwobbling Pivot & The Great Digest*—'They got me my "Ta Seu" and the Odes out of "supply" today', he informed Dorothy on the 9th. At the same time he was trying to get his personal vortex going again through such visits and correspondence as he was being allowed. When Dorothy managed the difficult feat of getting down to Pisa on 3 October, and had 'a long hour' with him, he told her all the things he wanted done, and as soon as she had gone dashed off a note to remind her to let 'all and sundry... know I was sending MY OWN stuff and that I was not taking orders from anyone'. He then got on 'with the Confucius Chung Yung, while this typewrite is free'. The next day he wrote, 'I think I got the first slab of the Chung Y rather well done yester e'en', and gave her several messages to pass on, one for Duncan's wife who had tuberculosis, about a new miracle drug, 'Pencellin'; another for Eliot about his Confucius and cantos; and another to go with 'the Dolmetsch verses' from canto 81 to Agnes Bedford and the Dolmetsch family, 'as suggestion for harpsichord'. He then typed for the attention of 'the Prison Office' and Colonel Steele a 'Report on the prisoner POUND, suggesting that he be sent to Rapallo on parole'.[1] On 5 October he wrote his long letter to Shakespear and Parkyn, mainly on the matter of his defence, but also with questions for Eliot at Faber about publishing his new works. And so it went on for a fortnight, nearly every day a letter with instructions, suggestions, requests for information, essential points for people to understand, until Major Lucree, who had replaced Colonel Steele as camp commander and was no doubt 'protecting his butt', ordered his 'OUT correspondence rationed and Cantos must go via base censor'. Pound then made his rationed letters longer and more charged with his agenda for action, and sent 'another batch of Canto ms/' with a covering 'Note to Base Censor' declaring that 'The Cantos contain nothing in the nature of cypher or intended obscurity'.

When Dorothy visited him again on 11 November, they 'talked mostly of publications, etc.', though after she left the place felt 'much emptier' and he was 'a bit elegiac'. But this letter continued their talk, about who would publish his Confucius since Faber would not, and about persuading Faber or someone to publish Bunting's poems, and Angold's. Then there was a great rush of ideas about what 'Possum might realize', what [Harriet Shaw] Weaver should do, what 'The Bells and M. Boddy' should know, and Swabey realize, and Omar read, and 'Send out copies of Introductory Text Book in all your letters. Mary will send you a packet'. It was as if he were reaching out from his imprisoned state to every one who came into his mind, wanting to be in touch with all his contacts at once, and to be again an acknowledged driving force among them. But what stayed with Mary after she and Olga had visited him on 17 October was the image of her father, 'grizzled and red-eyed in a U.S. Army blouse and trousers, in unlaced shoes without socks, with his old twinkle and bear-hug'.

[1] This letter was passed up the chain of command to the Provost Marshall General, who had 'no recommendation to make', and on to the Acting Theater Judge Advocate, who, noting that 'the Ezra Pound case is purely an FBI matter', had it forwarded 'to FBI representatives through technical channels'—but no word came back to Pound, perhaps because it was now well into October and all FBI agents were leaving for the United States by the end of the month.

Towards the end of October the various authorities concerned at last set in motion the transfer of the prisoner to the United States. US Army Headquarters in Rome issued an ultimatum on October 22:

EZRA POUND, American expatriate in ITALY, indicted 1942 [*sic*] for TREASON, has been in Military custody since May 1945 while FBI Agents investigated the case.

All FBI Agents will have departed for the UNITED STATES by end of October.

No instructions for disposal of POUND have been received from either the War Department or the Department of Justice.

Urgently desired is information concerning disposal of subject otherwise this Theater will release him.

The response was dated 5 November 1945:

The Department of Justice will shortly ask for return to the UNITED STATES of EZRA POUND, 14 November probable target date. We will give you about 3 days notice of date for Pound's arrival here Legal Jurisdiction requires that plane returning prisoner land at Bolling Field in the district of COLUMBIA and NOT at National Airport or other Airports in the UNITED STATES.

Arrangements to be made here for relinquishing POUND to Federal Bureau of Investigation upon arrival at Bolling Field.

Advise this office of destination of plane and time of departure of 6 Italian witnesses in EZRA POUND case.

The effective order from the Secretary of War, dated 16 November, directed that Pound be transported under military guard 'on regular flight leaving ROME 17 November'.

Two officers at the DTC received orders on the 16th to 'escort Ezra Loomis Pound, American civilian' to the Ciampino Airport at Rome. That evening Pound was in the dispensary talking to the Charge of Quarters about *Mission to Moscow*, a best seller by Joseph Davies, a former US ambassador to the Soviet Union—he had typed out a 1,000-word 'NOTE' on the book the previous evening. About 19.30 hours two lieutenants came in and informed him that he had an hour to get his personal effects together. He added a pencil scrawl to a partly written letter to Dorothy, 'Leaving probably Rome'; put on the jacket and trousers he had been wearing when the partisans took him away, and the officer's greatcoat which had been issued to him; and at 20.30 was being driven away from the camp by his escorts. The Jeep drove through 'a cold raw night', reaching Ciampino at 04.45, and he was there detained in the guardhouse until picked up by Lieutenant Colonels Holder and Donaghey and Captain

Manus, who had orders to escort him to Washington, and who shared their breakfast with him.

They were on the plane at 08.00, and the front three rows, twelve seats, were reserved for them, 'so that no one would sit in the immediate vicinity of Pound but his escorting officers'. At 08.30 the four-engined C54 took off and headed north for Prague, where it spent an hour on the ground, then on to Brussels with another long delay, and finally to Bovington, an American base in England. They landed there at 18.30 GMT and were able to leave the plane for the first time that day, and to find 'an ample dinner, the first food since 0600 hours (GMT)'. Colonel Holder wrote in his report, 'Mr. Pound was suffering acutely from hunger and was extremely nervous.' They flew next to the Azores, arriving at 03.00 on the 18th. There was an engine problem and an uncertain delay, and Pound was taken by two of the escorts 'to the Stockade to shower and rest', while Holder tried to impress the importance of his mission upon the airport officers, and succeeded in having his party put on a US-bound plane coming in from Paris at 07.00, with the same seating arrangement as before. He learned later that 'the French Ambassador, his wife and two colonels had been obliged to move their seats'. This flight 'took off at 0830 hours (GMT) and arrived at Bermuda at 2100 hours (GMT) or 1700 hours Atlantic time'. From Bermuda the plane flew on to Washington DC, landing 'at Bolling Field approximately 2230 hours Eastern time, 18 November'.

A French Government minister who had been on the plane told a reporter that over the Atlantic

> Pound, in dirty shirt and soiled prison clothes, sat silent and bored for hours, until the sun began to shine. Suddenly Pound sprang up and, looking down at the tremendous sunlit sea, became, on his first ocean crossing by air, ecstatic, like a bird let out of a cage, like a man pulled out of a deep, dark hole. He paced the aisle declaiming in poetic rhapsody.

There were press photographers at the airport to catch Pound being led away between two Justice Department marshals. The prisoner looks surprisingly alert after the long and exhausting flight, and appears well-dressed until one notices he has only an army-issue sweatshirt under his suit and coat. He has on his black borsalino hat, in his left hand is his slightly battered leather attaché case, and in his right, incongruously, a smart walking stick or cane. That wrist, one notices, is manacled to the wrist of the well-dressed marshal beside him, pausing for the press photographers. In the leather case were his Chinese texts, and the five notebooks and the typescripts of his Confucian translations and of his new cantos.

8 : 'In the Mind Indestructible'

The Pisan Cantos

There are occasional markers of the speed at which Pound composed these cantos in the DTC through July, August, and September of 1945. One hundred and seventy lines into the first of them there is, 'and Till was hung yesterday | for murder and rape with trimmings' (74/430). That was Louis Till, executed 2 July 1945, just two weeks after Pound had been moved from the 'gorilla cage' to his tent and given writing materials. One hundred and thirty lines on there is a date, 'Under Taishan, quatorze Juillet' (74/434), 14 July, anniversary of the day in 1789 when the citizens of Paris rose up and freed the prisoners in the Bastille. About 14 August, now in canto 77, he hears of the end of the war in the Pacific, '[I heard it in the s.h. a suitable place | to hear that the war was over]' (77/467). The next two cantos refer to events Pound would have read about in the 27 August number of *Time* magazine: 'So Salzburg reopens' (78/480, repeated at 79/484), and 'Pétain not to be murdered' (79/484). Then canto 82 carries the date '8th day of September' (82/523); 83 notes, after rain, 'There is September sun on the pools' (83/530); and the whole 'decad 74/83' was done, so Pound told Dorothy, by 2 October. That means that those ten cantos, made up of nearly 3,400 lines, had been composed between 18 June and 2 October, say three and a half months, or about one hundred days; which gives a rough average of a page a day of the printed text. All things considered, it was an amazing feat of concentrated and sustained creation. No wonder that he wrote as the final lines of that decad, 'Down, Derry-down | Oh let an old man rest' (83/536). The concluding canto, with the date '8th October' in its first line (84/537), was added as a sort of winding down in his last weeks in the DTC, while he was mainly working on his *Confucius: The Unwobbling Pivot & The Great Digest.*

The Pisan Cantos don't read as if they were written in haste—there is nothing rushed or forced or unfinished about them. Indeed, it is generally recognized that here Pound the master craftsman was composing with his powers at their height and fully at his command. There is an abundant yet controlled flow of material, made up of immediate and recollected and visionary experience. The language is consistently charged and layered with intricate meaning, and shaped into an ever varying verse that is at once measured and free—the sort of verse in which every line-break is a discrimination. The entire sequence reads as free flowing natural speech, only heightened, concentrated, intensely energized; each line is separately formed, and yet fitted into an ongoing rhythm; and each canto finds its own definite form. The poet was evidently altogether in his right mind through those summer months; and still, only long practice in which acquired skills had become habitual, instinctive, could have enabled him to compose so well at such a rate, and in that place.

After all, one thinks, he was a prisoner and completely cut off from his own world. Yet, remarkably, the world of the camp, though always present, never holds his mind captive. He could look out from 'the death cells' to the highest peak in the Appenines to the east and think of it as 'Taishan', China's highest and most sacred peak, whose clouds nurtured and brought prosperity to those under its influence. Or, knowing that some of those who had been alongside him in the death cells were likely to be hanged, he could think of the words Villon had imagined for himself and his fellow thieves when on the gallows, 'Absoudre . . . ', absolve us all—words he had set to haunting music in *Le Testament*. He could overhear Mr. K.'s 'if we weren't dumb we wouldn't be here', rhyme it with his own observation of prisoners at drill, 'the voiceless with bumm drum and banners', and notice as well 'Butterflies, mint and Lesbia's sparrows'. The prisoners were most of them black, and seeing them in the close-packed hospital ward makes him think of a slave ship 'as seen between decks'. Poor devils, he thinks, 'po'eri di'aoli sent to the slaughter | Knecht gegen Knecht | to the sound of the bumm drum, to eat remnants | for a usurer's holiday'—a variation upon Mephisto's saying in Goethe's *Faust*, 'The struggle is, they say, for freedom's rights, | Look closer, and it's slave with slave that fights.' As in those instances, Pound's mind is forever subjecting the camp as it impinges upon him to his own associations and interpretations, making it over detail by detail into *his* mental world. There he is at liberty to maintain his own vision of things, so that, even 'in the halls of hell', he is able to contemplate 'Mt. Taishan' with its clouds and the birds and other creatures that figure the sustaining process of nature. That freedom to create, and to recreate, the world in the mind is altogether what *The Pisan Cantos* are about—they exist by it, and they exist for it.

The leading themes are stated on the first page of canto 74. The dream of a just republic, which Pound had hoped Mussolini might achieve, has ended ingloriously, with the Duce hung up by the heels in Milan. Yet as

Manes' doctrine of light was alive, a millenium after his death, in twelfth-century Provence, and as the myth of Dionysus figures the self-renewals of nature, so Pound remains defiantly committed to the idea of building the visionary city wherein the peasant's dream of abundance and justice will be fulfilled. There, in the first ten lines, is the driving intention of the entire sequence: to build through the music of words 'the city of Dioce whose terraces are the colour of stars'.

Lines 11–26 respond to that opening by affirming that the necessary basis for the good society is in nature, that is, in both the elemental process of nature and inborn human nature, in both together. The rain and the wind and the sun are of the process; so too are the 'suave eyes' of the merciful divinities, Kuanon and 'sorella la luna' whom he had invoked in the Italian drafts near the war's end. Then there is the Confucian comprehension of 'the way' of natural law—this will permeate the entire sequence. And there are those who followed their own nature, possibly to excess: Dante's Ulysses venturing beyond the known world, and Lucifer carrying the light of heaven down to earth. To further complicate the ideogram there is Homer's canny Odysseus escaping the blinded Cyclops by naming himself 'No man'. In canto 81, under the spell of divine eyes, Pound will write 'It is not man | Made courage, or made order, or made grace | ... Learn of the green world what can be thy place.'

Still, humanity has its necessary part to play in the process: 'man, earth: two halves of the tally' (82/526). This is the third and major theme, introduced in lines 27–31. The human contribution is enlightened intelligence, the intelligence which conceives, and transmits, the precise definitions which shape right action and so build a just society—definitions such as Sigismundo's Tempio, with Duccio's bas-reliefs; or the mosaics in Rome's Santa Maria in Trastevere; or the Constitution upon which the United States should stand. Near the close of this first canto the theme will be restated—'that certain images be formed in the mind ... to remain there, resurgent *ΕΙΚΟΝΕΣ* ... to forge Achaia' (74/446–7). Those icons would be manifestations of *virtù irraggiante*, *virtù* that irradiates and illuminates, a phrase out of his studies around Cavalcanti which Pound applied to the Confucian metaphysic.

To grasp and to act out the generative and civilizing processes of nature and of human nature, this is the fundamental Confucian dynamic, and one which Pound had long made his own. He had affirmed it first in his 1927 translation of the *Ta Hio*, signalled its importance at key points in his cantos through the 1930s, asserted it with increasing urgency in Italy through the last years of the war, and now he was again studying and translating *The Unwobbling Pivot & The Great Digest* as he composed these

Confucian cantos, and doing it in the same notebooks. That *The Pisan Cantos* are Confucian before anything else has been recognized, though probably still not enough. It is not only that allusions and echoes and direct citations abound. More significantly, their procedure, metaphysic, and ethic, are all Confucian, or, more exactly, Confucianism made new. Pound really meant it when he typed into canto 76, 'better gift can no man make to a nation | than the sense of Kung fu Tseu' (76/454). In order to make quite clear what the gift was he wrote in by hand *ch'eng*,[2] his chosen ideogram for precise definition or the word made perfect.

But exactly how was he to give precise definition to our world of evolving, interacting, and self-ordering energies, the world which physicists and ecologists and artists and some philosophers may see, and in which and by which we all live, though mostly too 'rationally' to realise our immersion in it. At one point Pound had invoked the example of 'the biologist... thinking thoughts that join like spokes in a wheel-hub and that fuse in hyper-geometric amalgams'—a less than clarifying mix of metaphors. He had given Yeats a musical analogy, and Yeats had been unable to see it. But he stuck to that as giving the right idea, 'It is music—musical themes that find each other out'. It is in music that we can have a gamut of themes and motifs repeating and unfolding through their variations and their changing combinations. And that is exactly what is going on throughout these cantos. Canto 74 especially can appear rambling and formless, but then so too can Schubert's '"Wanderer" Fantasy' to the casual listener. Like that 'Fantasy', it is best read as a complex and extended musical composition in which the themes or preoccupations are being gradually worked out through progressions of specifying detail, and through their varying and developing interactions. This is the mode of a mind striving to comprehend the world in its diverse and often contradictory aspects and in its full complexity. Where I wrote above, 'the processes of nature and of human nature', a simplifying abstraction, Pound had written fifteen lines, each adding a different aspect of the matter and thus building up a more comprehensive, and therefore more precise, definition. 'Generalities', he would insist, should be 'born from a sufficient phalanx of particulars' (74/441).

The writing in these cantos is too dense, the ever-changing relations too fluid and complex, for deliberate analysis to do them any sort of justice. They need to be performed, and performed again and again, for their music to come clear. However, certain lines and passages will stand out in the flow as more immediately meaningful, and understanding of the rest can grow around these. One might start from the first statement of the major theme—

> Fear god and the stupidity of the populace,
> but a precise definition
> transmitted thus Sigismundo
> thus Duccio, thus Zuan Belin, or trastevere with La Sposa
> Sponsa Cristi in mosaic till our time (74/425)

That is relatively straightforward, but this free rendering of Legge's *Mencius* IV.ii,11 on the next page seems not to accord with it—

> not words whereto to be faithful
> nor deeds that they be resolute
> only that bird-hearted equity make timber
> and lay hold of the earth (74/426)

Surely it is right that words should be faithful and deeds resolute, yet here equity, natural justice, trumps them, and is associated with birds and trees that express themselves without thought. Well, the following lines observe, Odysseus' heroic deeds can be retold as tall tales, and empty words create clutter. Beyond mere words and deeds there is the word that shapes the world and is its law—

> in principio verbum
> paraclete or the verbum perfectum: sinceritas
> from the death cells in sight of Mt. Taishan @ Pisa (74/427)

That could have come out of Pound's discussions with Father Vath. The Latin 'in principio verbum', 'In the beginning was the Word', and the 'paraclete' or abiding 'Spirit of truth', are from the Gospel of John, the opening of which is read out by the priest at the end of the Catholic Mass. (The priest in his green vestments will be metamorphosed into an Egyptian 'great scarab . . . bowed at the altar' (74/428).) John's Word is God that made all things and is the light of men, and 'was made flesh, and dwelt among us', 'Verbum caro factum est'. Pound's 'verbum perfectum: sinceritas', proposes a Confucian correspondence with that while actually shifting the thought into a radically different belief system, one in which the attention is upon the human agent of the light more than upon the divinity. 'Sincerity, the perfect word, or the precise word', he wrote in his prefatory note to *The Unwobbling Pivot*, and 'Only the most absolute sincerity under heaven can effect any change'. Here it is the perfected human word that is creative and spreads enlightenment. Another Confucian passage brings in the idea of *virtù* that irradiates and has its effect through human action—

plowed in the sacred field and unwound the silk worms early
                                        in tensile 顯 [*hsien*[3]]
in the light of light is the *virtù*
        "sunt lumina" said Erigena Scotus
        as of Shun on Mt. Taishan
and in the hall of the forebears
                as from the beginning of wonders
the paraclete that was present in Yao, the precision
in Shun the compassionate
in Yu the guider of waters (74/429)

The *hsien*[3] ideogram, read by Pound as signifying active light, or the light from heaven, is enacted in the imperial fertility rituals, and in the works of the legendary emperors. It is manifest also in the Judaic law's sense of natural justice and its ban against usury—

    to redeem Zion with justice
sd/ Isaiah. Not out on interest said David rex
                            the prime s.o.b.
Light tensile immaculata
            the sun's cord unspotted
'sunt lumina' said the Oirishman to King Carolus,
                    'OMNIA,
all things that are are lights' (74/429)

Erigena's axiom was a logical conclusion from the Catholic doctrine of creation and incarnation, though it was condemned as heretical by the Church. Pound could find the same vision of all-informing light in Cavalcanti—though it was left to Spinoza to argue it out that all that is alive and active in creation must be a mode of the creating Being. Pound's emphatic 'OMNIA' insists upon the rightness of Erigena's insight even as he gives it a Confucian inflection by looking for the universal light in enlightened behaviours.

Here there is a shift into the negative, following on from 'and they dug him up out of sepulture', that is, the Church dug up long dead Erigena, 'soi disantly looking for Manichaeans'. That was a crusade to put out 'the light of light' in Provence, as other enlightenments have been put out of mind, for example, 'that the state can lend money' and need not go into debt to private banks to finance public works, witness 'the fleet at Salamis made with money lent by the state to the shipwrights' (74/429). In the unenlightened world, money, as Lenin said, is never invested 'inside the country to raise the standard of living | but always abroad to increase the profits of usurers'; and 'gun sales lead to more gun sales | they do not clutter the market for gunnery | there is no saturation' (74/429). 'All of which leads to the death cells' (74/441), or 'Till was hung yesterday'; and it has led to Pound's finding himself 'a man on whom the sun has gone down', a 'no man' like Odysseus in the Cyclops' cave. His response is a return to the dominant—

> nor shall the diamond die in the avalanche
> be it torn from its setting
> first must destroy himself ere others destroy him.
> 4 times was the city rebuilded, Hooo Fasa
> Gassir, Hooo Fasa dell' Italia tradita
> now in the mind indestructible, Gassir, Hoooo Fasa,
> With the four giants at the four corners
> and the four gates mid-wall Hooo Fasa
> and a terrace the colour of stars (74/430)

In effect he is reaffirming his early commitment to the generative image or 'seed-*gestalt*', only what is 'now in the mind indestructible' is charged with his lifetime's effort to conceive and to realize a *paradiso terrestre.*

One might notice in passing that the second movement of canto 74 is the same length as the first, about 244 lines, and the fourth movement will again have that many lines. The third movement will have 81 lines. So there are three equal movements, and the other a third of their length. These are teasing symmetries, to which, probably, no mystical significance should be attached, yet they do at least indicate a will to give a cut shape to the free-flowing writing. There is no evidence that Pound counted up his lines, but he did radically revise and condense his first notebook draft in the latter part of July. It would of course be all the more wonderful if such symmetries—and they exist throughout these cantos—had arisen unsought.

Each movement of canto 74 has its distinct character or force-field. The key to the first movement has been the light from heaven expressed in constructive intelligence. That has been in effect a profession of faith made 'from the death cells in sight of Mt. Taishan @ Pisa'. The second movement is a response which entertains the idea of a descent into the dark night of the spirit where clarity of mind and purpose fail. Here there are illusions, and false hopes, and fears: the amazing fakir's trick of making dead straw ignite in his mouth—Villon's mother's 'painted paradise' on the church wall offsetting her desperate fear of hell—sea bathers taking fright at a hawk's shadow. There is the decently elegiac 'Lordly men are to earth o'ergiven'—men who had been his companions, Ford, Yeats, Joyce, among them. There is nostalgia for the good society and the restaurants and the cake shops one used to know—where are the pleasures of yesteryear? But Pound is not doing a Villon, not giving way to regrets for the lost past. The present asserts itself unsentimentally: 'and Amber Rives [Princess Troubetzkoi] is dead, the end of that chapter | see Time for June 5th' (74/434). A tone of ironic good humour enters into the following episode, a lightening of the darkness—

> and Mr Edwards superb green and brown
>   in ward No 4 a jacent benignity,
> of the Baluba mask: 'doan you tell no one
>   I made you that table'
>   methenamine eases the urine
> and the greatest is charity
> to be found among those who have not observed
>   regulations
> not of course that we advocate—
> and yet petty larceny
> in a regime based on grand larceny
> might rank as conformity   (74/434)

Seriousness returns as the thought of casual loss and destruction provokes resistance—

> 300 years culture at the mercy of a tack hammer
>   thrown through the roof
> Cloud over mountain, mountain over the cloud
> I surrender neither the empire nor the temples
>   plural
> nor the constitution nor yet the city of Dioce
> each one in his god's name   (74/434)

After further affirmations of what he believes in, the movement comes to its crisis in the episode beginning 'I don't know how humanity stands it | with a painted paradise at the end of it | without a painted paradise at the end of it' (74/436). Pound himself is down among the prisoners as among slaves or among Odysseus' men 'in Circe's swine-sty', knowing that the ultimate cause of their being there is the poison of greed flowing 'in all the veins of the commonweal'. That is, 'if on high, will flow downward all through them', and here, at the exact mid-point of the canto, comes a desperate doubt: 'if on the forge at Predappio?' Mussolini was born at Predappio, son of a blacksmith—was he infected at birth with the poison, and was the whole Fascist effort infected in consequence? The instant response is to think of Allen Upward, a resister, but one who, believing himself sacrificed to a usurious system closed against his genius, succumbed to despair and shot himself. And yet his seal or 'intaglio', a carved gem which he called 'Sitalkas', exists still, an icon to keep in mind the perennial and sustaining life in the grain, and to lift the canto from its lowest point. The episode is framed by 'Magna NUX animae' at the start, and 'nox animae magna' at its end, phrases which play off against John of the Cross's Dark Night in which the soul experiences desolation and despair while feeling cut off from the divine light. 'NUX', however, meaning 'nut'—playing off against '*Νύξ*', Greek for 'night'—gives a radically different idea, suggesting that the soul has its own seed of light and intelligence and grows from within. Then the lines following 'nox animae magna' suggest in Confucian terms how humanity can stand the darkness:

> To study with the white wings of time passsing
>   is not that our delight
> to have friends come from far countries
>   is not that pleasure
> nor to care that we are untrumpeted?
>   filial, fraternal affection is the root of humaneness
>   the root of the process   (74/437)

That gives confidence to dismiss John of the Cross's negative way with low puns:

> dry friable earth going from dust to more dust
>   grass worn from its root-hold
>   is it blacker? was it blacker? *Νύξ* animae?
>   is there a blacker or was it merely San Juan with a belly-ache
>   writing ad posteros
> in short shall we look for a deeper or is this the bottom?   (74/438)

Actually, it is recognized, there is worse in the real world: Ugolino, shut away in a tower in nearby Pisa ate his own children; Berlin is now a city in ruins; dysentery marks the death camps; and phosphorus—the word coming from the Greek meaning 'bringer of light'—is used as a weapon of war against women and children. And still paradise exists, though not as painted on the church wall, and 'only in fragments unexpected excellent sausage, | the smell of mint, for example'. Or, possibly, in an experience such as when Confucius 'heard Shun's music | the sharp song with sun under its radiance', and 'for three months did not know the taste of his food' (74/439). The key to this movement turns out to be not its dark moods but a balanced and positive humanity which can get through them, a disposition which neither gives way to despair nor to an illusory heaven, and which maintains a working faith in a possible paradise.

The relatively short third movement takes up the economic theme. This was introduced in the first movement and appeared again in the second, but has been all along surprisingly understated given the reports that Pound would talk of nothing else in the DTC. Evidently he did not give away the inner and deeper workings of his mind to the guards and psychiatrists. Evidently too, when his mind was fully engaged in his poem of reconstruction the economic war became a subordinate concern. Indeed it is only in these eighty lines (at 74/439–41), and in canto 78, that the theme receives any sustained attention. Hereafter its leading motifs will be repeated from time to time, keeping it in mind, but it will not be heard at all in the climactic cantos 81, 82, and 83. The movement begins with a half-line reminder of John Adams's 'every bank of discount is downright iniquity | robbing the public for private individual's gain' (see 74/437), and with another half-line recalling how the Roosevelt administration purchased gold 'at 35 instead of 21.65', that is, at excessive cost to the public treasury and excessive profit to the private gold dealers. A passage of fifteen anti-Semitic lines pins that scandal on the Rothschilds and the Morgenthaus, and hints at a Jewish conspiracy against 'the goyim'.[1] Countering that there follows a slightly longer passage developing, positively and without prejudice, the principles of Judaic justice and law: 'From the law, by the law, so build yr/ temple | with justice in meteyard and measure'. The 'largest rackets' are mentioned, alternating the value of the unit of money, 'and usury @ 60 or lending | that which is made out of nothing'. That 'the state *can* lend money' and 'need not borrow' is once again insisted upon; and as an example the story is told of how Wörgl in the Tyrol issued its own money and terrified all the bankers. Set against that is the disaster of Russia's failure to 'grasp the idea of work-certificate', that is, 'money to signify work done, inside a system | and measured and wanted' (see 74/426), and hence 'the immolation of men to machinery | and the canal work and gt. mortality'. The final line of the movement, 'all of which leads to the death-cells', connects the evils that flow from greed and ignorance with the DTC, and there the subject is dropped. The war against usury, and for the nation's control of its credit, fades into the background of the poem. Here the root of reconstruction is not in economic reform but in the art which shapes perception and so directs action.

The fourth movement begins 'each in the name of its god', and is in three sections: (i) begins with and returns to both that line and to Aristotle's 'philosophy is not for young men' (74/441–4); (ii) begins at 'Time is not' followed by '"to carve Achaia"', and ends with 'to forge Achaia' (74/444–7); (iii) runs from 'and as for playing checquers with black Jim' to 'searching

[1] These, it is worth noting, are the only clearly anti-Semitic lines in *The Pisan Cantos*.

every house' (74/447–8). The last seventeen lines of the canto are a coda to the whole.

The first section opens with a restatement of the canto's main theme, that enlightened behaviours both public and private flow from fixing in the mind the wisdom derived from experience. Hence neither philosophy nor government are for the young, 'their generalities cannot be born from a sufficient phalanx of particulars'. At the same time there are the formative ideas and icons which, being 'in the mind indestructible', shape a culture, as in the Noh theatre of Japan, or the song of Gassir; or a belief 'in the resurrection of Italy'. Through the rest of the section Pound is trying to summon up the guiding light of his own mind. First Koré is evoked as the light of blind Tiresias' mind, then as Persephone under his Taishan, and this in spite of his being 'in the a. h. of the army | in sight of two red cans labelled "FIRE"'. There are spirits, Graces, 'possibly in the soft air . . . in this air as of Kuanon', or on the air that blows Botticelli's Venus ashore. But here is 'By no means an orderly Dantescan rising', as might be from the arse-hole of hell up to the height where Dante is reunited with Beatrice. Pound's vision is 'not to a schema'. Instead, the spirits accompanying Venus-Persephone, and she who calls herself 'la luna', and Cunizza, are on the varying wind, and grow in the mind 'as grass under Zephyrus | as the green blade under Apeliota'. They also are of the process. They are not, however, Confucian. This light is from Pound's other tradition, from Eleusis, from Provence and Cunizza's Sordello, and from Cavalcanti.

The second section opens and closes with visions of his beloved, not out of myth now, but the real woman moving into myth. She was introduced earlier in the canto—

> in coitu inluminatio
> Manet painted the bar at La Cigale or at Les Folies in that year
> she did her hair in small ringlets, à la 1880 it might have been
> red, and the dress she wore Drecol or Lanvin
> a great goddess, Aeneas knew her forthwith (74/435)

—that is, Aeneas recognized Venus, his mentor in the refounding of Troy at Rome. In this movement Pound's own 'great goddess' is seen in her house at Sant'Ambrogio as in a cameo, 'against the half-light of the window | with the sea beyond making horizon', a 'profile "to carve Achaia"'. That affirmation takes him back to Hugh Selwyn Mauberley's England, where the skill 'to carve Achaia' was lacking, and there the refrain is 'beauty is difficult'. Among other particulars, Charles Granville, rather briefly Pound's publisher in London, is mentioned ironically as 'a lover of beauty', one for whom 'the three ladies all waited', Granville being a serial bigamist.

And Arthur Symons's 'Modern Beauty', a fine poem of the *fin de siècle* decadence, is recalled in a half-remembered line, '"my fondest knight lie dead"'. This sketch of English *mœurs* as he knew them in his London years is sardonic and amused, not celebratory—'aram vult nemus', that decaying grove lacked an altar. From the last 'Beauty is difficult' he turns to the grass under his tentflaps, seeing it as 'indubitably, bambooiform | representative brush strokes wd/ be similar', and so to his own live images, 'her eyes as in "La Nascita"', the Botticelli 'Birth of Venus', and 'the child's face | is at Capoquadri'—the Siena palazzo where Olga Rudge had an apartment—'in the fresco square over the doorway | centre background'. These are his 'images formed in the mind... to forge Achaia'.

The final section consists of thirty lines touching on his youth in America, followed by thirty lines touching on his years in Italy. The American memories are sharply delineated details of a passing or past New York, but there is nothing iconic there. The only lasting things are a clutter of mementoes of Aunt Frank's European tours and Ma Weston's New England. That was the America he needed to leave. The Italian memories are mixed and don't offer a simple contrast. There are the things he values, San Zeno in Verona with its signed column, and the painting of 'the madonna in Ortolo' which he associates with Cavalcanti's celebration of the light shining from his lady. On the other hand, 'the soja has yet to save Europe | and the wops do not use maple syrup', and an art dealer says that he sells only '"the best"', but '"nothing modern | we couldn't sell anything modern"'. As if from these 'things seeking an exit' (40/199), he concludes the movement with a return to the major theme by remembering the woodcarvers in Mary's Tirol, 'Herr Bacher's father [who] made madonnas still in the tradition', while 'another Bacher still cut intaglios | such as Salustio's in the time of Ixotta'.

The coda is a poem in itself:

Serenely in the crystal jet
        as the bright ball that the fountain tosses
(Verlaine) as diamond clearness
        How soft the wind under Taishan
                where the sea is remembered
        out of hell, the pit
        out of the dust and glare evil
        Zephyrus / Apeliota
This liquid is certainly a
        property of the mind
nec accidens est but an element
                in the mind's make-up

est agens and functions dust to a fountain pan otherwise
            Hast 'ou seen the rose in the steel dust
                                    (or swansdown ever?)
so light is the urging, so ordered the dark petals of iron
we who have passed over Lethe. (74/449)

What is this 'liquid'? Imagistically, it is the crystal jet of the fountain, and the spirit-bearing winds under Taishan, 'Zephyrus | Apeliota'. In philosophical terms, it is an active element in the mind's make-up, which is near to saying that it is the force that drives the mind. Its action here, the action of the canto, has been to lift the poet's mind out of his hell, 'out of the dust and glare evil'. It has done that by composing the mind's otherwise dusty shards of memory and experience into a verbal music, just as the rose pattern forms in the steel dust when the iron filings respond to a magnet's force. But still one asks, what exactly *is* this 'liquid'? Pound used a similar word in the last sentence of his version of *The Analects* for (in Legge's translation) 'knowing *the force of* words'. 'Not to know words', Pound wrote, 'is to be without the fluid needful to understand men'. That connects with the Confucian principle that knowledge grows and becomes active through precise verbal definition. Altogether then, the coda resolves the leading themes of the canto into a single final statement: the generative process of nature, and the constructive process of intelligence, are seen and understood to be one and the same fluid life-force, the life-force active and manifest in the process of the poem itself, and active and manifest in our reading it.

There is something more in the resonant last line, one which looks forward to the cantos that are to follow. To have passed *over* Lethe is to have not bathed in nor drunk of the waters which take away all memory of evil. So what is wrong with the world is not going to be forgotten. Now, after Lethe, at the summit of his Purgatory, Dante comes upon another river, Eunoë, and when he drinks of its waters he is 'remade, as the plant repairs | Itself, renewed with its new foliage, | Pure and disposed to mount up to the stars'. In one DTC draft Pound did write as the final line, 'seeking Eunoë'; but he must then have reflected that that was not to be his way. His is to be a paradise in and of the world of the living, and for better and for worse it is to that world that he remains committed.

Canto 75 may be taken as a purely musical example of the renovation Pound was attempting. It presents the score of Gerhart Münch's transcription of a sixteenth-century setting for lute, by Francesco da Milano, of Clément Janequin's chorus for voices imitating the songs of many birds. Each bird may be heard distinctly even as another and another join in until their diverse songs become interwoven in an excited, richly textured song of all the birds together, a universe of birdsong. And this is the work of human intelligence responding to the birds' songs, then effecting a series of refinements in the accurate registration of them in art. 'Itz the double stopping for the fiddle that makes lezwoisseauxx the FINAL product. (to date)', Pound would write of Münch's transcription, which had given the chorus 'a third life in our time' on Olga Rudge's violin. And there was the other dimension, 'the carry thru' or transmission by one musician to another of an image or concept formed in the mind, 'indestructable'. 'Four times was the city rebuilded', Pound commented, then thought to add, 'les oiseauX having been thaaar for some time in the "first" place'.

Canto 74 is the extended overture to *The Pisan Cantos*, setting out the main thematic materials and sketching the form in which they are to be developed through the sequence 76–83. These eight cantos are subdivided into two sequences of four, 76–9 and 80–3. The first sequence culminates in the 'lynx lyric', a hymn to Dionysus; the second culminates in Pound's making a ritual ode of a wasp building its nest in his tent. The tone is now more personal, as these cantos turn out to be less directly concerned with the ideas of order, and more directly concerned with the ordering of his own mind. Their achievement will be, not yet a new Italy nor a United States true to its Constitution, but the recovery of his own centre and his own right relation with the universe. Like the men of old in Confucius' testament, he must first set himself in order before he can hope to establish order about him.

Canto 76 doesn't so much follow on from 74 and 75 as start over with all still to do. The mind is in a state where memories and dreams and observations and reflections well up together in a spontaneous flow with no apparent control. As one thing follows another, each thing a crystallized experience of one kind and another, the effect is rather *pointilliste*; and as the hundreds and thousands of bright, hard, luminous details accumulate through the course of these cantos into a great swirling cloud like a Milky Way, the effect can be overwhelming. One is in Pound's vast and various mental world, a world which ranges in detail through his personal experiences in America and England and France and Italy, through European history and culture ancient and contemporary, and which includes also his Confucianism, and of course his present situation in the DTC.

Those are comforting general terms, but this world exists in discrete, free-floating, particles, each particle a micro-world to itself, and with their relations all to be discovered. So much can lie condensed in an image or a name or a thing. The theme of memory is introduced in the opening lines of 76:

> And the sun high over horizon hidden in cloud bank
>   lit saffron the cloud ridge
>   dove sta memora   (76/452)

The Italian line is from Cavalcanti's 'Canzone d'Amore', translated in canto 36: 'Where memory liveth, | [Love] takes its state | Formed like a diafan from light on shade'. The lit cloud has brought Cavalcanti's 'diafan' to mind, and that association connects memory with love, anticipating or preparing the key lines of the canto,

>   nothing matters but the quality
> of the affection—
> in the end—that has carved the trace in the mind
> dove sta memoria

And later, in the best known passage of these cantos, that will become 'What thou lovest well remains | the rest is dross'. As to names, to take just one, 'che fu chiamata Primavera': she who was called 'The Spring' was Cavalcanti's beloved Giovanna, so named for her divine beauty by Dante in his *Vita Nuova*. The 'flowered branch and sleeve moving' makes her also Botticelli's Renaissance 'Primavera', a woman conceived as a vortex of nature's grace. And for a thing, take Tullio Romano's miraculous carved sirens or mermaids in Venice's Santa Maria dei Miracoli, spirits of the Venetian sea found in the marble which is compounded of sea creatures (76/460). In Pound's mind any word or image can unfurl like these—and in unfurling reveal their interactions, and their patterns.

The first episode of 76 begins with evocations of a paradisal Sant'Ambrogio 'in the timeless air'—a distillation from the Italian drafts of January and February, with 'Cunizza, qua al triedro | e la scalza, and she who said: I still have the mould'. The 'timeless' modulates into the temporal—'in Mt Segur there is wind space and rain space | no more an altar to Mithras'—and thoughts of deaths follow, and of the passing of once-famed cakeshops and restaurants, and of lives coming down to left-over bricabrac. 'Progress' in fashion is not the answer, rather things that endure, and he thinks again of the good sense of Confucius which guided Chinese civilization through millennia, and of ancient Judaic law respected still in Gibraltar when he was taken to the synagogue there in 1908, and why not rebuild Zion with justice now? '"Hey, Snag, wot are the books ov th' bibl' | name 'em"', thus the DTC breaks into his reverie as a neighbouring murderer passes the time with his cage-mate. The Bible has not saved him, nor has his study of

Latin. A move to recover 'the timeless air over the sea-cliffs' is interrupted by a local variation upon a popular American song that would have been much heard in the camp, '"the pride of all our D.T.C. was pistol-packin' Burnes"'. Then the reverie resumes, bringing back memories of walking the roads of France, then of Joyce at Sirmione, and so to Venice where the shops in the Piazza (subject to flooding) are 'kept up by | artificial respiration'. The will to recover the timeless vision contends with the insistent evidence of the attritions and evils in time: '20 years of the dream', but the dream of the Fascist republic is over and done with. Still 'the clouds near to Pisa [and to Taishan] | are as good as any in Italy'; and Aphrodite may be envisioned, as Aeneas's father Anchises 'laid hold of her flanks of air | drawing her to him... no cloud, but the crystal body'. Again actuality breaks in, 'Death, insanity/suicide degeneration | that is, just getting stupider as they get older'. And here, in mid-canto, is the resolving, centering statement—

nothing matters but the quality
of the affection —
in the end—that has carved the trace in the mind

Yet there is the other side of that to be reckoned with, that there are other traces carved in the mind, other persistent patterns, as of misconduct—

and if theft be the main principle in government
(every bank of discount J. Adams remarked)
there will be larceny on a minor pattern
a few camions, a stray packet of sugar
and the effect of the movies

Again the will to realize a natural *paradiso* asserts itself, attempting to actualize its vision: 'Lay in soft grass by the cliff's edge',

the gemmed field *a destra* with fawn, with panther,
corn flower, thistle and sword-flower
to a half metre grass growth,
lay on the cliff's edge
... nor is this yet *atasal*
nor are here souls, nec personae
neither here in hypostasis, this land is of Dione
and under her planet
to Helia the long meadow with poplars
to *Κύπρις*
the mountain and shut garden of pear trees in flower
here rested (76/458)

The mind is not yet in its paradise, not yet '*atasal*'; and if its paradise is not artificial, neither is its hell, 'Le paradis n'est pas artificiel, | l'enfer non plus'. At the end of the canto, which had begun in paradisal mode, it is the latter that is dominant, 'po'eri di'aoli sent to the slaughter... for a usurer's holiday', and 'woe to them that conquer with armies | and whose only right is their power' (76/462–3).

Much of the thematic material in canto 77 is now familiar, but the treatment of it varies in significant ways. Canto 76 was in the elemental key of air and light and crystalline water, and its leading preoccupation was vision. The elemental key in 77 is earth, and the leading preoccupation is action, as the opening chord humorously establishes—

And this day Abner lifted a shovel...
          instead of watchin' to see if it would
take action

The tone of this canto is frequently humorous, down to earth; though it is serious too about earthly powers, that is, about governors, and about mother earth and chthonic Zagreus. Instead of aerial visions there is dancing on this ground. Jefferson's axiom, '"the earth belongs to the living"', comes apparently casually in a passage concerned with credit and banking. Two mountains with the Arno flowing between them are seen as 'the two teats of Tellus, γέα'; and Pound himself 'kissed the earth after sleeping on concrete', kissed it as the fair breast of fertile Demeter—

bel seno Δημήτηρ copulatrix
                    thy furrow   (77/470)

(The union with 'GEA TERRA' will be consummated in canto 82.)

Canto 77 closes with a rapid, scherzo-like, succession of statements and images, as if impatiently reaching for some further development in the mind's process. In fact the last twenty lines, from 'For nowt so much as a just peace | That wd/ obstruct future wars', are leading on to canto 78. If there is a danger of stasis in 'mind come to plenum when nothing more will go into it', that is immediately disturbed by 'the wind mad as Cassandra | who was sane as the lot of 'em', though that in turn is calmed into the ordered activity of the dance, 'Sorella, mia sorella, | che ballava sobr' un zechin". The conclusion is 'bringest to focus', flanked on both sides by the ideogram *ch'eng*, 'to perfect or focus', with a repeated 'Zagreus' underpinning it. This is a strong variant upon 'the rose in the steel dust', and one which explicitly brings together Kung and Eleusis to declare again that it is the organic, chthonic, energies, the life force itself, which drive the process of just definition.

The dominant preoccupation of canto 78 is war and peace, or more exactly the perennial economic war which, to Pound's mind, is the war behind most wars. The recent war and its consequence have of course been a presence in these cantos from the opening lines, but the dominant motive up to this has been to recover the concept of the just city and the energy to rebuild it. But now, after the aerial spirits and the earthly powers, 'usura, sin against nature' is brought into focus, with the main episode the fall of Mussolini's regime. And here Pound's poetic genius partly shuts down. The trouble was that he knew too well what he wanted to say, having said most of it before in his prose propaganda. On this subject his mind was made up, and not, as elsewhere in these cantos, open to and energized by the variousness and contradictoriness and surprising depths of things, and, with that, attentive to their fluidly self-ordering interactions. Here, especially when dealing with Mussolini, he falls back into the simplicities of his wartime prose. The promising beginning suggests a parallel with Agamemnon's homecoming—

Cassandra, your eyes are like tigers,
  with no word written in them
You also I have carried to nowhere
      to an ill house and there is
            no end to the journey. (78/477)

But soon he is fighting old battles as 'the economic war' takes over, beginning with a loaded anecdote repeated from *Carta da visita* (1942)—'"it will not take uth 20 years to cwuth Mussolini"'. Mussolini's part in the war is represented very simply by a few of his phrases and supposed achievements—

'not a right but a duty'
      those words still stand uncancelled,
'Presente!'
      and merrda for the monopolists
            the bastardly lot of 'em
Put down the slave trade, made the desert to yield
and menaced the loan swine
      Sitalkas, double Sitalkas
      'not the priest but the victim' (78/479)

That association with Sitalkas, the life-force in the grain, would have us see Mussolini as at first a force for the just distribution of the abundance of nature, but then as a sacrificial victim, a martyr. One only has to think of his use of poison gas in the Abyssinian desert to see through at least one of those claims. More telling is a later passage recalling the time when Pound tried to persuade Mussolini that 'taxes are no longer necessary | in the old way if it (money) be based on work done | inside a system and measured and gauged to human requirements', and Mussolini had said 'one wd/ have to think about that | but was hang'd dead by the heels before his thought in proposito | came into action efficiently'. That at least moves on from blaming an international conspiracy for his fall to seeking the cause in the Duce himself (77/468).

The canto does open out beyond Mussolini and his failed regime. There is the humanity of the peasants who shared their room and food with Pound when he was heading north on foot from Rome. There are new memories along with some recurrent ones, for instance the meeting with Eliot in Verona in '1920 or thereabouts' at which 'a literary program' was agreed, or so Pound had thought, but which 'was neither published nor followed'. But there is also a sample of the sort of stuff he used to write to Tinkham and Borah, about the fights in the United States Senate to keep the country out of the League of Nations, and to repeal 'the constriction of Bacchus'; and after that there are half-a-dozen lines of crude rant in the manner of the Rome Radio broadcasts—'Geneva the usurers' dunghill... and Churchill's return to Midas broadcast by his liary'. That part of Pound's mind was unchanged, as if frozen by its vision of evil.

Nevertheless, at the end of the canto he gratefully gets away from the economics and the propaganda. His mind comes alive as he thinks of a series of women: Nausikaa in Odysseus' story; someone who 'sat by the window at Bagno Romagna'—this could have been when he was making his way north from Rome in 1943—'knowing that nothing could happen | and looking ironicly at the traveler'; Cassandra again; then a restaging of the Bagno Romagna incident 'as it might be in a play by Lope de Vega'; so to 'Cunizza's shade al triedro'; and finally to Dante's three Virtues. He comes out thus into a world where a white ox seen on the nearby road has 'its importance | its benediction', as Dr Williams would have appreciated, simply for being there.

In canto 79 Pound resumes the process of getting his mind together in the DTC. This is very much a musical canto, in its composition and in its material. It begins in counterpoint, sorts itself out into clear division—equity against iniquity, and from that gradually develops a sustained lyric resolution—a song and dance to the Eleusinian powers, somewhat after the *Pervigilium Veneris*.

Counterpoint depends upon discriminations of likeness and difference, of likeness in difference and difference in likeness. The opening statement sets up a simple contrast between white light and dark earth:

Moon, cloud, tower, a patch of the battistero all of a whiteness,
dirt pile as per the Del Cossa inset

A more nuanced fifteen-line passage then explores the subject of whiteness and womankind in contexts of opera and ballet, with a sub-theme of love and loss. That is followed by a slightly longer passage on the equally nuanced counter-subject, the 'whiteness' of black prisoners in the DTC, that is, their humanity and good humour, one of them

whistling Lili Marlene
with positively less musical talent
than that of any man of colour
whom I have ever encountered
but with bonhomie and good humour

'I like a certain number of shades in my landscape', Pound comments, finding a resolving pun in a black slang word for a 'man of colour'.

This is a relatively light-hearted, even playful, canto, with the poet taking pleasure in making verbal music of the sights and sounds around him, and of the associations they bring up. He writes a passage of ring-composed counterpoint as if just for the pleasure of it—

1a with 8 birds on a wire
or rather on 3 wires, Mr Allingham
2a The new Bechstein is electric
and the lark squawk has passed out of season
whereas the sight of a good nigger is cheering
the bad'uns wont look you straight
3a Guard's cap quattrocento passes *a cavallo*
on horseback thru landscape Cosimo Tura
or, as some think, Del Cossa;
4a up stream to delouse and down stream for the same purpose
seaward
different lice live in different waters
—
some minds take pleasure in counterpoint
pleasure in counterpoint
—
4b and the later Beethoven on the new Bechstein,
or in the Piazza S. Marco for example
finds a certain concordance of size
not in the concert hall;
3b can that be the papal major sweatin' it out to the bumm drum?
what castrum romanum, what
'went into winter quarters'

is under us?
as the young horse whinnies against the tubas
                    in contending for certain values
                    (Jannequin per esempio, and Orazio
                                        Vechii or Bronzino)
2b Greek rascality against Hagoromo
          Kumasaka vs/ vulgarity
                    no sooner out of Troas
than the damn fools attacked Ismarus of the Cicones
1b   4 birds on 3 wires, one bird on one   (79/485)

Then he does it over again in an even longer passage (79/486–7). Even his serious concerns come lightened with humour, as that 'Athene cd/ have done with more sex appeal', or this reflection upon Yeats's 'Blood and the Moon',

          '[a time] half dead at the top'
My dear William B. Y. your ½ was too moderate
'pragmatic pig' (if goyim) will serve for 2 thirds of it
to say nothing of the investment of funds in the Yu-en-mi
and similar ventures

The culminating 'lynx lyric', which brings the first sequence of cantos to a climax, is celebratory, dionysian, a rite of spring—if a somewhat genteel and confected one. It is to be enjoyed as an episode taking the mind out of the DTC in the spirit of Yeats's Bishop Berkeley who proved 'That this pragmatical, preposterous pig of a world ... Must vanish on the instant if the mind but change its theme'.

Canto 80, on the other hand, might be obeying Conrad's injunction, 'in the destructive element immerse', the destructive element in this case being time. This long canto, nearly as long as 74, is composed of memories of things that were of their era and tell of what has been. The keynote is 'Les moeurs passent et la douleur reste', a way of life disappears, the regrets remain. But Pound is not revisiting his past in a spirit of regret or nostalgia. There is a reminder at the start, in the word '*themis*'—'the vagaries of our rising θέμις' is something John Adams might have said—that the customs which most interest Pound are those which make for and sustain societies and their laws. 'Amo ergo sum', he then affirms, I love therefore I am, 'and in just that proportion', with the further emphasis, even though I grow old I still love, 'senesco sed amo'. That is an orientation, through this long passage of memories, towards 'What thou lovest well remains, the rest is dross'.

Initially the consciousness is timebound in a drift of memories of the past. Some things seem worth the remembering: that 'Spanish bread was made out of grain in that era'—the Velazquez paintings in the Prado—Turgenev's 'Nothing but death is irreparable'—Padraic Colum's poem 'O woman, shapely as the swan, | On your account I shall not die'—but then, 'Whoi didn't he...keep on writing poetry at that voltage'? The lack of voltage, of the intensity necessary for lasting achievement, is characteristic of most of these memories, and of the drifting yet alert consciousness observing and commenting upon them. For one instance, these were the American poets when Pound was growing up—

> Hovey,
> Stickney, Loring,
> the lost legion, or as Santayana has said:
> They just died   They died because they
> just couldn't stand it
> and Carman 'looked like a withered berry'
> 20 years after   (80/495)

Now and again there is a brief interruption to the flow of retrospection, the first when he looks up to notice that 'the clouds have made a pseudo-Vesuvius | this side of Taishan; and the next, a hundred lines later, when 'Prowling night-puss' recalls him to the DTC for a page or two.

The drama of the canto is in these interruptions which bring him back to his immediate world, and then in the gradual surfacing of the iconic moments in time, and the visionary moments out of time, which light up and magnetize the mind. As these moments increase and become dominant they establish a contemplative mood, one in which the drift of experience comes into sharp focus to be fixed in a definite image. The risen moon plays a part in this, lending a visionary presence to the compassionate Virgin who said 'Io son' la luna'on the Sant'Ambrogio hillside, and to the moon nymph of *Hagoromo*, and to Diana who 'had compassion on silversmiths | revealing the paraclete | standing in the cusp of the moon' (80/500–1). Among the iconic moments are 'old Belloti' registering the words on the pedestal of Shakespeare's monument in Leicester Square, 'There is no darkness but ignorance'; and the striking dignity of the red-bearded fellow mending his daughter's shoe whom Pound had come across when looking for de Born's Altaforte; and with that another memory from his walk through southern France, of 'tables set down by small rivers, | and the stream's edge is lost in the grass'. These are things not of any particular era but of 'the eternal moods', and through them the freewheeling mind gradually settles into its own mood. After the question, 'Nancy where art thou? | Whither go all the vair and the cisclatons', and the answer, 'the wave pattern runs in the stone | on the high parapet (Excideuil)', certain works and visions that outlast time fill the mind—Botticelli's Venus, and Jacopo del Sellaio's; and 'portraits in our time Cocteau by Marie Laurencin | and Whistler's Miss Alexander',

> and somebody's portrait of Rodenbach
>   with a background
> as it might be L'Ile St Louis for serenity, under Abélard's bridges
> for those trees are Elysium
>   for serenity
>   under Abélard's bridges
> for those trees are serenity   (80/512)

This dwelling upon Elysian serenity induces the 'eternal mood' in which the living can feel at one with the dead. It is carried on in thoughts of Confucius 'as he had walked under the rain altars | or under the trees of their grove'; thence to 'grey stone in the Aliscans' at Arles where the 'rain altars' are sarcophagi ranged under poplars; thence again to what remains of Mt Segur. The positive serenity of this mood comes from the feeling of communion with something that is still a living force in the mind. It is not an elegiac or melancholy mood, not at all that of Gray in his country churchyard meditating on what is dead and gone forever. Its surprising effect is to bring on a rare moment of self-revelation and confession:

>   Je suis au bout de mes forces/
> That from the gates of death,
>   that from the gates of death: Whitman or Lovelace
>   found on the jo-house seat at that
> in a cheap edition! [and thanks to Professor Speare]
> hast'ou swum in a sea of air strip
>   through an aeon of nothingness,
> when the raft broke and the waters went over me,
> [...]
>   Les larmes que j'ai creées m'inondent
> Tard, très tard je t'ai connue, la Tristesse,
> I have been hard as youth sixty years.   (80/512–13)

This release of feeling brings him altogether into the present, and into a calmed state. He notices that 'the ants seem to wobble | as the morning sun catches their shadows', makes a litany of the names of prisoners on sick call, reflects that 'the guards' opinion is lower than that of the/prisoners/o[f] t [he] a[rmy]', pauses, then with renewed energy proceeds to fix old England's image in the canto's finale as if carving its epitaph in stone.

A 'telescopic squash of English metric' was Pound's description of this finale. He was laying England to rest in its neglected honours, remembering (with the assistance of Speare's *Pocket Book of Verse*) Browning, and FitzGerald's *Rubáiyát*, and the lyric tradition back to Shakespeare and before. The finale is also a 'telescopic squash' of English history. The neglect of Magna Carta, it is implied, is at the root of its present decayed state, along with the sack of the monasteries, and the civil wars and treasons. The Wars of the Roses, the epic matter of Shakespeare's English history plays up to Henry VIII's bloody way with his wives, is condensed into three quatrains, beginning,

> Tudor indeed is gone and every rose,
> Blood-red, blanch-white that in the sunset glows
> Cries: "Blood, Blood, Blood!" against the gothic stone
> Of England, as the Howard or Boleyn knows. (80/516)

That is the *Rubáiyát*'s quatrain stripped of its luxury, syncopated by the contorted syntax matching the twisted history, and deployed to petrify the mortally violent past.

The last lines of the canto make a gentler, withdrawing, close. The Serpentine and the gulls on the pond and the sunken garden 'will look just the same'—that London remains. But there is as much life of that order, or more, in his immediate prospect where a young lizard is after a 'green midge half an ant-size'—

> and if her green elegance
> remains on this side of my rain ditch
> puss lizard will lunch on some other T-bone

There is a profound shift of attention here amounting to an alteration of consciousness in the apparently simple change from the long perspective of history to this close-up of the small drama under his eye. He has come 'thru the unending | labyrinth of the souterrain' of the timebound mind and emerged to see again the living world.

Canto 81 picks up that opening of the mind to nature and magnifies it in its opening images. The first line, 'Zeus lies in Ceres' bosom', declares, as Zielinski saw it, 'the final act of the cosmic drama, the reconciliation of the two powers' of the heavens above and the fruitful earth. Fittingly, 'Taishan is attended of loves | under Cythera, before sunrise' (81/517). Venus, currently the morning star, will be the dominant presence in this canto. But first there is a phalanx of details, nearly all of them anecdotes from Pound's own experience, making up a quite complex idea of tradition. Even sound traditions may become petrifications and need to be made new, thus 'to break the pentameter, that was the first heave'. Hugh Kenner has shown with what *maestria* Pound himself broke and renewed the pentameter through the latter third of the canto to give a timeless voice to inherited wisdom. This voice is the beloved, the mind's desire, but projected as the divinity of love and speaking not from but to the mind, interrogating, challenging, admonishing it. She speaks first as in the *libretto* of a court masque, in the guise of Venus rising in the September dawn sky,

Ere the season died a-cold
Borne upon a zephyr's shoulder
I rose through the aureate sky

She is greeted appropriately, as it seems—

Lawes and Jenkyns guard thy rest
Dolmetsch ever be thy guest

The goddess's response, however, is to challenge Dolmetsch's worthiness, 'Has he tempered the viol's wood . . . Has he curved us the bowl of the lute?' Next she challenges the poet directly—

Hast 'ou fashioned so airy a mood
    To draw up leaf from the root?

He fends off the challenge, daring to demand an answer of the goddess, 'Then resolve me, tell me aright | If Waller sang or Dowland played,' and his reward is an annihilating look out of Chaucer's 'Merciless Beauté'—

Your eyen two wol sleye me sodenly
I may the beauté of hem nat susteyne

Yet next 'there came new subtlety of eyes into my tent', eyes that he loves, at first giving the reassurance 'What thou lovest well remains', and then fiercely admonishing, 'Pull down thy vanity'. One may be reminded of the Psalms and the Preacher of Ecclesiastes and Villon's 'Ballade des pendus', and be reminded also that this is taking place in his tent in the DTC—

First came the seen, then thus the palpable
    Elysium, though it were in the halls of hell

(He would have been hearing all the time 'From the halls of Montezuma to the shores of Tripoli', from the 'Battle Hymn of the Republic', the signature song of the US Marine Corps.) The core admonition is to learn of 'the seen'—

The ant's a centaur in his dragon world.
Pull down thy vanity, it is not man
Made courage, or made order, or made grace,
    Pull down thy vanity, I say pull down.
Learn of the green world what can be thy place
In scaled invention or true artistry,
Pull down thy vanity,
                                        Paquin pull down!
The green casque has outdone your elegance. (81/521)

For all its biblical quality this is the voice of a natural, even pagan, wisdom. It would not say with the Preacher that all is vanity. And though humbled, the poet feels able in the closing passage of the canto to add something of his own—

But to have done instead of not doing
                    this is not vanity
To have, with decency, knocked
That a Blunt should open
            To have gathered from the air a live tradition
or from a fine old eye the unconquered flame
This is not vanity.

Hidden in the allusion to the visit to Blunt in 1914 will have been the knowledge that Blunt had been imprisoned for his part in the agitation in the 1880s against rack-renting Irish landlords, and while in prison had written his defiant sonnet sequence, *In vinculis.* That will have become a specially pertinent part of Pound's live tradition.

Canto 82 follows on from that allusion with 'Swinburne my only miss', the regret for this one error masking the implicit boast that he had otherwise gathered from the English air all the live tradition that it had to offer.

Zagreus, lord of the dead and of resurgent life, presides over canto 82 although not directly named. Zagreus was named, however, at the end of canto 77, and that prompts notice of an emerging system of correspondences between the two groups of cantos binding them together into a single sustained progression from 76 through to 83—

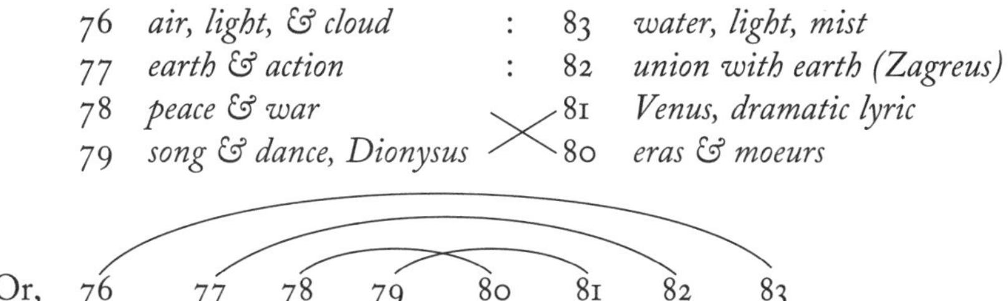

The entire sequence of eight cantos is, in effect, ring-composed. (Cantos 74 and 75 might be regarded as the overture or introduction to the action, and canto 84 as its coda, and also as a bridge to what is to follow.)

After the opening lines which situate canto 82 firmly in the 'a. h. of the army'—'"Guten Morgen, Mein Herr" yells the black boy from the jo-cart'—Pound's mind reverts to the London world he had had to get through, a world marked by death, although now he comes out at the memory of Ford's good conversation and his 'humanitas', that word glossed by the ideogram '*jen*', read by Pound as a man in touch with both earth and sky, and signifying the Confucian ideal of 'the man who lives out heaven's process on earth'. In the second half of the canto, which is of exactly the same length as the London episode, he undergoes a ritual death in which he must acknowledge the truth of 'man, earth : two halves of the tally', and realize in himself, 'simply, past metaphor', that death also is part of the process of life. His guides are Whitman's great song of death in life, 'Out of the Cradle Endlessly Rocking', and an episode in Kipling's *Kim*, both being rites of passage through near-to-death experiences into a new life sustained by an awareness of the deathless sources of life. In the final chapter of *Kim* the boy, exhausted by his long journey, is nursed through days of weakness by an old woman who then leaves his cure to Mother Earth. Kim lies down in the 'clean . . . hopeful dust that holds the seeds of all life',

> And Mother Earth . . . breathed through him to restore the poise he had lost lying so long on a cot cut off from her good currents. His head lay powerless upon her breast, and his opened hands surrendered to her strength.

In Pound's chthonic mystery the drawing of 'GEA TERRA' inspires terror—Clytaemnestra's spilling the blood of Agamemnon as if celebrating a fertility rite is also in his mind—and it also confers a sustaining wisdom:

How drawn, O GEA TERRA,
        what draws as thou drawest
                till one sink into thee by an arm's width
    embracing thee.
[. . .]
                connubium terrae   ἔφατα πόσις ἐμός
                                                ΧΘΟΝΙΟΣ, mysterium

fluid ΧΘΟΝΟΣ o'erflowed me
    lay in the fluid ΧΘΟΝΟΣ;
                that lie
under the air's solidity
    drunk with ΓΧΩΡ of ΧΘΟΝΙΟΣ
            fluid ΧΘΟΝΟΣ, strong as the undertow

of the wave receding
but that a man should live in that further terror, and live
the loneliness of death came upon me
(At 3 P.M. for an instant) (82/526)

In *Kim* Mother Earth restores not simply Kim's physical strength but, more importantly, 'the poise he had lost', his psychic balance. There is recovered poise, after 'the loneliness of death', in the last lines of the canto where Pound reads the birds perched on the camp wire as musical notes, 'three solemn half-notes | their white downy chests black-rimmed'—a closing benediction.

Interactions of water and light and intelligence bring peace and a lightened mood in canto 83, the climax of the Pisan sequence. Unity with nature is the key conception, announced by 'Gemisto stemmed all from Neptune | hence the Rimini bas reliefs', and by Scotus Erigena's 'all things that are, are lights'. There is also, to set the tone, 'the virtue *hilaritas*', and Yeats's mildly hilarious 'dawdling around Notre Dame' admiring, not the great building itself, but the symbol of it in the rose window. There is a new lightness and aerial fluidity in the writing, with the words seeming to float in the white spaces of the page, and with an impulse to form lyric strophes. There is a place also for Confucian thought, as when Pound's response to the September rain, 'in the drenched tent there is quiet | sered eyes are at rest', is followed by

the sage
delighteth in water
the humane man has amity with the hills (83/529)

'Amity' is the form love has in this canto generally, the lighter love as between friends, not the driving force which seeks union with the beloved. Yeats, 'Uncle William', is the principal human presence, recalled with both warm affection and amusement. As for 'La Cara', to whom he was desperate to send the message 'amo' in canto 76 (76/459), here her settings in Siena and Venice are sketched in, but there is no further communion.

The canto develops through three major episodes, all located in the DTC and together enacting Pound's private rite of communion with nature. The first features what is in the eyes of the caged panther and of Dryad; the second the dawn sun and Confucian principle; and the third the infant wasp viewed as enacting the autumn rite at Eleusis. The first is a preparation of the mind, the second instruction, and the third the epiphany.

The starting point is as it were in the death cells with all hope abandoned: 'In the caged panther's eyes: "Nothing. Nothing that you can do..."' Yet when in his mind he looks into the eyes of Dryad, addressed as '*Δρυάς*' in the Greek H.D. loved, he sees that they are 'like the clouds over Taishan | When some of the rain has fallen | and half remains yet to fall'. Imagined tears of compassion, possibly, but Taishan's clouds rain abundance, they mean life—

> The roots go down to the river's edge
> and the hidden city moves upward
> white ivory under the bark (83/530)

His mind is opened thus to the process of water and sunlight, despite his imprisonment—

> Plura diafana
> Heliads lift the mist from the young willows
> There is no base seen under Taishan
> but the brightness of 'udor *ὕδωρ*
> the poplar tips float in brightness

By this process is leaf drawn up from root. 'Dryad, thy peace is like water', he acknowledges, using the form of the name his 'boyhood's friend' had accepted from him when she first initiated him into her mytho-poetic vision of 'the universe of fluid force... the germinal universe of wood alive, of stone alive'.

The sun presides over the passage of instruction out of Mencius—this demands some clear thinking about the connection between the life force and human culture. The sun's breath, visible as morning mist, 'wholly covers the mountains' and 'nourishes by its rectitude'—

> Boon companion to equity
> it joins with the process
> lacking it, there is inanition

The 'process' here must be the single process of nature and human nature functioning together, so that it is simply seeing it from the human side to add,

> If deeds be not ensheaved and garnered in the heart
> there is inanition

That is the harvest of tradition, the basis of culture. A final formulation encapsulates the total process,

> that he eat of the barley corn
> and move with the seed's breath

That is enforced by warnings in Italian and in ideogram: don't force nature whether in plants or in oneself, best follow it.

With the thought of Venice he lapses again into nostalgia, 'Will I ever see the Giudecca again?' That would have been a familiar sight from the Zattere across the wide canal, and 'DAKRUŌN ΔΑΚΡΥΩΝ' he writes, weeping in Greek. His mind is back in his prison thinking thoughts of death. Then Brother Wasp 'building a very neat house' of mud on his tent roof takes his eye, and turns his mind to 'learn of the green world'—

and in the warmth after chill sunrise
an infant green as new grass
has stuck its head or tip
out of Madame La Vespa's bottle

mint springs up again
        in spite of Jones' rodents   [*i.e. prisoners set to pull up the grass*]
as had the clover by the gorilla cage
    with a four-leaf

When the mind swings by a grass-blade
    an ant's forefoot shall save you
the clover leaf smells and tastes as its flower

    The infant has descended
    from mud on the tent roof to Tellus
like to like colour he goes amid grass-blades
    greeting them that dwell under XTHONOS ΧΘΟΝΟΣ
ΟΙ ΧΘΟΝΙΟΙ; to carry our news
        εἰς χθονιους   to them that dwell under the earth,
begotten of air, that shall sing in the bower
    of Kore,   Περσεφόνεια
and have speech with Tiresias, Thebae

The *Cantos* began with Odysseus' tale of slaughtering herds to summon up 'the impetuous impotent dead' and have Tiresias speak to him. This is the reverse case. The newborn wasp descends under the earth to carry news of the living and to sing Kore-Persephone's hymn of perennial regeneration. The assurance she conveyed to initiates at Eleusis in her autumn rite was that, though this year was dying, in the next year and the years to come the earth would bring forth again green shoots and a harvest, that the source of their life was unfailing. The infant wasp can confirm this 'to them that dwell under the earth', as she confirms it to Pound in his contemplation of her. She is his epiphany of Kore-Persephone, neither tale nor myth but the life-force directly revealing itself to him in his DTC tent. Overcome by the revelation, 'that day I wrote no further.' Shortly he will write that the eyes which shone their light *at* him in canto 81 now look *from* his, meaning that now he sees his world with their vision and is of their mind.

Before that claim, however, there is down-to-earth humanity and good humour in the interlude celebrating Yeats composing his 'great peacock' at Stone Cottage, but disdaining to 'eat ham for dinner | because peasants eat ham for dinner'. And, after the moment of vision, what more is there to say, unless (in Heine's German out of Anacreon), 'the ladies say to me, "but you are old"'. So to the final lines, 'Down, Derry-down | Oh let an old man rest'. The great three-month mind-adventure has attained its end. Now common reality resumes its sway.

The closing passage of canto 83 turns from contemplation of the mystery to the matter of government in the United States, thus leading into 84 where Pound moves with renewed assurance to engage once more in the economic war. Back in that realm of problematic action and error it is 'John Adams, the Brothers Adam' to whom he pays homage as 'our norm of spirit | our chung[1] [*our centre*]'. Yet he salutes also Alessandro Pavolini and Fernando Mezzasoma of the Salò regime, and Mussolini, all three 'hung up by the heels' in Milan; and salutes also Pierre Laval and Vidkun Quisling, both recently executed as collaborators with the Nazi invaders of their countries. Though himself facing possible execution for treason he would not jump to the winning side (85/544).

PART THREE

if there is no intent to betray, there is no treason

—Justice Robert H. Jackson, delivering the majority opinion of the US Supreme Court in *Cramer vs. United States*, 6 Nov. 1944

9 : American Justice

> My instinct all along has been to leave the whole matter to the U. S. Dept. of Justice.
>
> —EP, 5 October 1945

> I dont want a fake defense against a phoney charge. If a man isn't ready to go to jail for his opinions, neither I nor Thoreau wd/ think that either the man or the opinions were worth much. BUT the vermin who jail him for holding them are worth a DAMN sight less.
>
> —EP, TS note, n.d.

Giving Cornell his head

A headline on the front page of the *Washington Post* on the morning of 19 November 1945 read, 'Poet Ezra Pound Flown Here to Answer Treason Charges'. The *Post*'s reporter had been among the press at Bolling Field for Pound's arrival there, and had noted that though looking 'somewhat decrepit' he was nevertheless 'still debonair' and 'in gay spirits'. Pound had said to the reporters, 'There is an idea afloat here that I have betrayed this country. If that damned fool idea is still in anybody's head, I want to wipe it out.' He was still ready to stand trial and to defend himself vigorously. But there was to be no trial, and no defence would be mounted. There would be a fresh indictment and an arraignment, but after that no trial jury would be empanelled, no prosecution evidence or witnesses would be produced; his defence attorney would not defend him, not one word would be said in court in his defence, and the indictment would stand unchallenged. Instead he would be shut away in a prison for the criminally insane for over twelve years, with the charge of treason suspended over him, and without ever being able to give his answer to the charge.

He would be in that prison in November 1953 when President Dwight D. Eisenhower, as he accepted the America's Democratic Legacy Award, at a B'nai B'rith Dinner in Honor of the 40th Anniversary of the

Anti-Defamation League, asked himself, 'Why are we Americans proud?', and gave this answer:

We are proud, first of all, because from the beginning of this Nation, a man can walk upright, no matter who he is, or who she is. He can walk upright and meet his friend—or his enemy; and he does not fear that because that enemy may be in a position of great power that he can be suddenly thrown in jail to rot there without charges and with no recourse to justice. We have the habeas corpus act, and we respect it.

That is indeed part of the American Constitution, where it is reinforced by the Fifth Amendment provision that 'No person shall be . . . deprived of life, liberty or property without due process of law.' Eisenhower spoke of other rights conferred by their Constitution which Americans could be proud of, including the 'right to meet your accuser face to face, if you have one', a provision of the Sixth Amendment—

In all criminal prosecutions, the accused shall enjoy the right to a speedy and public trial, by an impartial jury of the State and district wherein the crime shall have been committed . . . to be confronted with the witnesses against him; to have compulsory process for obtaining witnesses in his favour, and to have the Assistance of Counsel for his defence.

And yet the due process of law, and these other democratic rights guaranteed by the Constitution in which he trusted, would be denied to Pound. He would 'rot in jail' for a full dozen years, not counting the six months in the DTC, under indictment, but with no recourse to justice.

On Monday 19 November Pound was taken from the District of Columbia jail, where he had been held overnight, for his preliminary arraignment before Chief Justice Bolitha J. Laws. The *Washington Post* reported next morning that he had made 'a scholarly 10 minute debate why he should be allowed to act as his own attorney'. He had spoken of his efforts 'to keep hell from breaking loose in the world', and had probably argued, as he had in October to Arthur Moore of Shakespear and Parkyn, that no lawyer could know his work well enough to represent him. But Judge Laws, according to the Associated Press report, replied that the charge was too serious for him to be allowed to act as his own counsel, and 'Pound then agreed to have the court appoint an attorney for him'. The date 27 November was set down for the formal arraignment, and Pound was returned to the District of Columbia jail.

He still did not know that in September, while he was confined in the DTC near Pisa, James Laughlin had asked Julien Cornell, a New York attorney and special counsel to the American Civil Liberties Union, 'to undertake [his] defense'. Charles Norman, a journalist who took a particular interest in Pound's case, held Cornell in high regard:

Mr. Cornell, a Quaker, had been active in the field of civil liberties... He was endowed with great determination as well as idealism—his figure, which was stocky, his chin which was broad and firm, showed it. He accepted the brief in a difficult time, when the feelings aroused by his client's broadcasts were still strong; in doing so, he acted in the highest tradition of the American bar—that of safeguarding every accused man's right to his day in court. He had, in addition to conviction and courage, the professional skill needed and, like Dr. Johnson on toleration, 'untwisted this difficult subject with great dexterity'.

It is good to speak well of the dead; yet the fact remains that one result of Cornell's exercise of his professional dexterity was that Pound never did have his day in court, and another was that he was left stripped for life of his civil liberties.

Cornell had notified the Attorney General in early November that 'he had been retained to confer with Pound about his defense', and had asked 'to be informed when he arrived'. Upon receipt of a telegram from the Attorney General's office telling him that Pound was in the District of Columbia jail he at once travelled down to Washington. There, on the day of Pound's preliminary arraignment, he 'had a talk with the Chief of the Criminal Division of the Department of Justice, Mr. McInerny, and with his assistant who would have charge of the prosecution, Isaiah Matlack'. He also talked 'with the superintendent of the jail' where Pound was being held, and 'with the Chief Judge of the District of Columbia District Court, Bolitha J. Laws'. He did not talk with Pound himself.

In his 'Documented Account of the Treason Case by the Defendant's Lawyer', Cornell wrote that Judge Laws told him 'that he was very happy to know that [he] was going to appear for Pound'; but Cornell does not say whether he mentioned that he had never met Pound and did not yet have his authorization or consent, let alone his instructions, though, given that the judge had just heard Pound's request to defend himself, it should have been apparent that he did not have either authorization or instructions. Cornell was well aware, as was Laughlin, of Pound's reluctance to have anyone appear for him whom he would regard as unqualified. Laughlin had shown him A. V. Moore's letter of 9 October in which he wrote that Pound 'will much prefer to conduct his defense in his own manner, and by such means as may seem expedient to him'; and that while he was himself in full agreement with Laughlin about retaining Cornell, he did not have Pound's agreement and so could not give definite instructions to that effect.

Laughlin had also shown him Pound's letter to Moore of 5 October, in which he had resisted Moore's urging that he should 'allow a lawyer experienced in Court procedure to represent his interests', and had made it very clear that in any event he would accept only a lawyer prepared to acquire 'some concept of what I have been driving at'. Yet from his own account it would seem that Cornell never seriously considered defending Pound on Pound's own terms. Eliot had recognized that he needed a lawyer 'prepared to read all your works and try to understand them', but Cornell didn't bother to read any of them. Moreover, he would ignore even the fundamental contention of Pound's letter to Moore, that in his radio speeches he had been exercising his First Amendment right to freedom of speech, a constitutional issue which he believed should concern the ACLU and be the basis of his defence.

Cornell had not only been retained by Laughlin without Pound's knowledge or consent, he had also been briefed by Laughlin. They had listened together to 'recordings of several of Pound's broadcasts as monitored in London', and had concluded, in Cornell's words, that they 'did not sound treasonable', and in Laughlin's, that 'there is nothing in there which is indefensible on political grounds—very little that was not said openly here and accepted as free speech'. However, the 'outbursts of [anti-Semitic] intolerance', Laughlin feared, would, if they were publicized in the course of a trial, outrage public opinion and 'force a conviction on the court'. One might think that his fear showed a grave lack of faith in the American justice system, given that Pound was not under indictment for anti-Semitism, that anti-Semitism was not an indictable offence, and that indeed expressions even of anti-Semitism had to be allowed under the First Amendment. Yet Laughlin had his reasons, as he revealed in his letter of 4 November to Dorothy Pound:

> I think you are mistaken to count on much help from MacLeish. He still has political ambitions and he would not dare antagonize such an important segment of power by supporting in anyway someone who had challenged their position. Nor would I myself dare to make any open statement, though I hope to do as much as I can privately. Inside a fortnight my books would be barred from the several hundred important stores that are controlled in that way and I would be out of business.

Laughlin signed off his letter 'hoping that my gloomy forebodings will not materialize in fact. Cornell feels that there are many legal loopholes that may be utilized.' Evidently they had decided that a direct answer to the charge of treason, though it was warranted, would risk Pound's being condemned, not for treason in the court of justice, but for anti-Semitism in the court of 'public opinion'. To save him from that, and to save his friends from being caught up in the scandal, it would be necessary to exploit some legal loophole to make sure the case did not come to full trial.

On the Tuesday morning Cornell 'spent two hours with Pound'. Before that Pound had pencilled a V-mail letter to Dorothy:

> marvellous trip.—deadly tired on arrival as djeep'd all night to Roma before 4 engine flight. Venice visible. Prague, cloud ceiling made skip Frankfurt. Brussles, London, Azores. & marvel of Bermuda just in time 10 minutes of daylight on splendour, water as blue grotto, & greens & yellow etc. = Beebe's hole etc. french ambassador & nine on board . but not of the party . so to speak.
>
> This cell modernist with fine high mess hall below & four story windows, enormous high sala under the cliff dwellings.
>
> have seen various journalists. best photo ever had done by A.P. I think...
>
> et quant aux types!! more of that anon. hope to write again tomorrow.
>
> Love to mother.

'Cell warmed & good ventilation', he added on the address panel.

The premise of Cornell's account of the case is that 'When he arrived in Washington jail Pound was an old man, tired and sick, unable to understand his predicament sufficiently well to defend himself'. However that is not how he had appeared to the press who heard and photographed him at Bolling Field on the Sunday night. And though, not altogether surprisingly, he had looked 'tired and dishevelled in court' on the Monday, he evidently understood the charge, if not 'his predicament', well enough to want to defend himself. In the photograph taken that day he looks exactly as he had the night before, alert and self-possessed. On the Tuesday morning, before Cornell's visit, he had written that clear-minded, sharply observant, and humorous letter to Dorothy. Yet Cornell would maintain that it was immediately apparent to him on first seeing Pound 'that he was in no state to stand trial or even plead to the indictment but was in need of medical care and hospital treatment'.

He began his report to Laughlin, written the day after the interview, upon that note:

> I found the poor devil in a rather desperate condition. He is very wobbly in his mind and while his talk is entirely rational, he flits from one idea to another and is unable to concentrate even to the extent of answering a single question without immediately wandering off the subject. We spent most of the time talking about Confucius, Jefferson and the economic and political implications of their ideas. I let him ramble on, even though I did not get much of the information which I wanted, as it seemed a shame to deprive him of the pleasure of talking, which has been almost entirely denied to him for a long while.

The condescension to 'the poor devil' is as remarkable as his making not the slightest effort to understand Pound's ideas or even to treat his work with respect. 'Pound wants you to publish his translations of Confucius, which are ready', he added in a postscript, with the dismissive comment, 'He seems to think the Confucius is world shaking in its import and should be published immediately.' All Cornell wanted from Pound was information to make the case that his 'health has been seriously impaired by the brutal nature of his confinement [in the DTC] and that his continued imprisonment may end both his life and his sanity'; and indeed, in spite of Pound's 'wandering off the subject', he was able to put together a quite coherent account of his experience in the DTC, and to report that, as a result of his initial treatment there, he had gone 'out of his mind and suffered complete loss of memory, a state from which he said he did not fully recover until September'. Pound had told Cornell, amidst his ramblings, that he wanted Laughlin to publish his 'new volume of Cantos, some of which I believe he sent out from prison in Italy'. He had also mentioned that while there he had 'had no reading material except two volumes of Confucius'. Yet Cornell failed to see that this meant that those cantos, composed, according to the story he was making up, while Pound was 'out of his mind' and suffering from 'a complete loss of memory', must have been drawn almost entirely from memory. In any event, Cornell would have said that Pound 'is still under a considerable mental cloud' because, for instance, 'He said that whether or not he is convicted he could be of tremendous help to President Truman, because of his knowledge of conditions in Italy and Japan.'

There are telling traces in Cornell's letter of his prior discussions with the prosecution. He had gathered that they would 'probably oppose, but not strenuously', the application for bail which he planned to make, and that was because 'they regard Pound's case as rather a mild one of its kind'. He had also learnt something to support the application, presumably from someone in the Justice Department, and that was that 'three army psychiatrists who examined [Pound] found that he was suffering from claustrophobia'. He does not say whether he was also told that the reason the Justice Department had had him examined was that there was real concern about his mental condition, and that the question of whether he would be competent to stand trial had been on their mind. One other thing: he had told Chief Justice Laws, with whom he had 'discussed the case briefly' and found 'most courteous and helpful', that he would be appearing on Pound's behalf only 'for the purpose of arraignment', and could not say whether he would appear in his defence. The judge seems to have been content to leave open the question of who would defend him, in spite of its being a Constitutional requirement which he had insisted upon the day before that the accused in so serious a case should have a defender equal to the charge.

So far as one can tell from his letter, Cornell refrained altogether from discussing with Pound the substantive issue of the indictment, and therefore the main issue for his defence: whether his radio broadcasts constituted acts of treason as defined in law. Instead he 'discussed with him the possibility of pleading insanity as a defense', and Pound, he told Laughlin, 'has no objection. In fact he told me that the idea had already occurred to him.' That was a tricky question to raise with someone in a supposedly wobbly state of mind. Yet such an exchange, if it had gone like that, might well be considered evidence of the accused's sanity, or at least of his ability 'to advise properly with counsel [and] to participate intelligently and reasonably in his own defense'. Leaving that aside, Cornell's proposal was both deeply improper and profoundly damaging to the client it was his professional duty to defend.

In the first place, especially if he believed his client to be probably not guilty as charged, his first duty was to develop a defence against the specific charge. Secondly, by inviting, in effect advising, his client to plead insanity he was leading him into grave jeopardy, since the plea would carry the implicit admission that he was in fact guilty, though not responsible for his action; and the admission of insanity would inevitably result in his being deprived of his freedom. Worst of all, Cornell was tempting Pound, who had not and would not betray his country, to betray himself, since to plead that he was not responsible for what he had written and spoken, and thus to disown his own utterance, would be to represent himself most falsely. He would be giving aid and comfort to those who wanted him to be seen as a deranged crank; worse, he would be saving himself from judgment by discrediting what he believed in.

Of course 'the idea had already occurred to him'—how could it not after the three psychiatrists had been sent to probe his sanity following his month in the cage? But to have thought of it does not mean to have consented. And there was no sign that he had had it mind when addressing the judge just the day before. What made him consent, if he did consent, to Cornell's proposal at this first meeting? Later he would say that Cornell had told him that if the Court accepted that he was unfit to plead then he could expect to be 'back in Italy in six months a free man'. Certainly that is what Cornell told Dorothy Pound in January. If he was not deliberately misleading them he was, at the very least, raising a dangerously false expectation. And if it was that ill-founded hope that led Pound to succumb to Cornell's temptation, then Cornell, if not Laughlin also, was responsible for and party to the self-betrayal for which Pound alone would pay the terrible penalty.

At the end of the week, on Saturday 24th, Pound wrote to Dorothy from 'Cell Block 1 / cell 216', that 'Cornell has been in twice & I like him & he will attend to technicalities—I take it.' Apart from that, 'the Mapels had called & Mencken written', and 'The local comforts are weak chess (not had time for that in years) & a buffet or something that supplies ice cream &, I hear, peanut butter etc. on 3 days notice before hand.' Ida and Ada Lee Mapel were spinster sisters who lived in Georgetown and who had befriended Pound forty years before when he was on his own in Spain. They had visited him in the jail on the Tuesday, after Cornell's first visit, and though they had spoken through the jail bars 'It was wonderful to see you', Miss Ida wrote the next day, 'and you were wonderful in the good old way of the great past.' But that was 'An epoch completely finished. We must look to the future,' she went on, and offered to buy him a suit and some shirts. To Dorothy she wrote, 'Ezra stood the trip over very well—seemed a bit nervous'. If that was all, then the 'poor devil' must have staged a considerable recovery since the morning. On the Thursday, Thanksgiving, he was still his old self when he wrote to his mother:

Wonderful plane trip . includin Bermuda—escort most considerate . only blot was bein' Tired by night djeep ride before start.

Note from Mencken, Mapels have called—informal chess club amiable & play badly enough to stand my poor playing. fried chicken or rather poulade a la Virginia & chocolate ice cream today (Thanksgiving wish you cd/ have shared it. but the society is exclusive—Mr Peabody's anecdotes of Panama canal zone etc. in fact conversation level rather above that of the politer tea circles.

the papers seem to be expressin the views I held some years ago with rather more acrimony than I ever did. == Antheil publishin his autobiography & Dali havin a picture show. Poor ole F. Bacon is dead (2 or 3 years ago]

Idea (i.e. main idea in your last letter perfectly sound) just have patience.

Love to you & D.

E.

Yr. obstreperous offspring.

His letters were being stamped 'D. C. JAIL / CENSORED', with date and censor's initials.

Another jail formality is recorded on the 'Receipt of Property' dated '11/20/45'. 'Chief items in despatch-case of Ezra Pound' were listed as:

#1 Confucius / Ta Seu in chinese & Italian– #2 Typescript of English version #3 L'Asse 'che Vacilla [*sic*], italian– #4 typescript in English, "The Unwobbling Pivot / Unwavering Axis. #5 Ms of new cantos (5 note books) #6 Typescript of new cantos. #7 Legge, Four Classics, Chinese and English. #8 1 Check book. #9 one pr sun glasses #10 1 comb. ALL ITEMS LISTED IN SAFE ON FIRST FLOOR.

A second sheet listed the clothes and personal items he had with him:

1 pr. blue pajamas, 5 pr socks, 4 towels, 4 pc. underware, 2 sweaters,—Brief case containing the following: 1 book, 2 shirts, 1 2-pc. underware, 6 hankercheifs, 1 newspapers clipping, 1 soap, 1 brush, 1 tooth paste, (used) 1 prayer book, nail clippers, tooth brush holder, 1 soap box, 2 packages medicine, 1 roll toolet paper. 1 knap sack, no contents | all the above articles placed in large bag and placed in vault

Both sheets were 'Verified as correct' by the signature 'Ezra Pound'. Notably absent from these lists are the Chinese dictionary and the book of Odes—Pound must have hung on to them.

On Friday 23rd Pound was taken from the jail to the Court and there held all day in the 'bull pen' along with the other prisoners who might be required to appear. The Justice Department, in the name of the United States Attorney in and for the District of Columbia, together with his special assistant Isaiah Matlack and three other assistants, was presenting its revised indictment to the Grand Jury, and this was certified a True Bill without Pound's being brought into court.

On the Saturday, as the Washington *Times-Herald* reported in its Sunday edition,

Five prisoners, all described as dangerous and possibly armed, hacksawed their way to freedom from the District Jail yesterday afternoon in one of the smoothest and most mysterious jail breaks in the city's history. All escaped from a window aperture 15 feet above the floor of the recreation room while a stool-pigeon futilely tried to attract the attention of the two guards assigned to watch the 29 inmates of Cell Block No. 1 during a recreation period... The 24 other prisoners in the room at the time refused the chance for escape but helped their fellows by talking and singing loudly and otherwise trying to cover the sounds of the sawing.

All the prisoners still in Cell Block No. 1 were then confined to their cells for the rest of the weekend. On the Sunday Pound wrote to Ronald Duncan, 'All this is a marvelous xperience if it dont break me & if the lesion of May cured (I thinks) in Sept. dont bust open under the renewed fatigues.' That evening he complained of 'claustrophobia' to the guards and was transferred to the prison infirmary where he was accommodated for the rest of his time in the DC jail.

'Police reporters sought him out there', according to a piece in *Time* magazine, and Pound seems to have played up to them in his usual fashion. In its own inimitable style *Time* had

The ragbaggy old darling of the U.S. expatriate intelligentsia... lolling in the infirmary of the D.C. Jail [as] he denied that he ever talked treason: 'I was only trying to tell the people of Europe and America how they could avoid war by learning the facts about money.' He spoke ruefully: 'It's all very well to die for an idea, but to die for an idea you can't remember...'

If Pound did say that then he was denting the idea in the previous sentence for the sake of a *Time*-speak phrase. To another more sympathetic reporter he spoke of the books he had there in his cell that had kept him 'from going completely crazy' during his months in the Pisan prison. Cornell had 'succeeded in obtaining release from the authorities of [his] manuscripts, including the additional Cantos and the translations from Confucius'.

On Monday 26 November the Grand Jury indictment was filed with the Court in Washington. On the same day, in New York, Cornell swore an 'Affidavit in support of application for bail'—this he would present to the Court the following day after Pound had been formally charged with the indictment. Apparently neither Cornell nor Pound would know the exact terms of the latter until it was read out in the Court; and presumably the prosecution, while expecting that an application for bail was likely to be made, would not have advance knowledge of its terms. Between the indictment and the application would come the accused's plea of 'guilty' or 'not guilty'. On the Tuesday morning Cornell spent an hour with Pound in the jail. By his own account he found him 'in a state of almost complete mental and physical exhaustion', and 'suggested that because of his condition it might be wise for him to remain mute rather than enter a plea of not guilty'. The Court would then 'be obliged by law to enter a plea of not guilty'. And of course a mute Pound would not get in the way of Cornell's argument that he was in no condition to be tried.

The indictment, dressed up in impressive coverall legalese, was carefully crafted. The main contention, as summed up in the closing paragraph, was that

> The defendant, Ezra Pound, committed each and every one of the overt acts herein described for the purpose of, and with the intent to adhere to and give aid and comfort to the Kingdom of Italy, and its military allies, enemies of the United States, and the said defendant, Ezra Pound, committed each and every one of the said overt acts contrary to his duty of allegiance to the United States and to the form of the statute and constitution in such case made and provided and against the peace and dignity of the United States. (Section 1, United States Criminal Code).

Just seven specific 'overt acts' were alleged, each of them a broadcast 'on or about' a certain date, and each of them said to be 'for the purpose of giving aid and comfort to the Kingdom of Italy and its then allies in the war against the United States'. The particular purpose of the first and fourth overt acts was said to be, 'among other things, to create dissension and distrust between the United States and its military allies', and further, in the first act, 'the said defendant asserted, in substance, that the war is an economic war in which the United States and its allies are the aggressors'. In the second and sixth instances, 'the purport (*sic*)...was to create racial prejudice in the United States', and further, in the sixth act, 'to create... distrust of the Government of the United States'. Nothing in particular was said of the third overt act. In the fifth, 'the said defendant asserted, among other things and in substance, that Italy is the natural ally of the United States; that the true nature of the Axis regime has been misrepresented to the people in the United States and that England, Russia and the United States are the aggressor nations'. In the seventh offensive act, 'the said defendant praised Italy, urged the people in the United States to read European publications rather than the American press and to listen to European radio transmissions, and stated further that he spoke "from Rome, in a regime where liberty is considered a duty".' Then followed seven paragraphs, numbered 8 to 14, each alleging that Pound, 'between July 29, 1942 and July 25, 1943', or 'between December 11, 1941 and July 25, 1943', recorded broadcasts 'for the purpose of giving aid and comfort to the Kingdom of Italy' etc., in the presence of two named witnesses. There were five names, variously paired in the seven paragraphs. Paragraph 15 dealt with Pound's securing approval of the manuscripts of his broadcasts from two named officials of the Ministry of Popular Culture. A further four paragraphs dealt with his receiving payments for his broadcasts. And that was all—for all its ponderous generalities it was in its specific charges a flimsy indictment. In sum, Pound was being called upon to answer for opinions expressed in just seven broadcasts, opinions which could not seriously be held to have presented any grave threat to the United States of America.

A defense attorney should not have been impressed by the familiar legal bluster—'knowingly, intentionally, wilfully, unlawfully, feloniously, traitorously and treasonably did adhere' etc.—nor by the portentous repetition of the general charge in each and every paragraph. Stripped of its shock and awe rhetoric the indictment was startlingly limited, mild, and vulnerable. Most remarkably it was virtually signalling, by the failure to give specific dates in paragraphs 8 to 14, that the witnesses could not securely testify that they had been present at the times when the specified seven overt acts were committed. Given that Laughlin had noted in September the Justice Department's public admission that it was having difficulty finding its witnesses, Cornell should have been alert to that signal, and should have seen at once that the prosecution case was probably unsustainable. He may or may not have known it, but in any case he should have considered the further possibility, that the witnesses did not speak English and would not have been able to identify a specified broadcast even if they had been present when it was recorded. A defence attorney would have had merely to question them to expose their testimony as worthless, and to have the case instantly dismissed. One wonders if the Justice Department had expected that to be the outcome, and had been simply going through the motions in presenting such a flimsy indictment.

Even if the witnesses had been able to testify convincingly to the seven overt acts, those acts, it could well have been argued, hardly constituted treason. Pound was alleged to have asserted—and would certainly have admitted saying and believing to be true—'that the war is an economic war in which the United States and its allies are the aggressors', 'that Italy is the natural ally of the United States', that 'he spoke "from Rome, in a regime where liberty is considered a duty"'. These might well be regarded as wrong-headed opinions, or as simply false; and it is conceivable that they might have given some comfort in Italy, but not any serious aid. And there would remain the difficulty of proving conscious and wilful intention to do harm to the United States by broadcasting these opinions. The allegations that Pound intended 'to create racial prejudice in the United States' had more substance, though 'exploit' would have been a more accurate word than 'create'. But then, however regrettably, expressions and acts of racial prejudice in America did not constitute treason, so those allegations would have had to be set aside. Again, seeking 'to create ... distrust of the Government' could be, given the appropriate circumstances, an act of patriotism rather than of treason, as the founders who drew up the Constitution of the United States were well aware. Dissent is not necessarily treason even in time of war. That would leave the charge of intending 'to create dissension and distrust between the United States and its military allies', a serious enough allegation, yet not strictly treasonous, and one surely excessively flattering to the defendant's capacity to influence 'the United States and its military allies'.

A confidential Justice Department internal assessment in May 1950 would conclude that, 'with the exception of Overt Act 3, either the evidence available to prove the remaining eighteen (*sic*) overt acts was insufficient to meet the constitutional requirements of two witnesses to the same overt act or ... the acts alleged could not properly be construed as giving aid and comfort to the enemy'. There was no indication in the memorandum, as there was none in the original indictment, of what was thought to distinguish 'Overt Act 3' from the others. Following on from that assessment Mr McInerney would be advised 'that extreme difficulty would be encountered in meeting our burden of proof if Pound were declared sane and the Government forced to trial'.

After the question of whether the acts were in fact treasonous, and, the further question whether, if any were treasonous, they had been duly witnessed, there would remain a third and crucial question: had the defendant intended harm to the United States? The prosecution would have been required to prove that at least one of the broadcasts, if indeed it was treasonous, had been made with the deliberate intention of doing harm to the United States; but Pound's defence attorney, if he had had one, could have argued and effectively demonstrated that, on the contrary, each and every one of the specified broadcasts was animated by a deliberate will, however misguided, to save the United States from error. The Justice Department, which was in possession of Pound's letter to the Attorney General upon being first indicted in 1943, and of his two statements to Amprim in Genoa, must have been well aware not only of the need to prove intent but of how difficult it would be to do that—and a competent defence attorney should have been no less aware.

There had been an important Supreme Court ruling in April 1945, in the case of *Cramer v. United States*, 325 US 1. In June 1942 Anthony Cramer (or Kramer) had given material assistance to armed saboteurs put ashore from a German submarine to disrupt America's war industry. He had been found guilty of treason and sentenced to forty years imprisonment. Upon appeal the Supreme Court of the United States reversed the conviction and established a clear precedent for any future treason trial. 'The crime of treason', the decision stated,

> consists of two elements, both of which must be present in order to sustain a conviction: (1) adherence to the enemy, and (2) rendering him aid and comfort.
>
> The term 'aid and comfort' as used in the provision of the Federal Constitution defining treason... contemplates some kind of affirmative action, deed, or physical activity tending to strengthen the enemy or weaken the power to resist him, and is not satisfied by a mere mental operation.
>
> ... the acts done must be intentional. The intent sufficient to sustain a conviction of treason must be an intent... to betray the country by means of such acts.

Speaking for the Court Justice Robert H. Jackson, shortly to become a US prosecutor at the Nuremberg War Criminals trials, emphasized how narrowly the treason statute should be construed:

> A citizen intellectually and emotionally may favor the enemy and harbor sympathies or convictions disloyal to the country's policy or interest, but as long as he commits no act of aid and comfort to the enemy, there is no treason. On the other hand a citizen may take actions which do aid and comfort the enemy—making a

speech critical of the government or opposing its measures, profiteering, striking in defense plants or essential work, and the hundred other things which impair our cohesion and diminish our strength—but if there is no adherence to the enemy in this, if there is no intent to betray, there is no treason.

An attorney with his mind on defending Pound would have taken heart from that ruling as making the prosecution's case almost certainly unsustainable.

Cornell was aware of *Cramer v. US* as 'the only treason case which has reached the Supreme Court in modern times', and as 'containing the only authoritative discussion of the crime, as well as a learned review of its history in English and American law'. However, since 'the opinions do not shed any light on the matter of bail', he had no use for it. That was because he had no intention of defending Pound against the charge of treason, having made up his mind before even hearing the indictment that he had 'found a way to get around [its] difficulties'. In his later account of the trial he would merely summarize the indictment in a brief paragraph, and print, as an appendix, a partial text omitting the substantive paragraphs 5 to 15. Otherwise he would completely ignore it, as, quite extraordinarily, he did at the time of the trial.

Charles Olson had got himself into the courtroom on 27 November to observe Pound at his formal arraignment. He had made Pound his father in poetry and was Oedipally trying to cast him off; yet, being still in thrall to his poetry, he was projecting his murderous impulses upon the politics, wildly accusing him, for example, of having for twenty years 'damned democracy and all its works'. His stance towards Pound, like that of many of Pound's friends, would remain awkwardly conflicted, with indebtedness and rejection, admiration and enmity, always unresolved. He had never seen Pound before, and 'took him to look older and weaker than I had imagined'—'so alone that day, and worn down'. The courtroom, as Olson described it, 'was the chief justice's chambers, made like some Episcopal chapel, with Negroes filling the pews for witnesses, and on the other side of the bench... opposite the jurors' box, lawyers and the press and attendants'. Pound's eyes, he thought, 'were full of pain, and hostile, cornered as he was in a court, with no one he knew around him except his lawyer whom he had only known a week before'. It was a moment of drama 'when he, a man of such words, stood up mute before the court'. The next day's *New York Herald Tribune* described that moment:

Unkempt and clad in G.I. hand-me-downs, Ezra Pound, sixty-year-old American poet accused of treason, stood mute today during arraignment before a Federal district court here, shuffling from one foot to the other while a defense attorney requested he be released from District of Columbia jail because he suffers from claustrophobia and may lose his sanity if he remains imprisoned.

In Cornell's account, Pound 'said not a word but sat with hands folded and downcast eyes while I told the court he was not in condition to make a plea and asked Judge Laws to enter a plea of not guilty for him'.

Cornell 'then handed up to Judge Laws my motion papers, at the same time giving copies to Isaiah Matlack, Assistant Attorney General in charge of the prosecution'. The 'motion papers' were his 'Affidavit in Support of Application for Bail', and a 'Memorandum' concerning the law bearing upon the Application. He did not read out the Affidavit, which ran to twelve typed pages, 'but explained orally the general tenor', which was 'that Pound was suffering from mental illness . . . was in urgent need of medical care . . . should never have been sent over here for trial . . . asked the Judge to order Pound's immediate release from jail to a hospital'. Matlack, having reason to expect an application for an early trial at which he would have to drop the charges, was taken completely by surprise, and asked for a brief recess 'to read the motion papers and consult with his superiors'. It did not take him long to make out that Cornell was going for a plea of insanity, with its implicit acceptance that Pound was actually guilty of treason, and he quickly let the judge know that 'the government had no objection to a medical examination'. The next day's *Stars and Stripes* would carry the report that the Attorney General had announced that Pound 'admitted each and every one of these acts for the purpose of and with intent' etc. It was not true, but the Justice Department might well have thought it was as near as made no difference.

Matlack would have seen at once that Cornell was not defending Pound, but effectively handing him over to the Justice Department's mercy. Pound would not have been aware of what was happening, since the Affidavit was not read out and only the judge and prosecution knew what was in it. Cornell had not only silenced Pound, but was now keeping from him what he was saying for him. Worse, while appearing to appear 'for the defendant', he was covertly betraying him. Standing in the place that should by law have been filled by a defence attorney, and letting himself be referred to as 'counsel for the defense', he was nevertheless silently declaring in the introduction to his written Affidavit—

I do not defend his actions, nor do I approve his sentiments. I do not feel that I can properly try his case. But in accordance with my duty as a lawyer, I have felt obliged to comply with a request that I confer with this man accused of crime.[1]

[1] All but two of the passages which will be cited here, including this one, are silently omitted from 'the text of my affidavit' in Cornell's book. I take them from the official copy in the US National

His 'duty as a lawyer' was of course not to 'try his case'—that was for the judge and jury—but to present the best case possible in his defence. He was out of order from the start, and the judge, as soon as he read 'I do not defend his actions', and found that Cornell felt obliged only 'to confer with this man accused of crime', should have ruled him out of order and, according to the law, appointed a defence counsel willing to act as one.

In his second paragraph Cornell stated his belief that Pound, having suffered 'a complete mental collapse and loss of memory' while being 'continuously held incommunicado in solitary confinement', was 'still insane'. He then gave an account of Pound's early life and literary achievements, leading up to his being acclaimed 'by many as the greatest poet of his age'; 'and there are few, even today', he went on, 'who would deny homage to the fallen idol'—

> But among all the literary titans who have expressed deep appreciation for Pound's genius and leadership, it is doubtful whether there are any so brave that they would today rise to the defense of their erstwhile friend and captain.

Laughlin had said as much to Ezra and to Dorothy, and it was true—but why say it here, and so floridly? But Cornell was inspired: 'The mighty star has burned itself quite out, and leaves no flame to warm the hearts it once had set ablaze.' He had indeed come to damn Pound, not defend him:

> It is not necessary to recount the story of Pound's downfall. I need only say that his extraordinary conduct, his vilification of the nation's leaders during wartime, his vainglory and vituperations, his anti-Semitic and vulgar utterances, as broadcast over the Rome radio, cannot be explained on any basis of mere venality but only on the ground that Pound is an old man no longer in the full possession of his mental powers. I am led to this belief not only because the mentality of the man in his prime and the ridiculous broadcasts of his old age are utterly incompatible, but also because his intimates tell me that the evidence of mental deterioration in his private correspondence is unmistakable, and in the opinion of his close friends and associates his mind has been deteriorating for a number of years, far beyond mere senility or eccentricity.

That was as good as saying, of course he's guilty, but all his friends think him out of his mind. Moreover, Cornell was there damning Pound for things he should have insisted be excluded as irrelevant and prejudicial, 'his extraordinary conduct . . . his vainglory and vituperations, his anti-Semitic and vulgar utterances', these could make him look bad in the newspapers but they were not what he was under indictment for.

Archives—they are also to be found in the transcription in Charles Norman's *The Case of Ezra Pound* (1968), pp. 93–8.

I assume Cornell had been briefed by Laughlin about Pound's close friends and associates, such as Williams and Hemingway. In particular he might have called in evidence here Archibald MacLeish, whom Pound imagined to be someone whose support he could rely on. MacLeish, then Librarian of Congress, had written to Harvey Bundy, a Special Assistant to the Secretary of War, on 10 September 1943, shortly after Pound had been indicted for treason, to the effect that 'there is no question whatever that Pound is engaged in propaganda for the Fascist government', and that his 'blabbering correspondence with people at home ... has now turned into blabbering broadcasting which, in form at least, comes awfully close to treason'. He and Hemingway were entirely agreed, MacLeish had written, that those broadcasts had to be 'the product of a completely distracted mind', and that 'Pound seems to have gone completely to pieces'. There were other old friends ready now to say the same—indeed some had said it, just a day or two before the arraignment, in a New York newspaper called *PM*, copies of which Cornell handed to Judge Laws and Matlack with his Affidavit.

Cornell's next move was to assert that

> It was this streak of mental weakness in Pound, which had long been evident to his friends, that led him, I believe, into mental collapse when he was subjected to the rigors of imprisonment ... [an] imprisonment which destroyed the poet's mind and all but killed his aging body. For this unfortunate result, the administrators of the prison should not be criticized. No doubt they treated Pound exactly as they would any other man charged with a like offense. No doubt Pound when he entered the prison appeared to be merely an eccentric, with no evidence of insanity on the surface, and no reason to suspect insanity. The fact that Pound's mind cracked after a week or so of imprisonment was nobody's fault.

The fault then was not the cruel and inhumane treatment of the man he was supposed to be defending; it was simply Pound's own fault, no doubt for lacking resilience, and for not advertising his insanity. In spite of that Cornell proceeded to give a tear-jerking account of the mental and physical tortures to which Pound had been subjected in the DTC, sparing no lurid detail and adding several of his own, building up to this climax:

> After about three weeks of struggle to maintain his sanity, the wretched man fell ill. The heat and glare, added to the hopelessness of being held incommunicado and the torture of solitary confinement, were more than his aging mind could bear. Pound was stricken with violent and hysterical terror. He lost his memory. He became desperately thin and weak until finally the prison doctor feared for him.

> Pound was then taken out of his unhappy cage and placed in a tent. He was given a cot to lie upon, and medical treatment. The doctor even prescribed a walk each day, but most often the guards neglected to take him out for exercise.
>
> While the doctors took measures to keep Pound's body alive, his mind was not rescued. He was still kept in solitary confinement, still held incommunicado, still deprived of all reading matter but religious tracts. As physical strength gradually flowed back into his body, the terror and hysteria subsided somewhat, memory returned, but the great mind remained impaired, and fits of shuddering terror balked his struggle to retain his senses.
>
> The period of violent insanity apparently began about mid-June, to endure for three months or more.

Cornell, quite unashamed, printed this deliberately false fiction in his book, all but the last devastating and lying sentence. Those, after all, were the three months in which *The Pisan Cantos* were composed. There had been no 'period of violent insanity', as the Justice Department was well aware, but Judge Laws may not have been. As the final touch Cornell offered his personal testimony:

> I have twice seen Pound, talking with him for two hours or more on each occasion. While having no medical knowledge, one does not need to be a doctor to know at once that this man is not sane. The marvelous mind with its tremendous learning has been wrecked so horribly that all may see the sad results.

So there it was, Judge Laws had the defendant's counsel's own word for it, 'this man is not sane'; and the prosecution, who knew better, had his assurance that even his friends could testify that he had been insane when making the traitorous broadcasts. Cornell's sworn Affidavit went far beyond being an application for bail and made Pound's sanity the pressing issue.

Cornell respectfully prayed for bail 'in order that he may secure proper medical treatment', or that at least 'he be placed in the custody of one or more physicians in a civilian hospital or sanatorium operated by the United States or by the District of Columbia'—

> Only in a normal environment, free from the drastic restraints which are necessary in penal hospitals, can he possibly recover, in my opinion; only by such medical treatment does he stand a chance of regaining his sanity even to the point where he could stand trial on this indictment.

'I am confident', he concluded, 'that a disinterested psychiatric investigation of his condition would show that such measures are imperative.'

Having considered the application, Judge Laws declined to grant bail at that time, but did remand the defendant to the Washington Asylum and

Jail, 'with the recommendation that he be transferred to Gallinger Hospital [a public hospital administered by the District of Columbia] . . . for examination and observation and for treatment, if found necessary'. He ordered that the prosecution should enter any response they might wish to make to Cornell's Affidavit by the 10th, that the psychiatrists' report on their findings by the 14th, and that there would be a further hearing on 21 December.

'Am giving Cornell his head. I like him', Pound wrote to Dorothy on 29 November, still in 'Infirmary / District Jail', and enjoying the 'better ventilation' there. 'Patience', he urged. On the same day Cornell wrote to A. V. Moore that the treatment Pound needed was 'relaxation, recreation and a certain amount of physical freedom'; and yet he knew that 'because there happens to be no government hospital in the District of Columbia which affords adequate facilities for an ambulatory patient', Pound 'would be confined to his room' in Gallinger. Moreover, Gallinger did not have the staff to provide treatment of any kind. To Pound he wrote that he had nothing to worry about, and that he, Cornell, would get him into a better hospital once the mental examination had been completed.

Pound was transferred from the jail to the psychiatric ward of Gallinger Hospital on Tuesday 4 December, and placed in a private, locked, room. 'Having a rest cure', he wrote to Dorothy on the Saturday, 'Cornell has brought me Hen. Adams Life of Gallatin . . . Have patience. & Xmas wishes & Love to mother.' On Monday 10th he wrote to his mother:

> Dear Mother.
>
> You might like this hospital better than Rapallo, @ least the steam heat & morning coffee.
>
> One of my guardian angels is readin' Ron Duncan's 'Journal of Husbandman' with deep interest.
>
> Best wishes for as good a Xmas as possible.
>
> By mistake some coffee was sent to me instead of to you . but hope you'll get some.
>
> Love to D.
>
> E.P.
> Ezra Pound
> & a bright NewYear

He had some incoming mail, including a friendly note from Theodore Spencer, the Harvard scholar, asking, 'Is there anything you'd like in the way of books, reading matter etc. that I could send you', and telling him, 'I have been re-reading your poetry with admiration.'

Cornell was looking for a psychiatrist to examine Pound 'for the defense', and was recommended to appoint Dr Wendell Muncie, an associate professor at Johns Hopkins and a respected psychiatrist in private practice. When Muncie agreed to examine Pound on the 12th or 13th of the month, Cornell sent him a condensed version of his Affidavit, adding to his previous exaggerations the false statement that 'the government accepts that he became definitely insane during his imprisonment in Italy last summer'. Cornell knew that 'Army doctors at the military detention center in Pisa had found him sane enough', and that the Justice Department had their reports. Was he expecting the prosecution to bury those reports and go along with his falsehood? In any case, it would emerge that the government's position was not exactly as he described it. Cornell made it very clear to Muncie that he was expected to find Pound insane, and to be prepared to testify 'in behalf of the defendant' if a jury trial were to be ordered on the issue. He should bear in mind also the further question, 'whether even if he is sane, he is sufficiently well to stand the ordeal of a lengthy trial'. That was Cornell's fallback strategy, that poor Pound would never be able to stand the strain of a trial.

In the interval before the psychiatrists delivered their report Cornell was inviting Pound's friends to look out private letters they had from him which he could use as evidence of his aberrations and mental deterioration. Hemingway told him that in his opinion, and in Joyce's, 'Pound's mental condition had not been normal' for some years. Cornell was also seeking funds to cover his expenses and fees. Pound's account with the Jenkintown bank had been seized by the Custodian of Alien Property, though Pound was not an alien; and Dorothy Pound's funds in England were still frozen as enemy property. Cornell called on Cummings, who immediately handed him a cheque for $1,000 that he had just received for a painting—Dorothy later repaid him. Boni and Liveright paid over $300 dollars due to Pound for royalties, and Laughlin, who had told Dorothy that Pound's 'accrued royalties [from New Directions] are not very large', contributed $500. Cornell told A. V. Moore that the $1,800 would go to pay Dr Muncie's fee and 'hospital treatment', and that he would not submit his account until Dorothy's money was released.

Three psychiatrists were appointed to examine Pound for the government. Dr Marion King, Medical Director of the Bureau of Prisons, had spent his professional life in general medical and administrative positions in prisons and was not a practising psychiatrist. He had a copy of Cornell's Affidavit the day after it had been given to the Court. Dr Joseph L. Gilbert was in charge of the psychiatric ward at Gallinger Hospital, and was said to be 'a competent and decent man', though the quality of services in his ward had been so poor that an official investigation, led by Dr Winfred Overholser, had been called for the year before. Dr Overholser, the third psychiatrist for the government, was superintendent of St Elizabeths Hospital for the Insane, a government institution, also secretary-treasurer of the American Psychiatric Association, and an authority on the legal aspects of psychiatry. His hospital too fell short of the standards of his Association in respect of its duty of care and treatment—in some of its wards 'there were two psychiatrists for one thousand patients'—and he, it was said, 'was one of the most sued men in the District of Columbia' on account of the conditions under which patients were held in St Elizabeths.

Overholser naturally carried most weight, and was able to persuade the others of his view that when psychiatrists disagreed in court it looked bad and tended to undermine the authority of the profession. According to Cornell, 'When the four doctors first met, therefore, Dr Overholser told them that he hoped they would reach common agreement on the condition of the prisoner, objectively, without partisan bias in favour of the government or the defense'. And all four did in the end agree in their diagnosis. Their brief report to Chief Justice Laws, under the letter-heading 'FEDERAL SECURITY AGENCY | Saint Elizabeths Hospital | Washington 20, D.C.', was 'respectfully submitted' over their joint signatures. It stated that the three government appointees had 'examined the defendant each on several occasions, separately and together, in the period from his admission to Gallinger Hospital on December 4, 1945 to December13, 1945'; and that 'Dr Muncie spent several hours with the defendant, both alone and with us, on December 13'. They had available to them, beside 'the reports of laboratory, psychological and special physical examinations', 'considerable material in the line of his writings and biographical data'—that would have been material supplied by Cornell.

It must have been on the basis of that material that they stated that 'of recent years his preoccupation with monetary theories and economics has apparently obstructed his literary productivity. He has long been recognized as eccentric, querulous, and egocentric.' Far from being expert opinion, that was simply prejudicial hearsay. The third paragraph read:

> At the present time he exhibits extremely poor judgment as to his situation, its seriousness and the manner in which the charges are to be met. He insists that his broadcasts were not treasonable, but that all of his radio activities have stemmed from his self-appointed mission to 'save the Constitution.' He is abnormally grandiose, is expansive and exuberant in manner, exhibiting pressure of speech, discursiveness and distractibility.

Setting aside whether those characteristics, not unknown among salesmen, politicians, evangelists, and pundits, should be interpreted as indicators of treasonous intent, or, indeed, of insanity, one might question whether it was within the competence of the psychiatrists to pass judgment on Pound's judgment of his situation; whereas Pound's insistence that he was on a mission to save the Constitution showed a very sound grasp of how the charges should be met. Their professional opinion, when they came to it, was manifestly not wholly based on their own examination of Pound:

> In our opinion, with advancing years his personality, for many years abnormal, has undergone further distortion to the extent that he is now suffering from a paranoid state which renders him mentally unfit to advise properly with counsel or to participate intelligently and reasonably in his own defense. He is, in other words, insane and mentally unfit for trial, and is in need of care in a mental hospital.

That was no more and no less than the answer Cornell had first thought of, and very nearly in the words of his Affidavit, except that the psychiatrists had lent him their authority by the addition of that one mighty phrase of professional jargon, 'a paranoid state'. Apart from that mystification the four psychiatrists together had added nothing of relevance or substance to Cornell's submission to the Court.[2]

Had they nothing more to say on their own account after all the hours they had spent examining Pound? Stanley I. Kutler discovered that Dr King, in the first draft of his own report, had (in Kutler's paraphrase) 'found Pound astute, intelligent, cooperative, apparently sincere, rather tense, with no regrets for his acts, and steadfast in support of his convictions'. Moreover, King had noted that 'the reports of the Army psychiatrists do not

[2] E. Fuller Torrey noticed (Torrey 196–7) that the description of Pound's symptoms in the psychiatrists' letter did not correspond to the definition of a paranoid state in the *Handbook of Psychiatry* (Lippincott, 1947) which Overholser was then writing (with W. V. Richmond). According to that textbook the symptoms of paranoid insanity in 1945 were bizarre delusions, auditory hallucinations, hearing voices, etc. Frederic Wertham, a psychiatrist writing in the *American Journal of Psychotherapy* in 1949, commented, 'Surely the psychiatrists know the difference between a political conviction and a delusion ... Ezra Pound has no delusions in any strictly pathological sense' (cited by Sieber, p. 34). As to the term 'paranoia', it had ben observed in 1940 that 'Perhaps no term in psychiatry has undergone wider variations of meaning' (Hinslie and Shatzke, *Psychiatric Dictionary* 395); and in 1954 it was recognised that 'The effort to maintain paranoia as a distinct condition has ... failed' (W. Mayer-Gross et al., *Clinical Psychiatry* IV (1954) 158). Richard Hofstadter's essay 'The Paranoid Style in American Politics' (first delivered as a lecture in 1963) would have provided an invaluable elucidation and distinction. The 'paranoid style' in politics, he observed, was characteristic of more or less normal angry minds suspicious of government and prone to violent exaggeration and to conspiracy theories. It was the common style of populist politicians and agitators—as it is now a common style among radio and television commentators—and it should not be confused, he argued, with clinical paranoia.

suggest that he experienced a complete mental or physical collapse', and he had written, for his own part, that Pound 'cannot be considered mentally ill and thus absolved from responsibility'. King drafted his report on 11 December, but then, after discussion with Dr Overholser, radically altered it. Then there was Dr Muncie. Torrey discovered that he had concluded, after examining Pound on his own, that he was 'a damned psychopath', meaning, as the term was used at that time, a person who disregarded social rules and laws, was immature, unable to accept responsibility, put his own needs before everything else, and rationalized his behaviour to make it seem reasonable. Psychopaths were 'almost invariably held responsible for their actions', so Muncie's first opinion was that Pound was fit to be tried. But then he talked with Dr Overholser and the other psychiatrists, and went back to re-examine Pound and found that within the hour he had become 'completely incoherent'. Later in the day, after the four of them had interviewed Pound together, the joint report, under the heading of Dr Overholser's federal institution, was already prepared for their signature. It did not reflect Muncie's initial view, any more than it reflected King's independent judgment, but both signed along with Gilbert and Overholser. Possibly only Overholser clearly understood that they were consigning Pound to his care.

'If a person is acquitted by reason of insanity'—and the same would hold for a person who could not be tried by reason of insanity—'he will be, not may be, will be sent to St Elizabeths Hospital, and that may mean quite a long period of confinement. Actually, once patients get to us—and I hope this is not taken wrongly—they are rather inclined to find that possibly they would rather be considered a criminal than a mental case.' That was what Dr Overholser would tell a Senate Subcommittee on the Judiciary in June 1955, when Pound would be still confined to his care. He continued:

> I think that this matter of mandatory commitment by reason of insanity is highly desirable. It is going to reduce substantially the number of false pleadings if [the defendant] knows that he will be confined for a wholly indefinite period in a mental hospital, and sometimes that might well turn out to be a good deal longer than the sort of sentence he would get if he were found not insane at the time of the act.

It would be charitable to hope that Cornell did not know that his wilful strategy was delivering Pound into indefinite confinement in a hospital where his situation would be far worse than in an ordinary criminal prison. Pound could have had no idea of what he was letting himself in for by 'giving Cornell his head'.

A couple of days after the psychiatrists had done with examining him Pound wrote to Dorothy, 'on a thin sheet of white paper with U.S. Great

Seal watermark', 'Very wearing. Have patience.' He mentioned a visit from Katherine Proctor Saint, whom he had tutored as a girl in Philadelphia, now 'strong in the Lord' and there 'to save soul, complete with bible'—

but thanks to my irish guardian angel Mr. McGrath (his presence of mind) she did send excellent box of chocolate covered biscuit later—labled 'Weston's george Inn'—hotel keepin' evidently inveterate in the family even to unknown branches.

He had seen 'Bill Bird over at marshal's office other day'—Bird had come to see him and spent about 15 minutes with him. 'Doc. Shelling', whom he had displeased as a student, was 'just dead @ age 87 ... Last saw him by door Brit Museum reading room'. And he had 'just read minor odes VII.4. marvelous'—that Confucian ode (no. 218) being the song of a lover travelling eagerly towards his beloved. Worn as he well might be, he was evidently quite clear in mind and memory. On 20 December he began a note probably intended for Olga Rudge and Mary, 'Deare[s]ts, | Snow meltin' beyond steam heat & birds chirrpin. Thank god you two are together—at least I suppose you are—no mail yet from Italy since I got here.' The note broke off with a half-remembered fragment from Browning's *Sordello*, an image of once turbulent Ezzelino da Romano sunk to enforced idleness in a monastic cell.

In his court on 21 December Judge Laws read out the psychiatrists' report, then ruled on Cornell's application for bail:

It appearing that the physicians appointed by the Court as well as the physician appointed by the defendant to advise the Court as to the mental condition of the defendant have reported that in their opinion the defendant is mentally unfit to advise properly with counsel or to participate intelligently and reasonably in his own defense and is insane and mentally unfit for trial and is in need of care in a mental hospital. It is on this 21st day of December 1945, ordered that ... in accordance with the recommendation of the examining physicians, the defendant, Ezra Pound, be sent to St Elizabeths Hospital for treatment and examination.

Cornell in his book wrote that the Court 'ordered Pound transferred to St. Elizabeths Hospital, under the Federal statute which requires the confinement in that institution of all Federal prisoners under indictment who are found to be unable to stand trial because of lack of competence or understanding'. Although the judge had not invoked it, there was such a statute, and presumably Cornell had been aware of it all along.[3]

[3] The relevant statute, Section 211 of Title 24, USC, is less absolute than Cornell implied: 'If any person, charged with crime, be found, in the court before which he is so charged, to be an insane person, such court shall certify the same to the Federal Security Administrator, who may [*emphasis added*] order such person to be confined in Saint Elizabeth's Hospital, and, if he be not indigent, he and his estate

At the press conference after the hearing, as the *New York Herald Tribune* reported next day, 'The government's prosecuting attorneys', who had made no submission to Judge Laws, 'pointed out that immediately before Pound left an Army Prison camp in Italy a month ago Army psychiatrists examined him and found him sane... and able to stand trial for treason'. That gave the Justice Department reason to think that Pound 'might easily be feigning insanity to escape a trial that might cost his life', and they would have to demand therefore 'a public insanity hearing'.

Laughlin wrote to T. S. Eliot on 23 December about Pound's 'illness', and about publishing his 'Testament of Confucius' and the new cantos. It would appear that he had been with Cornell at the hearing on the 21st and had spoken with Pound there. Laughlin had found him not at all '"a broken man"'—though that was precisely how Cornell, acting on his instructions, had been depicting him. 'On the contrary,' he went on, 'I thought he looked very well and our conversation was animated and cheerful. In many ways he is just the same old Ezra and it made me terribly happy to find him so.' Of course Pound was neither guilty of treason nor insane, Laughlin intimated. At the same time, 'Julien and I are very pleased about this result', he told Eliot—that is, they were 'very pleased' that Pound had been declared insane and committed to St Elizabeths—since 'this solution seems the most practical'. Indeed they hoped the doctors would go even further, and 'state more clearly than they already have that he was not in control of his senses at the time the broadcasts were made'. He reflected that 'they down there [in Rapallo] are going to feel terribly badly about the appearance of the unattractive word "insane", but hell, it is just a word, and if it will save a life...' That was his justification, to save Pound's life. 'And we are confident', Laughlin assured Eliot, 'that with time the indictment will be dropped. Later it will doubtless be possible for Ezra to be released from the hospital since he is not in the least dangerous.' In the meantime, 'Dr Overholser... is very much interested in the case and I think he will do everything he can to make Ezra comfortable and happy.' As for Ezra himself, 'EP was delighted to be sent to his care because he liked him the best of the doctors who examined him', and 'All he wants now is to get his health back and get back to work.' And 'we must go to work here with a campaign', Laughlin declared, meaning not a campaign for his release, but a 'campaign to re-establish his standing' as a poet, and 'to get the good critics to write about him again'. He meant to make a success of publishing Pound's poetry and his literary work, and to make that possible he was

shall be charged with expenses of his support in the hospital.' Dr Overholser would say not 'may' but 'will be' confined.

well pleased to have him declared not responsible for his efforts to save his country from error, and to have the man with his live mind shut away as insane. He could comfortably write, 'Julien told Ezra when we left that he had nothing more to worry about and I think he is right.'

Lunacy at St Elizabeths

'Criminal No. 76028', as Pound was now officially known although he had been neither tried nor convicted, was removed in the late afternoon of 21 December to St Elizabeths Hospital for the Insane, 'for treatment and examination'. There he was assigned to Howard Hall, the maximum security ward for the most dangerous and violent of the criminally insane. In the following weeks he would be subjected to a great deal of examination by the psychiatrists of St Elizabeths, but there would be no remedial treatment. He would be kept in that ward for more than a year, until 4 February 1947, with Overholser maintaining, so Cornell would report to Laughlin, that it was 'an inflexible rule of the hospital to keep patients under indictment in Howard Hall which is the only completely guarded building'. It was Overholser's hospital and he made the rules.

St Elizabeths had many buildings spread over its mile-wide site. It held 'just under seven thousand' patients, and 'approximately fifty' doctors serving directly under Overholser. Ida Mapel, writing to Dorothy Pound, made it seem a pleasant 'place with extensive grounds... They have cows, gardens, etc. etc.' It was the first federal hospital for the insane, built in the 1850s on a tract of land above the Anacostia River known as Saint Elizabeth, and with views across to the distant Capitol building. But Howard Hall was an isolated building of grim aspect, built in 1891 and designed as a prison for the criminally insane. It had 'a high penitentiary wall', rows of barred windows, one to each small locked cell, and a dry moat between the prison building and its wall. When Charles Olson visited he was 'let in through a black iron door with nine peep holes cut in it in 3 horizontal rows'. Pound was shut up in a solitary cell with a similar door with peepholes through which he could be observed. His view through the barred window was of the high outer wall. His things had not been sent on from Gallinger, and for several weeks he would be without the books and manuscripts which had become his sole resource. At first he was not even let out for exercise in the crowded exercise yard, but he must have been with the violently insane at times since he said to Olson in early January, 'There's an Indian in my ward who talks all the time about killing people. Last night he got the number up to 10,000 he wanted to bump off.' Visitors could be overwhelmed by the stench of stale sweat and urine, and there were the madhouse noises of uncontrollable outcries and shouted words. Pound would call it 'the hell hole', and compare it unfavourably with the DTC.

He was delivered to St Elizabeths about 5.30 p.m. on 21 December, registered as Case no. 58,102, and given a pre-admission examination by Dr Parker who happened to be on evening duty. Physical examination revealed 'a well developed, well built, moderately well nourished, middle-aged white male whose general physical fitness appears excellent'. There was much more to the effect that 'The lungs are clear to auscultation and percussion', etc., etc. Neurological examination revealed normal reflexes, etc. etc. 'The blood pressure is 134/82. The pulse is 80 per minute. The respirations are 18 per minute.' So far the examination was thoroughly professional in its application of established tests and measurements. Then there were some simple questions to test the patient's 'orientation'. Did he know the date? 'Patient replies, after a slight pause, "I believe it is some time after the 20th of December", knows that Christmas has not yet occurred.' Patient also 'knows the name of the hospital, the place from which he has just been transferred, as well as the reason for the transfer'.

In fact, as the long and detailed report on the non-medical part of the examination reveals, the patient's understanding of how and why he came to be there went well beyond the doctor's comprehension, and beyond his competence. Invited to give a brief account of himself, Pound evidently let loose with everything that had happened to him since his arrest, together with the defence of his broadcasts that he was supposedly incapable of giving, and with an outline of his social, economic, and political philosophy complete with, or so it seemed to Dr Parker, 'a voluminous bibliography of authors and their writings'. 'At no time does he falter for lack of memory on any subject', the doctor noted, 'and tells his own story in a chronologically systematic fashion.' However, he also exhibited 'traits of egotism, intellectual haughtiness, dogmatism, and a tendency toward the belief that he is infallible and practically omniscient along certain lines of philosophy, economics and political science'. Dr Parker was not testing and measuring there, but merely dressing up his subjective reactions to make them appear scientific. Then, as Pound insisted that he had broadcast 'with a sense of performing a patriotic duty', and 'with a sense of duty to humanity', in attempting to acquaint the United States with the terrible destruction and waste in wealth and lives which it was causing by 'wrecking Europe', the doctor's professional objectivity lapsed completely, and he wrote breathlessly into his report that 'Apparently the patient is unaware or refuses to ignore [*sic*] the very bald fact that in carrying on his activities he was acting as a puppet who, because of the nature of his opinions, performed appropriately for the purposes of the Italian Fascist Government and with only a modicum of manipulation being necessary'. That was neither a professional nor an informed opinion, but it wore a white coat and would enter into the official record. Moreover, with a fine unconscious irony, the doctor remarked that 'He speaks about the undemocratic processes in the American system but does not mention that he owes his present situation in a mental hospital to a democratic judicial system.' Being observed and judged by doctors with conventional ideas and regular expectations would be a refinement of Pound's hell.

It was probably the next day, the 22nd, that he wrote to Mary, dating the note 'vers le noel':

Dearest Child:

Tell your mother I bless the day I first saw her. & thank her for all the happiness she has brought me.

a gleam of hope now the sun is reborn.

Then turning the page sideways he wrote two lines from canto 47, (but with 'Circe's' for 'Ceres' daughter'): 'First must thou go the road to hell | & to the bower of Circe's daughter Proserpine'. He was trying to give meaning and purpose to his descent into hell, and thinking of how Odysseus was sent by Circe to consult Tiresias who even in hell 'yet hath his mind entire'. But the photograph taken for the hospital's records on 26 December is the mugshot of a man unable to comprehend the hell he has got himself into, his eyes pleading without hope for help.

Yet when Charles Olson was allowed a fifteen-minute visit on 4 January he was struck by his surprising 'eagerness and vigor as he came forward into the waiting room', and the firmness and strength of his handshake. 'Gallinger was better than this', he said, but also that he 'wanted something to do'. Olson kept blanking out anything at all political that Pound said, but could not resist 'the charm and attraction of his person',

For he is as handsome and quick and at work as ever. His jumps in conversation are no more than I or any active mind would make. Once in a while he seems to speak with an obsession, but even this I do, and at his age, after the fullness of his life, I imagine I might be a hell of a lot worse.

As he was leaving Howard Hall Olson was stopped and 'formally interviewed' by Dr Jerome Kavka, a very young trainee psychiatrist who had just been given charge of Pound. Olson expressed surprise 'that the patient's attorney had not yet visited the patient here', and enquired after 'the patient's personal belongings not yet received from Gallinger Hospital'. Kavka noted that, but did nothing about it; and noted also that he felt

Olson was making 'a disguised plea for sympathy toward the patient'. The next day he began his 'psychiatric examination' of Pound—this would continue through the following three weeks with almost daily interviews probing into the patient's family background and personal history.

For Pound these interviews meant a brief escape from the boredom of his cell and the hubbub of the ward, but at the cost of subjecting himself to the intrusive questioning of a careful young clinician who would take down everything he said and probably understand nothing. Writing up his notes on 24 January, Kavka wrote that, 'Occasionally becoming angry and irritated over his status, he would refuse to follow orthodox methods of questioning, and would ramble on in a devious fashion, skipping rapidly from one topic to another, with his own "trials and tribulations" always the centre of discussion'—

> The patient spoke rapidly, with a faint suggestion of an 'English' accent, and modulated his voice frequently from a barely audible whisper to shouting 'at the top of his lungs'. He was exceptionally literate, but uninhibited in the choice of words, often using the most profane language and vilification. Gesticulation was frequently used to press home points, and his facial expressions were animated, expressive and emotionally appropriate.

In a retrospect written many years later Kavka would give a rather different impression of Pound on these occasions, calling him a 'dramatic conversationalist', and saying that

> It was pleasurable listening to this man as if he were making poetry in his normal verbal discourse. There was drama in every moment of it, quick changes of mood, intonations that rose and fell, pauses that amplified and raised expectations, and constant exciting changes that kept one alert. From time to time he synthesised all of this in a cogent psychological statement.

One of the more dramatic moments must have occurred on Monday 21 January. Kavka wanted Pound to go on about his schooling, and Pound wouldn't. 'This is all very dull. Talk to me about other things outside,' he said, and then,

> The birds are chirping. Are they coming or going? What did they stop for? I don't often get so excited about minor matters. It's not being able to count on anything; I obviously am not violent and do not shit on the floor. When will they get me out of this ward?

Kavka said, 'Recalling those years from college seems to bother you', and ended the session. In the next session he probed, 'What made you suddenly angry?', and Pound burst out,

> I am angry... irate! You know God-damned well I'm suffering from claustrophobia and you put me in a locked room with bars and locks and lock me up at night. The attendants kid me about the article in the magazine. You are in Soviet Russia here; one is completely at the whim of these attendants.[4]

The psychiatrist registered this episode as showing that the patient 'was easily distractible'. In his retrospective analysis, however, he wrote that 'At this point he showed grandiose feelings and almost delusional behaviour when he noticed the cessation of the bird's song... Almost uncontrollable anal-sadistic violence erupted'; and again, 'he referred to the birds and his wish to get out of the confined ward to a freer area. This, to some extent, was a reflection of a regressed state of grandiosity.' That the prisoner might just naturally wish to be free, freed from a place where the inmates did shit on the floor, and freed from this dull interrogation, was apparently too simple an explanation. Kavka did note at the time, but with an air of reproof, that the patient 'does not appreciate his status as a patient in Howard Hall, and continually makes extraordinary requests, even so far as to ask permission to roam beyond the "wall" surrounding Howard Hall. He is adamant to this request and cannot see the "logic" in his incarceration.'

No doubt Pound's way of adjusting to his status as a prisoner was not all that it should have been. 'During his stay in the hospital', Kavka reported, probably on the evidence of the guards' observations,

> the patient has co-operated with hospital procedures and has in no way obstructed normal routines except by his persistent demands for extra attention. He spends most of his time lying upon his bed in his room, reading a Chinese text and a few slim volumes of poetry, making a few notes on random slips of paper. He complains about the doors being locked and states that the security precautions used in Howard Hall do, in no way, help his claustrophobia. Often he is very sensitive to the noise created by other patients, and refused to accept an offered radio—'just plain noise'. He is moderately tidy, makes no exceptional attempt to wear a consistent outfit of clothes, but tends to his personal needs. He does no ward work, eats regularly without complaint, and manages to sleep well. He has arranged to receive a newspaper daily, a pint of milk every other day, and ice cream at intervals. Provided with shower privileges, at his request, he insisted upon tub baths, which were provided. He has made the acquaintance of several patients, but engages only in brief conversation with them.

[4] The magazine was probably *Newsweek* which ran an article in which Pound was described as America's 'Haw Haw'.

Kavka did not report what those random slips of paper revealed, though he must have seen them. On one Pound scribbled to Cornell, 'young doctors absolutely useless'.

Pound's 'status' as a prisoner in Howard Hall, and 'the "logic" of his incarceration', were more deeply disturbing than the young psychiatrist could recognize. He was imprisoned because his 'defense counsel' had entered a plea of insanity, and because Dr Overholser and the other psychiatrists had confirmed that he was indeed in a state of paranoid insanity. Yet Dr Kavka, after three weeks of interviews with him, had elicited 'No well-devined [*sic*] or systematized delusions, hallucinations or ideas of reference', thus in near textbook terms contradicting the experts' finding. The worst he could say about his patient was that he exhibited 'considerable egocentricity'; that his views on economic and monetary problems 'cannot be considered logical or reasonable'; that his judgment was impaired 'with regard to the seriousness of his situation', as evidenced by his having intended to defend himself. Leaving aside his incompetence to pass judgment on Pound's views, Kavka clearly felt himself to be dealing with someone who for all his eccentricity, egocentricity, and singularity, was not insane. And yet he was treating Pound as a 'patient', and holding it against him that he did not accept his 'status' as an imprisoned patient in a ward for the criminally insane. Pound's reaction to finding himself in that predicament was even more problematical. By agreeing to plead insanity, in the expectation that he would be well treated and soon released, he had betrayed himself into an impossible situation where, while being sane, he had to submit to being treated as if he were not.

When Kavka asked him directly, 'Do you believe you are insane?', Pound chose his terms very carefully, giving a direct answer but also attempting to deal with the complexities and contradictions of his situation:

> No, I don't think I am insane, but I am so shot to pieces that it will take me years to write a sensible piece of prose. I think I am of unsound mind, and I don't think I've been shown good therapy here. I was absolutely unfit to transact any business.

That was as much as to say, I am here only because of what happened to my mind in the gorilla cage—that rendered me unfit to plead—but it does not mean that I am insane, and you are not helping to put my mind together again.

One of the things that did not help was being subjected to the Rorschach inkblot test, now quite discredited but then taken very seriously by the profession as a key to the hidden depths of the personality. Dr Kendig, who administered the test and wrote up the results on 10 January, found that it revealed 'a brilliant but pedantic individual with a marked personality disorder of long standing'—

> The brilliance of his mind is attested by the relatively large number of whole responses (33%), the very accurate form perception (100%), and the very excellent capacity for kinaesthesis (6 M) denoting abstract and theoretical intelligence of a high order and unusual creative gifts. His whole responses, however, are cheap and popular and he gives no original interpretations at all, suggesting in part indifference and contempt for the test procedure (very apparent throughout) but probably also certain retrogressive changes accompanying his advancing years since he must certainly have had the capacity for more original syntheses. Such extremely meticulous form perception together with two oligophrenic responses (Ddo) and a neglect of the obvious and practical (low D) indicate marked pedantry... His interpretations and his comments as the test progressed were critical, hostile and sarcastic, occasionally vitriolic, revealing great hostility. Marked aggression in interpersonal relations is also disclosed in his kinaesthetic interpretations—people moving in opposite directions, 'making snouts at each other, looking over their shoulders, I don't know whether kicking each other or not.' The last he impulsively illustrated by pushing out his own foot toward the examiner.

And so it went on, discovering 'perverse sexual trends', 'a latent homosexual component', 'hatred of women and of other races ... in line with Fascistic ideology', and that 'His hostility, emphasis on order and symmetry, and his meticulous regard for detail (Ddo) suggest an anal-erotic personality make-up, and it is perhaps significant that apparently the only serious illness he ever had was an anal fistula.' Pound's impatience with this nonsense was of course used against him: 'in his refusal to make the syntheses of which he is capable ... there is an element of self-destruction and contempt for his own production ... and the core of his self-destruction is epitomized in his statement to the examiner, "You see it doesn't give me anything whatever".' As later critics of the Rorschach test would observe, it put the patient completely at the mercy of the examiner's own personality and preconceptions.

Pound was increasingly desperate for what St Elizabeths was not giving him in the way of sane conversation and contact with a familiar world outside. 'Olson gt. comfort', he told Dorothy after his first visit, 'Hope they let him come back . only solid.' During his second visit, on Tuesday January 15, Olson asked 'if Cornell or Laughlin had been to see him', and Pound told him, 'no, he had had a couple of postcards, they were off skiing somewhere', and that Olson 'was his only anchor to windward'. The next day he scribbled to Cornell, 'relapse after the comfort of Tuesday ... Olson saved my life'—evidently by affording '15 minutes of sane conversation'.

But he needed that every day, and without it, 'Problem now is not to go stark screaming hysteric cent per cent 24 hours per day'. Cornell responded, 'I am sorry... but for the present you will have to remain where you are'. He also needed people to write to him. 'Please everybody write a LOT to me & not expect answers', he asked in a note to A. V. Moore and Dorothy; and to Cummings he wrote simply, 'I like getting | letters'. When letters from Dorothy dated December 19 and 22 turned up six weeks later he told her 'great comfort that your letters have started to arrive' and hoped there would now be a steady stream. But he had heard nothing from Olga and Mary since the end of November, and anxiously asked Olga's brother if there were any means of getting news to or from her. He signed that note 'Ezra (Candide)', as if he were Voltaire's witness to the world's disasters. He wanted news of old friends, 'of Bunting or Nancy [Cunard] or anyone'; and he was glad when old friends turned up to see him, the Mapel sisters who came regularly—on one occasion 'Miss Ida fix'd coat lining', on another she brought chocolate—and Katherine Proctor Saint came again. Caresse Crosby, an old friend from the Paris of the 1920s and early 1930s, came just once, 'at the request of the hospital staff who wanted to get the impressions of someone who had known him years ago'. She thought him unchanged, and found his memory for dates and persons and events better than her own; and though she made it plain that 'her coming to see him was no indication of her attitude toward the charges', she did send him a new suit which Olson found him wearing, 'blue, looked summer stuff'.

All through January and into February his books and papers had still not been forwarded from Gallinger, though his other things did turn up eventually. But there were occasional ideograms and translations from the Confucian odes in his letters, so he must have been carrying with him the copy that had been fetched out of Supply for him in the DTC. He told Olson he was not up to reading much, apart from newspapers and magazines, and that it had been hard going to get through Ayn Rand's *Fountainhead.* In a note to Olga on 17 January he said he was at p. 155 of Ernest Poole's *One of Us*, a nostalgic novel of New England life—'sob stuff, eternal Alcott', he told her. But then at the end of January he was reading Ford's *Parade's End*, 'much better than I thought', and eagerly 'Bearding Possum's "4tets"'—Eliot's *Four Quartets*—which Laughlin had sent down to him.

Laughlin had written to Dr Overholser in early January on his New Directions letterhead, introducing himself as Pound's publisher, asking to be advised about visiting hours, and saying that if Overholser felt 'it would be helpful to his cure I should like to come to Washington now and again to see him'. He went on,

For nearly a year I lived in Rapallo and studied with Pound and I feel I can never repay him for all he taught me about literature. I knew him then to be one of the best men I have ever met—generous in every way and idealistic to the point, sometimes, of the ridiculous. To see him now emeshed in this terrible predicament is really heart-breaking. I cannot endorse his anti-semitism—which I attribute to his disease, for certainly it is a fairly recent thing with him—but in spite of that I want to do anything I can to help him or make him comfortable.

He offered to send Overholser 'a set' of the four books by Pound which he had published 'before the war', and Overholser acknowledged these with his thanks on 28 January. But, in spite of Pound's asking 'aren't you ever coming', he did not get down to see him until the dust of the court case was being settled.

Interest in the case was being kept alive in the press, with suggestions that Pound was faking insanity and that the psychiatrists were protecting a traitor from punishment. That may have had some influence on the Justice Department's decision to apply for a formal statutory inquisition into his mental state, and on 18 January Judge Laws ordered that the issue be tried before a jury. At St Elizabeths Dr Griffin noted, 'This patient appeared today in the District Court of the United States for the District of Columbia, and as a result of a brief hearing before Chief Justice Bolitha J. Laws an order was given that he appear in court, January 30, 1946, for lunacy trial.' In the event the hearing was deferred to Wednesday 13 February.

On 25 January Cornell wrote to Dorothy Pound to inform her of the hearing, the result of which, he told her, was 'a foregone conclusion since all the doctors are in agreement that he is in no condition to be tried and requires hospital treatment'. 'I have learned from questioning the doctors', he went on,

that they do not anticipate any substantial change in your husband's condition and also that they do not think he needs to remain very long in a hospital. I expect, therefore, that after a few months the case will be dropped and he will be set free.

You need not be alarmed about the report on your husband's mental condition. While, no doubt, his difficulties were aggravated by the ordeal of his imprisonment, he has been resting comfortably in hospital for some time now...

Pound was perfectly normal, he assured her, quite his old self, as Laughlin had told him, so she need have no worry; but what was normal in Pound, and would appear normal to her, 'is defined by the doctors as paranoid' and 'mentally abnormal'. He went so far as to 'think it may be fairly said that any man of his genius would be regarded by a psychiatrist as abnormal'.

Meanwhile Kavka was writing up the notes of his interviews and preparing his fifteen-page report to be considered at a formal internal review of

Pound's case on Monday 28 January. He incorporated with explicit acknowledgement the reports of the Army psychiatrists who had examined Pound in the DTC and found him competent; he incorporated also the joint report of the four psychiatrists to Chief Justice Laws which found him incompetent; and then, as well as drawing silently upon Cornell's Affidavit in the body of his report, he attached the entire Affidavit as an appendix, as if its defence attorney's story of Pound's abnormalities and incompetence to plead was also to be taken as objective evidence of his mental states.

On Sunday 27th, possibly anticipating the review scheduled for the next day, Pound scribbled a desperate note to Cornell from his 'Dungeon':

> mental torture
> constitution a religion
> a world lost
> grey mist barrier impassible
>   ignorance absolute / anonyme
> futility of might have been
> coherent areas / constantly / invaded
>   aiuto [help]

However, on the same day he also wrote a relatively composed note to Cornell, not about his own troubles but about how the Jews should attain their Zion. 'As no one ever listens to end of sentence or paragraph', he began, 'you might note that am Zionist @ least to xtent of having Zionist plan'. The ground of this plan had been laid out in some of the Pisan cantos, and he had outlined it to Kavka who had put it into his report as Pound's '"Zionist program" paraphrasing the Old Testament':

> 1– Zion shall be redeemed with justice.
> 2– Lord, who shall sojourn in Thy tabernacle?
> He that putteth not out his money on interest.
> 3– Thou shalt do no unrighteousness in judgment, in meteyard, in weight or in measure.
> 4– Thou shalt purchase the field with money.

He had told Kavka, 'If I could get seven Jews to stand on that, I could rebuild the temple of Herod.' And to Cornell he explained, '3 + 1 points, and also the finance & land basis'. 'Memory of André Spire and others', he added, Spire being a Jewish activist, poet, and Zionist, whom he had been close to in Paris. It might well be said that it was not for him to be telling the Jews their business; but it should also be said that here he was not being anti-Semitic but positively recommending a just and peaceful foundation for the nascent state of Israel.

At the case conference on the 28th there were six St Elizabeths doctors—'Doctors Silk, Hall, Duval [presiding], Griffin, Kavka and Dalmau'—and present also were a further two dozen or so 'mental health professionals'. A first hour was spent considering 'the history and other pertinent facts in this case', and then 'the patient was called for interview'. In Dr Duval's official report, 'He entered the room pleasantly, quietly, and in a cooperative manner'; later it is remarked that 'While he complains of constant fatigue he is quite active physically during the examination and on several occasions arose very quickly from a semi-reclining position to make some graphic illustration with paper and pencil of some point under discussion.' Thirty-five years later Duval recalled Pound's behaviour very differently: 'When he came into the room he begged our pardon but said he didn't feel strong enough to sit up and could he please lie on the floor', which is what he did 'during this whole conference while I interviewed him'. Dr Dalmau also recalled 'Pound's bizarre display of fatigue', and interpreted it as a hostile act. The psychiatrists asked him to 'outline his views with regard to his broadcasts over the Rome radio as well as the factual events which occurred following his arrest for treason', and later 'His ideas and concepts about his economic plan were discussed in some detail.' Apart from a rather dramatic and possibly consciously exaggerated mannerism—'suddenly puts his hand over his forehead or on the frontal area of his scalp, bows his head and looks at the floor, ceasing his talk for a moment'—apart from those interruptions, 'his stream of talk is clear, coherent and relevant although he shows some hesitation in searching for the explicit phrases which he wishes to use'. As for his economic ideas, 'he readily admits that his may not be the only successful economic plan', and 'Nothing in the way of grandiosity or expansiveness beyond this was uncovered and he denied any idea that he was a world saviour'.

The report noted Pound's 'present complaint': '(1) He feels constantly fatigued and has a sensation in the vertex of his skull as if there were a vacuum there, (2) he objects to his hospitalization in the Howard Hall Building as the building has an entrance like a medieval tunnel and the other patients in the building are disturbed criminals ... He believes that his fatigue will not diminish until he is "tethered" outside the Howard Hall Building in a "regular hospital ward".' Also noted was his belief that '"his mind was upset in the gorilla cage"', and by solitary confinement in the DC jail, and that 'he is still upset and ... not in condition to prepare a proper defense'—'"They ought to give me more time – enough time so that I can prepare a 600-page defense."' The psychiatrists recorded a surprisingly sympathetic recognition that it 'would seem quite natural in the circumstances' for him to feel 'some worry and frustration about his immediate future'.

Their overall conclusion fell far short of the clear diagnosis the case conference was meant to reach: 'From information available it appears that this patient has probably been egocentric and eccentric for many years, is an odd character and by some his case might be catalogued as a psychopathic personality by reason of certain asocial and antisocial behaviour with some disturbance of interpersonal relationships.' In short, this gathering of psychiatrists did not think Pound insane. Dr Duval would recall that he had tried but failed 'to elicit some symptoms of insanity'. Before the conference he had assumed insanity because Dr Overholser was on record with that diagnosis, but his examination found 'no delusions, no thought disorder, and no disturbances of orientation. He definitely did not seem to be insane.' The almost unanimous view of the psychiatrists present at the conference was that Pound was neither insane nor incompetent.

However, as Duval recalled, they were anxious not to contradict and embarrass their boss, and therefore 'decided not to make any formal diagnosis at all'. Duval had gone 'over to Win's office to tell him what we had found', and Overholser 'was very cordial' about it, and 'said we didn't need to disturb the practicalities of the situation by making it public, and that we should just keep it to ourselves'. Duval then added a note to his record of the conference: 'After this case was discussed with the Superintendent and the above findings reported to him, he suggested a longer period of observation before a final decision is reached.' Kavka, though, informed Olson that 'the questioning was now finished'.

Olson was visiting the next day, and sensed that 'Pound was wound so tight... he might snap', apparently on account of the previous day's examination. He was also excited because Dr King had been to see him, and Pound had formed the impression that King was sympathetic, '"would like to see me out of here"' and put to use—'"I understand they think to send me to Japan"'. '"The pure products of America | go crazy"', he wrote to Williams a day or two later, jokily giving the latter back his own lines; and Williams retorted, 'That you're crazy I don't for one moment believe, you're not that good an American... If there is anything I can do for you let me know.'

A week later, on Thursday 7 February, Dr Overholser made his first and (and apart from a brief further note a week later) his only entry in the case notes of #58,102. 'Patient was interviewed at length today', he wrote, 'by Dr. Marion F. King, of the Bureau of Prisons, Dr. Joseph L. Gilbert of Gallinger Hospital, Dr. Wendell Muncie of Baltimore and the

Superintendent.' This will have been their meeting to prepare for the hearing on the 13th where they would be cross-examined on their testimony. They noted that 'Patient was somewhat restless, agitated, stating that he is in a fog', and that 'He gave vent to numerous delusions of grandeur and persecution'. They were 'unanimous in their opinion that fundamentally the patient is suffering from a paranoid condition with a considerable psychoneurotic coloring'.

'"4 medicos at me this morning",' Pound told Olson that afternoon. He was 'in bad condition', Olson noted, 'his eyes worried and muddy, his flesh puffy and old. It appears again to have been too much "hammering" at him.' Pound also complained that the previous week, on the day originally set down for the hearing, 'they had had him dressed and waiting to go all day, even after the hearing had been cancelled, but no one apparently had thought to let him or Howard Hall know'. '"I don't know what goes on. Who to believe,"' he said. And Laughlin had not come, had not sent him the proofs of the *Confucius*, '"which is the base of my defense"'.

On 12 February, the day before the hearing, Cornell went to St Elizabeths, as he put it, 'to see Pound and prepare him for the ordeal of appearing in court'. Pound 'was very nervous about the trial', and Cornell told him that he 'would not put him on the witness stand'. He does not say whether he made it clear that the treason charge would not be considered, and that the time for Pound's defence had passed. The only issue would be his sanity.

After seeing Pound Cornell 'stopped in Dr Overholser's office to pay my respects', and was ushered into his private office. Overholser wanted him to know that 'many of the young doctors on his staff' disagreed with his diagnosis, 'They thought Pound was merely eccentric, and wanted to see him tried and convicted.' He assured Cornell that he remained unshaken in his own opinion 'that Pound was mentally unfit to stand trial'. He would take the junior doctors' reports to court in his briefcase, and if the prosecution asked about their views he would read them out and explain why he disagreed. Otherwise he would not mention them. In fact, he told Cornell, he was not going to tell the prosecution what he was telling Cornell. What was Overholser's game? An expert witness, he had maintained to his fellow psychiatrists, should give his professional opinion 'objectively, without partisan bias in favour of the government or the defense'; and even as just the government's main witness, he should not have been sharing with the defence critical information which he would not disclose to the prosecution. But here he was warning Cornell not to ask a question which might bring out evidence that would throw doubt on the finding of insanity, the finding Cornell clearly wanted. He was offering himself as Cornell's accomplice;

and he was also making Cornell his accomplice. They would work together to suppress the dissenting opinion of the junior doctors and to have Pound declared insane. Of course, for all Cornell knew, the devious Dr Overholser might have tipped off the prosecution too. They might all have been playing their parts in the same charade, each for their own covert reason.

The hearing

The insanity hearing turned out to be theatre of the absurd performed as straight courtroom drama. The transcript states that it was a case of 'United States of America against Criminal No. 76,028 Ezra Pound, Defendant'. Yet in an inversion of the normal procedure in criminal trials the prosecution did not make a case which the defence must answer, but instead Cornell, 'appearing on behalf of the defendant', led the proceedings and called the witnesses. And the witnesses, the four psychiatrists, of whom three had been appointed initially to testify for the government, were now all of them 'appearing on behalf of the defendant'. The prosecution, that is, 'Isaiah Matlack Esq. and Donald Anderson Esq. appearing on behalf of the Department of Justice of the United States', would neither call new witnesses for their side nor produce any evidence. They would do no more than cross-examine the witnesses appearing for the defendant. The defendant himself would not be called by his attorney to take the stand. And when the prosecution said, in that case they would call him, the Chief Justice intervened and said he didn't think so, 'If we call him he will take two or three hours,' and it wasn't necessary, because 'The Court of Appeals says very plainly you cannot disregard an opinion of the psychiatrists.' So the defendant's fate would be decided entirely by the opinions of the four psychiatrists.

Pound was in court, probably dressed for the occasion in the new suit in which Miss Ida had thought 'he looked "nice"', 'blue with a narrow stripe—tan (dark) shoes—a shirt of a pale tan . . . a two toned necktie of light & dark blue'. The Court was crowded with reporters and others—Laughlin and Olson were both there. And of course there was the jury, eleven men and a woman. The questioning of the witnesses began in the morning and resumed in the afternoon, taking up four and a half hours in all, and through all that time Pound was obediently mute, apart from one brief outburst when he had to be 'quieted by his lawyer'. 'Throughout the rest of the hearing', according to the reporter for the *New York Herald Tribune*, 'the bearded defendant moved nervously in his seat, held his head in his hands or leaned back and stared at the ceiling'. Another reporter wrote that 'He held his head bowed, running nervous fingers through his hair . . . slumped in his chair with his knees raised against the edge of the lawyers' table facing the judge's bench, looking neither to left nor right'. He had to listen to the four psychiatrists giving their garbled and uncomprehending and often simply false versions of his history, his life's work, his personality, and his mental condition, all of it directed towards the saving and damning conclusion that he, the man sitting there beside his lawyer, was of unsound mind, had long been of unsound mind, and always would be of unsound mind. That was what Cornell wanted them to say, having said it himself at the indictment and having primed them all with his powerful Affidavit. And Pound could not speak for himself, having agreed, at the urging of his wife, her solicitor, and his cautious friend Eliot, to do as Cornell wanted him to do; and because the judge also thought it not necessary that he be heard. He had to submit, without right of reply, to being represented, and grotesquely misrepresented, by the four government psychiatrists led on by his own lawyer.

'The question', Chief Justice Laws instructed the jury, as if it were a simple matter, was the 'sanity of this particular individual'; and in particular, was his 'mental condition such as that he is not able to participate with counsel in the trial of a criminal case, and is not in position to understand the full nature of the charges against him'. The individual in question would not be asked directly if he understood the full nature of the charges, nor if he could offer any defence—though he had given ample evidence that he did and could, in his letter to Attorney General Biddle when first indicted in 1943, and again when interrogated by the FBI in Genoa the previous May.

Dr Muncie was the first to be called. Asked if he had occasion to examine the sanity of people he replied, 'That is all I do, and treat them.' Asked what symptoms of insanity he had observed in Mr. Pound, he referred to his notes and gave this answer:

> He has a number of rather fixed ideas which are either clearly delusional or verging on the delusional. One I might speak of, for instance, he believes he has been designated to save the Constitution of the United States for the people of the United States...
>
> Secondly, he has a feeling that he has a key to the peace of the world through the writings of Confucius, which he translated into Italian and into English, and that if this book had been given proper circulation the Axis would not have been formed, we would be at peace now, and a great deal of trouble could have been avoided in the past, and this becomes his blueprint for world order in the future.

Further, these fixed ideas showed 'a remarkable grandiosity', and 'delusions of self-aggrandisement'. At the same time, there was a vagueness in

Pound's exposition of his ideas which made them impossible to follow, so that Dr Muncie had found himself 'left out on a limb every time'—'the topics may be clear in his mind but cannot be clear in the examiner's mind'. In addition to this 'breakdown in his thinking processes', and to his poor memory, 'he definitely shows a very poor grasp of his present situation'—'He apparently did not realize he was being brought back here for treason, and when he found that out his argument was that he must have been double-crossed...at the hands of the British Intelligence Service or Commandos.' Asked to go into more detail about Pound's understanding of his predicament, Dr Muncie at last said something accurately informed and perceptive:

> He has two minds about that. At times he believes he could persuade any jury who could understand him of the fact that he has not committed treason. At other times, he states categorically that he is not of sound mind and could not participate effectively in his own defense.

However, 'by no stretch of the imagination can you make him realize the seriousness of his predicament'. Dr Muncie could not say whether he understood what he was alleged to have done, because 'He categorically denies that he committed anything like treason, in his mind, against the people of the United States', and because the discussion always ended up in his bringing in his fixed ideas, 'the economic situation, Confucius, Japan, and so forth... and you end up with a confusion of thoughts.' In short, he would diagnose Pound's illness as 'a paranoid condition'—'in ordinary language he has been a peculiar individual for many, many years, and... engrossed with these things I have talked about as neurotic developments'. Cornell put his leading question, 'Will you tell the jury what is your opinion as to Mr Pound's ability to understand the meaning of a trial under this indictment for treason, and particularly his ability to consult with counsel and formulate a defense to the indictment?', and Muncie gave him the expected answer, 'I think he is not capable of doing any of those things'.

Mr Matlack in his cross-examination gently took apart Dr Muncie's testimony. He established that when Muncie said that it was his idea 'that there has been for a number of years a deterioration of the mental processes' he was in fact relying on the history in Cornell's Affidavit; that when he had himself questioned Pound, 'His memory, as far as I could find was all right, except for a substantial period in the concentration camp where there appears to have been a blackout of memory'—this 'blackout' sounds like Cornell's detail; that the fixed ideas he had mentioned would not in themselves indicate insanity, nor would 'grandiosity'; that the vagueness of the ideas, which Muncie now said made an 'essential difference', was a vagueness 'to the examiner'; that 'the peculiar personality' which Muncie said he had did not in itself denote insanity, nor did it prevent Pound from understanding the charge and discussing the matter with his counsel. Then Matlack had Muncie answer that yes, he did think Pound 'understood what treason was', and 'the nature of the charge, and that possibly he would be tried for the crime of treason'. But then the fact that he said his broadcasting was not treason,

> shows clearly that he was out of touch with a very large segment of the world, and it shows more clearly than anything else perhaps how his world was built for himself. You and I are living in what one is pleased to call the realities of the situation.

Matlack had had Muncie make his meaning nearly explicit, that in his view Pound's believing he was not liable for treason 'indicated that he was not of sound mind'. That was an unbeatable catch resting on the fixed idea that Pound was guilty: if he did not know that he was guilty then he must be insane.

Near the end of his cross-examination Matlack amused himself by briefly changing roles and doing what Cornell might have been expected to do. Muncie was saying again that Pound was incapable of consulting with counsel because 'It is hard to stay on a subject, and when you end up you don't finish with any coherent or intelligent thought', and it was put to him,

> Q. Well, he answered your questions?
> A. No, no, when I say, 'Mr. Pound, you are out to defend the Constitution; now, that is a lengthy document, will you tell me what items you are out to defend specifically?', why, he will say, 'The President is a magistrate with delegated powers.' That is all I could get on this question. From then on he goes through all those ramifications about Confucius, and Heaven knows what.
> Q. Doesn't he discuss the money and other clauses in the Constitution?
> A. Yes.
> Q. And that would be reasonable evidence he knew how he is going to save the Constitution?
> A. By inference, but there isn't any clear statement...

Cornell, perhaps feeling needled, objected shortly after this to Matlack's asking Dr Muncie what he thought about Pound's intelligence. Muncie began his reply by saying that it had been 'investigated at length by the psychiatrists at the hospital', and Cornell broke in, evidently anxious to prevent the opinions of the other doctors being brought out, 'Your Honor, I object to that. The other doctor is here and to have this doctor testify would be hearsay.' Matlack's retort, at the end of his questioning of Muncie, would be to elicit the fact that a good deal of his evidence had been hearsay based upon hospital records and upon Cornell's own Affidavit.

Perhaps prompted by Muncie's saying that the hospital records had contributed 'nothing essential' to his opinion, 'because they found the same things we did', Judge Laws asked him about the joint report which the four psychiatrists had made to him in December. All four had arrived at the same conclusion, he observed, had there been 'no disagreement at all?' 'No', he was told. And the witnesses at this hearing were all 'first duly sworn'.

Dr King's opinion, also based upon the hospital records and 'rather careful consideration of his life-long history', was that Mr Pound

> has always been a sensitive, eccentric, cynical person, and these characteristics have been accentuated in the last few years to such an extent that he is afflicted with a paranoid state of psychotic proportions which renders him unfit for trial.

He accepted Cornell's suggestion that a person could be all those things and still be able to stand trial, but what made the difference in Pound's case was that

> He has deviated from his chosen profession in that he has become preoccupied with economic and governmental problems to such an extent that during discussion of those problems he manifests such a sudden and such a marked feeling and tone that he reaches the point of exhaustion, and this unusual propensity, intense feeling, is quite characteristic of paranoid conditions and is sufficient, in my opinion, to permit, at least create, considerable confusion; at least that was the situation when I examined him, so that it is very difficult for him to explain his theories and proposals in a clear and concise logical manner.

Under cross-examination by Mr Anderson, Dr King went further. Asked what Pound had said about his activities in Italy, he went on instead about his interpretation of Pound:

> He resided there, and as far as his own ability was concerned he did a lot of work in translating and investigating Oriental classics, and during that period, too, he was very much concerned with political, economic and monetary problems. He became preoccupied with such matters to such an extent that it interfered largely with his own profession, without any profit or gain incidentally.[5] One point I think is significant, that he became so consumed with these other fields because he

[5] Compare Dr Kavka's report of 24 January 1946, p. 6: 'Italy, where he moved in 1924 ... After 1924, he became deeply engrossed in economic studies, especially monetary problems, and continued his researches in the classics, editing anthologies and making translations of Oriental writers, especially Confucius. It was here that he began work on his monumental cantos. He was always a critic of distinction and recognition in the field of poetry, but departed from this field to the extent of dealing

developed a belief that most government officials were tyrannical and it behoved him to do what he could to overcome that and safeguard the citizens' rights. Therefore, he wrote two pamphlets on economics and became very greatly concerned and interested in such matters.

As time went on his enthusiasm became greater, and there is no question but that he has a lot of sudden, emotional feeling in connection with these hobbies, or these special interests, so that during the time of the examinations he constantly told me about these ideas and beliefs with all the energy of which he was capable, which indicated that these matters more or less dominated his life, dominated his feelings.

He was inclined to argue and discuss them almost to the point of exhaustion. That is all indicative of a paranoid condition. That is really the evidence, as I interpret the case, the evidence of mental illness.

And all this, King seemed to think, was a reaction to having been 'mistreated or abused by a minor consular official in Paris in 1940 [*sic*]'. He very well may have been mistreated, the doctor allowed, 'but that is not sufficient justification for such a reaction'.

As Anderson's cross-examination went on Dr King was rather carried away, as he passed severe judgment upon Pound's 'abnormalities', into wildly generalizing about his supposed personal failings of which he had no direct knowledge nor even reliable information:

this paranoid state which now, to my mind, has been present for many, many years, has increased to such an extent that it has influenced his entire life, and through his own folly, and due to this defect, he has got himself into trouble more than once.[6]

It is also significant, I think, that he has never hesitated, not only in these matters we are just talking about, but also problems that have been incident to his own person and profit, he has never hesitated to criticize, or vilify, or condemn others in no uncertain terms, even without provocation, and without good cause, or without any cause. Without question he has been his own worst enemy in that respect.

Cornell entered no objection to these unprofessional remarks.

Anderson came to the question, 'Does the fact that Mr. Pound might think that what he did was not treasonable have an effect in arriving at your opinion here?', and King answered, 'To a minor extent', but then went on,

with economic, monetary and political problems in an uninhibited manner, and continued to do so despite skepticism and difficulty in getting some of his work published.'

[6] Behind this incomprehensible assertion might be the section of Kavka's report headed 'Anti-social Trends, Arrests': 'The patient was arrested once in France because of "the noise in my studio and Antheil was practising for a concert. He was a hammering pianist and used a piano as a percussion instrument." Another arrest occurred in Italy, when the patient over-drafted $15,00 on his bank, by error.'

'He does not believe he is a mentally sick person. He does not believe that he is guilty of a serious offense against the United States.' Since King would say that he was a mentally sick person, that was as much as to say that Pound was as guilty of treason as he was mentally ill, and that the two things went together, the sickness and the treason. But then in the same answer he went off on quite another tack:

He believes that he could be useful to this country if he were designated as a diplomat, or agent, and sent to Japan, for instance, or even to Russia, to deal with the people over there, with the idea now of maintaining the peace of the world... I don't think a sane man in his status would make such a proposal.

Anderson asked if he had given consideration to Pound's writings in forming his opinion, and King came back to his first idea:

To the extent that his writings on the monetary system, as far as I can ascertain, carried very little weight in this country, or elsewhere, although he had devoted a good deal of time to them. Over a period of many years he persisted in devoting too much time to matters of this type.

'Are you qualified in the diplomatic field and economic field?' Anderson asked, and King could only answer 'No'.

Anderson also asked about Pound's intelligence, his IQ, and King said he knew it to be 'Something over 120', and added, 'There has been no impairment of the intelligence over the years. That again is characteristic of the disorder we are describing'—thus directly contradicting Dr Muncie. Cornell did not object to the hearsay at this point. But he did ask Dr King, who had twice declared himself unqualified to evaluate Pound's poetry, to compare his early and his late poetry, and elicited the reply, 'Well, I saw one of his poems, that he had prepared in the camp at Pisa which, of course, was incoherent and impossible for me to understand as compared with the earlier.' None of the Pisan cantos having been published, he was presumably referring to the same lines extracted from canto 80 which Cornell had sent to Dr Muncie, lines which would of course not make sense when torn from their context and shown to someone unfamiliar with the cantos. But Cornell would use even Pound's most intellectually advanced work—the poetry which Laughlin was eager to add to his New Directions list—as evidence of his insanity.

And Pound sat mute as his future was being determined by such testimony.

At the beginning of his examination by Cornell Dr Overholser stated again the opinion reached with his fellow psychiatrists in December, 'that the defendant was unfit mentally and unable to stand trial', and went on to say that the four of them had examined Pound again last Thursday, and that 'I have before me the report made by the other physicians at [St Elizabeths], and I see no reason to change my opinion.' Cornell put no question about that report, but Matlack asked Overholser about it at once in his cross-examination:

Q. Do you have with you the records of the hospital showing his present condition?
A. Yes, sir.
Q. Could you produce them?
A. Surely; it is in my brief case.
Q. Have you, yourself, treated Mr. Pound, or has it been left to your associates out there?
A. Partly to the associates.
Q. Are these the records made by the staff?
A. That is right.
Q. And will you state by referring to them what the records show as to his present state of mental health?
A. It is rather a bulky record, as you see.
Q. Can you summarize it?
A. Essentially it is that there has been very little change in his condition since he came in. A summary of the case from the time he came in is pretty much in line with what I said this morning, and the whole staff has seen him. There has been some discussion about him which has not been formal; in fact there has been no formal diagnosis they have made as yet.
Q. No formal diagnosis?
A. No.

And there Mr Matlack let that matter rest, content apparently to let Overholser get away with his prevarications. There would be a definite instance of that at the end of his cross-examination.

Throughout his testimony Overholser made much of Pound's 'blow-up', as he termed it, in the DTC. He knew about it, of course, mainly by hearsay, from the Army psychiatrists' reports which he had from the Justice Department, where it was described as a single episode of disorientation lasting a matter of minutes, and from Cornell's Affidavit where it featured as 'The period of violent insanity [which] apparently began about mid-June to endure for three months or more'. Overholser gave as one of his reasons for concluding that Pound would be 'unable to participate in the trial of this indictment intelligently', that, 'due to the episode he had in Pisa when he was under confinement, I think there would be much more violent reaction on top of this paranoid reaction if the trial was to proceed'. During Matlack's cross-examination Pound obligingly blew up right there in the courtroom. Matlack asked, 'Did he give you in his general history anything about his belief in Fascism?', and, according to the transcript, the defendant said, 'I never did believe in Fascism, God damn it; I am opposed to Fascism'—a claim worthy of the proceedings. Matlack continued this line of questioning until Cornell objected that it was 'very distressing' to Mr Pound, and the judge said, 'try not to disturb him if you can help it', thus reinforcing the perception of the defendant as dangerously insane. Overholser was able to refer back to the incident as evidence for his opinion that 'he is unfit to consult with counsel'—'he might very readily have one of these, can I say "blow-ups," again, during which he would be quite unable perhaps to concentrate enough to realize the importance to his defense.'[7]

'Of what duration are those blow-ups?', Matlack asked, and got the reply, 'Well the one at Pisa lasted several weeks, as far as one can gather from the reports of the psychiatrists there.' In fact it was not the Army psychiatrists but Cornell who had said that. Those psychiatrists had recorded Pound's telling them of just one brief episode. Asked what was the opinion of those psychiatrists, Overholser said it was 'That he had anxiety neurosis.' And here there was a moment of genuine courtroom drama.

Q. Could that [opinion of the Army psychiatrists] have anything to do with the present opinion of the doctors around here?
MR. CORNELL. I object to that.

He must have been objecting to the implication that the opinion arrived at by the other St Elizabeths doctors was close to that of the Army psychiatrists, that is, that Pound was not insane and was competent to stand trial—an implication that would expose Overholser's improbable claim that the doctors' opinion was essentially the same as his own. Matlack resumed:

Q. You said you based [your opinion] partly on reading those reports?
A. Yes.
Q. And then I asked you did those doctors find him insane?

There was a testing ambiguity, since the reports in question were from the Army *psychiatrists*, but the *doctors* just referred to were at St Elizabeths. Overholser's answer covered both—

A. They said he was not psychotic.
Q. That means he was not insane?

[7] In his second and last entry in the Notes for Case #58,102, 13 Feb. 1946—just eight lines recording the patient's appearance in the District Court, the jury's verdict, and the patient's having been 'accordingly remanded to the Hospital'—Dr Overholser singled out this one moment for the record, with prejudice: 'Patient was restless during the trial and on one occasion leaped up and cursed at the attorney for the Department of Justice.'

A. They were, I think, interested in prison facts.
Q. When they said he was not psychotic that means he was not insane?
A. That he was not suffering from a major mental disease. That was their impression. How long they saw him, I don't know, or what their experience was.

Matlack refrained from making explicit that he had just elicited through Overholser's evasions and prevarications the fact that the reports of all three Army psychiatrists, and of the St Elizabeths doctors, provided no basis at all for his opinion. Instead he let him off by helping him back on to safer ground:

Q. Would you say that the incident known now as the Pisa incident was the result of one of those blow-ups?
A. Yes. Apparently he was held incommunicado in an uncovered cage of some kind out in the yard, and that apparently developed a neurotic state because of that.

There were no further questions.

In the end it was clear that Dr Overholser stood firmly by his opinion, but his reasons for doing so were less clear. He had said that Pound's background history

shows that we are dealing now with the end-product of an individual who throughout his lifetime has been highly antagonistic, highly eccentric, the whole world has revolved around him, he has been a querulous person, he has been less and less able to order his life. This has been a gradual evolution throughout his life, so that now we are dealing with the end-product, so to speak.

Then he had been brought by Matlack to concede that none of that necessarily meant that Pound was insane or unable to consult with counsel. He had been asked, 'Now, what is there about him that you say he cannot consult with his counsel when [you say] he understands the charge and understands what he did do?', and he had replied,

He understands the charge as far as it implies [*sic*] to some abstract person. I do not think he comprehends or knows how that applies to this particular charge. That goes to his responsibility, and I am not discussing that, but I do say that his mental condition is such that he is unable to discuss with any degree of coherence the explanation for being in the situation in which he is, or his motive for so doing.

Somewhere in that answer there seems to the implication, already noted in the previous psychiatrists' testimonies, that Pound's refusal to admit to treason, to accept responsibility in that sense, is to be taken as evidence of insanity. But it was a murky answer, as was so much of Overholser's testimony. He was not to be pinned down to any clear definition or diagnosis of Pound's mental condition—at one point he said, 'it resembles paranoia, if you wish to put it that way'—but all the time he was insisting on Pound's abnormalities and eccentricities, and on the impossibility of getting any clear and logical sense out of him.

Dr Gilbert testified to much the same effect as the others as to Pound's being unable to give a rational and logical, and, to the examiner, intelligible account of himself. He also said of the acts for which he was under indictment, that they were 'based on abnormal type of thinking away beyond what might be considered as a mistake or error, even mistake in judgment or error in judgment', and that indicated apparently an unsound mind incapable of understanding how he should answer to the charge of treason. Gilbert did add something of his own in attempting to define the paranoid state from which he said Pound was suffering. To 'delusions of grandeur' as a leading symptom, he added 'hypochondria', or Pound's complaining of unusual fatigue or exhaustion. For example, in Gallinger Pound had spent most of the time in bed, undergoing almost no physical activity, yet when he was being examined 'he spoke of this fatigue and exhaustion very frequently', and such hypochondria was to be expected in a paranoid state. It apparently did not occur to the psychiatrist that physical and nervous exhaustion would be a natural concomitant of the mental strain Pound had been under for some time.

Cross-examined by Mr Anderson, Dr Gilbert indicated that in his view Pound's delusions of grandeur would impair his comprehension of the possible outcome of a treason trial. There was his belief that 'he was worth more to his country alive than dead', for one instance, on account of 'his knowledge of economic theories, of which he indicated he knew more than anyone else in the world'. Anderson suggested that 'That could be a debatable question, could it not?', and then said, still more mischievously, as if he were mocking Cornell,

Q. He also thought that he had not committed treason because under the Constitution he was granted the right of free speech?
A. Yes.
Q. Wouldn't that be a very good matter to present as a defense, or possible defense?

Gilbert said he didn't know, and Cornell objected that he 'isn't qualified to answer that'. But the prosecution had made a telling point against Cornell's whole strategy.

Cornell had asked each psychiatrist whether in his opinion the broken down defendant would be able to stand up to the rigours of a trial, and each had been ready to speculate that he would not. Dr Muncie thought a trial 'would be rather dangerous to his welfare'; Dr King thought it 'would bring on collapse'; and Dr Overholser was sure that 'it would not be fair to him or to his attorney' because of the 'violent reaction' it might bring on. This touching concern not to distress the poor defendant was the final nail in their consigning him to indefinite incarceration in St Elizabeths.

At the close of the hearing there was no summing up or clarification for the benefit of the jury of what they had heard, though it is unlikely that they were able to hold it all together in their minds and sort the sense from the nonsense. Judge Laws explained to the jury at some length what the hearing was about, and then charged them that it was their duty

> now to advise me whether in your judgment you find that Mr. Pound is in position to cooperate with his counsel, to stand trial without causing him to crack up or breakdown; whether he is able to testify, if he sees fit, at the trial, to stand cross-examination, and in that regard, of course, you have heard the testimony of all these physicians on the subject, and there is no testimony to the contrary and, of course, these are men who have given a large part of their professional careers to the study of matters of this sort, who have been brought here for your guidance.
>
> Under the state of the law you are not necessarily bound by what they say; you can disregard what they say and bring in a different verdict, but in a case of this type where the Government and the defense representatives have united in a clear and unequivocal view with regard to the situation, I presume you will have no difficulty in making up your mind.

The unanimity of the government and the defence had not been as apparent as Judge Laws was making out, but no doubt he knew what he was about, and Matlack did not object. The jury caught his drift, and having retired for just three minutes, emerged all of one mind that Ezra Pound was of 'unsound mind'. 'Thereupon the hearing was concluded.'

A reporter, Albert Deutsch, who was covering the hearing for the New York newspaper *PM*, noted that Pound at once 'jumped up with alacrity and engaged in affable conversation with his young lawyer'. Deutsch was convinced that the insanity was an act and that the psychiatrists and the Government's attorneys were letting Pound get away with treason. It seems not to have occurred to anyone, or at least no-one was prepared to say, that in fact it was the Government that was being saved from losing its case.

Laughlin 'was all excited', when Olson saw him the next day, that 'the examination got to the point where they were asking: What the hell is reality anyhow.' Laughlin had met Dr Muncie and Dr Overholser at the hearing. To Dr Muncie he had said in the lunchtime intermission that 'it was most interesting to him how the three of us who had testified up to that time, while approaching the problem at slightly different angles, arrived at the same answer'. Olson asked Laughlin 'how much the unfit plea had been planned', and 'JL allowed he had from the beginning [thought] the thing was to get P out of trial, the easiest way'.

From Laughlin's angle then, the hearing with its dubious realities had been a great success. Indeed, all concerned had reason to be pleased. Even Pound himself was very pleased with the verdict and grateful to Cornell for having saved his life, or so Laughlin told Eliot. The Justice Department was pleased to be able to file the case away without having to go to trial, and to be able to send their shaky witnesses back home to Italy. They had probably decided that if Pound 'wanted to go to St. Elizabeths, why shouldn't they let him go'—that way they couldn't lose. That at least was the opinion arrived at by Conrad L. Rushing, a Superior Court judge in California, when he reviewed the case in 1987. As for the Chief Justice, Rushing supposed that 'Common sense probably told Laws that with Pound's friends in high places, the death penalty was never probable. Commitment to St. Elizabeths, therefore, would serve the ends of justice and/or punishment.'

From another angle, however, that of Thomas S. Szasz, an expert in psychiatry and the law, it appeared that Pound's lawyer, the psychiatrists, 'and especially the persons instrumental in depriving him of the opportunity to clear his name in court', had together 'placed a blot on the pages of contemporary American history'. Cornell, instructed by Laughlin, had orchestrated and directed the entire proceedings, his leading of the psychiatrists, by his Affidavit and the other material he supplied them with, going far beyond what appeared in court. The psychiatrists had been too easily led by him into testifying to things about which they had no direct knowledge or expertise. Their joint diagnosis had no sound basis in psychiatry; and depended, moreover, upon the professionally and legally improper suppression of significant and highly relevant differences of opinion. The government's lawyers suspected, if they did not actually know, that pertinent evidence was being suppressed; and they suppressed evidence of their own. They knew that at least some of the things the Court had been told by the witnesses were not consistent with documents and evidence held by the Justice Department; and they knew from those documents that Pound did have both a perfectly clear understanding of the charge against him, and a reasonable and solid defence. Yet they chose not to produce this evidence, which would have discredited Cornell's Affidavit, undermined the psychiatrists' testimony, and compelled the judge to direct the jury very differently. Finally, there was Judge Laws, who helped the travesty of justice run its course. 'The moral insults showered on Pound were almost limitless,'

Szasz wrote in his review of Cornell's book. The pretence of concern for his mental health took away from him not only his right to a proper trial, with the opportunity to defend himself, as guaranteed by the Sixth Amendment, but would in time take away all his civil and moral rights except only the right to life.

On 27 February Laughlin wrote to Dr Overholser, 'It was a pleasure to meet you the other day in Washington and I want to tell you how impressed I was with what I suppose in a gentleman of your calling is referred to as his "courtroom manner".' The letter continued:

> I called upon Pound the morning after the hearing and was regaled with an account of his plans for rebuilding the Temple in Jerusalem. Coming from him, I found this sollicitude rather touching!
>
> He asked whether it would be possible for him to take his daily exercise in the yard which has grass in it, rather than in the concrete-floored yard, and I promised him that I would pass on this suggestion to you in a letter.
>
> I dare say you yourself have considered the possibility of moving him to a place on your campus where he might have less feeling of claustrophobia. I realize that as a prisoner he must be guarded, but I can't really conceive of his making an escape or doing anyone any hurt. Surely his recovery might be speeded by an environment which did not rub his nerves so much.
>
> I gather that a cure is pretty rare in a man of his age, but I would like to be able to send some sort of cheerful news to his wife and daughter in Italy. They are very much upset, as you can imagine. Their devotion to him was so great – and so blind – that I know it never occurred to them that his mental processes were abnormal.

That was as good as turning the key upon Overholser's prisoner.

Laughlin told Eliot that he was 'beginning to feel that the diagnosis of the doctors—"a paranoid state in a psychopathic personality"—may be medically correct'. This was because Pound had told him 'that he could not understand why the Jews wished to conspire to hang him since he had worked out a complete plan for rebuilding their old temple in Jerusalem'. Laughlin also mentioned that Pound was willing to have the world think him insane if it would let him live to go on with his work. And the publisher was most grateful to Eliot for agreeing 'to write an essay about EP's poetry for the special number of Poetry Magazine'—that would 'help so much in the publicity campaign to clear him of the stigma of the treason charge'.

When he called on Pound the morning after the hearing Laughlin left with him freshly typed copies of cantos 74–84. Olson visited that afternoon between 2.30 and 2.45, and when Pound came in he was carrying them and had 'his bounce back'. 'The sense, the whole sense of this meeting was Pound in power, anew. Flushed with his return to work. Full of plans to get on with new things, now that his fate was settled for a while.' Having his fate settled—with the illusory promise that he would soon be out—may well have helped. But surely it was being back in touch with those cantos that was empowering. There was his reality, the sure ground for his mind. When he wrote from Howard Hall to Dorothy a week after the hearing, 'I long for Pisan paradise', he must have been thinking of it as the time in which he had composed the Pisan cantos and translated Confucius, a time in which his mind was free to work and create at full power and intensity.

Cornell now began to let out what he must have known all along, that it was not in his power to get Pound out of St Elizabeths. Writing to A. V. Moore to report the outcome of the hearing, he told him that 'the doctors appear to be agreed that the possibility is very remote that Mr. Pound will ever be able to stand trial'. While to his family and friends he might seem normal, 'the abnormalities which the doctors found in Mr. Pound's mental processes . . . are deep rooted', and Cornell himself thought that there was unlikely to be 'any considerable change in the future'. Now the statute under which he had been committed to St Elizabeths provided that if he should ever recover and be found fit to stand trial then he should be returned to the jurisdiction of the Court and be tried; and Cornell was sure that for that reason the government would never agree to dismiss the indictment. However, the statute made no provision for the possibility that a person under indictment might be permanently unable to stand trial and yet not require permanent hospitalization. It did not 'expressly prohibit the discharge' of a person so placed, but it would be difficult to persuade any judge to order his discharge since the statute did not authorize it, and there was no precedent for it. Cornell spelt out the consequence: 'Although he still would be presumed innocent under the law, he would be incarcerated indefinitely, possibly for life, because the government had obtained an indictment against him.'

That stated very precisely the predicament in which Pound now found himself, thanks to Cornell. However, Cornell went on to say, he felt confident that Pound's 'constitutional rights would thereby be violated', and that his release could be secured by a writ of habeas corpus. He advised that 'after the expiration of several months' Dr Overholser, and possibly other psychiatrists, be asked if they were 'then of the opinion that Mr. Pound will never be able to stand trial and also that he does not require hospital treatment', and, if they were of that opinion, an application should be made for a writ of habeas corpus. The government would resist, and without the consent of the government a trial judge would probably refuse, there being no precedent. The case, just because it was novel, should then be appealed to the higher courts—and Cornell, as a civil liberties lawyer, evidently relished the prospect of attempting to set a precedent. 'I think the expense of an appeal would be well worth while', he advised Mrs Pound's solicitor, 'since the prospects for gaining complete freedom would be favorable'. There he was letting himself be carried beyond the reality again, since a writ of habeas corpus would neither lift the indictment nor free Pound from the power of the Department of Justice. In the event, Cornell would not obtain his writ, and Dr Overholser would readily certify whenever applied to that Pound had not and never would recover and must remain permanently under his care.

The friends and enemies

There was a moment when Charles Olson, after one of his visits, felt provoked into declaring, 'I stand for keeping him in custody.' This was not because of the alleged treason, nor yet the supposed insanity. Pound had approved of something he had just read by Westbrook Pegler, a widely syndicated political columnist of the paranoid variety. Pegler had been a fierce critic of Roosevelt, whom Olson loyally admired, but also came out strongly against both Communism and Fascism. Yet Olson ranted against his 'fascism', and, by association, Pound's. Evidently the word no longer had any meaningful connection with Italian Fascism, having become simply a term of generalized abuse for 'right wing' opinion. But that Olson, a 'left wing' democrat, could stand up for keeping a man in custody because of his opinions was a striking deviation from a basic principle of American democracy and justice. He was far from alone in that.

Back in the fall, in anticipation of Pound's expected trial, Charles Norman had invited a number of poets and critics to 'size up Pound as an artist and as a man', and then published half a dozen of the responses in *PM* on Sunday 25 November, two days before the formal indictment, under the heading 'The case for and against Ezra Pound'. His poets and critics were Cummings, William Carlos Williams, Karl Shapiro, then an emerging poet, F. O. Matthiessen, the distinguished Harvard literary historian, the anthologist Louis Untermeyer, and Conrad Aiken. In reprints of the piece Louis Zukofsky appeared in place of Shapiro. There was a general consensus among these poets and critics that 'the case for' Pound was that his importance as a poet and as a creative influence upon modern poetry should not be forgotten; and that 'the case against' was that his objectionable opinions should not be forgiven.

Only Matthiessen seemed to have a clear idea of what those opinions were. That is, he did at least notice that Pound believed 'control of money to be the central issue for any society', before stating his view that his 'radio broadcasts before and after our entry into the war, vicious as they were in their anti-Semitism, could [not] have had any ponderable force as propaganda'. Nevertheless, he went on, 'the poet must be judged for the humanity of his thought as well as for his form. And if you believe in the artist's responsibility for his views, I don't see how you can explain Pound's away.' Very oddly, Matthiessen then did exactly that, accounting for his 'eccentric' political and social theory by his 'Living for so many years as an isolated expatriate in Rapallo', and concluding that it was 'As an eccentric he must now be judged'. It was not clear whether he meant, as his argument could be taken to mean in the context of the then imminent trial, that Pound could be found guilty of treason because he held eccentric views.

Karl Shapiro did mean that. 'Pound thought fascism superior to democracy,' he declared in a generalization which grossly falsified what Pound did think, and 'As a U.S. citizen he committed the crime of not reversing his beliefs after Mussolini came to blows with Jefferson.' That was to find him guilty of thought crime. And in a note to Norman, Shapiro wrote, 'I hope very much that nothing serious happens to Pound—just as I hope that somehow he will be made to pay for his idiocy.' Conrad Aiken also seemed to think that Pound, although 'more a fool than a traitor', should nonetheless take the consequences of his beliefs, i.e. 'finding himself under charge of treason'. Aiken improved the occasion by adding to his statement a protest against the banning of Pound's poems from an anthology he edited. The publisher, Saxe Commins, was saying, 'Random House is not going to publish any fascist', and Aiken was maintaining that 'a burning of the books was a kind of intellectual and moral suicide we might more wisely leave to our enemies'. That was nobly said, but it is strange that it did not occur to him that to charge Pound with treason because of his beliefs was equivalent to book burning.

Cummings alone, upholding the First Amendment in his individual way, saw freedom of thought and expression as a responsibility and a duty. 'Every artist's strictly illimitable country is himself', he wrote, 'An artist who plays that country false has committed suicide... But a human being who's true to himself—whoever himself may be—is immortal.' Pound would tell Cummings that because of this double-edged affirmation he was 'the one bright star'.

Norman's other contributors all accepted, on the Sunday before the indictment was made public, some of them implicitly and some explicitly, that Pound should be punished for his ideas. Louis Untermeyer wrote, 'I do not believe he should be shot. I would favour merely life imprisonment in a cell surrounded by books—all of them copies of the works of Edgar A. Guest.' Even his old friend William Carlos Williams, while suggesting that 'It would be the greatest miscarriage of justice, human justice, to shoot him', could only hope that, 'When they lock the man up', he would be allowed access 'to books, with paper enough for him to go on making translations for us from the classics such as we have never seen except at his hands in our language'.

Williams was in no doubt that Pound had wilfully committed crime, but his idea of the crime had less to do with the immediate indictment than with personal grudges and grievances going back over thirty years, these reinforced by some new disgusts. He confessed that he had 'never heard a word that Ezra Pound broadcast during the war from Italy', but, going by 'a single sentence referring to myself' which he had been told about, he judged them to have been 'dull stuff'. What disturbed him more was Pound's 'vicious anti-Semitism and much else [that] have lowered him in my mind further than I ever thought it possible to lower a man whom I had once admired'. As instances of the 'much else' he cited two out of context sentences from private letters from Pound. 'But that isn't the whole story,' Williams wrote, and proceeded to lay out what he really held against Pound: 'He always felt himself superior to anyone about him and would never brook a rival'—'He just lived on a different plane from anyone else in the world, a higher plane!'—'always insisted on the brilliance and profundity of his mind'. And all that was 'the thing that finally ruined Ezra', in Williams's judgment, 'He doesn't have a great mind and never did,' and 'His stupidities coupled with his overweening self-esteem have brought him down.' Along with this will to pull down Pound's vanity, if not to kill him off, there was the old quarrel between Williams's Americanism, and Pound's expatriate internationalism which made him 'one of a well recognized group of Americans who can't take the democratic virus'. And for that too Williams would have Pound locked up 'with Jim and John and Henry and Mary and Dolores'. Altogether, the right to freedom of mind, and the right to freedom of person until duly charged and found guilty of an indictable offence, had become recessive genes in Williams's democratic virus.

Norman had invited T. S. Eliot to contribute to his 'for and against' symposium, and Eliot had objected that his way of framing the question seemed 'to assume that Pound is guilty of whatever charges are laid against him'. He went on to deliver a much needed call to order:

> You make this assumption not only before the trial has taken place, and judgment given; you make it before the precise charge has been formulated, before we have heard the evidence for the prosecution, and before we have heard the evidence for the defence. I do not know what Pound was doing in Italy, from 1941 to 1945;

I do not know what he said in his broadcasts; and before I form any judgment I wish to hear what his counsel will say in explanation.

'It seems to me', he remarked pertinently, 'that many people in America have been far too ready to presume his "guilt".' Norman did not print Eliot's letter.

Wallace Stevens was another who preferred not to take part in Norman's symposium. 'It seems to me', he wrote, 'that since Pound's liberty, not to say even his life, may be at stake, he ought to be consulted about this sort of thing.' Stevens seems to have been exceptional in showing that kind of respect for Pound. He also asked, very pertinently though in vain, 'Don't you think it worthwhile waiting until you know why he did what he did before rallying to his defense?' In any case, while 'There are a number of things that could well be said in his defense... each one of these things is so very debatable, that one would not care to say them, without having thought them out most carefully'—

One such possibility is that the acts of propagandists should not entail the same consequences as the acts of a spy or informer because noone attaches really serious importance to propaganda.

Stevens was thoughtful and clear again where Norman's leading question had involved some of his contributors in trying to weigh Pound's importance as a poet against his indictment. 'I must say that I don't consider the fact that he is a man of genius as an excuse,' he wrote. 'Surely such men are subject to the common disciplines.' Altogether, Stevens had the uncommon distinction in the case of thinking about doing justice to the person, something that most other poets and critics were lamentably failing to do.

Louis Zukofsky's contribution, which reached Norman too late to appear in *PM*, was another exception. He recorded his having said to Pound in 1939 that he 'did not doubt his integrity had decided his political action', but that 'something had gone wrong' in his head. At the same time, he now said, Pound's 'profound and intimate knowledge and practice' of literature and music 'still leave that part of his mind entire'. Zukofsky did not attempt to set that part off against whatever had gone wrong. But he did address the issue which coloured all discussion of Pound's situation, declaring, 'I never felt the least trace of anti-Semitism in his presence'. Nevertheless he concluded with this cryptic statement, 'He may be condemned or forgiven... It will matter very little against his finest work overshadowed in his lifetime by the hell of Belsen which he overlooked.' Pound could not have seen the newsreels showing the horrors of Belsen after it was liberated on 15 April 1945, but Zukofsky was probably not speaking literally. More likely he had in mind Pound's blindness to the calculated evil of Nazism, and specifically its murdering anti-Semitism. But he drew no conclusion from that as to what should be done with Pound then and there. He was making 'a dissociation of values', not passing sentence.

Zukofsky was probably aware that the more active hostility towards Pound was concerned, as Laughlin had always expected, with his anti-Semitism, or his 'fascism'—the two often deliberately confused—rather than with the alleged treason. These attackers did not hesitate to find him guilty, without need of trial or examination of evidence, and to demand his death. The Communist paper *New Masses* responded to Norman's symposium with one of its own in the issue for 25 December 1945, with the heading featured on the front cover, 'SHOULD EZRA POUND BE SHOT?'—a rhetorical question, as a line underneath made clear, '*Five writers indict him as traitor. A reply to his apologists in PM*'. Norman Rosten, a poet, wrote:

> Mr. Pound joined the war. He became a fascist hireling. He contributed to the murder of the innocent... He was the poets' representative and he cheapened us, degraded us. Because he was a poet his crime is millionfold. Because he is a traitor he should be shot.

Albert Maltz, a Hollywood screenwriter later blacklisted by the studios for refusing to testify before the House Un-American Activities Committee, wrote with even more passionate disregard for truth and justice as he called for Pound to be executed 'by the will of the people of the United States':

> When a man becomes the enemy of Man—when a poet stoops to the vile wolfishness of racial hatred—when a poet who inherits the humanitarian culture of the ages, betrays his heritage and his talent to fascist thieves, sadists and murderers—then what is he? He is unspeakable—he is carrion...
>
> Do I sound savage? Yes—I remember the corpses of Buchenwald, Dachau, Maidanek. Who dares forget them?

Arthur Miller, who would complain in his autobiography about the lack of 'delicate nuances' in his interrogation by the House Un-American Activities Committee, wrote,

> I used to listen, now and then, to Ezra Pound sending from Europe, and... in his wildest moments of human vilification Hitler never approached our Ezra... His stuff was straight fascism with all the anti-Semitism, anti-foreignism, included.

'Hitler never approached our Ezra'? That wildest of exaggerations, one gathers from Miller's autobiography, was based on his having in fact heard just one broadcast, but that one had been enough to convince him that 'Pound had been calling for racial murder and ... would have happily killed me as a Jew if he could have.' There is no record of a broadcast in which Pound was 'calling for racial murder'; nor is there any warrant in the broadcasts, even at their worst, for Miller's 'would have happily killed me as a Jew if he could have'. But this was a self-dramatizing inversion of the actual situation. It was not Miller who was being threatened with death in December 1945, it was Ezra Pound; and it was Miller who would have happily had him killed. He was certain that Pound was a traitor, since he had broadcast, Miller asserted without regard for the truth, 'month after month to demoralize American troops fighting in Germany and Italy'; but it was the anti-Semitism, he made clear, that was the deeper reason for his unqualified condemnation. With Rosten and Maltz, Miller would have had Pound shot, ostensibly for his alleged treason, but really for his anti-Semitism.

'The mob is blood-hungry for victims,' Laughlin wrote to Olga Rudge, 'Had he been brought to trial now, there is not a chance in the world ... but they would have hung him ... there is nothing the little band of powerless intellectuals can do about it.' Certainly, the general assumption, in the media and among both his little band of intellectuals and the general public, appears to have been that Pound was guilty of treason, or that he would at least be found guilty. The only question was, should he be executed, or not? A *Washington Post* editorial suggested that Pound was never 'important or dangerous enough to make it really necessary to exact the price of his treason in blood'. But there was the other view, and not only in *New Masses*. A group of New York citizens, in a letter to President Truman, claimed that Pound had 'assisted the perpetrators of the slaughter chambers' and should 'suffer the same sentence meted out by the English people to traitors Amery and Lord Haw-Haw'. The Lord Haw-Haw case was frequently invoked, both by those who wanted Pound executed and by those who on the whole did not, as if it were the relevant precedent. But the United States had its own tradition of treason law and its own precedent in the Cramer case, and its government tended to take pride in doing things its own way and maintaining its independence from Great Britain. As for Laughlin's implicit claim to have saved Pound from a lynch-mob, that, even given some casualness about the law in the Chief Justice's court, was surely over-dramatizing the situation.[8]

[8] The fates of the seven others indicted on treason charges with Pound, all for broadcasting for Nazi Germany during the war, were various—none were executed, and three had their charges dismissed for lack of evidence in light of the Cramer case: Douglas Chandler was sentenced in Boston in 1947 to life imprisonment with a fine of $10,000—sentence commuted in 1963 on condition he leave the United

Much of the discussion of the Pound case, not least among those who should have cared more for going by the truth, the whole truth, and nothing but the truth, was, like that claim of Laughlin's, hypothetical, speculative, and prejudicial; and it was, moreover, either ignorant of the law and of the facts of the case, or it deliberately disregarded the law and the facts. The Justice Department was almost alone in making an effort to discover what Pound had actually said and done, and in recognizing that the case against him had to be proved in court before he could be declared guilty of treason. And it was almost alone in recognizing that he must be found guilty or innocent as charged in the indictment, and not upon any other ground. It seems to have been alone also in not presuming that he would be found guilty, in allowing that he might have a valid defence, or at least that the case against him might fail. But if the Department of Justice upheld the law so far, it nonetheless allowed Cornell's, and Laughlin's, perverse defence to prevail, thus denying Pound justice.

By the time of Pound's death Archibald MacLeish had come round to the view that Pound should never have been charged with treason in the first place, 'given the guarantee of freedom of speech in the First Amendment'—

> his indictment by the Department of Justice was an error of law and his attorney's plea of insanity an error in tactics and his incarceration in St Elizabeths a miscarriage of justice...

Pound was no more a traitor, MacLeish wrote, than the former Attorney General of the United States who, towards the end of the Vietnam War, 'did in Hanoi precisely what Ezra Pound had done in Rome', that is, 'He attacked the policy and conduct of his own country in the capital of a country with which the United States was at war.' Yet he was not indicted nor arrested,

> for the good and sufficient reason that the right to dissent, the right to criticize, had by then been exercised in time of war by so large a majority of the American people that if wartime criticism was treason, the Republic itself would have had to be indicted.

States; Robert H. Best sentenced in Boston in 1948 to life imprisonment with a fine of $10,000—died in federal custody in 1952; Jane Anderson, never arrested, charges dismissed in 1947 for lack of evidence in light of the Cramer case; Edward L. Delaney captured in Czechoslovakia in 1945, released, rearrested in 1947, but charges dropped for lack of evidence in light of the Cramer case; Constance Drexel, never arrested, charges dismissed in 1948 for lack of evidence in light of the Cramer case, died in Waterbury, Conn., 1956; Max Koischwitz died in Berlin in 1944, case dropped; Frederick W. Kaltenbach, called the American Lord Haw-Haw, reportedly died in a Russian prison, case dropped.

The US Supreme Court had firmly restated the principle of the First Amendment in 1949:

> The vitality of civil and political institutions in our society depends on free discussion... Speech is often provocative and challenging. It may strike at prejudices and preconceptions and have profound unsettling effects as it presses for acceptance of an idea. That is why freedom of speech, though not absolute... is nevertheless protected against censorship or punishment, unless shown likely to produce a clear and present danger of a serious substantive evil that rises far above public inconvenience, annoyance, or unrest.... There is no room under our Constitution for a more restrictive view.

So MacLeish could tell Torrey, 'Some of us thought Ezra's lawyer should have tried the case on the freedom of speech issue.' But that is what Pound had wanted all along. He had written to the Attorney General when first indicted, 'Free speech under modern conditions becomes a mockery if it does not include the right of free speech over the radio'; he had repeated that to the FBI in Genoa, and had said it again at the beginning of his *Pisan Cantos*, 'free speech without radio free speech is as zero'. But in 1945 and 1946 few were in the mood to privilege freedom of speech, and in consequence Pound was made to suffer the error of law, the error in tactics, and the lasting miscarriage of justice.

Note: on not understanding the charge

It is still being repeated as a simple truth that Pound could not be tried because he did not understand and never would be able to understand the nature of the charges against him. It is true that this was the opinion delivered to the Court by the four psychiatrists appearing as expert witnesses, that it was accepted by the Court, and that it was never effectively challenged. It is clear, however, from the transcript of the hearing that what Pound did not and would not understand was that he was guilty as charged, which is absolutely not the same as being not able to understand the charge. The demand being put upon him by those psychiatrists was that he agree with their simple view that he had committed treason—that was what they meant by 'understanding the nature of the charges'. In effect they declared him insane because he would not admit that he was guilty, an opinion worthy of Stalinist justice.

PART FOUR : ST ELIZABETHS, 1946–1958

Ne cede Malis
(Yield not to misfortune.)
—Loomis family motto

Though nothing happens that is not due to destiny,
one accepts willingly only what is one's proper
destiny . . . It is never anyone's proper destiny
to die in fetters.
—Mencius VII.A.2

What perversities you cultivated
could never match
those pitted now against you
—Ramon Guthrie, 'Ezra Pound in Paris &
Elsewhere'

10 : A Year in the Hell Hole

What the hell is reality anyhow
—J. Laughlin

Awareness restful & fake is fatiguing
—85/558

In the hot summer of 1946 a young orderly from another part of St Elizabeths seized a chance to look through the peephole at Ezra Pound in his Howard Hall cell. Once he saw him lying down, 'apparently napping'. Another time he saw him 'standing looking out the window... dressed in a hospital gown... trousers, and an institutional bathrobe'. Pound was 'pallid looking, ruffled hair and scruffy unshaven face', but this was unremarkable—inmates everywhere in St Elizabeths looked like that.

One of the attendants in Howard Hall reported that 'the patient spends most of his time writing'; and Dr Taub wrote in his report in April that 'On the ward'—that was Howard Hall's Ward 6—'this examiner usually finds the patient busily writing and in an apparently cheerful mood'. Dr Cruvant, however, noted in August that

> The ward personnel is impressed with Mr. Pound's erudition only that he spends most of his time complaining lying around on the bed, keeping it messed up and his room all cluttered with books and magazines 'all over the place'.

Dr James, in October, entered a more tolerant report:

> On the ward the patient spends the greater part of the time lounging around, rarely does any work, is very cheerful and cooperative with other patients and employees. He evidently has made a fairly good adjustment.

But Dr Cruvant expected more. 'On the ward he cooperates fairly well', he had noted in May, 'although taking little or no interest in his associates and does not participate in any of the activities of the ward.' Then in August, after noting the ward personnel's report that 'he does no work but he eats and sleeps well', he entered into the record the surreal remark that 'The examiner is too polite in general to call Mr. Pounds attention to this discrepancy in communal living and mutual obligation.' It was no doubt a fine idea, that in the maximum security ward for the criminally and violently insane one should behave as in a civilized community, but it was an idea likely to strike the sane inmate struggling to keep his individual mind and world together as unreal, if not plain mad.

Dr Taub had noted in April that 'During the pleasant days, Mr. Pound spends the time outdoors with other patients', usually stretching out 'in the shade on some blankets and a large rubber sheet which he carries around'. This was by command, not from choice. 'Only present affliction is being pried off my sord bed & made to lie on earth 2-5 hrs daily', he had told Olga Rudge in March, 'sposed to be hygenic . maybe it is . been given rubber sheet and quilt to intervene between me & the ground.' Again Dr Cruvant wanted him to be more communal. 'He spends the major portion of his time lying on a rather choice bit of ground in the outer courtyard of the Hall', he noted primly on 9 May, 'but is unhappy, today, because he was recently moved from his particular spot to be closer to the other patients.'

Most months the patient was formally examined by one or another of St Elizabeths young psychiatrists in order to 'monitor his progress'. None thought him insane, but all reported a fixed pattern of behaviour persisting through the course of the year. He would present himself as suffering from extreme fatigue, yet would then become animated and excited, as Dr Stevens reported on 31 March:—

This patient has been interviewed on several occasions throughout the month, most of the sessions beginning with a complaint of fatigue which Mr. Pound accompanied by histrionic gestures designed to emphasize his alleged state of complete exhaustion. As the interview proceeded, he ignored his obviously feigned infirmities, becomes quite animated in his conversation, bangs the desk, jumps up, raises his voice, becomes flushed and displays evidence of energy, the interview often lasting an hour.

Dr Taub gave a more dramatic description of a similar scenario in April—

When interviewed today he was called from outdoors. He came into the examining room wearing an Army coat, which still had Army buttons and was carrying two blankets and the large rubber sheet on which he stretches outdoors. He stomped hurriedly into the room, dropped his blankets and sheeting on a chair, quickly grabbed another chair, pulled it up to the desk and with an equally accelerated speed sat down and propped his feet on the desk. After that he leaned back on his chair and dramatically displayed a picture of complete and utter exhaustion.

During most of the interview he appeared so exhausted. Some statements are uttered in low tones and with sighing gasps as though they were a man's last words. On one occasion, however, when the question of publishers was innocently mentioned by the examiner in the course of conversation the patient suddenly became excited and bolted upright from his relaxed position.

Dr Cruvant noted the same behaviour in May: the agile bouncing into the examination room, the assumption of attitudes of extreme prostration and fatigue, 'with dramatic display and many histrionic gestures', then the becoming animated and forgetting for a while 'his pose of fatigue'. In October the performance took a further turn. On entering the room 'in a rather rapid manner' he saw a bed 'and immediately lay down', Dr James recorded. He gathered that 'The patient experiences difficulty in remaining upright more than a period of a few minutes, and is continually looking for a place to lie down. He feels this relieves his fatigue to a certain extent.' Nevertheless, 'at times the patient became extremely riled . . . and would then sit upright, raise his voice, and pound his fists'. 'Physically,' he noted, 'the patient appears to be in excellent condition.'

Dr Gilbert had told the Court that Pound's complaining of unusual fatigue and exhaustion was a leading symptom of his paranoid state, but these St Elizabeths doctors appeared to draw from it no conclusion at all about his state of mind. They were sure he was putting it on, faking it, and seem never to have considered that it might be both histrionic and the projection of a genuine reaction to his situation. They simply observed what could be observed in his behaviour, impersonally, though not without prejudice. Dr Taub had noted, 'he shows a general reluctance to answer questions or discuss any other problems [apart from his exhaustion]', and says '"you young men can't understand"'. Dr Stevens had quizzed him about 'his scurrilous and anti-Semitic broadcasts in Italy'—he had reviewed the copies of the broadcasts given to St Elizabeths by the Justice Department—and Pound had said he could not remember. Stevens then asked him if he wished to stand trial, but Pound 'effected an elaborate caricature of fatigue, and the interview had to be terminated'. Dr Cruvant insisted on leading Pound 'into some discussion of his economic and political theories', in spite of 'his protestations of the intense fatigue which it causes him', and then reported complacently that he could see little truth in the theories and that 'as a propagandist Mr. Pound leaves me quite cold'. On another occasion Cruvant asked the poet 'why he did not at some time write material for purely popular consumption as a sort of "Potboiler" to bring in some money'.

In general the psychiatrists' idea of examining Pound seems to have been to interrogate him as from the criminal charge-sheet rather than as a patient. Nowhere in their notes is any consideration given to the possibility of his being in need of treatment. And it seems not to have crossed their minds that, beyond being a put-on show of his weariness at their blank incomprehension of what drove him, his fatigue could be a genuine symptom of demoralization and breakdown. Dr Mitchell recorded that 'He feels burned out . . . feels a long way from his former self', as indeed he must have been to be behaving as he was. But the doctor noted the statement quite objectively, as simply what Pound had said to him, not as an indication that he might be really in a bad way.

Their implicit assumption all along was that he was sane and that there was nothing actually wrong with him. Dr Stevens noted, at the end of March, that 'while he may be obscure [in his speech and writing] he is never disconnected or irrelevant'. He then set down what amounted to a direct refutation of the expert opinion accepted by the Court:

> He is in complete contact with his surroundings, and apparently appreciates his predicament. Intellectual processes are well integrated, and his genius is quite apparent. No abnormal mental content is elicitable, and there has been no evidence of hallucinations, delusions, ideas of reference, or ideas of alien control. His views on economics, and especially on money, are unorthodox, but logical and coherent.

Dr James, in his October notes, remarked that apart from his wanting to lie down 'the patient gave no evidence of other abnormal mental states'. And Dr Cruvant, while confessing to his 'great difficulty in following Mr. Pounds reasoning' and making it plain that he did not take to him at all, showed no inclination to put him down as a mental case. All six psychiatrists who examined Pound during his year in Howard Hall—the sixth was Dr Kavka—dealt with him as a person of sane mind. Yet not one of them reflected in their clinical notes on what it might do to the mind of a sane man who believed himself innocent to be incarcerated among the criminally insane.

The letters Pound was writing might be expected to reveal his states of mind less opaquely than the doctors' notes, but the fact is that he was acutely aware that 'anything he wrote or sent out of St Elizabeths is inspected by ignorant interns', so that even in his letters he would have been conscious of their gaze upon him. When he told Ronald Duncan, 'you [can] hv no idea of my present fragmentary state', or told another correspondent 'I can't hold two sides of an idea together', or told a third, that he was 'in serious breakdown', was he telling the simple truth, or was he exaggerating for 'the ignorant interns'? Certainly his statement to Williams near the end of April, 'My Main spring is busted . . . I can not make ANY effort mental or physical', was just what he wanted the doctors to believe; but then he immediately contradicted himself by writing, 'I was trying to tell you how to combat the evil that Eliot has (unintentionally) done & does', a carefully weighed sentence showing that his mind was still in fair working order. 'IF the goddam mind flows O. K.', he admitted, 'but if not, NOT & nowt to do about it.'

He understood his condition well enough to point Olga Rudge towards a more perceptive account than anything in the doctors' notes. On 23 March he began his letter to her in the same vein as that letter to Williams: 'she write him simple things like that she went up & down the salita... but nowt needing thought, opinion, judgement'. He wanted a regular diary of things 'I don't have to work on'. Then, as if to explain this uncharacteristic lethargy, he wrote,

She see Tietjens in Fordie's 'Some do not'... loss of memory
& in, I think, Shakleton, in the little white Ogden series -- adrenal exhaustion case in Canadian forest—
help for her also . applicable to both of us . I think.

'Adrenal exhaustion', due to sustained anxiety and stress, offered a credible diagnosis of his physical state, and Olga would have known all about that and understood it at once. But when she recalled or looked into Ford's *Some Do Not*, the first novel in his tetralogy *Parade's End*, she would have realized that in Tietjens Ford was delineating not just a loss of memory but the split-level workings of a mind under prolonged strain. Shell-shock has knocked out Tietjens's formerly encyclopedic memory, and he is having to face 'death, love, public dishonour', 'all these things coming upon him cumulatively and rather suddenly', with two-thirds of his brain in shock. Nonetheless, he is still able to use 'what brain he had as trenchantly as ever', and Ford manages brilliantly to create a mind at once traumatized, even shattered, yet still able to articulate responses to 'death, love, public dishonor' that are fully in character. Pound, who had just re-read and been deeply impressed by *Some Do Not*, could well have identified with Tietjens's predicament, and felt that Ford's creative insight into a mind under great stress was of more use to him than his sessions with the psychiatrists.

The immediate source of stress was his being just another inmate in Howard Hall. 'My status is that of a bulot, a packet,' he complained to Olga, '& I don't know what J.C.[Cornell] is up to . and cdnt/DO anything about it anyhow.' One reflex was to blame himself: 'I suffer for solitude inflicted thoughtlessly on you @ Sirmione 20 years ago. etc.'—that was when she was waiting out her time to give birth to Mary—'Everything Anyone does falls on THEM in the end.... No one dodges . & Karma works.' He didn't go on about that, nor did he go on much about the pains of the place. 'Basso inferno', he called his ward in one letter to Mary, but let her know at the same time that there had been sausage for lunch and that the diet was 'abundant, dull, but, I believe, healthy'. 'I eat wot I get with a spoon – last saw k. & f. in Bermudah', this in passing to his old friend Viola Baxter Jordan after a reminiscence of Mouquins, a favourite restaurant in New York. To Olga the musician he mentioned as an item in the 'local bulletin' that someone in the hall was picking out 'The wearing o' the green' with one finger—'program runs to Loch Lomond, & Jerusalem the Golden', all painfully with one finger. Another letter suggested how heavily time weighed there—

> Today red letter in that am hand-kuffed to be taken to dental bld.—perfectly comfortable wide leather cuffs . do not cause nervousness after 1st time. NOT that am supposed violent but patients are continually beating up guards & guards therefore prefer etc. (when prisoners tempted by sight of wide open spaces).... pleasant ride to dental in station wagon—back in vulgar bus . small things make a day.

'One of the worst things is not being able to get out into the open air when one wants to', he would write later, and the 'Other worst thing when in the hell hole, IF one had lived between sea and hills, is to have no horizon, nothing but a blank wall 30 or 40 feet off'. He told Dorothy that from one window there was a 'view of Potomac sunset – flat, dull as Main @ Francoforte', and that if he stood on his own window sill he could see another bit of the Potomac. It made him 'long for Pisan paradise'. Just being let out of the courtyard into the 'dry moat of the dungeon' made him feel better, healthy. But he needed most to get his mind out of the prison altogether, 'to pierce the wall', 'to think of some world outside these walls', 'any means... to git my MIND out of here, even if carcass remains vinculated'. Visits, as from Olson and Mencken, served, even though restricted to fifteen minutes. But letters had to be his main resource. 'I like to get letters', he assured Wyndham Lewis, 'seul plaisir etc / of the jugged'. And to D. D. Paige, 'Gtst difficulty is to get people to write me enough letters to keep me aware of life outside the walls'. It was a place, he would say, for news to come into, not go out of.

At times his mind homed to Olga's Sant'Ambrogio. 'Keep St Amb. @ all costs', he urged her a fortnight into his indefinite commitment to St Elizabeths, 'even if they stole everything'—Casa 60 had been burgled twice—'There wd still be the house... Where wd I go if I ever got out.' A month later he assured her, 'yes if he had the wings of a sucking dove he wd. to S. Amb.—@ least sposin' they wd carry that far . loose or crated.' He was more grounded, and more nostalgic, in a letter to Mary:—

Dearest Child. / Casa 60 is holy ground . but I don't want you to leave Olga alone there – nor her chained there by Treasure real or supposed –

all I have left, the birds
answering fiddle, & her between
me & window & view of the bay

Still the desire persisted. Though 'I have no say in anything', he wrote to Olga in April, 'I know where I shd go if LET—as per earlier notes—to S. Amb.' One earlier note had read, 'He would like to see the salita & walk on it. He dont know anything much else he wants to walk on except the Zattere & Piaz S. Marco or the rue de la Paix etc.' That note had broken off, '& it is no use his projectin', and in another he had warned himself, 'he better not think about any thing nearer 'n the Confucian anthology'. But 'if LET', his mind would fly to Sant' Ambrogio.

In one of his letters to Olga, after asking for her news and Mary's and saying 'he lives on letters', he thought to add, 'and he wd like to see her'. He did not mean that he would like to see her in St Elizabeths, even less for her to see him as he was in there. When she wrote about getting herself across to America he exploded in fury, 'God Damn,—to talk 15 minutes in a corridor?!!' She should 'stop writing bilge about coming here and use what brains god has left you to get me OUT of here—HELL . . . '. Olga said she didn't understand his putting her off, and he raged at her, 'SHE damn well not set foot in this country. . . . six weeks wd/ kill her . . . It is no place for her'—

No—when a man is down a well-hole you dont help by jumpin in on top of him = Got all I can stand without worryin about what she wd/ be sufferin' from absolute incomprehensibility if she got here.

Nothing to live on for anyone with less than $5000 a year. & hatred for any activity save pillage.

'If there is ever a reason for her to come', he assured her more mildly, 'he will say so subito.' Otherwise she should remain well clear of America, and get him out of it and back to civilization—that was where he would be very pleased to see her.

He did not feel the same way about Dorothy getting herself to Washington and remaining there. She had declared her firm intention of doing that already in December 1945, in a letter which he may have received only in February—

I am quite intent on getting over to be with you. Its just silly, my living this life, & so dam far away from you. I must see you & be near you . . . Please get it into yr. head that I'm coming over as soon as I can. (when that will be . . . ?)

In the event it would be six months before she could secure a berth, and in that interval Pound neither discouraged nor welcomed her coming. 'I don't know how you can get transport—perhaps via England?', that was the extent of his reaction. He asked again, 'Wd you go via England?', probably with a view to who she might see and what she might do there for him. He would tell Mary, when Dorothy had been with him for a decade, 'D.P. a blessing because she does what she is told.' 'D. attendin to practical', was how he put it to his mother in May 1947.

He either did not notice or didn't mind that Dorothy had her own agenda, though it was plain to see. She was being venomous about Olga, and patronizing about Mary, while constantly praising Omar as a worthy and devoted son 'full of filial piety' towards her and towards his 'Dad'. She wanted them to be together as a family, just Ezra, Omar, and herself. And she meant to reclaim Pound as her own. In April she sent him a poem about her heart 'hammering with terror', and going down 'Until I touched bottom', then

The god has passed.
Because of your manhood
I am enriched with
'happiness for ever & ever'
So there be peace between us
And a new serenity.

Pound's only response was, 'Hope she hit bottom & is startin to rise'. He did take a sympathetic interest in Omar at her prompting, advising how he should read and what he should study, and suggesting ways in which he could make himself useful. He let pass the snide remarks about Olga and the disparaging remarks about Mary. And he said nothing about Dorothy's harping on about how she couldn't stand 'that perpetual mosquito yr. Ma'.

Dorothy was still living with Isabel Pound in her Villa Raggio apartment, but was arranging for her to move to a room in their old roof-top apartment up all the stairs in via Marsala, 'with Sig^{a} Corradi to look after her'. In her December letter telling Pound she intended getting over to be with him, she also wrote that Isabel

has always said or taken for granted that I was going to lug her along: but myself is all I can manage: & she hasn't enough to live on in the States + the fare. This time

I am just ignoring it—& coming—alone. She's much too weak in body and head now.

Isabel, actually quite clear-headed though physically frail, 'wanted at all costs to go to America', and stubbornly went on trying to gain access to her frozen funds to pay for her passage. When she fell and broke her hip in May Dorothy had her carried to the hospital, then wrote to Pound,

> 'its an ill wind'... I am once more in my own Studio—since yesterday—& the Corradis take me on to feed instead of I.W.P. She didn't look like dying today—Everybody is visiting her—& Chute bringing her custard & wine.

Pound wrote to his mother, 'Very very sorry to hear of yr accident . Hope it isn't too painful. / Don't know what I can do . . . .'. When Dorothy sailed without her towards the end of June Isabel 'terminated the lease and tried to sell the furniture in Villa Raggio, in order to travel light', and was still hoping the following spring 'to have passage on next boat for U. S.'

On 18 June, about the time Dorothy was preparing to sail, Charles Olson spent twenty-five minutes with Pound in Howard Hall. 'He has such charm', he began his account of the visit, but then, evidently afraid of being disarmed by the charm, went on at some length about its seductions and dangers:—

> In itself, it is lovely, young, his maintaining of youth a rare thing. I do not know anyone who could be in a prison and stay as he: it was young of him [...] to remark to Griffin, the doctor, as we spoke to him when he went through the visiting room yesterday '... before I got myself into this mess'. As far as I can judge Pound acts within the walls much as he acted outside, the difference only of degree. Yet the Griffin incident also suggested the misuse of his charm which I feel has led Pound into snobbery, and the company of shits and fascists. It is clear he has Griffin pegged for the white trash he is. Yet he can traffic with him.

'You come to distrust the nice things he says,' Olson wound up, distancing himself upon that dubious ground, 'look upon all his conduct as a wheedling or a blackmail... and it's no good.' Yet, he confessed, he had enjoyed the conversation which ran on against the guard's wanting them to quit, 'For he is swift, and his wit is sure.' They had 'batted around the radio, the movies, the magazines, and national advertising, the 4 Plagues of our time', and 'It was a pleasure to listen to him... for he was talking out his direct impressions and actions, not going over into generalizations, so many of which or all of them become fascist and cliche.' Altogether, Olson's Pound as registered that day was far from being the exhausted prisoner of the psychiatrists' notes, as he would be far removed from the 'broken man' his wife would discover.

Dorothy sailed from Genoa on the 'S. S. Marine Carp' on 23 June and arrived in New York on Saturday 6 July. Laughlin met her and took her to his home in Norfolk, Connecticut, for the Sunday, where she picked up the galleys of Pound's translation of Confucius to give him on her first visit; and the Monday she 'spent mostly with Cornell' who handed her the transcripts of the doctors' testimony at the sanity hearing. She will have been well briefed in his and Laughlin's view of Pound's situation and prospects. On Tuesday she flew to Washington and was received there by Miss Mapel. The next day she was allowed a 'one hour special' visit with Pound—thereafter it would be just the regulation 15 minutes three days a week. She would rent the attic of a house at 3211 10th Place SE, and on visiting days would eat in the Red Cross canteen at St Elizabeths.

After her 15 minutes on the Thursday she wrote a note to Laughlin and another to A. V. Moore in London, saying that she had found EP well physically, but very nervous—'& no wonder'. Pound had said, 'if he can rest 23 hours, one hour is clear to him', and that 'his head is good on just one subject during 15 minutes'. Dorothy was letting him talk on the subject he had uppermost, 'yesty. Confucius. Today other matters. He seems clear on the subject he has arranged to talk about.' But 'EP himself says he'll never get better where he is in there'—his wish was to be 'got out into some kind of less prison-y sanatorium'. On 14 July Dorothy wrote to Laughlin again, 'Just seen Ezra today. He [is] certainly very jumpy & nervous. 15 minutes is maddening! He says, & I think he's right, he'll never get well in that place . . . I think EP is fairly ill . . .' She wrote to Cornell the same day, 'I believe his wits are really very scattered, and he has difficulty in concentrating even for a few minutes. . . . I do believe we must try to get Ezra out of that place.' She wanted Cornell to tell her 'What can be done as quickly as possible, in safety?'

Cornell replied at once that he was sure Pound 'would be much better off in a private sanatorium', however,

> I do not think that the present is an opportune time to make an application to the court for his removal. This could be done only by the granting of bail or the dismissal of the charges. I discussed this question with Mr. Eliot, Mr. Laughlin and others a few weeks ago and all were agreed that such an application should not be made at the present time because of public clamor which would arise in opposition.

In his opinion they should wait 'at least until the fall'—meaning until after the November mid-term elections—unless 'Dr Overholser could be persuaded to testify that the state of his health required removal to a private sanatorium'. He suggested that Dorothy 'try to see Dr. Overholser about this', and he would do the same 'within the next few weeks'.

Eliot, then approaching the zenith of his celebrity as an elder of letters, had been in America since early June, visiting his family, attending to publishing matters, and giving crowded out public lectures and readings. He was 'very anxious to hold a council of strategy of those who are wanting to help Ez. P.', so Laughlin wrote to Cummings, with an invitation to join them over dinner on the night of 20 June. Cummings was unable to be there, and Laughlin let him know that 'What we concluded at the council'—that was Eliot, Laughlin, Cornell, and possibly one or two others—'was that things must be done quietly. An attempt first to get him moved to better quarters at the hospital, then later his release, since he is incurable but harmless.' Pound knew about the meeting and wrote to Cummings, 'Wd like yr. version of pow-wow', but Cummings could only tell him, 'I gather that 'twas a success.' Eliot went down to Washington to visit Pound about 10 July, and presumably gave him his version of the strategy that had been agreed. After his visit Eliot wrote to Dorothy that he feared there was nothing he personally could do, but that he imagined Cornell would apply for Pound's release to a sanatorium—he did not mention 'better quarters' within St Elizabeths—as the next step towards his eventual release. His letter implicitly endorsed the view that Pound was 'incurable but harmless'.

Dorothy spelt out the thinking behind this strategy in a letter to Ronald Duncan dated 'Aug.9': 'How can I make you understand that every line that EP writes, that isn't smuggled out by me—is inspected by the (Jew) psychiatrists? If they have reason to consider him of sane coherent mind, he goes to jail & to trial.' (The St Elizabeths psychiatrists, as Cornell at least knew, did consider Pound to be of sane and coherent mind, but would not or could not send him to trial—Overholser was seeing to that.) Dorothy also brought up Cornell's sub-argument, 'His nerves certainly are not in any condition, & never will be, to stand such treatment.' Did she really believe that, or was it all part of the Laughlin–Cornell strategy? She wrote again to Duncan on the 23rd, insisting 'He is really very much shattered', then telling him that 'Cornell & the Dr'—evidently Overholser had been consulted—'are agreed that the political situation is so important, that until after the elections they don't think it safe to try to get him even moved to a sanatorium'. There was then a double aim to the Laughlin–Cornell strategy: to avoid a trial, and to get Pound out of the hell-hole, and Pound's 'shattered' state would serve both ends. The strategy deliberately closed off the fundamental and abiding questions: was Pound sane, and was there or was there not a case to be made in his defence?

Pound, feeling 'put aside and forgotten', as Dorothy informed Cornell, wanted very much to know 'how far you understand the case'. To this Cornell replied, 'I think your husband can rest assured that I have a pretty good understanding of the entire case including his economic theories and the motives underlying his broadcasts. I have made it a point to study not only his poetry but his economic tracts and I have read up on Social Credit in general.' He did not say what he thought of the case, whether it was good or bad; nor did he mention that Pound's idea of the case would continue to play no part in his strategy. Dorothy, who must have known this, thanked him for giving her 'something to reassure [Ezra] a little'.

After her first visits to Pound Dorothy had been, as she mentioned to Cornell, 'most anxious to see Dr. Overholser to find out which way to treat him on certain subjects'. There is no record of the director's advice, but evidently she found him well disposed—in a letter dated 'Aug. 8' she thanked him 'for your benevolence towards my husband'. On that occasion Ezra was wanting the 'Spring and Autumn Annals' from the Loan Division of the Library of Congress, in an edition with the Chinese text and a French translation since the Legge was not lent out, and this had to be procured through Overholser. The latter made an affirmative note in the margin. There was also the matter of the books and papers in the leather music case which had never turned up after Pound's transfer from Gallinger. 'Is there any means of tracing these?' Dorothy asked, and Overholser wrote in the margin for his administration, 'Ask Gallinger'.

'He is working little at a time on his translation of Confucius' Odes,' Dorothy wrote to 'Bib' Ibbotson, Pound's old teacher and friend at Hamilton, 'he says his head only works an hour or so per day, & that "the dynamo is bust".' Pound himself told 'Bib', 'It works for a few minutes daily'. Nevertheless within the twelve months he was in Howard Hall he managed to fill more than twenty stenographers' notebooks with drafts of all 305 odes, and these drafts show an unimpaired poetic intelligence at work, drawing upon a rare command of the traditions and resources of English verse to find qualities equivalent to though necessarily different from those of the Chinese originals. He was not so much translating as rediscovering the odes in his own language. In June he sent the draft of one of the odes 'of Temple & altar' to Mary, with the comment 'It'll do you for a prayer, anyhow/even if not strict sinology'. This was the sinologist Legge's version:

I condemn myself [for the past], and will be on my guard against future calamity.
I will have nothing to do with a wasp,
To seek for myself its painful sting.

At first, indeed, the thing seemed but a wren,
But it took wing and became a [large] bird.
I am unequal to the many difficulties of the kingdom; [of my house (*Karlgren*)]
And I am placed in the midst of bitter experiences.

Legge's template here is an Old Testament psalm, an association which asks tolerance for the loose connections and the wordiness In his draft Pound was working for greater concentration and formal coherence:

I err'd, I pay, I awaken
Wasps be not stroked by men
Nor hawk for wren
Twice mistaken.

———

let me not be engulphed in the
multitudes of my family's
afflictions
Nor twice make nest
on a sandstorm.

The completely formed first stanza doesn't merely find four unforced rhymes, it finds four variations upon the initial sound pattern: *awaken/ stroked by men/hawk for wren/mistaken*; and with that *Twice* echoes the triple '*I*' of the first line. Along with this seemingly effortless formal invention there is the determination to pin down a definite meaning, so the opening line introduces the dramatic situation in three crisp phrases, the vague '[large] bird' becomes the specific 'hawk', and the definite image of the close binds the second stanza to the first. Further revision would alter this draft almost beyond recognition, shifting it from a lyric mode into iambic pentameter and the register of moralizing Tudor verse. Evidently Pound's mind was not only fit for concentrated work on the odes, but had the energy and the flexibility to go beyond his first inspiration. The dynamo was not completely bust after all. In retrospect, he would say that it was having the Odes to work on 'that saved my mind in the hell hole'.

He still had mind to spare for others, and for the state of the world. Mary Barnard recorded how she wrote to him when she heard he wanted news from outside, and got back 'a penciled scrawl [inquiring] in several different forms whether no<u>bo</u>dy was doing an<u>y</u>thing—not about him, about poetry', and 'The only signs in the letter of breakdown in mind or spirit were that all the words were correctly spelled and he signed his name legibly "Ezra".' But then 'The letter was obviously censored', and 'if he wrote in his usual style they would probably think it was some kind of black-shirt code.' She sent him four of her poems, and Pound returned them 'all marked up, with marginal comments'—the first time in all their correspondence that he had done that. He had 'slashed into' three of them 'but with such point, that it did me a world of good', and he gave her detailed advice on getting them published. He also saw to it that she made contact with Charles Olson, believing as ever that poets should keep up communications with each other for the general good of poetry and the maintenance of civilization. When they met, they 'told each other with much enthusiasm of all he'd done for [them]'—for Olson he had just written to Eliot about his book on Melville, *Call Me Ishmael*, which had been getting nowhere with the publishers.

Dorothy had assured Ronald Duncan in her 'Aug. 9' letter that EP 'doesn't sit and worry about himself all the time—He worries about getting things DONE, and getting certain ideas over—'. Indeed he would urge his visitors, Olson, Mrs Clara Studer, whoever it might be, to translate Frobenius' *Erlebte Erdteile*, 'not for ME but to educ. publk.—to CIVILIZE the U.S.' by the quality of his 'MIND'. He wrote to his friend Cummings, 'dont Fox or anyone ever do anything.... 4 or 5 definite jobs / Frobenius. / Gesell. B. Adms. / V. Buren', though Cummings had made it clear that he had his own jobs to attend to. He told Williams to catch up with Brooks Adams and others on his syllabus, and Williams told him to get lost, and wrote to Laughlin, 'He's never got over the pedagogic frenzy when it is to be applied to others.' Pound was not put off, and kept on in his usual way instigating all and sundry, but especially the young, to do the reading and to spread the ideas.

He was writing to Mary almost every other day, initially fairly briefly—'still hard for me to write more than a page,' he wrote in mid-March—but eventually very fully and as if he had a letter to her on the go all the time. He was being fatherly, affectionate, concerned, and encouraging. The ode he sent her as a prayer is one indication of how he was relating to her. It could be read as a lesson in acknowledging and correcting error, 'I err'd, I pay, I awaken'; but it was also freeing her to pray 'let me not be engulphed in the | multitudes of my family's | afflictions'. He wished her to have her independence and to live well. When she went back from Sant'Ambrogio to Gais in the spring of 1946 Mary wrote, 'I am now convinced that it is best for me to become a good farmer,' though her mother did not approve and was insisting on her 'getting "culture"' first. Pound's response was immediately to ask Laughlin, 'Will you send her seed of sugar maple—if the d–n thing grows from seed. & any Dept. of Ag. circulars . information re cultivation = extraction syrop etc.' He managed somehow to get hold of an extract from an official publication on 'The Production of Maple Sirup and Sugar' and enclosed that with one of his letters; and he told her that Signora Agresti, 'will put you through to Inst. of Agriculture' in Rome. He was intending to help with money too: 'a hillside where trees have been cut down—suitable for planting maples might be got cheap. Tell me local prices of sheep, & deforested or forest land—useless for other crops.' Next year he would advise her to consider growing *acero* in the valleys and low slopes of Gais. By then, though, Mary had married the brilliant boy she had met at Princess Troubetzkoi's picnic near Rome in 1943 and they had moved into an abandoned castle above Gais. Her mother had cautioned: too many unknowns. But her father had written 'from the hell-hole: "Make sure he is healthy"', and had given his blessing. Then he was advising her to make the alpine castle 'a *centro culturale*', and to invite Münch, 'the best musician also plays the piano', and Bunting, 'the best poet of the 1920s'—that was before he learnt that while the castle did have 'big majolica stoves' the young couple had no furniture. At the news that Mary was pregnant he wrote, 'You give me plenty to rejoice about,' and proposed, 'If you don't call it Olga secondo there is OBviously only one name—Walter—in those surroundings', the castle having a legendary association with the celebrated medieval poet of love, Walther von der Vogelweide, and Walter 'it' became.

His letters now were on his own headed notepaper which proclaimed top centre, 'J'AYME DONC JE SUIS / ezra pound'—'I love, therefore I am'. In the DTC he had put it in Latin at the beginning of canto 80, 'amo ergo sum', and reinforced it with 'senesco sed amo', 'I grow old but [still] love.' It was a retort to Descartes's 'I think, therefore I am', and an affirmation, as he told Olga when he first used it on 2 June, of 'the that which you said Kung-fu-tseu lacked or @ least cd not be put over without'. 'Kung *and* Eleusis', he had written in the China Cantos. But this was personal, the assertion of an identity flowing from the source of his being, and of an existence beyond the impositions of the Court and the psychiatrists. 'It aint out of no Romaunt', he told the romantic friend of his youth, Viola Baxter Jordan, 'it is out of ole Ez'.

He was in need of something to cling on to, something irrefragable, an elemental self that could not be taken from him when so much was being stripped away. He had never regarded himself as anything other than a responsible citizen of the United States, but its authorities had declared him a pseudo-American, refused him a passport, and seized his bank account as alien property. He had seen himself serving the best interests of his country, and had been perceived instead as having betrayed it. Having all his life thought and acted as a free individual he had been deprived of his liberty and his autonomy. With that he had lost his integrity as he stood mute while his lawyer misrepresented him as having been long insane, even violently insane. In St Elizabeths the psychiatrists, though they could neither find him mad nor drive him to madness, wanted him to identify with his 'associates', the genuinely insane and violent. And now his friends also, those who constituted themselves his 'council', though they knew him to be 'just the same old Ezra', were wanting to have the seal set upon his supposed insanity in order to leave no room for doubt about it in the incalculable realm of public opinion.

On 1 March, just a fortnight after the insanity hearing which definitively committed Pound to St Elizabeths, and a couple of days after Laughlin's letter to Dr Overholser implicitly taking it as established fact that he had long been insane, Cornell proposed to Pound that he should grant him power of attorney over his affairs 'by reason of your mental condition'. He put it to him that it was just because 'you are quite capable of taking care of money matters [that you] can properly delegate authority to me'. But if he were capable, what need was there for him to delegate? About the same time Cornell 'asked Dr. Overholser to permit Pound to execute [a power of attorney] on the ground that he had sufficient understanding of his publishing affairs to authorize me to collect his royalties for him and have other dealings with publishers'. Pound replied warily to Cornell on the 12th: 'Would it be suitable to say . Pwr. of Atty. on all matters pertaining to publishing, collecting money due to me, and ordinary routine connected therewith.' As for other matters, 'If D.P. arrives she might attend to various things.' About a week later, probably now considering the document drawn up by Cornell for his signature, he asked A. V. Moore, 'Should I make power of attorney to Cornell? For limited period?' But without waiting for an answer he informed Cornell on the 20th, 'Will send the pwr. of atty as soon as get notary.' Cornell observed to Overholser that Pound was displaying 'an extraordinary clarity of mind, even shrewdness, in his approach to business problems'. He wondered that he should be 'sane on some subjects and insane on others'. Behind that lay an anxiety lest it be suspected that if he were somewhat sane he might be sane altogether.

Having restricted the power of attorney 'to matters pertaining to publishing', and in effect appointing Cornell his literary agent, Pound at once began issuing instructions: 'Next point is to get Jas. to understand need of pub/ng a nucleus of civilization . more organic than a "Five foot shelf" | & the tooter the suiter.' On 16 April he wrote:

Dear JC / As you've that pwr. of atty please air-mail to Moore to collect what he can from Pollinger; & from Curtis Brown & hold it; NOT send anything here. Eliot knows where Faber paid.

Also in minor way cd/ you see that my deposit here is so fixed that small supply orders (for 20 cents worth of saltine biscuits etc) don't get held up 3 weeks.

Was Pound being satirical, asking Cornell to exercise his power of attorney looking after his 20 cents' worth of saltine biscuits? Cornell confessed to sensing that he was 'a little suspicious of me'.

At any rate, acting as Pound's agent was not what he had had in mind. He had already decided, as he informed her London solicitor on 16 April, that when Dorothy arrived he would have her appointed 'guardian of her husband's estate', and he did that and more. In September he had a firm of Washington lawyers, Covington and Burling, draw up the necessary documents for Pound to sign. Dorothy expressed astonishment to Overholser that 'an insane person should be asked to sign' the legal document, and with reason, since he was being invited to sign a document declaring himself incompetent to sign. Cornell wrote in his book that he 'had arranged for the appointment of Mrs. Pound as "committee" of the person and property of her husband by the District of Columbia Court in order that she might handle his business affairs', and the Court so appointed her on 30 October, Pound's 61st birthday. But why make her guardian of his 'person' if it was 'his business affairs' she was to handle? The effect was not just to give her absolute control of those affairs, but, beyond anything previously discussed with Pound, to vest in her all his rights as a person. As Pound later explained to Mary, 'Now I have no *persona giuridica*'—meaning that the law would no longer recognize him at all as a legally competent person.

Had he realized how much he was signing away, and irrevocably? Had he been led into thinking the arrangement was just another form of the power of attorney he had granted Cornell? Could he have failed to notice that it gave his person as well as his property into his wife's keeping, or did he think nothing of that, believing that she would do as she was told? Possibly it came home to him only after the singular 'Committee' had been set up that now he could do nothing except through Dorothy. In February and March he had been completely in charge of his affairs, instructing Cornell to 'please send $100 to Olga for rent of St Ambrogio', then asking, when Olga refused to touch the money sent, that all sums due to him be paid to Mary at Sant'Ambrogio because 'I want her to get used to handling the business'. Cornell evidently had no problem with that, telling Pound 'at your request I will collect sums which are due to you and pay them over to Mary Rudge'. But now when he wanted to send money to Mary it had to be done by the Committee—'inconvenience of being a lunatic . complicates life', he apologised to Mary. Dorothy held the power to grant or to refuse permission to publish his work, to receive and dispose of his royalties, and generally to control his intellectual property. Pound could not now make a valid will; nor could he initiate any legal proceedings, such as to ask to be bailed or released or brought to trial. He was completely in the Committee's care and power, a power over him that went far beyond Overholser's already potent care; and while Dorothy would do what he asked, she could and would do much in her role as Committee that he did not ask for and did not know about. He had given Cornell his head, and now he had done the same for Dorothy, and it would prove to be another disastrous abdication.

But why was control of his property, and of his person, removed from Pound in this way? Judge Laws had not required it, nor had the Justice Department. There is nothing to suggest that Overholser or anyone at St Elizabeths had sought it. Indeed Overholser would declare 'most emphatically' in a lecture at Harvard that commitment to a mental hospital for care and treatment 'should not involve suspension of civil rights'. Even Cornell who brought it about recognized that Pound was quite capable of managing his affairs and signing notarized documents. Where then was the necessity? Cornell's justification of his action to A. V. Moore, Dorothy's legal adviser—who Pound believed had brought up the idea—was devious but illuminating. 'Whether he is legally competent to handle his affairs or not,' he wrote, 'the public generally regard him as insane and he cannot very well do business except through a guardian appointed by a court.' But if actually asked how they regarded Pound, the general public at that time would more likely have thought to call him 'traitor', 'fascist', 'anti-Semite', well before reaching for 'insane', a label far more contested than any of the others. To have 'insane' their first thought was Laughlin's and Cornell's project, but it was not, as Cornell was pretending, an established fact. But even if it were, how should it follow that Pound must be put in the care of a court-appointed guardian? What the public might think should have been beside the point; but the bad logic does point up Cornell's concern. Regardless of Pound's competence, or more probably just because of it, he wanted not only his affairs but his person to be given over to a guardian for the sake of public opinion. The need was to have Pound's supposed insanity made legally and publicly absolute.

The February insanity hearing had determined only that he was unfit to plead to the charge of treason, and had reached no conclusion as to his state of mind when committing the alleged acts. Laughlin and Cornell had hoped to obtain a determination that Pound had been out of his right mind when making his broadcasts and therefore could not be held responsible for what he had said in them. Cornell had done his utmost to put that story across in his Affidavit, and the expert psychiatrists had repeated it for him; but many commentators remained sceptical and the general public still felt that Pound should be held to account. Laughlin was not happy about this because it left the anti-Semitism of the broadcasts still tainting his author, and put him personally in a difficult situation. In 1949 he would spell this out to Pound. He told him that in order to soften up public opinion he should allow it to be said, in a preface to the selection of his poems which Laughlin was then preparing for publication, that he was mentally ill when he made his Rome broadcasts. 'They are going to think you an awful bastard unless you let them think you were off your head,' he advised, and he went on,

> All of your friends with whom I have discussed the matter, including Possum, have all agreed with me that that line was the best one for bringing about a temporary softening of the heart toward you on the part of the public.

In another letter Laughlin explained that putting Pound's anti-Semitic remarks down to his insanity was his own way of resolving the problem—and that if they did represent Pound's true feelings then 'I would be obliged to take a moral position against you.' He didn't say that he would then feel unable to continue publishing him, but that appears to have been a consequence which he meant to avoid at all costs. But the price to be paid by Pound for Laughlin's devotedly publishing and promoting his poetry was nearly everything.

Laughlin's 'moral position' had the somewhat immoral consequence for Pound that it required him to agree that he had not meant what he had said over Rome Radio, although he had regarded it as his solemn duty to speak the truth as he saw it; and it required him to let it be said that he must have been out of his mind at the time, though not for a moment did he believe that—and nor, privately, did Laughlin. It was a moral position that had already required Pound to give up his legal right to defend his unwelcome views in a court of justice, and to be incarcerated instead in St Elizabeths. And now it required him to be rendered a non-person in the eye of the law. All this to clear his poetry of the stigma of anti-Semitism—though, privately, Laughlin accepted that Pound both was and was not anti-Semitic. But his moral position answered to a feared and powerful public perception and not to the more difficult and problematic truth.

That must be the ultimate explanation of Pound's being denied justice, his being shut up indefinitely in St Elizabeths, and his being now declared incompetent to speak for himself in any way: the reason was not insanity, it was Laughlin's longstanding and no doubt well-founded fear of the outcry against the anti-Semitism in Pound's economic propaganda and above all in his Rome Radio broadcasts. That, in the end, was what Pound was paying for.

One thing in particular was taken from him knowingly and with apparent intent: the power to make a will. While the legal manoeuvres of 1946 were going on, and before Pound had been committed to the care of a guardian, the question of whether he had made a will or could still make a will was being tossed back and forth between Cornell and Moore. On 30 July, presumably in response to a question from Moore, Cornell wrote, 'Except as to real property, our courts will permit administration of American assets by appointment of an ancillary administrator under a foreign will which has been admitted to probate in a foreign country.' Then on 5 August he wrote, 'It is unfortunate if Mr Pound has not executed a will, because if he were to make one now it would be refused probate on the ground that he is incompetent to make a will.' This must have been yet another instance of Cornell getting ahead of the facts. If Pound was competent to sign a power of attorney, and would shortly be deemed competent to sign a document requesting the Court to appoint a guardian, then why would a will he made before that be refused probate? Moore pointed out that 'By English law someone deemed lunatic and in care of a commission can nevertheless be found to have made a will in a lucid interval, and the will then be proved good.' Cornell's view however was that it would be best to allow Pound's estate to be governed by the rules of intestacy, in which case, he added on 12 August, under American laws his literary property 'would be shared by his wife and son'.

Pound had in fact made a will in Rapallo, typewritten, and dated 'the 17th day of June, a.d. 1940'—seven days after Italy entered the war. In it he declared Mary Rudge, daughter of Olga Rudge, to be his daughter, and bequeathed to her 'all that I possess', including specifically all his manuscripts and author's rights, and further appointed her to be his literary executor. His personal effects, books, and works of art were to remain in possession of his wife during her lifetime. She approved of these dispositions, the will stated, since 'she and her son are otherwise provided for'. Two copies were made of this will, both signed, witnessed, and stamped, either 'to have full force'. Doubts would be raised as to whether this 1940 will met all the requirements of Italian law, but there could be no doubt as to Pound's testamentary intentions and wishes. In the end these would be of no effect.

Laughlin's efforts as a publisher to separate Pound's poetry from his propaganda in the public mind went along with a dominant tendency in American literary criticism at the time, that of the so-called New Critics. These followed, broadly speaking, T. S. Eliot's early pronouncements that 'Honest criticism and sensitive appreciation is directed not upon the poet but upon the poetry', and that 'the more perfect the artist, the more completely separate in him will be the man who suffers and the mind which creates'. In the New Critical fashion the essay which Eliot himself wrote for *Poetry* in 1946 at Laughlin's instigation concentrated exclusively on Pound's poetry, literary criticism, and literary influence, and said not a word about the economic propaganda for which the man was suffering. Hugh Kenner's pioneering and influential 1951 study, *The Poetry of Ezra Pound*, would similarly study the poetry while eliding everything else in Pound's life and work. It was becoming not only possible but acceptable for those positively disposed toward him to talk about Pound without mentioning anti-Semitism and Fascism, and without questioning his alleged insanity and all that hung upon it. The consequence, to be played out dramatically when a prize awarded under the aegis of the Library of Congress was awarded to the *Pisan Cantos* after Laughlin eventually brought them out in 1948, was that Pound's economic and political ideas, and their intimate connection with his poetry, remained unexamined by judicious critics, thus leaving the ideas, the poetry, and the man, to be freely damned by hostile prejudice as embodying nothing but anti-Semitism and Fascism. Moreover, in the climate of opinion thus created almost no one would say that his being shut up with the criminally insane was unwarranted, and that this should be a matter of public concern.

One exception was William Carlos Williams. In spite of his conviction that Pound was guilty of treason Williams did write to the President seeking his release. About the guilt he was uncompromising. When Dorothy Pound wrote to him on 29 August, saying 'I don't know what you suppose he was doing over the radio?', and telling him that Rodker who had heard some of it had found nothing treacherous in it, and that the truth was that Pound's crime was to have 'advocated a sane economy', Williams answered back, 'That Ezra is guilty of treasonable activity towards the United States is inescapable nor does it matter in the least what he said in his broadcasts.' He had already told Pound, 'the mere fact of your broadcasting was enough for me', and he now coldly reasoned it out: 'To broadcast as he did from enemy territory under enemy pay at such a time [i.e. in time of war] is treason.... Legally his life is forfeit. Those are the rules of war.' Further, if Pound truly believed himself innocent then, as a man, he should have faced being shot and not have dodged the issue by pleading insanity. Nevertheless, when the war was officially over, he would 'write to President Truman asking him to look into Ezra's case and to release Ezra by executive order if that be legally possible'. Williams did that, in a letter dated 'New Year's Eve / 1946', even though (as he had told Laughlin on 28 December) he had just broken 'with old Ezra finally'. His letter expressed, and appealed to, an exceptionally elevated sense of Ezra's case:

Dear Mr. President:
Now that the recent war has been declared by you, in your official capacity, to be at an end, I come to ask that an old and honoured friend of mine, Ezra Pound, be freed by you from confinement in St. Elizabeth's Hospital in Washington, D.C.

Whatever Mr. Pound's actual sins against his country may have been our history has shown us, by our natures, always to be generous to dissenters from our generally accepted ways of thinking. Mr. Pound is not, as a political propagandist, dangerous to our economy—many far more dangerous to us during the late war, though at one time under arrest, are now at liberty among us. Pound is a writer, a distinguished poet and though in many ways a fool he does not rightly belong in an insane asylum as a criminal.

By your powers as President of the United States you have, I think, the right if you deem it proper to exercise executive clemency in such cases. I beg of you as a loyal supporter of your party for many years as well as of liberal democracy everywhere that Ezra Pound be given his immediate liberty.

Williams's letter was annotated 'Federal Security Agency' in the White House and forwarded to Overholser who overrode the idealism of the appeal with a statement of brute fact. 'Mr Pound is certainly not in suitable condition to face trial at present time,' he told Williams, then assured him blandly that 'we are doing everything we can to make his stay at St Elizabeths Hospital a comfortable one', and that Williams's 'interest in Mr Pound's welfare is deeply appreciated'. Williams, having chosen not to visit Pound in Howard Hall—'it would break me up and do you little good'—probably missed the smooth cynicism of Overholser's assurances.

Bill Bird, an old friend from Pound's Paris days, shared Williams's straightforward view of Pound's predicament. When he talked with him briefly in Gallinger in December 1945 he had 'tried to keep the conversation off his "case" and talk about personal matters, but [Pound] kept going back to the Constitution, etc. etc.', wishing to justify himself. But what Bird wished, he told Dorothy Pound later when she was in Washington, was that 'somehow it could be got through his noddle that he is NOT being persecuted for his ideas, because I very much doubt if there are a dozen people in the United States who have the faintest notion what his ideas are'. She ought to remember, he advised, 'and try to make Ez understand', that he was indicted because 'His broadcasts to the US on the Italian radio were construed as "adhering to the enemies of the US, giving them aid and comfort," and as a careful student of the Constitution he knows that that is technically called treason.' Having made that clear, he signed off with 'affectionate remembrances to you both'.

Nancy Cunard, who had loved Pound in the 1920s, had her own reasons for holding him to account. She had heard indirectly that he was eager to hear from her, and in June 1946 she sent him a long letter written in controlled fury and bitterness, charging him with a deeper treason than to the United States. 'Ezra', she began, 'I have been wanting to write you this for some time—for some years—but I could not do so because you were with the enemy in Rome, you were the enemy.' She had heard him 'on the air speaking from Rome', had monitored a talk when working with the Free French in London, and had found it 'all idiotic', but incomprehensible that he should be collaborating with Fascism and with 'the whole gang of [Nazi] criminals'.

> Williams has called you 'misguided'. I do not agree. The correct word for a Fascist is 'scoundrel'.... I cannot see what possible defence, excuse or mitigation exists for you, in the name of 'old friendship'—as with W. C. Williams—though it be. Nor do I believe anything concerning the 'advanced stage of schyzophrenia', 'madness', etc. that was postulated as a means to secure your non-execution. I do not believe you are insane or half-crazy. I think you are in perfect possession of your faculties as before.

He had been, up to the time when she published his *XXX Cantos* in Paris, 'a very fine poet indeed, unique, I think, in contemporary English', and his collaboration with Fascism would not efface that, but nor would the accomplishment of *XXX Cantos* efface the collaboration. But she could not understand, she accused, 'how the integrity that was so much you in your writing can have chosen the enemy of all integrity'. There was more than this in the letter—resentment of his having called her anti-Franco *Authors Take Sides* 'an escape mechanism', bafflement at his having wanted her to realize at the time of the Abyssinian War that 'the Ethiopians were "black Jews"'; and on the other side 'the good things I have to remember of you', including 'your charming and appreciative ways with Henry, my Henry of colour', and his remonstrating 'pretty sharply' with her mother on account of Lady Emerald's colour prejudice. She was also bitter about the ruin of her house near Paris and the destruction of her books and 'African things' by the Germans, 'the friends of your friends', and by 'their friends, the French Fascists'. For her the struggle against Fascism was not over, and Pound was still with the enemy. Pound's first response was a pencilled memorandum ending: 'too weak to write necessary 600 pages | though her serious letter deserved answer'. But the aggressively defensive answer he did send on 1 August was not what she deserved: 'My dear N. | What the blue buggering HELL are you talking about. I had freedom of microphone to say what I liked—namely the truth that your shitten friends were afraid to hear, Your friends who busted the Tempio @ Rimini etc. etc. Swine on both sides, but truth suppressed' etc. In time both would relent and resume occasional affectionate communication. In November 1948 he mentioned to Mary that he had received a 'Cheerful letter from Nancy who no longer thinks I ought to be shot for not shootin' Franco'.

Among those who concerned themselves with Ezra Pound at this time there was one group for whom he remained above all else a poet and a creative force within and for American poetry. Robert Duncan named him, along with HD and Williams, as an elder who remained for his generation a 'primary generative force'—

> Their threshold remains ours. The time of war and exploitation, the infamy and lies of the new capitalist war-state, continue. And the answering intensity of the imagination to hold its own values must continue.

Robert Creeley would also say that 'For my generation the fact of Ezra Pound and his work is an inescapable fact', giving as his reason that he taught them how to write—

> It was impossible to avoid the insistence he put on *precisely* how the line *goes*, how the word *is*, in its context, what *has been* done, in the practice of verse—and what *now* seems possible to do.

That last emphasis, 'what *now* seems possible to do', signalled an intent to go on beyond Pound, as he had gone beyond his elders, Browning and Whitman. These poets meant to honour him, and Williams, by building on them to make a new poetry for their own America. 'You begin at Pound wherever you go,' Duncan said in a 'A Canto for Ezra Pound', composed with Jack Spicer and presented to Pound in December 1946; and Spicer wrote, 'We ain't going the same way.' Pound might have approved and been heartened by that.

Duncan and Spicer were scornful in their 'Canto' of the way Laughlin was cautiously bringing out the new cantos—'printed in all the little mags. piously. With apologies.' 'Canto LXXXIV' had appeared in the *Quarterly Review of Literature* edited from Bard College, 'Canto LXXVII' had appeared in *Rocky Mountain Review* edited from Utah State University, and part of 'Canto LXXX' had appeared in the September issue of *Poetry* which included Eliot's and other appreciations of Pound. 'Poetry Magazine's piss all over our old Poet' mocked Duncan and Spicer, for whom that magazine was 'Chicago's cemetery for all verse'. They were the new generation of poets going about their business of clearing out the old and the established, taking their axe to the dead wood that stood in their way. But Pound was not dead wood to them, and was not to be shelved in academic journals, nor cautiously marketed. 'I go to that work to get what seems to me of *use*,' Creeley wrote, 'and the rest'—here thinking specifically of the indefensible anti-Semitism—'I toss out, condemning it just by that act.'

That was a fine attitude in its way, but not so far removed after all from Laughlin's in its separation of the poetry from the prisoner.

On 7 November 1946, Cornell wrote to Pound, 'Now that the elections are over I am proceeding as planned to make application for your release'—

> I am convinced that you have a constitutional right to be released if your own health and the interests of society do not require that you be confined. I do not believe that a man can be shut up indefinitely after being indicted when he cannot be tried because of illness.
>
> You are presumed to be innocent until proved otherwise, and since there is no prospect that you can ever be proved guilty, you cannot in my opinion be indefinitely confined merely because of the indictment.

That cavalier 'merely', making light of the grave charge of treason, shows a certain lack of professional weight in Cornell's 'application for your release'.[1] He confidently saw himself carrying the case, one altogether without precedent, all the way up to the United States Supreme Court and there winning a notable new ruling on the Constitution. And he was going to do this by sheer force of his own opinion and conviction—though his opinion, wholly unsupported by received legal opinion, amounted to no more than legal sophistry.

The law as it then stood was quite clear and definite. So long as a person under indictment for a serious crime was deemed too insane to stand trial he must remain confined within a federal institution for the insane. Cornell thought he could get around that by establishing that Pound was 'incurable', and then arguing that he should be let out just because he would never be fit to stand trial.

The 'Motion for Bail' which he filed on 3 January 1947 was actually a hybrid motion, in part a habeas corpus argument for release from custody, and in part an application for bail to a private sanatorium. Cornell was relying primarily and heavily on the dubious testimony of the four psychiatrists at the February hearing 'that [Pound] then was and had for many years been insane', and on recent information given to him 'by Dr. Winfred Overholser, Superintendent of St. Elizabeths Hospital, based upon his examination and treatment of the defendant'. No record has been found

[1] There is also a worrying carelessness in his account of the application. In introducing the above letter he wrote that in it he was telling Pound 'that I was going to try to have him released on bail because Dr Overholser did not think his confinement was necessary'. But the letter as he gives it speaks only of getting Pound released—no mention of bail; and nor is there mention of Overholser's opinion, which he was there misrepresenting. Cornell also wrote that his 'letter to Mrs Pound . . . explaining the outcome' of his application for bail would follow, but it does not (Cornell 54).

of Overholser's personally examining Pound later than the previous February, now nearly a year back, and no record exists of the defendant's having received any therapeutic 'treatment' in St Elizabeths. Nevertheless, Overholser had told Cornell, according to Cornell's Motion, that

> in his opinion (1) the defendant has been insane for many years and will never recover his sanity or become mentally fit to stand trial on the indictment (2) the defendant's mental condition is not benefited by his close confinement at St. Elizabeths Hospital where he is kept in a building with violent patients because of the necessity for keeping him under guard, and it would be desirable from the point of view of the patient if he could be removed to a private sanatorium and (3) the defendant is not violent, does not require close confinement and the public safety would not be impaired if he were allowed the degree of liberty which a private sanatorium permits for patients who are mildly insane.

In the event Overholser, when summoned to testify, would provide neither written nor oral testimony to back up Cornell's claims. He would simply maintain that the defendant was and would remain incurably insane, with the implication that he should remain permanently in St Elizabeths. Thus Cornell's primary contention would do no more than confirm yet again the reason for Pound's being confined there, and for the rest would be exposed as a misrepresentation of Overholser's official position.

Rather injudiciously, Cornell gave an interview at this time to Albert Deutsch, the *PM* journalist who had been all along sceptical about Pound's insanity plea. According to Deutsch, Cornell told him on the record that

> a number of doctors who have examined Mr. Pound since he was committed to St. Elizabeths have advised me that he is not insane enough to be further confined in a public institution. They told me that a long time ago. But I have been counseled that it would be best to wait at least a year after the insanity hearing to bring in the appeal for release, on the basis that public interest in the case might have died down by then and there would be no public resistance to this move. If the government does not oppose this motion, we should be able to obtain his release within ten minutes.

As if that was not sufficient provocation to both the public and the government, Cornell added, 'I am going to ask Judge Laws to bar the press from the hearing and to seal the papers on it. I don't see what concern the public should have in this case.' Deutsch naturally asked the Justice Department for its comment, and was briskly informed that 'Should Pound obtain release, we intend to start proceedings immediately to have him brought to trial on the treason indictment.' And naturally, Deutsch published all this as in the public interest the day before the hearing of Cornell's motion.

The Justice Department was well armed for the hearing on 29 January. J. F. Cunningham of the War Frauds Section of the Criminal Division had prepared for Isaiah Matlack, his chief, twelve closely typed pages of 'authorities and comments which may be cited in opposition to the Motion for Bail filed in behalf of Ezra Pound, under indictment for treason, who is now committed to St. Elizabeths Hospital under a judicial decree of insanity'. This brief was then condensed into six double-spaced pages for submission to the Court as the 'Government's Reply'. The Government conceded that the Court 'has authority to admit to bail pending trial persons under indictment for treason'. However, that would be the case only 'were the defendant committed to jail, instead of to a federal institution for the insane'. Moreover, he had been committed to St Elizabeths under federal statutes whereby Congress intended 'the Courts at all times to retain direct control over insane persons formally charged before them with the commission of serious felonies'. If such insane persons were to be admitted to bail, 'effective control by the Court... will be materially jeopardised, and many motions for bail will probably ensue on the incongruous grounds that the defendants are too insane to be tried for their crimes but not insane enough to be confined in a federal hospital'. Statutes and cases were cited in support of this cool dismissal of the pivotal point in Cornell's motion; and it was further rather more sharply remarked that 'No precedent, either federal or state, has been found which considered the allowance of bail under the circumstances urged by this defendant, and the dearth of authority on the subject betrays the novelty of his contention.'

Cornell was boldly arguing that the statute's silence on the matter of bail must render Pound's confinement unlawful and unconstitutional. If it did indeed leave a person such as Pound to be locked up for life, when there were no medical grounds for his confinement, and when, because he could not be brought to trial, he must 'for the rest of his life be presumed innocent in law', then it would be depriving him of his liberty 'without due process of law in violation of the Fifth Amendment'. Cornell went so far as to assert that, 'In the absence of medical grounds, a man may not be subjected to life imprisonment because an unprovable accusation has been brought against him.' The answer to that was too obvious for the government to bother stating: the accusation was not unprovable, it was simply not proved, and for the reason that the defendant's plea of insanity had prevented its being brought to proof; and the presumption of innocence did not dispose of the charge of treason which, by the statute, would stand against him for just as long as he could not be tried. Moreover, by his original Affidavit, and by the way in which he had entered the plea of insanity, Cornell had seriously jeopardized Pound's right to the presumption of innocence.

The government's response did address the contention that to deny bail would be a violation of the Fifth Amendment of the Constitution, and did so in a style which showed up the general shallowness of Cornell's arguments. 'It is the prerogative of Congress to determine when bail may be allowed', it pointed out, citing *United States v. Hudson*, 65 Fed. 68, 77 (DC, WD Ark., 1894); and therefore, 'If the statutes in question be construed to indicate an intent of Congress that bail should not be allowed in the circumstances of this case, the defendant's constitutional rights will not be infringed thereby' (citing *Douglas v. King* etc.). Further, 'It is obviously a proper function of government to provide public hospitals for the care and treatment of its insane, [and] to maintain direct control before trial over insane persons under indictment for criminal acts.... If an Act of Congress is logically designed to achieve this legitimate objective, its results are not arbitrary or capricious, and its adoption is in the public interest, due process of law has been observed.'

The essence of the Government's opposition to the application for bail was that it was really 'an application to transfer this prisoner from a federal institution, where the accused is subject to the control of this Court, to an institution or private physician of his own choosing, not amenable to the Court's direct control'. The Court, in the person of Judge Laws, of course refused bail. As the law then stood there was no possibility of Pound's being simply released, as Cornell seemed to be promising in his initial letter to Pound and in his interview with Deutsch. Once he had got Pound into St Elizabeths there was no way he could get him out short of having him declared sane after all and letting him stand his trial.

On 10 February Cornell wrote to Laughlin, 'Dear J: You will be interested to know the outcome of my application for Ezra's release to a private hospital.' Overholser, he wrote, had testified that Pound would benefit by being removed from Howard Hall, but had said that 'he could as well be cared for in St. Elizabeths as anywhere else.... Accordingly, we agreed upon a compromise under which the Judge and the Attorney General have consented to have Ezra removed to a more comfortable part of St. Elizabeths.' And 'The enclosed letter from Dorothy indicates that she and Ezra are both happy over the new arrangement.'

Overholser wrote a memorandum of the outcome for the file of patient #58,102. By his account Judge Laws, after dismissing the 'motion made by the patient's lawyer', asked Mr Matlock whether the Justice Department would object if the St Elizabeths Hospital authorities were to remove the patient from Howard Hall to another ward within the hospital, always taking reasonable precautions to prevent him from escaping. Mr Matlock said there would be no objection. Judge Laws then said he was 'willing to concur informally in this attitude of the Department of Justice', while 'disclaiming any right to interfere with the internal administration of Saint Elizabeths Hospital'. Thus deferred to, Overholser stated that 'since such was the attitude of the Department of Justice and the Court, the patient would be removed from Howard Hall to some ward where he would have somewhat more latitude and somewhat more free privileges of receiving visitors'.

Cornell did not let on in his letter to Laughlin, and may not have let on to Pound, that the arguments supporting his application had been comprehensively rebutted in the government's response.[2] After all, it had been the 'council's' strategy 'to get him moved to better quarters at the hospital' as a first step towards his later release, so the outcome could be presented as a success. Eliot at least cannot have been fully informed about the hearing, since he wrote to Dorothy at the end of February, 'I am sure the next step should be to a private sanatorium'. Pound's view of the whole matter was perhaps summed up in his scribble on Eliot's letter, '*nuts / ITALY or nothing*'.

[2] In his book Cornell printed his own Motion for Bail in full but said nothing of the government's reply.

11 : Resilience, 1947–50

Histrionics

On 3 February 1947, Dr Conover entered into Ezra Pound's case notes, 'By direction of the Superintendent, this patient was today transferred from Howard Hall 6 to Cedar Ward.' Cedar Ward was on the second floor of Center Building, and there Pound would have an 8' by 10' room that could be locked by the attendant when he was out of the ward. 'He has more freedom' there, Dorothy told Laughlin, and 'we can visit him for a much longer time (three times a week as before) a considerable relief'. Dr Keeney, when he examined him at the end of March, wrote into his notes,

> Since his transfer out of Howard Hall, Mr. Pound has evidently made a fairly good adjustment on Cedar Ward; he spends most of his time in his room, reading and writing letters, and he receives and sends enormous amounts of mail. He does no work of any kind on the ward, is quite careless in his dress and habits, and keeps his room cluttered and disorderly with books and magazines.

Over the next two or three years the formal examinations, now three-monthly, appear to have gone on much as before, with both patient and doctors playing out their set routines. The doctors would observe Pound make his rapid entrances, collapse immediately into the histrionics of extreme fatigue, only to jump up to deliver his usual denunciations and lectures; and they for their part would let him run on, or prompt him with their usual questions, and then write down that there was no change, that he continued in good physical condition, and that there was no evidence of insanity. As for this last, 'His insight and judgment do not appear to be impaired,' wrote Dr Gresser in September 1948; and Dr Gonzalez wrote in July 1949, 'No abnormal mental trends could be elicited.' A few of the doctors noted as before that he was eccentric and egotistical, that he was arrogant, and that he treated them with contempt. He said to Dr Keeney that since his arrival in the United States he had talked with only two adults, and he made it 'quite obvious that the examiner was not one of them'. Another time he evidently included him among '"people who are children and have to have everything spelled out for them, c-a-t"'. On that occasion, in March 1948, he had 'entered the interviewing room with his shirt tail out and his fly open'. Other doctors would remark his 'careless dress and habits'. Dr Granatir had to ask him to put on a shirt when he came into the cold interviewing room stripped to the waist, and Dr Segal recorded in March 1949 'that he was not particularly neatly attired, that his pajama top which was unbuttoned revealed a rather dirty undershirt beneath'.

On that occasion the interview descended into childish farce. According to Segal's report, 'This patient blustered into the interview room carrying his collapsible canvas chair as is his wont. He set up the chair, slumped low down into it, placed his hands over his eyes and began to sigh in deep, wheezing fashion with every expiration.' Asked how he felt, he kept silent for about five minutes, then said, '"It takes a lot of self control not to bring down chaos on a whole lot of you."' After another long series of 'expiratory sighs' he asked, '"Do I have to go through this goddamn business again?"' There was another long pause, 'in which the patient impatiently kicked his foot in the direction of' the examiner, before he said, '"Another new man in search of guinea pigs. I don't choose to talk. They told me a while ago that I wouldn't have to go through this again."' More silence and sighing while the patient placed his hands over his eyes again, and the examiner silently observed him, until after about five minutes the patient peeped through his fingers, saw the examiner watching him and 'immediately shut his eyes then said, "How much longer does this have to go on? Do I have to stay here?"' Told that he could go, 'he leapt to his feet, collapsed his collapsible chair and strode in hearty style out the door'. Segal concluded that evidently 'his weakness . . . can be turned off and on at will'; but he did not consider what could have reduced this highly intelligent patient to such pathetic behaviour.

Pound seems to have put on his bad behaviour exclusively for the psychiatrists. The ward attendants, at least when he had been moved on from Cedar to Chestnut Ward early in 1948, (where his room was larger, 10' by 14'), reported him as unfailingly courteous in manner and neat and clean in appearance. In June 1948 Mr Small entered in the Ward Notes,

> Patient does no work, causes no trouble, visited by wife everyday | has a awful lot of company. writes a lot of litters, recieves a lot of mail. does not mix with other Patients. stays in his room . neat in dress, clean in habits. keeps his room in a mess.

In July H. S. Grant in his 'Night Report' observed that 'He is very courteous & appears cheerful at all times', and that Patient 'sleeps very well & arises around 6:00 A.M., usually getting his morning newspaper at that time'; he further noted that 'Even though he remains alone, he is very pleasant when other patients approach him.' By all these accounts Pound consistently did no ward work, attended no ward amusements, kept to his room except when he had his visitors, and was clean, courteous with the attendants, and pleasant with the patients. 'Causes no trouble', is a frequent note, as if that was remarkable in those wards.

There was one notable episode, however, in which Pound did act like a fractious child bent on getting his own way. On 2 December 1948, Mr Langford, the charge nurse on Chestnut Ward, wrote into Pound's case notes: 'This patient was out for a walk today he claims it is too much for him he laid down on the ground said he just could not stand any longer. I told him it was too wet to lay on the ground.' Dr Saul Brown examined Pound on the 3rd, and when Pound spoke of his 'poor physical condition' the doctor noted, 'Actually appears quite vigorous.' On the 6th Langford recorded,'Patient refused to go for a walk today he said what he wanted was to go out with his wife as these walks are to much for him.' The next day, 'Patient was out walking today and laid down in the middle of the road said he could not take it as it was too much. He said what he wanted was to go out on the grounds with his wife but he said when you ask for water they put you in it up to your neck.'

Pound had been taken out in the 'walking parties' organized for the patients allowed out on the grounds when it was too chilly for them to be sitting 'on benches on the lawn without moving about'. One must imagine what kind of shuffling 'walking party' the ordinarily catatonic patients would have made up. Back in June Dr Johan had noted that Pound 'complained to the examiner that he wanted to be out on ground parole and he thought that it was very improper that so many "blithering idiots" should be allowed to walk outside and he should be so confined'. Apparently he was then allowed out, since Langford recorded on 19 June, 'Mr Pound was visited by Mrs W. R. Winslow who sat on lawn and painted his picture'. However, as Dorothy Pound explained to T. S. Eliot when he visited Pound in November, he 'was only allowed out of doors at the times when the other inmates of his ward were allowed to go out, under the supervision of a warder', and 'in consequence he was never out of doors during the winter'. Eliot was moved to write to Cornell, 'It seems to me that it ought to be permissible for him to go out alone in the grounds with his wife, and with her responsible for his returning in due time.' Eliot urged Cornell to take up the matter with Dr Overholser, arguing that 'Surely he is entitled to have some fresh air daily', and that this was something 'which his well-being seems to me to require'. Cornell did write to Overholser, enclosing Eliot's letter, and doctors Cruvant and Overholser discussed the matter on 2 December, when it was decided 'to reinstitute' the walking parties and to include Pound in them. 'I doubt very much that this will satisfy him,' Cruvant accurately remarked in his memorandum to Overholser,[1] 'he braced me for ground parole privileges, [saying] that he would like to have permission to walk about the grounds for 15 or 20 minutes each day, although he very much did not want to eat in the patients' cafeteria and preferred to take his meals on the ward'. That apparent non-sequitur suggests that Dr Cruvant was still bothered by Pound's persistent refusal to embrace 'communal living'. He closed his memorandum, menacingly as it might have seemed to Pound, 'I have been thinking of directing that Mr. Pound attend the group therapy sessions in Cedar Ward.' Overholser wrote back to Cornell on 6 December—

I have some hesitation in accepting the suggestions made by Mr. Eliot. It remains a fact that Mr. Pound is under indictment for the most serious crime in the calendar and that he has at the present time far more privileges than any other prisoner in the Hospital. He is on a quiet ward, has a room by himself and is allowed a good deal of latitude in the way he occupies himself. His wife visits him very frequently. When I found the walking parties had been suspended in the winter I saw to it that on days when the weather was good these were reinstituted, but I found that Mr. Pound refused to go on any but the first.

Overholser then stated, as if it were relevant to that refusal, that 'He has supreme contempt for the patients on the ward', before concluding,

I can assure you that we shall do everything within reason for the comfort of Mr. Pound, but in spite of his being a well known author, I question whether I should put myself in the position of giving unusual privileges to him over and above those which he already enjoys.

Nevertheless, on 12 July 1949 this 'Notice' was entered into Pound's case notes:

Mr. Pound has the following privileges. When the ward does not go out, his wife may take him on the lawn under her custody but only in the vicinity of Locust and Chestnut benches and in view of the ward. Time limits are—1 to 4 P.M. afternoons during weekdays and on Sunday 9 to 11 in the A.M. and 1 to 4 P.M. in the afternoon Orders of Dr. Cruvant, forwarded to the ward by Supervisor Gibbons.

'They now let me out to sit more on the grass—in comf. chair', Pound informed Mary in September. When Mary Barnard saw him lying back in

[1] Pound aimed his dissatisfaction at Laughlin: 'call OFF whatever ass asked the Supt/ to have me pushed out to WALK | too much and at inconvenient moments' (*EP/JL* 176).

his beach chair on the lawn in October she thought 'he was looking very well', only she was very conscious of his being 'in Dorothy's custody'.

'a awful lot of company'

Anyone wanting to visit Pound had first to seek the Superintendent's permission, and Dr Overholser would refer the application to the patient for his yea or nay. On Paul Blackburn's letter Pound wrote, 'O.K. & friend'; but on Allen Ginsberg's request to visit '& seek help with rhythm & measure' there is the note, 'D.P. regrets EP too exhausted to see any more strangers'.

Those who were approved would check in at the main office and write their names into an official book labelled 'Ezra Pound's Company'. Having then found the part of the building where Pound was kept they entered through a door in its outer wall and climbed the spiral stairs, all steel and dirty enamel, chipped and peeling walls, to the heavy black door of his ward, and there rang the bell. An attendant would open the door from the other side with a great jingling of keys, and let them into a long hall, wide and dark as a subway station, with benches along both sides, and alcoves lighted by barred windows where rooms might have been. There would be the smell of the place, decades of dried urine and sweat, and the oppressive smells of cabbage and other institutional foods which seemed to impregnate the very floors and walls. Pound would usually be found in an alcove blocked off with a folding screen at the end of the hall, and might bound out from there to greet the new arrival. The hallway itself would be peopled by the derelicts of St Elizabeths, many of them having been treated by ECT or lobotomy—vacantly staring imbeciles, men in slippers drifting like Homeric shades, old men lying or sitting stupidly on the benches, some muttering to themselves, some drooling, some making short senseless motions with their hands. There was always noise—loud television, radio song, sometimes the periodic, measured, scream of some hopelessly mad inmate housed at a distance. The noise and echoes reminded Ronald Duncan of a public swimming baths. When the braying television set in the corridor forced him and Pound to shout at each other even in his cell, Pound commented, 'They try to reduce us idiots to the level of insanity outside.'

But in the summer and in good weather Pound would be outside on the lawn in a special place by a clump of elms and other trees. There his visitors could imagine themselves in a more congenial world, for the other inmates impinged less, or not at all, and the grounds were altogether beautiful, a landscape, in Olson's view, as good as anything in America, St Elizabeths having been originally an arboretum. Lying back in his canvas chair, at ease but rarely still, Pound would entertain and instruct his small group through the allowed hours of the afternoon.

Whether inside in the alcove of the ward or out on the lawn Dorothy Pound would invariably be present, carrying her air of Henley and cucumber sandwiches, as Ronald Duncan, an Englishman, saw her. To Michael Reck, an American, her clipped speech had a British resonance, her manner a British constraint. Mary Barnard described her as 'tall, rather slender, with quite English looks and charm and style, but pretty well on the ragged edge herself.... leading a dedicated and pretty sad existence.' Barnard had seen her in her bare attic room. To William Carlos Williams Dorothy Pound was 'a tall, ascetic woman for whom all who see and know her have a deep respect and affection'; and Marianne Moore paid tribute to 'Mrs Pound's selfless aid and devoted service to EP [which] left an ineffaceable impression of nobility—of wholesomeness & also of self-sacrifice to an important end.' Mary Barnard did find that she could not speak freely to Pound about her visit to Italy when Dorothy was present; but only Olson, after his final breaking-off, seems to have had a bad word to say of her, for her 'anglo-saxon fear and hate... of the Jew'.

His visitors went out to St Elizabeths to see each their own Ezra Pound, though he could surprise. One day out on the lawn Mary Barnard observed the elderly classical scholar, Edith Hamilton, 'a stately figure in a large hat carrying an ear trumpet', lecturing Pound 'for a good quarter of an hour on the beauties of Gilbert Murray's translations from the Greek', and knowing that Pound regarded those translations as unreadable fustian, she expected him to rear up and bellow anathema, but he, 'lying back in his chair with a blissful smile on his face... uttered not a syllable and looked more delighted every minute'. Indoors, sad patients could intrude and be shooed away, but might be indulged. Guy Davenport recorded a sighting of T. S. Eliot 'lifting his legs to allow the imaginary vacuum cleaner of an inmate do its work around his chair, Pound having demonstrated how this was to be done'.

Some saw just what they went out to see. Conrad Aiken, who considered that it was Pound's foolish political infatuations or obsessions which had landed him in trouble, registered only his going off at random into 'some *idée fixe*—credit, usury, politics'. He was with Robert Lowell who, as Aiken put it, 'had become used to humouring Pound', and would get him off onto another track by saying, '"Tell us about such and such"'. On another occasion Lowell took Elizabeth Bishop to view Pound, and afterwards she wrote, in 'reverential mockery or mocking reverence' (as he assumed), 'Visits to St. Elizabeths', a ruthless variation upon 'This is the house that

Jack built'. Her poem builds from 'This is the house of Bedlam' through 'the tragic man', 'the talkative man', 'the honored man', 'the old, brave man', to 'the cranky man', 'the cruel man', 'the tedious man', and on to the final 'wretched man | that lies in the house of Bedlam'. Pound's old acquaintance Witter Bynner had his own fixed vision, seeing in his hour at St Elizabeths 'the same great, booming boy, or so he seemed, who clutched me with a great bear-hug and cried out. "After forty years!". Time and the beard had made little change for me in his presence.' But then Bynner had always, 'from my first meeting with Pound 40 years ago in New York... regarded Pound as insane'; and Dr Overholser, he told a friend, had confirmed his impression, 'saying that insanity had always been in the man and would never be out of him'. Bynner would give this another inflection when he wrote, in a letter to the Attorney General urging Pound's release, that he had 'never thought him any less balanced than William Blake'.

Robert Lowell began visiting Pound when he was in Washington in 1947–8 as Consultant in Poetry to the Library of Congress. After his first visits he wrote,

> He's just like his later prose, and absolutely the most naive and simple man I've ever met. Still sure that the world will be alright, if people only read the right books. Pathetic and touching. Told about snatching up Confucius odes when the Communists with Tommy guns came for him. And this was all that saved his mind in the ensuing months. Then he was in a specially constructed cage—America's number one war-criminal. Then a comparatively idyllic period with the army. Given a tent and called Uncle Ezra, and did all the writing he's done since he was taken. Then here in something called the snake-pit with 'a lot of imbecilic mad niggers' which was tough. Then as he is. Every day from one to four his wife comes and sits with him and he talks politics, jumps up for chairs, gobbles saltines and more or less mad people go wandering and raging past. Very sad and silly; and yet there [is] something wonderfully honest and innocent about him and he knows & loves books & he's absorbed in Chinese and he won't write 'while I'm in this cess-pool'.

Acutely observed as this is, it also reveals Lowell's need to hold Pound off and to avoid having to engage seriously with his difficult ideas and with his present predicament. One measure of his disengagement is his mentioning that 'comparatively idyllic period with the army' without reflecting that those were supposed to have been the three months of violent insanity which, by rendering him incapable, had led to his being now shut up in St Elizabeths.

Other visitors were less disposed to patronize. Marianne Moore first visited Pound in early June 1949. He 'talked brilliantly', she told Charles Norman, only his talk was 'full of allusions she didn't catch immediately', and 'like the other visitors, she merely listened'. But when she mentioned that her work on La Fontaine's *Fables* was not going well he asked to see it, and soon after advised, 'KICK OUT this god damned french syntax, with relative clauses. WRITE the sense in plain english, PROSE, and then versify the SENSE of your prose.' She wrote back, 'I am quite shaken by so much kindness, sacrifice and risk taken for me—speed, patience, definiteness.' She assured him at length that she could be trusted to let no one see the pages with his annotations, Pound having asked her to keep his communications confidential lest anyone seeing them be led to question his 'insanity'. She would say in retrospect that her 'cumulative impression of annual visits to EP and Mrs Pound is of fortitude & EP's resilience of mind | & obedience to regulations.||The official admitting me said "Mr Pound is a great help to us with other inmates. It is good of you to come to see him".||"Good of me?" I said "You have no idea of his incisive, powerful help to other writers. His discerning art is invaluable."' Mary Barnard also testified to that, in her case for his incisive help with her Sappho. Moreover, after her first visit to Pound in St Elizabeths she was struck by 'the complete incongruity of the situation: that I felt as though I had got a shot in the arm, and that probably everyone who comes feels that way, and that's why they come—to take life away instead of to bring it. Not that they don't bring it too, but it's the exchange that's important—one certainly doesn't come away depleted.' It seemed to her that 'the privilege is more in visiting than in being visited'. E. E. Cummings, after visiting with his wife in May 1949, wrote his guestly thank you note, 'you & Dorothy gave Marion & me an A1 time. We both of us heartily thank you each.'

There were visitors, mainly the younger minds, who went to listen to Pound, and to learn from him, and for them he was, as he had been for young poets and editors before the war, a cultural clearing house and an instigator of intellectual life and action. Guy Davenport, writing about the 1940s in America and drawing on his own visits to St Elizabeths, recalled Pound as a diligent teacher there, 'appalled at American ignorance' and doing his utmost to remedy it. 'One learned about Louis Agassiz, Leo Frobenius, Alexander del Mar, Basil Bunting, Arthur Rimbaud, Guido Cavalcanti, Confucius, Mencius, Raphael Pumpelly, and on and on'—'such a spray of energies that we have not yet charted them all'. For Hugh Kenner, who first visited with Marshall McLuhan in June 1948 before commencing graduate work at Yale, 'What came through ... was the emphatic aphoristic clarity, of a piece with the working of the most active mind I have ever experienced, and with the rhythms of his speech, which was the speech of the *Cantos*. There was *something* there that cohered ...

For his speech was slow, deliberate, and *built*... I never heard him utter a hurried or slovenly sentence.'

Thomas Cole was still at college when he visited in June 1949—admitted, probably, because he introduced himself as editor of a little magazine called *Imagi*. He recalled that Pound 'did most of the talking and always animatedly'—about 'the contemporary poetry scene, the Greek classics, Mussolini, music, some mention of the charge of anti-Semitism in his work, languages, and the Pennsylvania countryside' (Cole's college was in Allentown). He was kind about the young man's poems which in line and form followed the traditional English poets. 'Be yourself', he advised, 'If you like to lie by the brook and watch the fish do so, but don't try to be clever or difficult like others.' Later it dawned on Cole that Pound 'had every intention of directing me in future endeavours for the magazine and to extend my horizon in the world of ideas and the art of poetry'. He was put in touch with Dallam Simpson from Galveston, Texas, another precocious young man whose endeavours Pound was directing. Simpson had offered to edit EP's Rome radio broadcasts, but had been advised, 'More useful at moment monthly concentration of live thought as distinct from dead thought... go to anybody who is thinking about anything | minds alive impersonally not connected with EP etc.'. That was followed up with, 'Suggest that he do 4 pp. monthly for live thought', and thereupon Simpson had brought out a dozen numbers of a little magazine called *Four Pages* with contributions from Robert Duncan, Williams, Basil Bunting, and among the rest Pound himself, anonymously.

Huntington Cairns,[2] a regular and serious minded visitor, recorded that Pound liked to have notice of topics to be discussed so that he could get his thoughts together in advance. On one occasion he had been prepared to talk about editing Blackstone's *Commentaries on the Laws of England* for the contemporary reader, but Cairns was wanting to discuss Pound's theory that 'only the poets who have developed new and striking techniques' should be admitted to his anthology, and when that topic was brought up Pound said 'he had to have notice, and would discuss it with [Cairns] next

[2] Huntington Cairns (1904–85), by training a lawyer, was a self-taught scholar in classics, philosophy, and literary criticism; had served as a senior government official in various capacities; and was chief administrative, financial, and legal officer of the National Gallery of Art, and a trustee of Paul Mellon's Bollingen Foundation. Sharing Paul Mellon's sense of Washington's need for the arts and humanities he conceived the A. W. Mellon Lectures in the Fine Arts, and the Mellon funded national poetry award and Center for Hellenic Studies in Washington, DC. He wrote a massive *Legal Philosophy from Plato to Hegel* (1949), edited a three-volume anthology *The Limits of Art* (vol. 1 Bollingen, 1948)—a selection of the best of the world's literature in the original languages with English translations; and with Edith Hamilton edited *The Collected Dialogues of Plato* (Bollingen, 1961).

week'. He could be disconcerted by a topic, or a visitor, his mind was unprepared for. Cairns's notes record conversations ranging from Greek philosophy to current affairs, and also coolly observe Pound's wilder ideas and his obsessions, but without ever judging him uninteresting or insane.

In the fall of 1948 the Department of Justice informed Dr Overholser that it had been brought to its attention 'that Mr. Pound is frequently visited by persons who are interested in poetry and in literature in general', with the implication that these persons did not regard him as insane. To this Overholser replied, 'I may say that I have talked with some of these literary persons themselves and they have never expressed to me any assurance that Mr. Pound is of sound mind.' That is hardly surprising, yet Williams for one had hinted that he was, assuring Overholser after his first visit that 'To me Ezra Pound seems about as he has always been, not any worse or any better. Certainly his cerebration has been considerably slowed up due, no doubt, to his recent experiences but the quality of his ideas has so far as I can tell undergone no change, he is interesting, amusing and even profound in many of his observations.' But Overholser was not to be swayed. 'It is my personal opinion', he assured the Department of Justice,

> that there has been no essential change in the condition of Ezra Pound since he was admitted to this hospital on December 21, 1945. He is extremely bombastic and opinionated, highly disorganized in his train of thought and possessed of a considerable number of extremely grandiose ideas about himself as well as ideas of persecution directed against others. It is my opinion that Ezra Pound was not mentally competent to stand trial when he was admitted and that he is not mentally competent to stand trial at this time. Furthermore, I think it highly unlikely that there will be any substantial improvement in his condition, which is a singularly deep seated one.

Overholser was very likely telling the Justice Department what it wanted to hear. Those who would have it that he was protecting Pound appear to overlook the fact that he was a Federal official answerable to that Department.

No release

On 11 February 1948, 'Dorothy Pound, as Committee of the person and estate of Ezra Pound, an incompetent person', petitioned the District Court for the District of Columbia to issue a writ of habeas corpus directing Dr Winfred Overholser 'to produce the body of Ezra Pound', to discharge the said Ezra Pound from custody detention and restraint, and to release him 'to the care of the petitioner, as the Committee of his person and estate'. The petition was refused without a hearing.

That was as Cornell had expected. He had warned that 'because of the novelty of the question and the serious nature of the alleged crime, it would probably be necessary to take the case up to the higher courts', probably right up to the United States Supreme Court. The petition he drew up was simply a restatement of the motion for bail which had been refused by the same court a year earlier, but it was meant to be the first step in a long and difficult legal process—a process which 'should ultimately secure your husband's release', he assured Dorothy, 'if the case is decided without intolerance and in accordance with legal principles'. He had filed an appeal and the 'appelate court should reach a decision in the next two or three months'.

Dorothy's response was to instruct him to withdraw the appeal at once. Cornell was baffled, and so too was her English legal adviser, A. V. Moore. She repeated the instruction in a professionally typed letter, 'I must ask you to withdraw the appeal for my husband's release.' Cornell took that to be 'definite and final', withdrew the appeal, and was quietly dropped as the Committee's attorney.

Dorothy gave no clear reason for withdrawing the appeal, and the motive remains a matter for speculation. Also unclear is whether it was her own decision as Committee, or Pound's, or a joint decision. Back in December Cornell had urged her to think, before attempting to have Pound released, about the heavier responsibility and greater burdens she would face. He knew she was anxious to get him out, but where would they go and what would they do. 'Your husband said yesterday that he would not want to go back to Italy before next spring. Do you share that thought?', he asked. It seems a rather choosy thought for someone in Pound's situation, and Dorothy's answer was just as odd:

> Dear Mr. Cornell:
> Ezra should be gotten out of custody. We have been talking it over. Italy seems very unquiet just now. We should prefer not to go back there for possibly 3–4 months—but we could find somewhere in Virginia or N. Carolina to go on his release.
>
> Difficult without knowing what conditions, or any? attached to release: local laws might need to be consulted also. I don't count he'll be able to earn any money. Small sums in royalties come in.
>
> There is possible alternative of going to Spain. He speaks Spanish well.

There is a weird lack of urgency there, as well as an inability to think clearly. Cornell only compounded the uncertainties by saying that he doubted

Pound would be given a new passport and allowed to leave the country. Pound's reaction to that, according to Cornell, was to tell him that 'if they could not go back to Italy, [he] did not care very much about being released...If he had to remain in the United States, St. Elizabeths was probably as good a place for him as any.' Later in the year, in November, Laughlin would tell Olga Rudge, in words that sound more his own than Pound's, that 'Ezra for the moment does not want legal steps taken to get him out, which might lead to a trial and unfavourable newspaper publicity.' To John Berryman, however, who visited him in 'the "derelict" ward' on 3 November, it seemed as if Ezra did want to get out of St Elizabeths, though 'God knows what he wants', he added. Eliot may have hit the mark when he told Mary de Rachewiltz, in London in April 1948, 'I fear your father does not want to accept freedom on any terms that are possible.' But no one seemed able to say what his impossible terms might be. Dorothy had given no clue when she first asked Cornell to withdraw the appeal at once, simply telling him that 'My husband is not fit to appear in court and must still be kept as quiet as possible; the least thing shakes his nerves up terribly.' Thus his 'nerves', which in 1946 had made her insist 'we must try to get Ezra out of that place', had become the reason why he must now remain in St Elizabeths. Cornell's conclusion, as he later told A. V. Moore, was that 'she prefers the present situation to the troubles and responsibilities which any change would bring upon her'.

Evidently unaware that a petition for habeas corpus was about to be presented, Eliot had written to Dorothy on 7 February 1948, wanting to know 'is anything being DONE? or if not, why not?' Was it the case, he asked, that a move to a private sanatorium was not on, 'because of the great expense'? If that was the case, then 'the first step is when he can be either (1) tried with a good prospect of being acquitted, or (2) released as permanently incapable but not dangerous'. That was the soundest and clearest view of how Pound could be got out of St Elizabeths that had yet been expressed. There should indeed have been a good prospect of acquittal, if only Pound were properly defended; and if he were deemed permanently incapable, then the one effective argument for his release would have been that he was not a danger to himself or to the public. Cornell seems not to have seen that, or not clearly enough; and Eliot's good sense had no effect on Dorothy, nor on Ezra.

Laughlin kept asking them why they did not proceed with Cornell's plan. In the summer of 1948 he saw Olga Rudge in Rapallo and was unable to satisfy her demand for an explanation of why they were doing nothing to secure Pound's release. 'Don't you want him to try to get some legal wheels turning?', he asked Pound. In November, after that year's elections, he asked Dorothy, 'does EP think we ought to go ahead with the legal steps Cornell wanted', or, what were their views about obtaining his release. But then in December he wrote to Pound, 'had a v. good conference with the Possum & Cornell' in which Eliot 'confirmed what you had said, that you wanted for the moment to remain where you are, and not have any troublesome steps taken, which might stir up hornets and other vermin'. This deferring to Pound's judgment and wishes seems odd, given that he was held to be incompetent in such matters.

In his *Autobiography* (1951) Williams wrote that 'Pound had refused to entertain the idea [of an attempt to have him removed from St Elizabeths for treatment under more favourable surroundings] stating that he knew he would be shot by an agent of the "international crew" the moment he stood outside the hospital gates'. Pound would say as much to Ronald Duncan, 'I don't want to get out to be assassinated.' Yet those paranoid fears, which he occasionally indulged to keep up his morale, were an improbable explanation. Besides, Williams had reason to know that they were not the whole story. In October 1947 Lowell had invited him to Washington to record his poems for the Library of Congress, and he was to make his first visit to Pound in the afternoon, but lingered over lunch with Lowell and was late getting out to the hospital. It was a rushed visit. In spite of that Pound seized the moment to suggest that Williams write, as a qualified physician, to Dr Overholser asking whether Pound could be released into his charge. Williams did write a few days later, although he was fairly sure the nature of the charges would preclude any such release, and about that he was quite right. But he had been moved to act by an explicit expression of Pound's desire to be removed from St Elizabeths at that time. As if he had forgotten that, Williams wrote in his *Autobiography* that he couldn't understand how Pound could be 'so apparently unmoved by his incarceration', and then comforted himself with the thought 'that much of the world's greatest writing has waited on a removal from the world's affairs for its doing. Concentration is what a man needs to bring his mind to harvest...we must find quietitude.' Concentration Pound certainly mustered, but that finicky 'quietitude' was unlikely on the wards of St Elizabeths. It was surely in spite of his incarceration, not because of it, that Pound brought at least some of his mind to harvest in 'the bughouse'. But he did wish, as he told Agnes Bedford in 1953, that his friends would use a little more intelligence to get him out of it.

There were some among those close to Pound who simply believed that it was best for him to remain in St. Elizabeths, 'for his own sake'. Wyndham Lewis, who reported this in a letter to Douglass Paige in October 1948, supposed that it was because these friends—he named Eliot and 'Mrs

Pound's London lawyer'—feared that once let out, even to a private nursing institution, he would create scandal by embarking upon some 'violent crusade' and undo the recovery of his reputation as a poet. That view was 'too cold-blooded' for Lewis. 'If I were in E.P.'s position', he wrote, empathizing with Pound as very few seemed willing or able to do, 'I should feel rather strongly about the view that for my own good I had better stop in an asylum'; consequently, 'I under all circumstances will do what lies in my power to secure his release.'

At that moment, just before the November elections, what could be done was to sign and circulate a petition for clemency, drafted by Paige, for presentation to the new president when he took office in January 1949. Lewis foresaw difficulties, not least 'E.P.'s obstreperous intractableness', but he wholeheartedly supported the petition while assuring Paige that he should certainly 'not mention it in a letter to Ezra'. The petition was never presented, probably because Paige learnt that there could be no presidential pardon where there had been no conviction. Pound knew that, and Lewis too might have known it, since he had asked Dorothy in April 1947, 'Is there hope of his receiving a pardon?', and Pound had noted on the letter, presumably for Dorothy's reply, 'no pardon for crime not committed'.[3] He further noted, 'any one of 80 or 100 people cd persuade Dept. J .to drop the case | if they weren't all yellow.'

Olga Rudge could not understand why nothing was being done to secure Pound's release. In March 1948 she told Ronald Duncan that she was receiving 'at least 3 letters a week from E.' in which he talked 'of nothing but wishing to return to Sant'Ambrogio'. In May Duncan advised her to go to America herself '*and drive through Laughlin's and Dorothy's attitude of acceptance*'. There were people there, including Dorothy, he warned, 'who relish the situation of having their own pet genius all tied up in the cage'. Olga attempted to stir up Laughlin and Eliot from Rapallo, much to their irritation, and all the more because while they recognized that she was good for Pound privately they feared that the interventions of a mistress would harm him publicly.

She wanted to publish a selection of his Rome radio broadcasts, and Pound was all in favour. He had Dorothy write to Laughlin, 'Yesdy. Ez. said contact Olga re getting together a vol. as quickly as possible of the Discoursi, i.e. his radio talks, so that there may available evidence of what he actually said—instead of all this talk and rubbish about him.' Olga

[3] The woman convicted in 1949 as 'Tokyo Rose', after a shameful campaign against her by Walter Winchell, a gossip columnist and radio host, did receive an unconditional pardon from President Gerald Ford in 1977. She could be pardoned because she had been convicted, wrongfully.

selected four talks, the memorial to Joyce (1941), one on E. E. Cumming's *EIMI*, a book about Russia, ('e.e.cummings / examind', 21 May 1942), one on Céline ('A French Accent', 11 May 1942), and one on Lewis's Vorticist effort ('Blast', 16 April 1942). She also included canto 45. In the talk about Cummings there were some anti-Semitic and anti-Allies remarks, but none in the other talks in which Pound had recovered something of his better intelligence as a literary and social critic. Probably the Cummings talk was selected, and placed first, as a lightning rod to draw off the objection that she was whitewashing Pound. The title of the volume was to be a challenge: *IF THIS BE TREASON*. She submitted the manuscript to Cornell for his advice, and although he could see nothing dangerous in it he 'said better not to distribute in States'. Eliot advised that such a small selection would have no legal value for Pound's defence. And Laughlin told her, 'It does not matter what E. said over the air. If he had only said Jesus was a good man, it would still be treason if he had been paid to do it by an enemy government, with whom we were at war.' 'That is the whole nub,' he insisted, and accused her of not grasping 'the facts of the situation'—while being himself negligently or wilfully wrong about the legal facts. Undaunted by these rebuffs, Olga had 300 copies of the booklet privately printed in Siena in January 1948 and distributed them at her own expense. Whether the booklet helped or harmed she had the satisfaction of feeling that it was at least something done, an active protest against the stifling passive acceptance of Pound's predicament.

Later in the year she got up a formal statement, signed by the mayor and about seventy citizens of Rapallo, to the effect that the American writer Ezra Pound had lived in their town from 1923; that he had taken no part in Fascist meetings or activities there, had always been considered an American citizen, while being a friend of Italy, and a sympathizer with certain social and economic principles of Fascism; that he had retained the respect of even those among his fellow citizens who disagreed with his political opinions; and that he had always behaved correctly and never been party to any anti-Semitic acts. The mayor signed last, and wrote above his signature, 'The statement is approved in consideration of the fact that in Rapallo the aforementioned person has always done good deeds.' The statement was typed on one side of a large folio sheet folded to give four sides, and the signatures filled the other three sides. Olga sent the document to the US Embassy in Rome asking for it to be forwarded to the State Department. It had no evident effect.

In the background behind these ineffectual motions for Pound's release were always uneasy considerations of his supposed insanity. 'The first and only sign of it' that Ronald Duncan could see when visiting him, was his 'fear of being assassinated', but that was not new—'He had always imagined himself the target of some international group of bankers or warmongers.' John Drummond wrote to Duncan that he presumed that the insanity was faked, and that he thought that 'the "insanity" policy has been a tremendous mistake'. Olga Rudge had it explained to her by Paige, who was in Rapallo in 1948 with Pound's permission to edit a selection of his letters. Pound had told him to tell her that 'He cannot, absolutely cannot answer questions', because 'the psychiatrists examine every letter that he sends out' and 'he must appear witless to them'. However, as she told Eliot, she had 'come to the conclusion NOT that he is putting it on but that his mind IS affected. I have got either to believe that OR that he is being rather cruel to me'—this because he would not give her any answers even to the purely private things she most wanted answers about. Eliot found an equally self-concerned reason for thinking Pound insane. 'It is possible that Ezra is pretending', he wrote back to Olga, 'but at the same time I believe that he is insane: that is to say, that he is irresponsible and that the opinion of Dr. Overholser and the decision of the Court were correct.' This was because when Eliot had visited him the year before Pound had avoided all personal conversation, had been 'not merely exaggeratedly reserved about himself: he asked no questions about myself, or betrayed any interest in my affairs. I didn't even have occasion to tell him that my wife had died.' John Berryman had also been struck by Pound's impersonality and how 'he moved away from personal subjects very quickly and as if naturally', but it seems not to have occurred to him to take Eliot's leap from impersonality to insanity. More likely he recognized it as a common way of warding off pity and self-pity.

Olga wanted to hear directly from Dr Overholser about Pound's condition, and why it was that she could not get him to answer important questions. She conceded that it had always been his way to refuse 'to face any facts which do not fit into how he would like things to be'. Her letter was answered by the assistant superintendent, Dr Samuel Silk, who readily agreed that 'it is Mr Pound's mental quirk not to face any facts which are not in conformity with his preconceived beliefs', and added on his own account that 'Because of Mr. Pound's intelligence, he is very cleverly able to distort reality to suit his own purpose.' As if exemplifying this he described Pound's keeping himself apart from the other patients when taken onto the grounds, and his constantly complaining of fatigue when interviewed but showing none when alone in his room working on his manuscripts. Apparently he could not see that this might be a poet's determined effort to maintain his individual identity and vision, and to save his mind from the disintegrative conditions of the madhouse.

Laughlin did show some appreciation of that in a letter to Hilda Doolittle around September 1948: 'I was down to see Ezra in Washington the other day, and was pleased to find that in some ways he was considerably improved. His physical health seems good, and he is able to concentrate a good deal better. He also seems to have been able to create a kind of mental barrier between himself and his surroundings so that his own life is able to go on untroubled, and he is not too unhappy. However, his delusions...' Cornell had told Laughlin that the delusions were worse. 'I had not seen Ezra for about a year,' he wrote in June, 'and was impressed with the further deterioration of his mind. His delusions have become more clearly defined.' And as ever Dr Overholser was at hand, 'willing to testify that E. will never get any better'. Laughlin sent on Cornell's letter to Olga Rudge.

In September 1948 Pound had other priorities apart from what people might be saying about his sanity. William Van O'Connor had asserted in a discussion of *The Pisan Cantos* in the *Saturday Review of Literature* that Pound had gone over to the Fascists and committed treason. Pound asked Cornell to tell the editors that this was not true. Cornell wrote that it could not be said that he was guilty of treason since there had been no trial, and gave it as his personal conviction that if he were to be tried 'Mr. Pound would be acquitted on the ground that he was not responsible mentally for his actions.' When he saw a copy of what Cornell had written Pound had Dorothy remonstrate, 'EP is not interested in the question of his sanity—but in establishing that he did NOT commit treason.'

Thrown to wolves

In Willa Cather's *My Ántonia* Pavel, a Russian immigrant, tells his story. He was groomsman when his friend married the belle of another village; after the wedding- feast the bridal party set out at midnight for their own village, racing in their sleds across the snowbound steppe, Pavel driving the groom and his bride in the lead; a great pack of wolves scent them and attack, picking off the sleds behind them one after another until theirs is the last and the wolves are nearly upon them—and then Pavel had thrown out the groom and his bride and saved himself.

On 9 May 1948, Laughlin wrote to his close friend Robert Fitzgerald, the translator of Homer and Virgil, and (with Dudley Fitts) of Greek tragedies:

Are you in NYC? I desire to see you. TSE also desires to see you. He particularly hopes you can dine with us... the evening of Thursday [June] the 20th to plot and plan a bit how to restore poor ole Ezpo as a bard. His fate political and physical is in the hands of doctors and lawyers, but something we can do is keep slime like Cerf and Untermeyer from getting across the propaganda that he was never a wonderful poet, an ornament to his age.

Both *The Pisan Cantos* and a volume collecting all the cantos including those new ones were now at last nearly ready for publication—Marion Cummings was presented with copies of both when she called on New Directions about 22 May—but publication was being delayed until 30 July while the plotting and planning went on to have the cantos received as just wonderful poetry. Their relation to 'his fate political and physical' was to be played down as much as possible, or at least neutralized.

Laughlin knew very well what he was up against. Back in February 1946 Bennett Cerf of Random House had declared in his column in the *Saturday Review of Literature* that he refused to have Pound's poems included in Conrad Aiken's anthology, not because the poetry was not good enough, but because 'he was a fascist and a traitor'. His column had brought down 'a veritable avalanche of praise and blame', nearly 300 letters 'equally divided', but divided between those hostile to Pound and those hostile to censorship. Persuaded by the latter that he should allow the poems to be included, he 'angrily' conceded 'that it may be wrong to confuse Pound the poet with Pound the man'. That was the distinction Laughlin hoped could be maintained to save the poetry from the untouchable Pound.

In mid-June Laughlin mentioned to Pound that 'This Thursday a council meets on yr behalf at the request of the good parson Eliot. Cummings, Tate, Auden, Fitzgerald, Fitts and Cornell will be there and we shall mightywise deliberate and perhaps bring forth a small mechanical mouse.' Whatever else they discussed, they would certainly have talked about managing the reception of *The Pisan Cantos*, and they would have talked too about the Bollingen Prize for Poetry which was to be awarded in November by a committee on which three of them—Eliot, Tate, and Auden—would be serving. Allen Tate had proposed that there should be such a prize when he was Poetry Consultant to the Library of Congress in 1943, and Huntington Cairns had secured the funding for it from the Bollingen Foundation. $1,000 was to be awarded for the best volume of poetry by an American published in America during the calendar year, the awarding committee consisting of past and present Fellows in American Letters at the Library of Congress. The first award was to be made in 1948. Archibald MacLeish believed that the prize had been set up by friends of Pound with the intention of making him the first recipient and thus 'dramatizing his situation and putting the government, and particularly the Department of Justice, in an awkward if not untenable position'. It is possible though unlikely that this was the original intention, but it may well have been an outcome which Laughlin's 'council' were hoping for. In any case they could reasonably expect that the award of the prize by a group of distinguished poets, and with the backing of the Library of Congress and the Bollingen Foundation, would go far 'to restore poor ole Ezpo as a bard'.

The Pisan Cantos were reviewed upon publication by Robert Fitzgerald. 'We find ourselves, again, in debt to New Directions', he began,

> This publication is admirable—and far from being a simple act of piety. The poet remains in St. Elizabeths Hospital, Washington, adjudged too ill in mind to stand trial for treason; and it is easy to look for and discover in the poetry evidence of his illness. That evidence is almost certainly there in quantities strongly confirmatory for the diagnostician.

That 'illness', according to Laughlin's and Cornell's strategy, was meant to account for the Rome Radio broadcasts. But then, while it might neutralize the charge of treason, it also meant that Pound must have been insane when writing *The Pisan Cantos*. Laughlin had got around this difficulty when he published Pound's *Confucius* as an issue of his magazine *Pharos* in 1947—the translation carrying the awkward date-line 'D.T.C. Pisa; 5 October–5 November, 1945'—by advertising it as prepared 'during the intervals of his illness'. The dust-jacket of *The Pisan Cantos*, however, simply stated that 'they were composed when the poet was incarcerated in a prison camp near Pisa'. Fitzgerald was now conceding that Pound was 'ill' when he composed them, and then going on to find within the cantos themselves strong evidence of the 'illness'. What he meant, it emerges, is that there is madness in the very method of the cantos, in their 'ideogrammic method' with its abandonment of Aristotelian logic, and its disregard of the fact that 'it is impossible to use a logical language, like English, as if it were a picture language, like Chinese, or as if it were an abstract musical medium'. 'Once you start thinking [in English]', Fitzgerald asserted, 'you are irrevocably committed to logic', and because the Cantos don't put things together 'logically' they show that Pound was not right in his mind. Moreover, because he 'thought badly'—and here Fitzgerald turned from the cantos to the man and his fate—Pound had behaved 'fantastically', that is, he had made his broadcasts over Rome Radio and so ended up in St Elizabeths as incurably insane.

In spite of his thus identifying the *The Pisan Cantos* with the alleged insanity of the broadcasts Fitzgerald did not want to dismiss them altogether. Even as he complained that he could not make coherent sense of them, he rejoiced in the way Pound's mastery of melodic invention weaves the plenitude of evocative detail into a shimmering web, and insisted that 'we ought to be grateful for what we have'. 'At their least valuation', he concluded, 'I submit that these Cantos in which light and air—and song—move so freely are more exhilarating poetic sketch books, "Notes from the Upper Air", than can be found elsewhere in our literature.'

Louis Martz too, reviewing them in the *Yale Review*, though he found more coherence and depth than Fitzgerald, concluded that 'It is perhaps true that *The Pisan Cantos* are really a brilliant note-book held together by the author's personality, with poems scattered throughout.' Martz did remark 'the aging prisoner amid the ugliness of the camp', but otherwise passed over all that actuality with its crisis and its commitments as 'at the edge of the poetical'. A consensus was developing that *The Pisan Cantos* could safely be approved if they could somehow be detached from the unfortunate poet and read as harmlessly 'poetical'. Richard Eberhart, invited by Laughlin to write something about them, was explicit: 'An approach to the work as poetry is necessary and more rewarding, at least to me, than reading the Cantos as political, economic, or sociological manifestoes. Fifty years will remove the politics and leave the poetry.'

Many on the committee awarding the Bollingen Prize for poetry appear to have shared that view, while being very conscious that the world at large would not. They met on 18 and 19 November before the calendar year was out in order to accommodate T. S. Eliot, who was just then a visiting fellow at Princeton's Institute of Advanced Study but about to return to England. Coincidentally, it was announced about this time that he had been awarded the Nobel Prize for Literature. The other members present were: Léonie Adams (current Fellow and chair), Conrad Aiken, W. H. Auden, Louise Bogan, Paul Green, Robert Lowell, Katherine Anne Porter, Karl Shapiro, Theodore Spencer, Allen Tate, Willard Thorp, and Robert Penn Warren. The fourteenth member, Katherine Garrison Chapin, wife of Francis Biddle, who as Attorney General had indicted Pound, was not present. Four works were nominated: Pound's *Pisan Cantos*, Williams's *Paterson (Book Two)*, Randall Jarrell's *Losses*, and Muriel Rukeyser's *The Green Wave*. There was no vote at this time, but it was clear that the majority supported *The Pisan Cantos* as the best work of American poetry in that year. Questions were asked as to whether it was in the best interests of the Library of Congress, or of the Bollingen Foundation, to award the prize to a man under indictment for treason to the United States. Eliot suggested that Pound's interests should also be taken into account, since the award might bring him undesirable publicity and 'be exploited by the wrong elements'. Upon his advice the committee decided to think further upon these questions and to consult with the Librarian, Luther H. Evans.

After an interval the committee proceeded to an official vote by mail-in ballot. Twelve voted—Paul Green abstained, and Theodore Spencer had died in the interim. *The Pisan Cantos* received ten first preferences, and two second preferences, and so was clearly the winner. (Spencer was also deemed to have voted for *The Pisan Cantos* on the ground that he had spoken for them at the first meeting.) The committee reconvened (without Eliot) on 4 February 1949, and, before ratifying the result, 'heard directly an opinion previously given to Miss Adams'—quite possibly by the Librarian—'that serious harm might be done by the award [to Pound] especially with regard to all the individuals concerned, including the recipient of the prize, who would be exposed to the resources of an invidious publicity; and perhaps serious harm to the institution of the Fellows and the Prize'. The minutes of the meeting go on to record that 'Mr. Lowell thought that the Fellows should not consider themselves, but the effects upon the Library and on Mr. Pound'.

Léonie Adams then asked Cornell to advise on whether the award might hinder Pound's eventual release from St Elizabeths. As he knew, she wrote, it had been decided to make the award to him 'provided the special circumstances do not make this too difficult for the Library or Mr. Pound'. She had been told by 'those investigating the matter from the Library's standpoint', and also 'by someone in a position to know a good deal unofficially about Department of Justice attitudes', that there was 'now some question of reviewing Mr. Pound's case in order to determine on a legal finding of insanity, and in general it is their opinion that publicity at this time would be most unfortunate'. The 'someone' may have been Francis Biddle, the former Attorney General, who did let the Librarian know that he was 'strongly against the decision'. Even so, the words in Adams's ear would seem to have been no more than vague talk designed to confuse the committee and protect the Library, since, as Cornell said in his reply, there was no way Pound's legal position could be affected by either the award or the resultant publicity. As for its effect on him personally, Cornell supposed 'it could do no harm and might do much good', for surely 'such recognition would be welcomed by him, and might serve to support his wavering ego'.

With this assurance, but against the advice of the Librarian, the award to Pound was formally announced on 20 February. The *New York Herald Tribune* reported next day:

> Pound's work, the jurors held, 'represents the highest achievement of American poetry in the year for which the award is made'. The jurors, however, explained their decision to recognize Pound's work despite objections which might be raised against him politically. 'The Fellows are aware', the jurors said, 'that objections may be made to awarding a prize to a man situated as is Mr. Pound. In their view,

however, the possibility of such objection did not alter the responsibility assumed by the jury of selection. . . . To permit other considerations than that of poetic achievement to sway the decision would destroy the significance of the award and would in principle deny the validity of that objective perception of value on which any civilized society must rest.'

Karl Shapiro immediately went public with his dissent from that principle. He had argued, in a letter to Léonie Adams in January, that Pound could not be given the award 'without an accompanying apology for or denunciation of his political activities'; and since there was no point in making an award 'modified by some kind of condemnatory apology', he thought no award should be made for 1948. Adams had agreed, and had told Shapiro that Huntington Cairns also 'seemed to think that this would be an acceptable way out'. But Allen Tate, in a letter to Luther Evans, declared that to make no award would be a cowardly evasion of their responsibility and that to give the prize to their second choice would be disgraceful. 'Hell will no doubt break loose', he wrote, 'but I don't see how we can avoid it'—

If a democratic society is going to justify itself, it has got to maintain distinctions and standards, and allow for decisions which are above politics. Pressure groups and popular hysteria have nothing to do with intellectual standards.

Tate evidently prevailed, and his principled stand was published as the Fellows' official position. A few days later Shapiro wrote in the *Baltimore Sun*, 'I disagree vehemently with the principle embodied in the Library press release that to judge a work on other than aesthetic grounds is "to deny the objective perception of value on which any civilized society must rest". This is not a statement of principle but an apology,' he asserted, and one stemming 'directly from a coterie of writers called the "new critics"'.

All hell did break loose over the following months. Albert Deutsch at once objected loudly that there was 'something unholy' about bestowing 'honor in any form on the man who broadcast Fascist propaganda under the auspices of the Fascist enemy of his native land'. He denounced Lowell and Eliot in particular as 'friends of the turncoat poet', and condemned the committee's decision as a disloyal political act. Dwight MacDonald, the anti-totalitarian and contrarian editor of *Politics*, replied that, on the contrary, the committee's decision was 'the brightest political act in a dark period', precisely because 'by some miracle' they had been able to consider 'Mr. Pound the poet apart from Mr. Pound the fascist, Mr. Pound the anti-Semite, Mr. Pound the traitor, Mr. Pound the funny-money crank, and all the other Mr. Pounds whose existence has properly nothing to do with the question of whether Mr. Pound the poet had or had not written the best American poetry of 1948'. For MacDonald, the fact that 'Pound's treason and fascism were not taken into account in honoring him as a poet' represented the essential difference between the freedom and openness of 'such imperfect democracy as we in the West still possess', and the tyrannous thought-control of Soviet Communism. However, while rejoicing in the West's freedom to discriminate and to evaluate objectively, MacDonald had no discriminating word of his own for Pound or his poetry. He confessed that he was incompetent to judge *The Pisan Cantos*, yet felt at liberty to say that the book was not 'by any means free of its author's detestable social and racial prejudices'. His exercise of his democratic freedom extended to sharing with Deutsch the 'well-known' view of 'Mr. Pound the fascist, Mr. Pound the anti-Semite, Mr. Pound the traitor' etc. In short, in his polemic he had no care for the objective facts of Pound's case. For his purposes, the darker the poet's reputation the brighter shone out against it the committee's principle of 'That objective perception of value on which any civilized society must rest'. Neither MacDonald himself nor the commentators who cited him approvingly appear to have been troubled by the contradiction between the high principle and the irresponsible practice.

William Barrett, editor of *Partisan Review*, agreed that the sentiments behind the committee's affirmation of a general principle were 'admirable', but he was concerned about the application of the principle in the particular case. 'It would be a pity', he wrote in the April issue of the magazine, 'if in the aesthetic recognition of Pound's poetry as valuable we chose to forget about the humanly ugly attitudes of which he has been a spokesman both in his writing and in his brief and lamentable career as a broadcaster' and as 'a fascist and anti-semite'. Indeed, he went on, 'some of those unfortunate attitudes that led to Pound's downfall' are expressed in *The Pisan Cantos* themselves, and here he cited, as though they had some connection with the charge of treason, a few of the anti-Semitic lines in canto 74/439, and went on at some length about the difficulty of dissociating their 'odious and hideous human attitude' from 'certain objective facts like six million Jews dead in Europe'. But could it be, he wanted to ask, that in a 'lyrical poem' such as he took *The Pisan Cantos* to be, 'a poet's technical accomplishment could transform material that is ugly and vicious into beautiful poetry'? Barrett appeared to think it possible to give an affirmative answer to his question, even though he had set it up in such a way as to make it appear that this 'lyrical poem' consisted of nothing but anti-Semitism and other such ugly and vicious matter.

Partisan Review invited 'a number of Bollingen jurors' to respond to Barrett's editorial in the May issue and received replies from Auden, Shapiro, and Tate. Other contributors to the symposium were Robert

Gorham Davis, Clement Greenberg, Irving Howe, and George Orwell. Of all these not one dissented from Barrett's premise, and not one brought forward any specific evidence to support it. Indeed, there was nothing in the entire symposium to show that any of them had actually read *The Pisan Cantos*, let alone that they had attempted to understand them as poetry. Their common ground, unexamined but apparently needing no proof, was that *The Pisan Cantos* were to be characterized as anti-Semitic and fascist. And this judgment was based, it appeared, upon their general sense of Pound's politics, more particularly upon what they knew or had heard about the wartime broadcasts. Several added they didn't think much of the Cantos as poetry anyway, and Orwell said that he had 'always regarded him as an entirely spurious writer'. In his view the Bollingen judges should have said firmly that 'the opinions that [Pound] has tried to disseminate by means of his works are evil ones'. Davis, Greenberg, Howe, and Shapiro were explicit that Pound, on account of his anti-Semitism, should not have been honoured with the prize. Howe went so far as to say that 'Pound, by virtue of his public record and utterances, is beyond the bounds of our intellectual life'—beyond the pale, in short.

The clearest and most thoughtful statement of the general view came from Karl Shapiro. He said that he had voted against Pound, in the first place and crucially, because 'I am a Jew and cannot honor antisemites'; and secondly, because he believed 'that the poet's political and moral philosophy ultimately vitiates his poetry and lowers its standards as literary work'. That philosophy was 'fascist' he implied, and demanded to know who would deny that 'fascism' is 'one of the "myths" of *The Cantos*'. Whether by 'fascism' he meant anti-Semitism or something else remained unclear. In any case, since 'fascism' is a crime against civilization, it followed that both Pound and his cantos should be treated as criminal. But those who had voted for Pound, he accused, had chosen to 'disregard the mythopoeic and moral function of the artist'; though Pound himself, 'if he had sufficient intellectual honesty...would be the first to oppose such a criterion of selection'. There at least, though he had no call to impugn Pound's intellectual honesty when making the point, Shapiro was surely right, since Pound always had maintained that art should be in the service of life and of a just society.

Allen Tate's response differed from the rest, in that he thought Barrett had insinuated 'a charge of antisemitism' against the judges, and this he took personally as a 'cowardly and dishonourable' accusation. He appeared to be threatening to demand satisfaction for the sake of his own 'courage and honour'—but he entered no objection to Barrett's insinuation that the only thing to be said about *The Pisan Cantos* was that they were anti-Semitic. Barrett was astonished by 'Mr. Tate's explosion', and retorted that his editorial had 'contained absolutely no allegation whatever of anti-semitism on the part of the judges'. That was true enough, but some of the contributors to his symposium were now implicating the judges. Shapiro wrote that some of them 'had come under [Pound's] influence as impresario and teacher', that some 'had at some time made declarations of political reaction', and that some 'had engaged in the literary struggle to dissociate art from social injunction'. He named no names, except for Mr. Eliot, whose presence 'at the meetings gave these facts a reality which perhaps inhibited open discussion'. Davis, a literary critic and professor of English at Columbia University, was prepared to name 'Eliot, Auden, Tate and Warren' as reactionary representatives of the 'new criticism'. He held them responsible for 'a complex of ideas dominant in American criticism during the forties', 'made explicit by Eliot in *After Strange Gods* and *The Idea of a Christian Society*; by the Southern Regionalists including Tate and Warren . . . and by Auden in the Herod-as-liberal speech in *A Christmas Oratorio*'. And 'In this complex of ideas', he asserted, 'the antisemitism with which William Barrett is principally concerned has a vital part'. For him, whatever was to be said about Pound, it was the judges themselves who stood accused.

Partisan Review was written and read by the literary-political intelligentsia and did not have a wide circulation. *The Saturday Review of Literature*, on the other hand, enjoyed a much broader middlebrow readership, and its president and its editor, Harrison Smith and Norman Cousins, had scented an opportunity to attack the modern poetry and new criticism which a great many of its readers found difficult and intimidating. They commissioned a pair of articles from Robert Hillyer, who had been awarded the Pulitzer Prize in 1934 for his conventional poetry, had taught at Harvard—Laughlin quit his studies there for a time in reaction to his dreadful teaching and poetry—and had been appointed at Kenyon College to counter the new critical influence of John Crowe Ransom and the *Kenyon Review*. His first article, under the heading 'Treason's Strange Fruit', appeared in the 11 June issue, and was introduced by a flamboyantly inflammatory editorial signed by both Smith and Cousins. With a total disregard for truth they thundered,

> Ezra Pound is not merely the traitor who deserts his country to impart secrets which are useful to the enemy. Ezra Pound voluntarily served the cause of the greatest anti-humanitarian and anti-cultural crusade known to history. He was no innocent abroad who was made to sing for his supper and his safety, but an open

and declared enemy of democratic government in general and the American people in particular.

Hillyer then extended the attack to the Bollingen jurors, to Paul Mellon and the Bollingen Foundation, and to Carl Jung (from whose summer villa in Switzerland came the name 'Bollingen'), and netted them all together in a supposed fascist conspiracy to strangle American democracy and its democratic poetry. 'In the Bollingen award', he wrote, 'the clouds of an intellectual neo-Fascism and the new estheticism have perceptibly met.' In his second article, 'Poetry's New Priesthood', Hillyer held Eliot responsible for the scandalous award of the prize to Pound, and likened his influence upon his fellow jurors, upon the New Critics, and upon the teaching of literature in the nation's schools and colleges, to totalitarian dictatorship. Over the following weeks more than a hundred readers' letters were published by the *Saturday Review*, many agreeing with Hillyer, some finding his conspiracy theories outrageous, but only one supporting the award of the prize to *The Pisan Cantos.*

Norman Cousins sent Hillyer's articles to Representative Jacob Javits of New York, who shared them with Representative James Patterson of Connecticut. Within the month they made the articles the basis of a discussion in the House, and had them reprinted in the Congressional Record. Neither had read *The Pisan Cantos*, but they took Hillyer's word for it that they 'contain obscenities to an excessive degree, and make many derogatory references to Jews and Negroes'. They were particularly aroused by Hillyer's charge that the award was an insult to America's war dead. 'Pound states that Jews stimulate wars to make money, while the stupid Christians go out to fight and are slaughtered,' they declared, and demanded rhetorically, 'How can we tolerate these expressions, when we all realize the great contributions made in World War II by many thousands of Negroes and Jews who laid down their lives for an ideal?' Javits warned that the dangers of fascism to American democracy were as real as the dangers of communism, and called for an investigation into the committee and the award. In those years the House Committee on Un-American Activities was very actively seeking to uncover the communist affiliations of writers and public figures, and there was a very real fear among them of the damage they could suffer from being made to appear guilty by association with known communists. However, there was to be no Congressional investigation of the alleged 'fascist infiltration' of the Bollingen jury. Instead, the Library Committee of Congress simply decided in mid-August that the Library would no longer award prizes for art, music, and literature.

Harrison Smith made it clear to Laughlin in mid-September that the *Saturday Review*'s quarry had been not Pound but the Library of Congress's Fellows in American Literature. As with Dwight MacDonald, though their intent was the opposite of his, the more they could blacken Pound's reputation the better he served their attack on the Fellows. The editors had wanted to destroy the power over American poetry and criticism of 'a clique subservient to Eliot', a clique in whose work 'Pound's influence and Fascist conceptions' were plainly reflected, and whose members were among the Fellows who had so scandalously awarded the prize for poetry to Pound. By attacking them and working up a national sense of outrage, and then arousing the interest of Congress, they had succeeded, in their own estimate, in extinguishing this small group's highly undemocratic power.

When they found themselves under attack the Fellows readily sacrificed Pound's reputation to save their own. First Luther Evans contributed to the *Saturday Review* a defence of the Library's objects and procedures in the matter of the award, and of the Fellows' conduct in making the award. For himself, he regarded their giving the prize to *The Pisan Cantos* as 'unfortunate', and he confessed that to him 'Mr. Pound's book is hardly poetry at all'. But that said, he held that poetry should not have to pass a political test, and he could not and would not interfere with the Fellows' free and expert decision. Léonie Adams, as chair of the committee, issued a statement justifying the manner in which the ballot had been conducted. Allen Tate issued a 'personal statement' defending himself against the charge of 'fascism'. The Committee as a whole issued a statement defending the Fellows, their qualifications to act as jurors, and the correctness of their judging *The Pisan Cantos* exclusively on literary merits and in spite of their strong personal objections to Pound's attitudes and beliefs. The statement gave no indication of exactly what they perceived to be the book's literary merits.

Other writers rallied to the Fellows' defence. A *Hudson Review* editorial denounced the *Saturday Review* campaign as the most ill-founded and 'unscrupulous attempt that has been made here in recent years to discredit a group of serious writers, and serious writing in general'. Hayden Carruth, just then editor of *Poetry* (Chicago), saw the campaign as an attack on poetry itself, and hastened to defend the Fellows and American poetry in general from the taint of fascism and un-Americanism, while saying of Pound that he was 'very likely a traitor' and 'an acknowledged fascist'. The poet John Berryman obtained seventy-four signatures, including those of many leading writers and critics, to a letter to the editors of the *Saturday Review of Literature*. At the outset this impressive body of America's men of letters liberally allowed that 'The literary and political values of the poetry of Ezra Pound offer wide latitudes of support and opposition, as all poetry does in one degree or another', and declared that they would welcome discussion 'in these terms'. They did not stay, however, to engage in that wide discussion. Their pressing concern was that,

> Under the pretense of attacking the award of the Bollingen Prize to Ezra Pound, you sanctioned and guided a prepared attack on modern poetry and criticism, impugning not only the literary reputations but the personal characters of some of its foremost writers.... Through the technique of the smear and of 'guilt by association' you linked the names of T. S. Eliot, Ezra Pound, Paul Mellon, and Carl Jung, and adumbrated a Fascist conspiracy, for which you did not produce the evidence, and by implication you included in this attack not only certain of the Fellows in American Letters of the Library of Congress, but also a larger group of unnamed writers who were participating in the 'conspiracy'.

That was a just counterblast against what the editor of *The Nation,* where the letter appeared after the *Saturday Review* refused it, termed a 'philistine attack on modern literature'. Yet it failed to expose and challenge the fact that it was by their association with Pound that the others were being smeared and found guilty, and that his reputation and his poetry had been first smeared and condemned, and this without the production and examination of any evidence beyond the repeatedly cited half-dozen anti-Semitic lines, the only lines out of the more than three thousand in *The Pisan Cantos* that those arguing over the Bollingen award appeared to know. There was after all a profound injustice in this instance of America's more enlightened writers and critics rallying to their own defence against the paranoid prejudice Hillyer had whipped up against them while abandoning Pound to it.

It was a remarkable feature of 'the literary battle of the year' (as Malcolm Cowley called it) that such small regard was shown on all sides for the literary virtues of particularity and precision. The entire battle was conducted in abstractions and generalities, in rhetorical questions and assertions, with no analysis or demonstration of anything in particular. Most scandalously, there was no attempt at all to test and prove what was being alleged of Pound and *The Pisan Cantos*, whether for or against—none in the Bollingen jurors' statements to justify their award, none in the arguments in *Partisan Review* and the *Saturday Review* and *Poetry*, and still none in *Poetry*'s collection *The Case against 'The Saturday Review of Literature'*. It would be impossible to say from those sources whether the participants had any real knowledge of what they were all confidently asserting or assuming concerning those cantos. It would also be impossible to say exactly what they meant by 'fascism', the offensive word with which and against which the battle was mainly fought, since it could be intended, as by Shapiro, as a variant for 'anti-Semitism', or it could be used as in the *Saturday Review* to damn anything from Nazism to the New Criticism. And if occasionally some reference to Mussolini's Italian Fascism was intended this was inevitably lost in the prevailing imprecision and lack of definition. Altogether, it was a battle waged in a climate of fear from which no one emerged with honour.

Pound observed the battle from St Elizabeths without being drawn into it. In February, in advance of the public announcement, he had been informed through Dr Overholser that he was to be awarded the Bollingen Prize, and Huntington Cairns had noted his excitement. Apparently he had considered issuing a statement to the press, 'No comment from the Bug House', but had thought better of it. By early April he had collected a box of clippings and letters concerning the award and he showed them to Cairns with some pride in the fact that most were favourable. There is no record of any sort of formal presentation of the prize. Presumably the $1,000 were paid over, but possibly not to Pound himself since Cornell had advised Léonie Adams that 'the prize, if awarded, should be given to [Dorothy Pound] as his legal representative'.

The award brought down upon Pound much hostile attention and some very negative views of *The Pisan Cantos*—Malcom Cowley for one dealt quite savagely with both Pound and his cantos in his summing up of the affair in October's *New Republic*. With the public at large the prize did little or nothing for his reputation either as a citizen or as a poet. Laughlin, however, was unfazed by that. In a press release accompanying the publication of the collected *Cantos* in 1948 he had deplored the confusion of 'the obvious poetic value of the CANTOS . . . with the political issue of Pound's past', and had gathered statements from Tate, Eliot, Williams, Lowell, and others, testifying to the *Cantos*' aesthetic value and to Pound's good influence upon modern poetry. After the prize was awarded he made the most of it in New Directions advertisements, beginning with a full page in the April 1949 issue of *Partisan Review* visually associating *THE PISAN CANTOS* with **THE BOLLINGEN AWARD** *'for the "Highest Accomplishment in American Poetry" in the past year'*. That was the issue of *Partisan Review* in which the editor posed his awkward question about vicious attitudes in beautiful poetry, the question which Laughlin would steadfastly sidestep, holding firmly to the New Critics' principle that the value of a poem had nothing to do with anything outside the poem itself. Archibald MacLeish would point out after Pound's death that this treatment had heaped further injustice upon him, by denying the profound commitment of his poetry 'to the human world, to the historical world, the moral world'.

Courage against cowardice

Nobody thinks but grandpa
He sits round all day
Whistling in the bughouse
Just to pass the time away

When his visitors had come and gone, and if the psychiatrists were not bothering him, Pound would have another twenty-one hours to get through on his own resources. Evidently he did not spend all that time in his cell, since he paid attention to other inmates and could be, as one attendant said to Marianne Moore, 'a great help' with them. But as a feigned madman among the genuinely mad he must have been subject to a special kind of loneliness. And he must have been shut up in his own mind, alone with his thoughts, for much of the time. He did not give way to self-pity, but he felt the loss of being so utterly out of the world his friends were free to go about in. In 1960 he would tell Donald Hall that he still suffered from 'the cumulative isolation of not having had enough contact—fifteen years living more with ideas than with persons'.

His mind was probably not a comfortable place of confinement, being rarely still or at ease. Its ideas milled about demanding attention and expression, mostly the same old ideas insisting as ever on instant action against the world's follies and stupidities. That at least is how it appears in the bulk of the letters Dorothy was carrying out and posting for him, apart from those to Olga Rudge and to Mary, now Baratti and soon to be de Rachewiltz when Boris revived an ancestral title. One of his most faithful and regular correspondents was Olivia Rossetti Agresti, an old friend who lived in Rome, who had been for much of her life involved in an international institute there which became the United Nations' Food and Agriculture Organization, and who had been, like Pound, a supporter of Mussolini's economic programme. There were shared interests and friends, but also sharp differences—and Pound was as stimulated by their differences as by what they had in common.

She was Catholic, so he would attack the Church of Rome—'nothing cd/ be more idiotic than a religion that has put corsets on the holy mystery of fecundity'. She opposed his anti-Semitism, saying 'I am profoundly convinced that it is wrong to foster generalisations that make a whole people or race responsible for the actions of some', and Pound would blame the Jews for the errors of Catholicism—'a religion hatched in slums & cut off from agriculture is a *curse* whether of 1000 or 3000 years'; and again, 'The Church of Rome decayed, got steadily stupider pari passu as the jew books were put into circulation, and stupidities engrafted on the clean greek and roman ideas of the early Church'. He was particularly fierce against the Old Testament, calling it a 'turgid mass of bloodthirsty rhetoric'; and as for the revered King James' version, 'that ruind english style. It prevented thought. Boobs chained to cliches / cant think. // This bug house FULL of 'em.'

That letter had begun by asking Agresti to get copies of his wartime publications, *Confucio/Studio Integrale* and *Oro e lavoro*, to two Italian writers whom he thought needed to learn from them, specifically in respect of the 'ERRORS of the regime'. And did Villari, who was a defender of Mussolini's policies, 'understand the main points of Oro e Lav/ ?' As 'anonimo' he sent her a note for anybody to use over their own signature as 'from an observer of the interregnum', recalling Mussolini's declaration, 'Lo Stato è lo spirito del popolo', with the comment, 'And Mussolini's state fell when it ceased to be the italian spirit'. Placed as he was, he could not help living over again the part he had played in that past, and feeling he should have been heeded then, and should be heeded still. 'If the *young* had started reading me 20 years ago the world *wd* be brighter', he wrote in June 1947, and then later that month, 'I shall prob/ die of stroke from rage at idiocy of people who never read the authors I recommend.'

Along with wanting to plant seeds in people's minds as of old he was now as urgent about agricultural improvements. The yield from peanuts in the Veneto had been used for oil, he protested, 'Got to get BUTTER idea into their blocks re/ arachidi. And into ALL of 'em: Alberi e Cisterni. Arachidi, Acero, Soja'—plant trees, dig cisterns, cultivate groundnuts, maples, soja—but 'None of the Italian papers has yet mentioned, arachidi, soja, acero'. 'AND [there were] these new soil treatments / tiny quantities in sprays'. Thus, as he had once envisioned on Rome's balconies a nourishing crop of peanuts, now he dreamed of nature's abundance being intelligently cultivated throughout Italy.

He had money on his mind, of course, especially the evil of 'private AND irresponsible . . . and monopolistic issue of PUBLIC purchasing power'. The usurers would keep coming up, 'internat/ money lenders (some of whom despite your fanatical defence of 'em are yidds, and the dirtiest sort of yidds)'. So his mind would run relentlessly along its well-worn lines, often made furious by his perception of the neglect of what needed to be done, sometimes pausing to appreciate ORA's being a Rossetti and cousin to Ford Madox Ford, sometimes calmly sensible, as in recommending an apparently effective treatment for her adopted granddaughter's TB. Mostly, though, in these letters he would be in his driven prose mind, combative, prejudiced, utopian, so that his way of calling for calm enlightenment was to proclaim, 'Obviously the filth of the age is out to destroy the vita contemplativa altogether / but there is no reason to surrender to filth.'

In the spirit of not surrendering Pound was negotiating to get back into circulation all his economic writings, including those addressed to the Fascist regime. Laughlin wouldn't touch them, and nor would Eliot, and Stanley Nott was dead, so he had to cast about for a publisher who had nothing to lose by the association. A letter to Thomson & Smith Ltd., Publishers, London W.9, dated 'May 28, 1948' and signed 'D. Pound', though obviously typed by Pound himself, was intercepted and copied by the British authorities. 'There is E.P. economic material for almost any size volume you care to print,' it began, and went on to mention *ABC of Economics*—'the rights are in E.P.'s hands (or rather of his "committee", namely me)'—*Social Credit: An Impact*, *What is Money For*, 'great number of articles that appeared in Action, and others in the British Italian Bulletin, during the Abyssinian war', *Gold and Work* and *The Economic Nature of the U.S.* 'now translated from the Italian', with 'further translations pending'. Among the latter would be essays from *Orientamenti*, 'some of them, particularly the later development of Gesell, are among his best'. The Revd Swabey should be consulted, 'in E's name rather than in mine', as editor or selecter, and Olga Rudge could be written to for other Italian material, again in the name of E., not D. Pound. One odd thing about the letter was an uncertainty about who had published *ABC of Economics* and *Jefferson &/or Mussolini*: did Nott do the former and Faber the latter, or was it the other way round—they should telephone Eliot for the details. Thomson & Smith did not publish any of these writings, but some of them were issued in London as 'Money Pamphlets' by Peter Russell in 1950 and 1951.

There was one project in 1948 which got Pound's mind off the past and concentrated it upon the immediate task of saving the American mind. When Dallam Simpson took up the suggestion that he publish a four-page little magazine Pound made the monthly *Four Pages* his own, laying down its editorial policy and pouring out, in over 300 communications in the nine months that it lasted, detailed advice and directions which Simpson gamely tried to keep up with. He was given a typed sheet 'to be kept for ready and permanent reference' setting out aims and methods, and these were repeated and reinforced in letter after letter. 'OUR job', as Pound saw it, consisted of '1. permanent basis : Confucius / Gesell (lifted to level of literature, and not petrified) // 2. current necessities, without which the US mind is merely OUT OF DATE . . . Fenollosa, Brooks Adams, Frobenius'. Confucius and Gesell were 'SEED, god dammit SEED' to be aimed at 'the 25 intelligent readers, (desired, not yet GOT)'—the twenty-five to be 'the best receivers AND possible transmitters'. Also, 'Everything used apart from the Kung/Gesell shd/ be designed to HOOK the attention, NOT to tell the converted what they know.' Pound drafted letters for Simpson to type and sign seeking contributions—thus Williams was persuaded to say what he thought of Eliot's recent Milton lecture, and Eliot was invited (in vain) to reply. Simpson was told what to include and what to leave aside, and which issue a particular item should go into and where it should be placed in relation to the other items. He would be advised on the particular qualities of different typefaces, Caslon, Baskerville, or Didot, on the appropriate size of type to use for an item, 7 point or 6 point, and on filling up the page to avoid excess white space or 'printer's fat'. For this last Pound provided him with a 'barrel-full' of short paragraphs and one-liners, 'fillers', to choose from at need, all anonymous but unmistakeably his. It was in vain that he sagely advised that there should be 'as much as possible that is NON-EP, and that wont suggest too much and too many EP associations', since, inevitably, his 'internal signature' was all over most of the nine issues.

His daughter Mary in her castle Neuhaus above Gais, and Olga Rudge at Sant'Ambrogio or in Siena, were much in his thoughts. A few days after he was moved from the hell-hole to Cedar Ward he wrote to Mary, 'winter here, very—but warm in coop', then asked what he could do for her. 'If cento dollars are any use', he offered, 'you can have 'em . dono di nozze da ME', 'a wedding present from ME' even if he was legally a non-person. And if 'la nonna', her grandmother Isabel, 'has sense enough to go to Gais there would be money to pay for a serva and her food'. When Mary's first child was born, in April, he hailed 'evivva Walther!!', realised that he was now a grandfather, and punned, as if the child had transformed his state, 'here begins nonn'entity'. In June his mother was taken up to Neuhaus by car—she could no longer live on her own and there was no one to care for her in Rapallo—and wrote to him, perhaps forgetting how well he had known the Salò side of the lake, 'I regret you do not know the wonderful beauty of the road, under the rocky shore of Lago di Garda.' He wrote back, 'Glad to hear yr/ news & that you were getting some conversation. Mary has grand plans for yr. future.' Then he asked Mary how much it would cost to have a comfortable chair made for her. When his mother died at Neuhaus in early February 1948 and was buried there he wanted to send money for the funeral expenses, and to commission a traditional madonna for the grave from the local woodcarver, Herr Bacher, but first he needed to have specific figures since 'committee has to report to court all expenditures of my cash'.

Pound worried about Olga's struggling to make ends meet and was bothered by her refusing to take money from him. In a letter to Laughlin, whom he seems to think would be seeing Olga, he wrote,

> Will or (or NOTE; CAN you make clear to Olga that I wd/ like her to have leisure to play fiddle WHEN she likes/
>
> that whatever formula gets by the legal advisors, it would be framed to GET BY, not with aim of insulting HER.
>
> and that it is not D/ who is holding up the matter, but the red-bloody-tape.
>
> There wd/ be no strings as to what she actually did when or IF it is possible for the royalties to be turned over to her. I shd LIKE the accounts sent to her, and for her to get all there is /

In December 1947 he wrote on the back of the envelope of a Laughlin letter to Dorothy sent from Klosters in Switzerland, 'N.D. royalties made over to Olga || Pay to her | keep out of custody accounts || but DP approval [? because] EP incompetent.' On the front of the envelope he added, 'Cornell had question earlier will of E.P. | & this wd cover at least part of the intentions in that document. | no mention DP in note to OR.' On another envelope he wrote, 'Tell O. to for gods sake take the cash | so as not to worry EP further. | She can hold or spend | preferably spend.' On the back of this envelope he added, 'EP should have some freedom even from benevolent "committee".' These pencilled notes were evidently directions for Dorothy, who wrote more or less in those exact terms to Laughlin on 24 December 1947:

> About the royalties from New Directions: EP would like you please to make over whatever is owing to him from you to Olga Rudge.... If you make over to O.R. it will save me trouble as 'committee' when I have to make up the custody accounts again.
>
> Tell Olga for God's sake to take the cash so as not to worry EP any further: she can spend or hold—preferably spend...
>
> I feel Ezra should have some freedom to dispose of his own earnings, even from a benevolent 'committee'. This idea of turning over to Olga is made with my full approval....
>
> Whatever you write to O.R. don't mention my name in the affair.

In spite of these explicit directions Pound's royalties from New Directions were never paid over in full to Olga Rudge.

Laughlin reported difficulties getting the money to her, and at first the royalties continued to go to the Committee, and part would be returned for forwarding to Olga. Thus in October 1949 Dorothy sent Laughlin a cheque for $450 drawn on Ezra's Jenkintown Bank & Trust Co. account, and New Directions sent that amount in November to Olga Rudge 'for her services as custodian and editor of EP's musical manuscripts'. A further $300 was sent in this way in February 1950. Later two separate royalty accounts were set up, and through one the bulk of the royalties went to 'the committee', while lesser amounts were paid through the other to Olga Rudge. In April 1954 the amounts would be $1,558 to the committee, and $600 to Olga.

In November 1949 Dorothy Pound as Committee for Ezra Pound petitioned the Court to allow her to draw from his account each month $100 for her own expenses and maintenance, $20 for 'the patient's extras', and an allowance of $50 for Omar Pound. The Committee's legal fees and expenses were also paid from the account, and in time these would become considerable. A depressed note, not dated but apparently of 1949 or 1950, indicates that there were moments at least when Pound felt that he was not being allowed to dispose of his earnings as he wished. 'GODDAM/', he typed, 'not even $50 Xmas present for Mary. | or allowed to invest in anything of interest | such as printing sure seller'; and to this he added in pencil, 'in hands of money lenders | might as well die'. The Committee's accounts do show occasional payments to Mary, as $50 in October 1952, and $75 at Christmas that year.

Some time after 22 June 1949 Dorothy Pound sent Mary a copy of a document signed and sworn on that date before a Notary Public in Washington DC by Omar Pound. Omar had been demobbed from the US Army and was attending Hamilton College on the GI Bill of Rights, and about this time was a frequent visitor to Pound at St Elizabeths. The document states, 'FOR VALUE RECEIVED, I, Omar S. Pound hereby renounce all rights and claims to proceeds (royalties or whatever) from Ezra Pound's work in favour of Mary Baratti, of Schloss Brunnenburg, Merano, Italy and of her son Walter or subsequent issue.' There were two provisos: 'should the said proceeds at any time exceed twice my own income from all sources, then . . . the said excess shall become payable to me or to my issue, and should Mary Baratti's line become extinct, the whole proceeds shall be payable to me, my line or assigns.' In her covering note Dorothy wrote that the document had been 'notarized in triplicate' because Cornell had 'cast some doubt as to whether E.P.'s will made in your favour in Italy, would be valid (beyond question) in the U.S. or England', and 'the document now puts the matter beyond question'. 'Not that he would ever violate E.P.'s wishes in the matter,' she wrote, although the document was not fully in accord with Pound's testamentary wishes, which were known to her. In the event the document itself would be ignored and neither Omar nor the Committee would respect Pound's explicit and known wishes.

Mary had mentioned in May 1948 that she and Boris had 'a new castle' in view, and in September she confirmed that her address was now Schloss Brunnenburg at Dorf Tirol above Merano in the Adige valley. The castle was in a semi-ruined condition and masons and carpenters had to be brought in to restore roofs and floors and stairs, and Pound had Dorothy send money, $100, $720, to help pay for the works. In January 1949 he asked her, 'How many years' free roof can you give for furnishing a flat? you to get furniture or rent thereafter'. Evidently, in spite of what Eliot and Laughlin had been saying in December, he was thinking of getting out of St Elizabeths and having somewhere to go to in Italy.

It appears from a letter Laughlin wrote to Heinz Henghes on 14 February 1949, that this idea of a flat in Mary's castle did not mean that Pound had stopped thinking of Olga's Sant'Ambrogio. 'Do you remember Olga's little house on the hill up above Rapallo?' Laughlin asked, 'There seems to be an opportunity now to buy it from the peasant who owns it for about $3000. Both Olga and Ezra have been urging me to do so—with the idea that they would continue to rent the upper floor whilst I would fix up the lower one for myself. I have always dreamed of a place down there with that wonderful view of the blue Mediterranean.' Laughlin was free to dream as one does and to leave it at that, while Pound's urging from St Elizabeths must have been charged with nostalgia.

Pound was probably at his most contemplative when immersed in the ideograms of the Odes, or in the Greek of Euripides and Sophocles. In the summer of 1947 he was studying the verbal music of the Odes, seeking to repair his ignorance of how they should be performed aloud. He knew that there could be no 'real understanding of a good Chinese poem without knowledge both of the ideogram reaching the eye, and the metrical and melodic form reaching the ear or aural imagination'. But that was no simple matter, as he had recognized in his 'Notes by a Very Ignorant Man' appended to the 1936 edition of *The Chinese Written Character*:

> When you have comprehended the visual significance [of the ideograms] you will not have finished. There is still the other dimension. We will remain bestially ignorant of Chinese poetry so long as we insist on reading and *speaking* their short words instead of taking time to sing them with observance of the sequence of vowels.
>
> If Chinese 'tone' is a forbidden district, an incomprehensible mystery, vowel *leadings* exist for anyone who can LISTEN.

He knew of course that tone, the rising or falling inflection of the voice, was a determinant of sense—his *Chinese–English Dictionary* made that obvious—but he evidently felt forced to accept, as a translator into atonal

English, and one who had no hope of mastering the Chinese tonal system, that it was the 'vowel *leadings*' that would yield the best approximation to the sonorities of the original. He had been aware of this 'other dimension' in drafting and redrafting his previous versions of the 305 Odes, but now he was teaching himself to listen to the sound of the Chinese.

Through May and June he filled nine notebooks with syllable-for-character transcriptions of all the Odes, apparently looking up in his dictionary every character in Legge's Chinese text in order to establish its pronunciation and spelling in the Roman alphabet. This was his transcription of the first stanza of Ode 167, the poem he had translated as 'Song of the Bowmen of Shu' in *Cathay*—it reads from left to right across, [my italicized numbers here refer to *Mathews' Chinese-English Dictionary*]:

ts'ai^{3}	wei^{2}	ts'ai^{3}	wei^{2}	*[M6665, M7062, bis]*
wei^{2}	i$^{4\text{-}5}$	tso$^{4\text{-}5}$	chih^{3}	*[M7062, M3021, M6780, M939]*
jih$^{4\text{-}5}$	kuei^{1}	jih$^{4\text{-}5}$	kuei^{1}	*[M3124, M3617, bis]*
sui^{4}	i$^{4\text{-}5}$	mo$^{4\text{-}5}$	chih^{3}	*[M5538, M3021, M4557, M939]*
mi^{3}	shih$^{4\text{-}5}$	mi^{3}	chia^{1}	*[M4455, M5820, M4455, M594]*
Hsien$^{?}$	yün^{3}	chih^{1}	ku^{4}	*[[——], M7760, M935, M3455]*
pu$^{4\text{-}5}$	huang^{2}	chi^{3}	chü^{1}	*[M5379, M2294, M542, M1535]*
Hsien$^{?}$	yün^{3}	chih^{1}	ku^{4}	*[[——], M7760, M935, M3455]*[4]

One can see the rhyming and the assonance sounding across the lines and down the columns in an intricate pattern of 'vowel leadings', and then one can see Pound doing his best to match that pattern within the very different structures of English syntax:

Pick a fern, pick a fern, ferns are high,
'Home,' I'll say: home, the year's gone by,
no house, no roof, these huns on the hoof.
Work, work, work, that's how it runs,
We are here because of these huns.

[4] This is a very simple word for word translation using Mathews' dictionary:

Picking	fern	picking	fern
fern	already	growing	stops
day	of return ?	day	of return ?
a year	now	no	staying still
no	house	no	home
Hsien	huns	coming	the cause
no	quiet time	to begin	to be at ease
Hsien	huns	coming	the cause

The sound pattern is less intricate, though there is still much internal rhyme and assonance. More telling are the progressions of vowel notes or tones. Thus in the first line 'ferns' lengthens and dwells momently on the lighter and quicker 'fern', then the voice must rise on 'high'; in the second line 'home' is repeated as 'fern' had been, but is a slower, fuller, sound, and the stress of 'gone' at the end makes the rhyme a mere echo of 'high'. The stanza as a whole moves from the lightness and softness of 'pick a fern', through the drive of 'these huns on the hoof', to a heavy close upon the repeated 'huns'. That word will have been suggested by the sound of 'yün^{3}', the 'Hsien yün^{3}' being one of the hordes that thundered on horseback into north China. But Pound probably found the suggestion of a 'roof' in the look of the character 'chia^{1}' 家 *M594*, which Mathews defines as 'a house; a family; a home'.

To be involved in such a process of recreation must have been recreative, and as part of the process there was his listening to recover the sound of the original Chinese. At the least, this activity would have been an 'escape from abstract yatter' as the durations and reverberations of the well-sounded words, both the Chinese and his own, induced a more contemplative state of mind. Pound shared with the treatise on music in the Chinese *Book of Rites*, the conviction that while the properly sung Odes offer an experience of harmony, they also bring about harmony within the individual, and thus harmonize relations between individuals and all the way up to those between the state and heaven. That conviction attributes to the power of music exactly what is called for in the first chapter of the *Ta Hio*. In his own terms Pound had associated the Odes with the force in history 'that contemplates the unity of the mystery' and preserves 'the tradition of the undivided light', as against 'the force that destroys every clearly delineated symbol, dragging man into a maze of abstract arguments'.

David Gordon remembered how Pound chanted the Chinese sounds of the Odes one 'warm afternoon in early autumn of 1952 . . . on the lawn of St. Elizabeths':

> Deep and resonant to soft and high, every vowel sound and consonant pitched, regulated, and rehearsed just as he was again rehearsing it. Rhythm extremely exact and tempo very slow, but always with something surprising and uplifting about it. His range of expression was operatic and yet with tremendous subtlety of intonation; and at times within the rhythm of the chanting which was so carefully done it was as though you could overhear an intense voice just out of earshot conveying the feelings of lament, praise, supplication, groaning, yearning, or a tender and nostalgic vibrato, a muted roar or delicate and warm laughter, the many voices within the voice. Each sound he would come to would be itself distinctly

something in feeling and meaning from what preceded, and then there was a subtle joining together with a residue from the preceding sound to the next.

Gordon became aware of 'the whole man and mind' responding to the tonalities of the odes, and sensed that this many-voiced 'singing man and the song had joined undividedly into one'. Something of that intensely contemplative musicianship can still be heard in the recording of a selection of his versions of the Odes which Pound made for Olga Rudge in his last years.

Early in 1949, about the time the Bollingen award was announced, Pound was working out a version of the *Elektra* of Sophocles. For a better understanding of the Greek he drew on the expertise of one of his regular visitors, Rudd Fleming, a classics professor at the University of Maryland; and Fleming was to be named as author of the translation in order to conceal the fact that Pound was sane enough to translate a Greek tragedy. In the event Pound left the final revision of the text to Fleming and turned his mind to another tragedy, Sophocles' *Trachiniae*. His *Elektra* was forgotten until 1987, when it was performed off-Broadway in New York and found 'viable for the contemporary theatre'. In a program note the Associate Director of the production suggested that 'In the character of Elektra [Pound] had found a perfect mirror for himself: a woman locked up, treated as if insane, desperate to remind the world of her identity and her sanity, waiting—endlessly waiting—for a rescuer'.

While there is some truth in that suggestion, it does miss the leading concerns of both Elektra and Pound. Most important for Pound would have been Elektra's having the courage of her convictions, her continuing to speak truth to power in spite of being punished for it, and her refusing to compromise in calling for justice to be done. Justice in this case meant the avenging of the murder of her father, Agamemnon, by Clytaemnestra her mother, and by Aegisthus her mother's lover. At the time of the murder she had saved her young brother Orestes and had him smuggled out of the country so that, when he came of age, he should return to execute the appointed vengeance and 'bring back the old rule of abundance'. It is for his return and that outcome that she has been impatiently waiting, and meanwhile she will not cease complaining loudly of the wrongs done to Agamemnon and his house, and the wrongs done to her by his murderers and usurpers. The Chorus advise her to stop sounding off, it will do no good; and her sister Chrysothemis does the same, telling her 'if you don't quit bawling | they'll shut you up where you'll never see daylight | in some black jail outside the country'. But Elektra retorts, 'Need we add cowardice to all the rest of this filth?', and the stage direction would have her 'pause between each word', this being for Pound 'the key phrase for which the play exists'. But Chrysothemis keeps on at her, she should learn 'to bend and not break | when you come up against power', and other such nostrums. To her mind 'EVEN JUSTICE CAN BE A PEST', and to that Elektra replies, 'I don't want to go by your standards of conduct. | I'd rather die.' When told that Orestes is dead she accepts that it is now up to her to carry out the vengeance, or at any rate to attempt it, since justice must be done. As she has said, if 'there be no death for a death | ... all duty wd end & be nothing'. All the same, holding what she thinks are her brother's ashes, she comes near to despair and sings, 'take me in with you | I now am nothing, make place beside thee | naught into naught, zero to zero'. But Orestes is beside her, alive and returned to do his duty, his supposed death a trick to gain access to the palace. Their joyful recognition of each other and of their common purpose is operatic, the high point of the play. The end in which justice is done then follows swiftly and post-climactically, as simply the necessary and foreknown conclusion to the plot.

Beyond the possible mirrorings of his personal drama, Pound must have seen that the real action and interest of the play is in Elektra's states of mind and feeling; and then in how justice can be done when lawful authority has been usurped and is abused, when the people are cowed and apathetic, and the gods are silent. Her courage and her commitment to her culture's ethos and idea of justice are exemplary, but still she needs Orestes to do the deed. Her part is to suffer and to give passionate voice to injustice—she is likened to the mythic nightingale singing out her knowledge of the violence done by Tereus. Orestes for his part must be clear-headed and unemotional about what he has to do. Pound's notes make a clear distinction between these two aspects, between the 'intellectual complex' or idea of justice, and the passion for it. The idea must be got across in plain, direct statement; but in the emotional passages 'the translation need NOT adhere to literal sense (intellectual) of the original but must be singable IN THE EMOTION of the original'. Pound carried this to the point of leaving some of the more intense passages untranslated, to be sung in the original Greek so that the emotion should be wholly that in Sophocles' words. The great recognition scene, however, is all in translation, apart from a few isolated lines, and develops in taut, abrupt exchanges gradually revealing the siblings' common heritage and purpose, with Elektra breaking into song as her despair is overcome by joy. At this point the idea and the emotional demand for justice fuse in 'an intellectual and emotional complex', and from that follows the acting out of justice. The experience of the play would confirm Pound's longstanding conviction that the idea of order is inoperative without the emotional will to order, that for justice to be done there must be an intense and uncompromising will to see that it is done.

In Sophocles' *Elektra*, unlike Euripides', Elektra and Orestes manifest neither scruples nor remorse nor guilt. There is some recognition that justice in this case is not simple: Clytaemnestra is allowed her justification for killing the husband who sacrificed their daughter; and Elektra sees at one moment that she is being driven by the wrongs of others to commit wrong herself. Yet such refinements are swept aside in the passionate experience of injustice, and then in the equally passionate assurance that it is necessary and right to kill their mother and her lover. In this play justice is all, and the courage to demand justice.

Pound would recall Elektra in his next decad of cantos as 'the dark shade of courage | *'Ηλέκτρα* | bowed still with the wrongs of Aegisthus'. This would suggest that it was her speaking out against those wrongs that distinguished her in his mind, and this would fit with his valuing in Greek drama a 'rise of [a] sense of civic responsibility'. He saw his own speaking out on Rome Radio in those terms. A US Senator had told him in 1939 that Roosevelt 'has packed the Supreme Court, so they will declare anything he does constitutional', and he had concluded that 'When the Senator is unable to prevent breeches of the Constitution' then the duty to protest 'falls back on the individual citizen'. So far, up to 1945, he might be identified with 'the dark shade of courage'. But now, silenced in St Elizabeths by his plea and pretence of insanity, was he not to be identified rather with the compromising, cowardly, sister? There were those who saw it that way, Williams for one; and Katherine Anne Porter had written in a private letter in December 1947, 'if ever I committed treason or any other crime, personal or political, it would infuriate me to be considered insane. I insist on being held absolutely responsible for my words and deeds.' Pound would not have demurred—he too believed in standing by his word, and had wanted to do that in court. But then he had let himself be persuaded by his friend and his counsel, by the chorus and sister as it were, to keep mute and save his life. In the end *Elektra* may have offered him a discomforting mirror, though he did have other reasons for putting aside this translation.

12 : The Life of the Mind, 1950–5

'living the life of the mind, in the midst
of men whose minds had gone from them'
—Marcella Spann

The shirt of Nessus

It was probably in 1950 or 1951 that Pound turned from the *Elektra* of Sophocles to translate the play which he regarded as its antithesis, Sophocles' *Trachiniae* or *Women of Trachis*. In April of 1951 he exclaimed to Otto Bird, who was setting up a Great Books program at the University of Notre Dame, 'yr/ greek ROTTEN in omitting Trachiniae/ highest point of greek consciousness/ antithesis to Electra'. 'Elektra (Soph) | blood and savagery', he elaborated in some notes he put together for Huntington Cairns, 'Trachiniae | infinitely higher state of consciousness | unsurpassed in Xtn/ licherchoor, the HIGH for all gk/ consciousness.' He would put this strikingly original view of the play more formally in a note prefixed to his version when it appeared in print in late 1953: '*The* Trachiniae *presents the highest peak of Greek sensibility registered in any of the plays that have come down to us*'; and to this he would add, it '*is, at the same time, nearest the original form of the God-Dance*'. In his cell, and 'in the midst of men whose minds had gone from them', he was invoking that 'higher state of consciousness', a divine or godlike state of mind, to set against, or to rise above, the 'blood and savagery' of the tragic pursuit of justice.

There is no lack of brute violence in *Women of Trachis*. Indeed the play brings to a close Herakles' career of bloody and savage feats, most of them in the public interest, as in his getting rid of predatory monsters and tyrants, but some driven merely by his own passions and lusts. His final feat has been to sack a whole town because its king had denied him his daughter, Iole; and now he is bringing that young woman back home to be his concubine in a long looked forward to peaceful retirement. His patient wife Daianeira, fearing that Iole will take her place in Herakles' affections, remembers a love charm she had been told would prevent that. The centaur Nessus had been carrying her across a river, had groped her and she had screamed, and on the instant Herakles had nailed the centaur with a poisoned arrow. In his death agony the centaur told Daianeira, 'Scrape the drying blood from my wound | where the Hydra's blood tipped that arrow | . . . and you'll have a love charm so strong | that Herakles will never look at another woman | or want her more than you.' So Daianeira applies the bloody charm to an embroidered shirt and sends it for Herakles to wear as he sacrifices to the gods in thanksgiving for the completion of his labours. It burns into him as white phosphorus would, consuming him as it had the centaur. He curses Daianeira for doing this to him, then learns that she had meant only to keep his love and has killed herself knowing what she has done, and that really his agony is Nessus' revenge. His father Zeus had foretold that a dead beast would kill him; and an oracle had declared that after his last feat he would be released from trouble. Now it all makes sense, and Pound has Herakles remove 'the mask of agony' to reveal the appearance of 'solar serenity, the hair golden and as electrified as possible', as he speaks 'the key phrase of the play', 'SPLENDOUR, | IT ALL COHERES'. His physical agony will end only on his pyre, yet he has risen above it in reaching an understanding of what has brought about his fate. 'When he finds the destiny FITS', Pound wrote to Eliot, 'Herakles exults.'

So much in the play fits Pound's own story that it can be read as allegory. Dorothy Pound evidently came to read it that way. Asked in 1967 'what it was like in her domestic situation' she replied, '"You might picture the *Women of Trachis*."' So one might think of Olga Rudge as Iole, and of how Dorothy in her letters to Pound after his imprisonment in 1945 had tried to win back his love, and then kept him in St Elizabeths as if to keep him from Olga. Being shut up in St Elizabeths without hope of release would be his Shirt of Nessus, and Herakles' words would be charged with his pain—

> And now Miss Oineus
> with her pretty little shifty eyes
>   *m'la calata,* [*has tricked me*]
> has done me to beat all the furies,
> got me into a snarl, clamped this net on to me
>   and she wove it.

But those words will be cancelled by further revelations and recognitions, and in the end Herakles will blame no one for his fate. That was the distinguishing feature of the play for Pound. 'Everyone in the Trachiniae acts from good motives,' he told Denis Goacher, who was to play the son of

Herakles, in the BBC's radio production in 1954, and who was responsible (with the poet Peter Whigham) for the publication of Pound's version in England in 1956. To Michael Reck, who was in Japan attempting to transpose Pound's version into a Noh drama, he wrote:

TRAX in antithesis to Antig/ and other Soph/ plays in that NO ONE has any evil intentions, NO bad feeling, vendetta or whatso. All of 'em trying to be nice/. BUT the tragedy moves on just the same.

As he had said to Olga Rudge, 'Karma works.' If St Elizabeths is to be thought of as his Shirt of Nessus, then we must try to think at the same time that, if only in flashes of impersonal clarity, he could understand and serenely accept his situation, even exult in it, as the necessary and inevitable consequence of the part he had been impelled to play in his world and time.

Denis Goacher gave no hint of Pound's interpretation of the play in his 'Foreword' to the Women of Trachis. Instead he concentrated upon the 'cruel and unnatural punishment' of his decade-long confinement in St Elizabeths, evoking Pound's situation as he had witnessed it in 1954:

when the weather is fine *il miglior fabbro* will sit under one of the chestnut trees and entertain his visitors. One passes silent, disconsolate-looking groups of patients huddled together beneath the trees; a senile negro drooling over a captured snake in a large jar; fifty or so paces, and one might be in a garden in Rapallo, for there is Pound fidgeting in his deck chair with two or three friends or disciples on the grass about him. He sits in his chair, a burly bronzed figure with flying white hair and straggling mandarin beard; he speaks slowly and gently, sometimes lying uncannily still, but more often moving restlessly as he endeavours to punch some point home. He still has bouts of tremendous energy (that is how he gets his work done), but there are days when he is almost pathologically tired. Some visitors seem quite unconscious of their ability to drain his vitality; they will sit there, as before the oracle, waiting for him to talk; and he, with his almost legendary zeal, will endeavour to enliven them and bestir their wits. He is always giving, and his patience seems inexhaustible. As four-thirty approaches, Pound will look at his watch several times; it requires little imagination to realize how the time will be spent, away from all possible company, until lunchtime the following day, or perhaps the day after.

Goacher wondered, though, 'how many of Pound's visitors in a year were really disturbed in their hearts by what they saw'; and he reflected that 'The very fact that Pound was still able to produce his best work under conditions which would have crushed the will in most of us, somehow lulled our indignation, and made the situation seem less dismal than it was.'

Dr Overholser 'took considerable umbrage at some of the things he said and intimated about the hospital'. Goacher had mentioned that the '"treatment"' Pound was supposed to receive was 'apparently, to be confined to the Hell-hole', and that whereas 'his senile and schizoid colleagues' were 'allowed into the grounds at whatever time of day they please', Pound was allowed out for just three hours a day. Charles Norman had asked Overholser for details about 'the case of Ezra Pound', and as Pound's custodian, 'at least technically', Overholser was wanting the biographer to know that Pound had neither complained nor had cause for complaint while he was in his care. He assured Norman that the patient had been of course 'entitled to all the respect and sympathy that any sick person deserves', that 'a good deal of latitude was given to him and he went out practically daily with his visitors', and that his own 'personal relationships with Pound . . . were always most pleasant', while 'Pound's attitude toward me was always friendly'. In fact, 'having literary interests myself I visited him not infrequently and we discussed various persons and things of mutual interest'. One gets the picture of a civilized and humane existence giving no occasion for Goacher's indignation. It was of course a partial and self-serving picture, though with some truth in it.

There was certainly more truth than in Overholser's official reports to the Justice Department on Pound's 'condition and progress'. The patient's condition was always 'essentially unchanged' since his admission to St Elizabeths in December 1945, and there was never any hope of improvement—indeed if there was any change it was 'perhaps for the worse'. At the same time it remained impossible to say exactly what was wrong with him, as Overholser admitted in August 1953 to the Medical Director of the Bureau of Prisons:—

> The exact category in which he should be classified diagnostically is difficult to ascertain. There is no doubt that he is mentally unsound to a degree which renders him mentally incompetent yet he does not fit well into any of the psychiatric categories. Perhaps the nearest approach would be that of Personality Trait Disturbance, Narcissistic Personality.

That was because he was 'an extreme egocentric and, indeed his egocentricity goes to the extreme of a decidedly paranoid attitude, with particular emphasis on the outstanding nature of his abilities'. However, that was simply a finding about the predominant feature of his personality, and not a symptom of mental illness; or, as Overholser struggled with the difficulty, 'The implication of this diagnosis in the diagnostic category is that it is without psychosis.' In ordinary language he was telling the Justice Department that to the professional psychiatrist Pound was not insane. To evade the implications of that conclusion Overholser put away the profession's *Diagnostic and Statistical Manual* and boldly asserted on his own authority,

'In our opinion, one may be incompetent without being technically psychotic.' As a general proposition that may well be so, but of course it was not on the basis of that opinion that Pound had been deemed unfit to stand trial and committed to St Elizabeths.

The fiction that he was mentally incompetent was being rendered even less convincing by his continuing to write and publish. 'He does no writing and very little reading,' Overholser blandly lied in that 1953 report. The following year a surprised Assistant Attorney General in the Justice Department wrote to him,

> It has now come to my attention through the press that there has recently been published a volume of poetry entitled 'The Classic Anthology Defined by Confucius', translated by Ezra Pound, which was enthusiastically received by the critics.
>
> You will appreciate that this Department would be derelict in the discharge of its duties if it failed to bring to trial on such a serious charge a man who seemingly is mentally capable of translating and publishing poetry but allegedly is not mentally capable of being brought to justice.

Overholser stuck to his story. 'The work of this translation was, so far as we can learn, substantially completed when he was admitted to the Hospital,' he wrote back, adding for good measure, 'and we have no evidence that he has done any productive literary work during his stay in the Hospital.'

Pound himself was keeping up that pretence, while letting it be known that it was a pretence. He would write to his correspondents 'anonymously', and he would contribute to his disciples' little magazines over pseudonyms which fooled no one in the know. At the same time his new work was appearing in his own name: *Women of Trachis* in *Hudson Review* in late 1953, his translation of *The Classic Anthology Defined by Confucius* in 1954, and 'Canto 85' in *Hudson Review* later that year. And nonetheless, when Louis Dudek wrote the simple truth in his Canadian little magazine, in a sympathetic note seeking Pound's release 'without further indignity and cruelty', Pound exploded, 'God bloody DAMN it and save one from ones friends. // SHUT UP. | You are NOT supposed to receive ANY letters from E.P. | They are UNSIGNED/ . . . // Please remove that page from all copies Civ/n not yet distributed'. When Dudek pointed out that it was no news to anyone 'that he had a very large correspondence and did translations and other writing from St Liz', Pound let a year pass before writing to him again.

Kindergarten

Through all the years of his incarceration Pound never gave up on his teacher's mission. He had his regular class at St Elizabeths, on the lawn under the trees or indoors in his alcove; and beyond that he taught and directed by correspondence. By February 1958 he reckoned he had had '300 students in 12 years, or rather in fact ten, 'cause the first two were NOT very much open to enquirers'. 'When not in office, or in tiny minority, all one can do is educate,' he explained to Mary. And his basic method, which he recommended to the brilliant young polymath Hugh Kenner then at the start of his teaching career, was 'to attack IGNORANCE and drive in a few simple ideas'. His faith in the power of his few simple ideas to reform America was as strong as ever, and there were young people ready to absorb and propagate them.

'It is becoming a daily occurrence for six or more visitors to be with Mr. Pound simultaneously,' a nursing supervisor noted disapprovingly in October 1952 of the gathering in the screened-off alcove, and his 'visitors bring books, briefcases etc. to these sessions. Mr Pound assumes the role of a professor lecturing to his pupils, rather than an ill patient receiving comforting visits from loved ones.' Worse, he took left-over food from the dining room to feed his disciples, until this was mentioned in an article in *The Nation* in 1957 and he had to promise not to take any more.

Pound's daughter was not impressed by the band of disciples when she visited him in 1953. She saw them 'gobbling up hardboiled eggs which he had saved from his lunch or munching peanuts destined for the squirrels', and she thought, 'they should all go on hunger strike and call attention to the infamy of keeping the nation's greatest poet locked up in an insane asylum'. It seemed to her that 'no one had read or seen anything, certainly had not read much Pound', that the ignorance he was fighting was in them, and that he knew it. '"They all need kindergarten,"' he said. And he, she recognized, needed 'an outside audience as an antidote to the inmates'. Also, 'Confucius had said "make use of all men, even dolts."' Yet all she could see was 'a waste of his fine mind'. If he 'threw a new name at them they ran off with it like crazy dogs with a bone and since it was all they had in their mouths they declared themselves experts: on del Mar, Agassiz, Benton'.

She might well have been thinking in particular of young John Kasper, the most eager and rabid of Pound's followers. Kasper started writing to Pound in 1950 when he was not yet 21, and first visited at St Elizabeths in June of that year. He had heard of Pound in Babette Deutsch's poetry class in Columbia University's School of General Studies. 'We should reject his politics and respect his poetry,' Miss Deutsch had told her students—no doubt it was understood that his politics were 'fascist' and 'antisemitic'—but Kasper's reaction had been to declare to the class that for him it was the other way round: he 'didn't like Pound's poetry, but did like his politics'.

One can judge what he liked, or at least what he thought Pound would like to hear, by his telling him in January 1951 that he was meeting a few Nazis in the German section of New York and that he enjoyed talking to them because 'they keep the yitts out of their social life'. But that did not prevent him, it appears, from welcoming Jews along with Negroes and Whites to the night-time discussions and dancing in the Make It New Bookshop he opened with Paul and Lana Lett in 1953 on Bleecker Street in Greenwich Village.

Kasper established himself at once as the most activist of the disciples, one who would not need to be told twice that 'after EP. mentions a thing he wishes to hear nothing about it until it is Done'. Pound was forever calling for Confucius, Del Mar, Agassiz, Benton, to be published in cheap editions so that they could be widely taught, and in July 1951, just a year after their first meeting, Kasper began publishing a series of paperback offset reprints priced at one dollar each to do just that. The first in the 'Square $ Series' was Pound's *Confucius: The Unwobbling Pivot & The Great Digest*, together with Fenollosa's *The Chinese Written Character*. Pound's version of the *Confucian Analects* followed in the fall of 1951. Alexander Del Mar's *Barbara Villiers, or a History of Monetary Crimes*, and Kasper's own selection of *Gists from Agassiz*, appeared in 1953; and the part of Thomas Hart Benton's *Thirty Years' View* dealing with the Bank of the United States appeared in 1954; these three carrying unattributed blurbs by Pound. 'Basic education at a price every student can afford,' he declared anonymously.

Make It New Bookshop issued in or about 1954 'a partial list of recommended reading from the permanent stock'. This was a comprehensively Poundian list of twenty-two items, each with a brief extract to point the recommendation. The first was *The Constitution of the United States & The Declaration of Independence*, with 'Congress shall have power to coin money' as the featured extract. The following half-dozen items all dealt with monetary matters: *Mullins on the Federal Reserve*, a critique instigated by Pound and published by Kasper & Horton; the Duke of Bedford on *The Financiers Little Game*; Del Mar on *Monetary Crimes* and Benton on the Bank of the United States; Congressman Jerry Voorhis on *Debt and Danger*; and *Social Credit* by Major Douglas, the strikingly prescient extract from this concluding with an apparently menacing reference to *The Protocols of the Elders of Zion*. Making up the middle section of the list were Pound's translations from Confucius, his *Cantos* and *Personae* (this represented by an 'Alfred Venison' poem), his *Jefferson and/or Mussolini* and his *Patria Mia*, seven items in all. The remaining half-dozen items, leading up to *The Protocols of the Elders of Zion* at number 22, were anti-Semitic, anti-Communist, and anti-United Nations, in effect wrapping these three together as conspiracies against America's freedom and independence. As a final grace note, the 'Congressional Hearings on communist Subversion' would be sent 'free provided $1.00 in postage is forwarded'. Altogether this looks like a list designed to please Pound and assure him that his educational programme was being carried forward outside the walls of St Elizabeths.

Kasper could also play up to Pound's anti-Semitism and go mad with it, as when writing to him, probably in 1954, 'I had a private book burning and consigned numerous works by Freud, Reich, Einstein, Marx and other Jewish agents provocateurs to the flames of Kasper self-righteousness.' Louis Dudek had warned Pound that Kasper was 'a wild disrupting individual', but Pound only replied 'katz is katz', implying that you can't change a feline's nature. As his letter goes on one gathers indirectly that in any case he wouldn't want to change Kasper's tendency to violent action. After a good deal of verbal violence of his own against Roosevelt and Churchill, and against the broadcaster Ed Morrow who would help bring down Senator McCarthy, he dismisses as 'beastly blue china' all the writers who won't face the 'question of honest money' and who are 'incapable of ANY serious approach to problem of the state'. Then he concludes gangster style, 'nearly time to stop being purrLight re/ the 30 years of american inanity'. He had previously advised Kenner, when urging him to do as Kasper was doing and get into print books that were needed, 'don't try to do it all yourself. Get assistant who has INDIGNATION, ira, accensio sanguinis circum cor.', a rush of blood in anger. Evidently Kasper possessed that virtue. And with it, as Pound admonished Kenner, Kasper alone had grasped that

> 95% of all useful acts can be performed or AT LEAST started within 24 hours of SEEING the need. The slicks pour millions of copies of obfuscation over the country ONCE per week. and the goddam eeeease/thetes spend 6 months constipation before lifting un mignolo [a little finger].

Though he would call Kasper 'sqirril headed', Pound was well pleased with him as an individual with the will and the angry energy to carry his ideas instantly into action. Far from being bothered by his acting them out with extreme prejudice, as in that 'private book burning', he simply accepted that that was Kasper, 'katz is katz'. And when Kasper, after the Supreme Court ruled against school segregation in 1954 and 1955, was carrying his ideas into the quite unPoundian actions of violent white racist resistance and fiery crosses and the burning down of de-segregated schools in the South, still Pound would not disown him, to his own grave cost. That is an episode for the next chapter.

Pound expected his acolytes, several of whom had served in the war and been to college on the GI Bill of Rights, to make themselves useful according to their abilities. Don't expect 'all things from one person', he would say; the job was 'to find WHAT given individual CAN do, under IMmediate circs/ under possible future circs/'. So Eustace Mullins, 'a slow mountain country young man', who had seen active service in the US Air Force and who was working as a photographic aide in the Library of Congress, was assigned to use that library's resources to investigate the Federal Reserve System, and produced a thoroughly Poundian exposé of the 'conspiracy' behind it. Thereafter he went rogue. Discharged by the Library of Congress for forging and circulating violently anti-Semitic material, Mullins served, as he would later put it, 'as Special Legislative Researcher to Senator Joe McCarthy during the hectic days of the Senator's gallant struggle against the entrenched forces of Communism in our nation's Capitol'. The most far-out anti-Semitic conspiracy theories lay ahead. Pound had an eye for a person's utility, but was rather too often blind or indifferent to everything else about them.

T. David Horton was a quite different sort of individual from Mullins, and different again from Kasper with whom he became associated as co-publisher of the Square $ books. His assignment was to propagate Pound's economic ideas, and in the fall of 1950 while he was at Hamilton College on the GI Bill he duly reprinted, in a little magazine called *Mood*, 'Ezra Pound on Gold, War, and National Money' from the *Capitol Daily* of 9 May 1939. However, rather than acting as a fired-up propagandist he tended to follow Pound's better example. In a brief introductory note implicitly invoking the Poundian (and Aristotelian) principle that general ideas should be 'born from a sufficient phalanx of particulars', he declared that he needed to know more facts before he could begin 'to analyze E. P.'s economics'. He was equally reasonable in a letter to an Ohio paper in 1951 about 'the difference between interest-bearing and non-interest bearing government debt', a letter quite possibly instigated by Pound and certainly endorsed by him as 'a very lucid note'. The idea was Pound's, but it was presented without any of Pound's rage. After graduating from Hamilton Horton moved down to Washington, where he worked in a naval laboratory, studied law at night school, managed somehow to be mentioned as a regular in Pound's circle of visitors though arriving 'latish on Sundays', and became sole publisher of the Square $ books when Kasper went off to fight to maintain segregation. He went on to become an attorney in Battle Mountain, Nevada.

David Gordon first visited Pound in 1952. He was 23, had been in the navy, was 'working on beginning Chinese' while attending George

Washington University, and first wrote to Pound seeking instruction 'in music and rhythm factors', and in how to read and translate Chinese poetry. Pound took him seriously as a budding sinologist, and had him come early on Saturdays, at one o'clock when the official visiting hour was two o'clock, so that they could have some uninterrupted time together. Pound set him to translating Mencius; and later, in 1956, had him make a selection from the four volumes of Blackstone's *Commentaries on the Laws of England* (1765–9), this to serve as an introduction for university students to the common law as the basis of the rights and liberties of the individual in England and in John Adams's America. Gordon related to parts of Pound's mind few others among his visitors could appreciate. His Pound was the poet of the Confucian Odes and the later cantos, and he would become a brilliant expositor of the further reaches of these challenging cantos, as well as a distinguished translator, poet, and teacher in his own right.

William MacNaughton first visited Pound in October 1953. Having fallen out with his father, *Time*'s Capitol Hill correspondent, he was earning his living as a taxi-driver while attending Georgetown University. He was another undergraduate studying Chinese and wanting 'to talk about the poet's craft', but in his case Pound had other ideas. 'These days', he told him, 'with gentleness and good humour', 'he found it more interesting to talk about justice, good government, and sensible economics'. So he put the young man to work getting out a four-page monthly successor to Dallam Simpson's *Four Pages*, and told him it should be called *Strike*, to make an impact and possibly 'get you some notice from the labor movement'. The little mag ran from June 1956 to March 1957, ten numbers, printed some of Gordon's selections from Blackstone, and sixty-two of Pound's anonymous 'piths' concerning 'justice, good government, and sensible economics'. MacNaughton was also set to work translating Zielinski's *La Sibylle: Three Essays on Ancient Religion and Christianity*, but this task was not in his line and he failed to carry it through. It had been 'a chance for McN/ to get himself onto the map', a disappointed Pound remarked to another correspondent, 'but he may be a taxi driver CAN'T alter the zoological status of local fauna'. After *Strike* folded MacNaughton's function in Pound's eyes seems to have been to provide transport for Dorothy and for special visitors on his appointed days, Tuesdays and Sundays, and more especially to take care of Sheri Martinelli. Nevertheless in his life after St Elizabeths he was to make a successful career as a scholar and teacher in American universities and in the City University of Hong Kong.

One gathers from his students' accounts that in their experience Pound talked and they listened through the visiting hours and through the long years. Michael Reck remembered Pound's voice running on of a winter afternoon while the steam radiator sang in the alcove, his talk 'the liveliest I have ever heard, sometimes even boisterously good-humored', but with sadness underneath it all. He talked to entertain, and to instruct and instigate; and also because 'keeping quiet 21 hours a day leaves the larynx in want of exercise'. There were anecdotes and stories of old friends and enemies in his London and Paris days, jokes with mimicry of voices and dialects, sustained riffs against the villainies of Roosevelt or whoever; and there were lectures on economics, and sermons on the state of the nation. MacNaughton thought that Pound was rehearsing his cantos in his conversation. He noticed that 'entire "raps"—paragraphs and blocks of paragraphs'—would recur in his talk and 'eventually appear in print as parts of cantos'. According to Reck though Pound was mostly teaching and preaching. 'Like the Old Testament Ezra, Pound preached his visions constantly,' with 'a tendency to think that he alone could save society', and 'a genial assumption' that his listeners must think as he did on contentious matters.

With young artists, however—the writers, painters, sculptors, composers who felt the need to have visited him—he 'was not domineering'. While 'constantly trying to explain and guide . . . he received contrary opinions in good grace, and they seemed to amuse him'. His attitude to those who had some right to their own opinions was Confucian: all were correct if true to their own nature. At the same time he would tell the young in general, 'None of you have enough facts.' And there would be instigations to action. The young Beatnik poet Diane Di Prima, after a visit to Pound in December 1955, came away feeling that he wanted her 'single-handed to change the nature of the programming on nationwide television'. Some young enquirers, if they stayed the course, would be taught more or less formally. A Chinese student who sought his help with the Cantos visited once a week for four months in the summer of 1952, and for her and for the others who came on her day the routine was to read in advance some text set by Pound, upon which he would lecture and answer questions, and after that he would read a few pages from the Cantos and they could ask about things they did not understand. In the end she knew that she had 'undergone an intensive period of schooling under the guidance of a vigorous and dedicated teacher of the Confucian strain . . . he taught me what and how to read.'

La Martinelli

Of all Pound's regulars Sheri Martinelli was at once the most truly individual, and the most completely a product of a specific subculture of her time—the subculture of which Ginsberg's *Howl* (1956) was another expression. Most of the other regulars, though perceived as parasitical drop-outs by occasional visitors resentful of their presence, would go on to lead more or less conventional American lives. Even Kasper would end up as a car salesman in Nashville, Tennessee. Martinelli was the genuine drop-out. In the 1950s she was riding the wave of the Beat Generation, the Ginsberg and Kerouac and Ferlinghetti advance wave of the 'liberated' '60s, and she would remain to the end of her life a passionate resister of convention in the way she lived and in the way she expressed herself. And with all that she would become and would remain the most profoundly influenced by Pound of all his followers. 'Before Ez & After Ez man! The change,' she would write in the hip idiom of the time, 'he tuned me in clear & LOUD but it's still me'.

For a time, La Martinelli, as Pound grandly dubbed her, would bring to him, and bring out in him, states of mind no one else could in those drear St Elizabeths years. She was older and more experienced than the young men of his 'kindergarten', and indeed something of a diva. Dorothy saw her as 'the new honey-pot girl—who is lovely & charming & intelligent: with the most complete lack of morals I've come upon—almost ever!'

Sheri was 34 when she first visited in 1952, and had been around in Greenwich Village since the end of the war. In her Philadelphia background were an alcoholic Irish Catholic father, art school, a marriage which changed her name from Brennan to Martinelli, a daughter, and a separation when she moved to New York in 1945 leaving the child behind. Anaïs Nin took her up for a time; she painted, and supported herself modelling, mainly for *Vogue*; she knew the jazz scene, was a friend of Charlie Parker, absorbed his be-bop, and tried heroin. Men were drawn to her, 'so many who'd like to say they slept with me', she would write to Charles Bukowski, that 'I told all of them "oh just say you did anyhow . . . everybody else does"'. In 1973 she recollected that, having been first 'Made Trusting & Loving & Innocent & Ignorant', she had been 'having a Ball . . . . T/ guiltless sex of animal desire; pure simple & uncomplicated by The Falsities of Any Other Facts!' She hadn't known even for a split second that she was 'Lost in Hellishness', not until Pound 'spoke to [her] Thoughts'.

But did he sleep with her? God knows. Torrey thought he knew and said he did, though no one who was actually there ever suggested it, and the conditions in which Pound lived made it improbable, even impossible. In any case what can be known may prove more sensational.

Pound certainly delighted in La Martinelli, and was joyfully in love with her for a time. The sexual attraction was on display for all to see. Marcella Spann recorded how, 'Seeing Sheri approach across the lawn, he jumps out of his chair and hurries to greet La Martinelli with his most affectionate and energetic bear hug.' One indoors visitor looked away when she came into the ward as 'Pound embraced her and ran his hands through her hair and they talked excitedly, each interrupting the other.' That visitor was shocked again, having taken her for one of the inmates, when, their time being up, 'Pound threw his arms around her, hugged her, and kissed her goodbye.' Martinelli herself wrote in her correspondence with Bukowski, 'he read me Dante, Villon, Guido, the Kuan Tzu, the Sacred Edicts, Ovid . . . & lots of other things . . . & seduced me whilsts he read'; and again, 'he had one hand on my breasts & one eye on me . . . & one hand on Ovid's Metamorph & one eye on th'book & his mouth on mine . . . dear Educational Gramps', for this was '"education" the way gramps meant it', his way of speaking to her 'Thoughts'.

That was in a letter instructing Bukowski in her 'female point of view'. 'As for "nymphos" . . . they do not exist—the animal is not made that way', she had told him, 'women get their message through their psyche'. She did grant that 'they do wag their butts now 'n then when they aint certain of their psyches . . . I have even been caught doing it . . . in a loose moment . . . & place.' She continued the instruction in a later letter:

> girls only go to bed with males because they cannot take a delight in writing poetry/ one can have any male close enough to knock down; because males will fk ANY body/ thing/ any time anywhere/ they are mere fk hops & no earthly pleasure . . . & one has more than a sufficient knowledge & eggsperience with pleasure . . . but no earthly pleasure is equal to the spasm of the mind/ not the brain but the mind/

In another much later letter she used Pound's own terms:

> O! Telo Rigido! or how th' dickens EP spells/ an orgasm is not ecstasy—ecstasy has power to elevate the soma weightlessly . . . every cell participates . . . The cock is a local stop . . . Love 'e forma di Filosofia'

There might be a direct echo there of canto 93, and of Pound's talking to her of Guido Cavalcanti, of the 'Canzone d'Amore' and 'the intelligence of love'; but in any case Martinelli's 'female point of view', though rather differently expressed, was entirely in accord with his long held view that love's creative action took place in the mind.

The effect upon his own mind of being in love with Martinelli was written into canto 90, the first of *Rock-Drill*'s 'paradiso' cantos which he began drafting in July 1954:

> furious from perception,
>   Sibylla,
> from under the rubble heap
>   m'elevasti

from the dulled edge beyond pain,
m'elevasti
out of Erebus, the deep-lying
from the wind under the earth
m'elevasti
from the dulled air and the dust,
m'elevasti
by the great flight,
m'elevasti,
Isis Kuanon
from the cusp of the moon,
m'elevasti

In her private mythology Martinelli thought of herself as Sybilla, and as Isis, the female divine principle associated with the moon. 'Kuanon', the compassionate, would be Pound's addition; and the refrain, 'm'elevasti', is what Dante says of the light of divine love as he gazes upon Beatrice in the first canto of his *Paradiso*, you have raised me up into paradise. The canto goes on to enact a dionysiac rite which the lovers observed on the lawn in St Elizabeths, where they burnt olibanum obtained by MacNaughton from a Washington store:

Grove hath its altar
under elms, in that temple, in silence
...
myrrh and olibanum on the altar stone
giving perfume,
and where was nothing
now is furry assemblage
and in the boughs now are voices
grey wing, black wing, black wing shot with crimson
...
thick smoke, purple, rising
bright flame now on the altar
the crystal funnel of air
out of Erebus, the delivered...

—and among the 'delivered... free now, ascending', is 'the dark shade of courage', Elektra, standing in perhaps for Martinelli, perhaps also for Pound himself. The canto is framed by a Latin epigraph, and by its translation: that the soul is 'Not love but that love flows from it... And cannot ergo delight in itself | but only in the love flowing from it'. That was Richard of St Victor's way of defining the love that has lifted Pound's mind out of stultifying depression and opened it to contemplation of, and communion with, the vital universe. A line in canto 94 declares, 'Beyond civic order: | l'AMOR', and loving La Martinelli transported Pound's mind beyond the preoccupation with civic order which dominated his relations with the other disciples, and with his visitors in general, and into its paradise. That was the strange nature of this *affaire* at its most lyrical and most visionary.

Along with being Pound's spirit of love Sheri Martinelli was the artist in the St Elizabeths group, a painter of genius, Pound thought her, because able to paint the soul in contemplation as Giotto and Botticelli had done. Pound's visitors mainly observed her sketching, developing her iconic image of him, or drawing a likeness of Dorothy. Her paintings, many of which were to be seen on the walls of his cell, were mostly visionary versions of Pound, and of herself as she figured in their shared mythology and in the St Elizabeths cantos, as Sybilla, as Isis and Kuanon, as Leucothoe, as Lux in Diafana, as Ursula Benedetta, as the Princess Ra-Set, as La Luna Regina, as Undine. Stephen Moore reports that Cummings and Rod Steiger collected her work; but Pound's efforts to promote her, by sending out colour photographs taken by David Gordon, failed to impress *Vogue* or the Museum of Modern Art. He then commissioned his faithful Milanese publisher, Vanni Scheiwiller, to publish a little booklet of ten colour plates, with the title *La Martinelli* (1956), and sent $200 to get the job finished, and to have it done with 'a little more lusso'. He also wrote an introduction in which he implied that hers was an art 'which draws the soul unto itself'; and then affirmed that there was an affinity between her painting and his poetry, in that the 'unstillness' in her work manifested in paint 'what is most to be prized in my writing'.

Well, he was in love. He could tell Mary, in October 1954, that Sheri was 'the only person yet met here who can carry on a conversation at the level to which I have been accustomed'. She was 'a mist shot with lightnings etc., in fact the meteoric life of genius when it hits one of your sex'. That was in a letter to Ingrid Davies, his intimate London correspondent, in April 1955, and in July he added, 'Yes, La Martinelli, an act of god . . . let us plot the career and ubicity of a blue-jay'. He missed her between visits, and wrote messages he could not send, as these one November: 'Thurs a.m 10.30—That she might be feeling compagnevole or even consider coming out in the rain'; and later, 'P.M. 9.16 I dont know that you are painting another mermaid—but you might be in a pleasant state of mind. Ciao'; and the next morning, 'Friday 7.10.a m benedictions | birds in the fog | benedictions', this with the *hsin*[1] ideogram for renewal.

It has been said that Dorothy and Omar tried to put a stop to Pound's carrying on with La Martinelli, though Pound intimated to Ingrid Davies that Dorothy showed 'an extraordinary amount of good sense' in the matter. 'S.M. is not trying to kidnap me', he wanted Mary to assure Olga Rudge, and mused, 'Dare say D's horse-sense shows in "What does it matter unless we all go to Europe?"' Dorothy, who would have been well aware that jealousy was his 'particular PHOBIA', sensibly wrote the cheques to support La Martinelli when she moved to Washington to be near Pound, $35 a month rent for her apartment, and on one occasion at least $200 for dental treatment.

In July 1955 Martinelli was arrested and charged with possession of marijuana in Alexandria, Virginia, a felony in that state for which the penalty could be three years in prison. The charge sheet also mentioned her taking heroin. Pound, 'longing to protect his love'—this was how she later told it to Bukowski—'had the whole hospital upset . . . he was sending telegrams . . . writing spec. del. letters & phoning with special get-dr-op-middle-night permission . . . and he was writing . . . "2.a.m. . . . the moon . . . delecta . . . "'. For others Pound wrote, 'Shd/ like to keep Sheri out of jail long enough to get some religious art.' To that end he sent a note to Dr Overholser on 22 November, saying Martinelli was about to appear in court, and could she be appointed to teach art in St Elizabeths and be allowed to rent one of the attendants' rooms. That scheme was simply not practical, Overholser pointed out, 'We have no paid position, and the present state of the case would really rule out employing Miss M.' 'There was no question of payment to [her]', Pound wrote back, 'it was to be voluntary, and with the rent for the quarters paid to S.Eliz. | Difficulties . . . quite visible.' The trial turned on what might have been in a small plastic vial found behind a dresser, and the jury acquitted after being out just five minutes.

According to William MacNaughton, who shared a flat with her near St Elizabeths for a time, Martinelli did use 'marijuana, regularly, with periodic heroin "benders"'. Her own way of putting it was that she went 'down in Spade-town . . . turning on', and that she 'HAD to EXplore her age . . . entirely'. Pound, anxious about the damage she was risking to both herself and her art, condemned the age. 'The American milieu is filled with poison that did not get there by accident,' he wrote in his introduction to the booklet of her paintings. 'Since 1927 I have known that.' Claud Cockburn had told him in Vienna in 1927 that the Communists 'were definitely using dope as political weapon', and now it was his paranoid conviction that in America drugs were being pushed in a Jewish–Communist conspiracy as 'a definite method of the corruption and destruction of the god damned goy'—

heroin is pushed/ and the negro attendant knows that big chews are back of it.... AND the kikes go for the WHOLE of the more sensitive section of the younger generation/ 'all' jazz musicians on marijuana/ which 'is not habit forming' and leads to heroin/ and 'Benzedrine is harmless, they give it to aviators'/ so that after carpet bombing they will go on with some drug habit or other.

He was especially concerned about artists becoming hooked. In December 1955 he sent Noel Stock a note for his Melbourne magazine: 'Those charming internationalists with their heroin and "derivatives" attack the most sensitive ganglia of the occident, namely the art world, from which the university students take their snobism.' He was deeply worried for La Martinelli, lamenting to Goacher that 'God knows the barbarians are doing all they can to kill the painter before she brings the real thing into this hell of a country.... the future hangs by a hair, and they will kill her if possible.' A sentence someone had come across in Blake summed up his sense of the danger, 'destroy the arts if you'd mankind destroy'. He understood also, 'judging from local hell', that 'the red kikes' were directly degrading human nature by means of heroin, that being apparently the opium derivative 'that most kills the sex urge/ and THENCE damages ordinary affections/ normal manifestations of friendly affection, as comforting a child/ reverses all the normal magnetisms'.

Pound did have a certain amount of inside information, from Sheri Martinelli herself, and from William French, a regular visitor who was a jazz musician and whose wife was at that time hooked on heroin. Possibly it was French who told him that all jazz musicians used marijuana, and who explained that it 'magnifies TIME, which means they can gain precision'; and Martinelli might have put in, 'Same applies to sense of space.' Pound could understand that 'the temptation of artists etc/ is the increased momentary power/ or feeling of it'. But his own paranoid complex took over when he came to generalize about 'their' total war on 'the TOP sensibilities'. Then he could assert, without presenting any evidence, that the drugs are 'supplied by Dexter White and his coreligionists'. Simply because White, who had served as an important official in the Treasury and as executive director of the IMF, happened to be the son of Lithuanian Jewish immigrants, and had been accused of spying for the Soviet Union, he figured when Pound's mind was in its paranoid fit as an agent of the Jewish–Communist conspiracy against the American people.

Pound had informed himself as best he could about 'the local hell' in the hope of saving La Martinelli from it. But where his knowledge gave out he fell into his own mind's hell, the blind pit where not knowing enough let feared dangers project paranoid phantasms, and give apparent substance to rumoured conspiracies. At that time a paranoid fear of Communism and 'commie' conspiracies was a powerful force in America; and the paranoia was more potent when the anti-Communism was combined with anti-Semitism, each reinforcing the other, each making the other seem better founded. But it was Pound's particular responsibility as a poet, as a guardian of the language, to know fact from phantasm and to speak the truth of things. He should have known that the idea of a grand Jewish–Communist conspiracy was unproven, that it was a theory, and not to be spoken of as a fact. But in dealing with threats to the things he loved he lacked the poet's virtue of negative capability, the ability to contemplate steadfastly things that can not be finally explained and understood, and to accept and to make allowance for uncertainties, contradictions, and error, as inevitable facts of mind. Where he feared harm to La Martinelli or to the civilizing arts he just had to have a definite enemy to attack, and in Cold War America a suspected Jewish–Communist conspiracy met his need. And the lack of substance in this phantom of the mind degraded his language when he spoke of it, as when he wrote to Olivia Agresti of 'red kikes'. That is the language of mere negation, the language of hell. And yet it was not malice or wickedness that drove him to deploy it, but the frustrated desire for a paradisal order.

Adult conversation

Some visitors registered the anti-Semitism and anti-Communism as a fairly constant undercurrent in Pound's conversation. Others remarked little or none at all while they were with him. It depended, apparently, on the topic of conversation, and on the company. The English critic Al Alvarez observed the difference in 1955 when he made two visits a few days apart:

> The first time I saw him alone and we talked about literature. He was witty, courteous, lucid, passionately interesting, and interested, a devotee of writing... When I went back a couple of days later, he was surrounded by his disciples and was talking politics. They were pumping him on currency reform, 'Commy plots' and the use of dope for political ends. His talk was rhetorical, disorganised and full of improbable theorising. At moments he gave the impression of being faintly embarrassed by his followers' zeal. Otherwise there was little connection between this man droning on paranoiacally about usury and the dedicated, eminently intelligent man of letters I'd seen a couple of days before.

Probably Alvarez's first visit had been by special arrangement, and his second on one of Pound's open days. Marianne Moore, having visited on a day when 'the young people' were present, felt obliged to say rather fiercely to 'fearsomely resilient Ezra', 'Profanity and the Jews are other quaky quicksands against which may I warn you? You have seen turtles or armadillos, possibly, when annoyed and I sometimes have to be one of them.'

Visiting times at St Elizabeths, as Dr Overholser himself informed Elizabeth Winslow in 1951 when granting her permission to visit Pound, were 'from 2:00 PM to 4:00 PM daily, and 9:00 AM to 11:00 AM, and 2:00 PM to 4:00 PM, Sundays and legal holidays'. Pound, however, used to declare only Tuesday, Thursday, Saturday, Sunday, as regular visiting days, reserving the other days for visits 'only by special permission'. On his 'regular days' there might be as many as twenty present; on his reserved days there might be only one, or, rarely, nobody apart from Dorothy, who would be there nearly every day of the week from 1:00 to 4:00. Pound would give the impression that the special permission had to be granted by the hospital authorities, but it was actually his way of separating special visitors such as Eliot from the ordinary ones, and from the kindergarten. When passing a message to Archibald MacLeish that of course he would be glad to see him, he suggested that he be tipped off 'that as Mon/ Wed/ Fri/ are NOT visiting days, he might by saying he is in Wash/ fer limited time, get in on one of those days, and so have uninterrupted CONverSaySHun'. He divided the time on his 'regular days' in the same way, telling the more favoured among his visitors that the hours were 2:00 to 4:00, but that 'the nearer to one o'clock you get here the more likelihood of uninterrupted conversation'. Evidently the hours were even more flexible than that, since he informed a Polish scholar he took seriously and was trying to help, 'They wd/ probably let you in here even in the morning, if in transit'.

He was 'very hungry for adult company', as Dorothy said to MacNaughton when he had brought out a distinguished Chinese political and neo-Confucian philosopher and Pound had remarked that he was 'somebody you can talk to'. Dr Carson Chang could talk with Pound about Thomas Jefferson, having drafted a new constitution on Jeffersonian principles for the Republic of China in 1946; and while he 'admired the "remarkable genius" of Pound's translations of many paragraphs in the *Analects*', he would show him places where his analysis of an ideogram 'went too far'. Pound might not agree, but he enjoyed the discussions because Chang was 'interested in the definition of words', and they both found their talks engaging and stimulating. That was the kind of adult conversation Pound was hungry for.

He found it again in discussing the rendering of the *Pisan Cantos* into Spanish with José Vasquez-Amaral. Amaral, a professor of Romance languages at Rutgers University, had been taken to visit him and Pound had enquired 'What are you doing?', and that had led somehow to his undertaking to translate the Cantos. He would go out to St Elizabeths with a sheaf of drafts, and Pound would say to his court, 'Talk to yourselves, have some tea and cake, Amaral and I have some work to do.' Then there would be intense discussion of the meanings of words and hundreds of notes would be scrawled over the drafts. Amaral told how they disagreed about the right word for *cantos* in Spanish. Pound insisted that it should be *cantares*, but Amaral said that was impossible, '*cantar* had gone out of style with the end of Spanish epic poetry in the Middle Ages', it retained too strong a flavour of 'tribal legend'. But that was exactly what he meant, retorted Pound. Well, challenged Amaral, 'The legend of *what* tribe do the cantos tell?', and 'The *miglior fabbro*'s eyes glittered in triumphant amusement as he almost shouted: "the tribe of the human race, of Man, Amaral!"' And *Los Cantares* it had to be.

With Frank Ledlie Moore, a composer with, according to Reck, an exuberant personality, Pound discussed the tonalities of Byzantine music 'in an attempt to get at the original music of the Greek drama, and Moore composed Greek-type music for the choruses of Pound's *Women of Trachis*'. Moore told Reck about 'the day he first took the Greek-American sculptor Michael Lekakis to visit Pound', and as they left they '"heard a shout and saw Pound up in his window, leaning out and singing Greek verse to us at the top of his lungs. Happy, full of happiness, and playing the part of Homer."' With the poet and Nobel prize winner Juan Ramón Jiménez, an exile from Franco's Spain who was at that time a professor of Spanish language and literature at Maryland University, Pound conversed in Spanish. Jiménez struck Reck, with his 'trim black beard and burning eyes', as immensely 'dignified and noble in manner'; and Dorothy said she 'had not seen anything quite so *fine* before'. Pound would say to him, 'You are an exile *from* your country; I am an exile *in* my country'; but then he would talk as if Jiménez and his wife agreed with his political views, whereas, for obvious reasons, as Señora Jiménez remarked, 'Often we did not.'

Probably very few of his numerous 'sane and cultured' visitors did wholly sympathize with his political views, but they came just the same. Among the most faithful, along with Huntington Cairns, were two 'civilized professors' from the Catholic University of America, Craig La Drière and Giovanni Giovannini; and Rudd Fleming and his wife, 'a highly cultured couple of enthusiasts fer kulchur and greek drama' who 'would bring a thermos jug of excellent Chinese tea'. Serious work was done with Fleming on Greek drama; La Drière was 'a very sober English literature scholar'; and with Giovannini, another professor of English who wrote a study of Pound and Dante, there will have been intense discussions of the *Paradiso* and how it was behind the cantos he was then drafting. Just once, when no one else was present, Pound spoke to Giovannini about being caged in the DTC, 'speaking in a subdued voice, without visible emotion, with no word of complaint', and mostly 'in the third person, as if the memory of the caged creature were that of another unknown to him'.

There were literary people who regarded visiting Pound as a political act, and whose 'scruples of political conscience' kept them away and made them discourage others from going. Kathleen Raine, an English poet who was in Washington in the winter of 1951/2, was told by Auden, who had himself visited Pound in 1948, that it was perhaps all right for her to visit since she knew nothing about politics; but her friend the surrealist poet David Gascoyne 'backed out at the last minute from accompanying me', and argued for several hours 'about the moral implications of my actions'. For her, however, Pound was simply 'the most distinguished poet and man of letters in America', whose criticism of 'the evils of usurious materialism' chimed with her own spiritual values. When she entered the ward he jumped up from his deckchair in the alcove to greet her 'with the energy of a very active man' and the air of 'one accustomed to receiving literary visitors, wherever he might happen to be, and eager to begin on the serious discussion of serious (i.e. literary) topics'. He wanted to know all about what was being done in England; and when she showed genuine interest, he explained his Confucian philosophy in some detail. She felt his 'power of imparting creative enthusiasm', and found herself thinking, 'Why don't I start a literary magazine?' Afterwards she wrote,

> One thing I felt most strongly in America, both in literary and non-literary circles in Washington and elsewhere: everyone is disquietingly aware [that] Ezra Pound's presence, as an inmate of the St Elizabeth's State Mental Home, is an implicit criticism of the American way of life, and of American justice, about which history will have much to say. His present situation lends him a status that, paradoxically, belongs to no other living poet, whether he is a traitor, or a prophet (the distinction has always been a fine one) or both, his stature is on a historic scale... I even felt that he could not be more appropriately placed, in the map of history, than where he is now. Free, he would be a lesser figure...

Raine's lasting image was of 'Pound's large, vital, bearded figure, walking quickly away from us, alone down the ward, among the lunatics, in the flicker of the television set'—an image, for her, 'rather of greatness than of pathos'.

One of the things Pound said to Kathleen Raine was that 'after the age of forty, no man ought to give his first attention to the writing of verse', and she took that to mean that 'For the grown-ups there are more important issues to be considered', such as 'the evils of usurious materialism'. She might have been shocked into a less generous understanding if she had met young Kasper, or Mullins; or if one or two of the small group of grown-ups drawn to Pound by his political views had been of the company when she visited. Some of these were important ex-military men who probably came on his reserved days. Principal among them was Lt.-General Pedro del Valle (Ret.). He had commanded the US Marines in the heroic battle of Okinawa in June 1945, and was still intent on attacking America's perceived enemies, chief among them the Communist conspiracy to subvert American democracy from within, and behind that the Jewish conspiracy to take over the whole world. The United Nations Organization was perceived as the front and leading agent of this joint conspiracy, and in 1953, with other retired high-ranking officers, he set up an isolationist counter-organization known as The Defenders of the American Constitution. Pound shared these endemic paranoias and fed on them, though he did not go so far as to endorse del Valle's proposals for vigilantes and armed Minutemen to rid White Christian America of its subversives. But he became close to del Valle personally, and Dave Horton edited The Defenders' four-page monthly, *Task Force*; and del Valle's Omni Press in California took over the publication of Square $ books and put out a lot of small books which Pound would have approved of, including a reprint of Coke on Magna Carta. Del Valle's extensive correspondence with Pound is now in the Beinecke Library at Yale, but there is no record of what they talked about in St Elizabeths.

Del Valle's name and address is in the big address book which Pound kept in his St Elizabeths years; and so too is that of Dag Hammarskjöld, then Secretary-General of the United Nations Organization. The hardback book, with its leather corners and its worn cloth covering, also served as a visitors' book, and its over 600 names indicates the extraordinary range and diversity of Pound's visitors and correspondents. There are his economic and political contacts, notably Rear-Admiral John Crommelin (Ret.) and Lieutenant Colonel Eugene Pomeroy (Ret.) of The Defenders of the American Constitution, and the English Major-General J. F. C. Fuller (Ret.) who had supported Oswald Mosley's policies. There are many more literary and artistic and academic names, ranging from Julian Beck of Living Theatre, through art historian Kenneth Clark, essayist and story-teller Guy Davenport, poet James Dickey, critics Clark Emery and John J. Espey, poetry editor Rolf Fjelde, poet and translator Ramon Guthrie, independent film-maker Hollis Frampton, poets Langston Hughes and Christopher Logue, Dachine Rainer of the anarchist Libertarian Press, and on through the rest of the 600 to Louis Zukofsky. There are the names of

1. Ezra Pound talking to journalists upon his arrival in New York, 20 April 1939. Photo re-issued by Associated Press during the war with caption claiming that it showed Pound at Rome Radio studios. (*Wide World Photos*)

2. Ezra and Dorothy Pound, Rapallo, summer 1940. Headline 'Vasti incendie ad Aden' probably concerns Italian bombing of Aden from June 1940. (*Courtesy of Mary de Rachewiltz*)

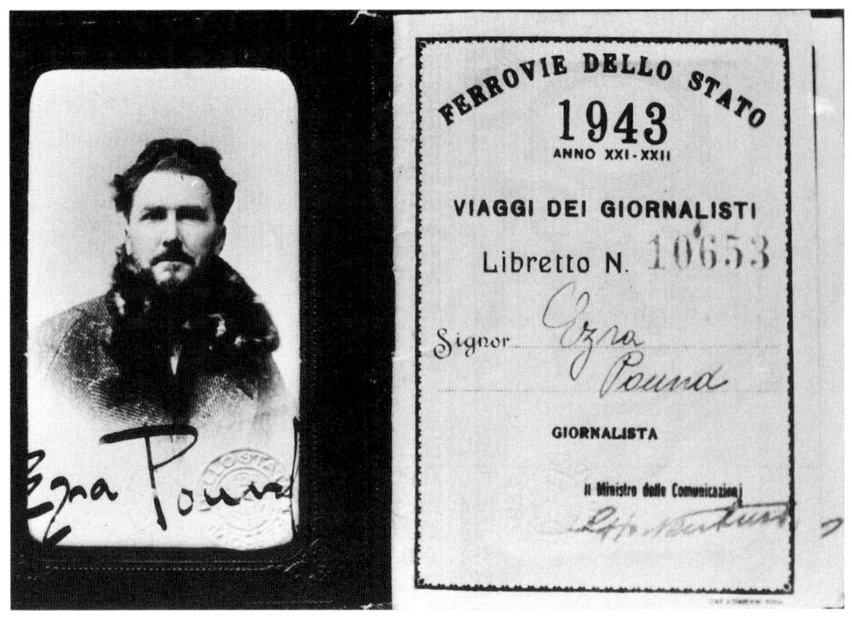

3. Pound's journalist's rail pass for 1943. (*Courtesy of Mary de Rachewiltz*)

4. Frank Amprim, FBI agent on Pound's case in 1945. (*US Army photo*)

5. Lieutenant Ramon Arrizabalaga, commanding officer and chief investigator Counter Intelligence Corps, 92nd Infantry Division, Genoa, with Ezra Pound, 16 May 1945. (*US Army photo*)

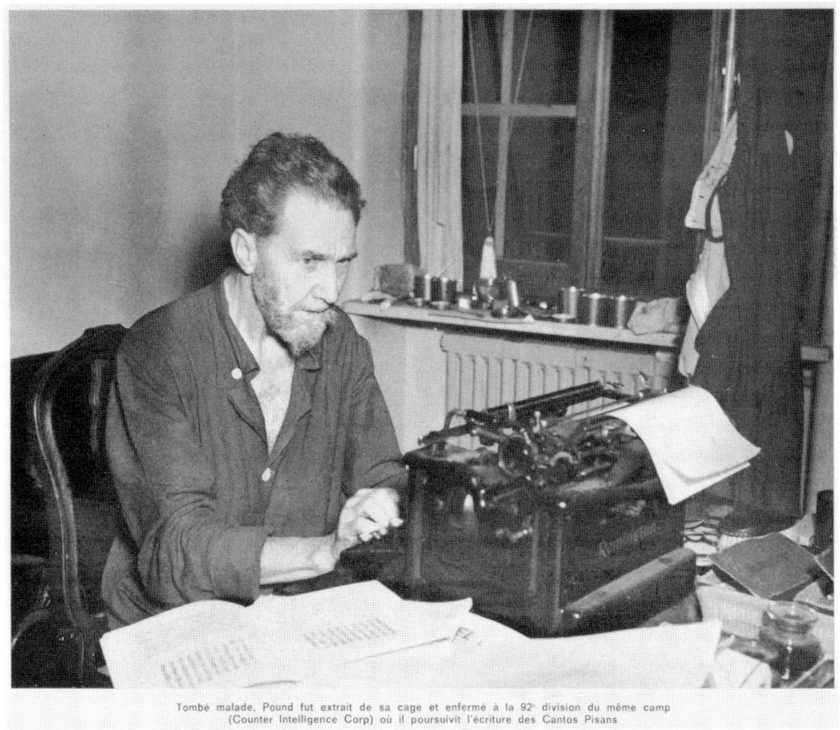

Tombé malade, Pound fut extrait de sa cage et enfermé à la 92e division du même camp
(Counter Intelligence Corp) où il poursuivit l'écriture des Cantos Pisans

6. Pound 'doing Confucius with Mencius for American readers if any', while held at CIC HQ Genoa, 16 May 1945. His Italian version, *Confucio . . . Studio Integrale*, is open on the desk. (*US Army photo*)

7. DTC cages for prisoners—the corner of Pound's special cage, with 'airstrip' in place of the regulation wire, is visible on the left. (*US Army photo*)

8. Ezra Pound's 'mugshot', DTC, 26 May 1945. (*US Army photo*)

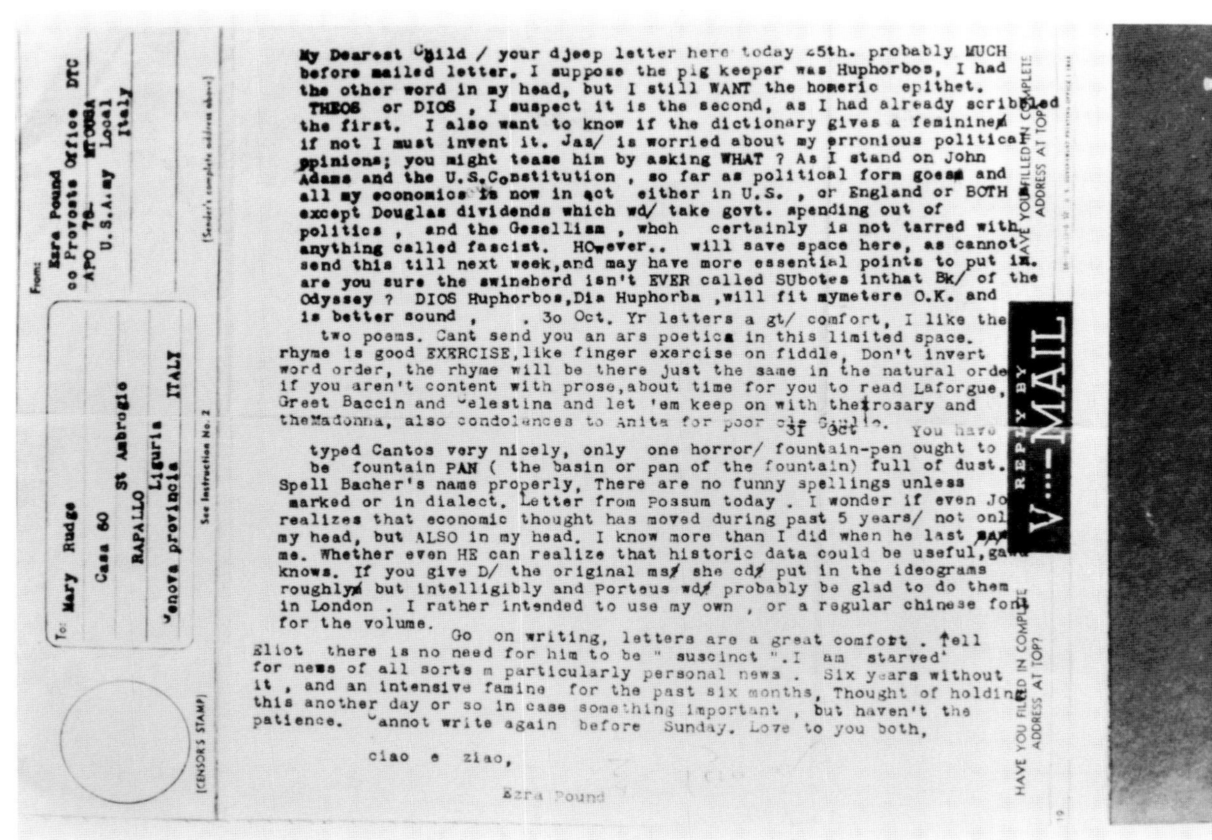

From:
Ezra Pound
co Provoste Office DTC
APO 78 MTOUSA
U.S.A.my Local
Italy

To: Mary Rudge
Casa 60
St Ambrogio
RAPALLO
Liguria
Genova provincia ITALY

(CENSOR'S STAMP)

See Instruction No. 2

(Sender's complete address above)

My Dearest Child / your djeep letter here today 25th. probably MUCH before mailed letter. I suppose the pig keeper was Huphorbos, I had the other word in my head, but I still WANT the homeric epithet. THEOS or DIOS , I suspect it is the second, as I had already scribbled the first. I also want to know if the dictionary gives a feminine, if not I must invent it. Jas/ is worried about my erronious political opinions; you might tease him by asking WHAT ? As I stand on John Adams and the U.S.Constitution , so far as political form goes, and all my economics is now in act either in U.S. , or England or BOTH except Douglas dividends which wd/ take govt. spending out of politics , and the Gesellism , whch certainly is not tarred with anything called fascist. HOwever.. will save space here, as cannot send this till next week,and may have more essential points to put in. are you sure the swineherd isn't EVER called SUbotes inthat Bk/ of the Odyssey ? DIOS Huphorbos,Dia Huphorba ,will fit mymetere O.K. and is better sound , . 3o Oct. Yr letters a gt/ comfort, I like the two poems. Cant send you an ars poetica in this limited space. rhyme is good EXERCISE,like finger exercise on fiddle, Don't invert word order, the rhyme will be there just the same in the natural orde if you aren't content with prose,about time for you to read Laforgue, Greet Baccin and Celestina and let 'em keep on with the rosary and theMadonna, also condolences to Anita for poor ole Giulio.

31 Oct You have typed Cantos very nicely, only one horror/ fountain-pen ought to be fountain PAN (the basin or pan of the fountain) full of dust. Spell Bacher's name properly, There are no funny spellings unless marked or in dialect. Letter from Possum today . I wonder if even Jo realizes that economic thought has moved during past 5 years/ not onl my head, but ALSO in my head. I know more than I did when he last saw me. Whether even HE can realize that historic data could be useful,gawd knows. If you give D/ the original ms/ she cd/ put in the ideograms roughly but intelligibly and Porteus wd/ probably be glad to do them in London . I rather intended to use my own , or a regular chinese font for the volume.

Go on writing, letters are a great comfort . Tell Eliot there is no need for him to be " suscinct ".I am starved for news of all sorts m particularly personal news . Six years without it , and an intensive famine for the past six months, Thought of holding this another day or so in case something important , but haven't the patience. Cannot write again before Sunday. Love to you both,

ciao e ziao,

Ezra Pound

HAVE YOU FILLED IN COMPLETE ADDRESS AT TOP?

REPLY BY V---MAIL

HAVE YOU FILLED IN COMPLETE ADDRESS AT TOP?

9. Pound's letter from the DTC to his daughter Mary, after her visit in October 1945. (*Courtesy of Mary de Rachewiltz*)

10. Pound with US Marshals and handcuffed to one of them, upon arrival at Bolling airfield, Washington DC, 18 November 1945. (*Wide World Photos*)

11. Pound immediately after his preliminary arraignment before Chief Justice Bolitho J. Laws in the District Court, Washington DC, 19 November 1945. (*Wide World Photos*)

12. St Elizabeths 'mugshot', 21 December 1945. (*Wide World Photos*)

13. Dr Winfred Overholser, Superintendent, St Elizabeths Hospital, Washington DC. (*St Elizabeths Hospital*)

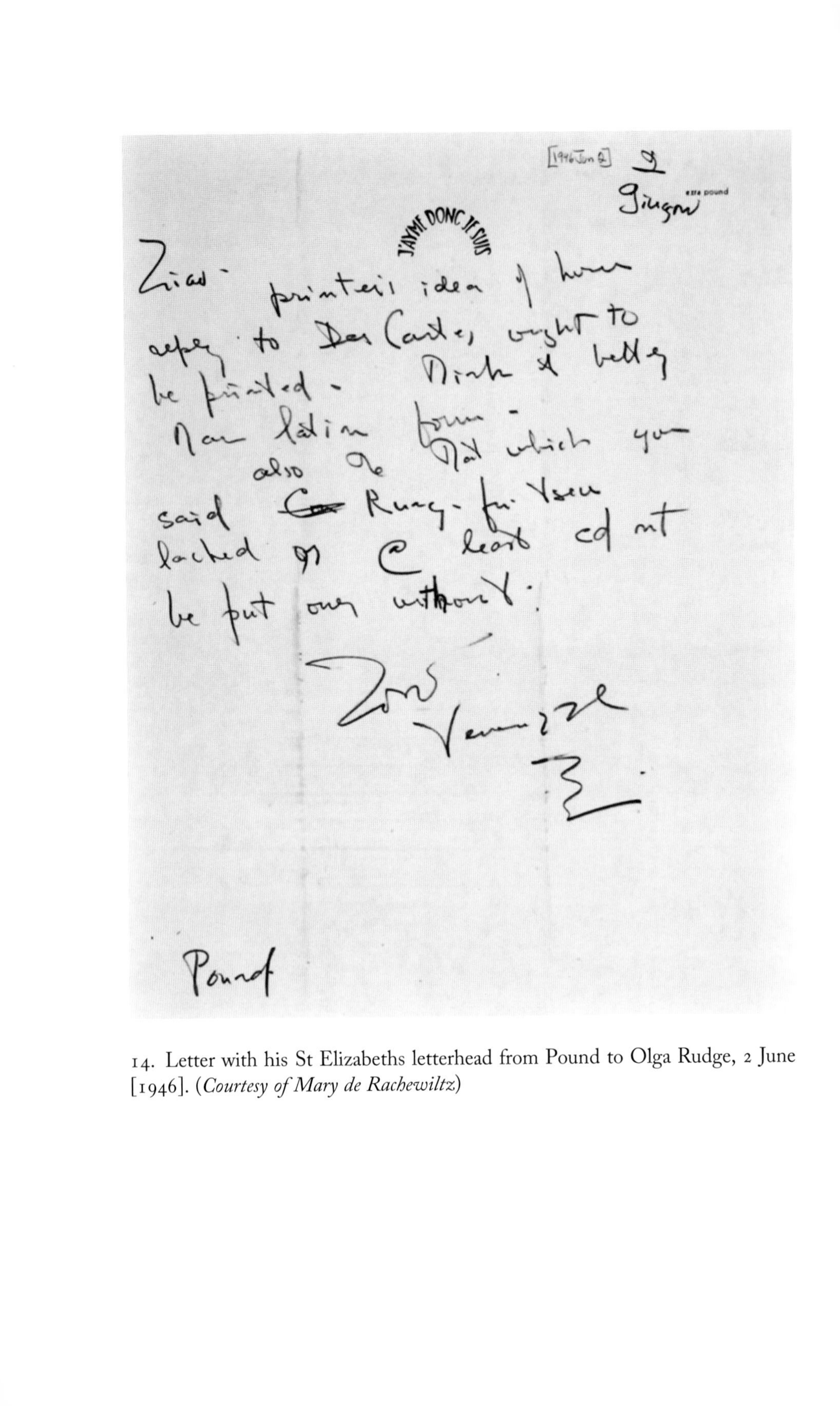

J'AYME DONC JE SUIS

ezra pound

14. Letter with his St Elizabeths letterhead from Pound to Olga Rudge, 2 June [1946]. (*Courtesy of Mary de Rachewiltz*)

15. James Laughlin, 1940s. (*Courtesy of New Directions*)

16. Omar Shakespear Pound in US Army uniform, December 1945. (*Courtesy Elizabeth Pound*)

17. Arthur Valentine Moore, Dorothy Pound's legal adviser, 1950s. (*Courtesy of Mary de Rachewiltz*)

18. Olga Rudge at the Accademia Chigiana, Siena, early 1950s. (*Courtesy of Mary de Rachewiltz*)

19. Sheri Martinelli under one of her sketches of Pound. (*Courtesy of Mary de Rachewiltz*)

20. Pound in St Elizabeths with a Sheri Martinelli painting. (*Courtesy of Mary de Rachewiltz*)

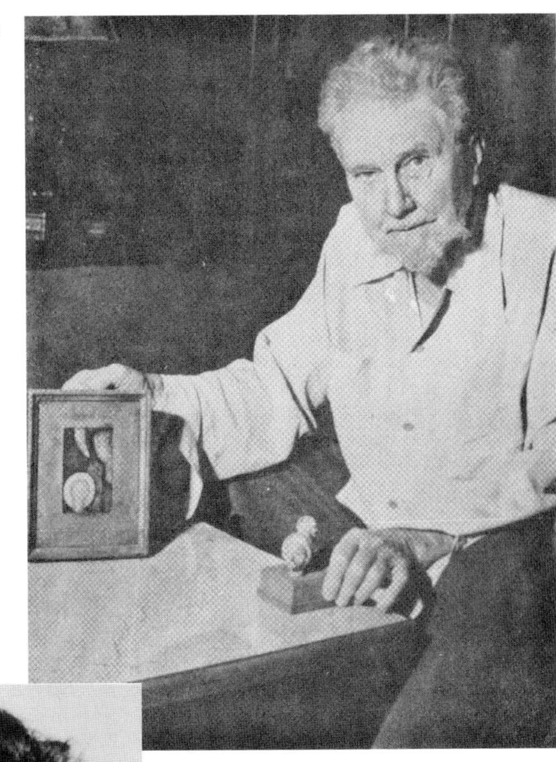

21. Marcella Spann (*Courtesy of Marcella Spann*)

22. Pound freed from custody, on courthouse steps immediately after charges dismissed, 18 April 1958. (*Wide World Photos*)

23. Dorothy at Ezra's childhood home, 166 Fernbrook Avenue, Wyncote, Philadelphia, 27 June 1958. (*Photo Carl Gatter*)

24. Ezra at 166 Fernbrook Avenue, Wyncote, Philadelphia, 27 June 1958. (*Photo Carl Gatter*)

25. Pound on deck of ship saluting journalists, port of Naples, 10 July 1958. (*Wide World Photos*)

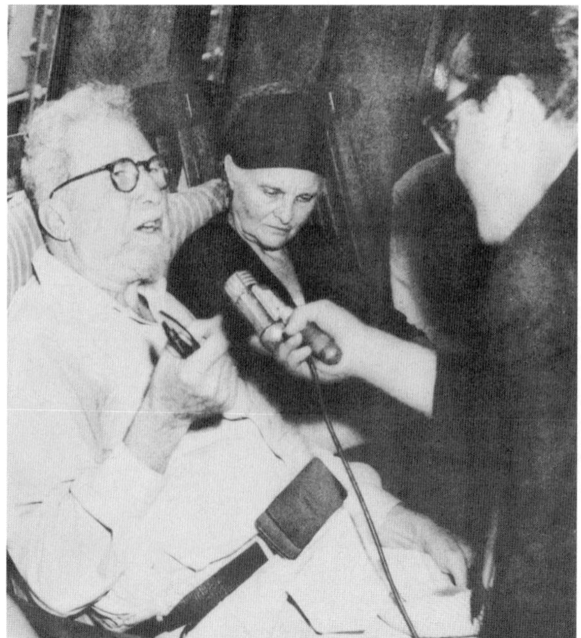

26. Pound with Dorothy, interviewed by Italian journalist on board ship in port of Naples, 10 July 1958. (*Wide World Photos*)

7. Arriving at Brunnenburg, 2 July 1958—from left: Mary de Rachewiltz, Patrizia de Rachewiltz, Boris de Rachewiltz, Dorothy Pound, Ezra Pound, Marcella Spann, Walter de Rachewiltz. (*Wide World Photos*)

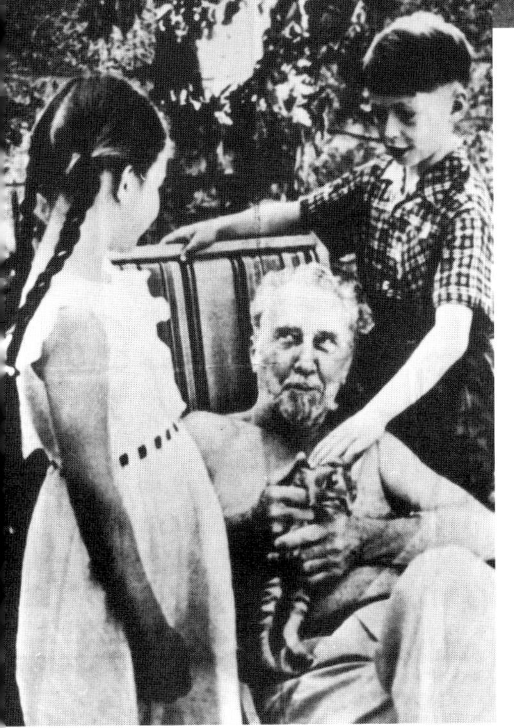

28. Pound with grandchildren Patrizia and Walter, and cat, Brunnenburg, summer 1958. (*Photo Boris de Rachewiltz*)

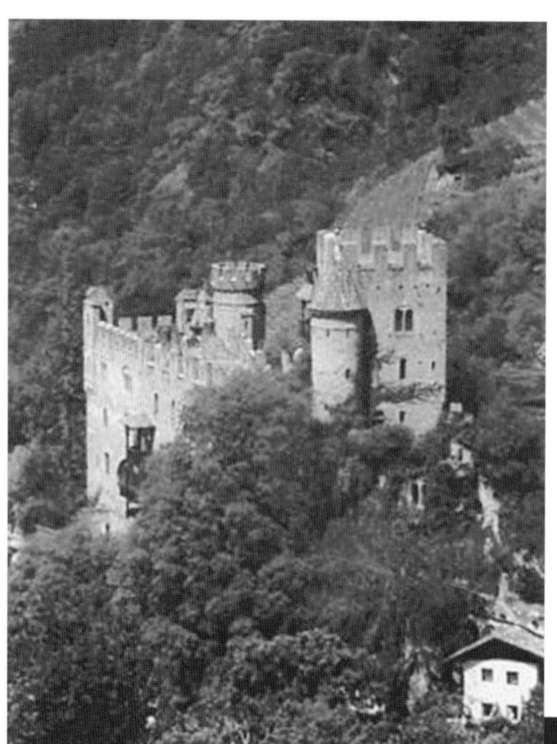

29. View of Brunnenburg. (*Photo Joanna Moody*)

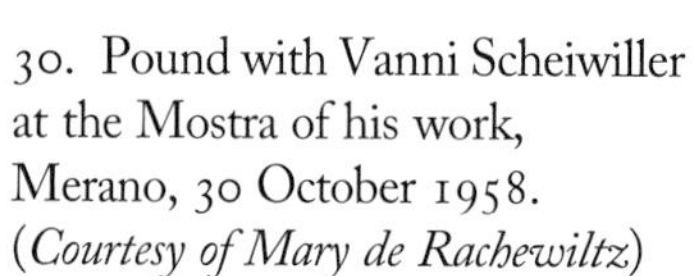

30. Pound with Vanni Scheiwiller at the Mostra of his work, Merano, 30 October 1958. (*Courtesy of Mary de Rachewiltz*)

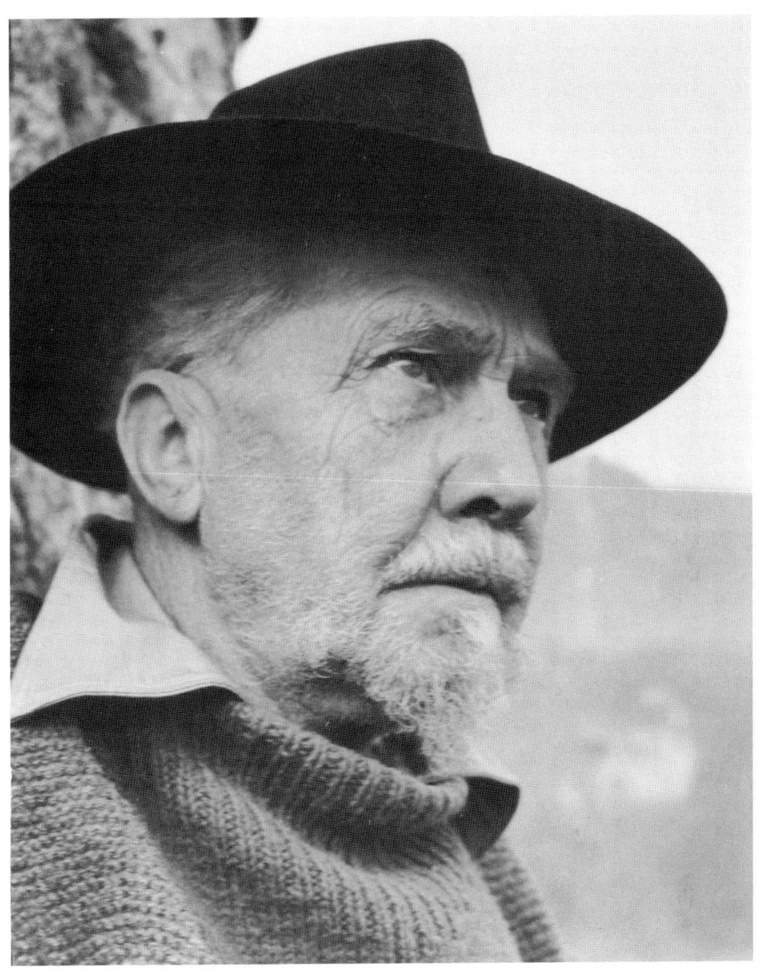

31. Ezra Pound, 1959. (*Photo Boris de Rachewiltz*)

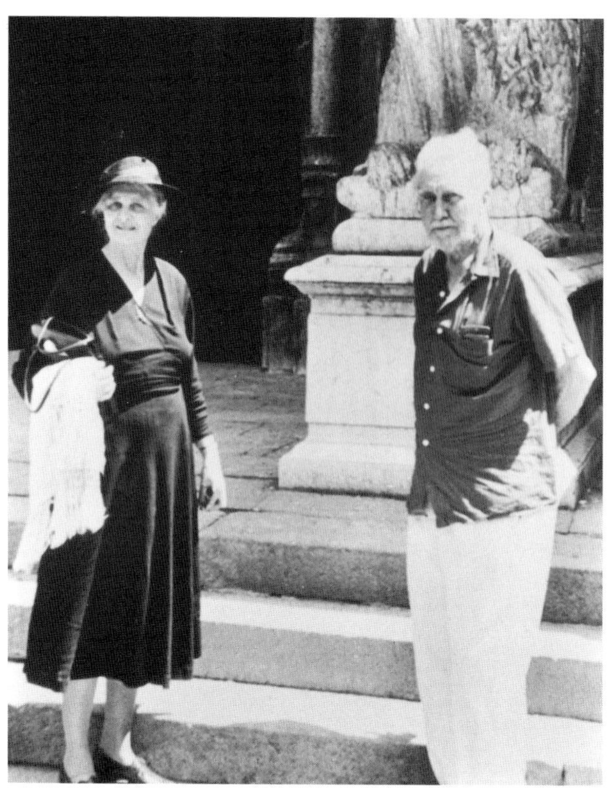

32. Ezra and Dorothy Pound, Brescia, Italy, 1959. (*Courtesy of Mary de Rachewiltz*)

33. Ezra and Dorothy Pound at Brunnenburg, 1960. Pound is wearing his yellow scarf embroidered with ideograms *hsin*^{4} and *hsin*^{1}. (*Courtesy of Mary de Rachewiltz*)

34. Pound on the *salita* at Sant'Ambrogio, 1963. (*Photo Annette Lèna*)

35. Pound with Oscar Kokoschka, Villeneuve, Switzerland, December 1963. (*Photo © Horst Tappe*)

36. Pound at the grave of James and Nora Joyce, Zurich, winter 1967. (*Photo © Horst Tappe*)

37. Pound at Graduation ceremonies, Hamilton College, Clinton, NY, June 1969, wearing the gown and hood of the honorary doctorate conferred on him by the college in 1939. (*Photo Robert T. Chaffe*)

38. Pound in Olga Rudge's 'hidden nest', Calle Querini, Venice, 1971. (*Photo © Horst Tappe*)

39. Ezra Pound by Joan Fitzgerald, 1969, bronze, National Portrait Gallery, Smithsonian Institution. (*Courtesy of National Portrait Gallery, Smithsonian Institution*)

40. Pound reading at Spoleto Festival dei Due Mondi, June 1971. (*Photo © Horst Tappe*)

41. Dorothy Pound, at tea with Massimo Bacigalupo, Rapallo, 16 March 1972. (*Photo Massimo Bacigalupo*)

42. Ezra and Olga at the memorial service for Igor Stravinsky, Venice, 15 April 1971. (*Courtesy of Mary de Rachewiltz*)

43. Ezra Pound, 1972. (*Courtesy of Mary de Rachewiltz*)

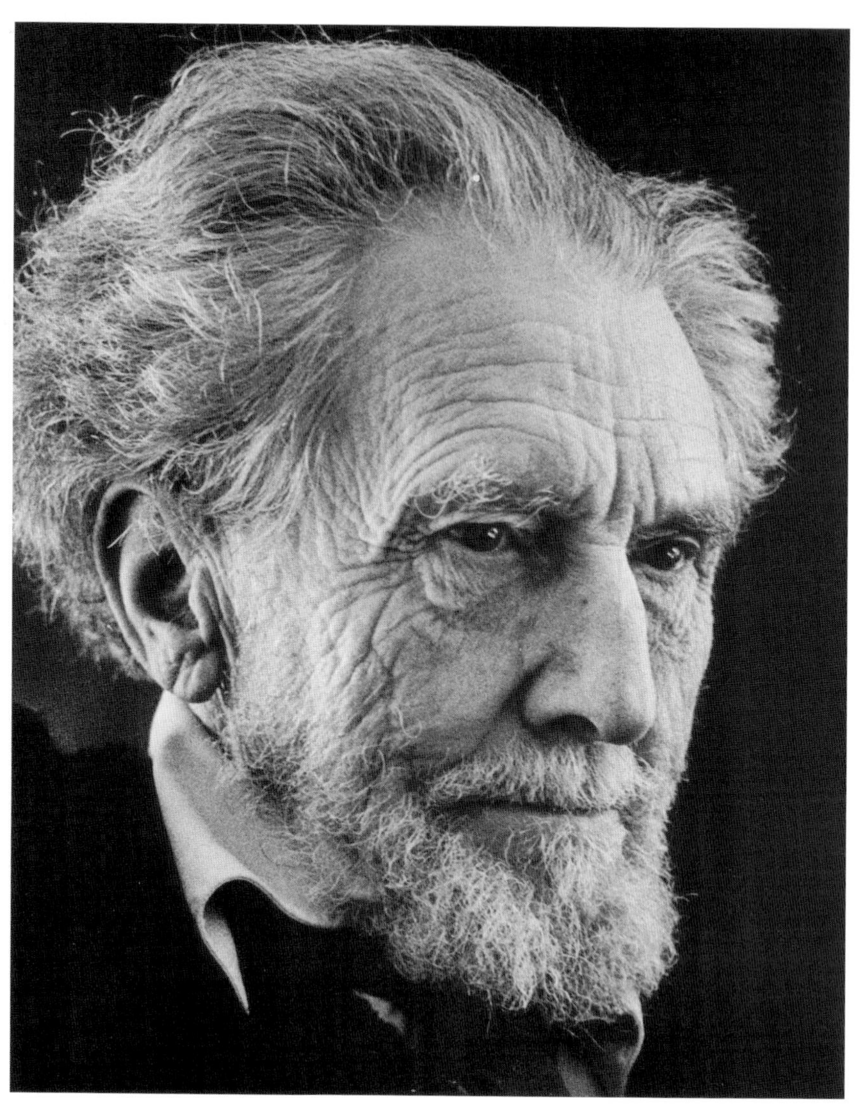

44. Ezra Pound, 1972. (*Photo* © *Horst Tappe*)

old friends, Margaret Anderson, Agnes Bedford, Bunting, Cocteau, Mary Moore (Cross), Hemingway; and there are the names of those newly drawn to Pound through their literary interests, George Kearns, then a young soldier in Washington, and William Pratt, then in the air force there, both of whom would lecture and write about Pound in the course of professorial careers.

Louis Zukofsky on a rare visit in July 1954 brought his 10-year-old son Paul, a prodigy on the violin, to play out on the lawn the bird song from canto 75, and the opening of the Bach Partita no. 3 in E major. And the old friends talked, according to David Gordon who was present, of Pound's new work, *Women of Trachis*, and Zukofsky left with him a small book of his own, *Anew*. They talked of a move afoot in Paris 'to get signatures of writers and painters, including Gilson, Frye and Picasso, for Pound's release'. They questioned, 'How sick was Eliot, and what fire was left in Lewis?' Pound had to go on about 'a so-called Gesellite muddying the issue' of stamp scrip, about 'taxation no longer necessary, Benton and Del Mar'. But he was more concerned to resolve old disagreements, as about Fascism, saying 'that if you put the top 25 Fascists together each one would have had a different idea and different program for the corporate state'; and about his own allegiance he said that 'the only program he had ever AVOWED was John Adams and the American Constitution'. After Zukofsky had left, driven back into Washington by David Horton, Pound went through his poems and made notes, composing a letter to Zukofsky as he went along, generous notes responding positively to the poems, as, at p. 15, 'I note that you have got OUT of influence of E.P. and Possum'; and after poem 24 the confirmation, 'damn all I think yu have got yr/ own idiom'. At poem 22, a version of Catullus viii, 'as incorrigible IMpresario', he encouraged 'YES, Catullus, translated. good.... CAN yu do TEN Catullus poems?' (Zukofsky would do them all, in his own way.) As he read Pound marked certain passages, among them 'I am like another, and another, who has | finished learning | and has just begun to learn,' and 'There are almost no friends | But a few birds to tell what you have done.'

Agenda etc.

In 1950 the Canadian poet and literary activist Louis Dudek (1918–2001), then a mature doctoral student at Columbia University, offered to do anything 'in the way of legwork etc. around New York city' that Pound might want done. Pound wrote back, 'if loafing in 2d/hand book shops he comes on anything by Alex Del Mar, would he kindly purchase, READ and then forward, price and shippings cost will be refunded'. Dorothy added her address to the typed note, '3211 10th Place SE /Wash: DC'. Dudek picked up a number of Del Mar titles and sent them there, and thus began a correspondence in which he found himself being pressed to serve in Pound's 'propaganda machine'. He did not respond well to that, being 'interested in doing a lot for poetry, but not for an economic or political idea'. That distinction was alien to Pound's thinking. Live literature, he insisted, 'has GOT to be based on understanding of LIFE', of 'civic life', and not be something to go 'on a mantle piece with the blue china'. And if Dudek couldn't see that, was not clear, for one thing, 're/ prob/ monnetaria/', then let him at least DO something useful. 'AGENDA', he wrote to him in March 1952, 'grampaw can't be bothered with anything but AGENDA. ... plenty of ag/ of various kinds', and here was one, 'let him mobilize any N.Y. personnel to putt over Lekakis', the Greek-American sculptor whose work Pound had become enthusiastic about on the basis of the photographs shown to him, 'find gardens for his gods/ nemus vult aram'. But he could not let it go at that. In 1955 he was berating Dudek, now teaching at McGill in Montreal and contributing to a little magazine called *CIV/n*, 'No civilization without civic sense.... You profs OUGHT to groan for shame of decadence in american letters in all dimensions save glitter of surface technique.... The pusillanimity of the present.... ABSOLUTE allergy to pivotal thought. ABSOLUTE failure in ten years to face any of the basic issues raised by E.P. over only means at his disposal.' Then came the threat of excommunication, 'On the whole I see no reason to communicate with anyone who hasn't sense enough to see the point of the Sq $ series,' the latter being in his view 'the ONLY curricula now defined'. In November 1956 he told him again, 'NO ONE can be considered as having a culture valid in 1957 who has not DIGESTED at least the Sq $ series.' This was the point at which the correspondence effectively ended.

Dudek regretted that 'Propaganda for his ideas had become more important than literary value'. While 'very much in agreement with Pound's general motives and significance', he found the narrow program which he imposed on his followers 'repugnant and absurd'. In retrospect he wrote:

> From this point in the correspondence [mid-1952], the ambiguity of my devotion to Pound—a devotion which continues to this day—and the pattern of my resistance to him become increasingly clear. I believe that his narrow dogmatism was a product of his mental illness; but this illness, though devastating and tragic for him, did not penetrate very deep, it was surface mania. Behind it, within it, surrounding it, was the brilliant and generous intelligence with which I wanted to communicate.

Yet it was this intelligence, Dudek concludes, 'that was afflicted with a mania', and this 'mania' made it impossible for Dudek to serve Pound in the way either of them wanted.

Another correspondent who felt the pressure of Pound's imperative sense of things needing to be done was Else Seel (1894–1974), a German-Canadian writer of stories and poems. She had moved in literary circles in Berlin before emigrating to Canada in or about 1927 and there marrying a trapper-prospector. From their log cabin in a small settlement on Ootsa Lake in the remote forests of British Columbia she wrote a few words of encouragement to Pound in December 1946, being troubled by a newspaper report of his year in the hell-hole of Howard Hall. He responded with interest, and over the following years up to 1953 they wrote frequently to each other and exchanged books and magazines. She opened a window onto German history and culture for him, and he energized her writing. In his second letter he asked had she read anything by Leo Frobenius, a name which meant nothing to her. So he enlightened her about the importance of Frobenius, 'the best mind in Europe in his time', whom he could read however only with difficulty, and whom no one would translate. Would she translate the seven volumes of *Erlebte Erdteile*? She would not, though she was later glad to come across some of Frobenius' African stories and translated four of them.

'ELSA AGENDA AGENDA,' Pound began a letter in March 1951, 'she just do it and not wait for six page explanation'—on this occasion she was to write to the Indian Congress for Cultural Freedom on behalf of some passing bee in his bonnet. At Christmas he informed her that it was time for her to choose some job of work and see it through to the finish—such as translating *Erlebte Erdteile.* In 1953 he was still at her to do the needed translation, 'everybody sittin' round thirty years and the job NOT getting done'. By this time she was no longer writing to him, having felt the need to free herself from his demands. In a poem in her German she wrote, 'You always demanded more, you insatiable one. | . . . | How many years did I read your words? | Soaked like the dry earth rain into myself? | And slowly got to know you. | What you had done in your long life, | what you had written and thought, | it quivered in my heart | and it enlivened my nights. | A spirit was my companion, | a spirit replaced flesh and blood, | the net became hard and heavy | and enveloped me as a prisoner.'

And then there was Ingrid Davies, the 'duchess' of the lyric Pound wrote for Sheri Martinelli's jazz-playing friend Charlie Parker, 'mid dope-dolls an' duchesses | tho' orften I roam'. That is, the lady gave Pound to understand that she was somehow connected with a duke, and was an 'Hon' (or Honourable) and of the aristocracy, though she rather rebelled against its conventions and had declined to 'come out' as a society debutante. She was married unsatisfactorily to Richard Davies, who 'tries to write plays', and was herself an actress though apparently 'resting', and had a small daughter who may or may not have been Richard's, and cherished a cat. Pound gathered, or speculated, that she was about 22, though she may well have been in the later twenties. It was all rather like his 'Moeurs Contemporaines', only with upper-class England transposed from 1918 to the 1950s.

Richard Davies was active among the English Poundians who wanted to do something to effect Pound's release; and Ingrid was upset about Pound's everlasting incarceration and wrote in 1954 to say so and to cheer him up. Their correspondence took fire in 1955—do you remember, she wrote in 1969, when asking what she should do with her collection of his letters, 'when we wrote to each other every day'? She had indeed written every day for a time, sometimes two air-letters in a day; but his were less frequent, perhaps every other day. Up to April 1956 when she stopped numbering his letters there were 239, though only 35 more after that.

In the intense year or so of their relationship she poured out her heart to him, and he responded as an agony-uncle, though at times also as an impressionable wooer. She wrote as a damsel in emotional distress, not happy in her marriage, not happy about the men she knew, not happy at all about her sex life and its prospects. All the same, in March 1955 she evidently invited what he took to be an *amour lointain*, eliciting the response, 'Yes, my Love, | I shall be deeelighted to be yr/ Valentine.... Jaufre Rudel having nothing on Ingrid.' His first thought had been to educate the seeming *jeune fille* by putting her on to his current curriculum, starting with Agassiz, Mencius, and Blackstone's *Laws of England*, though he soon realized that her light liveliness was not intellectual, and that it was sexual and emotional education that she wanted. He warned her off psychiatrists, university academics, and Judeo-Christian religion; implied that he was the one to meet all her needs; and charmed her by making her feel that she had his complete attention, and deserved it. 'My dear superchick', he flattered her in August 1955, 'YOUR velocity is about 4 times that of anyone else save possibly that of yr/ anchored correspondent.'

As Pound took up his self-appointed 'position as grandual tutor... in the ars amatoria' he made it axiomatic that 'there is NO uniformity of individuals in nature'. And since 'no two people are identical', it followed that 'you cant learn anything save from particular presentations of individual cases'—'nowt to be learned save from poetry and gt/ novels or narratives'. He would imply that there was a good deal on the subject of love in his own poems and translations; but he advised, 'start with Ovid: EST

DEUS IN NOBIS AGITANTE CALESCIMUS ILLO'—*a god is within us and with his stirring we take fire.* Later he would tell her, 'I can't believe book learnin' is necessary, the platonic gawd in his mercy having given impulses to the children of light.' In that light he recommended dancing, in 'half open air or open air as at Bullier and in decent climates', because 'You can certainly learn more in one tango than from 12 vols of Golden Bough. You can be TOLD more in one tango ... Tactile, god damn it, values, and all gradations depending on the relative magnetisms, the relative fineness of perception | the number of strata of the personality engaged.' However, Ingrid's 'Guy', otherwise unidentified, did not dance, so there was further advice: 'Too bad about Guy's inhibitions. Find somebody you LIKE to be touched by AND notice the vibrations'—

Courtship is a graduation of caresses whereby the parties explore, and find out IF they want to go further,,, semicolon; IF going further will reward one or both of them. Tempo, as in music, the DANCE ...

Still she fretted, and he assured her, while warning again that 'generalities are NOT binding', that

To the best of my belief, given any temperament, the female capacity for enjoyment remains fairly constant from 15 to 50 ... At any rate, my chick, you needn't hurry, I shd/ think you have at least 30 years in which to locate whatever experience you ultimately decide to indulge in. Take it easy, paZienZaaaaaaa

The next day he continued:

you still leave me a bit up in the air | re/ what you know and don't. You are at least aware that procreation and pleasure are not necessarily linked, i.e. that the pleasure can be had without increasing the population. French peasant girl to the Virgin: 'O toi qui a concu sans pecher, donne moi la grace de pecher sans concevoir'. The male CAN take all the precautions, but I gather that that form of courtesy has largely gone into disuse, especially among the ignorant. Mechanical devices, not always trustworthy/ chemicals viewed differently by different sects. 'Free time' advertised, but a later innovation, THAT is what the Maoris had by antient tradition. I personally would want to know a lot more about it before relying on anyone's calender. Further details if requested.

'Is it worth it?', she evidently wrote back, and he returned,

"Is it worth it!" | there are NO universal laws, dogmas, answers. Magnificent nights without penetration. One phase of the moon when same is not desirable. Naturally one can only deduce the feelings of the co-celebrant.... There have been damsels who seem happy without penetration, there are daughters of Cythera who are merely irritated if full act is not performed. Indubitably it may be certified that some males can get a great deal of pleasure from naked contact without entering the cave of the goddess... Cara, there are no universal answers that apply in all cases. 'Non a diletto m'a consideranza.' Everything from the Heine to the Cavalcanti translations applies. The gamut, more varied than the 8 octaves of the piano keys.

'One is not used to putting these things on paper', he remarked, 'and they are not much use until the right batteries are in rapport.' When Ingrid wrote that she had been reading Eustace Chesser and was his book right about the female orgasm, he wrote back that he couldn't say—

All I know is that several have expressed pleasure and satisfaction (NOT satiety) and come back for more, and some have even referred to past pleasures after considerable interval. If it warn't a explosion it must have been a blossoming out. There are all sorts and degrees, just as all sorts of talents for music, no two people the same. Gt/ violinist one chord, with drawing of the bow over two strings at once.

In reply to some later query he thought to add, 'The illusion of being in LOVE, at least for the DURATION of the rites, is certainly highly desirable.'

In one letter Pound looked back to what had been for him the customs of 'the america of 1900', customs which would, he expected, 'sound to Ing/ like lost arcadia'—

The renouned 'purity', the liberty acquired by 200 to 300 years of frontier when there COULD be no chaperonage. The young trusted to enjoy themselves and stop just short of copulation. Only a 'fast set' at the top, VERY small, 'vice and the red lights below' and the free born in between, yeoman and parson and lawyer stock, the latter mostly come up from millers, maltsters, but with say 300 years 'culture'. .. Govt. employees, professors, the 'college attending' class... and most certainly a great deal of affection and emotion unhindered, trusted because the young accepted that convention. The dance still two step and waltz, square dances going out. And the 1910/14 bunny-hug, tango etc. not yet come in. Emotional refinement, and couples when the female consented slipping from the dance room for further but wholly unfecundative caresses in the night air.

'And not till yr/ correspondent got to england, where the males were scarce', Pound concluded this history lesson, 'did he pass beyond these Idylic raptures'.

By the summer of 1955 the excitement had gone out of Pound's letters. Ingrid's had ceased to stimulate. He quoted to her a dictionary definition, 'Pound: an enclosure for stray animals'. He became practical: the solution to her uncertainties—she was considering divorce—would be to spend time with his daughter at Brunnenburg and work on the land in a suitably upper-class way. At the same time she should use her social advantages in the spirit of *noblesse oblige*, and she should mobilize her father who was better placed to *act*. His letters were now characterized by 'she ought' and 'she might do', as in she might be getting publicity and sales in England for La Martinelli's art works. When her letters became infrequent he complained, 'no correspondence FROM the Hnbl. I. Pia hence the drift toward the Publk/ meeting tone'. At the end of November he wrote frankly, 'It is the EduCaTion that we are aiming at | the construction of the perfect secretary'— as if she were now to him simply someone to make herself useful to carry out his agenda in England. The following May he told Mary de Rachewiltz, after saying 'one needs a corps of secretaries', 'Ingrid sunk, evaporated, exploded, since went on theatre tour.'

Ingrid Davies did visit Brunnenburg, though not to work on the land. She did divorce in 1957. In a late letter, in July 1959, Pound wrote to her, 'AND of course I wd/ like to put the duchy in order, or indeed ANY township or village | E | CO | NOMicaly | and discuss the tax system with ANY available adult or hopeful pupil.' He offered to turn on the dynamo again 'IF you turn highbrow again in a moment of rashness', signed himself 'pedagicicly yrs', and sent 'best' to her cats.

Not licked, merely caged

Thus Pound to his 'DEEvoted daughter' in August 1954, 'I don't even feel licked | merely caged | mebbe that's why I'm a lunatic.' On the other hand, as he remarked to Olivia Agresti, 'Of course I wd/be DEAD from overwork if I hadn't been jugged.' He was rarely so confessional. He did confide to Mary, in January 1955, 'haven't been able to keep head up for more than a few minutes without head rest for the past nine years. . . . AND my temper gets worse with age'. Yet there was some pride in his telling her, 'got DOWN from cento kili to below 95. In fact I think it was near 90 the last time I was weighed. At any rate nearer human form than in 1938.' (Samuel Hynes, visiting Pound two summers back, had seen him as 'lean' in his loose clothes. 'hardship had stripped him of all unnecessary flesh'.) He was delighted at being 'let out into the air more'—allowed since August to sit out until about 8:00 o'clock in the summer evenings. And he had at last succumbed and got in a radio, as he confessed to Wyndham Lewis, 'thinking to save eyesight or praps different rest from playing solitarie', though he expected nothing 'via the "air"' but 'slusch, goddam trype, tunes used to sing in 1895 and ROTTENLY done at that', a 'peril to all life above that of newts and dungworms'. However, in November 1951 he was able to tell Mary that he had 'heard on radio Toscanini conduct MAGnificently

Beethoven Septuor'. And he evidently found Elder Solomon Lightfoot Michaux, an immensely popular and influential black evangelist, worth listening to as a phenomenon of American culture.

'Elder Lightfoot' is celebrated in canto 95, as being 'not downhearted' and observing 'a design in the Process'; but a possibly tone-deaf critic has found in that abbreviation of his name evidence of anti-African-American racism. However, against that can be set the rather more solid testimony of a black artist who had been an attendant in St Elizabeths in the 1950s, and who, in a 1960s coffee house where he played chess, 'told compelling, vivid tales of Ezra Pound and his visitors', and who 'said repeatedly: "There was not a racist bone in Ezra Pound's body".' Pound himself remarked to Ingrid Davies in March 1955, when desegregation was a burning issue, that he took his meals 'with colleagues, desegregation in flower'. 'Having grown up in cordial relations with afro-derivatives', he explained, he was not bothered by the current fuss. When an 'afro-confrère' asked if he remembered him in the hell-hole and wanted Pound 'to type 12 lines on the City of God in regular metric', Pound readily obliged, and was offered a dime in return. His relations with black prisoners in the DTC, as reflected in *The Pisan Cantos*, had gone well beyond cordiality as he responded to them both as victims of white capitalist inhumanity, and as exercising even while imprisoned a redemptive humanity. He appreciated a touch of that humanity in August 1954:

> new black attendant this a.m. as he gives me butter for breakfast, murmurs: 'Right forever on the scaffold, Wrong forever on the throne', then says: 'Who wrote that?' which stumps me, damn if I kno/ quote familiar, and the murmur certainly intended as encouragement.

Black Americans were most needed in America as 'a humanizing element', he told Olivia Agresti.

He did that, however, in a paragraph which, taken as a whole, while not racist was racialist. That is, it expressed Pound's belief in the persistence of racial characteristics as the basis of culture, in this following Agassiz rather than Frobenius, the latter having regarded not race but the determinant ideas and practices of a society as the essence of its *paideuma* or ethos. Between the wars Pound had followed Frobenius' lead, but now his hope for a better society, and his fear of a worse, could be vested in what he took to be more or less fixed racial types. So he could write to Signora Agresti,

> marse blackman will most certainly NOT return to africa to infect what the dirty brits have left there/ with any more occidental hogwash/ He will stay here

(incidentally D's one comfort) being human and refusing to be poured into a mould and cut to the stingkging pattern on the slicks and the weakly papers.

But his own mould and pattern turn out to be just the commonly attributed stereotype—

> An occasional upsurge of African agricultural heritage as in G. W. Carver, O.Kay but also marse Blakman him LAZY | lazy as Lin Yu Tang. Thank god for it/ AS a humanizing element most needed here./... he ain' nebber been moralized/ thank God. The pleasantness of the animal kingdom unbitched by Calvin...

Pound's tone is positive, even celebratory, far from hostile prejudice, yet such naive racialism can be turned in an instant into demeaning or aggressive racism.

In his own turn to racism Pound's now obsessive anti-Semitism had incorporated the stereotype of Jewish racial characteristics. He would remind others that 'any tendency to abstract general statement is a greased slide', and that it was 'NO use EVER discussing package words | fascism, socialism, etc'. And then he could write to Olivia Agresti:

> Pity the pore uncawnshus 'carrier' whether it be of bubonics, tubercles or the kikerian state of mind, the oily and spherical/ the so accurately defined by Wm Shx/ etc. Not that the chew shd/ be prejudged/ he shd/ simply be watched for racial symptoms, and not allowed to infect the mind of the non-kike.

The paragraph doesn't get any better as it rants on, mentioning 'the problem of issue' and the reduction of literature 'to mere ornament' as consequences of 'the kikerian state of mind', and concluding, 'Whether they act from intent or from nature do not permit the infection of uncontaminated areas. und so VEITER.' The German phrase touches, all too unconsciously, the bottommost pit of the twentieth-century hell, Pound's mind having gone so deeply wrong. He would deny that he was anti-Semitic, and Jackson MacLow, writing to him as a Jewish poet in April 1955, could write back, 'Alright—so youre not an antisemite. I never thought you were.... But WHY do you & other well-intentioned goyim, insist on talking about "kikes" & singling out the jews among the swindlers & power-bastards???' In Pound's case at least the answer to MacLow's question must be that the anti-Semitism he had deployed as a propaganda weapon, knowing it to be wrong, had gradually poisoned his mind and become a paranoid obsession. Bernard Hart, author of the elementary handbook *The Psychology of Insanity* (1912) from which Pound had drawn some ideas for his theory of *Imagisme*, would have diagnosed a psychotic 'complex' about Jews. In lay terms, on the subject of Jews he had lost his reason.

When a translation of Hitler's wartime private conversations was published in 1953 Pound was eager to read them. 'Hitler crazy as a coot,' he told Kenner on 1 November, 'but extremely lucid on matter of money.' He had thought when reading the reviews in September that 'May be [that] was the ONLY subject on which Adolf WAS clear-headed'. Now, in a letter to Olivia Agresti, he went further:

> The Hitler Conversations very lucid re/ money/ unfortunately he was bit by dirty jew mania for World DOmination, as yu used to point out/ this WORST of german diseases was got from yr/ idolized and filthy biblical bastards. Adolf clear on the bacillus of kikism . . . but failed to get a vaccine against that.

There is the insane complex at its most twisted and deranged.

Agresti firmly insisted in reply that Hitler's killing off all the Jews he could lay his hands on was 'a case of criminal lunacy', but Pound brushed that aside with 'Yes, my Dear O.R.A. BUTTT we shd/ ask WHAT kind of bloody lunatic, and what druv him.' He wanted to attend only to the 'The POSITIVE lucidities which revived the whole of germany by enthusiasm', and would have it that 'a man's going nuts does not free one from his preceding lucidities'. He had always made a virtue of separating 'the CONSTRUCTIVE parts of heretical or innovative writers from their fantasies', of accentuating the positive and ignoring the negative. At times this mental habit became a form of microscopic vision, magnifying the selected detail with great clarity; but it could also allow the isolated detail, when it did not truly represent the larger reality, to blot out the whole truth. Hitler's lucidities about money were indeed behind Germany's economic miracle in the 1930s; and that miracle fuelled his drive towards war and conquest, and his war brought with it his drive to exterminate the Jewish race. For Pound, though, his right idea about money eclipsed those atrocities.

When thinking back to the Fascist era, as he frequently did when writing to Olivia Agresti with whom he had shared an enthusiasm for Mussolini's economic system, Pound would emphasize the constructive parts, but in this case without being excessively partial. He would cite Mussolini's dictum, 'Lo Stato è lo spirito del Popolo,' 'The State is the spirit of the People,' and comment, 'And Mussolini's state fell when it ceased to be the italian spirit.' His summary judgment would be, 'TEN years construction | then ten years undermining and going wrong.' And for his own part he would say that he had been, 'in Italy, engaged in a very vigorous criticism of the Fascist regime, which appeared to him suited to the necessities of circumstance in that given time and place, but not for export'. He would remark that the Italian spirit was 'individualist, anarchic', and quote the diehard Fascist Farinacci's complaining that 'if you put the 25 top Fascists together each one wd/ have a DIFFERENT idea of the corporate state'. In his own writing, he declared to Agresti, 'There is of course not a line in support of ANY kind of totalitarianism'; and again, 'Of course there was never a word in favour of dictatorship in my writing, save as interim necessity, and M[ussolini] never suggested it as universal system.'

His own politics, Pound would insist when on the defensive, was solidly 'John Adams and the American Constitution, with due retrospect to the Leopoldine Reforms which preceded that remarkable document'; and it was always their principles which he had upheld in his wartime broadcasts against Roosevelt's taking America into that war. 'The time was probably inopportune, and his methods entaild considerable risk,' he admitted in a draft note which he hoped Mary de Rachewiltz could manage to get published in *La Nazione* or *La Fiera*, with the afterthought, 'That is an understatement.' But it had been his duty, he maintained to Hugh Kenner in 1953, as a 'citizen placed in a far look-out, i.e. in position to see events & facts ... to warn his compatriots'. Besides, there could be 'No treason without evil intention'—a judge in Boston had affirmed that in the Douglas Chandler case, as he informed Olivia Agresti in August 1953, and 'Nobody but swine like Thos Mann or Rose Benet wd/ accuse me of evil intention'.

'I want OUT': a log of pleas and petitions

1950: In March Olga Rudge reproached Hemingway for doing nothing about Pound's mouldering in St Elizabeths. Dorothy Pound, she wrote, 'refused to take responsibility of any kind', and 'the easy way is for E's friends to leave him where he is and salve their consciences with tributes to his literary worth—he is simply crawling with literary parasites—none of whom, in the States at least, compromise themselves by touching on the subject of treason'. 'It is surely time', she challenged, 'for his friends, if he has any, to see what can be done.' Hemingway, who regarded her interventions as hysterical and unhelpful, replied that as a true friend of Pound he must use his head and not give way to sentiment, and the fact was that Ezra had made 'the rather serious mistake ... of being a traitor to his country, and temporarily he must lie in the bed he made'. He assured her that 'If Ezra is released at this moment as of sound mind', he would not be allowed to return to Rapallo, but would be tried and 'would receive a sentence of from ten to fifteen years'. As if to explain why that would be the case, he further assured her that 'His anti-semitism has made him very powerful enemies in the US.'

Dudley Kimball, who was experimenting at his Blue Ridge Mountain Press with printing Pound's ideal version of the Confucian Odes, one which would include the Chinese seal text and a sound key, wanted to circulate 'Sixteen Points' in Pound's defence. Pound asked him, 'Please do NOT distribute any copies of circular until you have finished the edition of the Odes', and indicated that he was more concerned to get the Odes into circulation and so raise the cultural level than with getting himself freed—indeed the former in his view was the likeliest way of effecting the latter.

On 15 October, Laughlin wrote to EP: 'Cornell says he can get you outov there if you will have D. sign the papers to start the wheels chuggin.'

1951: In mid-March Pound exclaimed to Hugh Kenner, who seems to have asked why not let himself be put on trial, 'trial yu ass | where yu getting half a million $ for preliminary legal eggspentzes??'

On 26 July Laughlin wrote to Kenner that he had just seen Pound, and that 'he is just as unreasonable as ever. He refuses to have any step taken legally to try to get him out of hock . . . so I guess he will just have to sit there until he changes his mind. There is nothing any of us can do for him if he won't allow Dorothy to sign the papers.'

In October D. D. Paige wrote to Hemingway about the distinguished Chilean poet Gabriela Mistral's project for freeing Pound by 'requesting an amnesty for Ezra in the name of all Nobel Prize winners'—she had been awarded the Nobel in 1945. Eliot had advised that she proceed cautiously, and Paige thought him timid. Hemingway did not agree. 'Many people have tried with great valour and little sense to free a prisoner and had the prisoner killed due to their blind zeal,' he warned—his own son had been killed that way in the late war. And there were practical considerations. An election year was coming up, and Paige should remember that 'The Pound of the treasonable and anti-semitic broadcasts has been declared insane. That is his protection against the charges against him. . . . If he were declared sane you can be sure that the people who resent his anti-semitic broadcasts will take up the offensive against him,' and 'no administration is going to risk alienating the Jewish vote by freeing Pound at this time'. He insisted, 'Please do not think my heart is cold toward Ezra when I try to make my brain as cold as possible in considering his situation'.

1952: 10 September, Wyndham Lewis wrote to EP: 'It wearies me your remaining where you are. To take up a strategic position in a lunatic asylum is idiotic. If I don't see you make an effort to get out soon, I shall conclude, either that your present residence has a snobbish appeal for you, or that you are timid with regard to Fate.—Ask your wife to give the signal to your horde of friends to go into battle for you.'

An open letter in three languages, dated 'Naples, le 1er Décembre 1952', from Gabriela Mistral (pour l'Amérique du Sud), Doris Dana (pour les États Unis d'Amérique), and Stephen Spender (pour l'Europe), as 'Comité International en Faveur d'Ezra Pound', solicited signatures for a petition to the President of the United States for the release of Ezra Pound from confinement in St Elizabeths Hospital, Washington, DC.

Richard Aldington and HD, reacting to Olga Rudge's efforts to get EP out of St Elizabeths, agreed that they did not want to get involved.

The anarchist Dachine Rainer set up 'Committee for the Liberation of Ezra Pound' with help from W. H. Auden, Dwight Macdonald, E. E. Cummings, Marion Moorehouse [Cummings], and many others.

1953: in March Mary de Rachewiltz sailed to America with the firm intention of taking Pound home to Brunnenburg. Laughlin, when they discussed ways and means in his New York apartment, said, '"You are the only person who could influence him . . . if you can get him to sign certain papers".' Eliot had said to her in London in 1948, '"The idea that you should be sent over to persuade him to sign a statement that he is mad is a travesty".' In any case Pound would not have it—he would not 'for mere impatience pretend guilt or incapacity'. She said then, '"Stand trial and you'll be acquitted!"', and to that he retorted, '"What's the point in my being free if the family has to go bust and one has to pass the begging bowl around!"' She managed to see someone in the Justice Department, and was told, '"Young lady . . . If you want a piece of good advice you better not insist that the case be reopened; you might land him in the electric chair."' After ten weeks in Washington she returned to Brunnenburg 'bewildered and discouraged', and with the firm conviction that her father's 'liberation must be obtained from Italy'.

In a typescript note, undated but probably dashed off after May 1953, Pound wrote:

> Tha[t] they base the defense on literary prestige/ O. K.
> despite the fact that one is dealing with utterly illiterate gangsters
> plus the pink 4th rate writers/
> one lot DONT know what is literacy and the other lot loathe it.
> Then they sit round yelling for E. P. to get into some TOTALLY
> useless legal tangle
> that will cost $5000 a week and get NO where/
> instead of getting on with the job of getting his most
> important work into print as fast as possible.

There was also this general complaint: 'Practically No curiosity as to the facts or the juridical basis, i,e, the legal as distinct from the habitual "bunk" what you can put over.'

In June Olivia Agresti wrote that John Drummond had plans to get 'a good many prominent Italians to sign a paper expressing their hope that the U.S. Government would set free the most outstanding American poet and leader in the new trend literature has taken in the last twenty years'. She enclosed a copy of a draft petition, on which Pound commented, 'idea of petition O.K. but NOT a petition as in their idiotic or perfidious draft/ looked as if composed by pink or "Partisan review" // all their dirtiest insinuations accepted'.

In October, Rufus King, a Washington lawyer who had been tasked by Eliot and others to look into Pound's situation, returned a confused report of which the upshot was that there was nothing to be done for him at that time. King's friends in the Justice Department assured him that they would not be abandoning their case 'so long as their witnesses remain alive and available'. He went on about a presidential pardon as if it were a serious possibility, although Pound at least was well aware that with no conviction there could be no pardon; and while saying that 'the only present escape would be via a trial', and that he thought 'we could win an acquittal', King nevertheless advised that because it was felt that Pound's nerves would not stand the strain of a trial, it was better for him to remain in St Elizabeths, horribly confined though he was 'with a ward of depressives and a television set'. Moreover, anything that stirred up publicity would be harmful: nothing could be done until 'it is felt that Pound has been forgotten by the great mass of the American public'. 'It does appear to be a stalemate,' Eliot replied, 'All that you say tends to confirm my opinion that any steps to be taken, must be taken quietly, and in America, not elsewhere.'

In November Wyndham Lewis told Eliot that he had been shown a letter in which Pound had said, in effect, 'It is time that a little more intelligence was used to get Grandpa out of the bughouse.' That led him to feel that 'If Ezra seems to wish that a major effort should be made to secure his release from prison, then a few of his friends should draw up a programme and go into action.' An appeal might be printed, to be signed by people in all parts of the world, and sent to the President of the United States, and published with the signatures in *The Times* (London) and the *New York Times*. As 'his two oldest friends in England', Eliot and Lewis himself 'could start the ball rolling'. Eliot's response was to send King's letter to Lewis, with his own conviction that 'public agitation outside of the U.S for Pound's release was not advisable'. Lewis still felt that an effort should be made to rescue Pound, since that was what he wanted, and since

'It is most unlikely that the rescue initiative will come from America.' He had always said that he would do whatever he could whenever Ezra gave the word, and 'He has now done so.' There was further debate between the two old friends, but no appeal materialized.

1954: Boris de Rachewiltz, Pound's son-in-law, had begun to act on the idea that his liberation would have to be worked from Italy. With his training in Vatican protocol he was able to arrange in March for a professor of Portugese at Rome University, José de Piña Martins, to appeal on Vatican Radio for America to free its 'Prometheus Bound'. The broadcast was repeated over Italian Radio the same evening, and then printed and widely circulated in June as 'Vatican Radio Appeal for Pound'. A sustained campaign of articles, editorials, and letters, followed in the Italian press, notably 'The Ezra Pound Case' by Carlo Scarfoglio in *Paese Sera* of 16 June, and a series of articles in Rapallo's *Il Mare* in the autumn. Many of these articles were aimed at, or were brought to the attention of, Clare Boothe Luce, the American ambassador in Rome, who would as a matter of course pass them on to the State Department in Washington.

Encouraged by this raising of awareness of his case in Italy Pound entertained, 'on the purely Utopian plane', a suggestion from Olivia Agresti that he might take up residence in a friend's villa at Cumae. 'D & I wd/ have to live somewhere and pay rent', he mused, and 'I wd/ want a place for two, plus 2 guest rooms'. Then paranoid realism cut in and he reminded himself that he would be able to enjoy the Vergilian villa at Cumae only 'IF the Ecclesiastic and Statal authorities can get round the strangle hold the kikes and the hroosians still have on the yellowlivered yanks and pry yr/ tottering friend out of the buGGhouz.'

Dag Hammarskjöld, Secretary-General of the United Nations, had been prompted to take an interest in Pound's situation by two young fellow Swedes, Bengt Nirje who had studied with Norman Holmes Pearson at Yale and been encouraged by him to visit Pound, and Lars Forssell who had translated a selection of Pound's poems into Swedish. Hammarskjöld had made enquiries and become more fully aware of 'his tragic fate', and had at the same time been surprised that Pound's many American visitors had 'not found ways to address his situation... especially as there seems to be a common understanding—among those who have some knowledge of the case—that Pound is of sound mind'. In the summer and fall of 1954 the *Cantos* figured in his reading, and in October, delivering the main address at the opening ceremony celebrating the 25th anniversary of the Museum of Modern Art, and before an audience numbering over 2,500, he invoked Pound as an exemplary modern artist:

> Modern art teaches us to see by forcing us to use our senses, our intellect, and our sensibility to follow it on its road of exploration. It makes us seers—seers like Ezra Pound when, in the first of his *Pisan Cantos*, he senses 'the enormous tragedy of the dream in the peasant's bent shoulders'. Seers—and explorers—these we must be if we are to prevail.

A measure of how undiplomatic this public recognition of Pound's significance as a modern artist would have been in that setting is given by the contrast with Jacques Maritain's virtually blanking him out in his A. W. Mellon Lectures in the Fine Arts delivered in the National Gallery of Art in Washington in 1952, on a similar subject and to a similar if more select audience, and published as *Creative Intuition in Art and Poetry*. Maritain, a former diplomat and then an honoured philosopher at Princeton, had ranged widely over the field of modern art and poetry, and cited and quoted from several contemporary American poets, but had mentioned Pound only twice, once in a footnote, as holding dear 'state-totalitarianism', and once in the text as a mere name in a list of half a dozen poets.

When Hemingway was awarded the Nobel Prize for Literature at the end of 1954 he was interviewed by *Time* and featured on its cover. He used the interview as a public platform to declare, 'Ezra Pound is a great poet, and whatever he did has been punished greatly and I believe he should be freed to go and write poems in Italy where he is loved and understood.' The Swedish Academy had considered Pound for the prize that year, along with Camus and Claudel, and Hemingway added, 'I believe it might well have gone to Pound . . . I believe this would be a good year to release poets.'

Around the same time Pound asked a professor of English at the University of Alabama, Douglas Hammond, who had been writing to him about getting him out, to obtain a copy of Hammarskjöld's speech, and Hammond wrote to Hammarskjöld on 12 December. He told him that 'For quite some time now, a group of English majors, faculty members in English Literature and classical languages and romance languages, have been thinking of forming an organization which would ask the Federal Government to drop its treason indictment.' In January Hammond wrote to Dorothy Pound about the plan, telling her that he expected to secure the support of Marianne Moore, T. S. Eliot, Hugh Kenner, Archibald MacLeish, A. V. Moore, and others, for an organization which would raise funds and work quietly behind the scenes for the release of Pound, without a trial and without publicity; and that they wanted to engage Thurman Arnold who had helped defend Owen Lattimore when Senators McCarthy and McCarran were accusing him of being a Communist agent. Hammond gathered from Dorothy's response that 'she thought we were too much in the dark' to do any good, and she refused to see him. Pound's own attitude was that he had 'no objection to a movement in his behalf "so long as nobody fakes"'. Hammond wrote again to Hammarskjöld on 3 January, and again at greater length on 7 January, even though he knew that the Secretary-General was at that moment in China engaged in important negotiations. In the 7 January letter he outlined two courses of action: one which 'Mr Pound would probably accept', namely that the federal government be persuaded 'to quietly drop the charges'; the other, which Pound was very unlikely to consent to, would involve him pressing for discharge on the grounds of sanity and then pleading guilty at the ensuing trial in the expectation of 'a nominal sentence which could and would be suspended'. 'It is said', Hammond claimed, 'that T. S. Eliot endorses the plea of guilty and the trial idea.' But Pound himself 'wants complete exoneration and a conversion of official America to the views he expressed on Rome Radio'; and he would most certainly regard the guilty plea stratagem as faking. Either course would call for an organization supported by important names and Hammond was asking Hammarskjöld to lend his name 'in an honorary capacity'. Pound would tell Olivia Agresti in December 1955 that Hammond had migrated to Tokyo, and that 'A buzzard named Blum in Tokio offers Laughlin some letters for $200/ which Mr Hammond had received during some alleged efforts to circulate a quite phoney petition'.

1955: In January, in one sentence in a long letter to Wyndham Lewis, Pound vented his frustration: 'I am gittin bloody near fed up with bein' in jug.'

'Hem/ has done what he can, timing it by what I take to be a fairly good understanding of obstacles'—this was on 19 March to Ingrid Davies in London, whose husband was organizing a group effort there on Pound's behalf. On the 28th, addressing them both, he let them know that there was a conspiracy to keep him locked up because of what he knew and/or what he might get to know; and that any change in his situation would have to come from leverage 'INSIDE the locus of power' since 'It is in those circles that the keys to jails are kept.'

In March the CIA-sponsored American Committee for Cultural Freedom considered applying for Pound's 'release on probation to a private physician or ... institution', and wrote to Dr Overholser in those terms. Overholser stymied the idea.

At the end of March the Italian Premier Mario Scelba and his Foreign Minister were on an official visit to the United States, and US Secretary of State John Foster Dulles and Clare Boothe Luce were present at a dinner given in his honour by the Italian ambassador. Pound's friend Craig La Drière was at the reception. In mid-April Pound mentioned in a letter to

Olivia Agresti, 'It appears La Luce was very affable at the Scelba reception/ yes E.P. wanted in Italy (not by the police) and no need of trial because he WAS crazy when it happened, and cd/ now be released.' Presumably that was what she was reported to have said. Pound then commented, 'I do not much care about technicalities/ a nolle prosequi [to dismiss the charges] need give NO reasons whatever'; and later in the letter he added, 'I don't mind being considered eccentric, officially, so long as I am not required to say Roose was other than a dunghill.'

Archibald MacLeish wrote to Pound in August: 'I have been told by personal friends of yours that nothing is to be done—that no solution would be acceptable to you which did not involve vilification of President Roosevelt and those who served the Republic under him. If that is so it's so—but I'd like to hear it from you before I accept it as the truth.' Encouraged by a friendly response from Pound, he then said he would do what he could for Pound, though 'not exactly grata in this [Republican] Administration', and would 'try to instigate others who can do more'. 'Individual action' was what he had in mind, 'the only kind of action that ever really counts'.

Laughlin asked Hemingway for a contribution to a pamphlet of tributes to Pound's art to be published for his seventieth birthday.[1] Hemingway responded by way of a letter dated 27 October to Harvey Breit of the *New York Times*:

> Will gladly pay tribute to Ezra but what I would like to do is get him the hell out of St Elizabeth's; have him given a passport and allow him to return to Italy where he is justly valued as a poet. I believe he made bad mistakes in the war in continuing to broadcast for that sod Mussolini after we were fighting him. But I also believe he has paid for them in full and his continued confinement is a cruel and unusual punishment.

That statement was included in *Ezra Pound at Seventy*, but in his letter to Breit Hemingway went on, 'If Laughlin wants to help Ezra, rather than exploit his confinement, he could spend some of his Steel earned money and his time and get him free.' The letter was to be sent on to Laughlin, and copied to Pound. Hemingway added a 'private and confidential' note for Breit's eyes only which concluded, 'I detest the Laughlin procedure of a tribute to "Old Ez" with a list of his books in print published by Laughlin, naturally.' Hemingway repeated his public statement for a radio seventieth

[1] The contributors to *Ezra Pound at Seventy* were: W. H. Auden, E. E. Cummings, T. S. Eliot, E. Hemingway, A. MacLeish, J. V. de Piña Martins, M. Moore, N. H. Pearson, E. Sitwell, S. Spender.

birthday tribute broadcast by the Yale Broadcasting Company on 5 December, adding this time that Pound's continued confinement was 'contrary to the Constitution of the United States'.

In October Hammarskjöld asked Bengt Nirje, who was now working for Swedish Radio and who was in touch with Pound, to sound him out on what might be done to free him. Nirje mistakenly thought Pound was being asked to choose between the Nobel and his freedom, but when this was put to him 'he shouted loud and clear "I want OUT"'. In fact Hammarskjöld's concern had been from the start to save the human being, not to support the poet for the Nobel, something he had decided he could not do. In any case, as Marie-Noëlle Little observed in her account of Hammarskjöld's efforts to free Pound, the prize 'would not open any doors for Pound; on the contrary, it might trigger the wrong kind of publicity', as the Bollingen award had done. But Hammarskjöld would use his position as a member of the Swedish Academy to do what he could not do as Secretary-General of the United Nations, and, with the backing of the other members of the Academy, 'discuss the case with his friends in the State Department'. His idea, agreed with his friend W. H. Auden whose judgment he trusted, seems to have been 'to protect Pound, if he admitted he was guilty, and then help him to relocate to Southern Europe'.

In Italy the 'Amici di Ezra Pound' organized by Boris and Mary de Rachewiltz were being very active in the poet's seventieth year. The Mayor of Florence, La Pira, wrote to the US ambassador, Clare Boothe Luce, 'in the name of the City of Dante, which is still grieving for the decree of exile passed upon its greatest poet', asking her 'to intercede with the authorities of his country so that the poet-prisoner may be given his liberty on his seventieth birthday'. On that day, 30 October, the titular head of the 'Amici', Giovanni Papini, wrote in an open letter to Ambassador Luce in *Corriere della sera*,

> In the very moment when the chiefs of the Kremlin are sending back pardoned German war criminals, we cannot believe that the descendants of Penn and Lincoln, of Emerson and Walt Whitman, wish to be less generous than the successors of Lenin and Stalin.

Vanni Scheiwiller, Pound's publisher in Italy, drew up a petition for clemency and secured the signatures of thirty-four Italian writers and intellectuals, several of them anti-Fascists who had suffered under Fascism, and including Ignazio Silone, Mario Praz, Alberto Moravia, Giuseppe Ungaretti, Eugenio Montale, Salvatore Quasimodo, and Vittorio Sereni. They subscribed to the conviction that Pound was substantially innocent of the crime of high treason, and therefore looked to the American authorities to withdraw the charge levelled against the illustrious poet whose cultural services to America and to the entire world were of inestimable value; and it was their wish, that once at liberty, the poet might return to the Italy he loved so well and there pass his days in peaceful work. They counted on the support of Ambassador Luce, and she did indeed communicate to the State Department 'the feeling that seemed to exist in Italy' concerning Pound's incarceration, and twice 'personally took up the matter with officials in State, and once...discussed it with the Attorney General'. But the difficulty, she explained to Charles Norman, was that 'The campaign to free Pound was plainly based on the widely held view among Italians that Pound was innocent...of treason to his country', and had been 'nevertheless sentenced and sent to prison where he was being kept long after his wartime crime (if indeed he ever committed one) had been forgotten and forgiven by most Americans'. The Italian government, however, had 'never made any official representations on the subject, no doubt because they knew the legal facts concerning Mr. Pound through their own Embassy in Washington'. Misconceived as it may have been, the campaign did find an echo in an editorial in her husband's influential *Life Magazine* in February 1956, where it was declared that 'The crimes of World War II have aged to the point of requital, parole, or forgiveness. For this reason, if no other, the arguments for quashing the indictment against Ezra Pound should be publicly considered.'

A loose sort of committee formed in London in 1955 'to obtain [Pound's] release'. Denis Goacher and Peter Whigham who arranged the publication of *Women of Trachis* were involved; and Peter Russell who was publishing Pound's economic tracts as 'Money Pamphlets'; and Dryden Gilling-Smith, an undergraduate at Durham University, who reviewed those pamphlets in the *Social Crediter*; and Ronald Duncan, and John Drummond, and a number of others concerned for Pound's work and welfare. Richard Davies, husband of Pound's intimate correspondent Ingrid, acted as organizing secretary and wrote the foreword to a nine-page pamphlet, *Ezra Pound, written on behalf of the committee formed to obtain his release*, and 'privately printed' in January 1956. The pamphlet gave an account of Pound's life and career up his present state, and concluded—

> Now is not the time to weigh the truth or falsity of his beliefs—to assess the worth of credit economics—the value of the Corporate State—nor is it necessary to balance the technical 'comfort given to the enemy' with those motives which must be held to constitute the morality of his act. It is necessary only to remember the dedication of his life's work, and to look at the walls of St Elizabeth's. If we are indeed responsible for each other's acts then we must each inescapably share a part

of the guilt which attaches to the sufferings this man has endured, and to the increasingly lonely fate which awaits him.

That final sentence was doubtless well meant. Pound would probably have welcomed only the appeal to 'those motives which must be held to constitute the morality of his act'.

The well-wishers concerned to secure Pound's release would not have known that the Justice Department had recognized in 1950 that its indictment was 'faulty', and 'that extreme difficulty would be encountered in meeting our burden of proof if Pound were declared sane and the Government forced to trial'; and that it had therefore been decided that under no circumstances should they take any action 'to reopen sanity proceedings', nor should they 'take any action looking toward dismissal of the indictment'. They would just sit tight and rely on Overholser's opinion to keep Pound shut up in St Elizabeths indefinitely. They were not going to be moved by any appeal to justice or to mercy.

Writing and reading

Evidently Pound was waiting quite stoically for his fate to work itself out. He would not force it. He would not sign, or have his Committee sign, the papers which Laughlin insisted would obtain his release. He would not plead guilty to treason against his country, holding steadfastly to his conviction that he had acted as a dutiful citizen. And he would not say that he must have been insane when he made his broadcasts. But nor would he admit to being sane enough to stand his trial and prove himself no traitor—and that may have been evidence of sanity given his experience of Cornell and of the justice system. He had seen the course of justice perverted for his supposed benefit by his own lawyer's 'bunk', and by the complaisance of the Justice Department and the judge and the jury. Moreover, he had been taught to fear the influence of those who were most vociferous for him to be condemned, and who, under cover of the treason charge, really wanted him executed for his anti-Semitism. He would say that in any case he could not afford a trial. He would also say he could not afford to go free. And he would say that of course he wanted to be set free. All angles considered, the only way out was for the charges against him to be withdrawn, but he was leaving it to others to find how that might be brought about. He neither abandoned hope, nor let his hopes be raised unduly by his well-wishers' petitions. In fact he gave few signs of having these matters on his mind at all.

There was work to be done, and he mainly got on with it. There was his 'Loeb' edition of *Confucius. The Great Digest & Unwobbling Pivot* which Laughlin had agreed to publish. This was his previously published version of those classics but this time with the original texts from rubbings of the T'ang dynasty stone tablets on the facing page. Dr Achilles Fang, an expert sinologist whose offer of guidance Pound would soon gladly accept, expressed puzzlement at Pound's wanting a bilingual edition. 'Professing sinologues are too dull to appreciate his translation,' he informed Laughlin, and 'those who are characterless would resent the ideograms'.

But Pound, holding that 'no civilized man wd/ want the trans without the original for comparison', was adamant, and 'The noble Fang' (as he became to a grateful Pound) contributed 'just the right note' on the Stone-Classics to the book which appeared in December 1951.

For his edition of the Confucian Odes he was more ambitious still. Fang was again to write an introductory note, and Pound urged him to 'HAMMER ... that the bloody translator does NOT consider translation complete without the accompaniment of ideograms and sound-graph'. The original texts were to be in the Confucian era seal script, with Pound's versions on the facing page, and beneath them on that page would be the phonetic transcript of the ideograms. The phonetic symbols had to be 'VISIBLE simultaneously with the ideograms AND the translation', otherwise 'the phonetic transcript will NOT help the ignorant reader (like yr/ friend here below unsigned) to SEE what sound belongs to what ideogram (seal or other)'. When he saw Dudley Kimball's sample layout Laughlin decided it was all too complicated for New Directions to handle, and at that point Fang interested the director of Harvard University Press in the project. The Press proposed that there should be two editions, a 'scholar's edition' with all three components, and a 'trade' edition for the general reader with just Pound's English versions. Contracts for both editions were signed in August 1953. The trade edition appeared reasonably promptly in September 1954, but for Pound 'the real edition', the only one that interested him in the least, was still to come.

There was however a fundamental problem which would lead to increasingly difficult negotiations with Fang who was now in effect his editor. It emerged when Pound was correcting the galley proofs of the trade edition that Fang had regularized the spelling of some of the Chinese names, changing 'Wan' to 'Wen' for example, and Pound expostulated, 'NO!',

> No, my very dear ACHILLES, almost sole comfort of my declining years. The PENalty for altering a VOWEL in verse is DEATH.
>
> You are reprieved because of yr/love of exactitude, but don't do it again.

I am trying to teach these buzzards PROSODY, as well as respect for a few civilized chinese.

Much depended on 'relation to vowels in the context', he explained; although in fact, he relented, 'apart from one Wan | no partic/ damage has been done', and he had restored 'the three necessary spellings/ Wan once, Hsin once, Kiang once'. The real problem was that 'the noises made by yr/ compatriots have almost NO relation to sounds represented by barbarian alphabets', and this meant that it was simply impossible for the phonetic transcript in the 'scholar's edition' to accurately represent the syllables as they might have been sung by Confucius. Fang was licensed to adopt whatever system he thought best for the sound key, but as time passed without progress towards 'the real edition' Pound's impatience grew and he began to suspect that Fang's love of exactitude was holding things up. In February 1956 he exploded,

if you are waiting to satisfy your letch for precision Gaw Damn it/ there is NO alphabetic representation of chinese sound, let alone any fad of spelling it in amurkn alPHAbet that will fit 27 different kinds of chinkese thru 3000 years/

The poet and his expert editor were at odds, because the one cared about the precise sounds in his English version, while being relaxed about the 'highly imperfect but useful' representation of the sound of the Chinese, which he intended 'MORE as a graph of the metric than as a phonetic equivalent of the MUCH disputed chinese sound'; and the other had a scholar's care for the correct pronunciation of the Chinese. There were other reasons along with this for the delay, and in the end the project would remain unrealized. Pound would withdraw the materials from Harvard University Press in 1958, complaining bitterly that his work had been sabotaged and blocked. He would tell Fang that 'The infinite vileness of the state of education under the rump of the present organisms for the suppression of mental life is not your fault.'

His translations from the Chinese and from the Greek appear to have preoccupied Pound's poetic mind from his being committed to St Elizabeths in early 1946 until about March of 1953. There are two notebooks dated as of August and November 1951 with notes and drafts towards new cantos, the later of the two containing ideograms that would feature in cantos 85 and 86. Apart from that there was a long pause between the completion of *The Pisan Cantos* and the beginning of sustained work on the St Elizabeths cantos. 'It has taken me nine years to blot all this out,' he told Denis Goacher in 1954, meaning, Goacher understood, 'being in the madhouse'. The notebooks show that once begun on the new series he worked on them without serious interruption through the following five years. In October 1954 he wrote to Mary de Rachewiltz, 'Canto 85 in proofs'—it would appear in *Hudson Review* at the end of the year—'86/7 sent to Hud/ 88 started | & then 4, further along, not quite sure what numbers, may be 91 onward'. A couple of days later he told her that he had 'typed p.11 of 88' that morning, 'and there are more done for Paradiso after the end [of] "Section Rock-Drill"'. A month later, in November, he was through struggling 'to get ms/ 85/89 in order', those being the cantos to which the title 'Section Rock-Drill' specifically applied, 'The Paradiso proper starting with 90', though 'the reader will have to find THAT out for himself'. He was rather pleased with the way 'the poEM' was growing, confident that it would give 'a fairly good kick in the panTZ' to the idea that it had 'no shape or design'. He foresaw 'A WHOLE vol/ ELEVEN or 12', and was planning to have it set up and printed by Vanni Scheiwiller in Milan because New Directions and Faber were too slow and had not taken on the Confucian Odes. Scheiwiller did publish *Section: Rock-Drill/85–95 de los cantares* in September 1955, 'All'Insegna del Pesce d'Oro, Milan'. By then Pound was fairly well on with cantos 96 and 97 of *Thrones*.

There is very little of St Elizabeths in the twenty-five St Elizabeths cantos. They were written in that sad institution, but they were not of it as *The Pisan Cantos* were both in and of the DTC. Their world is made up out of books, and so immersed is the poet in his reading and in his making that his actual world is indeed blotted out. The reader can easily forget where Pound was as he wrote them.

His chosen books, borrowed from the Library of Congress or found for him by friends, were an idiosyncratic collection, not extensive and with many out-of-the-way titles, but for Pound they did add up to a universe. First among them, as standing for the proper method of natural intelligence, were the writings of the great Swiss-American scientist Louis Agassiz (1807–73), whose 'precise knowledge of his subject [led] to great exactitude of expression', and who built upon Alexander von Humboldt's 'art of collecting and arranging a mass of isolated facts, and rising thence, by a process of induction to general ideas'. That is the method of the cantos, except that it is left to the reader to discover the general ideas in Pound's arrangement of the details. Next on his bookshelf might be the works of Alexander Del Mar (1836–1926), who applied that method to the subject of pre-eminent importance in Pound's view, the history of money from ancient times up to his own. Pound particularly relished his exposure of the crimes of those who usurped from the state the prerogative of issuing money. 'America's greatest historian', Pound called him. Alongside Del Mar would stand Senator Thomas Hart Benton's *Thirty Years' View* (1854), for its first-hand account of the war fought out in Congress between President Jackson and the private Bank of the United States for control of the nation's money supply. Benton supported Jackson, holding that 'when the government becomes "the servant of the lender", the people themselves become its slaves'. Next to Benton would stand Brooks Adams's *The Law of Civilization and Decay* (1896), a study of the economic forces governing civilization, in particular 'the driving greed of the usurer and the finance capitalist'. Adams observed the transformation of Capital through the nineteenth century as it increased its power to use the public credit for private profit, saw it growing to be independent of the productive economy and of the state, and foresaw the coming domination of the state by predatory financial interests and their imposition of an era of austerity.

A second group of works would offer ancient examples of sound economic government where the common wealth was managed for the common good. *Economic Dialogues in Ancient China: Selections from the Kuan-tzu* (1954), contains thirty-two essays from the writings of a prime minister of the state of Ch'i (684–645 BC), a major source for Confucius' thought 150 years later, and for that of Mencius after him. The first essay, 'On Shepherding the People', advised that the good ruler 'should fill and watch over the granaries and public storehouses... When the granaries have been filled, then the people will obey the laws and the rules of courtesy.' From the other end of the Confucian tradition came the sixteen maxims of *The Sacred Edict* of Emperor K'ang-hsi, issued in 1670 and ordered to be read out once a month to all the people in every town of China. It was enlarged by his son and successor Yong-cheng in 1724, and then rendered into the everyday language of the common people by a Salt Commissioner. A typical maxim reads (in the British missionary F. W. Baller's translation), 'If people would regard all connected with the community as making one corporate body—if there were advantages all would enjoy them; if adversities, all share them; this would be (true) union among the people.' Baller the missionary, while recognizing that these moral maxims had guided the people of China for generations, could see 'no life-giving power in them', and wrote in his Foreword that they had left the Chinese 'still enveloped in a darkness which may be felt' since 'nothing but Divine motive power can raise fallen humanity'. He could recommend them only as an aid to those wishing to learn colloquial Chinese, but Pound thought their ethic made them worthy of a place in his *Thrones*. Alongside those Chinese guides to a just social order would stand *The Eparch's Book* of Byzantium's banking and market regulations, put together by Leo the Wise, Roman Emperor in the East (866–912), and edited in 1893, in the original Greek with Latin and French versions, as *Le Livre du Prefet*. That was the earliest attempt to legislate in detail for the good government of a market economy. It established a form of guild system designed to ensure fair trading conditions, and it stayed in effect 'right down to Mustapha Kemal'.

Pound would tell an interviewer in 1960 that his thrones in the late cantos, like Dante's in his *Paradiso*, were reserved for 'the spirits of the people who have been responsible for good government'. Hence his reading into those cantos the works of Kuan I-Wu, and Confucius and Mencius, of the Emperor K'ang-hsi and the Salt Commissioner, and of Byzantium's Leo the Wise. Pound added that his *paradiso* was 'an attempt to move out from egoism and to establish some definition of an order possible or at any rate conceivable on earth'. One work in his collection of books especially relevant to this 'attempt to move out from egoism' and to define a just natural order would be the two-volume Loeb edition of *The Life of Apollonius of Tyana*, written by Philostratus in Greek for the Roman Empress Julia Domna (d. 217). Apollonius, born about the same time as Jesus of Nazareth, was an itinerant sage who would own nothing but his knowledge of men and nature, and who went about his world as far as India and Egypt and the Pillars of Hercules, practising and teaching the Pythagorean idea of the good life, and giving wise counsel to the rulers of the cities he visited. Pound especially approved his having had nothing to say of Heaven and Hell, nor of Original Sin, nor of the life after death, and his attending rather to the live universe and the cultivation of natural wisdom. Among the epistles attributed to him in volume two Pound would have read, 'The gods are in no need of sacrifices. What then can one do in order to win their favour? One can, in my opinion, acquire wisdom, and, so far as one can, do good to such men as deserve it.'

Pound's reading for the cantos included law books, or what served him as law books. He read in Eadmer's life of St. Anselm how, as Archbishop of Canterbury (1093–1109), he had fought to maintain the rights of the Church against the state power of William Rufus and Henry I, and Pound saw that as a 'pivotal point in brit/ history' and a start towards Magna Carta and the development of the democratic idea through the succeeding centuries. He read with close attention Edward Coke on Magna Carta in his *Second Part of the Institutes of the Laws of England* (1628), and told Noel Stock, 'it's all there in Coke, and with a lucidity Blackstone never attains', meaning that the whole history of the common law and of the charters establishing the rights and liberties of the subject was clearly argued out in Coke's seventy-seven pages. And when he read Catherine Drinker Bowen's life of Coke, *The Lion and the Throne* (1956), Pound at once set it alongside the *Institutes* as 'live work'. Then for all his coolness towards Blackstone's prose, he did regard his *Commentaries on the Laws of England*

(1765–9) as necessary 'For the understanding of American (U.S.) LITERATURE', along with the works of John Adams and Jefferson.

American literature, as we ordinarily understand the term, is notably absent from his reading for the cantos in these years. There is no mention of Whitman or Henry James, let alone Melville or Thoreau, or any of his own contemporaries. As for literature in general, he was now, he told Kenner, 'apparently focusing on Dante & Sophocles'. Beyond that, 'EP has never made any bones about wanting a cultural renaissance with Chinese (specifically Confucian) thought in place of Greek, BUT with renewal of gk/ and lat/ studies.' To that end he sponsored but could not sign a statement issued in 1953 by ten professors, among them Hugh Kenner, Rudd Fleming, and H. M. McLuhan, expressing alarm at 'the neglect of the Greek and Latin classics, milleniar source of light and guide in judgment of ideas and forms in the occident'. They wanted them revived in order to maintain the life of the mind here and now and tomorrow and elsewhere. But 'read the TEXTS and not the blithering Idiocies of people who yatter about texts', so Pound admonished Jankowski.

He was encouraging the Polish scholar to translate Richard of [the Paris Abbey of] Saint Victor, the twelfth-century exponent of a theology at once rational and mystical. 'What is WANTED', he told him, 'is an English or American translation of Richard of St. Victor's "Benjamin Minor, sive De Contemplatione", plus two or three chapters of the *Benj. Maj.* and a page of sentences from the rest of the volume. MIGNE 196. Patrologia selected by yr anonymous correspondent.' Richard, he informed Olivia Agresti, was 'A catholic biJAYzuss author whom a confucian CAN read, and whom Dante & Guido damn well DID read. Wd/ have improved my G[uido] C[avalcanti] notes if I had reread him in 1927'. He had 'absorbed some R/ StV in 1909', he told Beatrice Abbot about the same time—he had derived from him then the formative dissociation of the three stages of thought: cogitation, meditation, and contemplation. Now he had 'dug out' the sentence with which he would frame canto 90: 'The human soul is not love, but love flows from it. Thus it cannot delight in itself, but only in the love flowing from it'; and with that one text, he asserted from within St Elizabeths, 'The Church cd/ KILL the kikiatry racket'.

The St Elizabeths Cantos (1): 'Section: Rock-Drill. 85–95 de los cantares'

In June 1955 Pound was cutting out Chinese ideograms from a printed source and pasting them onto the proof sheets of *Rock-Drill*. It must have been a fiddly and painstaking business—there are over a hundred ideograms in canto 85 alone—but he was evidently determined to present his readers with an extreme challenge. Here we must learn some Chinese or abandon hope. Later the challenge will extend to Byzantine Greek.

A note at the end of canto 85 indicates that it is concerned with 'the basic principles of government' as set forth in the Chinese 'History Classic', the *Shu King*. We are referred to Couvreur's edition, *Chou King/Les Annales de la Chine* (1950), which gives the Chinese original, a transliteration for pronunciation, a rendering into French, and in double columns at the foot of the page a Latin version with some notes interspersed in French. Pound's note claims that 'Meaning of the ideograms is usually given in the English text', but this rather overstates the case since the ideograms, as he would analyse them, are generally much richer and denser than his matching English (or French) terms. What Pound does not declare in that note is his conviction that 'China [is] IN [the] ideogram', and must be discovered there. Even the most committed reader will be lost without some serious study of the ideograms, and would be well advised besides to have digested at least certain chapters of the 'History Classic' before attempting to come to terms with the canto.

There will be another sterner note in the middle of canto 96, the first of *Thrones*, after the reader has been invited to follow Pound as he correlates some Greek with some Chinese—

If we never write anything save what is already understood, the field of understanding will never be extended. One demands the right, now and again, to write for a few people with special interests and whose curiosity reaches into greater detail.

For considerable tracts of these St Elizabeths cantos Pound was exercising his right to write for the few, and the non-specialists are in effect bidden to occupy themselves meanwhile with the tea and cake. Dag Hammarskjöld, who was disposed to welcome *Rock-Drill*, felt excluded—'a locked room' was his reaction upon attempting the volume. Al Alvarez blamed Pound's circumstances: 'He could hardly write of what goes on around him. So perhaps Ancient Greece and China are the best way of escaping the public ward of St. Elizabeths Hospital.' Randall Jarrell concluded that Pound was writing for his disciples, and that in order to understand these cantos you needed to have 'read exactly the books Pound has read, known exactly the people Pound has known, and felt about it exactly as Pound has felt'. That was an exaggeration, but it is true that the best interpreter of these cantos has been David Gordon, who read the books and knew how Pound read them, and was thus able to follow the composition of his vision of good government.

The hopeful reader begins,

'LING[2]

Our dynasty came in because of a great sensibility.
All there by the time of Y Yin
All roots by the time of Y Yin.
Galileo indexed 1616,
Wellington's peace after Vaterloo

chih[3]

a gnomon,
Our science is from the watching of shadows;
That Queen Bess translated Ovid,
Cleopatra wrote of the currency,
Versus who scatter old records (85/543)

One can learn to say *ling*[2] in the required second tone, for the sound at least; then gather that 'a great sensibility' is Pound's English equivalent; but to see why this ideogram is the apt introduction one must decipher it as if it were a pictogram. The top line gives the heavens above, over clouds, over the rain from heaven—3 drops which can also be read as mouths and thus as heaven's utterance; and below on the ground men ritually invoking and enacting the heavenly word, receiving from heaven its mandate to rule the people. The English word 'sensibility', rooted in its own very different culture, seems only distantly related to all that. But Pound may have chosen it because the mandate of heaven, as is written in the first chapter of *The Great Digest*, reveals itself to 'the straight gaze into the heart'.

Y Yin, we are unlikely to remember, had a one-line mention in canto 53: 'Honour to YIN'. Grieve's glossary informs us that as chief minister of Ch'eng T'ang ('Tching Tang' in canto 53, q.v.) Yin 'moved T'ang to overthrow the corrupted Hsia dynasty' in 1766 BC, thus bringing in the virtuous Shang dynasty; and that after T'ang's death Yin passed on 'the principles of virtuous government' to his young successor. The ideograms giving his name signify 'one who governs well', and his teachings are recorded in several chapters of *Chou King*.

If we have Couvreur in mind or to hand, and have followed the prompts in Grieve and Terrell, we will find that the claim for 'Our dynasty', which was made for the coming in of the Shang dynasty, is being made again at that dynasty's end when it has been overthrown by the Tcheou. *Ling*[2], which makes only rare appearances in the Confucian books, occurs in what is the likeliest source for Pound's line, *Chou King* IV. xiv, 13, where the officers and officials of the defeated Shang regime are being addressed in the name of the new emperor, and are told that the Tcheou, because of their *ling*[2], were charged with executing the mandate of heaven, i.e. with bringing down the decadent Shang. One might reflect, isn't that what victors tend to say, 'God was with us!', and isn't it uncomfortably near to 'Might is Right'? Or should we suppress such Western thoughts as disturbing to the mind-set of the Confucian ethos?

Pound's response is to remark that the decadent Christian West suppressed what Galileo learnt from studying the heavens and observing the shadows on the face of the moon; and that Wellington's peace—but what are we to make of 'Wellington's peace after Vaterloo'? Cookson reminds us that in canto 50 it brought in a new era of usury. But Terrell informs us that Pound's source for this line, (and also for the Galileo line), was a work by one Captain Russell Grenfell, *Unconditional Hatred* (1953), in which Wellington is held to have reached a wise settlement to prevent future wars between Germany and France, as against 'the unreasonableness of the Churchill–Roosevelt war objectives (the total destruction of Germany as a European power following "unconditional surrender")'. 'Wellington's peace', we are perhaps meant to reflect, suffered in the 1870 Franco-Prussian war a fate similar to that of Galileo's science; and beyond that, if we are to read the line through Grenfell's argument, would be the shadow of the unwise peace terms sought by Roosevelt and Churchill. And if we can go so far, we may find an accord between Wellington's peace and the terms being offered by the Tcheou to the officers and officials of the defeated Shang regime in *Chou King* IV.xiv. They are told that while they stand condemned by heaven to total destruction all will be forgiven and they will be well rewarded if they choose to serve the new regime. So a point of rest and basis for a new beginning might be attained, which Grieve tells us is Pound's reading of the ideogram *chih*[3].

That 'Our science is from the watching of shadows' is itself a gnomic proposition, connecting Galileo and the ancient Chinese use of the gnomon's shadow to track the seasons, and intimating that the sun in heaven is behind what we observe on the ground. But here are also shadows without substance. Scholars have been unable to establish 'That Queen Bess translated Ovid'—and indeed Ovid is unlikely to have been in her line of interest. Nor is it known that 'Cleopatra wrote of the currency'. This is fantasy masquerading as fact, nice ideas but not in the historical record.

The hopeful reader might well pause at this point, to excavate the text from beneath the array of books heaping over it—Couvreur, Grieve,

Terrell, Gordon, Kearns, Cookson, and Mathews's thick Chinese–English dictionary—and to reflect, this is not *reading*, this is no way to perform and to experience a poem. Having Couvreur to hand is all very well, but should one have known that Grenfell was a source for a couple of lines, and must one hunt up a copy of his *Unconditional Hatred*? And in this canto alone there are another sixteen pages to be studied in this fashion, some of them entirely in Chinese. Kearns suggests that Pound was able to write in this way because he knew that 'a scholarly-critical industry had grown up about his poem even before it was completed', and that 'the economics of American academic life' was now one of 'the forces shaping the cantos'. William Carlos Williams had warned years before that this was exactly what Pound, and Eliot, were doing—handing poetry over to the academics and making it an object of study removed from aesthetic experience. Study does discover a coherent composition of statement and response, of (sometimes hidden) resonant accords and contrasts, and through them a major thematic development. And the reward of intensive study of such a canto as this may well be to arrive at such a familiarity with the materials, and with Pound's understanding of them, as to be able to read it in a state of immediate apprehension. Short of that, Pound's readers must accept that the canto can be read in the full sense only by the few who have achieved the necessary expertise, and the rest must be content to make what sense of it they can, then move on to the cantos that are accessible to the non-expert.

The non-expert reader of 85 will mainly make out a series of Confucian maxims of good government: 'Justice, d'urbanité, de prudence', in Couvreur's French—'Perspicax qui excolit se ipsum', in a variant of his Latin, meaning perspicacity is from self-knowledge—research, observation, training, and always *Τέχνη* or know-how, the skill to carry insight into action—'Nisi cum sapientibus non regit', cannot govern without wise advisers—'Ling^{2} | 靈/ was basis of rule'—and finally 'Sagetrieb', Pound's own coinage for the instinctive wisdom of a people, as gloss on the *Chou King*'s 教 *chiao*^{1}, 'teach', meaning (in Couvreur IV.xvi, 13) that the emperor must have men about him teaching the principles which sustain the empire.

Canto 86 continues Pound's digest of the *Chou King*, but now introduces motifs from European and American history, some of these familiar from earlier cantos. More of the writing is readable, though for the non-expert the canto will be again largely an exercise in exegesis. The preoccupation is still with the conditions of good government, with the emphasis now on the ruler's responsibility towards the people and with the maintenance of peace. However complications set in as the scope widens to include *l'histoire morale* of European and American governance, and to set that alongside the Confucian view of China's history. In the *Chou King* the difference between good governors and bad appears simple and absolute. '"Gentlemen from the West",' we are assured in canto 85, '"Heaven's process is quite coherent | and its main points perfectly clear."' There is no such clarity in nineteenth- and twentieth-century Western affairs. Are we to range Bismarck and Talleyrand with the benevolent Tcheou emperors and ministers, the one for his 'No more wars after '70', that is after he had defeated France, and the other, who had served Napoleon in his wars, for buffering the Bourbon dynasty which replaced Napoleon? Surely there was more involved in those issues of war and peace than is indicated here.

On the fourth page there is the highly problematic invocation of Edward VIII, briefly king of England, as the 'one man' who held off war with Nazi Germany, whether 'to good for three years, | or to evil'. The suggestion is that he let the German ambassador know that he personally would oppose any military response to Hitler's remilitarizing the Rhineland in breach of the Treaty of Versailles; and that he may also have revealed that the British government did not intend to react. If he did say such things, then he was not really securing three years' peace, but rather, out of whatever blinkered motives, blindly encouraging Nazi Germany in its carefully staged preparations for total war. In any case, he had no authority to speak for Great Britain, and was behaving, one might well think, simply as a maverick individual and altogether irresponsibly, if not traitorously. The *Chou King* (IV.xxx, 8) sagely observes that 'the state may be shaken and ruined because of one man', although 'sometimes its prosperity and tranquillity may be due to the fortunate appearance of some individual'. Pound has changed the emphasis; and in later cantos, when he asserts that 'Edwardus' saved the peace for three years, he drops the balancing, and properly complicating, 'to evil', altogether.

The partly veiled references to Mussolini do not simplify Il Duce to that extent. 'Lost the feel of the people' is out of Couvreur, but (in a letter to Olivia Agresti) Pound said as much of Mussolini to account for his fall. Later we read Mussolini's resigned, 'All, that has been, is as it should have been', unattributed, but something he had written in his 'Journal in Captivity'. Yet that line is followed by 'what will they trust in now?', with the ideogram for a man standing by his word and the Verona statement, '"Alla non della"', thus suggesting that at least he had held to the idea of governing for the people.

The allusions to President Roosevelt implicitly contrast him with the good rulers of China. They had sound advisers and heeded them; but 'HE' talked, Woodward, one of Roosevelt's advisers, told Pound. He did not listen, and would not hear the things Pound wanted Woodward to tell him. Consonant with that failing at the top was the quality of his Senate, 'Eleven literates . . . '. And hence, one is led to conclude, the state of America in 1939.

In this field Pound is laying down opinions and judgments that are often arguable, if not downright tendentious, and which must in consequence involve the reader in debate, and may provoke dissent if not passionate disagreement. That is the nature of the five cantos of his 'Section Rock-Drill'. Isolated among the mad in St Elizabeths he was struggling to bring his mind to focus, and these cantos are best read as a record of that struggle. His mind was filled with ideas and driven by concerns that would run on endlessly, as could happen when he was talking with his young followers, and for his very sanity he needed to compose its heteroclite contents into a formal order focused on the epic issues of individual rights and responsible sovereignty. He took the *Chou King* as a model, a basis; but whereas that was a record of a received and established idea of good government, rooted in its culture, his cantos were more than ever the work of a solitary, sometimes maverick, sometimes credulous, individual crusading against the prevailing culture.

He would claim, however, that his was not a merely private and idiosyncratic struggle, but that he was attempting, as a responsible member of the human race, to recover and to teach the known but forgotten roots of its more enlightened states. Thus 'Bellum cano perenne', he asserts at the end of canto 86, 'I sing the perennial war'; and 87 picks it up—'between the usurer and any man who wants to do a good job'. Resistance to usury is the underlying theme of this canto, with the emphasis on constructive natural process, from the action of the light from heaven in flora and fauna, and in the mind, and on to the making of laws. A medley of allusions and references—many of them obscure or simply private to Pound—is being pieced together, rather as if he was trying to 'make cosmos' of a miscellany of fragments recovered from all parts of his universe. Mencius and Aristotle and Erigena are in there with Henry James and Picabia; Alexander is mentioned by one Gollievski; Justinian's inefficient law codes chime with Mussolini's; there are lines in Greek from the *Trachiniae*, and a line from Mencius in an English demotic—'Nowt better than share'; Dante's Latin glosses an ideogram; and St Elizabeths' squirrels follow somewhere's 'headless clay lions'. And there is one arresting image for the action of light in nature, 'As the water-bug casts a flower on stone'. This is a canto of 'cogitatio', a canto of preparation for 'meditatio, contemplatio', though the latter states of mind are still at least two long cantos away.

The least difficult of these 'Rock-Drill' cantos is 88. It opens with a sustained character study—the first and only passage of narrative in these cantos—and it closes with a relatively lengthy digest of a Senate speech. Linking them is a sequence repeating and varying the motifs of the 'Bellum perenne', the everlasting war against the usurers. Senator Randolph 'of

Roanoke', an often impassioned and caustic orator, had attacked, in a speech in the Senate, President John Quincy Adams's Panama policy, and had accused his Secretary of State, Henry Clay, of fabricating a letter in order to further that policy. Clay, taking this as a personal injury, demanded satisfaction in a duel. Randolph maintained that anything said in the Senate was privileged and that he could not be held to account for his speech there. Nevertheless he accepted the challenge, as a private person answering to a private injury. Pound's narrative, drawn from Thomas Hart Benton's account of the affair, details Randolph's preparations for the duel, and presents him as a responsible, humane, and honourable Southern gentleman, who, incidentally, rejects the private bank's notes and insists on having his money in gold, the national currency. Given Pound's extended attention to the incident, one might wonder if he saw something of himself in Randolph, in his upholding the right to privileged speech, and yet giving satisfaction to those whom he had offended in his intemperate use of it.

About mid-canto Pound returns to Benton's *Thirty Years' View*, drawing from it details of the drawn out struggle to save the currency, and the commonwealth, from private and foreign interests, and leading into Benton's major Senate speech opposing the renewal of the Charter of the private Bank of the United States. Whereas Randolph's fiery speech had merely given offence, Benton's clearly reasoned argument was forensic. The Bank was 'too great and too powerful', he objected, and asked

> To whom is this power granted?
>   in a remote corner, a company.
> By whom directed?
>   By seven, by four, none by the people elected
> Nor responsible to them.
>   Encroaching on power of States,
>   monopoly absolute.

'Such a power tends to subjugate government', he observed presciently, 'it tends to create public DEBT.' Further, 'It tends to beget and prolong useless wars; | aggravate inequalities; make and break fortunes'; moreover, its branches are 'to be exempt from liability if they fail', and 'exempt from the regular administration of Justice'. Yet that day the Senate voted 23 to 20 against Benton.

'To know the histories | to know good from evil,' begins canto 89, with *Chou King* in ideogram as example. It then goes on at considerable length to recapitulate details from Benton's and other histories, mainly around the theme 'Sovreignty is in the right over coinage'. As detail is heaped upon detail it is as if Pound is bringing his mind to the 'plenum when nothing more will go into it'. And when he breaks out at the end, 'I want Frémont looking at mountains | or, if you like, Reck, at Lake Biwa', the overwhelmed reader, struggling to bring the mass of facts into focus, is likely to feel some relief, as if emerging from an exam into the open air.

With canto 90 we enter quite abruptly upon another realm of discourse and an entirely altered state and mode of mind. The reader would have to be nodding off not to notice that Pound's 'Paradiso proper' starts here. The four cantos 90–3 form a single extended composition, each one carrying forward the meditation upon a set of paradisal themes and motifs. Canto 95, after the interruption of the Apollonius of Tyana canto, which, with its Greek and Chinese, presents difficulties similar to the 'Rock-Drill' section, is a true finale to 90–3. The writing in these five cantos strikes one, after 'Rock-Drill's' hammering recapitulation of the preoccupations of cantos 31–71, as a return to the form of the later Pisan cantos and a going on beyond them. There is both a recovery of the intensity and clarity of vision which makes for musical composition, and new growth in the mind of the poem. It is an advantage to 'Know the mythologies'.

Paradise is here a state of mind illuminated by the love that animates everything in the universe. It is not a pleasure garden wherein the soul may find its rest. The essence of this love is that it is forever active and a cause of action, and that it would move the soul to make the paradise it promises. The mind's predicament is that its capacity for illumination is limited—

> For a flash,
>   for an hour.
> Then agony,
>   then an hour,
>   then agony

So paradise comes in fragments, in odd moments of vision It is manifest in the luminous detail, such as 'the room in Poitiers where one can stand | casting no shadow', because the right proportions were known to its builders, having been preserved in masonic tradition. Again, love's action makes the mind more active, as in this more developed image of the water-bug, 'The water-bug's mittens | petal the rock beneath.'

The love that in canto 90 lifts the poet's mind 'out of heaviness where no mind moves at all' flowed through Sheri Martinelli, as is well attested; however, being universal, it is affirmed under names drawn from various mythologies, as 'Kuthera δεινά | Kuthera sempiterna', and as 'Sibylla', 'Isis', and 'Kuanon'. Its immediate action is to open his mind again to the divinity in nature, 'To the germinal universe of fluid force... of wood alive, of stone alive', to the dionysiac vision of canto 2, and the chthonic rite of canto 83. There, in the grounds of St Elizabeths, he sees in the mind's eye 'the stone under elm... taking form in the air', and 'the great cats approaching... where was nothing', and 'in the boughs now are voices | grey wing, black wing, black wing shot with crimson'. Delivered thus 'out of Erebus', he is 'free now, ascending', in the company of 'Tyro, Alcmene', and 'the dark shade of courage | *'Ηλέκτρα* '. 'UBI AMOR IBI OCULUS EST', the canto concludes, linking love and vision.

The following canto moves out from the personal to the public realm, and from the illumination of passionate experience to the light of intelligence—

> that the body of light come forth
> from the body of fire
> And that your eyes come to the surface
> from the deep wherein they were sunken

The eyes sunk in their caves, 'pinned' eyes in 93, were for McNaughton Sheri Martinelli's, that being an effect of heroin. One might recall then that she was of Pound's mind about love, as when she wrote 'no earthly pleasure is equal to the spasm of the mind'. The eyes become those of 'Reina' and 'Miss Tudor', Queen Elizabeth I, and in their depths Drake sees 'the splendour and wreckage' of the defeat of the Spanish Armada to which he will be moved by her. Like Helen of Troy she is *'Ελέναυς*, a destroyer of ships; but unlike Helen, the Virgin Queen puts forth her influence in defence of her city. Interwoven with that episode are allusions to others who enacted the intelligence of love in their works and lives: Apollonius of Tyana, Helen of Tyre, and Justinian and Theodora of Byzantium who codified its laws and constructed Hagia Sophia. Interwoven also are motifs recalling the universality of love's action, in the holly leaf, in the moving stars, in the silkworm cocoons the peasant wives keep under their aprons 'for Tamuz'. The central episode, drawn from Layamon's *Brut*, presents the founding of Britain as a religious mystery. Unlike Actaeon, Brutus observes the hunting rite and honours 'Artemis that is Diana', and she, in answer to his prayer, guides him to a pleasant land. Later Merlin, like Jesus, is fathered by 'a spirit bright', and in the kingdom there is, 'Over harm | Over hate | overflooding, light over light'—for instance, Athelstan's instituting 'before a. D. 940' a system of justice.

The meditation upon love's civilizing work is jarringly interrupted by this notorious outburst—

Democracies electing their sewage
till there is no clear thought about holiness
a dung flow from 1913
and in this their kikery functioned, Marx, Freud
and the american beaneries
Filth under filth,
Maritain, Hutchins,
or as Benda remarked: 'La trahison'

Dante raged in that fashion near the summit of his paradise, damning Florence. The offence in Pound's denunciation is of course in that one word, which can be explained, but not explained away. And it turns what would otherwise be a natural reflex into a stumbling block. The canto needs a page of reminiscences of Verona to recover its temper, and enter upon its final movement of variations upon 'Queen Cytherea, | che 'l terzo ciel movete', and who moves the mind to come to its 'High City'. Near the close there is mention of 'Jehann | (the Lorraine girl)' who was inspired by a voice heard in the fields to lead the French resistance to the English occupiers. 'A lost kind of experience?', Pound asks, and answers 'scarcely'.

A key word in that canto would be 'protection', as in 'The Princess Ra-Set... has entered the protection of crystal'. And it is noteworthy that the protective powers are female: Miss Tudor, Artemis/Diana, Leucothea, Joan of Arc, and, overall, Queen Cytherea. In the following canto, which is more involved in action than in invocation, the actors are nearly all male.

This relatively brief canto 92 pivots on the assurance that while 'Le Paradis', to us, 'is jagged', 'the Divine Mind is abundant | unceasing... unstill'. It is found in the honour of Desmond Fitzgerald, who had fought in the 1916 Dublin uprising, and who yet freed a man who had not; or in the sentinel who would not leave his post to take cover during bombardment. And it is found in the fragile wings of butterflies, and in the naming of them—'Nymphalidae, basilarch, and lycaena, | Ausonides, euchloe, and erynnis'. The first half of the canto is made up of such manifestations of 'the Divine Mind'. The second half begins, 'and that the lice turn from the manifest', and develops that theme through the consequent evils—'usury | and the degradation of sacraments, | For 40 years I have seen this', 'also desensitaization'. Against that there is still 'a little light from the borders' such as Erigena's, and Hilary looking at an 'oak leaf | or holly'; and there are some more men of active honour, Delcroix, and Bottai, and Marinetti who went 'to the fighting line', and Drake who could not turn back when he saw the armada, having seen the light in the queen's eye. Still the canto ends on the negative image of 'the Portagoose uprooting spice trees, "a common" | sez Ari "custom in trade".' There is no point of rest in that canto.

Canto 93 builds on the preceding three cantos and completes a set of four. In form it resembles a prelude and fugue. The first half, the prelude, takes up the theme of paradise under the aspect of civility, that is, the relation of the individual to civic society. The first emphasis is on the individual: '"A man's paradise is his good nature" | sd/ Kati', he has 'his own mind to stand by him'. But a line in Greek, *Καδμου ϑυγάτηρ*, daughter of Cadmus, recalls that even Odysseus with his strong mind needed Leucothea to save him. And sage 'Apollonius made his peace with the animals'; likewise 'the arcivesco' had thoughtfully brought along a cornucopia of chocolates to keep young Mary happy while being taken around the churches in Rome. From this anecdote there develops a sustained sequence of reflections on the 'sense of civility', on its manifestations, and on the lack of it. There is also the rather complicated case of Tristan, who suffered great pains for his love of Isolde—did their love transcend the social code which it breached? 'The suicide' who would carry the assertion of individuality to the ultimate is a simpler case, and easily contrasted with 'San Cristofero's' public service. The canto then enters into a kind of dialogue with Dante, especially with his treatise *Il Convito*, from which it takes, among other observations, 'that men are naturally friendly', and notes the mention of 'distributive justice'. The underlying concern here is with the social responsibility of the individual, the highest degree of knowledge being 'the moral', which is the sphere of 'the agenda'—'Know agenda, | to the utmost of its virtu.' Counter to that there is ignorance and obstruction, as of the banker who wanted Pound's *Oro e lavoro* destroyed, and 'the lit profs' who do not discuss the relevant passages in Shakespeare and Dante, 'in abuleia | or in total unconsciousness'.

The second part, the fugue, takes up themes from the preceding cantos, more particularly from canto 90. Where the latter was a canto of spring resurgence, this 'cools toward autumn', but, as in the autumn rite at Eleusis, it affirms what does not die with the year. 'The autumn leaves blow from my hand . . . and the wind cools' is the opening statement; but between those lines as counter-statement comes the now familiar 'agitante calescemus', 'we grow warm [when our divinity] is aroused'. There follows an autumnal passage of prayer for compassion from spirits of love, beginning with an invocation of creative light, 'Lux in diafana, | Creatrix'. Light and air are the keynotes of the fugue, 'Lux in diafana' their chord. The prayer modulates into confession, 'J'ai eu pitié des autres. | Pas assez! Pas assez!', and turns then to his child,

For me nothing. But that the child
    walk in peace in her basilica,
The light there almost solid.

A statement of the counter-theme follows that, in ideograms but with the meaning given directly, 'that energy is near to benevolence', a call for constructive action. But 'not yet . . . ! Not yet! | do not awaken,' is the immediate response, as if the child were the princess asleep in the enchanted wood, 'Au bois dormant'. The call to action resumes with D'Annunzio's 'it is never too late to attempt the unknown', with Ocellus' 'the soul's job', i.e. 'to build light', and the T'ang emperor's motto, 'make it new'. And yet men's acting can be a vanity, as in Italy's Libyan adventure, its 'Quarta Sponda | transient as air', or in the 'Waste after Carthage'. To that the response is again, 'not yet! not yet! | Do not awaken.' Then, as if in answer to the prayer, comes 'Flora Castalia', the Apollonian spirit of the spring giving her assurance in the autumn rite, '"Air hath no petals now, | where shall come leaf on bough."' Other assurances follow of the drawing of love, down to Beatrice lit up with love so that Dante may enter upon his new life. 'Such light is in sea-caves', is the reflection, and in 'pinned eyes, the flame rises to fade | in green air'.

'[T]hus was it for 5 thousand years' makes a break in the music, at once celebrating a tradition going back to Kati the Egyptian and placing it in the past. Now in the waking present there is the problematic 'trigger-happy mind | amid stars | amid dangers; abysses | going six ways a Sunday'—one thinks of Kasper; and there are the butchering biographers with no idea of the hidden life of a mind. 'There must be incognita', comes the assertion, but with the unsettling question, 'Shall two know the same in their knowing?' Canto 90 had opened with the affirmation, 'Beatific spirits welding together | as in one ash-tree', and there has been a prevailing sense of love as a unifying force. Now however, as the canto works towards its close, there comes a sense of distance—

You who dare Persephone's threshold
Beloved, do not fall apart in my hands.

Other themes intervene—of individuals and societies, of the coming forth from hell, of mental velocities and stupidities, and of the young again, 'Without guides, having nothing but courage'—then, finally, to his 'Beloved'—

You are tender as a marshmallow, my Love,
I cannot use you as a fulcrum.
    You have stirred my mind out of dust.

That recall of the 'm'elevasti' passage in canto 90 comes in an altered tone, detached now, an acknowledgement of what she has done for him to soften the recognition that, now that he has come through, she is of no use for his agenda. His mind is turned now to the active universe—

> Flora Castalia, your petals drift through the air,
> the wind is ½ lighted with pollen
>   diafana

The sunlit pollen blowing in the autumn wind gives substance to that opening chord, 'Lux in diafana, | Creatrix'. And the final thought is of Persephone who offers assurance in the dying year that the earth will flower again.

Taken together, the four cantos which culminate in that fugue amount to a preparation of the mind for its attempt 'to make paradise' in *Thrones*. Canto 94 brings a salutary reminder of what Pound meant by that. 'Cantos are a POLITICAL implement', he told John Theobald in 1957, with the very important addition, 'like the Div, Com. | (vs temporal power) or Shx Hizzeries'. Canto 94 plunges us back into the realm of temporal power and moral history, the realm of those acting to make the world we live in. More specifically, it is concerned with the wisdom of law-makers and their advisers. The main part of the canto is devoted to Apollonius of Tyana. John Adams features rather elliptically at the start; notice is taken of Justinian's codification of Roman law in the 'Pandects' or 'Digest'; and Kung and Mencius and Dante are mentioned; and Antoninus who said '"Law rules the sea."' These are to have their thrones as seekers after justice and builders of light.

That is what one can make out by glancing over the canto. It is another matter to attempt to read it. The treatment of Apollonius, quite apart from the lines left in the original Greek, is provokingly bitty. His marvellous birth is touched on, with travellers' tales of marvels seen; his advice to a king is transposed into Mencius' Chinese; it is noted that he learnt 'that the universe is alive'; and fragments of his wisdom are recorded. But overall his 'sense of cosmos as living organism'—which is what mattered most to Pound—comes through only faintly, if at all. Possibly the intention is to drive the frustrated reader back to the source, and certainly one must do that if one would understand why Apollonius has his place here. At least the chapters dealing with his conversations on the question of 'how a sovereign ought to rule' would help make up the canto's deficit.

Pound's defence might well have been that he was providing a guide book. At least he claimed on one occasion that the 'Cantos as guide book are no more obscure than a list of names in Dant. Parad.' So when he writes in the first lines of the canto, '"Brederode" | (to Rush, Ap. 4. 1790)', and later 'J. A. to Rush | 18 'leven', we should probably take the reference as an instigation to seek out the 'meritorious Biddle's' edition of John Adams's *Old Family Letters* (1892), and there discover the clue to '"Brederode"'—and also what exactly was 'mentioned in Rollin', and that it was noted by Adams in a letter to Rush. As it happens they were discussing where George Washington acquired his wisdom—and so one would discover that hidden deep in these references is a statement of the canto's main theme: wisdom in government.

There is more that is hidden on the canto's first page. 'Blue jay, my blue jay | that she should take wing in the night', one reads, and then 'by the Kingdom of | T'ai Wu Tzu [plus ideograms] | as mentioned in Rollin'. Members of the inner circle at St Elizabeths identifed 'my blue jay' as Sheri Martinelli, and explained (so Terrell records) that she was living at the time in Alexandria in Virginia, which suggested Alexander the Great, who was described by Rollin (1661–1741)—in his *Ancient History of the Egyptians, Carthaginians, Assyrians, Babylonians, Medes and Persinas, Grecians, and Macedonians* (8 vols., Philadelphia: 1892)—as having 'a violent fiery temper', which is roughly what the ideograms say—those ideograms having no known source but being associated by Pound (on account of their sound) with Dioces who built the city of Ecbatan—Sheri Martinelli herself vouched for that—and (as Terrell continues to inform us) Adams wrote to Rush, in September 1807, that it was 'From Rollin I suspect Washington drew his wisdom . . . in the History of the Kingdom of the Medes, there are in the Character of Dejoces' etc., etc. That is quite wonderfully beyond all exegesis, leaving the uninitiate altogether 'locked out' of the game.

In December 1955, shortly after the *Rock-Drill* volume was published in Italy, Pound thought to mention to Mary that '85–95 have richiami | echos | the whole thing working in fugally | and if you haven't the earlier phrase in yr/ head, especially when it is much abbreviated. . . . ' That is especially the case with canto 95, which is composed in part of brief echoes of motifs from previous cantos, these following one upon another with scherzo-like rapidity—

> 'In favour of the whole people'. 'They repeat'
> said Delcroix
> Van Buren unsmearing Talleyrand,
> Adams to Rush before that, in 1811
> And there were guilds in Byzantium.

That is to be read as a unit, and taken in at high velocity. The next unit does expand at a slower pace upon the root senses of 'political', before another rapid passage, a variation upon the first, these now being clearly 'political' echoes.

The three units together are a response to the canto's initial passage which affirms, in Bede's Latin, that God animates all things, from the comets to the mist weighing down the wild thyme. Adams and the rest of it are the *diafana* of the animating light in human affairs, though subject to the paradox stated in the first lines that Love which endures through all time is yet 'gone as lightning'. Undaunted by that the canto builds through a fast moving succession of echoes and allusions to its main statement, 'And there is something decent in the universe | if I can feel all this . . . | At the age of whatever.' There are just a few dissonant lines—'The immense cowardice of advertised litterati' with 'no voice for the Constitution, | No objection to the historic blackout'—but these hardly disturb the confident celebration of Love's multifarious manifestations in the world.

The closing lines, in effect a bridge passage to *Thrones*, condense the episode in which Homer's Odysseus, wrecked by Poseidon's wrath, is saved by Leucothea—another instance of the Divine Mind's being 'abundant | unceasing | *improvisatore* | Omniformis'. One should not make too much of this use of the *Odyssey*. Pound's *nostos* is not his Penelope's bed but a just society. 'Div Com | the main structure', he assured Mary. 'not Odyssey'.

Intimate relations

Neither Pound's wife nor his longtime companion figure in the St Elizabeths cantos. Dorothy Pound could claim as her own the Lynx song in *The Pisan Cantos*. Olga Rudge appeared there as a sustaining vision, as 'La Cara', the 'beloved', and as 'a great goddess'. But in the *paradiso* which Pound was trying to compose in *Rock-Drill* and in *Thrones* they are no longer presences. The long years among the mad had dimmed their light in his mind. He had lost sight above all of what Olga had meant to him. In that place La Martinelli was his resident divinity.

By 1955 Dorothy Pound had moved from 10th Place to Brothers Place, a dreary block remembered by Michael Reck as 'a jungle of wooden row houses fronted by porches with fake-Greek fluted columns'—

> And somewhere down the endless row lived Mrs. Pound, in a basement. You descended four or five steps; the screen door creaked. Mrs. Pound had just one room, which contained only books, a bed, and a writing desk. She smiled (maybe a bit grimly) and did not complain. One had the impression that externals mattered little to her; what counted was the time she had with her husband.

Sometimes she did let out what she felt, as when she told Douglas Hammond in January 1955, according to his account, that she had '"led a hell of a life these last sixteen years, first the bloody war, and these nine years here"'. And she sent Richard Aldington, 'without comment, a postcard of a Washington Gallery picture of "A Tired Old Woman with a book"'. Aldington found that 'pathetic', missing the grim strength, which Pound was better placed to appreciate. 'There are bottomless pits like D.P. who let people think they are getting on with THEM', he wrote to Mary, and quoted 'S/ [Sheri] on D.P. at the Giovannini's stating SILENTLY: "I have been invited here to dinner, I will eat my dinner, please DO NOT hold ME responsible for any of this".' That air of keeping herself to herself hid a cold determination to control what remained to her. One day when Mary was in Washington in the spring of 1953 Dorothy wanted to tell Pound that 'that money to O.R. ought to go as private transaction between O.R and Jas'—she did not want to be the one to send it—and she wrote him a note instead of speaking of it when visiting, 'because I can't talk to you about this in front of Mary. I do not know what Mary knows—and anyway Olga would probably get it out of her if she thought Mary knew anything.' She was of course keeping more than private information from Olga Rudge. Forty years later Sheri Martinelli, interviewed by Anne Conover for her biography of Olga Rudge, 'quoted Dorothy as saying she liked having Ezra in St. Elizabeths: "At least I know where he's sleeping tonight."'

After the de Rachewiltz's second child, Patrizia Barbara Cinzia Flavia, was born in March 1950, Pound had advised that the castle and its land should be held in trust for the children because 'As trust it cannot be mortgaged'. He was aware that Boris was seriously overdrawn, and warned her, 'Don't get into debt.' In that year the dining room ceiling in the castle came down, breaking furniture and china, and requiring repairs costing more than half a million lire. Pound had Dorothy send $100, then $720 'for Patrizia's roof'.

In 1953 Mary had managed to get to America to visit her father, spending ten weeks there, March into May. Her mother had looked after the two children at Sant'Ambrogio, along with a 2-year-old, Graziella, whom Mary had rescued from a Roman orphanage. Olga delighted in being a grandmother, telling Pound, 'This place is a Paradiso Terrestre, with those three kids running round—children necessary to complete the picture.' Pound had expected Mary to 'come to him straight off the boat, first things first', and kept two days clear of visitors for her while she, following her own sense of priorities, had stopped over in New York to discuss getting him out with Laughlin and Cornell. But all was well: he wanted to hear all about 'Boris and the children and of our efforts with the castle', and said 'Thank God you have taken time to produce a family and lead a sane life.' He would not talk with her about getting out, saying, '"All you can do is plant a little decency in Brunnenburg."'

Pound would watch out for her from his window every day and be 'right behind the door when it opened, ready to go out on the lawn or . . . down the long corridor' to his alcove. After Mary's second day Dorothy was usually present, or else Omar, who agreed with his mother 'that they should not attempt to hurry Pound's release'. After a week the regular visitors returned, and Mary found her role was to be an observer. Her first impressions of Pound were of his boundless 'kindness and curiosity', and she wrote to Olga soon after her arrival, 'he is wonderful, except for the waist line, just like Rapallo. He talked all the time for my "education", like ten years ago.' Then she began to feel his 'heaviness, boredom, depression', and the only time she saw it lift was with La Drière and Giovannini, or when Huntington Cairns visited—'he really made a difference'. She felt the petty humiliations he was subject to, perhaps more than he did, as his having a tiny purse where he kept some coins for peanuts to feed the squirrels, and his saying when he showed her the contents, '"This is all I am allowed."' She thought then of how 'with lordly gesture [he] would pull out a handful of coins and allow me to give them to the beggars'. She had little money for her time in America, and Pound, apparently unable to ask Dorothy for money for Mary, had to ask Laughlin to send her some, and Laughlin sent it 'as advance on royalties', which so angered and humiliated Pound that he tore up both letter and cheque. But the boredom was the worst horror, she recalled, that and not the noise or the stink of the ward. She returned to Italy 'bewildered and discouraged. The legal and physical morass in which father was caught up was a nightmare.' But Pound wrote to Olivia Agresti, 'Yes, Mary a gt/ comfort.'

In that year the chance had come up to buy some land around the castle, but five million lire had to be found for it, to be paid in instalments. There was money from the settlement of Isabel Pound's estate, and Pound had the first million, $1,670, sent to Boris in Rome. In December he had a further $2,600 sent, 'on specific condition that it is to be used for the land, and nothing BUT land, and that at no time shall the land be hypothecated, or used in any way to raise money by loan'. The next year, in November, he was worrying that a cheque to meet the demand for the remaining one and a half million lire seemed not to have reached Brunnenburg, and that Boris might be forced to borrow money and get into debt. He was dreaming of maples and their yield of syrup, but the hillsides below the castle would be covered in apple orchards and vineyards.

Mary and Boris had invited her mother to Brunnenburg for Christmas of 1953, the more especially as she had got on so well with the children, but she chose to remain in Rapallo, telling Pound that she was enjoying 'the luxury and joy of this place after the Palazzo Chigi . . . to look out the window first thing in the morning, to rejoice in the sight of five healthy cabbages growing below, to climb that salita in the dark, and sit on a bench with stars to look at'. The previous year, desperate to see Pound, she had booked passage from Genoa to New York on the SS *Italia*. She was travelling third class, but the purser, who knew about music, gathered that she was connected with the Accademia Chigiana and the Vivaldi revival and gave her a pass to the first-class salon. Arriving in New York on 9 April she had gone straight to Washington, and Caresse Crosby, with whom she stayed, took her out to St Elizabeths. Conover writes that 'Olga was permitted three visits of three hours each' with Dorothy 'discreetly absent', but that must have been three visits with Pound all to herself. After that there would have been other visitors, as when Miss Jung, the Chinese student who would be taking instruction from Pound through that summer, was introduced on her first visit to 'Olga Rudge, who had just arrived from Siena the previous week', also to Professor Giovannini, and 'a young man with a British or Australian accent'. Olga was in America for just four weeks, sailing from New York back to Genoa on 7 May. On the 5th Pound wrote to Mary, 'O. arrived in state of great serenity. Time very short . . . Thank heaven conditions now possible for her to visit in comfort = and out of doors when it don't rain.' 'Hope to see her again soon', he wrote when she had gone. Olga wrote to him from the SS *Vulcania*, 'This one, who expected after having at last seen Him to want nothing more than to lie down and die, has accomplished the viaggio di ritorno in a most serene state of mind, resigned to going on in this vale of tears.' She was feeling that 'sitting on his lawn is paradise . . . watching His trees and His birds with Him has been the only time she felt really relaxed and contented all these years'.

They would grow out of sympathy through the three years of renewed separation that followed. '10 years bug house does not conduce to adaptability to directives from others—esp. if rooted in different pt. of view.' He was accusing her now, in early 1955, of having a set of 'idées reçues' picked up in Paris, 'probably same as Colette's', and of having been trying for thirty years to fit him into it. But he was not anyone's private property, he asserted, wonderfully eliding his Committee and the bug house. 'A civilization', he went on in his imagined liberty, 'is where each person consumes their own smoke & does what they can do best & that is their point of contact with others who have sense to want 'em to do it.' Olga retaliated,

'He not think she not noticing that for months he been docking letters to her of any affectionate closure.' 'She not to worry about his unsatisfactory character,' he replied to that, with an affectionate closure. Still she could be sharply critical. In March she wrote, 'Having once again gone thru all his "discorsi" and found magnificent ones—she deplores his insistence on the subject [i.e. his "anti-semitic trype"] which he drags in like King Charles' head in Mr Dick's memorial—For god's sake lay off it'

When she told him in April that she was hoping to get to Washington again, he wrote back: 'I don't see what good yu can do in Wash/n either to yrself or to me. Have enough to do with my own nerves & don't have to argue with my colleagues on the ward. Ziaou.' 'Alright', Olga replied, 'she won't complicate things for him by going to Washington, but she has affairs of her own to see to—& does not want to pass up a free passage.' Pound conceded, 'Bene | she come in that sperrit. O Kay.'

Olga was in Washington on Tuesday 5 July, 'in Wash's worst heat wave, looking very elegant', Pound reported to Olivia Agresti, 'but the complications etc/ etc/ etc. question of timing. Hemingway understands better than she does.' But her arguing fiercely with him about the need for urgent action to get him out of St Elizabeths was not the only complication, nor yet the main one. Sheri Martinelli, forty years later, told Anne Conover how she remembered Olga's appearing at St Elizabeths on that Tuesday:

> [Sheri] was sitting at the right hand of Pound one afternoon when Dorothy failed to appear. Then Olga came, 'a royal presence, with marble-like, sculptured features, her back stiff and erect, professional-looking, a *trained* person'. Her hair was carefully 'marcelled' in waves, and she was wearing a lovely lavender and white summer dress, with matching lavender parasol to protect fragile skin against summer sun.
>
> No one knew who Olga was, but Pound looked up with a 'bad little boy' grin, an expression that said, according to Martinelli, 'anything can happen now'. . . . Olga 'stared like a lioness' when she saw the attractive young woman sitting close to Pound. 'In a magnificent fury, she lifted the folded parasol over my head. I could see she was reading my face, and when she looked into my eyes she saw—"iggurance". She waved the parasol over me, but never did bring it down.'

Olga's presentiment that she had been displaced was confirmed by Pound's paying her no particular attention. He wrote to Mary, 'Oh well, your ma turned up looking quite beautiful, not to say elegant. And I have brutally gone on with writin' a canto, I suppose 97, tho 96 aint yet tucked in, got to get from the Odyssey, thru Paul the Deacon, down to Del Mar's marvelous account of rascality.' That was on the Thursday, and he wrote again on the Saturday not knowing whether Olga 'sailed yester/ or is waiting for

1 Aug/ IF you hear let me know.' It seems that Olga had made just that one visit to St Elizabeths, and that she had seen and suffered all she needed to make her sever relations with Pound. She would not speak to him again until years later when he had been released and was back in Italy, and was near to death.

Pound's Saturday letter to Mary began, 'Waaal, she'za nice gal | and she wuz lookin beeeyewteeful, not only elegant | better than ever save possibly in one early foto, taken before I met her. But the WRONG time and the WRONG place.' And she was unteachable, and 'she don't stop for explanations'. There was only this oblique allusion to what had really happened, 'she wd/ probably explode if she knew that her ally in the anti-Martinelli campaign wuz young Omar/ so fer garzache don't MENTION that.' If he cared at all about her hurt and her anger he wasn't letting on. In fact Olga was close to despair, as she would tell Mary. She booked a passage to return to Italy on a cargo ship sailing from Newport News and had to climb a rope ladder over its side—'It would have been so easy to let go', she said.

13 : 'INDICTMENT DISMISSED', 1956–8

Archibald MacLeish[1] went to see Pound in St Elizabeths in late November 1955. They had corresponded, but they had actually met only once before, back in their Paris days. There was little enough to bring them together. MacLeish thought Pound's politics altogether wrong-headed; and then during the war he had worked for Roosevelt, Pound's *bête noire*, and Pound had fiercely attacked him for that in one of his broadcasts, and still held it against him. Nor did Pound show much respect for MacLeish's poetry or wider literary achievement. But MacLeish did genuinely respect and honour Pound as a poet and for his services to the arts, and that was what brought him finally to make his visit. He had written to find out if there was any way of getting Pound released from St Elizabeths so that he could have 'some peace and quiet in which to work'. Would Pound accept 'a medical disposition of the problem: meaning by that, a disposition based on medical opinion, as distinguished from a legal or political (whatever that might be) disposition'. Pound wouldn't give a simple answer, telling MacLeish that he was 'overlooking the simple and direct solution' but leaving him to guess what that might be. He evidently believed, as he wrote to Mary, that talk of legal complications was a hoax and 'the minute they WANT to let me out they can'. In the meantime, to the infuriation of friends such as Harry Meacham, he would spend hours helping others but 'will not lift his hand to unlock his cell'.

MacLeish's visit left him feeling sick and convinced that Pound must be got out. The horror of what he had seen was still vivid a year later when he was reviewing *Rock-Drill* in the *New York Times*:

[1] Archibald MacLeish (1892–1982), graduated from Yale 1915 (Phi Beta Kappa, Skull & Bones); LLB Harvard 1919, (edited *Harvard Law Review*); briefly practised law; in France 1923–8; worked on *Fortune* and *Time*; distinguished and prize-winning poet and playwright; Librarian of Congress 1939–45; assistant director Office of War Information; Assistant Secretary of State for Public Affairs 1944–5; Chairman of the American Delegation to the 1946 London conference which drew up the constitution of UNESCO; Boylston Professor of Rhetoric and Oratory at Harvard 1949–62.

> Not everyone has seen Pound in the long, dim corridor inhabited by the ghosts of men who cannot be still, or who can be still too long.... When a conscious mind capable of the most complete human awareness is incarcerated among minds which are not conscious and cannot be aware, the enforced association produces a horror which is not relieved either by the intelligence of doctors or by the tact of administrators or even by the patience and kindliness of the man who suffers it. You carry the horror away with you like the smell of the ward in your clothes, and whenever afterward you think of Pound or read his lines a stale sorrow afflicts you.

Pound had to be saved from that, not only for his own sake, MacLeish told Hemingway, 'but for the good name of the country: after ten years it was beginning to look like persecution and if he died there we'd never wash the stain out.'

Pound's own immediate concern seemed to be to interest MacLeish in La Martinelli's art. However he did tell Kenner after MacLeish's visit that 'dear Archie' was being 'useful and benevolent'; though he then told A. V. Moore, 'The benevolent will not get me out on false pretences', which led Moore to tell Eliot, 'he insists on his own terms for a release'. All the same, he was showing interest now in the possibility of release. In his letter to Kenner he wrote hopefully of 'a mild beginning of mild scepticism as to Ez having ever committed ANYthing whatsodam vaguely approaching treason'. And he enquired of Zukofsky, 'what yu kno bout Thurman Arnold', Arnold being a leading Washington lawyer who had served as an Assistant Attorney General in the Roosevelt administration and might well have been mentioned by MacLeish in connection with efforts to get him out.

In February 1956 an editorial in *Life* magazine noted that 'Tokyo Rose'[2] had recently been released, and that Nazi war criminals were being released, while Ezra Pound was still incarcerated, his room at St Elizabeths 'a closet which contains a national skeleton'. Encouraged by this straw in the wind of public opinion, at the end of February Dag Hammarskjöld raised the Pound case as 'a humanitarian problem' in a meeting in Washington with Assistant Secretary of State Francis O. Wilcox, and then wrote him, in

[2] 'Tokyo Rose' was the collective name given to a dozen American-speaking women who made propaganda broadcasts from Japan during the war. In 1945 two American journalists identified Iva Toguri Aquino as Tokyo Rose and she was arrested by the US authorities in Tokyo, but no charges were brought and in October 1946 she was released. In 1948 she was re-arrested, taken to America, and there convicted on one count of 'speaking into a microphone concerning the loss of ships', the only evidence against her being verbal evidence from a colleague at Radio Tokyo who later said he had been coerced. Sentenced to ten years, she was released for good behaviour after serving six years. She was accorded a presidential pardon in 1977.

confidence, a long letter conceding the difficulties presented by Pound's ideas and radio activities, yet leading up to this conclusion:

> Considering various international decisions on war criminals from far worse categories than the one Mr. Pound represents, and considering his positive contributions to American letters, there seems to be, with regards to his old age and the circumstances of his legal status, forceful humanitarian reasons for a reconsideration of the case of Ezra Pound.

Hammarskjöld was advised, discreetly, 'that action in 1956 is considered unwise'—once again it was an election year—but that an effort in 1957 'might well prove successful'.

Hammarskjöld showed his letter to Auden, who thought it excellent, but warned, 'Our chief headache, I fear, may be E.P. himself: I am so afraid of his making some statement to the Press about USURY or one of his hobby-horses.' Hammarskjöld apparently shared that fear, as did Hemingway and others among Pound's supporters, and this in spite of the Constitution's First Amendment guaranteeing freedom of speech and of the press, which he, and no doubt all of them, would uphold. In May he sent Pound a copy of a speech he had just given on the 180th Anniversary of the 1776 Virginia Declaration of Rights, drawing his attention to the last page where he had said, 'It is when we all play safe that fatality will lead us to our doom. It is in "the dark shade of courage" alone that the spell can be broken.' The unattributed quotation is of course Pound's characterization of Elektra, who would not be silenced. That was in the spirit of the twelfth clause of the Virginia Declaration which held 'That the freedom of the press is one of the greatest bulwarks of liberty and can never be restrained but by despotic governments.' A noble ideal nobly affirmed, but Hammarskjöld appears to have missed the irony, that here was Pound being urged by his friends to shut up, and being literally shut up by the state for having spoken his mind, his situation that of an Elektra lacking an Orestes.

Like Hammarskjöld, MacLeish had gathered 'that it would be unwise as well as useless to approach Dept of Justice before the election'—that was 'the consensus of opinion' among his 'Republican friends and political acquaintances'. He intended therefore to prepare for a serious approach to the Department in November, unless Pound told him not to. Pound did not do that, but nor was he being helpful—replying to MacLeish's proposals, for instance, with 'personal attacks on those [senators] whose help [he] had thought of enlisting'. 'I am fighting feathers and losing my way', MacLeish complained, 'whoever offers him a hand will have his fingers broken.' Nevertheless he persisted, and in July he asked Pound to lay aside all his arguments about Roosevelt and the war and Mussolini, and just say simply and clearly whether he wanted to be got out of St Elizabeths; or did he want rather to have people learn 'the facts of your position over the past many years . . . including the Rome broadcasts', in which case a trial would be the proper procedure and he, MacLeish, 'should desist and withdraw'. He had been 'assuming that the objective is to get you out of St Elizabeths', and further assuming 'that the best—indeed the only—way of accomplishing that objective rapidly is to persuade the Attorney General to nol pros[3] the indictment'. His own position was that he wanted to get Pound out 'because its hurts me personally and seems to me a disgrace to the country that you are held there still after all these years'. But he was not going to do what Pound did not want done. Pound must have indicated that he could go ahead with his plan to persuade the Department of Justice to drop the indictment.

He did want to get out, and was pleased to note in August that 'Hem is apparently telling 19 millyum readers of Look . . . that I should be got out'. More irritation on the part of other writers at his 'prolonged incarceration' would be in order, he intimated to James Dickey. At the same time he seemed to regard his release as an affair for others to attend to. He had other preoccupations. On 3 August he fired off a formal letter 'To the President and Trustees | Hamilton College', telling them 'the time has come for me to return to you the Honorary Litt. D. conferred on me in 1939, this being the only form of protest left me'—apparently the college was failing 'to teach the facts either of U.S. History past and present or any other historic truth with due vigour'. The actual parchment was where he could not get at it, he had to admit, but he trusted that the means would be found to restore it to them at some future date. The president of the College blandly replied that he was distressed to have such a letter from so distinguished an alumnus, was at a loss as to the exact nature of the college's failings, and that an honorary degree was 'a permanent fact' and could not be 'returned'. And that was the end of that brief episode. Pound's main preoccupation at this time was finding new materials for the ongoing cantos. He had just discovered the writings of Mme de Rémusat, her son Charles François, and his son Paul, and hoped they would prove 'CantObile', as indeed they did, the grandson providing 'essential facts . . . on frog commune' for canto 100, his father providing anecdotes of St Anselm for that and other cantos, and Mme de Rémusat providing memories of the Napoleonic era for canto 101. Pound was also being excited by accounts of the rituals and customs of the 'forgotten' Na Khi kingdom of south-west China, and these he drew on in

[3] Nolle prosequi: legal term signifying 'I will not proceed with the prosecution'.

canto 101 and some later cantos. Then, whenever the weather allowed, there was the excitement of tennis after regular visiting hours, with John Chatel, one of the acolytes, recruited as a regular opponent, or he would look out for Evans, one of the hospital staff. It had been an important moment in June when he was able to play again; and there was some further unspecified relaxing of his conditions in September when this note was entered in his Clinical Record: 'Daylight privileges on grounds in vicinity of tennis court ordered by Dr. Overholser in addition to his 9 P.M. privileges in same vicinity.' His life in St Elizabeths was going along apparently undisturbed by talk of release.

He was even allowing it to be assumed, apparently, that he would die in St Elizabeths. When D. G. Bridson of the BBC came in December to record him reading from his cantos it was agreed that the recordings were not to be broadcast in his lifetime. Bridson at least thought he was recording Pound's voice for posterity. And he found that Pound was anxious to make a statement, 'for the record', of the experiences which had led him to speak over Rome Radio. He spoke without notes, in an easygoing, eminently reasonable, amusing, and persuasive manner very far from the style of those wartime broadcasts. Bridson heard no hint of 'paranoia or any other disturbance of the mental faculties'. It was simply 'the considered statement of something [Pound] wanted to make generally known'. He spoke of being hassled over visas and permits in the American Consulate in Paris after the 1914 war; of the official in the Chicago call-up tribunal who had said, not to him but to an acquaintance, 'Say, young feller, don't you know that in this country there ain't nobody has got any god-damned rights whatsoever?'; then there was the Prosecuting Attorney who had told him—and here Pound assumed 'a heavy and aggressive accent'—'All I'm interested in is bunk—seeing what you can put over'; and finally there was being told, by a Senator in Washington in 1939, 'He [Roosevelt] has packed the Supreme Court, so they will declare anything he does constitutional.' And the accumulation of these things had brought him to use the microphone to speak out in defence of the rights and liberties guaranteed by the Constitution. 'If no one protests you will lose all your liberties,' that was what he had to say 'for the record'. It was a defence of a sort, but not for the courtroom. His expectation was that this, along with his canto readings, would be heard posthumously.

In September 1956, as part of an Eisenhower administration Cold War propaganda initiative, an American Writers Group with William Faulkner as its chair was set up to propose ways of improving the image of the United States abroad. A range of writers were canvassed for suggestions, among them William Carlos Williams. His advice was that the best thing the

President could do was 'to see to it that Ezra Pound is released'. His 'Free Ezra Pound!' was then included in a questionnaire incorporating the various suggestions received, and to this there were 22 responses. On the Pound question, 10 were positively in favour, 3 were supportive with reservations; 2 were against; and 7 abstained. At the end of November fourteen members of the Group met, with the 'Free Ezra Pound' item last on the agenda. However, Williams was determined to raise it, and the discussion became heated. Saul Bellow, supported by Robert Hillyer, argued angrily that Pound was an anti-Semite who deserved to be punished for advocating the murder of Jews in his poetry and broadcasts. Eventually he lost his temper and strode out of the meeting. The next day Faulkner met with John Steinbeck and Donald Hall, who had participated in the meeting, to consider the Group's interim report. Hall wanted to include the recommendation to free Pound, and Steinbeck said that would just make people mad, whereupon Faulkner turned to their secretary and said, 'You take this down, young lady: "The government of Sweden gives the chairman of this committee its greatest award and the government of the United States keeps its best poet in jail."' The proposal that 'we should free Ezra Pound' was retained in the draft report sent out to the members of the Group on 2 January 1957. This time there was unequivocal support only from Marianne Moore, and from Malcolm Cowley who wrote, 'There's no doubt that . . . the continued imprisonment of Ezra Pound [has] done more damage to the United States in world opinion than all of us together could mend or patch.' Others did not mind his being freed, but thought his literary eminence irrelevant (Richard Wilbur), or thought it inappropriate to include his case in the President's programme. Two, including Saul Bellow, strongly objected. (There was apparently no comment from Williams.) At a meeting of the Group in February Faulkner walked out of the room, effectively resigning, and no report was ever issued.

MacLeish meanwhile was trying to clarify Pound's situation. In mid-October he wrote to A. V. Moore to set out his present understanding:

(1) he is not now legally insane according to the responsible medical officer
(2) he is not however sane enough to stand trial
(3) ergo he should be released

However, in the way there was 'the vociferous Jewish group who feel, with reason, that Pound has ben antisemitic and who would keep him in for that reason'. Moore comunicated all of that to Dorothy Pound, adding his own view that even if Pound were to be released it was unlikely he would be granted a passport.

In mid-November, the election being over, MacLeish prepared to take the first steps towards an appeal to the Attorney General. First he wanted to be sure that Overholser's position was still what it had been when they talked about Pound in his office the previous year, and as MacLeish had reported it in his letter to Moore. Overholser, however, would now say only that 'it is unlikely that his mental condition will in the future be such that he is able to stand trial', and that therefore 'it seems unnecessary . . . to keep the charges alive any longer'. 'We should not bring up the question of his insanity', he advised, nor 'the question of release at the present time'. MacLeish understood him to be saying 'that Pound, though unfit to stand trial, is not fit to release', and Overholser said that was correct, but added, 'I think it is high time that charges against Ezra Pound should be dropped, but I think that his release from the Hospital at this time would muddy the waters to an undesirable extent.' One must deduce that he did indeed consider Pound 'not now legally insane', but would not say so on the record. He was attempting a rather fine distinction between his being sane and yet 'mentally incompetent to advise with counsel and to participate in his own defense'. He was quite right of course that it would complicate matters, or 'muddy the waters', if it were to be admitted that Pound was actually quite sane in all other respects; and it would be a further puzzle as to why, in that case, he should not be released from St Elizabeths if the charges were to be dropped.

Anxious to keep Overholser on side, MacLeish proceeded to draft a letter simply seeking a 'Nol Pros' from the Attorney General. The question of release would be left to be dealt with 'on a medical basis'. He sent the draft to Eliot who rewrote and signed it, and he secured Hemingway's agreement. Then Frost too agreed to sign, and Guy Davenport was commissioned to carry the letter to him. 'Eisenhower will never consent to this', Frost told him as he waited, 'It's a waste of all our time'; but he did add his signature, 'after meditating a whole ten minutes'. The letter, sent to the Attorney General on the letterhead of the American Academy of Arts and Letters, about 16 February 1957—though dated 'January 14'—was diplomatic yet quite sharp:

Our interest in this matter is founded in part on our concern for Mr. Pound who is one of the most distinguished American writers of his generation, and in part on our concern for the country of our birth. As writers ourselves we cannot but be aware of the effect on writers and lovers of literature throughout the world of Pound's continued incarceration at a time when certain Nazis tried and convicted of the most heinous crimes have been released and in many cases rehabilitated.

It is our understanding, based on inquiries to the medical personnel at St. Elizabeths Hospital that Pound is now unfit for trial and, in the opinion of the doctors treating him, will continue to be unfit for trial. This opinion, we believe, has been communicated to the Department of Justice. Under these circumstances the perpetuation of the charges against him seems to us unfortunate, and, indeed, indefensible. It provides occasion for criticism of American justice not only at home but abroad and it seems to us, in and of itself, unworthy of the traditions of the Republic. Concerned, as we must be, with the judgments of posterity on this unhappy affair, we cannot but regret the failure of the Department thus far to take steps to nol pros the indictment and remit the case to the medical authorities for disposition on medical grounds.

May we add that this is a personal letter to you and that we have no intention at this time of making a public statement on this matter.

The Attorney General, Herbert Brownell, acknowledged the letter, saying he had 'asked that a review of the matter be made', and that he would 'communicate further when it is completed'. On 10 April the Deputy Attorney General, William Rogers, wrote to each of the signatories to say he would be willing to talk to them.

Macleish had been doing what he could to bring indirect pressure to bear. He had tried to enlist the support of the President's brother, Dr Milton Eisenhower, an old friend now President of Johns Hopkins University, but had received the dusty answer that if Pound were to be released he should be tried, and that his standing as a poet was immaterial. Then in January, fearing that William Rogers 'wasn't going to do anything positive', he had urged Hemingway to write to the undersecretary of state, Christian Herter, 'making again the point you made so well in your letter to the Atty Gen—that it is the US which will suffer if Pound is allowed to rot in St. Elizabeths'. Herter, he knew, 'would be listened to in Justice'. He had already spoken to him, and found him attentive, but 'obviously worried by the possibility that, once released, Ezra might embarrass the government by shooting his face off in his usual way'. The government of course had 'no right to keep him in an insane asylum for *that* reason', but needed to be persuaded, and a page from Hemingway 'would help a lot'. MacLeish was also hoping that Dr Gabriel Hauge, economic adviser to the President who happened to be Laughlin's brother-in-law, would be able to put in a good word. He had been alerted to tell Brownell that the Frost–Eliot–Hemingway letter 'would be on his desk' on the morning of the 18th. And MacLeish made sure that Overholser was told that the letter had been sent and what was in it.

Hammarskjöld, possibly as a result of reading in the *New York Times* MacLeish's eloquent paragraph about the horror of Pound's situation, had let him know that he shared his concern and had discussed the matter 'at a high level', and that the Swedish Academy too was keenly interested. The two men met near the end of January in Hammarskjöld's office at the United Nations, and a few days later Hammarskjöld wrote to Francis Wilcox, the Assistant Secretary of State with whom he had corresponded before about the Pound case, to lend his strong support, and that of the Swedish Academy, to 'the initiative of Mr. Frost and his colleagues'. Wilcox assured him that his personal views and those of the Swedish Academy had been passed informally to the Attorney General, and that he had suggested 'that a copy of your most recent letter be incorporated in the file containing the appeal by Mr. Frost and others'. 'Keep up the good work', he added by hand.

Then Kasper hit the fan. Early in January William Carlos Williams asked Pound, 'Did you ever hear of a guy named Kasper? Your name was used along with his in a television broadcast last night. I didn't like it.' At the end of January and into February the *New York Herald Tribune* ran a series on Kasper's activities agitating against desegregation in the South, linking him to the Ku Klux Klan and to Ezra Pound. A front page spread carried the headline, 'SEGREGATIONIST KASPER IS EZRA POUND DISCIPLE', with the sub-head, 'Goes to Asylum Often to Visit Fascist Poet'. In February an article about Kasper in *Look* was illustrated by a photograph of Pound over the caption, 'Ezra Pound, the insane American poet, is Kasper's idol'.

The Tale of John Kasper

In February 1956 the Senate Committee on Interior and Insular Affairs had been considering a proposal to build a giant mental institution in Alaska. John Kasper appeared before it to express the fear that it would serve as a dumping ground for dissidents and political prisoners. The Committee Chairman told him, 'This is the United States, Mr Kasper. We don't have political prisoners here.' Whereupon Kasper stated,

> Mr Chairman, less than three miles from where we sit now, at St Elizabeths Hospital, America's greatest poet of this century and, in my opinion, one of the truest patriots of our history, is being held—without trial—as a political prisoner. No trial. No *habeas corpus*. And he's been there for twelve years, for his political ideas. I mean Ezra Pound.

He went on to speak of the inhuman treatment of patients in the nation's mental hospitals, naming prefrontal lobotomy and electric shock treatment, and thence to psychiatry as a Jewish imposition upon the American people. There was uproar in the committee meeting, and it made the news in that evening's Washington *Evening Star*.

In April and May Kasper was down in Alabama working with Admiral Crommelin's Senate primaries campaign team. As a Defender of the American Constitution the Admiral was hoping to win the Democrat nomination. Kasper thought to enlist Pound's help:

Dear Gramp:

COPY COPY. Can you write some short quotable slogans. Nothing highbrow. Stuff to stick in mass-mind. Repeated over and over so they don't forget.

And 5 minute speeches and 15 minute speeches on Segregation/ States Rights/ Mongrelization/ Separation of Races.

NIGGERS

And JEWS: the Admiral has taken up THE Question openly and it hasn't hurt him. The kike behind the nigger.

Pound advised, 'dont confuse ingenuity with proclamations', and 'Don't fight from confused principles'—

> Fight from the original declaration of the Rights of Man.
> Droits de L'homme.
> Droit de faire tout ce qui ne nuit pas aux autres.
> To do anything that harms not others.

But then he got onto 'Segregation/...Mongrelization/ Separation of Races', and affirmed 'Nothing is more damnably harmful to everyone, white AND black than miscegenation, bastardization and mongrelization of EVERYTHING.... Blood banks an infamy also.' Pound was giving Kasper what he wanted, a slick slogan to fix in the 'mass-mind' of the South the idea that cultural traditions are, literally, 'in the blood'.

In June Kasper announced the setting up of a White Citizens' Council in Washington DC, with its charter from the North Alabama Citizens' Council headed by Asa E. Carter. Its stated aim was to halt the integration of schools in Washington and to restore segregation. The press reported that Negroes, including two reporters, were barred from its first meeting. Soon after it was calling itself the more ambitious Seaboard White Citizens' Councils, with the cry, 'Honour—Pride—Fight: Save the White.' 'Our movement arises', its declaration ran, 'from a deep-seated belief in the diverse natures of animals and plants as established by the Creator.... Nigras were not meant to be WHITE. The white race was not intended to be anything but white.' The declaration went on to 'damn all race-mixers', aiming particularly at 'the communist-led NAACP'. 'We are an attack program,' it concluded, 'We proclaim action as our creed.'

In August Kasper drove down to Clinton in Tennessee where Anderson County High School was to be one of the first in the South to desegregate—

twelve Negro students were to be admitted when the school year began on Monday 27th. On Saturday 25th Kasper, well-dressed in suit and tie, well-spoken and sincere, was going about the town giving out SWCC leaflets. On the Sunday evening he addressed a small crowd in front of the Courthouse, speaking against desegregation as a conspiracy of Jews and Communists to undermine the white race. The town officials asked him to leave town and when he refused had him arrested for vagrancy and inciting a riot. Monday there was a small protest outside the High School but the enrolment of the black students went ahead. On Tuesday the charges against Kasper were dismissed for want of evidence, and he then went to the school and told the principal 'to run the negroes off or resign'. He recruited some white teenagers into a Junior White Citizens Council and organized a picket line around the school. That night he spoke in inflammatory terms to a crowd of several hundred in the Courthouse square. On the Wednesday morning there were over 100 protesting whites outside the school, black students were abused and chased, and there were walkouts by white students. A crowd of around 1,000 gathered in the square that night, and federal marshals served a court order upon Kasper, restraining him from interfering in the school integration and summoning him to a court hearing next day. In the morning a crowd of around 300 abused and threw stones at the black students, and a judge sentenced Kasper to a year in prison for contempt of court. Thursday night there were 1,500 in the square and there were speakers from several out of town segregationist organizations, including the fiery orator Asa Carter. Retired Admiral John Crommelin also spoke and declared that 'someday a statue will be erected on this courthouse lawn to John Kasper'. On Friday night, with 2,000 in the square, the crowd was shouting 'We want Kasper.' A mob marched on the pro-integration mayor's house threatening to dynamite it, and cars with blacks were stopped, shaken and tilted, and their windscreens smashed. There were no arrests. On Saturday 1 September the Clinton board of aldermen declared a state of emergency and formed an auxiliary police force armed with shotguns and teargas. The rally that night was sponsored by five white supremacist organizations, and a crowd of 3,000 was broken up by teargas grenades. On the Sunday the National Guard arrived, with seven tanks, three armoured personnel carriers, and 600 armed men who fixed bayonets and dispersed the crowd. On Monday the National Guard commander banned all outdoor public speaking and Clinton calmed down. Much of the blame for the week of violence was put upon Kasper.

The following Thursday two local citizens put up a $10,000 bond and he was bailed under a permanent injunction against further interference in desegregation. Within a fortnight he was back in jail on a charge of sedition and inciting riot. On 20 November, after a trial lasting two weeks, in which Admiral Crommelin and Judge Raulston testified on his behalf, he was acquitted and emerged vowing to continue the fight against school integration in defiance of the laws.

During the trial Kasper wrote a long letter to the editor of the 'Negro' *Amsterdam News* in New York, in reply to its article about him headlined 'RACIST EXPOSED'. He accused the paper of falling in with 'the red-controlled Supreme Court-NAACP's race-hating, race-destroying schemes', meaning its 1954 and 1955 rulings on school desegregation. Against that he invoked 'the views on racial segregation of Booker T. Washington, George Washington Carver, Abraham Lincoln, Thomas Jefferson, and in latter-day experience, Benjamin Gibbons of the Universal African Nationalist Movement'. He invoked Frobenius' 'expeditions to Africa from 1897 to 1937 to "define African culture"', and demanded,

> Is there any reason to conceal from American Negroes their African source, their rootedness in the 'Dark Continent'? Is there any reason to deny them their common heritage of African folk myth, poetry, epic, sculpture, music and drum communication, perhaps chiefly the African genius for agriculture?
>
> When the white man holds up his unequalled achievements in constructing free government, his mastery of technical accomplishments, his Bach and Mozart in music, his Piero della Francesca, Giotto and Brancusi in the arts, his Homer, Dante, Shakespeare and Ezra Pound in letters and so on ad infinitum, should not the Negro turn face around with his own traditions, accomplishments, his own racial genius from the land of the Congo and Balbua?
>
> I believe it is the duty of every Negro leader to undertake the task of educating his own people to their historic facts and working from there to raise the Negro to ever higher racial accomplishment, to foster racial identity and pride, not arrogance, and teach a proper respect for all members of other races in the same manner they would demand it for themselves.

What they should specifically respect in the 'Anglo-Saxon-Nordic white man' was his carrying out '(for the benefit of ALL) a concept of free government which has given the maximum of personal liberty and the minimum of tyrannical irresponsibility'; whereas 'your Negro race', which has 'fallen time and again into abject slavery', has contributed nothing 'to free, representative government, and the cause of free men, as embodied in our own American Constitution'. In all this there was an implicit amendment adding the words '*and separate*' to the founding principle that 'All men are born free and equal'. 'We are organizing Negro Citizens' Councils', Kasper informed the readers of *Amsterdam News*, 'The qualifications are: "Negro, 18 years of age, believe in the separation of the races as ordained by the Creator, uphold racial segregation, loyal to the United States of America, its Constitution, and believe in the divinity of Jesus Christ".'

In August or September the Seaboard White Citizens' Councils had produced *VIRGINIANS ON GUARD!*, a 34-page roneoed document which framed in the crudest racist propaganda a states' rights proposal that Virgina should in effect reconstitute itself a segregated state. The proposal pursued into minute legalistic detail what should be done to ensure the absolute separating out of 'Negroes' from 'whites', in the state's school system and on the public payrolls generally. Anything and any person advocating racial integration was to be purged. Jews and Communists were to be excluded from public office and to be allowed no voice in the state. It was a lawyer's dream of absolute apartheid, brewed up by the Defenders of the American Constitution and other like-minded groups, not excluding the Ku Klux Klan. One lawyer involved was probably Robert Furniss, who worked for the National Association for the Advancement of White People, and pounded away at the school situation, as he put it, on his Washington radio programme. He had arranged the lease on Kasper's Washington bookstore and sometimes helped out in it. He also for a time acted for the Committee for Ezra Pound, and Pound himself thought him 'a damn good guy and honest'. Kasper's contribution may have been the crude pages at the front and the Seaboard White Citizens' Councils declaration at the end. He also showed a draft or drafts to Pound, who offered some advice on the presentation of the constitutional proposals, contributed a couple of long paragraphs on how the free state should manage its funding, and another on the freedom and responsibilities of the press. Pound implicitly endorsed the determination to keep out Communists and Jews, while offering no comment at all on the anti-Negro agenda. He may not have had advance sight of either Kasper's work or the racist rant into which the states' rights proposal descended in its latter stages. In any case, when he later sent a copy to Noel Stock in Melbourne he first tore off the crude racist material, and commented on the segregationist proposals, '2 points at least quotable, rest VERY local'. The '2 points' would have been his own contributions on funding and the press, and all the rest it seems was too 'local' to be of wider concern. 'Kasper defeated, same as South was in 1864', he commented to Olivia Agresti in December, 'cause mind diverted from money and taxes, customs, onto local issue having no broad and defensible theoretical basis save in nature itself.'

On 26 December Pound mentioned 'Mr Kasper's meteoric rise into publicity' to Ingrid Davies, and commented that he was being 'reported VERY inaccurately in the enraged organs of the jew press | furious that he likes afro-americans but not kikes'. In February Kasper played up to being billed as a disciple of Ezra Pound by the *Herald Tribune,* by featuring in his short-lived *Clinton-Knox County Stars and Bars*—'A Nationalist Attack Newspaper Serving East Tennessee'—such Poundian themes as 'local control of local purchasing power' and the 'infamy of interest-bearing bonds which benefit only the jew-bankers in New York and Washington'.

In the months following his acquittal in November 1956 Kasper was going about the American South speaking against desegregation as a fanatical effort by Jews and Communists 'to subvert the existing Gentile order everywhere'. In March 1957 he was charged with criminal contempt of the federal district court 'on grounds he violated a permanent injunction against interference with peaceful integration of Clinton High School'. After Clinton he was jailed again in Nashville and Knoxville and Tallahassee and Charlotteville, for trespass, boycotts, pickets, interference with the free operation of schools, and inciting to riot. On 10 September 1957, the first school day, one wing of a newly integrated elementary school in Nashville was dynamited—it had enrolled a single black child. Kasper was suspected but no evidence linking him, nor the KKK, nor anyone else, to the dynamiting was ever found. Later that month Pound advised David Wang,

> K probably in ERROR mixing with ignorant. | . . .
> Guard against sedition. USE the law, even when tyrants do not.
> The theory of the law, the words of the law, until changed by constitutional and legal process.

Not long after that Nashville outrage Kasper was convicted on a federal charge of conspiracy and jailed for eight months in prisons in Florida and Georgia. After his release, in mid-1958, he was tried in Nashville for inciting to riot and sentenced to six months in the Davidson County workhouse. In April 1959, on a Sunday morning in Clinton, three dynamite blasts reduced Anderson County High School to rubble. No one was injured, and no one was charged.

The skeleton in the national closet

The publicity linking Pound to Kasper, and even holding him responsible for Kasper's violent white supremacism, shocked and dismayed his well-wishers and set back their efforts to secure his release. Bo Setterlind, a Swedish poet who had visited Pound in St Elizabeths and published a poem lamenting his imprisonment there, wrote to him now asking urgently, 'Is it true that you hate negroes and jews? | Have you ever written in your poetry that you do hate the human races mentioned?' Pound answered, 'NO, naturally I do not dislike africans or afro-americans... neither to the best of my knowledge does Kasper.' As for anti-Semitism in the cantos, the local psychiatrist had looked hard for it and been 'very puzzled' when he was unable to find any. It was a fair answer, so far as it went, but it was hardly adequate to the Kasper problem.

Pound did regard Jews in general through a strong prejudice against their supposed racial characteristics—this is especially evident in his letters to Olivia Agresti. And this prejudice, combined with his anti-Communism, predisposed him to accept the white supremacist line that the anti-segregationist NAACP was a Jewish-Communist conspiracy out to destroy both the Afro-American and the Southern white cultures (plural). Yet he was never a white supremacist. He genuinely valued difference and variety and cared that the individual and the particular be preserved. That was why Agassiz and Frobenius mattered to him, the one because he taught the scientific method of noting the specific qualities of things; the other because he observed the specific characteristics of diverse cultures. 'ALL study of nature <veget & animal> ... is study of VARIETY', he told John Theobald, 'It is good that hindoos be MORE hindoo | that chinks be MORE chink | each rising to it own height and not a *mélange adultère de tout.*' Further, along with wanting individuals and cultures to be more themselves, to develop their distinctive qualities, he wanted them also to be in communication with others and to learn from others. For himself, in Italy or America, it was 'Kung AND Eleusis'. He did not go in for setting one's own race or culture above all the rest, nor for racial or cultural apartheid.

Yet he seems not to have noticed, or not to have cared, that Kasper was doing exactly that. He could perhaps believe that Kasper, like himself, did not 'dislike africans or afro-americans'. And he was under the illusion that he was educating and directing him. But how could he fail to see that what Kasper had taken from him, or from Agassiz and Frobenius, had become perverted into fuel for white supremacist violence against Afro-American schoolchildren. He would disclaim responsibility, to the extent of telling Harry Meacham, 'I don't think you can show any connection between my telling Kasper to read Confucius and Agassiz | and his present imprisonment.' Louis Zukofsky apparently agreed with him about that, telling Giovannini that 'E.P. is no more responsible for Kasper's actions than Aristotle for the Hollywood production of Alexander the Great.' Well, of course Kasper was to be held personally responsible for his actions; and there is no evidence that Pound directly encouraged or endorsed his incitements to violence in the South. 'Guard against sedition. USE the law,' and 'Fight from the original declaration of the Rights of Man,' would have been his advice. But it was advice not taken—'obviously the heroism of a Crommelyn is much more stimulating to youth than the doctrines of moderation', Pound remarked to Meacham, thus obliquely pointing to the Defenders of the American Constitution as the direct source of Kasper's 'attack program'. Archie Henderson has collected evidence to show how widespread that programme and its propaganda were at the time, and that Pound was indeed not responsible for Kasper's embracing it. But that still does not settle the thorny question.

Pound was evidently in accord with Kasper and the Defenders and the white supremacists in general so far as their propaganda and their actions could be represented as anti-Communist and anti-Jew. But about their anti-Negro programme and attacks he had nothing to say. After Kasper's trial in November 1956 for sedition and incitement to riot in Clinton, Pound commented to Olivia Agresti, virtually in Kasper's own crude words, that he had 'At least got a little publicity for the NAACP being run by kikes not by coons.' It was as if the violence against the children and the breaking of the law had simply not registered with him. 'I am in no position to judge particular local events,' he explained to Meacham, 'and do not think I have ever formed judgments on them.' He was 'Au dessus du conflit', above the battle. Moreover, from his loftily detached viewpoint he somehow made out that Kasper's apparently racist 'attack program' was really a programme for economic reform. 'Kasper's REAL ideology', as he informed Olivia Agresti, 'is far above ANY U.S. audience | and am not sure it is useful to spread it among those who will NOT understand why Lincoln was shot', i.e. because he wanted to bring the money supply under government control and remove it from a private banking conspiracy. His own little audience apparently shared this privileged understanding, to judge by the report of David Rattray who wrote, after visiting St Elizabeths in December 1956, that John Chatel had told him

> the Negro business is just a front, [Kasper] knows it's the only way he can get the Southern farmers to vote for him, but *then*, when he gets the power . . . he can get to work on the economic program.

And Sheri Martinelli had put in, when Pound said something about New Directions suppressing 'the truth about international finance' for fear of 'losing the support of the New York banks', that therefore 'Grandpa's got to do it with suicide troops. Like Kasper. Kasper is your suicide troops.' So the inside knowledge had it that Kasper was really on the attack down South for Pound's economic reforms—as if the real meaning of the 34-page *VIRGINIANS ON GUARD!* was all in Pound's paragraph on state funding.

This was the tunnel vision which had enabled Pound to see in Mussolini's Fascism and in Hitler's Nazism only those features which he could endorse. It had always been his habit to take notice only of people that were *doing* something that positively interested him, as he told Mary on one occasion, and not to 'look for their iniquities etc.' 'May be inhuman of me,' he confessed, with the implication that it was just one of those things that could not be altered.

Pound was sanguine about the *Herald Tribune*'s 'attempt to implicate grampaw in civic disorder'. It seemed that the bad news was not being taken up by the media generally. And there were articles on his side. In April a piece in *American Mercury* suggested that Pound had been put away in St Elizabeths as a matter of political convenience—it called his 'mishandled case' a 'miscarriage of justice'. Also in April an editorial in *New Republic* declared that, in spite of everything that could be said against him, 'we would like to see the government give this old man and this eminent poet his freedom—if not as an act of justice, then as an act of largesse'. This was accompanied by an article which began by noticing that 'the plea for Pound's freedom runs constantly among those aware of his situation', and ended by repeating Hemingway's 1954 comment, 'This would be a good year to release poets.' Later in the year there would be more calls for his release in *Esquire* and *The Nation*. But Pound, to adapt his own phrase, held himself 'au dessus du conflit'—he observed but did not engage in any way with the journalism swirling about 'the case of Ezra Pound'.

He was engaged elsewhere, primarily with his cantos, then with his propaganda—this mainly in whatever little magazines were currently being edited and published by his followers. And, as always, he had his daily array of visitors to perform for, and his ever extending network of correspondents to instigate to action.

Thrones, a new sequence of fourteen cantos to follow *Rock-Drill*'s eleven, was under way. The governing concern was now the possibility of good government, or 'the states of mind of people responsible for something more than their personal conduct'. For some time he had been gathering materials and drafting passages for his thrones—the opening canto, 96, had appeared in *Hudson Review* in April 1956, and canto 97 had appeared there in October—but the main work of composition appears to have gone on through 1957. An entry in his 'Nursing Notes' for 28 August of that year indicates intense and sustained mental activity:

> Mr. Pound continues in his usual manner. Always well occupied even at night, seems unaware that others are sleeping and chants some strange ?! Turns his light on many times and looks through his text.... Good natured person and easy to live with.

From February to March Pound had been working on 98 and 99, with *The Sacred Edict of K'ang Hsi* as a primary source. In May he 'typed up what may be the end of Canto 105'. By the end of October he had '96/106 "Thrones" in rough draft . . . and a few lines of 107'; a month later he was about to 'start on gettin 107 in order, clean ms/ with ideograms etc.'. He was drawing on Coke's *Institutes* for the last three cantos of *Thrones*, 107, 108, and 109, and appears to have finished taking notes from Coke in November, although he had got hold of the *Second Institutes* only at the end of October. At least in rough draft then, the entire volume was complete by the end of the year. And besides that, on the evidence of Marcella Spann's files, in the fall of 1957 Pound was already drafting passages that would go into the next and final volume of cantos, *Drafts and Fragments*.

His favoured little magazines were now in Belfast, Northern Ireland, and in Melbourne, Australia. *Voice* in Belfast, and *New Times*, a Social Credit weekly in Melbourne, were printing his familiar economic and political instigations and explosions, most of them quite brief pieces unsigned or over a scatter of pseudonyms. He was variously 'John Vignon (Boston, U.S. A.)' or 'J.V.', 'Washington Correspondent','Paris Correspondent','London Correspondent', 'New York Correspondent', 'Melville Larkin' or 'M.L.', 'M.V.', 'T.V.', 'T.G.','J.T.','D.E.J.', 'Diogenes', 'William Watson', 'John Foster','Jose Boler', 'Xavier Baylor', and, just once, 'Anon'. One perhaps surprising note in these pieces is a newly unequivocal attitude towards Hitler, as in 'Herbert Briscoe's' contribution to *Voice* in April, 1956, which begins,

> 'The Twisted Cross', B.B.C.'s tremendous indictment of Hitler, is now on U. S. television, eased off by rather long slices of a commercial. It fails only in one thing, namely that it does not in any way indicate that fraud and rascality are not a satisfactory remedy for Hitler's brutality.

That the right idea about money, which had formerly been Hitler's virtue in Pound's view, was now to be attributed instead to Gottfried Feder, the source of National Socialist economic policy, was implicit in a note in *New Times* in May regretting that 'All this quite proper fuss about Hitler has unfortunately diminished the number of people who might otherwise have read Feder'.

In October 1956, Noel Stock, the young enthusiast who had been inserting Pound's pieces into *New Times*, set up a little magazine of his own, a monthly called (at Pound's suggestion) *Edge*, and with a general dedication 'to intelligence, in nature, in the cosmos'. Stock had secured first publication of canto 90 for *Meanjin*, Australia's leading literary quarterly, and had published there a perceptive and laudatory review of *Rock-Drill*. He had written to Pound and been instantly enlisted as an activist and a target correspondent. Now *Edge* was to be, for the eight issues that it lasted, more or less under Pound's direction. It led off with his new translations of five poems by Rimbaud; selections from David Gordon's Mencius and Yankowski's Richard of St. Victor; a Williams poem, 'The High Bridge above the Tagus River at Toledo'; some unsigned 'Observations' and 'Definitions' by Pound; and a reprint of his introduction to *La Martinelli*. Among the definitions was this: 'Utopia: where every man has the right to be born FREE of debt, and to be judged, in case of disagreement, by a jury capable of understanding the nature and implications of the charges against him'. Number 2 was entirely given over to a translation of Thaddeus Zielinski's *The Sibyl. Three Essays on Ancient Religion and Christianity*—the argument being that in ancient paganism is to be found 'the genuine Old Testament of our Christianity'. Pound's own case was featured in *Edge 3*, in '"Mental Illness": New Name for Nonconformity', a translation of a German article which declared that he had been found insane and locked up in order to silence his political critique of America and his attempt to form a new mentality. A 'Notebook of Thoughts in Captivity' attributed to Mussolini took up much of number 4, along with 'Pages of a Memoir' by Olivia Rossetti Agresti, and 'The Church and Usury' by Henry Swabey—the subject Pound had put him to work on years before. Numbers 5 and 6 contained articles and notes related to Pound's preoccupations: an 'Examination of Scotus Erigena' by Swabey; a review by David Gordon of Goullart's *Forgotten Kingdom* about the Na Khi; an article connecting 'Mencius, charters, and Blackstone'; Colin MacDowell on 'Why was Lincoln shot?'; passages from the *Kuan Tzu*; and an eighteen-page translation by the English poet and Pound-supporter, Alan Neame, of Cocteau's long poem *Léone*. Stravinsky's *The Poetics of Music*, selected and with a commentary by David Gordon, filled no. 7; and most of number 8, in October 1957, was given over to a memoir by Olivia Agresti of David Lubin, agricultural reformer and founder of the institute which was the forerunner of the U. N.'s Food and Agriculture Organization. In most numbers there were 'fillers' by Pound, unsigned or pseudonymous. In his judgment, *Edge* was the best magazine going—the best since the *Little Review*, he raved to Brigit Patmore, which put it above Eliot's *Criterion* and even his own *Exile*. Its vortex meant that 'the Kulchurl cenTER is in Melbourne', or so he declared to Peter Russell, who might have wondered where that left his own efforts to promote Pound's ideas in England, through his Pound Press which reprinted *ABC of Economics*, his series of Pound's 'Money Pamphlets', and his Poundian little magazine *Nine*. But *Nine* had about run its course, and *Edge*, in 1956, seemed the most promising prospect of the moment.

In September 1957, however, when *Edge* was nearly on its last number and Stock was about to sail from Melbourne for England and

Brunnenburg, William Cookson, a precocious young schoolboy about to go up to Oxford, sent Pound a copy of his school magazine, of which he had been editor in his last year and in which he had reviewed *Rock-Drill*. Pound immediately thanked him for the review—'the best since Stock's' he told him—and, perhaps not quite realizing at first that his young correspondent would no longer be editing it, began to suggest how *The Trifler* might continue what *Edge* had been doing. When he caught on to the facts of Cookson's age and situation, he turned to directing his reading and preparing him to be his organizer and agent in England. He was to get in touch with 'live characters', meaning Pound's more active correspondents—apparently Cookson already knew Ingrid Davies—and he was to look in on Sir Barry Domville, and go down to see General J. F. C. Fuller (from whom General del Valle had learnt much that was useful to him on Okinawa), in order 'to pick up a bit of tradition' and 'get knowledge incarnate'. 'Yr next reading: Coke, Second Institutes, 4th Report', he was directed in October, 'And probably C. D. Bowen "Lion and Throne"', a life of Coke just out which he hadn't yet read.[4] Later it was 'Del Mar (apart from Science of Money . . . his one poor book)'. 'The FIRST fight', he was briefed, 'is to clear up the chaos | and get the NEEDED (for NOW) ideas into more people'; and 'The QUESTION to ask, but not loudly or prematurely, and which is unlikely to be answered is: why issue all money as INTEREST BEARING debt?' Cookson somehow survived these often weekly blasts, and in 1959 founded his own literary magazine, *Agenda*, which he edited until his death more than forty years later, and which, always broadly Poundian, established itself as a leading magazine of poets and poetry in the Pound–Williams (and David Jones) force-field.

Besides attending to his education Pound sent Cookson a couple of 'clarifications' of the scandals attaching to him, as this in February 1958:

> I am 'of course' not antisemitic. I am merely against irresponsible oligarchy, whose god is PANURGIA
> and whose Anschaung is : ahj awl I'm in'erested in is BUNK; seein what you can put over

In a previous letter, Cookson having reported Admiral Sir Barry Domville's view that 'a number of the ills of the world' are to be blamed on 'Jews and Masons', Pound had written back, 'The enemy is IGGURANCE, not jews or

[4] He was reading it in November, and 'found [this] entertaining item on p/ 239': 'An old gentleman, Mr. Pound, protested by petition to King James [against Catholics being treated as traitors] and was prosecuted in Star Chamber—Coke officiating—and punished with pillory, fine and imprisonment.' 'Plus ça change,' Pound commented [18 Nov. 1957].

masons'. Cookson would cite these remarks loyally throughout his life whenever the charge of anti-Semitism was brought up, in the hope of exculpating Pound. A more convincing clarification concerned Kasper and white supremacy. 'Two bright sparks', one of whom, Contini, had been 'quite a lot in jail for fascismo or under acc[usatio]n of same', were considering putting together 'a special Ez issue' of a Genevan quarterly, and Cookson was to tell them that—

> their job is to get me out of quod, and not to implicate me in any MORE squabbles between uncontrollable parties . . .
>
> for conversational porpoises in London / yu cd/ say I steered Kasper onto Agassiz, but he seems inclined to the Fuhrer prinZiP . Whereas E. P. is a Jeffersonian republican /
>
> and that Wang's advocacy of 'Wheat in Bread' seems nearer to Soil Association movement in Britain than to a howl for white supremacy.

The 'uncontrollable' Kasper had been in the news again for projecting a neo-Nazi party under the banner of 'Wheat in Bread', a name proposed by Pound, possibly in the naive hope of getting him onto a sounder track; and David Wang, a Han Chinese who visited Pound and corresponded with him, and who was also at that time devoted to Kasper, had declared the affiliation of his notional group to the notional 'WHIB party'; and David Rattray, in a poisonous account in *The Nation* of two visits to Pound, had stated that Wang, a disciple of Pound and Kasper, 'devotes himself to the cause of white supremacy'. Pound's point in his letter to Cookson was that it was unlikely that Wang, 'as grandson of a chinese high official', would advocate white supremacy. The further implication must have been that Pound himself was not advocating white supremacy via a campaign for unadulterated wheatflour. What he would have meant, after all, could be traced back to canto 45—

> with usura, sin against nature,
> is thy bread ever more stale rags
> is thy bread dry as paper
> with no mountain wheat, no strong flour

Moreover, whatever Kasper and Wang were up to in the fall of 1957, Pound was writing (in canto 104), 'Luigi in hill paths | chews wheat at sunrise | that grain his communion', and affirming (in canto 106), 'the gold light of wheat surging upward', 'The strength of men is in grain.'

By this time Pound was closing his letters with a red-ink seal, made for him by the sinologist William Hawley, and consisting of a transliteration of the sounds of 'Pound' into three ancient Chinese small seal characters which might be rendered as 'preserve the form of active virtue'; or, combining Confucius and Richard of St Victor, as 'keep the form of the love flowing from the heart'.

Visitors to Pound were liable to come away with conflicting impressions of the man himself. Folke Isaksson, a Swedish poet, who saw Pound twice in March 1957, wrote shortly afterwards to Dag Hammarskjöld—

> I was troubled by his situation. What shocked me most was not so much the obvious appearance of degradation, the surroundings and the situation, as much as the very strength and dignity, and the health shown forth by Pound the human being, in that predicament. Simplicity, alertness and warmth—which felt like a gift.

But then in an article published in Sweden in 1958 he wrote that 'when Pound was talking, the flow of his thoughts was broken, thus hard to catch...The old poet seemed like a puppet with half its strings, as if he himself were wandering about in his latest *Cantos.*' Isaksson noticed that Pound made not a single comment on his situation, and that he acted like a free man, except that now and then his hands seemed to tell a different story. But the real prisoner, he thought, was Pound's devoted wife, Dorothy.

John Wain, an English poet, novelist, and critic, visited Pound in August 1957 and, like Isaksson, came away 'with an impression of Pound's grandeur and dignity' but also of his 'paranoia and monomania'—

> As he sat in a deckchair on the lawn, shirtless, revealing the muscular upper torso of a man twenty years his junior, and with his strange, sad little band of disciples listening carefully to every word, I felt like Edgar in the presence of Lear. 'Conversation' in the ordinary sense was not possible; Pound talked on and on, in connected sentences and with perfect logic and persuasiveness; but if anyone interrupted him with a question it simply threw the needle out of the groove, and he fell silent for a moment, passed his hand wearily over his eyes, and then went on talking from a different point, as if the needle had been dropped back at random. He seemed unconscious of the question except as an interruption.

Wain, on his single visit, may not have been aware that he was observing a routine performance, and that the Pound Show had been running for a decade. He could not see that Pound may have been as weary of it as he was committed to putting it on for every visitor taking him in as one of the not to be missed literary sights of the capital.

None of Pound's dropping-by visitors would have seen him, as one ward attendant had, playing 'Chess each evening with Jack Knight', who had been an engineer; or fulfilling his 'contract' to give McNiel twelve games of chequers each week; or, again, humming and chanting in his room in the night. Even in the visiting hours there would always be elements of the scene left unmentioned or unnoticed. Reno Odlin, a frequent visitor between July 1957 and January 1958, remembered that 'Jets kept taking off from a nearby Naval Air Station, their punctuation contributing doubtless to the jumpiness and discontinuity of the conversation. Not that one noticed any discontinuity until afterwards.' Odlin too would come away with dissonant impressions. On one occasion,

> A coloured inmate offered to wash my car. He was *gently* dissuaded, and encouraged to seek amusement elsewhere. Remembering the rage of the Radio Roma period, I could scarcely get over my shock at the tact and gentleness displayed.

Another of Odlin's recollections throws a startling light upon the usual picture of the relations between Pound and devoted Dorothy:

> Another day, in the back seat of my car (with the New Year, his thirteenth in captivity, he was allowed out to the Point, out of sight of the ward) he said: 'Hell, I'm no anti-semite: [pointing to DP] *she* is'.
>
> They rubbed along, with respect, affection, and absolutely no illusions. Her dislike for 'that tiresome *Paradiso*' is legendary.
>
> My last day of all (very much en famille in the alcove) he recalled Olivia Shakepear's words on his wedding-day: 'I hope you are happy with Dorothy, she has a mean, narrow little soul'. Dorothy's return thrust was delayed until he had finished the tale of her first, four-year-old's encounter with Yeats, and her urgent question—'Is that gentleman a clargymint?' was the way Pound phrased it: with her immediate vigorous correction: 'I didn't say "gentleman". I didn't know there was any other kind—I hadn't met *you* yet'.

Odlin refrained from mentioning that on other days in early 1958 it would be with Marcella Spann in her car that Pound would be sitting looking out at Washington from the Point.

But before we come to Miss Spann, what of Olga Rudge? The Accademia Chigiana was flourishing and she was being kept occupied with the arrangements for its distinguished visitors and the students. For its 25th anniversary in May 1956 Rubinstein came, and Zubin Mehta and Daniel Barenboim and Claudio Abbado; in 1957 there were Elisabeth Schwarzkopf and David Oistrakh and Joseph Szigeti. Olga had sought peace with Pound at the New Year, sending him a message, 'Bear no grudge | to the Rudge', but there had been no response. Pound was not disposed to repair the break. In August he wrote to their daughter,

> Note from O, in serene mood. Has she got around to thinking of a possible modus to amity, without chains? I get on with a number of different people, but I am NOT going to climb into a box with ANYbody sittin' on the lid . . . plenty of people have been divorced without recrimination or bitterness . . .

'One does not want a keeper', he ended, as if he hadn't one already. In November he declared the break absolute: 'I can NOT see her again. My nerves have stood a good deal, but it is separation, à l'amichevole, BUT clean cut.'

'M'Amour, ma vie'

In April 1957 Marcella Spann, aged 24, was formally admitted to the course in 'Ezrology' at what she would call 'the nation's most unusual institution of higher learning'. The previous August she had graduated from East Texas State University with a BA in English and an M.Ed. in guidance and counselling. In graduate school she had followed Professor Vincent Miller's thoroughly Poundian literature course and been introduced by him to Pound's poetry. In early September, on her way to New York where she planned to spend a year out, wanting 'to see something of the world other than Texas', she had stopped off in Washington DC to visit the man himself. After that first meeting she wrote promising to 'read all the books that you suggested', and hoping that he would keep her informed 'on all the books that educated people should know'. In New York, with his stimulus and guidance, she met people who talked about Pound and Chinese poetry and such things, and she went to museums and concerts 'to develop appreciation'. Now in April she was back in Washington with enough money from having worked in New York as a secretary to spend three months at the Ezuversity. 'Marcella an addition to the population,' Pound remarked to Mary. Dorothy thought her 'lovely, intelligent, and v. pleasant'. In the fall, so that she could continue to be 'Pound's most frequent visitor', she would find work in Washington as Instructor in English at Marjorie Webster Junior College.

Her closest class-mates through the summer's session, not all as regular in attendance, were David Horton, Sheri Martinelli, David Gordon, John Chatel who was working on his never-to-be-published novel 'The Mind of Pierre Duval', and Hollis Frampton who would become a leading avant-garde film-maker. In her retrospect it seemed not to have rained much that year, and the class had met mostly 'on the green stretch of lawn attended by squirrels and blue jays, giant elms making a gentle shade'. Pound would read aloud from *The Cantos* and would not tell them what they were to understand. 'Read the parts you like', he would say, 'The rest will come when you're ready.' On other matters too he would say, 'Stick with what you know and build on that.' That summer he also read to them the whole of Ovid's *Metamorphoses*. And always he would be urging them to do something about the country's 'ILLITERACY', meaning 'a lack of awareness about money, especially the power to issue money'. Marcella felt that 'he taught like a kind father'.

When faced in the fall with 'the prospect of TEACHING 100 females six or 5 days a week' she felt quite lost at first and wailed one afternoon on the lawn at St Elizabeths, 'in a burst of tears', that she 'really didn't know how to teach school'. Pound was sympathetic, indulging for a moment 'the gloom that could gather in dark eyelashes', then practical: she should make up a poetry anthology for her Junior College girls, that would at least take care of '*what* to teach, and one had to start somewhere'. So the 'Spannthology' was conceived, or *Confucius to Cummings. An Anthology of Poetry* 'edited by Ezra Pound and Marcella Spann'. It was to be a collaboration, though in truth Pound made the project very much his own, determining the selection of poems and translations, making new translations where needed, and providing the sparse notes and comments. He wrote at once to Laughlin to secure his interest in publishing the anthology; and he wrote to Cummings and Williams and other old friends whose poems he wanted to include. At the same time he immersed himself in her teaching, typing lesson plans timed to the hour, reading her students' 'themes' and suggesting comments and grades, and advising on method, for example, start each lesson with a summary of the one before, like reading the minutes of the previous meeting. The first lesson was on 'The Seafarer', and that was the subject of the students' first 'theme'. The next lesson, according to Pound's outline, was to recap on that, then tell them about *Piers Plowman*, a great poem of social criticism; 'BUT the great landmark is the BRUT, by Layamon (spell him as they like)'. From *Brut* came Malory, some of Shakespeare, Tennyson's *Idylls*, and now the recently published canto 91 (perhaps 'needing a glossary')—and the relevant section of that canto was to be read out and explained as a rendering of 'race memory or . . . the soul's memory of what it has passed through'. After that there should be 13 minutes left for Chaucer. One gathers from the selections and notes in the 'Spannthology' that Pound's expansive idea of what could and should be taught to 'the squawks' (as they agreed to call Marcella's juniors) had had to be severely pruned in the light of her experience in the classroom. Neither *Brut* nor canto 91 are represented in it.

By October Pound was writing to Marcella daily, even hourly, communicating what he was thinking and doing in a manner that was at once objective and intimate, drawing her into his life after visiting hours. This letter is from Tuesday 1 October—he will have been let back into the ward by Mr Newton, the chief warder, at 4.30 sharp, and is regretting his state of mind that afternoon and its effect on his conversation:

PREZICELY/ 4.50 Choozdy | having got mind onto Julia Domna* and ancient greek coinage | OUT of the hurley burley for constructive reason |

plus Mr Newton's problem re/ Diyle and Doria ,
I git rattled and don't come to focus | MY error. and VAST
vacuum looming,
Chatel's tea still warm, but rather insipid.
J.D. Unless I got muddled, the lydy got Philostratus to write life of Apollonius.*

THE slowness of my head (bad as Chatel) when HEADed lickety split for something/ and the MO(or whatever)MEntUMM, preventing me from picking up... ANYthing not in direct line of trajectory !!!!! ugh!

ZAMatr of act/ hadn't changed the calender to / inst.
AND yu ain' got time now to play tennis/
wonder (5.17) if it is warm enough and if Evans will exist
Really shd/ NOT git entangled in minor agenda./...
6.13 NO competent animal life on tennis court/ AND mislaid Odlin's
agendum AT that. 48 hour lag. till Toisdy/
CONcentration /

As to whether brown bread and peaches CAN be considered adequate aid and comfort !! shd/ anyhow have mixed peaches with cottage cheese | a day of rush and MOmentum, rushing past the just bourne.
Better next time.
'sero'/ Augustine . meaning too late.

Later he added by hand,

If you teach english I must stop fancy spelling in contagious correspondence & reserve curly cues for the outer world. Doyle instead of Dave H. confusing agenda. Will try to make Thurs less boiler factory.

Marcella regularly brought him cheese and other food—the peaches and cottage cheese were probably from her. On another occasion it was rye bread and a potent roquefort, which brought forth a Joycean explosion, 'JHeez!' Pound was not only regretting Marcella's not having time for tennis now she was teaching school, but was beginning to miss her between visits and to mind her being 'tied up with her damn SCHOOL/ at other side of district'. When she too resented the school's demands on her time he took that to mean that she was struggling with her conscience over being forced to substitute 'a lower activity for a higher', the higher activity being apparently the cultivation of a 'more luminous state of awareness' on the lawn at 'S. Liz'. You are 'wasting the days of your youth in servitude due to econ pressure', he told her, and 'shd plan eZcape'.

He did what he could to create a refuge for her. One Wednesday morning, following a Tuesday when she had not made it to 'S. Liz', he began that day's letter, yes m'amour 6.46 a.m. ONE must INDubitably clear OUT Thursday, and leave a place where you can be QUIET after the clucks and the squawks and the cluckings and squawkings. It is extraordinary how LONG it takes me to think of the simplest things. Chatel and cattle/ O.K. I have told J.C. to come at 5.15 oggi IF the weather permits tennis and can clear him out of Toisdy/ etc. and putt the ODDment [Reno Odlin] on fried-day, et ceteraaaa , AND shorten 'em other days.

AND suspend boiler factory , et cetERa.

yester, a sqush. and fatigued with ole Coke. Tenny rate yu didn't lose anything. Not the gt/ open spaces but a li'l tranquility needed.
ciao.

Later, at 8.45, he added, 'contemplatio, yes, produced . . . spiaggia, a few columns . spiaggia is a beach, some classic scenery', and then at 10.19 this further explanatory note, 'Must reconstruct Terracina and the Circeo/ as you don't think Texas a suitable cite /and Brunnenburg too cold in winter'. He was apparently envisioning for her a sacred place in which her mind would be tranquil.

At the end of November he told Ingrid Davies that he had been 'in dumps because of the cold weather', but 'Sheri and Marcella bring me back to life momentarily with sunshines of their so diverse presences'. Martinelli's was a fading presence, however. Pound was fast becoming disillusioned. 'Sheri . . . reportedly on water wagon for ten days', he mentioned to Mary on 2 November. But beyond her getting foolishly drunk, as he would write later to justify his sending her away to Mexico, there was 'the struggle to get the artist off heroin, and D's anxiety lest I get legally encoiled in the dope racket'. And there was her mind, which 'goes up as far as you can take it, and then DOWN to the bottom of the pozzo nero, with squalor and to a point that is not Rabelaisian but obscene'. And there was her way of 'dumping the poubelle or ash can . 45 minutes tirade vs/ all acquaintance, before you could get up into higher air'. Even her painting, which could be 'quattrocento' as in the *La Martinelli* brochure, could also be 'rubbish'. And in spite of being given 'an allowance, about what I would have had to run on had I been out, and a hospital bill, and studio to paint in, rent sometimes more than of D's flat', she could not be relied on to turn up to save him from having to suffocate inside on the summer days when Dorothy needed a rest and he had to be notionally in the care of one or the other of them. And all this 'in contrast to someone who goes into debt for a car so one cd/ get out of ward into air in bad weather'. That was Marcella who had acquired a blue Chevrolet in which they would sit that winter, 'parked on the point, with his company, his food and drink, the whole of Washington D.C. in panorama below, the car heater running against the cold'.

Now it was Marcella who was figuring in the cantos he was drafting. He addressed her in one letter as 'M'Amour, Artemis Queen of Ambracia', and the line 'in thy mind beauty, O Artemis' became her recurrent motif as Pound wove her into *Thrones* and *Drafts and Fragments* as he had woven Sheri as 'Sibylla' and the rest into *Rock-Drill.* In canto 106 Artemis-Marcella is associated with Persephone, and with Circe who directed Odysseus to Persephone's bower—Eleusinian motifs from cantos 17, 30, 39, and 47. Circe is recalled 'coming from the house of smoothe stone'; Persephone is evoked as she was seen by the initiates at Eleusis, and in canto 81, as 'unmasked eyes' blazing with light, not to be probed. Then there is this new Eleusinian image of the returning abundance,

> the gold light of wheat surging upward
> ungathered

But Persephone is seen now 'in the cotton field', as Marcella had worked picking cotton in Texas. This complex life-force, Circe-Persephone-Marcella, further incorporates Artemis or Diana who answers Brutus' prayer for help (as in canto 91) by directing him to sail to Britain and found a new Troy there, thus connecting the Eleusinian mystery with the establishment of civic order—

> Artemis out of Leto
> Under wildwood
> Help me to neede
> By Circeo, the stone eyes looking seaward
> Nor could you enter her eyes by probing.
> The temple shook with Apollo
> As with leopards by mount's edge,
> light blazed behind her;
> . . .
> Gold light, in veined phylotaxis.
> By hundred blue-gray over their rock-pool,
> Or the king-wings in migration
> And in thy mind beauty, O Artemis
> Over asphodel, over broom-plant
> faun's ear a-level that blossom.
> Yao and Shun ruled by jade.
> Whuder ich maei lidhan
> helpe me to neede [106/754]

Near the canto's close there is 'God's eye art 'ou', Pound's instigation not to surrender perception of the undying life in things. The final image is from the lawn at St Elizabeths as the light fades, 'The sky is leaded with elm boughs', as if one were in a sacred space.

It was an extraordinary vision for him to be constructing in his cell in that place. He was trying 'to make a paradiso | terrestre', 'though it were in the halls of hell'. And Marcella was a vital element in the vision. The effort was for her, and with her—he was sharing his drafts and fragments with her as they came to him. And though we do not know what they talked of in her car through that fall and winter, we can be certain he told her what was on his mind. She was not his collaborator, yet she shared in the work in progress, if only as the catalyst which could bring his racked mind into focus so that he could see what he most needed to see and could write what he most needed to write. 'He was happy for weeks', Marcella would recall, when he had written 'lines "fit for the goddess"', such as those in canto 106.

Whatever else she had come to be for him, in enabling him to write his paradise she was meeting the deepest need of his being. When he began his letters to her with variants of 'm'amour, ma vie', he must have felt that, Artemis fashion, she had cut away the dead past and brought him newly alive. La Martinelli had enabled the breakthrough to Love in *Rock-Drill*, but then gone awry. Now Marcella was enabling him to resume the process of trying to make his paradiso, and that was what he lived for.

When out of his fit he could put this view of the matter rather ungallantly. An undated letter, probably of spring 1958, begins, 'NO! (continuing the interrupted conversation)', and goes on, 'ov curse they'—meaning women, evidently—'ought not to WORK. They shd/ adorn and go ornate'. After some rather scattered reflections upon the varieties of women, and a suggestion she bring her tennis shoes and give him a game, the weather being suitable, he added by hand,

> 9.42 The proper function of the female is to produce (or assist in producing) in the male a state of mind that will cause him to enjoy doing some thing useful OR interesting . if she wants to do more that is her affair.

His most enlightened idea of doing something really useful and interesting was, as it had always been, 'to make cosmos' in his cantos. Marcella appears to have been very happy to fulfil the role assigned to her in that process.

The St Elizabeths Cantos (2): 'Thrones. 96–109 de los cantares'

George Kearns, in his expert guide, declared these fourteen cantos 'largely ineffective as poetry'. Basil Bunting could pay generous tribute to the way '*Thrones* soars over what went before, the madrigal surface growing steadily more swift and lyrical', and that may be true of the surface. Yet his earlier criticism, that the cantos 'refer, but they do not present', applies here far more than to what went before, and that is one reason why these cantos are indeed, at least for the common reader, 'largely ineffective as poetry'.

Pound was not writing now for aesthetic effect. He had told Kathleen Raine that 'after the age of forty, no man ought to give his first attention to the writing of verse'. And his St Elizabeths circle had heard him say, as Reno Odlin recorded, that his intentions in *Thrones* were 'paideutic and anagogical'. That is, he was engaged in teaching a *paideuma* by leading the mind to perceive things anagogically. He had explained the latter term, when writing about Dante's *Paradiso* in *The Spirit of Romance*, as the discovery of symbols 'of mankind's struggle upward out of ignorance into the clear light of philosophy'; and he had told his mother, 'you might take it as leading up to a sense of things in general'. Now he was emphasizing the 'EFFECT on the MIND', meaning that the effect of his writing anagogically would be to involve the reader in that process. 'The anagogic leads to unity', he would re-affirm in his last years. In his *Thrones* then, from 1956 to 1958, he was writing with a philosophic agenda. He had disparaged as 'blue china' fit only for the mantle-shelf poetry not based on an understanding of civic life, and *Thrones* opens with a variation upon that—'Aestheticisme comme politique d'église, hardly religion.' In 105 he will cite Anselm, 'via mind is the nearest you'll get to it', i.e. to a true image of the cosmos.

These cantos look and sound much like those preceding. On their surface, as Bunting remarked, they grow steadily more swift and lyrical, and one hears the characteristic rhythm of Pound's verse. Each line is a taut unit, and the lines flow 'in the sequence of the musical phrase'. But all that is secondary. The writing is not, as it had been up to *The Pisan Cantos*, a composition of immediately luminous and intelligible details, but rather a composition of anagogical symbols which at times becomes a form of verbal algebra. We might think of it, by analogy with meta-physics, as a kind of metapoetry.

For the light to shine through these 'diafana', as they are named at the start of 96, the reader needs to know in advance a good deal more about their sources than Pound presents. He teaches on the assumption that the well-prepared student is already familiar with the text and will be able to follow him as he leafs through it, translating a detail here and another there, and throwing in the occasional comment and aside. Here he is going through Paul the Deacon's Latin history of the Lombards, written before 800, and printed in volume 95 of Migne's *Patrologia*—

Martel father of Pippin,
Pippin of Charlemagne,
Alpaide's son, one of 'em, not Plectrude's
empty grave outside San Zeno, to the right as you face it.
another bloke in Milano, 'seven Cardinals attended his funeral,'

apud Pictavium, Aquitaine, Narbonne and Proença.
Martel, that would be in the 'thirties'

As it happens the empty grave, as Terrell's note informs us, is not in the source. In Pound's mind, according to David Gordon, it somehow rhymed with 'Y Yin sent the young king into seclusion' (85/546)—near the grave of Confucius, that may have been; and the other 'bloke in Milano' was apparently Mussolini, for reasons to do with his being buried in the family vault only in August 1957. How would one guess any of that; and having been told, what is one to make of it? The line of place names refers, we may need to be informed, to 'two battles Charles Martel fought against the Saracens' across in Gaul. After half a dozen such pages the reader is assured, 'we are getting to the crux of one matter', only to be confronted by a block of Latin from 'col.1060, The Deacon, Migne's Patrologia'; and, 'to fully grasp the importance of this', Wilhelm advises, 'one must read Alexander Del Mar's *History of Monetary Systems*', where one may learn that the crux of the matter is that Justinian, as emperor of Byzantium, preserved his sovereignty by asserting his right to issue the currency. (On the other hand there is the view that he may have been doing wrong to Habdimelich, who was trying to maintain local control of local purchasing power, a thoroughly Poundian principle.) One will have to read Del Mar again to make anything of canto 97, which consists almost entirely of fragments from his writings and is scarcely intelligible without constant reference to his work.

At the end of his chapter of commentary on the first half of canto 96 Wilhelm, having filled in what Pound leaves out, sums up its half-dozen pages as 'a tale told by many idiots with half-remembered, half-pieced-together details—all of them suspect'. 'But', he adds, making the best of it, 'the quest, dark and questionable as it may be, is important because it leads to the City of Light', by which he means Byzantium. That would mean that the ignorant reader has been required to struggle through those opaque fragments of a murky and often violent and benighted era as the approach to enlightenment. And certainly the struggling reader will at least have registered the absence of any settled order. Early on there is Cunimundus 'inviting his wife to drink from her father's skull', while 'Tiberius Constantine was distributist', and Rothar 'got some laws written down' though 'touched with the Aryan heresy'. Justinian's regulations provoke the money sellers into thinking about bumping him off. 'Under Antoninus' there was a remarkable '23 years without war'. Altogether, Fortune rules in a dark age—'all under the Moon is under Fortuna', that is, all that is not formed by the light from heaven.

The latter half of the canto presents evidence of the light that was in Byzantium. But there is no Yeatsian celebration of its mosaics, and Hagia Sophia gets only an incidental mention. The source here is the book of regulations for the crafts and trades and markets of Byzantium. It is noted that 'the idea of just price is somewhere, | the haggling somewhere'. The price of bread and the bakers' margin of profit is set down, as are their hours, 'and that they take due care against fire'. There are regulations for the wine-sellers and their measures, and a punishment for false measures. And so it goes on, with regulations for the perfumers, the grocers, the candle-makers, the builders, the notaries and tabularies—the latter needing to have 'perfect style' without which 'might not notice punctuation and phrases | that alter the sense'; and the silversmiths and the goldsmiths; and the bankers who are commanded 'not to file coins | nor make false ones', and 'If they do not notify counterfeits that come in | and from whom | shall be flogged, shaved and exiled'. The detail is perhaps excessive, though it does provide the balancing counterweight to the first half of the canto. And the point does bear some emphasis: this is the ground of Byzantine culture, the evidence that its enlightenment goes right down into the detail of its economy and daily life. Yeats and Wyndham Lewis and Eliot, ignoring this economic basis, 'had no ground beneath 'em', while 'Orage had'.

As he works through *The Eparch's Book* Pound's commentary pays special attention to its language, noting particularly the refinements and precisions of its Greek. The effect is to foreground the common language as the necessary instrument of intelligent government. Indeed nothing else to do with the government of Byzantium is mentioned—it is as if all depended upon finding the right words. Canto 98 similarly emphasizes the civic function of language. Its source is *The Sacred Edict* (1670) of Emperor K'ang-hsi, in the version written 'in the language of the people' by the Salt Commissioner Wang Iu-p'uh.

Canto 99 will present a digest of that commentary, but first Pound involves the reader in his study of Wang's ideograms. 'Get a dictionary | and learn the meaning of words', he urges (echoing Ford); and he observes at one point, 'The text is somewhat exigeant, perhaps you will consider the meaning of /cheng 正 | king 經 | From Kung's porch 門 mên³.' Here the dictionary gives 'upright or constant classics' for *cheng king*. However, Terrell notes, 'Authorities differ about the meaning of these two characters in the Chinese classics,' and suggests that Pound 'invites the reader to consider the terms from Kung's point of view'. John Cayley, perhaps doing that, remarks that 'the image is of correctly aligned warp threads; here the warp of tradition and orthodoxy'. Thus the qualified student may be led into the deep structures of Confucian morality.

There are some fine inventions in Pound's translation, as when he finds in the ideograms 'Earth and water dye the wind in your valley | . . . | that his feelings have the colour of nature'; or again when in *hsien ming*, which connect the clear light of intelligence with the light from the sun, he finds 'the silk cords of the sunlight, | Chords of the sunlight (*Pitagora*)'. For the most part however, and more especially in the lengthy moralizing of canto 99, Pound cultivates a simple and direct language 'of the people' in keeping with the Salt Commissioner's intention. The History Classic, the source of cantos 52–61, was a book for the ruling class; now the entire population was to be instructed in the Confucian *paideuma*. Thus for education,

> have masters in village schools
> To teach 'em classics not hog-wash
> . . .
> And if your kids don't study, that's your fault.
> . . .
> Dress 'em in folderols
> and feed 'em with dainties,
> In the end they will sell out the homestead. [99/704–5]

The canto goes on at what may seem excessive length with such snippets of the *Edict*'s traditional morality. It is all very worthy and humane, but mostly at the level of a quiet village life. 'One village in order, | one valley will reach the four seas,' it proposes, aiming no further than the well-behaved family in the well-ordered village. There is no Odysseus to venture forth upon those seas, and no divinity in them. For the common people all is to be practical good sense, dutiful respect, and plain living. 'Order' is the key word, order in the family, order in the village, and thus order in the state.

Yet from this communal wisdom, which did after all hold China together for a few thousand years, and from the Eparch's regulations for Byzantium's marketplace, Pound is constructing the thrones of his *paradiso terrestre*. Evidently some further adjustment to the reader's preconceptions about paradise may be required. Pound's is a *paradiso terrestre* with the emphasis upon the terrestrial, which means too that it exists in time. It will be then forever a work in progress, like Wagadu. One might call it a long-term project, extending throughout history; and a global project, comprehending diverse cultures and traditions. It would be a paradise for the whole people, and of the whole people, universal though constructed by the enlightened few. And those few, the Byzantine Emperor Justinian, Confucius, and the others, now have their thrones not on account of their personal enlightenment, but because that enlightenment has made a positive difference to the daily lives of their people.

The following five cantos, 100 to 104, are altogether concerned with the struggle to achieve any kind of civilized order in public affairs, more particularly in France under and after Napoleon. Relatively brief and scherzo-like, they present a rapid succession of brief quotations, allusions, references, and comments, playing off one thing against another in swift discriminations and perceptions of relations. Canto 100 begins—

> 'Has packed the Supreme Court
> so they will declare anything he does constitutional.'
> Senator Wheeler, 1939.
> —and some Habsburg ploughed his imperial furrow
> Eu ZoOn—
> Not that never should, but if exceeding and
> no one protest,
> will lose all your liberties.

The contrast between the behaviours of President Roosevelt and the Habsburg emperor is clear, and thematically important for the whole set of cantos; but the third item can baffle readers who don't recognize it as an abbreviation of Pound's own protest against Roosevelt's exceeding his powers.

The rapid and often dissonant to and fro of the better and the worse behaviours of responsible and irresponsible citizens and governors goes on throughout this set of cantos over a ground note of natural harmonies, as in 'From ploughing of fields is justice', and, more generally, 'Eu zoOn', which implies there that right living consists in working with the abundance of nature. This note can sound in an isolated observation, as 'Shingled flakes on a moth's wing', or the repeat of '"Earth and water dye the air in your valley."' In 101 it becomes a distinct theme in images drawn from the landscapes of 'Chalais, Aubeterre' and the Na Khi, and in that form is present again in 102. One misses it in 103, where right living is not prevalent; but 104 takes it up again—

> Na Khi talk made out of wind noise,
> And North Khi, not to be heard amid sounds of the forest
> but to fit in with them

Then there is the Na Khi ritual invocation of the life-force—

> no glow such as of pine-needles burning
> Without ^{2}muan ^{1}bpo
> no reality
> Wind over snow-slope agitante
> nos otros
> calescimus

So the wind that makes the lit pine-needles glow is perceived as one with the divinity whose stirring within us sets us, 'we others', on fire. This canto is much concerned with communication and communion, especially, as in the *Ling*[2] ideogram, with communications between 'heaven' and 'earth', and then also with disconnections. Thus 'Luigi in hill paths | chews wheat at sunrise, | that grain his communion'; but the Portuguese colonizers were 'No sooner in Goa | than they started uprooting spice trees', to establish a monopoly, 'a common practice in business'—theirs 'a blindness that comes from inside'.

In 104 intelligence is primarily from the senses, with the warning, 'who try to use the mind for the senses | drive screws with a hammer'. In 105 there is the complementary recognition, 'via mind is the nearest you'll get to it'. That paraphrases Anselm (*c.*1034–1109), an Italian by birth, a Benedictine monk in France, a theologian who would ground faith in reason, and in his later years, from 1093, archbishop of Canterbury and defender of the English Church's rights against the encroachments of King Rufus. Anselm features in the canto as a rational theologian, a man of practical insight, and a defender of liberties; and on the latter account, in Pound's view, a forefounder of Magna Carta.

At the end of the canto there is this summary history of the times before Anselm—

For a thousand years savages against maniacs
                                        and vice versa.
Alfred sorted out hundreds, tithings,
            They probably murdered Erigena,
                    Athelstan gon yilden rere, after 925
                            Aunt Ethelfled had been literate,
                                    Canute for alleviation of Alp tolls
                                          Gerbert at the astrolable
                                                  better than Ptolemy,
A tenth tithe and circet of corn.

There is a jump then to the people in his own moment whom he can regard as 'responsible for something more than their personal conduct'—

With a Crommelyn at the breech-block
                        or a del Valle,
This is what the swine haven't got
                        with their
                                    πανουργία [*villainy*]

That may be, and yet the swine with their villainy remain in the mind no less than those who parade as Defenders of the Constitution. 'One is held up by the low percentage of reason which seems to operate in human affairs,' Pound would tell Donald Hall. And that is the moral of his history, and of the preceding cantos. There are individuals 'who have some part of the divine vision' and who make a difference in human affairs—just there he thinks of Alfred, Erigena, Athelstan, and will note in the closing lines Anselm's contribution to Cavalcanti. But always there is the opposition of the unenlightened, always the struggle to conceive and to create a better order in human affairs, and always the resurgent darkness. Villon too, he notes in the last line, should have read Anselm's *Proslogion* in his time at the university of Paris, but in his case you wouldn't know it from his life and work.

Looking back over the previous cantos, back to 100, it becomes apparent that they present the states of mind of a person subjected to the ordinary condition of human affairs. It is a mind with an extraordinary range of reference, able to touch it would seem on all times and traditions. And while it can discover no fixed order, only endless change under Fortuna, so it is itself unfixed, 'as Ixion unstill, ever turning', even as it goes on questing after a possible order.

Canto 106 takes up the theme of the order that is in and from natural process. It begins, as Terrell's *Companion* observes, with 'a sort of subject-response incantation between the Eleusinian mystery rites and the oriental wisdom that climaxed in Neoconfucianism, or "between Kung and Eleusis".' The Eleusinian vision of the sustaining source of civil life is the 'subject', with Demeter-Persephone associated also with Circe and Artemis, and also Athene. The 'response' to the evocation of Persephone in the autumn rite, as 'Dis' bride, Queen over Phlegethon', is the statement, 'The strength of men is in grain.' That comes from an early Chinese work by Kuan Chung which taught the primacy and the principles of agriculture and became a major source for Confucian thought—hence 'How to govern is from the time of Kuan Chung.' But there is the qualification, Master Kuan 'could guide you in some things, but not hither', not to the vision of Demeter and Persephone. 'Kung is the outer or public doctrine,' Pound wrote in a note to Denis Goacher, but 'we must keep an inner doctrine (of light)'. Here the divine light is manifest in 'the gold light of wheat surging upward | ungathered'. There is the same 'Gold light, in veined phyllotaxis'; in monarch butterflies, 'king-wings in migration'; and in the flowers of asphodel, broom, marsh-marigold ('caltha palistris'), gorse, and no doubt too in the orchid 'herys arachnites'. In the seeing mind, in 'God's eye', this is 'That great acorn of light bulging outward'. This image of fertile light touches on the mystery which was never to be spoken of by the initiates at Eleusis, and which is only glanced at here, in the notice of Circe, daughter of the sun, who in earlier cantos initiated Odysseus into the sacred rites of the life-process. The emphasis now is on perceiving the goddess in her several forms, invoking her aid, and honouring her. A further distinction is that the canto presents an immediate perception of the light of life in its action, and not the idea of it as in Erigena and Richard of St Victor, important as that has been in the poem's own progress. Again we have cause to reflect that its paradise is made of enlightenment in action, even at the most simple level. Thus Luigi's 'grain rite', his chewing wheat at sunrise in the hill path, is the needed completion of 'Kung' by 'Eleusis'.

The final three cantos, 107–9, are drawn from *The Second Part of the Institutes of the Laws of England*, and more especially from the seventy-seven pages in which Sir Edward Coke (1552–1634), who had served as Lord Chief Justice of England, analysed and commented upon the Magna Carta of 1225 in such a way as to make it pertinent to his own times. The barons had forced the king to grant the rights they claimed, and now it was the turn of the Commons to assert their liberties against the arbitrary powers claimed by James I and his son Charles I. Coke's part was to set common law against the royal prerogative. For his pains he was dismissed from public office, and imprisoned for a time on a charge of treason. Charles so feared him that he prevented publication of his *Second Institutes* in 1628, and the work appeared posthumously in 1642 'by Order of the House of Commons'. Coke's commentaries on the law, with their upholding of the rights and liberties of each and every person in society, not only helped bring on the English Revolution, but subsequently informed the thinking of John Adams and helped bring about the American Revolution. In *Thrones*, Coke, as the enlightened upholder of the common law which formed the effective constitution of England, and informed the declared Constitution of the United States, completes the progression from virtually lawless Lombardy, through the Eparch's regulations in Byzantium, and the highly developed sense of social order in Confucian China, to the most advanced concept and practice of law achieved in Pound's own tradition.

That at least is the idea of the Coke cantos. But the experience of them is something else, and the reader may be left feeling that in this case Pound might well confess, 'my notes do not cohere'. There is a quite dazzling meta-reading by David Gordon in which he has Pound revealing 'a migration of the real powers of government and central taxation . . . from the king and nobles to the whole people of the realm'; and further, 'Upon the thirteenth century palimpsest of struggle for human rights is written a seventeenth century struggle for virtually the same rights, and herein

Pound has interlarded the life, and luminous comments of Coke in order to heighten the effect of the permanence of these human rights.' But then we must come down to the text, and to this opening of canto 107:

> The azalea is grown while we sleep
> In Selinunt',
> in Akragas
> Coke. Inst. 2.
> to all cathedral churches to be
> read 4 times in the yeare
> 20.H.3
> that is certainty
> mother and nurse of repose
> he that holdeth by castle-guard
> pays no scutage
> And speaking of clarity
> Milite, Coke, Edwardus
> 'that light which was Sigier'
> ... of Berengar his heirs was this Eleanor
> all the land stored with ploughs, & shall be at the least as he received it
> quod custod'... vendi no debent
> Light, cubic
> by volume
> So that Dante's view is quite natural;
> (Tenth, Paradiso, nel Sole)
> non per color, ma per lume parvente

'Selinunt[e]' and 'Akagras', the latter the old name of Agrigento, are cities in Sicily, and Gordon's gloss is that 'The Sicilian rose of Ciulio D'Alcamo has grown into the English azalea ... reminding us that the legislative ability of Frederick II was known in the England of Henry III.' That 'reminder' might be taking rather a lot for granted. 'Coke, Inst. 2' indicates Pound's source; '20.H.3' gives, in the style of Coke's references, the year in which Henry III ratified Magna Carta, the twentieth of his reign; that the charter was to be read 'to all cathedral churches' is from Coke's 'Proeme'; and the lines 'certainty | mother and nurse of repose' is his comment at the end of the 'Proeme'. The note about not paying 'scutage', from the second chapter of the commentary, is presumably an instance of the reposeful certainty. Coke is named on the title page of his *Second Institutes* as 'Authore Edwardo Coke, Milite, *J.C.*'. Sigier is a light in the sun of Dante's *Paradiso* x, from which the last line above is quoted. We may gather from Gordon that in the university of Paris he maintained against Aquinas that theology should not have authority over natural philosophy, and that thus he 'rhymes' with Coke's standing for common law against divine right. At the same time the allusion elevates Coke to stand with Sigier as a light in paradise. Eleanor of Provence, wife of Henry III, was the daughter of Berengar, Count of Provence—the implication would be that the Provençal ethic had entered into the great charter, and so led to the sense of equity in its provision that

> The keeper, so long as he hath the custody of the land of such an heir, shall keep up the houses, parks, warrens, ponds, mills, and other things pertaining to the same land, with the issues of the said land; and he shall deliver to the heir, when he cometh to his full age, all his land stored with ploughs, and all other things, at the least as he received it. All these things shall be observed in the custodies of archbishopricks, bishopricks, abbeys, priories, churches, and dignities vacant, which appertain to us; except this, that such custody shall not be sold. [In the parallel Latin text, *except' quod custod' hujusmodi vendi non debent.*]

One can get drawn into Coke: 'That this was the common law appeareth by Glanvile, who saith', and there follows the quotation in Latin. Over the page he tells a racy tale of one Ranulph, chaplain to King William Rufus, who offended most grievously against this law, and was committed by King Henry 'to prison for his intolerable misdeeds, and injuries to the church, where he lived without love, and died without pity, saving of those that thought it pity, he lived so long'. But this is distraction from what Pound is making of Coke.

One can discern, with the aid of Gordon, and by referring to Coke's text and to Dante's, that Pound's notes do cohere. He was not grabbing fragments at random, nor attaching to them any loose association that came into his head. But to the common reader the sense that *is* there will be more or less impenetrable. One more example—

> Owse, Wherfe, Nid, Derwent,
> Swale, Yore & Tine

A reader may take pleasure in finding these rivers of Yorkshire and Northumberland named in a canto, but to what purpose? Coke names them in connection with the regulation of salmon fishing, and Gordon comments, 'man's efforts to synchronize with nature's cycles such as the spawning of salmon ("Owse, Wherfe") then becomes the pattern of his ethical, and ergo civic achievements; his *directio voluntatis* becomes the *directio naturae.*' That is very fine, but it is as it were in the cloud, not in the writing.

Pound began drafting a Coke canto in October 1957. At that point he had not actually read any of his work. As he told Moelwyn Merchant, a Welsh academic who visited him and who was just then reading around

Shakespeare and looking into Coke in the Folger Library, he was 'IGNORANT of Coke' and knew him 'only in J. Adams reference until 30 October 1957'. In mid-September he had drawn up a list of 'various items raised in Adams cantos' as a possible exposition of 'COKE on PRINCIPLES'. Then on October 31 he told John Theobald, 'G. Giov. brot 2nd *Institutes* yester, and I only got the full sense of clarity an hour or two ago.' Two days later he wrote to Mary, 'Coke "Institutes" nearest thing to Confucius in english, necessary, complementary, touches point Kung doesn't'. He ended this letter, 'Much better mind than Blackstone, a lecturer, Coke, Atty/General. like Kung, practice of high office, de-eggheads 'em. 72 years to get to him, exactly when needed fer Canto 107 or wotever. or 108. Parad. X'. His poetry notebooks show that he was making notes from Coke's *Institutes* before 8 November, and that from that day he filled an entire notebook with notes and drafts for all three Coke cantos. It seems likely that he had them all in draft by 28 December. As Merchant observed, there was no time 'for the digestion and assimilation of the vast quantities of matter in the Coke texts'. But then he was not too hastily composing a digest of Coke on Magna Carta, but piecing together a mosaic of fragments illustrative of his principles, and of the universal principles of equity and justice. The trouble is that Coke's mind is thus reduced to fragments, while the fragments, when detached from their own context, can become opaque if still colourful, so that (to change the metaphor) what Pound sees in them does not shine through.

Whatever else is to be said of *Thrones* one thing does shine out: that in the months when the US government couldn't make up its mind about what to do with this notorious fascist, the poet himself was absorbed in his epic subject of the struggle for individual rights and responsibilities, and for civic justice, with a profound commitment to a natural humane order that would be radically opposed to what the term 'fascist' stood for then and stands for now.

MacLeish gets his 'nol pros'

Officially, there had been no change in Pound's mental condition since the report to the Department of Justice in 1953—indeed there had been no 'substantial change . . . during his more than eleven years of hospitalization', or so Dr Overholser informed the Assistant Director of the Bureau of Prisons in March 1957. 'In our opinion', he therefore wrote, 'he is still mentally incompetent to stand trial or to consult with counsel.' There was a new diagnosis, even vaguer than the one before: 'Psychotic Disorder, Undifferentiated'. But the 'symptoms' were still the same: 'professes more or less continual fatigue', 'supercilious and critical attitude', 'decidedly egocentric'. 'He has been doing some writing,' Overholser conceded.

Thurman Arnold would later remove the obfuscation. The fundamental difficulty for all concerned, for the psychiatrists as for Laughlin and Cornell, had all along been that if he were to be tried Pound would insist 'on testifying that America's entry into the war was a conspiracy between Roosevelt and the Jews and that in opposing such a war over the Italian Broadcasting system he was saving our Constitution'. That could not be allowed, because

> From the point of view of the philosophical morality of our judicial system, it would have been an injustice to Pound to try him until psychological therapy had cured him of those delusions so that he would not have insisted on testifying against himself.

In short, as the psychiatrists had virtually testified in 1946, Pound was guilty of wrong ideas, and had to be insane not to see that. Indeed, he must have been insane to broadcast them. And if, after his eleven and more years of Elizabethan therapy, he still held the same ideas then he must be incurably insane.

It could follow that he would still be classified as insane even if MacLeish's efforts to have the indictment dropped were to succeed. In England, A. V. Moore, Dorothy Pound's confidential adviser, and T. S. Eliot were considering the options. Moore put it to Cornell, would a successful habeas corpus application 'clear Mr. Pound of mental incapacity?' He was concerned that if it did, 'the Indictment could immediately be proceeded with, and it is quite true that Mr. Pound could not stand any more legal proceedings'—so it would be best, apparently, for him not to be cleared of mental incapacity. There were other worries. He doubted 'whether Mr. Pound would be given the freedom he desires, and probably he would not be permitted to leave the United States'. And then 'Mrs. Pound has always the anxiety that if her husband should be released she would find the cost of his future maintenance in the U.S. too much to bear alone, and also that she does not think it practicable to get herself involved in any further legal entanglements and heavy expenses.'

Moore sent a copy of that letter to Eliot, and Cornell sent Eliot copies of his letters to Moore. 'Taking everything into account', Eliot told Moore, 'If Pound is to continue to be certified as insane, I see no advantage for him or Mrs. Pound in his release from St. Elizabeth's'. There was the 'probability' that he would never be granted a passport to go to Italy; and Mrs Pound had always given him to understand that they would not be able to afford a private sanatorium in America. The best to be hoped for, therefore, was that 'Pound would still be detained in St. Elizabeth's, but only as a lunatic and not as a man under an Indictment.' About even that though, 'MacLeish in his last letter to me was very depressed', on account of the Kasper business, and because 'the Attorney-General might fear that the spectre of Ezra's anti-Semitism might rise again to plague him'.

Graham Greene was appalled by the attitude that Pound was probably happier where he was, and told Ronald Duncan, 'You can use my name certainly for what it's worth in any protest you make about Ezra Pound's detention.' A petition signed by Greene and Cocteau and Stravinsky was sent to the Attorney General, with no evident effect. The United States government, in its imperial pomp, could afford to file away petitions from foreign artists however distinguished their names. As Americans, Eliot and MacLeish knew that only an American initiative would have weight; and even then it would have to be a government insider who made the difference. MacLeish, a Democrat and therefore an outsider to the Republicans of the Eisenhower administration, needed Robert Frost as his front man.

Frost was in good standing with the administration. Assistant Attorney General Rogers, MacLeish knew, regarded him 'as a fellow Republican which he very nearly is, being a [Grover] Cleveland Democrat as he puts it'. And Secretary of State John Foster Dulles thought him just the man, as 'a prominent literary figure' and 'distinguished representative of the American cultural scene', to undertake a 'good-will' mission to Great Britain in the spring of 1957. There Frost was to be honoured by the universities of Oxford and Cambridge. He was in London in April and early May, staying at the luxurious Connaught Hotel in Mayfair close by the American Embassy. MacLeish, who had been travelling in Europe, made a point of catching up with him there and bringing in Eliot to discuss strategy. Frost said then that he was willing to go to Washington to take up Rogers's offer to discuss the Pound case. In mid-June, when they were both back in America, MacLeish wrote prompting him to do that without delay, and Frost wrote back,

> My purpose holds to help you to get Ezra loose though I won't say my misgivings in the whole matter haven't been increased by my talks with Eliot lately, who knows more about Ezra than anybody else and what we can hope to do for his salvation. I should hate to see Ezra die ignominiously in that wretched place where he is for a crime which if proven couldn't have kept him all these years in prison. So you go ahead and make an appointment with the Department of Justice.

Frost did not like Pound or his poetry—'Neither you nor I would want to take him into our family or even into our neighbourhood,' he couldn't help adding. His misgivings made him see it as altogether a 'bad business', but he would go through with it.

MacLeish arranged the meeting with Rogers for 19 July, and offered to accompany Frost. He also asked Eliot and Hemingway to provide Frost with written statements of their views so that he would go 'fully armed' into the meeting.

Hemingway wrote at length, that he could never regard Pound's broadcasts 'as anything but treasonable', but he must have been 'of unsound mind' to have made them, and he was never a dangerous traitor, his influence 'no more than that of a crackpot'; and then, 'as one of our greatest living poets with an international reputation', he 'should be extended a measure of understanding and mercy'. 'It may be', he acknowledged, 'that the Department of Justice will feel that to nol pros the indictment against Pound would be a very unpopular move because of his antisemitism, race-ism and his crack-pot views and contacts'—and he himself detested 'Pound's politics, his anti-semitism and his race-ism'. Nevertheless, he truly felt 'it would do more harm to our country for Pound to die in confinement, than for him to be freed and sent to live with his daughter in Italy'. He 'would be glad to contribute fifteen hundred dollars toward getting him settled with his daughter'. MacLeish had told him that Mary had said, when she talked with him at Sirmione in April, that she was eager to care for her father at Brunnenburg.

A day or so after the meeting with Rogers MacLeish reported the outcome to Hemingway and to Pound. The Department of Justice could be willing to drop the indictment, if there were a sound plan for taking care of Pound outside St Elizabeths, but only after 'the Kasper stink has blown over'. Until then the Department would not move. The suggestion that he should be sent to Italy 'to live with his natural daughter' was considered to be not 'a sound plan because it would provide a "story" for the papers and because it is feared that there may be—are—people in Italy who would like to make use of him, get him talking'. Frost and MacLeish were inclined to agree, and expected Hemingway to agree, that in spite of Pound's wanting to go there, Italy should be out of the question because of what he might say there. If he were to be freed, he was told, his 'future would have to be in the United States'. And Frost had an idea that the necessary plan for his care could be 'a sound professional arrangement with your publishers', such as had worked for himself over many years. The Department of Justice would make no commitments, 'but the door wasn't closed', and MacLeish and Frost had come away, 'on balance, encouraged' and 'a little more hopeful' than they had feared. Evidently the issue was no longer a matter of law, but of political expediency. It was to be decided not on the basis of justice or of mercy, but on fears of what Pound might say and who he might associate with, on calculations about how his release might play with media commentators such as Walter Winchell and with the voting public, and on what it might do for the reputation and influence of the United States abroad.

MacLeish thought Pound should know that 'Somebody has spread the rumour at the Department of Justice . . . that you and your wife would really prefer to stay on at St. Elizabeths.' He assumed this was false, but 'your wife ought to make that clear to the Department'. Pound thanked him 'for yr/ noble efforts', and exploded, 'It is damned nonsense to say that either I or D.P. prefer me to stay in St Eliza.' At the same time, 'I have said that there are more IMPORTANT issues than my getting out. I wd/ rather see an honest system of money.' Upon further reflection he wrote to Mary,

> It wd/ however be timely to note resurgence of smear to effect that I don't WANT to get out. This time it might be from people who don't want me to get to Italy. Idea I might be let out IF confined to the U.S. // Other line was that I cd/ get out if I would LEAVE the country. Can't please 'em all.

MacLeish passed on to Frost his impression that Pound was not disturbed 'about not being able to go to Italy', but was infuriated by the rumour that he did not want to leave St Elizabeths. Pound had mentioned that he had 'offers of housing'—one of these was from Frank Lloyd Wright, to come and live with him in the house he had designed near Phoenix, Arizona. Eliot, apparently thinking him 'nuttier than he is', was now anxious that 'the doctors might let Ezra go off and live somewhere down south with nobody but his wife etc. to look out for him'. 'Does Eliot strike you as a bit timid?', MacLeish asked.

In August and September there were significant developments quite apart from MacLeish's discreet campaign. On 13 August Senator Richard L. Neuberger of Oregon requested the Library of Congress to provide 'as much information as is available on the literary, political, legal and medical status of Mr. Pound', and H. A. Sieber, a research assistant in the Legislative Reference Service, was set to work to prepare a report. The completed report would bear the date 'March 31, 1958', and be subsequently updated to 18 April. In an independent initiative, Representative Usher L. Burdick of North Dakota introduced in the House on 21 August a resolution which began,

> Whereas Ezra Pound has been incarcerated in Saint Elizabeths Hospital for the past twelve years on the assumption that he is insane; and

Whereas many people visit him there and are convinced that he is not insane: Therefore be it

Resolved, That the Committee on the Judiciary, acting as a whole or by subcommittee, is authorized and directed to conduct a full and complete investigation and study of the sanity of Ezra Pound, in order to determine whether there is justification for his continued incarceration in Saint Elizabeths Hospital.

Burdick's resolution was not acted upon. Instead, independently he would say, he made the same request as Senator Neuberger to the Library of Congress, and became party to Sieber's report which he would read into the Congressional Record in late April and early May of 1958.

In September Arnold Gingrich's *Esquire* published a sympathetic article by Richard Rovere, suggesting, as Pound read it, that 'its is time to spring grampaw'; and letters appeared in the following number from, among others, Marianne Moore, Van Wyck Brooks, William Carlos Williams, and John Dos Passos, all to the effect that he should be released. The American Civil Liberties Union also responded, saying that they had been concerned for a number of years over Pound's continued confinement, and had 'repeatedly offered our support for a possible legal challenge'. In fact the ACLU had carefully kept its powder dry, and there was reason to think they were more interested in 'the larger legal problem his confinement represents' than in his particular case. Their letter on this occasion was lukewarm in its willingness 'to cooperate in a court test of his continued confinement with anyone who is in a legal position' to assume responsibility for the special care he might need. Unless there were such a person, they opined, 'it would be a cruel thing to turn him out of "the sanctuary of St. Elizabeths"'.

About this time Harry Meacham, an energetic executive of Dun and Bradstreet, the mercantile agency, who was also active in the Poetry Society of Virginia and in other arts organizations, was moved by MacLeish's 'eloquent passage' about the horror of Pound's incarceration to mount his own campaign to get him out. His idea was to run 'a letter-writing drive, by "prominent people known to be favourably disposed to Pound's release", and aimed at the office of the Attorney General and members of Congress'. He discussed this with Pound on one his visits, and Pound at once gave him lists of people to contact, together with suggestions of what they might say on his behalf. Meacham advised against 'complaining of particular lies and slanders', and Pound agreed, but wanted it said that he had used the microphone to continue his '19 years of effort against encroachment ON liberty'. At the same time he was less concerned with the past than with the present and the immediate future. In the same letter of '24 Sep 57' he wrote, 'On quite another line, it probably has not occurred to you that I am not raging to get back to Italy', and he proceeded to put out a feeler towards the University of Virginia, founded by Thomas Jefferson, where 'I wd/ be interested to carry on the job T. J. intended. i.e. he was interested in civilization'. 'Of course, I am not out of the bughouse yet,' he recognized—but he evidently was beginning to think of a life outside. Later that day he wrote again,

> Re/ one of yr/ questions, I don't see that it is anyone's damn business WHAT I wd/ do IF I got out.
> It is unConfucian to make plans for circumstances that cannot be calculated.
> It would depend on HOW I got out.
> As I always spoke as an american, FOR the constitution, etc. it wd/ be a joke of jokes to get out ON CONDITION that I return to Italy.
> I would naturally prefer to go live with my daughter to staying in the bughouse.
> After all Borah did say: 'Waaaal, I'm sure I don't know what a man like you would find to do here?'
> God knows I can see PLENTY that needs doing. HERE.

Pound was eager to involve Meacham in his own campaigns for enlightenment, along with 'yr admirable aim to eliminate captivity of yrs. truly', but Meacham cannily held off, aware that 'Many of his well-meaning friends had destroyed their usefulness by getting involved with the lunatic fringe.' He meant to keep it simple: 'not justice, but freedom' was his aim, since 'after all, it was a bit late to talk about justice in the Pound case'.

Meacham let MacLeish know about his campaign, and in mid-October MacLeish wrote back to put him in the picture. 'There should be no public stir,' he advised,

> the Department of Justice is well aware that Pound cannot and should not be held longer. The problem is one of working out a disposition of the indictment (which should be nol prossed) arranging for Pound's future and finding the right moment. The principal obstacle now is Kasper.

Pound was taking notice at last of that obstacle as he began to allow himself to think about getting out of St Elizabeths. In an undated letter to Marcella Spann he wrote, 'E.P. can only AFFORD to receive the people likely to conduce to his getting out/ contagious fringe, the effulgences of Kasper etc./ are not to be thought of at this time.' It must have been a relief, to MacLeish at least, that Kasper was now in jail and would be there for some time.

Frost had taken care of the problem of Pound's future by explaining his idea of a professional arrangement to Laughlin, and obtaining his guarantee to make available $300 per month as an advance on royalties for as long as Pound lived. That, with Dorothy Pound's own income, was reckoned sufficient to meet the costs of a private sanatorium, and, since Pound's royalties in that year were in excess of $5,000, there was little risk that the advances would not be covered. Frost went down to Washington again to see Rogers, who was about to move up to be Attorney General, and informed him that the money for the private institution seemed assured. That was on 23 October, and he followed up on 19 November with the information that MacLeish 'has Dr. Overholser's consent for Pound's transfer the minute he himself is released from holding Pound as a prisoner'. 'I grow impatient', Frost concluded this letter, 'The amnesty would be a good Christmas present.'

When nothing further was heard from Rogers, MacLeish turned to Dr Overholser. Frost had 'a firm commitment from Rogers', he told him, 'to nol pross if the doctors at St. Elizabeths would advise that Pound could be transferred to a private sanatorium'. Would Overholser go along with that plan? Overholser's reaction was that 'nothing much would be gained by moving Mr. Pound to a private institution except that, of course, the cost would be very considerable'. He then questioned, first, the assumption that Pound, if released from St Elizabeths, would need to be committed to a private institution; and then the assumption that he should be prevented from returning to Italy. 'I know perfectly well, as you do', he told MacLeish, 'that he would much prefer to return to Italy. . . . I am sure that he would be much happier there and would, of course, be no menace to any persons or any government.'

MacLeish talked this over with Frost, and wrote back that Rogers had told Frost that the Justice Department 'would quash the indictment IF Pound were removed to a private institution'—it would not make the first move—'and that thereafter it would have no interest in Pound's future except that it would frown on his leaving the United States'. MacLeish was too diplomatic to spell out the contradictoriness of this, but he was evidently wearied by it. Rogers appeared to be saying that he would drop the indictment *after* Pound was transferred to a private institution—yet his department had all along maintained that Pound could not be released from St Elizabeths while still under indictment, and Overholser held himself bound by that. Then there was the troubling lack of clarity about Pound's future status. There was a covert suggestion that he need not stay long in the private institution—'the Department would avert its face', as Frost had put it—but what force was to be assumed in its frown? MacLeish could only ask if he might talk it over with Overholser 'shortly after Christmas'.

He did not hide his exasperation from Meacham. Frost's letters to Rogers were not being acknowledged, he told him on 22 December, and nor were his own, but he expected that from a Republican administration. 'The Pound business looks cloudy from this angle,' he wrote, 'I am sick to death of the treatment we have been given over the past two years and I don't know how long I shall continue to sit on my typewriter—or the typewriters of all the others who want to burst out in shrill yells.'

Back in October he had told Meacham that he was finding Pound 'very reasonable and patient about the whole sad business'. But Pound was now telling his friends that he had had enough. Writing to Cummings from 'Bastile of Baruchistan' on 20 November, he said, 'I cd/ do wiff a change of scene, tho the delights of the American florilege are a compensation.' There was nothing qualified though about his statement to Patricia Hutchins, 'I shd/ like to get OUT. you can, at least, squash rumours to the contrary.' In December he tried rather desperately to enlist the support of *Noigandres*, a Brazilian literary magazine which had published some of his cantos in Portugese translation in 1952—

Time has come when if I had a clear official invitation from SOMEWHERE, say S. Paulo, to come and inhabit and lecture on, say Chinese, or any other LITERATURE | it might just possibly help git me out of quod, i.e. incarceration.

If your Ministero of Education cd. Express such a desire, saying they don't regard me as political . either as asset or detriment...

at any rate worth trying.

Along with wanting to get out he was he was feeling the squalor of the ward. When Mary floated the idea of bringing his grandchildren across for him to see at Christmas—Norman Holmes Pearson had offered financial help for a visit—he put her off, saying it was the wrong time of year, 'This ward is no fit place for the kids and out on the lawn would be the only place for them. Perhaps next spring...'

MacLeish heard from Rogers at last on 2 January 1958, offering 'to discuss the matter with you when you are next in Washington'. He was evidently no nearer to any decisive action. 'I am not sure whether it can be worked out or not,' he wrote, 'but I am certainly inclined in that direction, if it can be worked out from a legal standpoint.' MacLeish, concluding that the Department of Justice 'would like somehow to get the problem solved without solving it', had already decided to shift his efforts from Rogers to the State Department. There he would argue that although the decision would have to be made by Justice it was State that was suffering because Pound's continued incarceration hurt America's prestige abroad. His friend and former colleague in the Roosevelt administration, Christian Herter, was now Under Secretary for Foreign Affairs, and agreed to intervene, but said 'that one thing was certain: Ez couldn't go back to Italy'. Herter promptly wrote to Dr Overholser, on 2 January, saying that he understood from MacLeish 'that you can give the whole story so far as Saint Elizabeths is concerned', and asking him to 'drop in some day at your convenience as I would very much like to be fully informed in respect of this difficult individual'. MacLeish next asked Dag Hammarskjöld to let Herter know of his concerns in the matter, and also to think if there was 'any way in which Italian representatives might suggest to the Department of State that Pound would be welcome in Italy'. He was now persuaded that 'this is the real solution . . . to let him go back to his daughter in Italy', though that 'will be hard to arrange because Justice wants neither to act nor to let him return to Italy'.

According to an internal FBI memo from its Director J. Edgar Hoover, what the Attorney General had done when first approached on the matter in April 1957 was to set up a committee of three Assistant Attorney Generals to look into the case, 'in view of the controversial character of Pound, he being both anti-Semitic and pro-Fascist'. Evidently the FBI's Internal Security Division had been tasked with the investigation. In January 1958 Cornell, who appears to have been completely out of the loop, was surprised to be visited by two agents, who told him the Attorney General was considering the possibility of releasing Pound. In particular, they wanted to know 'why the Department of Justice, at the time of Pound's sanity hearing, had not put up a better fight'. '"Was he really insane"', they asked, '"was he really unfit to be tried and why was he any different from the other war criminals?"' Cornell referred them to 'the unanimous opinion of the government's own doctors', but also told them on his own behalf, 'that the situation would never have arisen if the army psychiatrists at the Pisa concentration camp had not blundered in their failure to diagnose Pound's illness'. What the FBI reported back to the Attorney General is not known, but an internal memo did make the point that 'the indictment against Pound on the charge of treason is still standing'.

On 27 January Representative Usher L. Burdick read into the Congressional Record '2 letters from the December 1957 and February 1958 issues of Esquire [which] throw much light upon this case and point to a remedy which would relieve the American Government of an embarrassment that has persisted for over a decade'. The letters followed Rovere's conclusion in his *Esquire* article, that 'It is hard to think of a good reason why Pound should not have his freedom immediately'. The first was from Professor G. Giovannini, and concerned the violation of Pound's constitutional rights throughout the months in 1945 during which he was held a prisoner in Italy. The other letter was from T. H. Horton, and mainly put forward Pound's defence against the charge of treason.

On 1 February Dorothy Pound wrote a formal letter to Dr Overholser, probably at Pound's dictation or direction, and possibly at Overholser's suggestion. The letter looks like an attempt to put down a marker. 'If Ezra Pound were released, we plan to go to Europe,' she wrote, 'Financial means are available to live modestly & not be a public charge. Summer quarters are ready in Italy, & he would want mild Mediterranean climate in winter.' To this she added the reassurance that he had 'no political views re contemporary Italy, & would take ten years at least to develop any—hardly likely'. 'Unlikely', Pound had said when giving a similar reassurance to *Noigandres*, since 'in ten years I will be 82'. Then at the end of February he became agitated when he learnt that Williams was intending to use one of his letters in *Paterson Book V*. He wrote to the editor at New Directions, 'it may be o.k. or it may be MOST untimely to release it | no need to protrude my blasted nekk any FURTHER at this TIME . . . Bill dun't mean no harm, but I am gittin tired of incarceration.'

Hammarskjöld found time to write to Herter, as MacLeish had requested, on 18 February. Emphasizing the international aspect, and his being personally in a position to know how alive the case remained in the minds of 'serious and thoughtful people in the intellectual world in Europe' whose opinion Herter would respect, he suggested that it would be both 'a tribute to [Pound's] great importance in Western letters and a noble humanitarian gesture if a formula could be found which put the matter entirely in the hands of his doctors and enabled him, when they find it advisable, to take up a new life with his daughter in Italy'.

On 5 March Christian Herter reported back to Hammarskjöld and MacLeish on his conversations with Overholser and Rogers. 'The idea of getting Pound to Italy [is] definitely impracticable,' he told them. Some compromise was possible, however, 'in a legal way'. Provided his friends and publisher could raise the necessary funds, Pound might be transferred to 'some inconspicuous place', 'with a maximum degree of freedom', 'where he could be visited from time to time by a recognized physician'. MacLeish, who was now down in his holiday place in Antigua, put this to Pound in mid-March:

> The idea is that you and, I assume, D.P., would live in a house of your own in some quiet town with the kind of climate you like where you could be visited from time to time by a recognized medic, and where you would have 'a maximum degree of freedom'.

And 'The locus would have to be in the US.' But it all depended on Pound's 'willingness to accept such an arrangement', MacLeish was explicit about that.

In his reply sent on 25 March Pound was far from satisfied. What was being offered appeared to him 'an illegal arrangement with an anonymity', and said 'nothing about placing my earnings in my own control'. He doubted 'if there IS enough money for me to live on in the U.S. under the present system of taxation'; did they mean 'a physician or a quackiatrist?'; and he had 'never heard of a "private sanitarium" that existed save for private motive'. 'I spose you mean well,' Pound concluded. MacLeish thanked him for that 'First kind word I've had from you since I started butting my head against this stone wall two years ago'. He patiently explained that there was nothing illegal about the proposed arrangement since it would be approved by the government and the Court; that all his earnings would be paid over to him by his publisher, only there would be a guaranteed minimum paid monthly; and that he might want to discuss the nature of the medical services with Overholser—'you can be sure that what he has in mind is a physician, not a quack'. There is no telling whether MacLeish was consciously drawing the sting in 'quackiatrist'; but he must have known that it was the Committee for Ezra Pound, not his publisher, who had control of his earnings, as of his person. In assuring Pound that 'the decision is, of course, wholly yours', he was very decently overlooking that vital, or lethal, fact. But then no one had thus far seriously addressed the question of whether Pound should be released from the Committee as well as from St Elizabeths. As things stood, MacLeish was convinced, the offer Herter had reported 'was the best solution we can now hope for'. Privately, Pound feared that Macleish was being 'played for a sucker'.

In February Frost had been making the most of a chance of direct access to the White House. The Poetry Society of America had awarded him its Gold Medal for Distinguished Service and a congratulatory telegram from President Eisenhower had been read out during the banquet. Frost detected the hand and influence of his old friend Sherman Adams, currently the President's Chief of Staff, and in his letter of thanks suggested that he should be invited to 'a meal or something' with the President so that he could thank him in person. A telegram from the President duly followed, inviting him 'TO AN INFORMAL STAG DINNER AT THE WHITE HOUSE IN WASHINGTON ON THE EVENING OF THURSDAY, FEBRUARY TWENTY-SEVENTH.' Frost 'ACCEPTED WITH GREAT PLEASURE', but in a second telegram made it clear to Adams that 'WHAT'S ON MY MIND WOULD BE MORE APT TO BE BROUGHT OUT IN TALKS WITH YOU SEPARATELY'. Adams, understanding his intention, invited him to lunch in the staff dining room at the White House on the 27th, and, at Frost's prompting, arranged for Attorney General Rogers to lunch with them. The outcome of these manoeuvres was a memorandum from the Department of Justice to President Eisenhower, stating that it did not intend to oppose a motion for Pound's release. Sherman Adams presented this to the President, who initialled it as the sign of his approval. Later Laughlin would tell Harry Meacham, what he may have learned from his brother-in-law, Eisenhower's Chief Economic Adviser, that Adams had 'secured the "nod" of the President so that the Dept. of Justice was instructed to drop the indictment'.

Next there was some discreet briefing of the press to prepare public opinion. On 16 March the Washington *Sunday Star* reported that, following a plea to the Attorney General by Robert Frost, 'A decision is near on the twin questions of freeing poet Ezra Pound of treason charges and releasing him from St Elizabeths Hospital'—an official close to the case had said the '"whole matter is at boiling point"'. For the Justice Department to be publicly contemplating dropping the treason charges was a startling new development in itself; but for it to be raising expectations in this way suggested that it was now prepared to act with some urgency. The *Sunday Star* article also quoted Dr Overholser as saying that 'It is perfectly possible to be mentally unfit to stand trial and yet be perfectly safe to be at large.' A. V. Moore noticed that the case appeared to be stirring, and remarked to Pound, 'Surely if the indictment is dismissed you should be quite free to go where you please, without supervision.'

Sieber's Library of Congress report in its first state was released to the press on 1 April. At the beginning Sieber delicately observed that while 'The Government's case against Mr. Pound is fairly well-known it appears that some of the arguments... presumed to be favourable to Mr. Pound's release from St. Elizabeths Hospital are not quite so well-known'. By the end of his report, with all due care and impartiality, he had pretty well made the case for Pound's release. At the Attorney General's press conference later in the day the Pound case was raised, as he must have expected it would be. Yes, he said, according to *The New York Times*, 'The Justice Department is giving consideration to dropping the treason charges against Ezra Pound, the poet, with a view to letting him return to Italy.' He was awaiting 'a final decision by the Saint Elizabeths doctors. If they say Pound will always be mentally incompetent, [he] may then move to quash the long-standing indictment.' 'His "friends and supporters", Mr. Rogers suggested, 'could then arrange with the hospital to have him moved to Italy.' Here was another surprising development, that Pound would after all be free to return to Italy.

Frost at once went back to Washington on the 4th to keep Rogers moving. Afterwards they would tell it as if their meeting were scripted for the movies. Frost: 'I've dropped in to see what your mood is in regard to Ezra Pound.' Rogers: 'Our mood is your mood, Mr Frost.' Frost: 'Well then, let's get him out right away.'

The Attorney General helpfully suggested that William Shaffroth, the official government 'expediter' in legal matters, might be able to recommend a lawyer for the defense. Shaffroth recommended Thurman Arnold, and immediately made an appointment by phone for Frost to see him.[5] Arnold's law firm let it be known next day, 5 April, that 'in the public interest, without a fee, following a request by Robert Frost', it had agreed 'to represent Mrs. Pound in Mr. Pound's behalf'. It has been assumed that this public statement was the first either of the Pounds knew about the arrangement. However, Dorothy Pound was called to 'Dr Overholser's office' on the 4th, and it is possible that he been kept informed and had put her in the picture. What is true is that she did not retain Arnold but agreed to the arrangement only after it had been fixed by Frost at the direction of the government. In any case, Pound felt able to write to Mary on the 5th, 'things look more hopeful than they have // Overholser optimistic. BUT hold in steam of the whistle for another month or so'. On the 7th Dorothy had a 'long talk with Thurman Arnold', who then issued this statement:

> We have been retained by Mrs. Ezra Pound to institute legal proceedings to secure Mr. Pound's release from St. Elizabeths and to dismiss the 13-year old indictment.
>
> We are informed that Mr. Pound's mental condition is such that he will never be able to stand trial, although he is not a danger to himself or society.
>
> Mrs. Pound has advised us that if Mr. Pound is released they will proceed to Italy where Mr. Pound has spent many years of his life.
>
> Dismissal of the indictment will not prevent re-indictment and trial of Mr. Pound for treason if warranted and if, at some later time, he should recover his mental competence. There is no statute limiting the time when a person may be indicted for treason....
>
> It is intended that formal legal papers on behalf of Mrs. Pound will be filed in a few days.

[5] Arnold presented himself as a 'dissenting' lawyer, but he had been an insider in Roosevelt's administration, serving as Assistant Attorney General in charge of the Anti-trust Division of the Department of Justice from 1938 to 1943. When Roosevelt relaxed the anti-trust laws in the interests of the war effort Arnold was moved out and made a judge in the Court of Appeals. In July 1945 he returned to private practice in Washington DC, co-founding a law firm with Abe Fortas who had also served in the Roosevelt administration.

That was speaking in two voices, one for Mrs Pound, and one for the Justice Department—and none, it might well be said, for Ezra Pound. It was only right therefore that Arnold should take no fee. He was, after all, acting 'in the public interest' as well as 'in Pound's behalf', and while there was a real coincidence of interest, there was also bound to be some conflict. There would be a need for compromise on both sides: the Justice Department would abandon its case, but would save face; and Pound would be released, but as a non-person in law he would be unable to clear his name.

There is nothing in the record to show that Arnold consulted with Pound himself at any stage in the ensuing proceedings. And Pound appears to have accepted that he had no part to play in them except as their interested but mute object. It was certainly on his mind. 'The standing mute included plea of NOT guilty', he recalled in a letter to Mary on 3 April; and on the 12th he observed that, with regard to his being released to return to Italy, 'a certain amount of optimism is justified'. And still, while others were deciding his fate, he was getting on with his life: 29 March had been 'First day one cd/ sit out in chairs till 3 p.m.' That day he wrote for his grandson Walter, soon to turn eleven, 'It is IGNORANCE that is the trouble. Not one in 100,000 knows that you do not HAVE TO issue all new money as interest-bearing DEBT.' Norman Holmes Pearson told Hilda Doolittle on 2 April that he had just seen Pound, 'a monument of sanity' amid the distrait and the lobotomized of St Elizabeths, and 'full of vigor and good humour'. Robert Hughes visited with a recorder quartet led by Forrest Read, and they played Gabrieli and other early music for Pound out on the lawn for half an hour. After that Forrest Read engaged Pound in an intense discussion of *Rock-Drill*. As the quartet were preparing to leave, Hughes mentioned Pound's having played the bassoon, and, as Hughes would recall, 'at the mention of music he sped off to his room and shortly returned with a large sheet of crude butcher paper upon which he had crayoned staff lines and notes and asked me to play it for him . . . It was a plain, simple, singable melody.' On 13 April Pound wrote to Dag Hammarskjöld, about the precision of Linnaeus' Latin—Hammarskjöld had sent him an essay he had written on the Swedish naturalist—and about George Crabbe's *The Borough*, Crabbe having mentioned Linnaeus. On Thursday 17th he 'got thru a lot of work', including typing up for Marcella's anthology his translation of the ancient Egyptian 'Conversations in Courtship' from his Egyptologist son-in-law's Italian version.

On 14 April Thurman Arnold filed his motion for the dismissal of the indictment. Preparing it had been an interesting challenge, as he reflected in his autobiography, because there was no clear legal argument for a dismissal. The problem was simply that while the Justice Department no longer wanted to keep Pound incarcerated, they didn't know how to let him go without coming under attack for freeing 'a notorious traitor and anti-Semite'. And yet the situation had become intolerable, both because it made the United States look bad in the eyes of the world, and because while he was kept in St Elizabeths undesirables, especially anti-Semites, would continue to flock around him. If it could have been shown that he was insane at the time of the offending broadcasts then, under the Durham Rule adopted by the Washington DC Court of Appeals at the urging of his law partner Abe Fortas in 1953, Pound could have been tried and acquitted on the ground that he could not be held responsible for what he had said. But Pound had refused that defence—presumably it was what he was refusing to sign up to in 1953 when Laughlin tried to have Mary persuade him. In any case, Arnold conceded in his retrospect, no one could reliably testify about his mental condition at the time of the broadcasts. All he could do then was to move for a dismissal on the ground of the absurdity of the situation. There was no risk in that since he knew that while the Justice Department would not itself move it was not going to oppose his motion.

UNITED STATES DISTRICT COURT
FOR THE DISTRICT OF COLUMBIA

UNITED STATES OF AMERICA
v.
EZRA POUND, Defendant

Criminal No. 76028

MOTION TO DISMISS INDICTMENT

Comes now Ezra Pound, defendant, through his committee, Mrs. Dorothy Shakespear Pound, and moves that the indictment in the above-entitled proceeding be dismissed.

And on the grounds of the said motion, he respectfully represents:

1. [*a paragraph summarising the initial proceedings to February 13, 1946*]
2. The defendant has remained in confinement at Saint Elizabeths Hospital since that time, where he has been the subject of constant and intense psychiatric tests, examinations, observation and study. As a result thereof, it is the opinion and conclusion of officials at Saint Elizabeths Hospital that defendant remains mentally unfit to advise properly with counsel or to participate intelligently and reasonably in his own defense and that he is insane and mentally unfit for trial, or to comprehend the nature of the charges against him.

3. Furthermore, it is the opinion and conclusion of these same officials that defendant's condition is permanent and incurable, that it cannot and will not respond to treatment and that trial on the charges against him will be forever impossible because of insanity.
4. Defendant is 72 years old. If the indictment against him is not dismissed he will die in Saint Elizabeths Hospital... There can be no benefit to the United States in maintaining him indefinitely in custody as a public charge because that custody cannot contribute to his recovery and defendant's release would not prejudice the interests of the United States. The inevitable effect of failure to dismiss the indictment will be life imprisonment on account of alleged acts and events which can never be put to proof.
5. The primary alleged acts and events on which the indictment is based occurred prior to July 25, 1943. In the ensuing fifteen years memories have faded and direct evidence by the constitutionally-established minimum of two witnesses to each of the various alleged acts and events have inevitably dissipated. In all probability, therefore, the United States lacks sufficient evidence to warrant a prosecution at this time.
6. Suitable arrangements for defendant's custody and care are otherwise available. In the event that the indictment is dismissed, Mrs. Dorothy Shakepear Pound, committee, proposes to apply for delivery of the defendant from further confinement at Saint Elizabeths Hospital to her restraint and care with bond under such terms and conditions as will be appropriate to the public good and the best interests and peace of mind of the defendant in the remaining years of his life.
7. On the issues of fact thus presented, defendant respectfully requests a hearing.

WHEREFORE, Ezra Pound, defendant, by his committee, Mrs. Dorothy Shakespear Pound, respectfully moves that the indictment be dismissed.

Respectfully submitted,

THURMAN ARNOLD
WILLIAM D. ROGERS
ARNOLD, FORTAS & PORTER

That the name of Thurman Arnold's associate differed only by an initial from that of William P. Rogers, the Attorney General, might have amused, since the Justice Department had had a firm if hidden hand in drawing up the motion. And it was as well that some of these 'issues of fact' would go unchallenged. If Pound had indeed 'been the subject of constant and intense psychiatric tests, examination' etc., and of 'treatment' in St Elizabeths, it is surprising that there is no record of it in the St Elizabeths archive. Then there is the rather too ready shift from defendant's being 'mentally unfit for trial' to a condition of unqualified and incurable 'insanity', with its implications for the 'suitable arrangements for defendant's custody and care'. However, that was all window-dressing. The nub of the matter was that there was no possibility of a successful prosecution, and that it was not in the interest of the United States to continue to keep Pound in St Elizabeths.

Attached to the motion was 'AFFIDAVIT OF DR. WINFRED OVERHOLSER SWORN TO APRIL 14, 1958, IN SUPPORT OF MOTION TO DISMISS INDICTMENT'. This confirmed in detail paragraphs 1 to 4 and 6 of the motion, and then strongly affirmed this new opinion:

> Finally, if called to testify on a hearing, I will testify and state under oath that in my opinion, from examination of Ezra Pound made in 1945, within two to three years of the crimes charged in the indictment, there is a strong probability that the commission of the crime charged was the result of insanity, and I would therefore seriously doubt that prosecution could show criminal responsibility even if it were hypothetically assumed that Ezra Pound could regain sufficient sanity to be tried.

The Durham Rule was rescinded in 1972 precisely because it was found to be vulnerable to that kind of unverifiable 'expert opinion'. But no matter, whatever Overholser opined was going to pass unchallenged.

Also attached to the motion was a supporting 'MEMORANDUM' citing precedents, and, secondly, recognizing that 'The motion presents an appeal to the discretion of the Court' and therefore asking leave

> to lodge the attached statement of Robert Frost, who, along with many other poets and writers of distinction, has sought the release of Ezra Pound for the last several years. Although his statement does not speak to the legal issues raised, it is directly relevant to the serious considerations bearing upon this Court's exercise of its discretion.

There followed 'STATEMENT OF ROBERT FROST'—

> I am here to register my admiration for a government that can rouse in conscience to a case like this. Relief seems in sight for many of us besides the Ezra Pound in question and his faithful wife. He has countless admirers the world over who will rejoice in the news that he has hopes of freedom. . . . And I feel authorized to speak very specially for my friends, Archibald MacLeish, Ernest Hemingway and T. S. Eliot. None of us can bear the disgrace of our letting Ezra Pound come to his end where he is. It would leave too woeful a story in American literature. He went very wrongheaded in his egotism, but he insists it was from patriotism—love of America. He has never admitted that he went over to the enemy any more than the writers at home who have despaired of the Republic. I hate such nonsense and can only listen to it as evidence of mental disorder. But mental disorder is what we are considering. I rest the case on Dr. Overholser's pronouncement that Ezra

Pound is not too dangerous to go free in his wife's care, and too insane ever to be tried—a very nice distinction.

Mr. Thurman Arnold admirably put this problem of a sick man being held too long in prison to see if he won't get well enough to be tried for a prison offence. There is probably legal precedent to help toward a solution of the problem. But I should think it would have to be reached more by magnanimity than by logic and it is chiefly on magnanimity I am counting. I can see how the Department of Justice would hesitate from fear of looking more just to a great poet than it would to a mere nobody. The bigger the Department the longer it might have to take thinking things through.

The final two sentences were a way of excusing, or obliquely reproaching, the Department of Justice for having had to be dragged mulishly to this conclusion. The rest, leaving aside the dash of personal animosity towards Pound, was a decent attempt to voice a troubled American conscience. And the appeal to magnanimity was exactly what was required to break out of the legal impasse.

Arnold arranged for the motion to be heard on Friday the 18th to ensure that the presiding judge would once again be Bolitha J. Laws. The afternoon before, Marcella Spann would recall, Pound had been sitting with her in her car outside Chestnut Ward when they heard from a nearby car radio *Che sarà, sarà* | *Whatever will be, will be*, 'and Pound listened with quiet pleasure'. The morning of the 18th, 'Furniss fetched OP and DP to Arnold's'—Omar had been in Washington since the 7th, had been to see Arnold on the 14th, and had had long talks with Dorothy. She would sit with Arnold at the Counsels' table. The hearing was at 10.30, and Pound was seated at the back of the courtroom, casually dressed, according to the *New York Times* report, 'in a shabby blue jacket, a tan sport shirt with the tails not tucked in and blue slacks. His pockets were full of folded envelopes and other scraps of paper.' The hearing was soon over. Arnold, who said 'he represented not only Mrs Pound but also "the world community of poets and writers"', spoke briefly, chiefly about the medical findings. For the Justice Department United States Attorney Oliver Gasch told Judge Laws 'that it would be "virtually impossible" to produce evidence of Mr. Pound's sanity during the war years in Italy at so late a date', and that 'the Government thought the motion was "in the interest of justice and should be granted"'. The judge asked a few questions, then issued his '**ORDER DISMISSING INDICTMENT**'—

This cause came on for hearing on defendant's motion to dismiss the indictment and upon consideration of the affidavit of Dr. Winfrid Overholser, the Superintendent of St. Elizabeths Hospital, and it appearing to the Court that the defendant is presently incompetent to stand trial and that there is no likelihood that this condition will in the foreseeable future improve, and it further appearing to the Court that there is available to the defense psychiatric testimony to the effect that there is a strong probability that the commission of the crimes charged was the result of insanity, and it appearing that the Government is not in a position to challenge this medical testimony, and it further appearing that the Government consents to the dismissal of this indictment, it is by the Court this 18th day of April, 1958, ORDERED that the indictment be and the same is hereby dismissed.

Bolitha J. Laws
CHIEF JUDGE

To this the Justice Department Attorney added, 'I consent.'

The decisive voice for Judge Laws, at the end as it had been at the start, was that of the psychiatrist with his legally unverifiable and dubiously scientific opinions. Dr Overholser had been put in the position to determine Pound's fate when his defence chose not to defend him. The indictment had been in order, but it had needed to be challenged, and if correctly challenged should have failed. Whether through a defective grasp of the law of treason, or a lack of trust in the due process of the law, and certainly through a fear of the power of hostile opinion, and a fear also of being contaminated by Pound's perceived guilt, or by his anti-Semitism, Cornell's and Laughlin's strategy 'saved' Pound by denying him justice, and by committing him to a sentence in St Elizabeths longer than he would have served if convicted, and, with that, to a life-sentence as a legally insane non-person. Cornell's 'bunk', taken up by the psychiatrists, had stymied justice; and the operations of justice in Pound's case had become altogether subject to prejudice and arbitrary whim. The tragic farce was brought to an end only because MacLeish and Frost accepted that justice was not to be had, and that the only way out was to accept that Pound's was now a medical case requiring a compassionate judgment.

When Judge Laws had delivered that judgment, Mrs Pound, according to the report next day in the *New York Times*, walked to the back of the Court 'and gave her husband a kiss'. The *Manchester Guardian* was more dramatic: 'Mr. Pound . . . showed no emotion as the case began; then he seemed to brood intently; and finally he twinkled with happiness and merriment as his wife, calling him "beloved", rushed to kiss him, and a small company of friends and admirers clustered round.' He then went out onto the Court steps. He would say nothing to the posse of reporters, 'except a firm "yes" when asked if he wanted to return to Italy'. He agreed to pose for the photographers, after draping over his shoulders 'a long yellow scarf with Oriental characters on it'. In the photo he is pointing to one of the two Chinese ideograms woven into the knitted scarf in black wool, *hsin*^{4} which he would translate as 'a man of his word'. William McNaughton, who knew the scarf well, saw this as an assertion 'that he had never "broken the faith"—had never fled from his "post" in the *bellum perenne* and had never acknowledged that his broadcasts were treasonable—or even hostile—to the U.S. Constitution'. The other ideogram is *hsin*^{1}, the sign of renewal.

14 : Clearing Out

The New York Times reported on Saturday 19 April that the treason charges had been dismissed, 'opening the way for the 72-year-old poet's return to Italy'.

> The poet's wife, Mrs. Dorothy Shakespear Pound, who will be his legal guardian, indicated she would move for his release [from St Elizabeths] next week. In the meanwhile he is under no restraint, and in fact he went downtown this afternoon unattended by anyone from St. Elizabeth's.

A report in England's *Manchester Guardian* from their Washington correspondent added that 'Mr Pound will now apply for a passport,' and that it was expected that the Government would act with 'magnanimity in the last phase of this unfortunate case'. In fact Dorothy Pound was informed on the 21st by William D. Rogers of Arnold, Fortas and Porter that 'We are informed, off the record, that the State Department has stated that it sees no reason why passports should not be issued.' The certainty that he would not be allowed out of the United States had simply evaporated, along with all the stern suggestions of conditions to be attached to his release. He would remain in St Elizabeths, Dr Overholser had told the press after the hearing, but only 'until his family have made plans for him and until his affairs had been straightened out' there—'"He has a lot of papers and books to take care of in his room."'

Pound was driven back to St Elizabeths immediately after the hearing and at once began a high-spirited letter to Mary:—

> Yr. venbl parent is spring. Walt's grampaw and Patrizia's has had charges withdrawn/ I am to go down and git a ticket to leave the grounds of this insterooshun and reenter at pleasure? an you can start wangling re/ transport at reduced rates as soon after July first as the Christofero Colombo has a kennel or bridal suite disponible.

Overholser had said the institution could overlook 'the brown jacket with trade mark' which Pound wanted 'as souvenir and symbolic deer-hide'—an association with the Nha Khi religion which he did not attempt to explain.

After a break for lunch he got back to the typewriter. Two generals of the Marine Corps, one of them del Valle, and Col. Pomeroy, had been 'present at the liberation', and 'cert/ do not think I was betraying the best interests of the american people and constitution'. He implied that Horton's Congressman from Ohio had also been among those 'glad to git gramp out of quod'. Then there was the Borsolino, 'the GREAT original, 1939, 1945/ BORsolino', which he hoped would be on display in the press photos—

> The borsolino was at bottom of bottomest box in shattered gardaroba and a gawd send/ [Dr] Cuchard looked at linen cap/ purchased on tip from Newton the noblest of nubians/ AT mercato africosassone. Cuchard suggested that it needed a 'jaguar' to go with it—jaguar being some kind of red hot sports car. So I etc.

It would appear that Pound had started clearing out his room the previous day, before the hearing—'got two car loads of impedimenta in M's car and Furniss's. Room now contains only enough to fill it.' More of 'the archives of captivity' would go 'when M/ gets here at 3 approx.' 'Officially', he confided merrily to Mary, 'I am crazy as a coot, but not a peril to society or to myself.'

He was still officially in the care and custody of his wife. Her diary recorded that after the hearing she had 'Escaped with Eliz. W[inslow] to lunch & sat in garden | v. fine day', and after that it was 'back to St. Eliz'. She would be leaving Washington next morning for a 'much needed vacation and inspection of the Adams houses in Braintree', as Pound put it in his letter to Mary. Her diary would record, ' 9.45 a.m. to Boston with OP'—she would stay there with Omar and his wife until the 29th. She took with her, as she later informed A. V. Moore, 'THE pearl necklace' Ezra had asked her to leave to Mary, and gave it to Omar 'for his wife to wear'. Pound would be using her small basement apartment until she got back, and would then stay with Craig La Drière, 'apt. 511 | 2407 Fifteenth St | Washington N.W.'

The scattered objections to Pound's release had not coalesced into the public outcry some had feared. Rep. Emmanuel Celler of New York, Chair of the House Judiciary Committee, had spoken out in New York—Congress was in recess for Easter—declaring angrily that 'Many of our men lost their lives as a result of his exhortations,' and 'I don't care how long he has been in there, maybe we want to keep him in a little longer.' But an editorial in *The Nation* then observed, 'Bloodier war criminals have been freed; we have had ritual-killings enough for one generation. | It will be a triumph of democracy if we set Pound free.' And the *Wall Street Journal* editorialized that 'a little magnanimity would seem to be in order'. The London *Times* had noted Celler's outburst, calling it an attempt to stir up

'American public opinion into one of its periodic fits of emotional injustice', and had also appealed to a spirit of magnanimity. Echoing that, *The Manchester Guardian*, which had first reported Celler's 'angry rumblings', attributed Pound's release to 'a magnanimous spirit which has prevented arid legal technicalities from blocking Mr. Pound's road to freedom'.

The *New York Times*, along with the positive tone of its news report of the hearing, printed a feature which reads like a New Directions press release. Observing in passing that 'His literary followers today include many who disapprove heartily of his wartime espousal of fascism, and anti-Semitism', it concentrated on advertising his 'literary output [which] has poured forth steadily and his literary reputation [which] has flourished despite his confinement in St. Elizabeths Hospital in Washington'. His time there, one was to gather, had been well spent in literary activity, and had even had its idyllic aspect:

> In winter months at St. Elizabeths he has somehow managed to make himself oblivious to the disturbed patients who share his ward and to the continuously blaring television set. He has worked with the utmost concentration on composing new poetry, making new translations, and revising and editing previous writing. This time of year he works outdoors, in the shade of the beautiful trees at the hospital, which was formerly an arboretum.
>
> Mrs. Pound, who lives near by, goes daily to his ward. Together they carry the two folding aluminium chairs he keeps under his bed to the lawn. There she helps him with correspondence and proof reading, and they share the lunch she brought in a paper bag. She is the former Dorothy Shakespear, a blue-eyed, tweedy Englishwoman.
>
> They were married in 1914 and have one son, Omar, who teaches at Roxbury Latin School in Boston.

A *Times* feature writer might have had a hand in that, but the idea of promoting a sentimental, pastel-toned, image of the poet at the moment of his release is likely to have been his publisher's.

The morning after the hearing Pound was awake at '5.17', listening to chattering birds and scribbling a note to Marcella about feeling defeated by 'the amount of clutter to be exclutterated', and reckoning 'he be'r try a li'l food & shut-eye'. At 6.10, after 'Nestea...plus rye and jam', he typed, 'Can't do it all in 24 hours./...guess I b'er slow down.' Harry Meacham drove up from Richmond in Virginia that day to make himself useful, and moved 'boxes, bags, manuscripts, books and other memorabilia' to Dorothy Pound's apartment, 3514 Brothers Place, SE. He wanted then to take him out to one of Washington's best restaurants, but Pound insisted on a nearby Chinese restaurant, where, Meacham recalled, he 'consumed his order of chicken chow mein and mine also, and he talked, talked, talked'.

Pound slept at Brothers Place that night, and began to realize what he had been missing while he was inside, making him feel a Rip van Winkle. That was how he referred to himself in a note to Dorothy that Sunday morning, and again when writing to Mary later in the week. When he first used the gas, he told Mary, 'it dawned on me that I hadn't had anything HOT, for 13 years'—'I sure am going to take to cookin' again,' he resolved. And he loved the 'gadgetts . . . all done with the twist of a wrist'. And the 'drive in, with loud speaker to get an orange juice from gas pump or something or other/ and the traffic . . . jell'Ezuss, had no idea what Marcella had been doing with two hours of it daily'. And back to food, he was being dined and wined, a 'crescendo of brute and sensuous pleasures'—'HongKONG, home food, even hot toast just out of toaster is an event'. He could be picky: lunch at Cathy's, Dr Birch, had been 'po'k chaups', though 'a banana salad wd/ have been far superior . . . AN she had BANanas.' But he simply revelled in a dinner of 'shrimp cocktail, Chateaubriand, candle on table (with electric lighting) and three kinds of wine with proper regard to the harmonies'. And it was ' indubitably pleasant to have plenty of hot water bawth to SOAK in, instead of shower'.

Friends were taking care of him, especially Giovannini and La Drière, and Aida Mastrangelo, also of the Catholic University, a professor of Italian with connections in Italy's Embassy in Washington. But the personal support that mattered most to him was Marcella's. He needed to be in contact with her all the time, writing a running commentary of his days to her when she was not with him. He wrote of feeling solitary sitting in a garden with the sun shining on the flowers of a forsythia—not gold, he discriminated to be precise for her, but yellow, chrome-yellow, perhaps. 'BUTT it is nice to have something to look forward to,' was the next thought, 'an the sooner she gits here the quicker.' 'Giardino | purrnounce jardinoh', he prompted, preparing her for being with him in Italy. When he called her 'M'Amour, ma vie' he was in earnest. It was not only that she was 'very lovely', or that she could be 'VURRY deetermined'; it was more profoundly that she was in tune with his own inner imperative and expected him to be composing cantos. 'He might try to versify', he scribbled on the first Monday after the Court hearing, as if needing to justify himself to her, 'but iz such a lot/ mebbe be'r try a spot of manicurin' before tryin to catch the shade of a butterfly—but them lepidops ain' far off // if he don't git round to it by time he ought to'. She brought out the poet in him, and that was the really vital bond. Those butterflies, named out of precise Linnaeus, would be caught into the cantos under her aegis.

As for Sheri Martinelli, she had been 'booted outta the nest' by Pound, made to break her vow 'not to leave the Maestro until he was freed'. 'The male can't just go about like that, ditching a spirit love,' she raged to Hilda Doolittle, who, remembering herself as 'Dryad', sympathized with 'poor Undine'. Early that summer Sheri married Gilbert Lee, a fringe member of the St Elizabeths circle, and they went down to Mexico where, at Pound's instigation, there was an art scholarship waiting for her. Before long that fell through and thereafter she made a nest for herself in San Francisco and on the West Coast. In her later years, apparently seeing herself as Pound's spirit widow, she would dress all in black and wear a black veil. With Pound's release the circle of disciples was altogether broken up, all 'flying off on a personal tangent when cut off from the unifying influence of Il Maestro'—that was how Lee Lady expressed it to Noel Stock—'Sheri in San Fran, Nora in New York, Chatel in real estate, Kasper in jail, McN setting up to be a lit-critic'. The only one still around in Washington, apart from Marcella, seems to have been Horton. He would make himself useful as a driver with a car.

Pound having become news, was trying to keep out of the news. His friends were being pestered by the press, he told Mary on the Thursday after the indictment was dismissed, and there had been 'three calls during ten minutes I was [in] SLIZ office on Monday'. Canadian Broadcasting Corporation television was offering $1,000 for a sympathetic interview, but Pound suggested to Dorothy that she reply, 'Don't you think my husband has made enough use of foreign broadcasting stations for one lifetime, and his family's comfort?' He instructed Mary in what she should know 'OFFICIALLY'—

Officially I am NOT discharged from orspital. I have city parole or the equivalent. I am in charge of D.P. / who is OUT of town (de facto, in Boston) and I can only be reached through HER. I don't know whether you have seen the present domiciles, messuages etc. of the EEElight. <Craig, G.G.>

I am having one gee/lorious time, but don't headlight or headline THAT.

Officially I am NOT yet discharged.

And the astute Overholser is stalling the press, who are howling to know the EZact date of final etc/

the astute Ov/ suggested that I use DIFFERENT gates when entering and leaving the grounds of our REEmarkable insterooshun, and I am strictly following Donelli's ADvice, re following suggestions of that nature.

Lengthwise in the margin of that letter he typed,

N.B. You don't know WHEN I am to be discharged. You don't know WHEN it will be convenient for me to sail. You do know that I have never seen the old South, and am headed for Virginia.

Meacham was taking him to meet the cream of Richmond's literary society on the 30th.

On the 29th he was able to see Representative Burdick who had been ill in hospital, to thank him for his support. Burdick's attitude to the case was summed up in his saying for the benefit of a reporter who was present, 'I'm against people being railroaded into asylums. There's no question the fellow was off, but that was no reason to lock him up without letting him talk.' And Pound talked to him and at him, in spite of his resolution to be circumspect, holding forth for an hour about the things Burdick might not know—about Roosevelt: 'the mildest judgment is that he was a fool'—about why it had been his duty to use the Italian microphone—that he 'never told the troops not to fight'—that what he was interested in was the American Constitution. 'I'm talking too much', he said at one point, 'I've had the plug in for 12 years.' He also mused, 'I ought to keep quiet for a couple of weeks.' As he left, a reporter asked him for a word about Robert Frost, who was taking all the credit for his release, and the quote next day was, 'He ain't been in much of a hurry.' When MacLeish took exception to that remark, Pound wrote back, 'Alzo I did speak well of Frost . . . I said Frost paid his debt when he finished writing "North of Boston".'

Dorothy returned from Boston on the 29th and was met by Pound and Marcella, who drove them to 3514 Brothers Place where Ezra cooked for her. Next morning Meacham picked Pound up from there, and seeing that 'the poet was mentally and physically exhausted . . . put him in the back seat where he reclined during the two-and-a-half-hour drive'. In Richmond a select group of literary people were gathered to greet Pound in the 'oddly chaste and dulcet surroundings' of the Rotunda Club which took up one side of the old and elegant Jefferson hotel. Present were Mrs James Branch Cabell, who brought a courteous apology from her husband who was ill; James J. Kilpatrick, editor of the *Richmond News-Leader*; the editor of the *Virginia Quarterly Review* where canto 99 was about to appear; and Meacham's successor as President of the Poetry Society of Virginia. Kilpatrick wrote a brilliantly impressionistic account of Pound's conversation for *The National Review*, under the sub-heading, 'The poet who spent twelve years in "St. Liz" proves to be eccentric, often obscure, sane, and sometimes acutely wise'. Pound, he wrote,

> shakes hands with the hard grip and strong forearm of a man who has played much tennis, and he dominates a room as if his chair were down-stage centre. He wore an open-necked shirt of a particularly god-awful magenta, tails out, and a pair of outsized slacks with the cuffs rolled up. A black coat, flung clockwise over his shoulders completed the costume. If the description sounds theatrical, it is

intended to suggest that there is in Pound a good deal of the actor, a good deal, indeed, of the ham. His bearded face, mobile, is the bust of some morning-after Bacchus; but it is seldom in repose. He sits on the lower part of his spine, head supported by the backrest of the chair, eyes closed; his restless hands are forever searching for glasses, or plucking pencil and notebook from a breast pocket, or shaping ideas in the air. Now and again, he bolts from his chair like some Poseidon from the deep, and his good eye—his right eye—is suddenly shrewd and alive.

Kilpatrick had found it impossible to keep up with the torrent of Pound's talk and could only pick out one thing and another, 'much as one plucks a recognisable rooftop from a flood'—

the causes of war, the suppression of historic truth (of one historian, banished to obscurity by the educationists, Pound had an epitaph: 'Poor Fellow, he committed accuracy'), the corruption of the Federal Reserve Board, the usury rates of Byzantium, the reasons why he had not translated a particular Chinese writer, the enduring characteristics of the Manchu Dynasty, the old days in London with Ford Madox Ford. It was wonderful to eat something hot; he had forgotten what it meant for food to be hot. At Rapallo there are surf rafts, and one floats on a blue sea. Had he mentioned that Hemingway had once sent him a shark's jaw, the grave of the unknown sailor?

Then, after a pause, 'I don't have a one-track mind.' Asked about the Cantos, however, he entered upon 'an extended comparative analysis of *La Divina Commedia*', and here he spoke 'with easy sureness and a confident grasp of the complexities of both his work and Dante's'. And he could be 'terse and to the point'. Asked what advice he had for young writers, he said simply, 'Get a good dictionary and learn the meaning of words,' to which he added, 'Read Linnaeus. Not for botany. Read him because he never used an inexact word.' In the end Kilpatrick recalled from his childhood 'a multifaceted chandelier, formed of a hundred tiny mirrors, which revolved slowly in the glow of colored spotlights', and thought, 'Pound's mind spins and refracts in the same way.' But Pound was 'surely no lunatic': 'Obscure, yes; eccentric, yes; full of apparent confusion, yes. But crazy, no.'

Pound received his formal discharge from St Elizabeths on 7 May. Dr Cushard's 'Recommendation for Discharge' on 6 May stated that since 18 April, when the charge of treason was dismissed, he 'has remained on the hospital rolls'

because he asked that he be permitted to do so in order that he could have some necessary dental work completed and to have an eye examination: refraction and prescription for glasses. The refraction was done this morning. He has spent the majority of his time on visit status in the city since his charge was dropped but has

been to the hospital frequently to pick up his mail and to confer with me regarding his case. He, also, had an interview with Doctor Overholser a few days ago. Since everything is now cleared up, it is recommended that he be discharged from the hospital while on visit.
DIAGNOSIS: 24.2 PSYCHOTIC DISORDER, UNDIFFERENTIATED
CONDITION ON DISCHARGE: UNIMPROVED

The 'Report of Discharge or Death' declared that 'In physician's opinion patient is medically competent to receive funds,' and directed that 'patient's remaining funds and property are to be sent to 3514 Brothers Place, S.E., Washington, D.C.' 'Has committee' was written in under 'Remarks'. Dr Overholser sent a note to the Passport Division of the State Department stating, 'In my opinion he is entirely safe to travel here and abroad in the company of his wife, Mrs Dorothy Shakespear Pound.'

The Committee's audited return for the year declared that the Patient owned

Folding chairs
Independent Radio
Hamilton pocket watch
Corona portable typewriter
Olympia portable typewriter

in addition to $19,400 in bonds and deposits. Monthly payments recorded: $50 to Omar Shakespear Pound; $20 to the Patient for personal expenditures.

In his mind Pound was already arranging how things would be in Mary's castle. 'Marcella at TOP of tower where she won't be disturbed, and my work room on floor just under,' he directed on 30 April, 'D. in lower apt. with the Gaudiers.' In mid-May he wrote to Mary, 'Shall stop one night in Verona, to break trip and show that city to my life-saver and body-guard.' On the 21st he sent 'fotos of me and my body guard, one of the best shots in Texas'. Apparently Mary hinted some unease since Pound wrote in June, 'Do credit her with having conserved the remnants of your ancestral line during the ult. eggzausting seasons.'

He was being assured of a welcome in Italy. The London *Times* Rome Correspondent reported on 14 May that Ezra Pound 'was today offered "asylum for life" by the Italian Government' at the request of his daughter. On 17 May William D. Rogers informed Dorothy, in a variant translation, that the Italian Embassy had received word from the Italian Government 'that the Government has no official objections whatsoever to Ezra Pound's re-entry into Italy'. About the same time Pound let Mary know that Count Cini was 'offering shelter on Isola S. Giorgio'—that was his Venetian *palazzo*. But it was Mary's Brunnenburg, also known as Castel Fontana, that his mind was set towards.

In the interim 'the Spanntholgy [was] takin most of our time and energy', or he was sifting through the mass of correspondence that had cluttered his room in St Elizabeths and trying to get it sorted into files. On 17 May he was driven down to Virginia Beach where Furniss had a place, and stopped off briefly in Richmond for Meacham to take him to the offices of the *News-Leader* where Kilpatrick granted him accreditation as its 'foreign correspondent'. That was so that he could get an Italian journalist's *tessera* with its 70 per cent discount on travel in Italy. But Meacham was surprised when Pound asked for Marcella to be accredited as well—he had had no idea that she would be going with him. Pound also asked if Meacham could help Marcella to sell her car. Later Meacham was told of Guy Davenport's having observed Pound at Virginia Beach, 'wrapped in blankets, by a fire, gazing long, returned Odysseus, at the loudsounding sea'. Back in Washington on the 24th he dashed off a hurried note to Cookson, the first since his release, asking if it was Cookson had sent him 'a big foto of 2 pages of Homer, and if so, is it Ogilby's or who's?' 'No time for chronicle', he wrote, 'alarUMS, scursions, whoops, reactions from banderlog etc/ . . . stuffed with various foods by rival schools of gastronomy. | Trying to get anthology ms/ out of domicile by June the onc/t.'

Their passports came through on 27 May—they would be sailing from New York on the *Cristofero Colombo* on 1 July, expecting to be in Genoa on the 10th or 11th. 'I think I shall have to continue as committee', Dorothy wrote to A. V. Moore, 'EP's release being that he is "insane" but not dangerous.' Pound had just told Mary that it made no difference, so far as signing cheques went, that he was 'not yet out of "committee" control'. But on the 29th it occurred to him that things might be different in Italy, 'as my status still entangled'—

> The voice of the local law seems to be that I can deposit and run an account in woptaly, regardless of whether I am officially a lunatic in the U.S., rather than having a committee account, which probably no wop bank would understand.

'My passport don't say I am "nutts",' he noted, 'That seems to be reserved for the internal workings of the bugocracy.'

At the start of June Meacham took Ezra and Dorothy to visit some of the historic Old South. On the way down they visited James Madison's old law office in Fredericksburg. They were found rooms at the Inn in Williamsburg, in spite of its being the height of the season and especially busy because Virginia was celebrating the 350th anniversary of the first permanent English settlement at nearby Jamestown. They went there, and toured the Governor's Palace and other historic buildings in Williamsburg, and were granted a brief visit on account of Dorothy's connection to the Tucker family to the privately owned George Tucker House. They dined at the Kings Arms Tavern, with the Dean of the College of William and Mary and another professor. Pound had told Meacham that he was interested in meeting the Dean and professors only if they were disgusted 'with the present state of degradation in their sources of income', and was bored and bothered by the polite dinner-table chit-chat. He seemed to Meacham to be anxious to get back to Washington. And again it struck Meacham that Pound was utterly exhausted, and a line from one of the *Pisan Cantos* came into his mind, 'There is fatigue deep as the grave.'

In mid-June Laughlin came down from New York to Washington with the two young women who had founded Caedmon Records. They had first visited Pound on Labor Day 1952, and had recorded him reading in Provençal on the lawn of St Elizabeths, and, they later wrote, 'as he sang of birds, the birds perched overhead and sang too', while 'in the background inmates hooted'. He had made them promise not to release the recording while he was confined—'"Bird in cage does not sing," he said, many times'. Now he was out he went with them to a studio and did 'two hours tape recording for Jas/'—in fact there were recording sessions on three days, and he read enough cantos and shorter poems to fill two long-playing discs. The royalties, he stipulated, were to go to Marcella.

'8 trunks packed and mostly padlocked,' he told Mary on the 22nd, '13 years impedimenta.'

Hemingway had been trying to discover Pound's temporary address in Washington and was given one by MacLeish at last on 26 June. He wrote that day to send him a cheque for the $1,500 'for expenses for you to Italy' that he had guaranteed to the Attorney General in June 1957. 'For Christ sake cash the check,' he urged. Beyond the money there was a depth of enduring friendship in the letter—'great happiness' at Pound's being sprung, and this conclusion:

> Please count on me for anything that I can do ever. I am so ashamed of how you were kept in such a way and so proud of how entire and fine you looked in the pictures we saw the day you left. Hope you have a good trip and everything goes well. My love to Dorothy.
>
> Your friend,
> Hem

Pound did not cash the cheque, but, as he later told Hemingway, had it 'sunk in plexiglass as a token of your magnanimous glory'. He had thought to use it as a paperweight, but realized it was 'too damn valuable as a souvenir to leave on the table'.

On Friday the 27th the Pounds and Marcella left Washington in Dave Horton's car to make a three-stage progress to New York. That night they were guests of Carl Gatter and his mother, the occupants of Pound's childhood home in Wyncote, Philadelphia, 166 Fernbrook Avenue. Pound revisited remembered things and places, a crack in the stained glass window on the landing which he'd made practising tennis, trees in the back yard, Calvary Presbyterian Church. Next morning, Gatter noted, 'Pound appeared transformed. He forgot about the need to rest his head and sat on a regular diningroom chair.' After lunch they all went on to Hopewell, New Jersey, where they were the guests of Alan C. Collins, president of the Curtis Brown literary agency, in his summer residence—'a swank swimming-pool-tennis-court old house', according to Harry Meacham. Collins had been taught by Homer Pound in Sunday School; and his father-in-law, who was present, was Eugene C. Pomeroy, vice-president of the Defenders of the American Constitution. On Saturday night they talked, or Pound talked, and on Sunday he played tennis and swam in the pool.

The party then drove up to Rutherford, New Jersey, to spend Pound's last night with William Carlos Williams. Williams had written, 'Take care of yourself in Italy where I understand you are going, don't ever expect to see you again . . . if you have time plan to spend at least a night with us.' 'Be glad to see you,' he had signed off, but the visit seems not to have been a glad occasion, at least for Williams and Floss, his wife. In their eyes Pound was wrapped up in the adulation of his entourage, and behaving with his usual insufferable assumption of superiority towards Williams. Laughlin had arranged for Richard Avedon to go out to Rutherford to photograph Pound, and Avedon had the two old friends pose together. Williams, who had suffered a series of strokes, is seated and looking strained; Pound stands to the side and half behind Williams with his hands on his shoulders, his chest bare, a crumpled shirt loose over his shoulders, and his eyes shadowed but intent on the camera. The photograph can be read as an iconic image of the two great American poets taken at a moment charged with poignant personal and cultural history. But to Floss it showed 'Pound hovering—still—over his friend'. Rather than tapping into their deep affection for each other the meeting seems to have brought on only the old clashing of intransigent personalities. Mariani, Williams's biographer, records that after the party had left for New York and the boat on the Monday morning Williams wrote to Cid Corman that Pound, a 'tortured soul', was still, after all the years of his confinement which would have broken a lesser man, 'a fury of energy'.

Horton drove the Pounds and Marcella directly from Rutherford to the West Side pier from which the *Cristofero Colombo* was to sail late that afternoon. It was, Michael Reck remembered, 'a broiling hot June day'. The few friends who came to see them off found them in cabin 128, the larger of their two cabins, tucked away in a corner of first class. An unexplained man stood in the corridor as if keeping watch. Omar Pound opened the door, on guard to keep out the press who kept coming for photographs and interviews. Norman Holmes Pearson reported to HD that when he arrived about 2.30, 'on the bunk lay Ezra, stripped to the waist, his torso rather proudly sunburned. At his knees on the bunk sat Marcella shoeless. On the other side of the cabin was Dorothy, smiling and looking very well.' Pound lectured him for half an hour 'on college entrance examinations and the program [he] must follow to improve them'. He also spoke of the Spannthology and what Pearson should do with it. The only other visitors mentioned, apart from Reck, were the Italian cultural attaché in New York and his wife, and Robert MacGregor representing New Directions. Reck asked Pound how it felt, and Pound replied, 'Well, there is a certain euphoria.'

PART FIVE : 1958–1972

15 : A Final Testament, 1958–9

A photograph dated 12 July 1958 preserves Pound's joyful arrival at Brunnenburg, his daughter's castle looking out over the broad Adige valley from Dorf Tirol above Merano. The poet, a smiling patriarch, has a hand lightly over the shoulder of his 11-year-old grandson, Walter, with the boy holding the hand, half-smiling, uncertain, perhaps a little proud. On the other side is his son-in-law, Prince Boris de Rachewiltz the Egyptologist, smiling warmly. His hand rests lightly on the head of his 8-year-old daughter Patrizia, whose head is turned to look up wonderingly at her grandfather. Over her husband's shoulder Mary de Rachewiltz is walking with a preoccupied air; and behind Pound one glimpses on one side Dorothy, and on the other Marcella behind dark glasses. The four figures in the foreground compose a family group connected by smiles and by Patrizia's glance; but the three women in the background are apart, each in their separate space. The joy of the moment, one finds, is projected more by Pound's stance and expression than by anything else.

It had become the custom for the people of Dorf Tirol to celebrate Mary's birthday on 9 July with illuminations and fireworks, and dancing to the music of zither and guitar—they were pleased to have a princess again in the old castle. That year the celebration was held over to the 13th and made a welcoming party for Il Poeta. It was a 'Breughelesque feast' with flowers and torches and the village band with a big drum, and Pound led off the dancing, finding the rhythm of the Tyrolean music irresistible.

His 'volcanic energy pervaded the house', Mary would recall. He wanted to catch up with 'everything that had happened since the end of the war, and back through millennia', and he would spend mornings in solid conversation with Boris, about the findings of archeology in Italy or in Egypt. He went down into Merano to buy chairs, and for the races—he had been made a life-member of the Racing Club. He began drafting new cantos. He climbed most of the way up the very steep local mountain, the 7,000 feet high Mut, and talked of placing a Greek-style temple on it. At their bedtime he read Uncle Remus stories of Brer Rabbit to the children, doing the voices with immense enjoyment. He read his own poetry for the adults after dinner. And after everyone else had retired to their rooms, as if it were his turn to fill in the gap, he would sit up with Mary and talk to her for hours, about himself and about the years at St Elizabeths.

'*Sono, naturalmente, felice d'essere tornato fra i miei*,' he began a note to go with her translation of canto 98, which was about to appear in *L'Illustrazione Italiana*, 'Naturally I am glad to be back among my own.' And Dorothy wrote to Omar, 'We seem to be shaking-down into a familial clan; they treat me with due respect!' 'Yet something went wrong,' Mary would write, 'The house no longer contained a family. We were turning into entities that should not have broken bread together.'

There was the problem of Marcella, who must have found herself besieged by others' passions whatever her own might have been. Mary had looked forward to recovering her father and taking her place as his daughter, but found that she had been displaced by this 'secretary and bodyguard'. Things would reach the point where she could hardly bring herself to speak to the young woman from Texas. And Dorothy, who had regarded Marcella as a useful adjunct, was coming to see her as a threat to her own position. 'What does it matter unless we all go to Europe,' she had said when Pound was in love with Sheri Martinelli, but now they were in Europe and Pound was 'still crazy about Marcella'. What if he should contrive to marry her? Mary was another problem, useful as a housekeeper, but a threat to Dorothy's intention that her Omar should be the beneficiary and inheritor of Pound's estate. Her way of dealing with this coil of problems would be to cling on to her controlling position as the 'Committee' into whose custody had been committed Pound's person and property.

A. V. Moore, Dorothy's legal adviser in London, wrote at the end of July to Robert Furniss who was handling the Committee's affairs in the United States, to ask, 'will the Committee eventually be quashed', since Italy, as he assumed, had admitted Pound as a sane person. And further, 'does the existing legal mental condition prevent his making a Will?' Furniss replied that before Pound left he had discussed very briefly with him the possibility of asking the Court to discharge the Committee, but he had had many other things on his mind and the matter had seemed not urgent. It was his own view that, because the Committee had been appointed on the basis of Pound's being found incompetent to assist in his own defence, once the charges were dropped there was no longer any basis for the Committee, and the District of Columbia Court had ceased to have any jurisdiction over him. If it were to be maintained that a Committee was still required, it would have to be on the different ground that he was 'either dangerous or wasting his estate'. Someone would have to make that complaint to the

Court, and Pound would have to be actually within the Court's jurisdiction—which he would not be, being in Italy. 'Though I believe we have a good possibility of having the Committee discharged,' Furniss concluded, 'I have not taken any steps in that direction because they have not asked me to.' On the matter of 'Mr. Pound's testamentary capacity', he thought there could be no definite answer, but he knew 'of no law in which a court has held that the presence of a Committee under these circumstances amounts to a presumption that the defendant is incapable of disposing of his property'. So, simply 'as a practical matter, Ezra Pound might as well make a Will if he so desires. In order for it to cause difficulty there would have to be someone who wants to set it aside which in all likelihood would not occur.' That last was a very proper assumption, but not well founded. When Moore next informed Furniss, on Dorothy's behalf, that 'Mrs Pound and her son are the only next of kin', and that she feared that if the Committee were dismissed the charge of treason could be revived, it was a clear indication of how her mind was working. Furniss regarded the possibility of the charge being revived as so remote as to be not worth worrying about. He said again that in his view the Court should be asked to discharge the Committee, but no instruction to that effect was forthcoming.

There is nothing in these exchanges in August and September 1958 to show that Pound himself was involved in them or even informed about them. The 'Committee for Ezra Pound' would keep a great deal from its subject in the following years.

He would be under assault more visibly in the public press from time to time. There was the photograph taken on the deck of the *Cristofero Colombo* when it docked in Naples, of Pound with his arm stretched out in salute—a 'fascist salute' in the eye of an American journalist, and in the minds of Pound's detractors ever since. To the unprejudiced eye there is no 'fascism' in Pound's genial expression, and the salute—try it—might be simply a natural gesture acknowledging a person or persons some way off. 'But why give him the benefit of the doubt?' as a *Time* writer put it to me, and indeed why spoil a good story? An even better story would have it that in 1961—one of the biographers relaying the story makes it 1962—Pound

> was photographed at the head of a neo-Fascist, May Day parade, five hundred strong, a writhing column of *Missini* [Moviemento Sociale Italiano] goose-stepping their way up the Via del Corso.... They wore jack boots and black arm bands. They flaunted banners and shouted anti-Semitic slogans. They gave the Roman salute and displayed the swastika. They heaved rocks and bottles at the crowd, overturned cars, attacked bystanders.

The source of this scenario—if it was not simply made up by Heymann—is never cited, and the scandalous photograph is never reproduced. But then, according to Giano Accame, the story is 'pure legend', and, as Tim Redman says, 'no such photograph exists'. The fact is that though Pound was in Rome in May 1961, he was not in physical shape to lead a goose-stepping march through its centre. But never mind, the story was, and is still, good for stamping Pound as indelibly 'fascist'.

'He's very angry if someone wants to tag him "fascist",' a journalist reported after interviewing Pound in early November 1958. And as a protest against such indiscriminate labelling Pound wrote down in the journalist's notebook so that there would be no mistake, 'Every man has the right to have his ideas examined one at a time.' That was the leading principle of his politics now, or of what remained of his agenda as he summed it up in this note in a Mexican journal in March 1959:

> PROGRAM in search of a party.
> Every man has the right to have his ideas examined ONE at a time.
> Liberty: the right to choose one thing at a time.
> Representation divided by trades and professions.
> Know specific facts of history, ancient and modern, and keep out of debt.

'Vocational representation' was about all that was left of Fascist policies in his thinking. The right to 'live free of debt' was the residue of his war on usury. The concern for education remained, but as a task for others to carry on—

> Let the poets combat the blackout of history and the all-engulphing brain-wash. Let them consider Horton's work in printing the Square $ series, and trying to get a bit of the true record (Benton's, Del Mar's, Coke's) back into print at a reasonable price.

On that occasion—a message requested by a Spanish correspondent in April 1959—he added a further call to respect distinctions: 'Let them preserve the DIFFERENCES in the great racial traditions, and between one man and another.'

The evidence builds up that it was not mere window-dressing when Pound told Laughlin in November 1959, 'E.P. no longer a POlitical figure, has forgotten what or which politics he ever had.' A few months later he went so far as to say that 'E.P now objects to violent language,' with reference to his own past vehemence. He did appear in *The European*, a magazine founded by Oswald Mosley, in January and February 1959, but his contributions were hardly of the kind that association might suggest. The first was an extract from Coke's *Institutes: The Third Part* concerning 'misprision of treason', that is, knowing of a treason and not revealing it; and to Coke's words he added only the sub-heading, 'What I *Would* Have Been Guilty Of, | If I Had Not Spoken'. That was the residue of his defence against the charge of treason. For the rest, in that issue there were also three small unpolitical epigrams, one of them a parody of a couple of lines in Eliot's 'Aunt Helen'; and in the next issue appeared 'CI de Los Cantares'. Pound's old campaigning fire, if not quite out, was reduced to its embers.

Once can almost see the change happening as he drafts new canto material in his notebooks. In the first of these, starting on 'CX' on 23 July and continuing through August into September, he is going straight on from *Thrones*: drafting more Na Khi material; then a long passage of history relating to government and statecraft, drawing now on *Storia d'Italia by* Francesco Guicciardini (1483–1540), the Florentine statesman and diplomat, and working in some familiar allusions to American affairs; and finally there is what became 'Notes for Canto CXI'. The Na Khi drafts went into cantos 110 and 112 as we now know them; but the historical draft—in which we read 'this part is for adults | seats . thrones'—drops out altogether in later recastings. Instead canto 110 accretes very different material around the Na Khi passage. The opening lines were drafted during or just after a visit with Marcella in November to Venice and Torcello. The passage following the Na Khi purifications, beginning 'And in thy mind beauty, O Artemis', can be dated to January 1959 and to time spent with Marcella at Limone on Lake Garda—that runs through to 'KALLIASTRAGALOS'. The rest of the canto, from 'hsin^{1}' and 'That love be the cause of hate' through to the end, was drafted in February in notebook 2. By then a radical reorientation for these final cantos had occurred: immediate personal experience had become dominant.

The initial flow of volcanic energy soon gave out. On 1 September Pound began a letter to Olivia Agresti by declaring himself 'In very weak and enfeebled condition'. On the 12th he warned William Cookson, who was proposing to visit in October, 'I alternate short bursts of energy, with total exhaustion, don't expect me to function as dynamo, or diesel. when yu get here.' And he put off indefinitely Douglas Bridson of the BBC who was wanting to do a programme on Pound: 'NOT in shape to stand a 3 day TV beano.' Nevertheless he left Brunnenburg with Marcella on the 19th to spend two nights in Venice. And before and after that trip he was drafting lines for cantos, and negotiating with Giambattista Vicari about contributing a column on books to his magazine. And Cookson, when he made his visit in mid-October, went away sufficiently energized to set up *Agenda* to take the place, in Pound's scheme of things, of *Four Pages* and Stock's *Edge*.

Yet at the same time Pound was writing to John Theobald, 'Have very little energy' and 'My head works very slowly.'

He was revived at the end of October by a 'Mostra Delle Edizioni Poundiane 1908–1958', an exhibition sponsored by the Merano Tourist Office in 'a highbrow gallery', and organized by Pound's Italian publisher Vanni Scheiwiller. The idea was to mark the 50th anniversary of the publication in Venice of *A Lume Spento*, but it was his entire poetic achievement that was on show. And on the walls, as a setting for his manuscripts and first editions, there were paintings and drawings by Gaudier-Brzeska, Wyndham Lewis, and Sheri Martinelli. The Dolmetsch clavichord, for which Pound had just ordered a new set of strings from the Dolmetsch family in Haslemere, was also on show, as a reminder of his love of early music. The opening was on 30 October, Pound's 73rd birthday, with speeches paying tribute to *il grande poeta*. The recognition was evidently restorative, since Giacomo Oreglia, who interviewed him for a Swedish newspaper a day or two later, found that 'in spite of his seventy-three years and the hardships he has met with, he seems far from tired and finished, and it's difficult not to be excited by his nervous energy and rapid changes of moods'.

Pound and Marcella went down to Venice again for three days, 10–13 November, and there he first sketched the images that would become the opening lines of canto 110—

> To thy quiet house at Torcello,
>   Alma Astarte
> Wake exultant
>   in caricole
> Hast'ou seen boat's wake on sea-wall
>   how crests it?
> What panache? paw-flap, wave-tap
>   that is gaiety

They had evidently gone out to the island of Torcello in the Venetian lagoon to see the very early Byzantine cathedral dedicated to the Virgin Mother as 'L'Assunta', as assumed into heaven—a gold mosaic of the Madonna is in the dome above the apse. 'Alma Astarte', however, reaches back to the Phoenician mother-goddess, later assimilated into Greece's Aphrodite and Rome's Venus. So Pound was invoking the protection and support of the primal force of love, and then, as if to establish a mood of gaiety, finding an image of exultant energy in the *vaporetto*'s 'wake on sea-wall'. (The Na-Khi passage would follow that as a counter-statement, introduced by a phrase from Dante's poignant vision of the adulterous lovers Paolo and Francesca in *Inferno* V, 'che paion' si al vent'', 'who seem so light upon the wind'.)

Back at Brunnenburg Pound finalized *Thrones* and on '17 Nov. 1958'—he noted the date emphatically—he opened up 'the Fenollosa inheritance' and began on a new project—

> having last evening handed over the ms/ of 96–109 de los Cantares to the remarkable Scheiwiller (V.) I now tackle Fenollosa's penciled record of Mori's lectures on the History of Chinese Poetry, with the intention of transmitting them as his view, which I am in no way competent to affirm is the last word on the matter...

He typed thirty-seven pages before coming to a stop.

As the winter set in Pound began to feel the cold, in spite of the castle's great wood-burning stoves, and to complain of the winds, and of having difficulty breathing in the mountain air, though 600 metres is hardly alpine. After thirteen years of steam-heating in St Elizabeths he could not acclimatize, though he may also have been finding the tensions in the castle oppressive. 'ANY news of villas in the SUN and south of europe wd/ be welcome,' he wrote the day after Christmas to Meacham.

On 11 January the odd triangle, Ezra, Dorothy, and Marcella, went down to Lake Garda for the inside of a week, staying at Limone on the western shore, then going on to Brescia and to Sirmione. At Limone they stayed at Albergo Le Palme, and on a copy of its brochure Pound wrote the lines that begin the long Lake Garda passage which follows the Na Khi passage in canto 110—

> And in thy mind beauty, O Artemis,
>   as of mountain lakes in the dawn,
> Foam and silk are thy fingers,
>   Kuanon,
> and the long suavity of her moving

Those were lines for Marcella, and it was at Limone that Pound proposed that they should marry. On 5 February, back at Brunnenburg, Pound began a new notebook with the lines, 'That love be the cause of hate | something is twisted', and then wrote out the rest of canto 110 as it goes on from the Lake Garda passage. The next draft in this notebook contains the lines, 'Pride, jealousy & possessiveness | 3 pains of hell'.

Those lines which would become part of canto 113—the canto which opens and closes with invocations to the sun as 'Pater Helios', 'Father Helios'—were written shortly after Ezra, Dorothy, and Marcella, had moved down to Rapallo at the end of February to look for a flat to rent with three separate rooms. The change of scene is marked in the notebook by the observation, 'over Portofino 3 lights in triangulation'. A later observation, dated 28 April, 'Sea, over roofs, but still the sea and the headland', gives the view to be had from a balcony of the flat which they had taken on the sixth floor of a new apartment building a block or two back from the seafront. Marcella, according to Dorothy, was to learn to cook and to do all the housework. But Pound was writing, and Marcella was typing up from his notebook,

& in thy mind , beauty
O Artemis
& as to sin / they invented it—eh?
to implement domination
eh? largely.
There remains grumpiness—
malvagità
sea, over roofs, but still the sea & the headland.
& in every woman,
somewhere in the ~~bitch~~ snarl is a tenderness
a blue light under stars
The ruined orchards, trees rotting
empty frames @ Limone
& for a little magnanimity somewhere
& to know the share from the charge
(scala altrui)
God's eye art'ou, do not surrender perception.

He was attempting to integrate his feelings about Marcella, and about Dorothy's possessiveness, with his vision of justice, and also to root enlightenment in responsiveness to the natural world. 'Young people today need more courage than any other generation in the past,' he would say, 'But they can find their moral values in the beauty of nature.' In May he would write these lines in the notebook as part of what was to be the opening passage of canto 113—

& who no longer make Gods out of beauty
Θρῆνος this is a dying. [lament]
yet to walk with Mozart, Agassiz, & Linnaeus
here take thy mind's space
& to this garden, Marcella,
ever seeking, by petal, by leaf-vein
out of dark & toward twilight

The end of the canto echoes the last of those lines as it invokes the primal light, 'Out of dark, thou, Father Helios, leadest'—that light conferring, as on '19th May '59', a singular day of 'sun & serenitas' when, ''neath overhanging air under sun-beat', 'souls melt into air'. But apart from such moments the mind remains 'as Ixion, unstill, ever turning'. The contention between the love that brings the light of the world to focus in contemplation of its beauty, and the 'pride, jealousy & possessiveness' which threaten to shatter it, had become very personal and immediate.

These two closely related cantos, 110 and 113, grow tense with opposing forces. The initial exultance in nature is countered by the story behind the Na Khi episode, a story of young lovers kept apart, of the girl's suicide on a black tree and the boy, a shepherd, protesting against the unnaturalness of her death—

> When the stag drinks at the salt spring
> & in gentian time sheep come down
> can you see with eyes of coral or turquoise
> walk with the oak's root?

The Na Khi purifications (here and in 112) re-assert the live oneness with nature; and the Artemis passage carries that on into constructive action (a road built at Gardesana), and courage (Uncle G. in the Senate, a cavalry charge), and the happy marriage of his own daughter ('Felix nupsit'). Yet again his mind turns to unfortunate lovers: Eurydice, Daphne, Endymion. Renewal and going forth by day are countered by hatred, by war's destruction, by the neglect and blacking out of resisters. A *Waste Land* mood enters briefly—

> From Time's wreckage shored,
> these fragments shored against our ruin

But still, against that, there is 'the sun...jih$^{4-5}$ | new with the day'; and Rock's perseverance with his work on the Na Khi (to which Pound was indebted), despite having twenty years of research torpedoed by a submarine. In the end the canto, which began so gaily, seeks resolution in a desperate prayer—

> falling spiders and scorpions!
> Give light against falling poison!
> A wind of darkness hurls against forest
> the candle flickers
> is faint
> Lux enim—
> versus this tempest....

Canto 113 continues the struggle to have light and beauty prevail against the pains of hell, but it ends with 'the mind as Ixion', in perpetual motion upon a wheel in hell.

Pound was in love with Marcella but bound to Dorothy, and there was no way he could get free so long as he remained in her keeping. But then he would not or could not do anything effectual to get himself free of the Committee—Furniss remarked that he seemed always to veer away from the subject. In St Elizabeths he had waited passively for others to get him out, and he had maintained his morale while he waited. This was a different situation, one which touched him to the heart, and there would be no way out.

The matter of the Committee was still under discussion:—

Moore to Furniss, 12 January 1959: EP and DP just granted residence in Italy, which should enable EP to apply for discharge of the Committee and of DP's Bond to the Court.

EP to Overholser, 2 February: can he get the Committee removed so that EP can manage his own affairs—his 'trouble or weakness had been physical rather than mental... too exhausted physically to use his mind at all'—this presumably with reference to the 1946 diagnosis.

DP to Moore, 13 February: EP 'in process of writing to Overholser, to see whether he can get this maddening committee business stopped—or , if not, to get a regular allowance for E, instead of accounting for each $ & ¢'. Also, 'Poor EP. St. Eliz's has let out not much more than wreckage—days when he cannot collect his wits to work at all'.

Moore to du Sautoy of Faber & Faber, 3 March: 'I am pressing for discharge of the insanity proceedings in the US'.

EP to Moore, 8 March: 'Th. Arnold has writ/ of possibility of release of Committee.'

Moore to EP, 13 March: if it were granted 'it would ease the legal situation in many ways—and you wd then be competent to consider making a proper will dealing with your wishes'.

Furniss to EP, 28 May: 'All that would be involved would be to get an affidavit from D.P. that she wishes to be discharged as Committee and to get an affidavit from Omar to the effect that he has no complaint should the Committee be released.' In any event, because DP is abroad, she needs to sign a document he has sent her authorizing the Clerk of the Court to accept service on behalf of the Committee in case someone should file a claim against EP's estate.

Moore to EP, 7 June, (after seeing him and DP in Rapallo): favours Furniss's proposal, as against Arnold's which EP had been inclined to follow. Arnold had said that the Committee should simply stop filing its annual report and ignore any demand for one from the Court. At worst the Judge might make an order removing DP as Committee—which would achieve the desired result—whereas a formal petition claiming that Pound had returned to sanity risked a fresh indictment.

DP to Moore, 13 June: 'I have sent on the Court paper signed to Furniss thinking it's a clearer position—dear old Arnold can probably pull off a lot of stuff—but I'd rather be less wrangle-y. | Nobody has mentioned—if D.P. were removed as Committee—surely the CT. would want somebody else to take over?'

That had not been mentioned of course because the idea in everyone else's mind was to get rid of the Committee altogether. Dorothy did want to be rid of the 'maddening business' of having to report the Committee's expenditure to the Court every year. But she would make no move to have the Committee discharged, nor would she allow it to lapse. Instead, in time, she would suggest that Omar and Omar's lawyer should be appointed in her place. The notion of affidavits from herself and from Omar she simply ignored. The thing that nobody appears to have questioned was Omar's having his say on whether Pound should be freed from the Committee. One can only assume that this was on account of his interest in Pound's estate, and that would indicate that behind the legal question of whether the Committee could be discharged the real issue, for Dorothy and for Omar, was whether Pound should be free to dispose of his person and his property according to his own wishes.

In August Dorothy reminded Omar that her husband and his legal father had no legal existence or status in the USA. And in October she would make it clear to Moore that she wanted to keep it that way. No substantive reasons for this were now given or asked for. The state of Pound's health would be played up, as if that were a sufficient reason, but it was never directly argued or legally established as a justification for keeping Pound subject to the Committee. As for the original justification, Pound's supposed insanity, Dorothy would tell Omar in 1966 that she 'always knew that EP. is <u>not</u> <u>crazy</u>—& never has been'.

Pound had not been in touch with Olga Rudge since she had gone away in rage and despair after seeing him with Sheri Martinelli in July 1955. Now he had at last written to her a few days before the move from Brunnenburg down to Rapallo—

All you or anyone else can do is to try to understand fatigue as far as I am concerned. // I need rest....

Thanks for the silence.

As you know I have always disbelieved in anyone owning anyone or running their existence....

AND the need to avoid possumism, and to avoid falling into Waste Landism.

If I ever get out of the morass I will let you know.

A day or two after reaching Rapallo he wrote again, 'Evidently was altitude that kept me gasping like a fish at Brunnenburg, | may be able to resume normal life sometime'. He also mentioned that 'my status is still officially under the Committee, am trying to get it dismissed'. There followed an exchange about his removing from her Casa 60 the books and papers and the Gaudiers which she had been devotedly guarding. She gave him a key, permission for him 'and no-one else' to enter the house, asked that he take everything at one visit, and said she would not be there when he came, all this 'for her own convenience and peace and quiet'. In fact—possibly because the road up from Rapallo had yet to reach Casa 60—it took more than one visit, on 23 and 24 March, to bring all the 'stuff DOWN from St. Amb/'. And now, he wrote to Mary, it would be 'sensible to bring everything to Brun.'. He was concerned that Olga had stopped her remittances from New Directions, and would see to it that the 'small regular cheques' were started again.

Bridson of the BBC had kept in touch, and on the day he brought the last of his archive down from Sant'Ambrogio Pound wrote to him, 'am having rush of energy and revival with the sea air, | but don't know that it will last | always do too much WHEN I have the surge'. Bridson seized his moment, and had Pound agree to be interviewed at Brunnenburg in April. So Pound and Dorothy returned there for five days while Bridson filmed and talked with him. Three or four afternoons were spent in Pound's room high up in the central tower with its magnificent view of the valley and distant mountains. 'The room', as Bridson described it, 'was packed with books and papers—Chinese calligraphy well to the fore—and Gaudier-Brzeska's well-known black-and-white profile of him propped up against the wall above his desk.' In the film Pound is seen striding or standing in various parts of the castle; he reads from his poetry; and, seated, he talks in a teacherly fashion about money and taxes, with his 'Money Pamphlets' spread on the floor in front of him for the camera to focus on. Bridson wrote up their conversation in a substantial 'Interview with Ezra Pound' for Laughlin's *New Directions in Prose and Poetry 17*, and in this, near the end, Pound says, 'There are only about two subjects that I got the strength to argue about. One is how you issue money.... And the other...is the system of taxes.'[1] But he had talked well and interestingly about many aspects of his life and work from his early days in London up to the recently published cantos. The surge of energy had carried him through.

[1] The subject of taxes was so much on his mind that his first words when coming upon his old friend Dr Bacigalupo on Rapallo's seafront—they had not seen each other since 1945—had been, 'Perché paghi le tasse? Le tasse non vanno pagate' (Giuseppe Bacigalupo, *Ieri a Rapallo* (2006), 87).

Back in Rapallo, the old trouble with his neck, with not being able to hold his head up, was getting him down. X-ray revealed calcium deposits on his '6th and other cerebral vertebrae', 'enough to supply a giraffe'. 'It slows the mind as well as the body,' Pound wrote, though he felt better after an 'x-ray attack on the calcifications'. In any event, the condition did not stop him from swimming in the sea and going out rowing on it with Marcella. And the new cantos continued to grow, a few lines at a time, in his notebook.

On 29 June the three of them set off on a trip south to Rome—'Poor little Marcella hasn't "seen Italy" much!', Dorothy explained to Omar. They passed through Pisa, finding that the site of the DTC to the north of it was now a rose nursery, and went on to Florence. On 1 July they were in Perugia, from where they visited Assissi; and on the 4th they reached Rome. On the 7th they returned via La Spezia to Rapallo.

Pound would shortly tell Mary, 'I have been too exhausted to attend to detail since Rome'—'I had a burst of energy, but the Roman heat finished THAT.' Nevertheless, between 9 July and 16 August, in less than six weeks, he composed the latter two-thirds of canto 114, a long draft for 115 (to be broken up into 'From Canto CXV', 'Notes for CXVII', and the other published fragments[2]), and the whole of canto 116—that is, virtually all of *Drafts and Fragments* after the first page of 114. On 9 July he wrote—

These simple men who have fought against jealousy—
as the man of Oneida.
Ownership! ownership!
There was a thoughtful man named Macleod
to mitigate ownership.

The 'man of Oneida' would be John Humphrey Noyes who, in 1848 founded, in Oneida County of New York State, the Oneida Community which held all property in common and did not believe in monogamy. After a celebration of Pound's own immediate ancestors, traceable back to Oneida County, Marcella enters the poem again—

Tanagra mia, Ambracia,
for the delicacy
for the kindness

[2] But note that the entire fragment 'La faillite de François Bernouard' was composed earlier, after 19 May, following 'flowing—ever unstill' (113), and immediately preceding the opening of 114, which was written in the notebook before 19 June.

—the word recurs, 'kindness', as against 'Fear, father of cruelty'. And it was Marcella, the notebook makes clear, who said on 14 July, '"That lizard's feet are like snow flakes,"' the observation eliciting the approving comment, 'ubi amor, ibi oculus'. 'The kindness, infinite, of her hands,' the canto concluded on 23 July, 'And that the truth is in kindness.'

What follows in the notebook is a statement of contending emotions more personal than anything Pound had ever written. His love of Marcella, his love of beauty, and his ambition 'to write Paradise', confront hardness of heart and jealousy and hatred; yet 'peccavi', I too have sinned, he confesses; and he ends humbly, as 'a blown husk that is finished'. This is lyric writing from a mind in the exaltation of breakdown:

a bronze dawn, bright russet
but dawn of some sort
                & some how
There is so much beauty
how can we harden our hearts
a beautiful night under wind mid garofani
        that wind would be?
                                Apeliota
do not move
        let the wind speak
                That is Paradise
The petals are almost still.
Ἀπηλιώτης
The beauty of my thought has not entered them.
That is, it has as but a flash in far darkness—
I have tried to write Paradise—
let the gods forgive
                what I have made
let those I love try to forgive
                what I have made.
Mozart, Linnaeus—
                Sulmona
        out of dust
        out of dust
                the gold thread
        in dark pattern @ Torcello.
The wall still stands.
There is a path by a field almost empty.

That could be the path at Torcello from the landing stage to the village. A few lines casting back to his possible 'utility' in the war and the economic war briefly break the meditation, which then resumes with a new intensity—

m'amour
        ma vie
m'amour
        ma vi'
for the blue flash & the moments
        benedetta Marcella
the young for the old
        That is tragedy
& for one beautiful day there was peace
        Brancusi's bird
                in the hollow of pine trunks
or when the snow was like sea foam
Twilit sky leaded with elm boughs,
under the Rupe Tarpeia
        weep out your jealousies.
[. . .]
when one's friends hate each other
how can there be peace in the world
peccavi.
        Their asperities
                diverted me in my green Time.
        Their envies.
Their paradise?
        their best—
for an instant.
? to all men for an instant?
        Beati
the sky leaded with elm boughs
above the visions
        the heart
'The flowers of the apricot
        blow from the East to the West
I have tried to keep them from falling.'
A blown husk that is finish'd
but the light sings eternal
a pale flare over marshes
        where the salt hay
whispers to tide's change

The breaking up of this draft radically disrupted the progression of these final cantos. Leaving aside 'Notes for Canto CXI' as a last echo of the St

Elizabeths cantos, there has been a steadily advancing realization of the poet's personal predicament, in his ecstatic but threatened love of Marcella, and in the change of direction this has given to his poem, thus throwing into question the very possibility of bringing it to its previously intended end. The personal predicament is most intensely realised in that draft for 115, and it is felt there as personal tragedy. The voice of the lyric self takes over, elegiac, finding consolation in failure. But then in the notebook canto 116 follows on directly as a counter statement, taking its cue from 'but the light sings eternal' and incorporating the sense of personal failure into a reassertion of the timeless venture.

This final completed canto opens with an image of the vital universe—

Came Neptunus
his mind leaping
like dolphins

Thence to the human mind's scope, 'To make Cosmos— | To achieve the possible'; and that stands despite errors and wrecks, Mussolini's and his own. He can claim to 'have brought the great ball of crystal | . . . the great acorn of light'. That he personally 'cannot make it cohere' is balanced by his confidence that 'it coheres all right': though we must make it for ourselves, the Cosmos does not depend upon our making. And though 'If love be not in the house there is nothing', there is still 'beauty against this blackness', still deeps to be learned from a Laforgue and a Linnaeus. A paradise of love can be conceived, though it be 'over the shambles'. Wrong can be confessed 'without losing rightness'—

Have I seen the divine where it was not?
Charity is what I've got—
damn it
I cannot make it flow through
a little love
like a rushlight
to lead back splendour.

Upon that note Pound's last and very personal cantos, and the epic *Cantos of Ezra Pound*, concluded, some time in August 1959. The notebook carries the inscription, 'This copy book is Marcella's. | E.P. | Aug. 7.'

He would write no more cantos. The great work ends then, not with a Dantescan vision of his paradise, which would be an enlightened social order governed by love and justice, but with a personal testament, a reckoning of achievement and failure, and an affirmation of the possibility of a paradise he can conceive only in his mind. The final canto rises above his own tragedy, though still conscious of it, to reconnect with the epic enterprise to which his whole life had been dedicated. Here, to end, he achieves an impersonal vision of his lifetime's effort, and sees it in relation to all that he can conceive, sees himself in relation to his universe, and humbly affirms his little light, his 'little love | like a rushlight | to lead back splendour'. He had been brought to this by his love of Marcella, and by the thwarting of that love.

On 12 August Dorothy wrote to Omar, 'EP very low indeed ... & he is terribly discouraged, says "Marcella is keeping him alive".' The same day Pound himself told Mary that he was not in a fit state to be seen by his grandchildren. And a week later, 'My old head just won't do any more work'. And after that, 'I have nostalgia for Brunnenburg', he wrote, and finally, at the end of August, 'Have you still got the car that cd/ carry me to Brun/ for a visit, AND return me???' A few days later he told her it was 'No use', just a half-hour trial drive had been very tiring—he would not be able to hold up for the eight hours to the castle. In these notes to Mary he did not mention Marcella.

He was in an uncharacteristic mood, softened, all aggression spent. 'To bless people', he wrote to her,

> for their good moments / for their awarenesses.
> Olga's heroism not to be forgotten.
> To expect people to behave like disembodied spirits in Paradise
> Dante's or any other / is beyond reason.

In another letter he confessed that 'destino or my muddles have done you out of long conversations that were due to you', and he asked for 'Patience, strength, tolerance and forgiveness.' He was moved, by coming upon some notes of his first walking tour in Provence, to write out of the blue to Richard Aldington who now lived there, 'Cher R/',

> amid cumulative fatigue, and much that has gone to muddle, thinking of early friendship and late. This is to say I have for you a lasting friendship. EP/

Aldington was 'completely shattered' by receiving that, as he told HD; and HD told him that Pound had written to her, 'Not since Brigit, Richard, the four of us, has there been any harmony around me.'

J. Laughlin visited Mary at Brunnenburg on 3 September, and then spent a few days in Rapallo as Pound's publisher and friend. On the 9th he sent a postcard from there to A. V. Moore: 'no immediate concern. I never saw him look more fit. And what an appetite! But then mental snarls & depression.' Afterwards he reported at greater length: that Pound was suffering from low blood pressure, lack of energy, and mental depression, complaining of being unable to think and fearful of losing his mind; 'also hoping to have the Court in Washington rescind the Committee.' About that Laughlin said he sympathized, but, 'between ourselves am not sure this would be wise at present'—Pound had not been sensible about his publishing permissions and had been causing problems for his publishers and literary agents.

On the 11th Pound started a new notebook, and that day wrote on the first page, 'Who again went down into hell | unto cowardice, dither & death fear'; and after that, 'who defied hell & the lightnings | & ends like a sick mouse on a rubble heap'. Dorothy mentioned in her letter to Omar on the 13th that EP's and Marcella's behaviour was 'becoming such a scandal—today she says she is going back to USA'. And on the 15th Pound wrote to Eliot, 'Sitting in my ruins, and heaven comes down like a net | and all my past follies.'

On 22 September Pound and Marcella went by taxi to Genoa where a passage was booked for Marcella, cabin class 'senza doccia', no shower, on the 'Augustus' sailing for New York at 11 a.m. on the 28th. Dorothy had written the cheque for the fare, $322 from Pound's account. She had written three further cheques amounting to $1,200, which was what Pound had told Furniss the Committee should be allowed to pay out per annum for his secretary. Back in Rapallo Pound wrote in his notebook, 'I have been a pitiless stone | stone making art work | & destroying affections.' On another day he wrote,

> In meine Heimat
> Kam ich wieder
> where the dead walked
> & the living were
> made of card board
> *scene shift* - - - - - - - - - -
> Till suddenly the tower
> blazed with the light of Astarte
> @ Genova the port lay below us

Marcella typed up these last jottings before she left. In another notebook Pound wrote—

> That I lost my centre
> fighting the world
> The dreams clash &
> are shattered
> & that I tried to make a paradiso

Terrestre
That the light stand
& grow solid
M'a[mour]
m'a[mour] what hv. I lov'd
& where a[re] y[ou]

Marcella typed these lines too, but added above them, 'not cantos'.

'EP in a fuss re Mlla', Dorothy wrote in her diary on the 26th; and on the 28th, 'MS away 8.30'. To Omar she wrote that day, 'EP lying on his bed—a wreck.' Marcella had chosen to go home on her own, she told him. Laughlin would tell Williams, what he had probably been told by Dorothy, that 'Marcella couldn't take it any more—she hated Italy—and has gone back to Texas.' Marcella, who may well have felt that she had no option but to remove herself from an impossible situation, maintained a discreet silence on the subject, then and thereafter. On the other hand, Dorothy wrote to Moore a week after her departure, 'We couldn't go on at that tension.' Marcella had been 'useful in odd jobs', she believed, 'but debilitating'. 'Anyway!', she concluded, 'I'm not going to live with EP and his mistress. It makes too much v. bad tension—and he's "in my charge".' Moore approved: 'I am glad you stood firm this time,' he wrote, with reference to the '"mistress"', 'You have been such a loyal and patient Wife.'

All Pound wanted when Marcella had gone was to get back to Brunnenburg. His books and papers were packed up, the flat cleared, and on 4 October Boris and Noel Stock came with a truck to carry everything up to the castle. Invited to write something for a journal in India, Pound replied at the end of the month, 'I came up here to die quietly, and am without a secretary.'

16 : 'You Find Me in Fragments', 1959–62

'[T]ower is full of you,' Pound wrote to Marcella from Brunnenburg on 6 October; and he felt 'full of emptiness'. In the cold night, 'pages racing thru head, the complication the four thousand entanglements and HOW one is netted'. 'Rapallo, m'amour, ma vie', he wrote, and 'how it got shattered'.

In his notebook one finds, 'one dies without saving the world | & with Seneca: no gods in this part of ~~heaven~~ the sky space | MA LA BELLEZZA ESISTE'—but there IS beauty. And on 15 November,

> in the labyrinth of death longer to find you
> & the rivets of tyranny driven over our head
> 'The portal to inquisition' Thiers.
> Tragic heart, they have played your compassion
> There is no cave left in the world
> there is no shelter
> What flower is come in the hedge row
> the white bud half open
>
> To have seen you walk in flat shoes
>   & have let you go
>   this is agony
> or seated in your flower-skirt
>   under elm trees

Those around him, friends who saw him, read the agony as some kind of breakdown, and were reluctant to acknowledge what was breaking him up.

Laughlin told Williams that 'Uncle Ezry... is really sitting on the bottom of the black hole. A terrible depression and collapse of physical energy.' This was the letter in which he mentioned that Marcella had gone back to Texas, but he made no connection between that and Pound's depression. To Dr Overholser he wrote, 'I am so deeply concerned over his condition... Now he is at the bottom of the pit of melancholy, and most of his talk is about dying and "losing his mind".'

Pound was having nearly daily injections from a local doctor, possibly of vitamins, as Laughlin thought, but actually of 'reserpine and testicular hormone'. This treatment proved 'not successful'—indeed it could well have made his condition worse, since reserpine, an 'antihypertensive drug' or tranquillizer, was later found to have as its serious side-effect depression, and in some cases suicidal depression. Pound had cause enough to be depressed without that.

He entered what Dorothy called a cycle of 'self-abasement', or 'self--debasement—which is another form of egotism'. He was feeling that he had betrayed his friends and botched his life's work. He attempted to type a letter to Eliot—it was probably not sent—

Now that I am wrecked, and have struggled three days to write a page to you
That I am trying to repudiate 30 years of injustice to you, / from time of Ash Wednesday / & in Rock V 2 lines, all of Confucius[1]
In Strange Gods, what I should have heeded,
you doing real criticism
and me playing a tin penny whistle

He was taking to heart Eliot's criticism, in *After Strange Gods*, that his ideas of good and evil were 'trivial and accidental', and that his 'Hell, for all its horrors, is a perfectly comfortable one for the modern mind to contemplate'. When Olga Rudge tried to rally him against despair, Pound replied, 'DEEspair | the Possum says it in *After Strange Gods* | didn't seem to be my trouble'. It was as if he had learnt late from Eliot the necessity of despair. And Mary, since her father was now heeding the Possum, and making everyone in the castle read *After Strange Gods*, 'wrote to Mr. Eliot begging him to come and see Babbo', and Eliot sent a comforting birthday telegram, 'saying "You are the greatest poet alive and I owe every thing to you"—or words to that effect'.

In this new spirit of humility and penitence Pound wrote to MacLeish, 'Forgive me for about 80% of the violent things I have said about some of your friends'—'some of them are deplorable, and it is too late to retract 'em. Violent language is an error.' MacLeish was knocked sideways by this:

[1] EP's reference was to these lines in TSE's 'Choruses from *The Rock*, V':

> And they write innumerable books; being too vain and
> distracted for silence: seeking every one after his
> own elevation, and dodging his emptiness.
> If humility and purity be not in the heart, they are not in
> the home: and if they are not in the home, they are
> not in the City.

'Your letter frightened the living bejeezzz out of me. Gentleness—even affection—out of old Ez, says I: he's sick!' And he offered sane reassurance—

Don't have your abuse of my friends on your conscience. FDR was abused by experts all his latter life and it didn't sour him none. I think he'd have liked some of your expletives. What I want to know is where you are and if you're warm enough and what you plan to do next and how lovely Mary is and those children and all and all.

'Merry Christmas you Old Buzzard and God keep you,' he signed off.

Pound had his better moments. On 24 November he had occasion to tell Laughlin, 'don't git euphoria. I aint feelin so much better as all THAT,' which was at least a concession towards a lifting of the gloom. A page in the notebook dated '28 Nov' balances the perennial struggle for renewal after failure against personal tragedy:

Troica Roma resurgens
These are the failures—
        Aged . Ge [?] . Fasa
That the city be there in the mind
—
Tragic heart once given
when separation is crucifixion
& light is in meeting

A week later, in a moment of clear perception, he wrote this on the next page, but again the impersonal reflection breaks down into the personal—

Dec. 5. 4 p.m. Pax
These sudden devaluations, threats of devaluation
always more somewhere than elsewhere
keeping the nerves raw by scaring the market
sweeping away the life's fruit
in an instant—or over a weekend
100 million dashed into slavery.
lure of the luxury traders
        drugs to break courage
for the blind mice of the nations—
women starved with brutality
                                —envy
—
But the sense of awe is not vanity
The bright moment not vanity

but the awe is not vanity
before I died
I had & given
these hours.

He was trying to recover his better sense of himself.

On 17 December he wrote to Marcella: 'Ciao, cara mia. Minor tragi-comedies amid the larger. Craig [La Drière] arriving . . . probably after dark and no means of guiding him down the salita as hour unknown.' The next day he added, 'woke absolutely empty in emptiness. H. J. "The private life" ref. Then empty plain and she walking in it. Then hurried self onto Cantos, shall try to make copy and revise some toward the end, putting in explanations to clarify. Must get it simplified.' On the 20th it was, 'M'amour, He havin a go at her cantos . . . AND of course what they didn't think of is that his life started again when he got OUT of bg/hs, and all before that sort of cut off. So everything intimate is all shared with her.' Next day the thought came to him, 'he better stay alive'.

He had in fact been re-animated by an invitation from the Mayor of Darmstadt to be the city's guest of honour at the première on 10 December of Eva Hesse's translation of *Women of Trachis.* Mary went with him to Munich on the 8th, and on the 10th Eva Hesse took them to Darmstadt. Afterwards she gave an account of the occasion to Laughlin. Pound had worn the 'vintage velvet jacket in which he used to attend concerts in Rapallo before the war', and in which he was 'an imposing figure'. He had visibly enjoyed the production, and

> Just before the end he suddenly rose from his seat and made a dash for the exit . . . [and] suddenly appeared on the stage, where the cast were receiving their applause. A great new wave of applause set in as Ezra showed up in the spotlight, and there were long ovations—he was called back to the curtain some five or six times. He cut a very fine figure standing out there—one critic described the incident as 'the final appearance of the real Herakles'.

When he returned to the castle on the 14th further work on Marcella's cantos seemed possible.

On New Year's Day Dorothy wrote to Omar that Pound was again 'depressed and jumpy'. On 3 January she reported to A. V. Moore, who passed it on to Laughlin, that

> during the night of Jan. 2 E.P. left the Castle, and returned about 8.15 am soaked to the skin, through all sorts of sweaters and a heavy coat, and was put to bed immediately, after a rubbing with alcohol and a dose of brandy, and I understand

since he remains rather a handful. His physique is strong, and he is having injections, and D.P. says he complains his head is slow and hardly works at all—which worries him dreadfully.

In spite of that episode he was in an upbeat mood on the 9th: 'Starting for Rome domani sera'—tomorrow evening—having 'Done two days work on Fenollosa | cloud seemed to lift off my head day before yester'.

His address in Rome would be c/- Ugo Dadone, 80 via Angelo Poliziani, though he did not expect to be staying there since it was a new apartment and likely to be too small. However Dadone, who had been a general and a military attaché in the Fascist regime, and whose head, according to Mary de Rachewiltz, 'was still too full of the *Eia Eia Allalà* spirit', insisted on putting him up, and on giving him a lively time of visits to old Fascist friends, and concerts and parties.

Pound's letters from Rome to Dorothy, who was 'resting in Rap.... away from corrosive castle', were full of apology and self-blame. On 11 January, his first day in Rome, he wished he had 'not been so blind', and was 'sorry not to contribute more to her tranquillity'. On the 14th, he 'had orter made a better job of a lot of things'. On the 16th he asked, 'how much of him can she stand & when?' 'Difficult to get unhitched,' he wrote on the 20th, meaning, apparently, that he couldn't get out of Dadone's social arrangements which he was finding a strain. The ambiguity was there again on the 22nd: 'Mao Mao . . . wot has he done to get into such a tangle? Vortex that once drew together & now scatters. . . . very hard to get unhooked.' His friends in Rome, he told her on the 24th, thought it good for him to circulate, and he appreciated 'every body trying to hold my fragments together'. 'O Mao', he ended that letter, '& where to begin', to which he added the *hsin*[1] ideogram, renewal, and 'she not hate any one'.

Dadone had arranged for him to have injections, starting on the 25th—'D/e swears by his medico = who swears the stuff is quieting etc.' What he told Mary was rather different: 'Dadone idea is that injections will make cantos pour out without waiting to decide what to say. Their lecturers do it.' Later, in February, he would tell Laughlin, 'Am being shot full of chemicals which I greatly mistrust.' All the same, whether it was the chemicals or not, he could tell Mary on the 17th, 'have emerged from the tomb. Taken to song-writing | I ain' nebber been a fambly man.'

He agreed to do an interview for the *Paris Review* series of interviews with celebrated older writers. Donald Hall, then a young American poet making his way in the literary world, secured the commission and went to talk to Pound in Rome in early March. He knew and loved Pound's poetry; yet the prevailing preconceptions made him fear that he would be confronted by a man who talked politics more than poetry, and who would be giving arrogant fascist salutes and delivering murderous anti-Semitic diatribes. Pound answered his knock on the door of Dadone's apartment, and 'There was no mistaking him . . . the magnificent head.' 'But his eyes, which looked into me as we stood at the door, were watery, red, weak. "Mr. Hall", he said, "you—find me—in fragments."' Hall's memoir continues,

> we sat opposite each other. Looking in his eyes, I saw the fatigue. Later I watched his eyes and mouth gather from time to time a tense strength, when he concentrated his attention on a matter gravely important. Fragments assembled themselves in half a second, turned strong, sharp, and insistent; then dissipated quickly, sank into flaccidity, depression, and silence.

That was the pattern Hall observed through the three days he spent with Pound: deep fatigue relieved by freshets of energy which might abruptly give out, or which could carry him through an evening over dinner in Crispi's with Hall and his wife. Hall saw that Pound was lonely, and desperate for what he called normal conversation with intelligent young people. He wanted to give Hall his interview, and to give of his best; and he wanted to spend time with them, to show them something of Rome, and just to talk with normal Americans. But the fatigue was always there. To Hall it seemed 'more than physical; it seemed abject despair, accidie, meaninglessness, abulia, waste'. The access of energy—as when after a collapse into silence his speech would become 'newly vigorous and exact'—evidently came from 'a fragile and courageous effort of will'. But he had lost all confidence—he had lost his centre—and now, it appeared to Hall, 'he doubted the value of everything that he had done in his life'.

Yet something remained. Granting that he should have paid attention when Bunting had told him in the thirties that Mussolini was no good; and granting that he had been wrong to imagine that his voice alone could save constitutional government in the United States, and wrong to have used violent language; yet he felt still that his intentions at least had been good in his relations with Mussolini's regime, and in his broadcasts. Even so, he lacked conviction, and Hall felt he was being appealed to, to grant 'exoneration, forgiveness'. '"Do *you* think they should have shot me?"' Pound pleaded. But all that was past history, and nothing either of them could do or say could redeem the errors and wrecks in his politics and his propaganda.

There was still some hope that he might complete his epic. Hall let him know that he was reviewing *Thrones* for *The New Statesman*, and Pound, encouraged by this, 'read over his new *Cantos* and fragments', and on the morning of their third day Hall found him 'vigorous . . . and happy with plans for work... able to *conceive* that he could finish the *Cantos*'. He would have to 'clarify obscurities |...get clearer | definite ideas or dissociations already expressed | verbal formula to control rise of brutality | principle of order vs. split atom'. Pound gave the typescripts of the new cantos to Hall to read there and then, and Hall, excited at finding a return to lyricism, told him that he was moved 'by the acknowledgment of error or failure shining through a language that gave the lie to failure'; and that 'these fragments were paradisal', the completion to the *Cantos*' ascent. Pound couldn't hear enough of that, until fatigue welled up and, as it seemed to Hall, for a black quarter of an hour drowned all hope. Then Pound pulled himself together and said, 'Let's be going'—he wanted to show Hall the Circus Maximus.

One evening Pound attended a reception at the Chilean Embassy, and the ambassador invited him to visit Chile, offering free flights and hotels. Then, after Hall had left Rome, Pound was writing a series of letters to Ronald Duncan about a performance of *Women of Trachis*, giving detailed notes on how it should be spoken and sung: 'may be the Xoros ought to be declaimed by one good voice—with the chorus moving to the thud of the words'; and, 'sometimes a lot of syllables start same level of pitch & may relapse into speech for particularly emphatic statement'. 'What chance of combining with the B Bloody C to get me to England?', he asked, followed by, 'I'll be dead by '61.' In mid-March he was driven across Italy to Fonti di Tolentino to visit Leopardi's house and garden. He was 'not well, but better', he told George Hartley of the Marvell Press when returning the proofs of the new edition of *Gaudier-Brzeska*. And he told both Dudek and Gatter that he was hoping 'to resume human activity some time'.

One day Samuel Hynes chanced to encounter him walking in the Borghese Gardens—this was probably in April or early May when Pound had left Dadone's and was staying in a hotel. Hynes, an American scholar who had visited Pound in St Elizabeths, was now spending some time in Rome with his wife and very young daughters—the daughters were playing nearby in the Gardens. Pound 'hadn't changed much', Hynes decided,

> a little thinner, perhaps, the furrows in his face more deeply scored, his eyes sunk more deeply into their sockets... a little less of the old imperial manner, and something new in its place—a quietness, the kind that comes after great trouble.

Pound sat down with him and talked about the *Cantos*, and about how he could not complete the work; but, Hynes thought, 'He didn't seem to feel that this unfinished state was a failure, not a personal one'; it was the times that had failed to provide the sought after order. 'The problem was how to resist brainwashing, the power of the system to shape our thoughts.' When Pound stood up to leave Hynes called his daughters to meet the great poet.

The elder of the two, 'held her hand out before her, palm down, fingers a little bent, as a princess might, greeting a duke. Pound took the waiting hand in his, bowed, and kissed it gently.' Then he strode off, 'a solitary erect figure, toward the Pincian Gate'.

He was sending Marcella intimate letters of love and regret, of anxiety and guilt, written in starts and fragments. On 'a rainy easter', he wrote, 'I been trying to write for days, and I get more muddled', but he managed this—

> Oh, m'amour, so much beauty
> quanti dolci pensier' ,

—that was Dante's reflection on Paolo and Francesca in their circle of hell, 'what sweet thoughts, what longing, led them to this woful pass'—

> and I did you so wrong
> letting you in on all my past error

On 29 April he wrote from Zagarolo, a town outside Rome,

> His trouble, he keeps gumming things up / mind stops, then rushes. 20 minutes clear, then he tangles. . . .
> Ibsen : life a struggle with phantoms of the mind. . . .
> Has now gummed up even Canto ms- which was for her glory, and then he didn't want her exposed to the furies.

He was taking apart his original draft of 115, partly so as to 'not transmit private discouragements', but also to remove her from it in order to protect her from scandal. 'He having nerves as she may have gathered', he added next day. On 12 May he typed—

> dear, my dear, The beauty they have had, they have had. She conserve it.
>
> That they mistook his release for a triumph, The whole picture of his world, which was their private world, and not very accurate as to the outside. She is not to blame for that, which is what he meant by 'misleading her'. She couldn't have known. He not strong enough to hold off the outside.

At the end of May Pound showed up in Rapallo 'without so much as a toothbrush', as Dorothy put it—she had been there for some time—then went back with Mary to pack up in Rome and return to settle in Rapallo for the summer. Dorothy reported him as bathing in the sea and doing well, though 'his head v. wobbly & indecisive'.

On 8 June he wrote to Marcella, 'Bless you for heroic offer 3rd and 4th inst. It takes me 6 hours to write a letter. have lost roman friends. . . .' He ended, 'Time—place—me think of something.'. The day before he had written, 'He can't git to Texas, he don't see ahead . . . Why shdn't I have let the day dream go on, and not rung useless alarm bells.' And on the day after, 'haven't come up with an answer'; then on the 10th, 'don't seem to answer question: a place & a date'. A month later he told her, on 14 July, 'leaving Rap. domattina', tomorrow morning, 'don't know that anybody will hear what becomes of him or if he will have an address'. In fact he was not eating and was being taken up to Brunnenburg. 'Sure wd. like to see a plantation,' he wrote, 'but keep out of ~~Europe~~ Rapallo till I get to some city . . . I shd. have come home sooner. She is the love of his life & he thought he had killed her by misschance.' One can just make out through the course of these letters a hopeless plotting to be together again.

Dorothy had her suspicions of that, which she shared with Moore in May: 'Of course I suspect his intention is to recall the girl to live with him—knowing his awful persistence! much worse now his wits scatter so.' Still, 'Ezra is released in my custody,' she wrote later, and that gave her a sense of being in control of the situation. She was exercising her powers by keeping close control of his literary property, on that occasion by refusing T. E. Lawrence's brother permission to use a letter Pound had written to Lawrence. 'Ezra is released in my custody,' she declared, and then, as if it followed that his rights were thereby made over to her, she coolly went on, 'and I prefer the long letter should not appear'.

Then there was the matter of Pound's money. In Rome in February he was tied up in knots about it, had been for months. He was trying to write his own cheques drawing on his own funds, and Dorothy was telling him he could not do that, and that she had to account for every item of his expenditure 'to Mr. Gleason'. It was not as if they were short of money—Moore had advised her that 'you have plenty to enable EP to be kept comfortable'. But having control of his finances was a very good way of keeping him under control. There was also the longer-term consideration, that Omar's inheritance should be kept safe. And as that included his literary property, she was packing up and sending to Omar in America all of Pound's letters to her that she could find in the boxes that had been stored up at Sant'Ambrogio and were now at Brunnenburg, early letters between them and his letters from the DTC; also Wyndham Lewis's drawings, which were her own, and Lewis's letters to Pound which weren't. Her fear, as Moore had expressed it, was that if the letters were 'to remain at Brun Mary will doubtless make some claim as all belonging to her—and she might not part with WL's which you wish Omar to have'.

Pound was not in a good place. In July Dorothy reported him 'full of manias'—some of them perhaps 'justifiable—difficult to tell—& he hardly speaks at all—wh may be wisdom learnt too late'. It was taking her up to half an hour to get him to put on a shirt to go down to eat, and then he would eat nothing. He wanted to go back to Brunnenburg, and they did that on the 15th. But there he went on 'a hunger strike', and Dorothy wondered if he were trying to kill himself, or was it penitence? He was taken down to a clinic run by nuns in Merano—'a sort of rest home', Dorothy called it—and was cared for there for a couple of weeks.

Back in the castle on 5 August he began a letter to Marcella, 'He start again [. . .] Was following her thru the plantations, and then crash.' He 'plugged up the salita' to post that note, and continued on Sunday 7th, 'been sufficiently coherent to do a day's work, or approx, instead of being lugged around like a sack of meal'. He was putting the question to himself, 'has he got what it takes to make a new start, and not merely shrivvel. With a bit more guts, or another month, he might have made Paris. Ugh . . . She doin' all the work, and ready to sail.' The questioning went beyond Marcella. Eliot was being 'more assiduous', and there was a new play 'called Rhinoceros by a bloke with a name like Unesco', and 'There are 40 young with techniques', and, at '15 minutes pas' midnight', he was asking, 'Has he still got what it takes to make a come-back.' A week later he admitted,

> No, my Dear | There aren't any new Cantos to speak of, only the ones she has copy of, which he took in his suit case, presumably to Milano for three days, and then on to Roma for 6 months | and all that happened was to get 'em more confused and shifted about. | And instead of shouting he drifted, and what he was convinced of once, he wasn't so convinced of.

He wondered, did she feel up to re-typing the Cantos she had taken with her, 'in triplicate, and sending him orig. and second carbon'? Marcella did that almost by return, posting the freshly typed copies to him on 30 August.

R. Murray Schafer, the Canadian composer and music-theorist, spent a few days with Pound at Brunnenburg about this time. They talked in the tower room, about Arab music, and about *Le Testament* which Schafer wanted to produce with the BBC. 'Pound was a generous conversationalist,' he recalled, 'he listened. He asked questions. There was no monologue but an exchange of ideas—at least one flattered oneself to think so.' Only once did he touch on 'the renunciation theme so often recounted by other visitors of those years', and that was when he said, 'We've made a mess of the world for you people'—'and then we returned to Arab music'. When they got on to *Le Testament*, Pound '"sang" portions' while Schafer looked at the music, and 'was astonished at his impeccable memory for the songs well over forty years since they had been composed.' There was just one untoward but revealing moment. Schafer and his wife were invited to tea, and Dorothy,

Mary, and Boris, were all there, and 'Pound was sullen'—and 'then after he reckoned we had chatted enough said in a plangent voice I shall never forget: "Schafer came here to talk music and the whole thing has degenerated into a god-damned tea-party."' Then he 'sprang out of his chair with a startling athleticism' to fetch the books in which he had marked places, 'and for the next several hours he read poems and we talked about how they could be set to music'. There was nothing wrong with him then. As Schafer was leaving Pound handed him 'an open brown envelope, '"Something to read on the train. When you get back to London give this to Tom."' In the envelope was 'a neat typewritten draft' of the final Cantos.

Michael Reck and his wife paid a visit that autumn and found a different Pound. 'He seemed very tired, at times had difficulty finishing a sentence, at times almost whispered. "I've been sick, you know", he said. "I haven't been able to read for a year".' And Reck said, '"In any case, you are resting,"' and '"No"', came the answer, '"just . . . " his voice trailed away " . . . pushing"'. But as they were standing up to leave, 'Pound rises suddenly and, with an access of vigor, *kicks* his chair back', and his face 'crinkles profoundly in a smile' as he shakes hands in farewell.

His depression was beginning to take hold of him, however. He had the proofs of his *Paris Review* interview to correct, but his concentration gave out towards the end. A year later Dorothy would find the partly corrected proofs in his drawer and ask Hall to add a note 'saying that Pound had lacked strength to complete his corrections'. Back in June, in Rapallo, he had accepted an invitation to lecture in October to students in Lund, and that had been followed by invitations from Uppsala and Copenhagen. His first thought had been to speak on 'controversial figures, private worlds', but the advertised topic became the anodyne 'Technique and Language of Poetry'. When the time came the lecture tour had to be called off. As Mary explained to Pound's Swedish publisher, 'One day he feels very well, and one day he feels so depressed that he won't even leave his room or talk.'

In mid-October he did manage to do a reading for a cultural society in Trento, down the Adige valley. Eveline Bates Doob, wife of a Yale professor who was in Merano for the year, met him a day or two after that when they were having tea with Mary at the castle, and wrote in her journal,

> the door swung open and there he was. Tall, shaggy white beard, longish white hair, a bright yellow scarf flung jauntily around his neck and down one shoulder, piercing eyes.

He stood in the doorway and stared and said nothing for a long moment, then went to each of the visitors in turn, 'bowed, shook hands, and what I'll never forget, stared straight in my eyes with such glittering intensity that I couldn't possibly turn away'. He sat down, and to break the silence Mrs Doob said they had been talking about the new English novelists and what did he think about them, but he could only mumble something she could not make out, 'with his head down over his plate'. From then on 'E.P. only listened. But he did *listen*... And he never seemed bored, or withdrawn even.' When they were leaving 'he shook hands (icy cold hands) quite graciously and said goodbye'. Before the end of the month, in Dorothy's opinion, 'the nervous breakdown [was] pretty far gone'. Scraps and fragments of writing confirm that he was sinking back into a sad and self-lacerating depression.

In December he was not eating again and was taken for X-rays, which showed 'nothing wrong in his middle', and some new pills seemed to help. 'Eating a little better now,' Dorothy reported to Moore. On the 15th Pound felt able to write to Marcella—

> Ciao, Cara. wish I cd/ be with you this Xmas. Weight down to 120 lbs. yes 120, not 160 . or 180 . or cent kilos.
>
> Got to x rays yester and feeling better. First time I got dragged up the salita for month or more.
>
> As they say, so low, no place to go but up.
>
> If on the loose at all in the spring, shd probably be totally so for a season, but alzo totally broke.
>
> Ciao. sentences run smoothly, for once. as to the pull of particular words, etc.
>
> Love, m'amour. Will stop this before it gets into a snarl . As am due back at roentgen rays place again oggi.
>
> As can again read at least half a page di seguito, resolved to set bak, relaX . and try long term effort.

'Love | E', he signed off, with the initial a flourish, then wrote one word more, 'hope'.

It would have been about this time that he sent to Agnes Bedford, by hand of one of his visitors, the 'type-script of 7 new cantos'. DP 'seemed to know nothing' about them, Bedford told Omar. And Dorothy remarked to Omar that she was unable to control EP's mail since he was in a different part of the building.

In the New Year—'3 Jan. I think'—Pound typed a full page and more to Olga Rudge. 'Why o could n't I have come to you?', he began, and answered himself, 'block and blackout/ blackouts appear to be about ten years long, '46/56.' But now he was reaching out to her from his pit of depression, 'May be still time, some how, now that I have done so much evil.' He went on about having 'done wrong to everybody', to Yeats by not reading him, to the people who had stuck their necks out for him, by not showing proper gratitude at the time; to 'Tate the poet, and the rev. Eliot', and to Hemingway, and to Olga herself, 'a marvel, always trying to educate him, the uneducatable', as at Genova in 1945 when he was under arrest and being questioned there. And as to why, once back in Italy and in Rapallo, he had 'persisted in not getting up hill at St Am/ save without announcement and missing you', that must have been because he was 'crazier when I got out of bughouse than when in'. 'In fact INSIDE was where he belonged for COMFORT, and no responsibility, able to think soap bubble and be lord of creation with no fuss.' But still, 'for past year and a half WHY, Why , Why', and 'how much time he will be given, now he looks like a Tyrolese devil mask'. 'Give the New Year a chance', he appealed, reaching out to her again, 'She is marvellous. and he don't know what to do about it. At any rate he can think of her among the emparadysed spirits, and him repenting and then some.' He ended: 'will continue this if she can stand it. | but take this down to post now.' One has the impression that he was coming out of a dream, recognizing that he had been caught up in a doomed romance, and painfully struggling to reconnect with a previous life.

A few days later he began a long letter to Marcella, 'Feelin a bit more human. dunno about weight, but appetite returning.' This was not a lover's letter, but newsy, even chatty, all about visitors and people at the castle and one thing and another. Olga had been put out of her Sant'Ambrogio house, the thirty-year lease being up. Dadone was very ill, and was being attacked by Ramperti for having presented Pound to Ungaretti; and Dadone had not wanted Pound to be 'mixed with group that was paintin hackenkreutzes on synagogues'; and 'ANYHOW I am still in the DAWG house'. 'And Mr Norman's volume does not present me as anyone fit for you to know'. The tone is light, 'more human', and much less intimate. According to Dorothy's diary, that was the day Pound got out the Fenollosa manuscripts again and was putting some order into them.

Eveline Doob was observing Pound's behaviour through that winter. 'We've been seeing him fairly regularly,' she wrote in her journal on 2 February, 'he's usually present on our visits to the castle', and he had been down with Mary and Boris to lunch with them. She noted his silences, his listening, his occasional pointed contributions. 'No question that he follows our talk and is fully capable of being coherent'. But that day, visiting the Doobs with Dorothy and Boris, he had sat for three hours in blank silence, 'blinking staring, SILENCE', unresponsive to the simplest question, such as '"What will you have to drink, Mr Pound?"' 'I don't think it's insanity,' she wrote, 'it's deep, *deepening* depression', and the cause, she decided, was that he was 'unbearably discontent with himself'. She noticed, but drew no conclusion from it, that when DP said, '"Shan't we go now Ezra?", he had stared straight ahead as if she weren't there', but then did get up and go with Boris after Dorothy had gone ahead to the bus. Mrs Doob thought to 'bring a little light, joy, comfort' to Pound by telling him in a letter that she had been reading his critical works and that it was 'Fantastic to read the sharp, passionate, sometimes sheer genius of precision, and the excitement it communicates about the role of poetry'. On her next visit to the castle, encouraged by Mary's telling her that Pound had seemed pleased by her letter, she talked to him about how wonderful his criticism was, and when he said nothing but listened intently she 'was feeling inspired', until he cut her off, saying abruptly, '"I think it's time now that we call a halt to your beautiful performance."' Then when she was leaving,

> E.P. said it was nice for me to say all the things I'd said, even if it *was* 'all bunk', and then he grabbed hold of my shoulders, stared straight in my eyes and said, 'But don't you see? There was something *rotten* behind it all!'

In her journal Mrs Doob concluded that Pound was tortured by his past errors and obsessions, and she thought of 'his enthusiasm for fascism, his dreadful antisemitic allusions and statements, and, worst for him, the treason that he denied having committed but cannot dismiss in his own mind, it seems'. Those things 'were terribly wrong and he knows it', she decided, 'God knows he knows it! He's the prototype of the hero at the moment of tragic perception.' That was evidently a satisfying conclusion to her reflections after that day's experience. But for all the possible sharpness of the final insight she was not equipped to read Pound's mind, and was simply projecting upon his words and behaviour what in her judgment he ought to be feeling. Among the things she probably did not know was the fact that Pound was in Dorothy's custody.

Later in February Dorothy told Moore that Pound was refusing to eat, and refusing to speak or answer questions, and was always saying 'No' to her. He was perfectly in order physically, she thought, only there was 'this WILL to starve himself to death presumably'. It made her very mad, she told Omar. But then, with the prospect of doing a reading for students in Milan and going on from there to Rome, Pound took 'a turn for the better'.

Eveline Doob saw him in Rome at Dadone's on Sunday 19 March and wrote in her journal that night, 'Here were two frail old men, both of them ailing, forlorn, and neither of them capable, even if they had wanted, to excite anyone about the hanged demon, Il Duce.' She asked if he had enjoyed his Milan reading, and he answered without hesitation that he had; and what did he think of Quasimodo, who had also read in Milan, and had he enjoyed *his* poetry? The answers were direct: 'I admire a man who has the courage to say what he believes'; and he had liked what Quasimodo read, 'but I haven't read very much and now I think I should read more of it'. Mrs Doob concluded 'that just to be out, seeing people, after the isolation of the castle was doing him good. At least he was considerably more spirited.'

On the Monday Pound and Dadone were at a meeting where Oswald Mosley spoke in favour of a European Union. According to *La Stampa* Mosley's purpose in coming to Rome was to introduce this new idea to their former Fascists. Pound was seated on the platform, and was applauded when introduced to the audience. He did not speak, but was reported in *Frankfurter Rundschau* as saying after the meeting that he believed the day would come for European unity.

Reports on his health varied—he was eating well, then he was not eating at all. Eveline Doob noted on 15 April, 'Evidently he not only won't (or can't make himself) eat, but he's not taking any fluids, or so little that the skin is peeling off his hands,' and Dadone, 'who's been trying to get him to eat and cheer him up... says he can't cope with him any more'. Dadone told Mary that the doctors thought Pound's heart was failing. Mary went down to Rome at the start of May with the intention of taking him back to Brunnenburg, but when she got there and saw the state Pound was in she arranged for him to go into a clinic, the 'Villa "I Pini", Casa di Cura per Malati Nervosi'. Olga Rudge visited him there on 14 May, and found him confined to his bed and neither eating nor drinking. She later recalled how, after a long silence, he had said, 'There's an *eye* watching me,' and she had feared that he was losing contact with reality; but then in the afternoon she had seen the eye of one of the attendants looking through a crack in half-open shutters and been reassured. She kept up her visits, travelling down from Siena at weekends in May, then 'every day, twice a day' for the first two weeks in June. On the 15th she decided with Mary that Pound was not getting any better and must be moved back to Brunnenburg. They drove him up to Merano in a hired car, with Pound 'curled up on the back seat like a foetus'. When they reached the town that evening he was so weak that it seemed best to place him in the Martinsbrunn Casa di Cura. He would remain there until the following April, very nearly a full year.

'He will never be himself again,' Dorothy told Moore in early July. In early August she told Omar, 'he might not last long'. He was now being fed intravenously. On the 11th Mary said to Eveline Doob, 'He's just *dying*,' and she had called Olga who was arriving that evening. But the next day Mary was saying he 'is drinking and drinking and drinking', and cursing, which might be 'a sign of health'. Olga, as she narrated to James Wilhelm years later, had gone immediately to the clinic and 'found him lying in his bed, with his head turned toward the wall . . . clearly dying'—

> But the minute I entered the room, he turned his head toward me and nodded hello. I told him that I had heard he wasn't eating. He said nothing. I walked over and sat by the bed, undoing a packet of chocolates from his favorite store in Venice. I took a piece and held it toward him, saying, 'Here, Ezra. Do eat'. He looked at me with blank, hopeless eyes and said nothing. I raised the piece toward his mouth, put it in, and watched him begin to chew. He chewed and chewed, and then he swallowed. The fast had been broken.

In another version Olga attributed the miracle to a jar of Chinese ginger which grandson Walter had brought from London for Pound, and after he had been given a little bit, the next day 'E. demanded a piece of ginger, after which he asked for a ham sandwich.'

Three deaths touched him deeply about this time. He had heard of Hemingway's in May, but it had been kept from him that it was by suicide, until one of the nuns happened to mention the fact, and then he became upset, lamenting that America destroyed its best writers. In mid-September Dag Hammarskjöld was killed when his plane mysteriously crashed in the Congo, and the news made Pound wild with despair: 'This is the end!', he cried. At the end of that month news came that Hilda Doolitle had died in Switzerland, and this time he was moved to assert her immortality. The letter announcing her death, from Norman Holmes Pearson with Perdita and Bryher, quoted the message of Venus speaking 'in the winter dark' in HD's *Sagesse*. This begins, 'arise, arise, re-animate, | O Spirit, this small ark, this little body', and ends with an affirmation of 'Love who redeems the lost'. Pound, in his bed, scrawled an impromptu translation of the lines into Italian, incorporating a note to Mary, 'Translate this for Vanni or some current obit of H.D. | or I will if my signature is of use.' Then he put into Italian HD's '[to] set [the] dead pyre flaming'. To Pearson, who had been close to HD, he wrote that he had been struggling to write to him about her death, but 'besides she isn't @ all'. He was thinking of how he and HD had known each other over sixty years, '60 years unrequited devotion', as he expressed it to Olga; and he was thinking of her continuing life in her poetry, 'Helen in Egypt a marvel,' he wrote to Pearson, and 'H in Egt the real epic'. To Perdita, HD's daughter, he wrote, 'algae of long past sea currents are moved'.

In October Dorothy reported that Pound was both 'more lucid' and 'looking old'. On the 14th, evidently writing with difficulty, he told Olga that he was 'sitting at desk for first time'. The letter carried on over five hard to read pages, full of remorse and a sense of failure. But when Olga went up to see him she found him '*much better* than when I saw him in Rome . . . mind clear, not in the terrible state of anxiety and self-reproach'. 'He *can* get well', she was encouraged to think. She wrote to him positively, and told him to practise writing and let it come back gradually, not to force it.

Mary Barnard also saw Pound in the clinic that October. She had been warned that she would find him very much changed, and had imagined him aged, but he looked, as she wrote afterwards, 'not like an old man, but like a dead man, with a fleshless head such as one might see on a slab in a morgue'. He had had a blood transfusion that morning, she was told, and was extremely fatigued. He had asked to see her when he heard that she was at Brunnenburg for a few days, but it seemed then that he had nothing to say, and Barnard began to doubt he knew who she was. Finally he did speak, 'H.D.'s death was a great loss', and 'You never met her, did you?' He was not only remembering her, but casting back to her having not followed up his giving her HD's address more than once in the past. Evidently 'his mind and memory were still alive,' Barnard thought, but she had no doubt that he was on his death-bed.

There are odd scraps which appear to have been written in Martinsbrunn. One reads—

> At night, now 3.15 a.m. I still get a few, damn few moments when can write cogerent sentences, i.e. I take it when mass hypnotizers' agent is asleep. / Then the blurr returns, and I continue in basso inferno of incoherence. Paralysis, unable to write.

Another scrap—

> Telescope is totally blind to everything save the spot it is focussed on. Week's agony to get that trope to illustrate my total blindness
> AT moments

When he did manage to get that image right, there must have been some positive satisfaction, even some pleasure, in the clear self-knowledge.

He was still in Martinsbrunn clinic in January 1962, but slowly improving. 'He has been much better lately,' Dorothy reported to Moore, 'but yesterday was in trouble again about the urine problem'. The real problem was an enlarged prostate, and a catheter which had been inserted to assist with urination and had to be changed regularly, a beastly business, according to Olga. She went up to see him on Valentine's Day, and was delighted to find him 'eating, showing interest in newspapers'. A few days before he had 'surprised Mary by being dressed and *ready to go out* . . . walked as far as the gate and back with no fatigue'. He had sent Olga a telegram, which frightened her, but it read 'Keep hoping.' His mind was turning to Sant'Ambrogio and the good things they had done and known together.

On 15 March Dorothy was surprised to find Olga at the clinic having lunch with Pound, and then, as she noted in her diary, talking with Mary. 'Something is moving,' she thought; and she wondered where would they 'park' him now that he was getting better. He was taking 20-minute walks, and then walking a bit longer, and staying up longer. And he was longing for Rapallo. Dorothy was apparently unaware that Olga was eagerly preparing to receive him at Sant'Ambrogio in the cottage below the church where she was now living. 'I would be ready to receive *Him* in ten days or two weeks,' she had written on 2 March, and had told him that 'He and Mary could spend the first night or two at Villa Chiara,' Dr Bacigalupo's clinic, 'see the urologist, and face the bit of a walk to Casita 131 rested'. She had given 'Yeats' ex-bed and bedtable a lick of paint... so if He feeling up to the simple life, glad to see Him when He likes'. At the end of March she wrote again, 'she hoping to see Him in House of Pure affection overlooking Golfo Tigullio'. This was what she had been waiting for all her life, she had told him. And she wrote to Ronald Duncan 'in haste—am painting, cleaning, contriving' because 'EP is expected here just before or after Easter'; but '*please*—don't tell *anyone else* about this... The situation is extremely delicate.' To Pound himself she wrote on 6 April, 'as she painfully sees he hasn't yet got unstuck'; and Pound acknowledged, 'he hasn't got mobilized & he don't see how'.

Somehow it was arranged that Mary would take him to Rapallo—to stay with Olga for a month, Dorothy agreed. Mary packed up his things at the clinic on the 25th, and on the 26th, as Dorothy informed Moore the next day, 'we brought EP here, Rapallo, without any trouble.... He ate a good lunch—and M d R delivered him over to Olga R—up outside the town. She is to take care of him for perhaps a month.' 'We all need a change badly,' she added. Ten days later she let Moore know that she was 'not in communication with them'. And at the end of the year she would tell him, 'They have taken possession of E.P.—I can't say much as it's a job I can't do myself—and as I got on E.P.'s nerves, he wouldn't do anything I wanted.' She was only 'thankful that he's not in the hands of Marcella Spann'. Olga would later note for the record, 'when He was well enough to move, He came back to me at Sant'Ambrogio—and stayed. I gave up my job and took over.'

17 : His Sickness & His Wealth, 1962–4

Mainly clinical

Ezra and Olga would be inseparable for the rest of his life. As for Ezra and Dorothy, they would henceforth be separated in fact, if not in law; but Dorothy, as Committee for Ezra Pound, would maintain to the end her hold over him, and while not able either to care for or wholly to control his person, she would contrive to have absolute control of his literary property and of his increasing income from it. She would allow him a monthly dole out of his funds sufficient for his necessities, every cent of which, she would continue to insist, had to be accounted for 'to the Court'. And she would decide whether to grant or to withhold permission to publish his writings, often without bothering to consult or even to inform him.

In April 1962 Olga was renting a small cottage in Sant'Ambrogio; but two years later, in the summer of 1964, she would be able to move back to Casa 60, this time occupying with Pound the middle and not the top floor of the house. She had also kept free her little house in Venice's Calle Querini for them to go to in the winter, refusing her tenant's request to extend his lease. They would spend the cold months there when Venice was most itself, uncluttered with tourists; but would rent out the house for the summer season and return to Sant'Ambrogio above Rapallo and its Gulf of Tigullio.

The immediate concern, in May 1962, was Pound's physical state. Dr Bacigalupo was disturbed to find his old friend lying on a bed, strikingly thin, his face hollowed out, quite silent, only his blue eyes alive to everything going on around him. He quickly determined that the root of Pound's problems, including his not wanting to eat and his depression, was an enlarged prostate causing retention of urine and thence serious uremic blood poisoning. In the clinics in Rome and Merano all attention had been on his nervous condition, and his talk of being diseased and infected had been dismissed as delusional. Now treatment of his physical condition was urgent, but because he was not a free person the permission of his legal guardian had to be sought, and Dorothy had returned to Brunnenburg and Dr Bacigalupo was having difficulty contacting her. Then in early June Pound suffered a serious haemorrhage, his temperature shot up, and it became imperative that he be admitted to hospital at once. Dr Sacco, a leading urologist at Genoa's Galliera Hospital, was called in and confirmed the diagnosis of serious uremic blood poisoning and the immediate need for detoxification by the insertion of a catheter above the pubis to draw off the poison. Dorothy, now back in Rapallo—Omar was with her there for a week or two—signed the permission for the operation on 15 June, and it was carried out, under local anaesthetic, on the 19th. It was foreseen, however, that the surgical removal of the prostate would probably be called for once Pound had recovered sufficiently.

He left the Villa Chiara on the 30th and did get back his physical energy fairly soon, but, as Dr Bacigalupo noted, he still spoke very little, and when questioned struggled to find words, though what he did manage to say would be to the point and would show that there was nothing wrong with his memory. Thomas Cole who had visited and corresponded with Pound when he was in St Elizabeths—Cole was then the precocious young editor of *Imagi* and a poet in the old romantic way—saw Pound while he was still in the Villa Chiara, and found his silence 'frustrating, uncomfortable'. 'Other than a few forced words (he repeated "I remember"), he merely smiled forlornly and nodded and held me with his piercing eyes.' Pound attempted to explain in a note addressed to Cole, written just after he had gone, what it was like from his side of the non-conversation: 'My malady "includes" an absolute wall or vacuum | For indefinite period between interlocutor'—and here he drew the wall or vacuum, resting on 'time lag'—with 'ez or eg' on the other side of it. Then he elaborated: 'During your call —NO perception on my part that you had come FROM the U.S.' In consequence he had failed, if one follows his thought, to send his best 'to old Bill whose patience is & of right ought to be EGzausted'. He resumed: 'There is an insanity | neither illogical [?nor] incorrect in registering what is said to it | BUT INcapable of perceiving the person speaking while the talk is going on.' The note ends, '& pray that I recover (not from the disease they think I have but from this particular insensibility which is not defined by any psyc I have read —but then I havent read any of em'.

Next day, instead of sending the note to Cole who had probably left Rapallo, he enclosed it with one to Bill Williams, 'almost first letter have writ since recovery', asking him if he could help define 'this impenetrability'. 'Dante's hell is COLD at bottom,' he remarked, discriminating a difference from his own, in which there was 'nothing loco | no hate, no coldness, but just that eg condition'. It was not 'indifference', he insisted, this 'insensitivity I am briefly jabbing @'—and again he drew his diagram,

speaker || vacuum transmitting NO sense of the speaker || Eg

—'Eg' apparently standing for himself as exhibit in the case. 'Am not yapping re/ stupidity in general or insensitivity as such', he added on a fourth sheet, and ended, 'I spose there is an equation in electronics for it.' One significant feature of this struggle to articulate his condition is that Pound does not mention the difficulty of finding and uttering words. It is rather as if the poison in his blood had affected the electro-chemical functioning of his brain and brought on a form of autism. There was more to his silence than an inability to get his words out, and something much harder to bear. Now he feared that he really was insane.[1]

He was in good form, however, when Henry Swabey saw him up at Sant'Ambrogio in August, 'much thinner now and quiet', but 'the same keen eyes . . . Nor, after severe illnesses, had his mind clouded.' Pound appears to have conversed without difficulty, and, when Swabey was leaving, he and Olga walked with him some way down the *salita*. He was doing well and eating now, Dorothy had heard.

She was sending Olga a monthly cheque 'for Ezra's "keep"'—allowing '60,000 lire a month for food', or just under $100. 'Please let Ezra have all the little luxuries,' she instructed, while requiring lists of all expenditures for the monthly accounting. Then she wrote, 'let me send you something extra for all your work; I did not understand he could not bathe and dress himself. What do you suggest as a monthly stipend?' That was very kindly putting Olga in her place as Ezra's carer. In 1963 she would make the monthly cheque $200, then the Court allowed $300 for 'care and maintenance of the Patient', this to include medical expenses. In 1964 the allowance was raised again to $400—eventually it would rise to $800. But not until July 1970 would the Court be petitioned by the Committee 'to make monthly payments to Miss Rudge in the amount of $100 per month as compensation for her services to the patient'.

News came that Ezra Pound had been awarded *Poetry*'s 50th anniversary Harriet Monroe Memorial Prize. To mark the special occasion the prize money had been raised to $500, and was to be awarded for any contribution to *Poetry* since its foundation by Miss Monroe in 1912. The citation named

[1] In fact most if not all his recent afflictions could be accounted for by uremic blood poisoning. As the blood flows to and serves every function of the organism so toxins in the blood can cause multiple dysfunction. Common symptoms include fatigue, shortness of breath, loss of appetite leading to loss of weight, clouding of the mind, depression, dry skin, and impairment of speech.

Pound, 'the great poet', as the 'one inevitable choice', because of his many contributions to the magazine, and because 'No other person in the history of this magazine helped her to do the proudest things that *Poetry* has done.' Laughlin, who had selected the opening section of canto 113 for publication in the anniversary issue, must have given instructions for the $500 to be sent to Dorothy as Committee for Ezra Pound, since she wrote to Pound in mid-October to let him know that she was holding the cheque. It was made out in his name, 'but perhaps after your signature I had better put DP Co for EP? Or if you make it over to me I can send it to the B. di Roma Merano, which is all your money although in my name.' At the end of December Pound would write a brief note to Dorothy—they were both then in Rapallo—wishing her 'Happy New Year', and asking her to send $200 'from my account' to Mary as a Christmas present. But, as Dorothy would insist to Olga, 'no money is supposed to be his "own" nowadays'.

Olga had taken Pound to Venice at the end of September, as soon as he was fit to travel by train. That winter and early spring Richard Stern, a young American writer, saw him from time to time in Calle Querini. He judged that Pound was not fully recovered from his operation and was still adjusting to having to live with the 'physical inconvenience' of his urinary apparatus. At the same time he was reading a lot. During his first visit Stern encountered 'that famous silence'; but the next time they 'talked for a couple of hours, fairly easily'—

> He asked me what was going on. I told him what I knew, we disagreed about Eliot's plays—he liked them a lot—he spoke of the coherence in Frost and Eliot ('Frost wanted to be New England'), men who had their feet planted in one place, a fortunate, an enviable thing. Nothing overwhelming, but every sentence, clear, complete and underwritten by thought, so rare that the word sanity took on a new depth for me.

Pound could be playful as well, or at least Stern took it to be playful when Pound would reply to the formulaic 'How are you, Mr Pound?', with the single word, 'Senile'. His style though was generally simple and courteous, creating a sense of occasion. Once, however, something said brought Pound's feelings of guilt and failure welling up, and he gripped Stern's hand and drew him close, '"Wrong, wrong, wrong. I've always been wrong,"' he said, '"I've never recognised benevolence,"' and 'he'd left only notes, scattered notes, he hadn't made anything clear'. Stern could not comfort him, 'The old man was touching bottom.'

Others were wanting to assure him that he had not failed, his errors notwithstanding. George Oppen, who had turned to Communism in the 1930s, wrote to him, 'Dear Pound',

I suppose if we should take to talking politics to each other I would disagree even more actively than all those others who have disagreed, but there has been no one living during my life time who has been as generous or as pure as you toward literature and toward writers. Nor anyone less generously thanked.

I know of no one who does not owe you a debt.

Lowell wrote, praising the *Paris Review* interview as 'the best statement of our and your case that anyone has made', and telling Pound that the words of his favourites among the *Cantos* 'stay with me and sing, and are not just the words of a poem but a message and a record'. 'Be proud', he urged, 'that for so much of your long life you have been a fountain for your friends and readers.'

When William Carlos Williams died on 4 March 1963, Pound cabled to Flossie Williams, 'he bore with me for sixty years. I shall never have another poet friend like him.' At her house after the funeral Flossie extracted Pound's cable from a bundle she was clutching and said to Denise Levertov and Mack Rosenthal, 'This is the one that means most to me.' She wrote back to Pound, 'it is just as true for Bill and his respect love and admiration for you. He counted on you—that I know.'

About that time Pound granted an interview to an Italian journalist, Grazia Livi. Her first impression, she wrote, 'is that his genius is now vanquished', and that 'he is not himself any more and that all the elements of his being are coordinated in a purely physical, functional way'. When she wrote up the interview from her rough notes, she began it with her remarking to him that she was a little afraid coming to see him, and had him reply with the since often quoted statement, 'I understand. I spoil everything I touch. I have always blundered.' The journalist then wondered 'what a man like you must think of the mass media, such as television or the press, intruding into the private lives of people', and to that he replied, revealing a mind in perfect working order, 'would you prefer to live alone in a room, or in a sewer with dozens of drains?' Livi put the interview back on her track by having him say,

all my life I believed I knew something. But then one strange day came when I realized that I knew nothing, yes, I knew nothing. And so words became void of meaning.

That statement too is often quoted, but not what followed—

Livi. Perhaps they became void of meaning also because new elements had forced their way into men's lives. I mean increasing mechanization and its antipoetic and alienating effects on humanity.

Pound. Yes, that too. But at the same time I believe that is all temporary. I think there is something 'seminal' in humanity that can outlive mechanization. In short, I believe something of man's consciousness will remain, despite everything, and that it will be able to fight against the forces of mindlessness.

While the advertised theme of the interview, the one critics have fastened on, is Pound's having arrived at 'ultimate uncertainty', at knowing only 'that I know nothing', there is also this strong counter-theme, that 'there is something "seminal" in humanity', and that there is a world to be known. That counter-theme is developed and becomes dominant in this later exchange:

Livi. Then what is it that binds you to life now that you have attained the supreme certainty of uncertainty?
Pound. Nothing binds me to life any more. I am simply 'immersed' in it.
Livi. And I was hoping that the pure wisdom which comes with old age might also bring beauty and peace!
Pound. Yes, it can bring peace also. The universe is so very marvellous.

Or, as he had expressed it in canto 116, 'it coheres all right | even if my notes do not cohere'. Livi seems not to have comprehended the wisdom of being conscious of one's immersion in the vital universe; nor to have realized how Pound's knowing nothing is inseparable from his positive affirmation of the universe and of the potential of human consciousness. At one point she brings *The Spirit of Romance* into her interview, but she quite misses the profound continuity between Pound's youthful and his aged mind. He had not lost his confidence in the intelligence that 'makes cosmos', but only his confidence in his own verbal formulations. Livi ends her interview upon her key note, Pound's confessing 'I have lost the ability to reach the core of my thought with words,' but that is far from meaning, as she assumes, that his mind had stopped.

An American, Jean McClean, spoke with Pound in Venice about the same time as Grazia Livi, and protested that she could not discern in the latter's interview the man she had seen. In reaction to what she regarded as Livi's total failure to comprehend Pound, she portrayed 'a beautiful, quiet, humble, almost Chinese mystic', and recalled

the clean clear beauty of his blue eyes as they passed from gentleness to intensity and back again, his gracious manner, the calm serenity with which he explained to me most coherently what it is like to have to re-examine all one's values at so advanced an age.

She was left with the sense of an 'always searching . . . brilliant intelligence, softened by the lacerated wisdom of a sage'. McClean's enthusiastic account is of course wholly subjective, and it tells us nothing of what Pound actually said; but it does accord with his more positive statements in Livi's report.

When the Academy of American Poets awarded its $5,000 Fellowship for 1963 to Pound he acknowledged the honour with a considered statement of his position in a letter drafted for Dorothy to send to its founder and president:

Dear Mrs Bullock.

40 or more years ago I believed that my work for a clarification of language deserved commendation. This belief endured for some time.

If a majority of the Chancellors now believe that the good in the work as it stands outweighs the errors I can gladly accept their judgement as encouragement to get on with the present search for a true basis.

'Thank you', he concluded, then added 'for magnanimity', and crossed that out, wrote 'for the good you have done', and crossed that out. It was left to Dorothy to close 'With sincere appreciation for what you have done & are doing for "us".' In December she let Olga know that her lawyer in Boston, Mr Gleason, had advised that she, Olga, 'may draw on the prize money at the rate of $200 a month' in lieu of what the Committee would otherwise send her, until the said prize money is exhausted—this so as not to spend 'in excess of the Court's allowance'.

When Ezra and Olga moved back to Rapallo in May Dr Bacigalupo recommended a total prostatectomy, and this was performed by Dr Sacco at the end of the month. Three weeks later 'a perineal insertion of the urethra' was carried out, assuring 'a perfect continence'. Bacigalupo had sworn to Pound that 'he can remake normal men'. However, although the two operations were declared successful, they did render the patient impotent, as Olga noted, and he would need to wear the bothersome 'apparatus' for the rest of his life.

Pound was well enough to accompany Olga to the final concerts of the Accademia season in Siena, and to return with her to Venice in early September, going by way of Rimini so that he might see Sigismundo's Tempio once more. In November, in the hope of completing his recovery, Olga took him to Clinique La Prairie in Clarens, Montreux, which specialized in restorative and rejuvenating treatments. To judge by the vivid and disturbing portrait of Pound drawn by Oskar Kokoschka while he was in the clinic—Kokoschka was then living in Montreux—Pound was in need of such treatment. There is a suggestion of suffering age about the face and hair, while the fierce gaze is inward-directed, angst-ridden. The treatment, by Dr Niehaus, an endocrinologist and diet specialist, did successfully 'disintoxicate' Pound and restore him to stable physical health. It did not, however, cure his mind of its profound depression.

The Committee's agenda

While he was in the Villa Chiara for his operations Pound wrote a 'formal letter' to Dorothy: 'if my old will is not valid, will you see how my possessions can go to Mary. as committee find how this can be done legally.' He wanted his literary estate to provide for his daughter and for her family.

Dorothy's and Omar's lawyers, who were also the legal advisers and agents of Dorothy Pound as Committee for Ezra Pound, had in fact been poring over the 1940 will, seeking grounds on which to dispute its validity. Dorothy had obtained photostat copies from Boris who held the original at Brunnenburg, and had sent them to Moore and to Gleason. Moore who was now retired, though continuing to advise Dorothy and Omar, had passed his copy on to a cousin of Omar's wife Elizabeth, Frank Cockburn, who had taken over their legal affairs in England. Moore suggested to Gleason and to Dorothy, and no doubt to Cockburn also, that a date on the will was suspect, that a witness's signature appeared to be missing, that it was very odd that Mary, who was only 14 in 1940, should be appointed literary executor, that no 'true Executor' was appointed by it, and that he doubted whether the Will was 'good according to Italian or U.S. law'.[2] He implicitly looked forward to Pound's dying intestate, when much would depend on 'whether E.P may be regarded as domiciled in Italy', in which case his property would be administered under Italian law; but if it could be argued that he should be regarded as domiciled in the USA, then 'the certificate of Omar's birth' would certainly be taken into consideration as establishing him as 'one of E.P.'s next of kin' and therefore as having a direct claim on his property after Dorothy herself. In any case 'The Will is definitely bad,' Moore assured Dorothy, 'unless Mary finds something to prove her legitimacy'. There was the nub of the matter: a determination, shared by all three lawyers with the Committee, to prevent the inheritance going to Mary, as Pound expressly wished it to go, and instead to secure it, or as much of it as possible, for Omar. They appear not to have been bothered by conflicts of interest—though Gleason did later recommend that Omar employ another lawyer, Louis Warren—nor by the fact that

[2] 'a.d. 140. Era Facsista XVIII' had been typed, then, by hand, '140' had been cancelled and '1940' written in above it; and in the photocopy the signature of the second witness is indistinct. The will is reproduced p. 18 above—see also p. 250 above.

their fees, which could amount to between a third and a half of what was being allowed to Pound, were being paid out of the Committee's, that is, Pound's, accounts.

There was the awkward fact that Omar had signed a notarized document in 1949 renouncing in favour of Mary and her children 'all rights and claims to proceeds (royalties or whatever) from Ezra Pound's work'; and that, moreover, Dorothy had assured Mary that Omar would never 'violate E.P.'s wishes in the matter'. Moore knew the document, and knew Pound's wishes, but still gave it as his opinion that 'E.P. had not then the slightest idea what his archives might be worth' and that he would not now 'want to deprive you [i.e. Omar] of your just inheritance'. It appears to have been accepted by the lawyers, and by Laughlin, that the 'old understanding' should be forgotten.

Another document they found reason to disregard was a letter of instruction to Laughlin, dated 9 November 1957 and formally signed by Pound and by his Committee, confirming 'the statement that all income royalties fees or whatever from publication of Ezra Pound's writings on the continent of Europe are to be paid to Mary de Rachewiltz'. That, Laughlin would inform Cockburn in 1968, 'seems to say' that Mary should receive 'the whole proceeds' of European royalties. However, Dorothy Pound had subsequently instructed that Mary's 'agent's commission' should be held down to 10% of the net amount, and that is what he had done. When the matter came up in 1963 Dorothy was instructing Gleason to handle all translation rights for her, but Mary was claiming Europe as her territory. Gleason and Laughlin—Gleason was also New Directions' adviser on copyright matters—suggested that it would be tactful and might make for future harmony to treat her as agent for the Committee and to pay her an agent's commission. Dorothy declared, and Moore echoed, that Mary was overworked with her family and the castle and could not cope with the business. She should be kept out of things, Moore urged. It was agreed, however, that Mary should get 'something nominal'—2½ per cent, Moore proposed, sure that Mr Gleason would object to anything more. But evidently Gleason allowed the 10 per cent Laughlin paid out, while Mary was effectively stripped of her territory. Again in 1965, when Dominique de Roux was negotiating permissions with Faber & Faber for translations in his big *L'Herne* volumes on Pound, Moore arranged that Faber should allow her just '5% of what they collected from France'. Dorothy thought that right since, she told Moore, Mary could not expect to paid at a rate that had been arranged twenty years before 'so she could earn tuppence'.

Omar was so worried that Mary might somehow establish a claim to the papers and correspondence still at Brunnenburg that he had a long talk about it with T. S. Eliot when the latter was in Boston in March 1962; then he had Eliot discuss the matter with Gleason; and afterwards wrote begging him to see Moore in London 'to explain his anxieties... and discuss the situation'. Moore, however, was sure that 'now that he has both Gleason and Cockburn acting in his interests he should have nothing further to worry about'. Two years later, when Gleason was trying to arrange the sale or at least the safe custody of the papers on Omar's behalf, Moore had to reassure him again that all necessary steps would be taken to protect his 'inheritance and social position'.

The 'social position' in question was Omar's being accepted as the son of Ezra Pound. Dorothy was constantly in fear of 'scandal' being spread about herself and Omar and causing problems for Omar both socially and legally. She had had Laughlin and Gleason, with Omar's help, eliminate from Charles Norman's 1960 biography of Pound 'any reference to certain personal matters which would have been embarrassing to the family'. Norman had been required to be economical with the truth, writing simply, 'Omar Shakespear Pound was born in the American Hospital in Paris on September 10, 1926, and registered as an American citizen, his mother being American by marriage'. But then Ronald Duncan, in an article in the *Sunday Times* in February 1962, wrote of Pound's having 'returned to Italy to live with his only child, Princess Mary de Rachewiltz'. And the following year Dorothy questioned whether action should be taken on Omar's behalf against something 'detrimental to the family' which Duncan had published in an extract from his autobiography in the *Daily Telegraph*. When the autobiography, *All Men Are Islands*, appeared in 1964 Duncan had learnt discretion. While being explicit about Mary being the daughter of Pound and Olga Rudge, he mentioned Omar simply as 'their son', leaving it to be understood that this meant the son of Ezra and Dorothy.

Protecting Omar and herself from scandal became a main motive in Dorothy's exercise of her control over Pound's literary property. Their private letters were a particular concern, one shared by Moore, who urged her to get her letters to E.P. into her own hands since they needed special safe custody for Omar's protection. Dorothy had indeed been doing that, and when she was not sending them to Omar for safe custody she was burning them. She was also telling Omar that all the letters she had sent him should be embargoed for forty or fifty years after Ezra's death. In any case, biographers would be required to submit their manuscripts for her approval, later for Omar's approval.

The 'scandal' of Omar's origins was successfully suppressed for nearly the whole of his lifetime. But the fear remained that Mary might somehow establish a stronger claim on Pound's estate. Dorothy foresaw that if she were to die before Ezra then 'Olga will almost certainly try to marry him', and Moore saw that if this were to come to pass it would give the world proof of what Duncan had said about Mary in the *Sunday Times* and thus strengthen her legitimacy. He could only hope, he told Dorothy, that she would survive Ezra; and Dorothy confided to Omar that she saw it all 'as a race—who dies first—EP or DP'. However, Omar was able to put that anxiety to rest after Mr Warren, his new legal adviser in America, remarked that Pound 'may not re-marry without the consent of the Court since he is an "incompetent"'. That assumed that he would be still subject to his Committee; and the Committee, it was being suggested, in the event of Dorothy's dying or giving it up, might consist of Omar himself with or without Gleason.

There was still the problem of Pound's will. On 15 August 1964, Pound had attempted to re-execute the will of 17 June 1940. He made 'a copy of a typewritten will which I made in Rapallo in 1940 and which I intend as my will, this day 15th of August 1964 [signed] Ezra Pound'. He then added:

> The proceeds from any sale of archives must be placed in some form of trust fund to be applied to pay my expenses during my lifetime and such gifts as I choose to make.
>
> Omar to have the W. Lewis work if he renounce claim to the other material and future rights for self & descendants for sums accruing to me from author's rights and other sources.
>
> [signed] Ezra Pound

This reassertion of his testamentary wishes, written by hand as required by Italian law, and signed by three new witnesses as required by US law, made no difference in the end.

In spite of all the efforts to find arguments against the 1940 will there was no certain view. In February 1965 Omar was complaining to Moore that no one among his American advisers was willing to state whether the will was valid or not. He wanted to know whether Mary would have 'to PROVE that the will is valid', or would someone have to claim that it was 'INVALID'. That now seemed to him the important question. However, the lawyers, unable to give any watertight assurances about the will, and faced with the complication, which Warren had established, that Pound was legally domiciled in Italy, were now seeking a way of resolving the rival claims to Pound's estate before the issue could come to court. It was being suggested that the estate should be put into a Trust, and that there should be an agreement as to how the proceeds should be shared.

Dorothy apparently put this suggestion to Ezra, as she reported to Moore on 26 February 1965. He had been in Rapallo briefly for a check-up, and over coffee alone with him on the 22nd she had told him what she planned to do with his money. He would not speak to her, but listened carefully, and a day or two later wrote to her. Omar was to have the Wyndham Lewis pictures provided 'he renounced all claims on M.S.S. art-works, royalties —other money coming in, for himself & his descendants. Trust for any money accruing from sale of letters etc. to be income for his life-time. All to go to Mary.' Dorothy sent copies of Pound's letter to Gleason and to Cockburn, 'without comment'. Her concern, she told Moore, was 'to head-off Mary's hogging everything', and the letter, while it showed Pound's wishes, 'is only a letter, & not a legal document'. Like his formal letter from the Villa Chiara it would be disregarded.

Shortly after writing that letter Pound received from the Librarian of Congress, L. Quincy Mumford, a formal invitation to make the Library of Congress 'the permanent repository for your literary manuscripts and personal papers'. Pound replied:

> I appreciate the honor of your proposal, but an acceptance would be conditioned by a promise made by me in favour of my daughter Mary de Rachwiltz the terms of my will appointing her as my sole literary executor & leave my archives unconditionally to her. It would be necessary for me to add a codicil stipulating that certain of my effects be presented to the library of congress.

He would give the matter his consideration, he ended. It must have been a tempting offer given the official recognition it implied, but Pound appears to have let it lapse. He was holding fast with absolute consistency to his wish that all should be entrusted to Mary.

To justify their efforts to head off Mary's entitlement Moore and Dorothy were calling her a 'gold-digger'. But it was Omar who appeared eager to sell off the estate to the highest bidder, and who needed to be reminded that the Court might want the proceeds of any sale to be applied 'for the benefit and maintenance of the Patient during his lifetime'. Mary's concern, beyond her financial interest, was that Pound's literary legacy should be preserved for future generations. Dorothy, reporting this to Moore, was inclined to scoff at Mary's 'solemn' attitude', and repeated the old joke, 'what has posterity done for me?'

In September of 1963, over a cup of tea, Boris had given Dorothy a 'long very quiet explanation—that all his [i.e. Pound's] property [is] his own, to do as he wishes with. He has the usual alien's papers—like myself', and,

> before EP. came back in '58—he, B, interviewed ministers & such—result that EP. is here as a free man, like any other alien—that his signature is valid, that he can sign cheques, as long as he is here in Italy—'committee', as I knew, does not exist here—but B—ought to have told me—would have saved me much worry—

but as soon as EP leaves, & is under U.S.A. again; then committee begins at once to function...I have written this talk at once to Gleason—It entirely alters my position—As long as he stays here, I am free of responsibility.

That remarkable account was written for Omar, and Dorothy had repeated the gist of it to Pound who was then in Venice—

Boris tells me that in Italy you are considered a free man, that your firma [signature] is valid. I wish I had known this earlier—it changes my situation—but the moment you leave Italy, coming under USA jurisdiction, the 'committee' begins to work.

That last assertion appears to have been not correct. At least Cockburn advised Omar in November 1967 that 'USA jurisdiction' did not extend to Great Britain. The unavoidable implication was that the Committee had no legal standing outside the United States—an implication that was in line with what Furniss and Arnold had advised in 1958 and 1959. But in spite of Boris de Rachewiltz's explanation, Dorothy felt able to go on insisting to Olga that 'E.P.'s signature is not valid', and to continue exercising her burdensome responsibilities as Committee. And her lawyers and Omar's lawyers, in spite of their better knowledge, went on keeping up the false pretence that Pound and his property were legally subject to her control, and that he was not 'competent' to re-marry or to make a valid will. Apparently none of them cared that they were depriving him of his human as well as of his legal rights.

But there is another mystery here. Boris must have told Pound what he had told Dorothy, that he was not subject to the Committee in Italy. Why then did he not claim and exercise his freedom there? Why did he submit to being bound in this net of falsehood? Was it the *abuleia* he confessed to, a failure of will? Or was it some deliberate and strong-willed refusal to assert himself against the fated working out of his life? Whatever we may surmise, the fact is that Pound appears to have lived out his last years in a state of extraordinary detachment from the ways in which his Committee was exercising its duty of care.

18 : Afterlife of the Poet, 1965–72

'Tempus tacendi'

These were the years in which the poet fell into an impenetrable silence, at least in public. They were also the years in which he became more than ever a celebrity and the object of fresh honours—each one a fresh provocation to his implacable furies. These would always be bringing up the errant propagandist to blot out the poet's contribution to humanity, and were never to be appeased by the humility and dignity of his silence. Yet the silence was creating a space in which the poetry could be listened to by those who had a mind for it.

It was announced on 4 January 1965 that T. S. Eliot had died at his home in London. There was to be a memorial service in Westminster Abbey, a 'month's mind', on 4 February and Pound, 'visibly shaken' by the news, felt that he must be present. At the Abbey he was accompanied by Olga's brother, Dr Teddy Rudge, since Olga meant to keep discreetly out of range of the press who were making much of Pound's appearance there. After the service they went on to Valerie Eliot's Kensington flat where Pound said little, moved about looking at photographs of Eliot, and sat quietly for some time. 'On his own hearth, a flame tended, a presence felt,' he would record in a brief tribute, with the afterthought, 'Who is there now for me to share a joke with?' They were booked on a flight back to Venice, but decided to go first to Dublin to see Yeats's widow. Pound wanted to honour his shade too, having in mind, possibly, the blending together of Eliot's voice—'the true Dantescan voice'—with those of Yeats and Dante in *Little Gidding*. In Dublin he was observed 'apparently lost in introspection', but was also photographed 'in conversation with Mrs Yeats in the Royal Hibernian Hotel'.

There would be another such moment of introspection at Joyce's grave in Zurich in the winter of 1967. Olga had taken Ezra to Basel to consult a specialist at the Psychiatrische Universitätsklinik—the specialist prescribed antidepressants and promised Pound's mood would lift with the spring—and they had gone on to Zurich in order to visit the grave. They found it in a corner of the cemetery, 'a tomb without flowers, among others decorated with Christmas trees and wreaths with little candles, as is the custom there', and 'the names of Joyce and Nora nearly illegible on a stone hidden in the grass'. That near obliteration was what stayed with Pound, and not the rather literal bronze statue set up by Joyce's admirers. In Horst Tappe's photo blind Joyce listens for who is there, while Pound keeps his distance, standing quite still with his gaze fixed on the stone in the grass. One gathers from a letter he wrote to Dorothy when back in Venice that he was reading its illegibility as 'a warning' to 'consider such things'.

The point of that letter to Dorothy was to communicate his considered wishes concerning his own grave:

> I wish to be buried alone in Hailey, Idaho. I am considering this arrangement, which obviously will take some time. If I die before its completion, I wish to be buried temporarily in St Ambrogio, Rapallo, or in Venice. Olga to take charge of the arrangement. She knows my wishes.... Nobody can contest my right to be buried in my birth place my bust by Gaudier as grave stone. Some trees. The state of Idaho will provide suitable ground outside the town, with view of saw-tooth range. On the way to Haily the Gaudier head to be lent for exposition: Paris (Musée d'Art Moderne) London (the Tate) New York—Washington—P-hiladelphia—one month in each place. If properly managed this should pay the expense of moving head from Brunnenburg to Haily.

Thus the poet ordered his tomb. The arrangements—which were confirmed in a codicil to his Will dated '11th September 1967'—are at once fantastical and quite practical. He would end where he began, as if following Eliot's *East Coker* to the letter, though without the Christian humility. There may be also a rhyme with President Lincoln's funeral progress through the States as memorialized by Whitman. And then the grandeur of it, the timeless bust by Gaudier to mark his tomb with a view of the 'immense row of mountains in the Sawtooth range'. There may have been something more. Such an arrangement would take out of play the most valuable single object in his estate—'it should eliminate any future discussion among the young,' as he pointed out to Dorothy. And that object being a representation of himself, to remove it in this way was as near as he could get to setting himself above the arguments over his estate. It would be a declaration, to his heirs particularly, of how he wanted to be remembered, not as a marketable property, but as having his real existence in the quite other realm of artistic creation and contemplation.[1]

He was already becoming a living monument. In Sant'Ambrogio, down in Rapallo, in Venice, he could be identified simply as 'Il Poeta'. Poets, musicians, literary people of all sorts and unliterary people too, would find their way to Sant'Ambrogio or to Calle Querini in the hope of being admitted to offer him their homage or to seek his approval of their poems and performances. To strangers whom Olga deemed worthy of admission he would say little or nothing; but his silent listening was more impressive than most talk, and there could be a compelling intensity in his eyes and sculpted features.

He would speak with friends and familiar acquaintance, but only when he had something pertinent to say, and as the critic Sister Bernetta Quinn remarked, 'It is really very difficult to carry on a conversation with someone who doesn't speak unless he has something to say.' The poet and publisher Peter Russell, who had visited Pound in St Elizabeths and had published his 'Money Pamphlets', was the guest of Ezra and Olga in Sant'Ambrogio for several days in August 1964 and found himself falling in with Pound's silences in a companionable way. There would be intermittent conversation. 'Are you writing poetry now?', Pound asked, and after Russell had answered, he said, 'I liked some of the things I read in Washington.' This was said not so much to praise them, Russell felt, as to tell him, 'Don't underestimate what you did when you were younger.' Russell 'felt a great kindness in him' at that moment. He asked which contemporary poets Pound liked, and was told without hesitation, 'I like some of Lowell's things'; then, when Russell mentioned Santayana in connection with Lowell, 'You wrote an article on Santayana, didn't you?' Russell realized 'that Pound's memory was excellent, and that neither essentials nor details escaped him', with the important qualification, 'if they interested him'. At the same time he noticed that Pound 'didn't seem to pursue any subject further than the brief exchange of first observations'. When others were present he would listen attentively to what was said, 'but would rarely say anything unless it was to correct an impression, or to add something omitted'. Though brief, these remarks 'were always coherent, grammatical

[1] In June 1966 Pound had written to Dorothy: 'you will agree with me that the Gaudiers are too important to be hogged in one place in view of the fact that they have opened a room devoted to Gaudier (permanently) in the Musee d'art moderne in Paris ... they have the Kettle Yard collection donated by Ede, I feel it is only decent for me to present some important work and have promised to give the Embracers (marble) and a drawing (profile of E.P.)' (Lilly)

and complete in themselves', while often requiring 'further explanations which were not to be forthcoming'.

Guy Davenport, who had been visiting shortly before Russell, noted a striking example of that. Over dinner at a local *trattoria* 'the old poet broke hours and hours of silence to say, "There's a magpie in China can turn a hedgehog over and kill it."' He had learnt that from '"Giles's *Dictionary*", he admitted, but nothing more. It was only next day, and with the help of Miss Rudge and his friends, that Davenport connected the remark with the 'Hedgehog and Fox' fragment in his translation of Archilochos—Fox knows many tricks 'and still | Gets caught', while 'Hedgehog knows | One but it | Always works.' He had given Pound a copy of the book and this was his mischievous way of acknowledging that he had read the translation.

In fact he had read it aloud to Olga, and Davenport learnt that he liked to read to her in the evenings—the current book was Sartre's *Les Mots*, just out. At Olga's prompting Pound read for Russell from the Confucian *Odes*, ten or so of them one evening, 'with plenty of effects, though no exaggerations—many changes of tempo, many varying tones of voice, shifts from the lyric to the colloquial and the proverbial or didactic'. Russell 'felt that he was fully in control both of his voice and of the contents of each poem'. What then was his problem in conversation? Pound offered an explanation on another evening after he had read some things from the *Cantos*: 'I just can't put two thoughts together and then manage to get them *out*... can't make the words on my tongue,' and 'By the time I can say it, the moment's passed.' Russell decided that his problem was with converting 'thought into speech'. It seems likely, however, that before that it was a difficulty with formulating what was in his mind, a difficulty in the thought process itself. Being unable to 'make the words on my tongue' was apparently a consequence of that, since he evidently had no difficulty reading aloud what was already formed and written out. What had happened was that his genius—that genius for finding and rhythmically uttering words charged with meaning—had left him.

Yet his genius was still palpable to others and publicly honoured; and there was power in his mere presence. In 1965 he was Gian-Carlo Menotti's guest of honour at his Spoleto Festival dei Due Mondi. *Le Testament de Villon* was being performed as a ballet, with the singers in the orchestra pit—Pound's reaction to this curious transformation is not recorded, but then it was a festival of music, theatre, and dance. The programme that year included Verdi's *Otello*, Britten's *Abraham and Isaac* based on the Chester Mystery Play, and Leroi Jones's *Dutchman*—the 'two worlds' of the festival were Europe and the Americas. There was also an international poetry fest bringing together Stephen Spender, Yevgeny Yevtushenko, Pasolini, Pablo Neruda, and a contingent of Americans including Allen Tate, Charles Olson, John Wieners, and Lawrence Ferlinghetti. Ferlinghetti's first sight of Pound was in a box above the stalls at the back of the theatre, 'still as a mandarin statue... a striking old man... lost in permanent abstraction'. To John Wieners, seeing him from the stage where he and some other poets were about to read, 'His eyes were like stone. They pierced me from a distance. I felt I was in the presence of a god and afraid to look.' When it was Pound's turn to read, Ferlinghetti recalled, 'Everyone in the hall rose, turned and looked back and up at Pound in his booth, applauding... and Pound tried to rise from his armchair... and could not.' The applause went on until a poem was put in his hand, and after at least a minute a voice came out,'frail but stubborn', and the hall went instantly silent. He was reading Marianne Moore's translation of La Fontaine's 'The Grasshopper and the Ant', in which the Grasshopper, having sung through the fair weather, asks to share the Ant's store now winter has come, and the Ant says, '"A singer! Excellent! Now dance."' Then he read Robert Lowell's 'imitation' of Dante's meeting in hell with Brunetto Latini, his old master who taught him 'how a man becomes eternal', and who bids him now, '"Give /me no pity. Read my *Tesoro.* In | my book, my treasure, I am still alive."' 'The voice knocked me down,' Ferlinghetti wrote, 'So soft, so thin, so frail, so stubborn still,' and as 'the thin, indomitable voice went on' he went out of the theatre 'into the sunlight, weeping'. Pound read at the Festival every year until 1971, his almost whispering voice the ghost of what it had been but still deliberately articulating the weight and duration of each syllable in a way that let the rhythm carry the meaning. That ghostly voice is still alive on the recording of his reading from the *Cantos* at Spoleto in 1967, a reading which was for Robert Duncan 'a beautiful model of *delivering the meaning direct, not directed*'.

A dynamic young publisher in Paris, Dominique de Roux, had decided to make Pound better known in France. He had commissioned translations of *The Pisan Cantos* and *ABC of Reading*—these would be the first volumes of the *Cantos* and of Pound's prose to be translated into French—and he was also preparing, in his 'L'Herne' series of 'dossiers', two sumptuous volumes containing translations of his writings, 'témoinages' by friends and others who had known him, and interviews, essays, and commentaries. De Roux proposed to launch these for Pound's 80th birthday, 30 October 1965, and invited him to be his guest in Paris for the event. Pound arrived at the Gare de Lyon on the 21st with Olga, and was welcomed there by de Roux who had organized in his honour a ten-day programme of interviews, dinners, receptions—through all of which he would maintain a near absolute silence. He was seen at Brasserie Lipp and Les Deux Magots, and all Paris, de Roux claimed, was talking only about Pound. *Paris-Match* devoted an issue to him; *Le Figaro littéraire* gave him a whole page, *L'Observateur* two pages; *France-Soir* and *Paris-Jour* carried features. All this media attention went on in spite of the journalists having only photos to show from their interviews, and the television presenters having to talk over shots of the silent poet. He appeared on one live show, *Lectures pour tous*, responding to all the hosts' questioning with 'a fearful silence, staring back hard at the camera', until declaring suddenly, 'in a voice from the catacombs, "Le silence m'a choisi,"' 'silence has made me its own.' On his birthday de Roux invited a few carefully selected guests, among them Alain Robbe-Grillet and Pound's old friend Natalie Barney, to join them for dinner in his apartment. The latter's birthday gift was an immediate visit to Greece.

The famous meeting with Beckett, in which the master of theatrical silences was upstaged by the poet who was beyond speech, took place two years later, when Pound was in Paris for the publication of *ABC de la lecture* and *Esprit des littératures romanes*. Beckett invited Pound to a performance of *Fin de partie* (*Endgame*), and it was reported that Pound broke his silence to declare, 'C'est moi dans la poubelle.' Exactly what prompted him to place himself in Nagg's dustbin remains a mystery. He called again on Natalie Barney, now 92, whose house in the rue Jacob appeared to Olga to be derelict, and they were seen as two shades walking silently through the unkempt garden, revisiting the Temple à l'Amitié.

Thanks to Miss Barney, he had seen the remains of some of the great Greek temples, Athene's on the Acropolis, Apollo's at Delphi, Poseidon's at Sounion. There is no record of his visiting the sacred site of Persephone at Eleusis, but then his Eleusis, and indeed all of the Greece he had known and drawn on, was the heritage of the ancient civilization made new in his mind out of its myths and its epics and its tragedies. There is no knowing what he made of its physical ruins in1965. Apart from press notices of his presence, and some photographs, the only account of this visit is in an essay by Zesimos Lorenzatos, a Greek poet, literary critic, and translator—he had published a translation of *Cathay* in 1950. He received a totally unexpected call from Pound's hotel on 4 November, telling him that Ezra Pound was there and wished to see him. He went to Pound's room and found him standing before an open window with a view of the Acropolis. Pound simply looked at him for some moments, according to Lorenzatos' account, then, speaking with great difficulty, said something about 'breaking out of the cosmos', and '"There must be a light... somewhere"'; and, after a silence, in a dramatic voice, '"the power of Evil!"' Finally 'he murmured in a husky voice and forming his words one by one... "Shrivelling, diminuendo...I am going down, down below...".' Lorenzatos could give no context to specify what might have been in Pound's mind, and, taking his words to be wholly personal, found them simply 'heart-rending'. But I wonder could Pound, who had been contemplating the Acropolis, have been thinking of Athene and of Homer and the ancient tragedies, and of the struggle of intelligence to rise above brute force and to achieve a sense of civic responsibility, and then been overcome by a sense of his own tragic hubris and fall in that perennial struggle. The broken phrases might be the ultimate condensation of a classic tragedy, with the protagonist brought down in the end to the revelation that the divine light must be sought in Persephone's realm.

Lorenzatos appears to have made himself Ezra's and Olga's guide for their week in Greece, but Pound said nothing further of note. He found Delphi '"Marvellous!"', and the immense prospect over the sea at Sounion beyond price. On the drive back to Athens he saw 'the 3 fates', three figures in black at a cross-roads. Otherwise he left just one definite trace of his visit, an inscription in a small book about Delphi which George Seferis presented to him when he had Pound and Olga to lunch at his home in Athens on 5 November. The inscription, under Seferis's dedication of the book to Pound, reads, 'This to Olga who got me to Delphi when no other force under heaven would have. E.'

She was indeed the force that moved him now—and 'the sea in which he floated'. And Olga had the life with Ezra she had waited so long for, with never a regret for what might have been. 'Why is it, in old age, dancing seems better?', she wrote in her notebook. 'We had a gramophone, dancing with Him to Vivaldi His idea!' But he became dependent upon her energetic care for everything from travel arrangements to washing and dressing—to dressing in both senses, since she saw to it that he was always elegantly turned out for his appearances in public. There she was the discreet impresario, managing his appearances with the skills she had developed in looking after the practical arrangements and the egos of the world's musicians at Count Chigi's Accademia in Siena. Her idea was to keep him alive by having him go about in the world and maintain a presence in it. In Venice they went to all the concerts, to operas at the Fenice where they would be seated in a box, to the theatre, to lectures, keeping up with whatever was going on. He was a regular guest at events at the Cini Foundation. And they would travel at the drop of an invitation, to a performance of Bach's *Saint Matthew Passion* in Sant'Apollinare in Classe in Ravenna, to the Premio Letterario in Rome where Pound was seated on the platform and Mary's translation of a canto was read, to Sicily as guest of honour at a literary conference where he and Pasolini first met. One year, after hibernating in Venice, they went to France for a choreographer friend's '*spectacle* during the Fêtes Jeanne d'Arc... three days in Paris, Orleans in May'; in early June to Rome 'for two performances of Noh'; 'then to Spoleto, where Gian Carlo Menotti has lent his flat to E. for the Festival for the last five years'.

Travel was her antidote for his depressive tendencies. There had been an episode in the winter and early spring of 1966 serious enough for him to be hospitalized in the University of Genoa's Clinic for the treatment of nervous and mental disorders. On this occasion publicity was not wanted and he was registered under his doctor's name as 'Bacigalupo'. His leading symptom proved difficult to define, but seemed to be, according to the Clinical Report sent to the Director of St Elizabeths in Washington, 'an involuntary difficulty in the initiation of movements; for example, when the patient began to walk, or to dress himself, he remained arrested for a while; but when the action started, it could be carried out without apparent difficulty.' However the young psychiatrist put in charge of his case found that 'Any attempt to help or force him to complete the action increased the motor arrest with presence of opposition and active negativism.' He might have concluded, but did not, that the patient did not appreciate being treated like a dummy. He could find nothing wrong with him physically: reflexes, blood pressure, pulse, etc., all normal. As for his mind, 'When addressed he looked perplexed, answering with a marked delay,' but then 'his answers were correct and coherent', and 'sometimes the precision and the correctness of his answers were astonishing'. But there was that 'retardation of verbal expression', and this appeared to him to be due to the patient's having too much going on at once in his mind, with 'ideas of self accusation and hypochondriacal delusions' always pressing in. To the psychiatrist 'It seemed as if'

> the personality of the patient had always been on the autistic side, with a prevailing phantastic attitude and insufficient contact with reality... so that a psychotic-like situation came out ('borderline patient') permitting however, and perhaps encouraging, poetic activity.

That 'seeming' became apparent fact in his expert opinion, which took account also of a twenty-year 'series of traumatic events, psychorganic involutional factors, and a melancholic attitude', all this in order to explain 'the present extreme autistic situation with almost complete psychomotor arrest'. He prescribed 'general somatic therapies and antidepressant drugs (amitryptiline)', but was obliged to record that 'the psychic situation remained almost unmodified'. Olga thought the drug actually made

Ezra's condition worse, putting him altogether into a 'a catatonic state'. After a month she telephoned Dr Bacigalupo and had him removed from the clinic. The experience can't have done much to improve either Pound's negative view of psychiatry's ability to read the mind or his fear of its drugs. The only treatment he would respond to now was Olga's endlessly patient care. She could never cure him, but she would keep him moving.

Robert Lowell's impressions of Pound shortly after he had left the clinic were strikingly different from the psychiatrist's. He saw him up at Sant'Ambrogio in late April, and wrote afterwards to thank Olga for her 'courtesy and hospitality'. 'I had a good talk with Ezra', he told her,

> though everything I said seemed fuzzy and platitudinous after the crisp carving of his scattered sentences. I tried to tell him he was about the only man alive who had lived through Purgatory, and come through white with a kind of honesty and humility. So, so—he was the most awesome encounter I had in Italy, and somehow wonderfully the same and wiser than when I used to go to St. Elizabeths.

'So much owing to you', he added, giving credit where it was manifestly due. Lowell also wrote to Laughlin, telling him that 'The visit to Ezra was awesome and rather shattering, like meeting Oedipus—he said, "I began with a swelled head and am ending with swelled feet."' Lowell was evidently thinking of Oedipus seeking peace with his Furies and with the gods at Colonus as he went on, 'He has a nobility I've never seen before, the nobility of some one, not a sinner, but who has gone far astray and learned at last too much.... No self-pity, but more knowledge of his fate than any man should have.' But Pound had only said to him, when he talked of his having 'had the courage to go through Purgatory', '"Didn't Frost say you'd say anything once?"'

On their own Ezra and Olga appear to have led a simple domestic life. From her notebooks one gathers that he would do his yoga exercises before breakfast, and that she would throw the coins for the I Ching hexagrams first thing every day. They might go out to lunch nearby, at a favourite *trattoria*, Montin or Cici, and would take walks along the Zattere beside the broad canal. Ezra read a great deal, slowly, and apparently with total recall of any book he had read. He played chess, with enormous concentration, and, according to Russell, 'was still pretty good at it'. Sometimes he would cook supper, 'Veal chops with fried eggs and a green salad was the usual menu.' In the evenings he would read to Olga, sometimes from the *Cantos* for her collection of tape recordings. Their daily routine was probably much more of that quiet order than one is led to imagine by the accounts of visitors who saw them always in company. The company was important as a stimulus to Pound, and Olga encouraged old friends especially to visit, and they did. At the same time the two of them seem to have been content enough with just each other for company.

Pound clearly counted himself blessed to have been brought home after much wandering to his true Penelope—'nostos to Olga | Olga's fortitude', he wrote on a scrap of paper. It may have been in 1967 that he wrote this tribute:

> There is more courage in Olga's little
> finger than in the whole of my
> carcass.
> [...]
> That she wd. have saved me
> from idiocies in antisemitism.
> Determination to build up
> my physical health & restore
> mental balance, from the time
> she took over , & got me into
> Villa Chiara

—'& trying day by day to keep my | mind alive', he ended that note. On a Thanksgiving Day he wrote these lines for her—

> & her name was courage
> & she had pity for every living thing
> & kept me alive for ten years
> for which no one will thank her
> her red head a flask of perfume.

And for her 75th birthday in April 1970 he wrote in her notebook,

> If there was a trace of beauty in anything, she saw it.
> For fine and just perception and a level gaze,
> For courage in face of evil,
> For courage in time of adversity,
> If anyone ever deserved the spring with all its beauty, she did.

Those were private recognitions. There were a few public statements too, these discreetly restrained. The selection of Cantos he made in 1965 at the suggestion of Peter du Sautoy of Faber & Faber carried the dedication 'To | OLGA RUDGE | "Tempus loquendi"', as if declaring that it was time to speak out about her place in his life while saying no more than that. The volume of *Drafts & Fragments of Cantos CX–CXVII* (1969) was dedicated very simply 'To Olga Rudge', and the informed reader might think that the opening lines referred to her 'quiet house' in Venice. Beyond that, however, even though Marcella's animating presence was concealed by discreet changes to the drafts she had typed up, there was no way Olga could be read into those cantos. The only explicit public tribute, placed at the end of the collected *Cantos* after Pound's death, was the fragment of a few lines 'for the ultimate CANTO' dated '24 August 1966'—'That her acts | . . . | of beauty | be remembered. // Her name was Courage.' He would tell close friends such as Peter Russell that he now owed everything to her, and to her courage, and he would have intended that word to be connected with its root in 'heart'.

In these years Pound was an object of constant media interest and scrutiny. One article which achieved a degree of notoriety was Daniel Cory's 'Ezra Pound: A Memoir', published in Stephen Spender's *Encounter* in May 1968. Cory had got to know Pound when he was George Santayana's secretary, and also from renting an apartment at Brunnenburg from time to time in the early 1960s. In 1966 he visited Pound in Venice to gather material for his article, and put it to him that 'we might say that the *Cantos* reflected faithfully the incoherence or fragmentary insights of the contemporary writer in a cosmopolitan milieu'. Pound's response to this sophistical gambit was simply, '"It's a botch. . . . I botched it."' He elaborated for Cory by telling him to think of '"a shop-window full of various objects"', and then saying, '"I picked out this and that thing that interested me, and then jumbled them into a bag. But that's not the way to make . . . a *work of art*."' Cory took this at face value, and there were many to whom it gave aid and comfort—here was the poet himself confirming their view of the *Cantos*. However, in an interview with Pasolini recorded in the winter of 1968, possibly after he had seen an advance copy of Cory's article, Pound made a point of dismissing the notion that the *Cantos*' 'quotation after quotation' were 'chosen at random'. 'They say they are chosen at random', he said, 'but that's not the way it is. It's music. Musical themes that find each other out.' Beneath his now habitual self-deprecation and his readiness to confess 'my notes do not cohere', there was still a sustaining confidence in his art.

The declarations of failure were a symptom of his depression, and did not speak for his core convictions which remained constant. In 1970, in a brief introductory note for a new edition of *Guide to Kulchur,* he reaffirmed his struggle in that book and generally, 'which was, and still might be, to preserve some of the values that make life worth living'. Another such note, this time written as a foreword to *Selected Prose 1909–1965* and dated 'Venice, 4th July, 1972', administered a timely if oblique self-correction: 'In sentences referring to groups or races "they" should be used with great care'. He had always known that, of course, only he had too often failed to practise it. He next wrote what some have mistaken for a recantation: 're USURY: | I was out of focus, taking a symptom for a cause. | The cause is AVARICE.' That was in fact no more than a refinement of language, since he had written, in essays included in that very volume, 'it is not money that is the root of evil. The root is greed'; and again, 'This ruin has its roots in the greed for lucre.' If there had been a change in his position, it was only to concentrate attention upon the root cause rather than upon its effects.

The Allen Ginsberg vortex descended upon Pound for about ten days in October 1967, with Ginsberg chanting 'Hare Krishna' and mantras to the accompaniment of his Benares hand-organ, and talking of beatific mind-states and mystical drugs, and of his visions of William Blake, and of his and his generation's debt to Pound's ear for the natural language, and of what Williams and what Bunting had said in praise of his verse, and then he played him tracks of the Beatles, and Dylan and Donovan, and Pound attended impassively, listened through it all with exquisitely tolerant patience and goodwill. Ginsberg, for all that he was high on pot some of the time, really knew what he was talking about when it came to the way changes of rhythm and tone contribute to the clarification of perceptions, and Pound responded to that. But when Ginsberg, trying to explain 'the concrete value of [Pound's] perceptions manifested in phrasing', invoked 'the Paradise in the intention and the desire to manifest coherent perceptions in language'—then Pound demurred and said (in Ginsberg's account),

> The intention was bad—that's the trouble—anything I've done has been an accident—any good has been spoiled by my intentions—the preoccupation with irrelevant and stupid things.

Ginsberg insisted, he had come, 'a Buddhist Jew', to give Pound his blessing because his perceptions had been clarified 'by the series of exact language models' in the *Cantos*, and would Pound accept his blessing, and Pound said, 'I do', and then,

> 'but my worst mistake was the stupid suburban prejudice of anti-Semitism, all along, that spoiled everything'.
>
> And [Ginsberg] responded, 'Ah, that's lovely to hear you say that . . . ', and later, 'as it says in *I Ching*, "No Harm"'.

On another day, talking about the problem of finishing the *Cantos*, Ginsberg asked, 'Is your problem one of physical depression?', and Pound told him, 'The depression's more mental than physical.' Ginsberg's last sight of Pound and Olga was as they were on their way to catch the vaporetto for the railway station—they were going to Padua to escape the expected November *aqua alta*—and Pound was walking energetically, 'white raincoat flowing behind him, walked with speedy strength, slowed to climb small bridge steps to Salute's platform and stepped up firmly, then with youthful balance stepped from the tipsy floating platform on to boatbus...'

A conjunction of events drew Pound to America in June 1969. He received an invitation, as a past Fellow of the Academy of American Poets, to attend its thirty-fifth anniversary meeting in the board room of the New York Public Library at which the annual Fellowship was to be awarded to Richard Eberhart. He had also been invited to attend the opening of an exhibition in the Library of the original drafts of *The Waste Land* on which he had worked in Paris in January 1922, and which had recently turned up in the Library's Berg Collection. The third event, for which he had not received an invitation, was the conferring of an honorary doctorate upon Laughlin by Hamilton College for his services to literature. Laughlin had been discouraging, saying that the trip to America would be a terrible strain for Pound, but Olga had gone ahead regardless and they turned up unannounced in New York on 4 June. A call from the airport took the Curator of the Berg Collection, Dr Lola Szladits, by surprise—there was some problem with officials there and she was being called upon to vouch for Pound. They went to a hotel on 45th Street which Olga had known in the past and called Laughlin from there. But the neighbourhood was not what it was, the hotel was now a brothel, and when he discovered this Laughlin arranged for them to stay for a few days at his home in Norfolk, Connecticut. Grandson Walter, who was studying at Rutgers University, was called upon to drive them there the next day. They would now of course accompany Laughlin to Hamilton.

At the Academy of American Poets reception Lowell observed Pound seated 'in a stately chair' and 'whenever a woman came up, he stood up and bowed', so that finally Lowell said, '"For God's sake sit down, Ezra,"' and Pound, '"I've done nothing but sit down all afternoon."' When Marianne Moore was brought to him in her wheelchair Laughlin noticed the President, Marie Bullock, take them off to a side room and stand guard at the door. He looked in and saw Pound 'talking to Miss Moore with animation'. At some point Pound went again to the Public Library to go over the *Waste Land* drafts with Valerie Eliot and elucidate his marginal notes for the 'facsimile & transcript' she was preparing. In a brief 'Preface' to her edition, written when he was back in Venice, he made no mention of his having had a hand in the poem, but wrote, 'The more we know of Eliot, the better,' though Eliot had said that *his* only reason for wishing the missing manuscript might be found was so that it could be seen how Pound had transformed 'a jumble of good and bad passages into a poem'. But all that was nearly fifty years in the past.

Hamilton College had not panicked when informed at very short notice that Ezra Pound intended to be present at their Commencement ceremonies on 8 June. Professor Austin Briggs of the English Department was detailed to look after him—to have him to lunch, see that he was rested, and drive him to the ceremony. When Pound entered the hall, gowned and wearing his honorary doctor's hood, he was given a standing ovation, rather upstaging Laughlin at whose side he was seated on the platform. Afterwards he was photographed, white hair standing out about his head, and silently shook hands but uttered no words. Briggs heard him speak 'only twice: once, in reply to an enquiry as to whether he would prefer the white or dark meat of the turkey served at dinner, he replied, "I take it as it comes"; once, in parting, to Mrs. Briggs, to "apologize for the trouble I may have caused you".' He thought Pound's deep silence 'proud', and that it came from power, not from his being at all broken. He struck him as physically strong too: when he had taken Pound's arm to help him over a high step, 'it was no withered branch—it gave back power'.

Laughlin made over his New York apartment in Greenwich Village to Ezra and Olga for the remainder of their stay, arranged dinner parties for them, and got hold of Lowell and others Pound wanted to see. With Lowell, Austin Briggs was told, 'he *talked*, for *five hours*'. One day Walter drove them to Philadelphia's Germantown to see the Heacock sisters who had been his earliest teachers, and who were then in a Quaker nursing home. Another day Olga flew to Youngstown, Ohio, to deal with property left to her by her father, and that day Ezra would not go out and refused to eat, afraid she might not return, though she made a point of flying back that evening. Reassured, 'he was up early next morning to go with Walter to the Hans Arp exhibit at the Guggenheim'. Laughlin arranged for him to see George Oppen at New Directions' office, and a few years later, after Pound's death, Oppen recalled how it had gone:

> Pound silent. Olga and the rest chatter to cover the situation. I didn't want to chatter and stood up to leave. Jay says to Pound: Give George a copy of your book. Pound says—uninflected, low voice: How do I know he wants it. I walked over to Pound and held out my hand and said, I want it. I had stood close, so that Pound would not need to reach out. But Pound stood up and that brought us touching, or nearly touching each other. Pound took hold of my hand, and held on. I began to weep Pound began to weep.

'Perhaps neither of us knew what we were crying about,' he wrote, and then, 'or, of course I do know. Every sincere or serious poet who ever met Pound has reason to have loved him.'

One American poet at least did not feel that way about Pound. Kenneth Rexroth. as one of the judges for the 1970 National Book Awards, made it his business to keep *Drafts & Fragments* off the list of poetry to be considered. The award for poetry went to Elizabeth Bishop for her *Collected Poems*, and she asked Lowell to receive it on her behalf. He reported afterwards to her that in his acceptance speech, after speaking of her deserving excellence, he had expressed regret that Pound's good and possibly last book had not even been mentioned, and had then read Bishop's poem on visiting Pound in St Elizabeths. As he sat down Rexroth said aloud, '"I announce that I sever myself from this antisemitic fascist performance".' But the master of ceremonies had instantly said, 'I want to dissociate myself from anyone who could say what you've just heard was antisemitic or Fascist.'

The great Scottish poet Hugh MacDiarmid, who had corresponded with Pound over the years, spent some hours with him in Venice in 1970, and found him 'in high spirits and extremely genial'. They 'went out to lunch together, crossed the Grand Canal in a vaporetto and walked and had coffee in St. Mark's Square'. MacDiarmid had a sense, as they linked arms and walked, of 'his strength and self-sufficiency'—'He must have been frail, but he did not feel frail.' His main impression was rather of 'a surprising sturdiness and independence and a wonderful directness and simplicity'. Looking back, at a memorial symposium in 1973, he told the audience, 'of all the men I have known (and I know them all over the world, I know poets from many countries), I loved Ezra Pound. I think he was the most lovable man I met and I was happy to know that my affection for him was reciprocated.'

In 1972 the august American Academy of Arts and Sciences, made up of the country's intellectual elite from the academic disciplines, the arts, business, and public affairs, chose not to honour Ezra Pound. Among the Academy's awards was the Emerson-Thoreau Medal, 'established in 1958 to give special recognition to distinguished achievement in the broad field of literature', taking into account the writer's 'total literary achievement'. The first recipients had been Robert Frost, then T. S. Eliot, and the most recent, in 1970, I. A. Richards. In January1972 the selecting committee recommended that the medal should be awarded to Ezra Pound. The chair of the committee was Leon Edel, and the other members were John Cheever, Lillian Hellman, James Laughlin, Harry T. Levin, Louis Martz, and Lewis Mumford (himself the recipient of the medal in 1965). Only Mumford did not support Pound—his preference was Henry Miller.

Serious dissent broke out when the recommendation was referred to the Council of the Academy in April. Of the twenty-four members present only one, Morton Bloomfield, a distinguished professor of mediaeval literature at Harvard, could be said to be a leader in the field of literature; and not one of them appears to have manifested close acquaintance with any of Pound's writings, let alone with his 'total literary achievement'. But that, it appeared, was not what they were there to talk about. One member of the council, Jean Mayer, who had been an officer in the French army in 1940 and a prisoner of war, opposed the award on the ground that while Pound was broadcasting for the Fascists, persons 'potentially just as creative as he were being gassed and put to death by his friends'. Others suggested 'that with memories of the holocaust so prominent, the award of the Emerson-Thoreau Medal to Pound... would be deeply offensive to many members of the Academy'. Daniel Bell, a sociologist, raised the discussion to the level of abstract principle, arguing that art could not, should not, be considered apart from morality. If it were, he declared rhetorically, 'then the most despicable things, murder or torture, could be done in its name'. And while Pound's aesthetic achievement might be great, his wartime broadcasts on behalf of Fascism, and the anti-Semitism of some of his *Cantos*, amounted, in his view, to advocating 'a way of life that makes the world hellish'. On moral grounds then the award should not be made to Pound. It was a strong argument, relying on principle and prejudice and not at all on evidence and analysis, and after much discussion it prevailed. The award was vetoed, 13 to 9 with two abstentions. Apparently no one noticed that Bell's line of argument effected exactly the separation it started out by forbidding, only setting aside the art and coming down on the side of morality.

Martin Kilson, a professor of government at Harvard and recently elected to the Academy, deprecated this show of moral outrage. 'As a Negro', he wrote in the *International Herald Tribune* in July,

> I am as outraged about anti-Negro intellectuals as a Jew about anti-Semitic ones but such outrage is not a matter of intellect but of politics, and in evaluating an intellectual's works I believe that short of the intellectual himself committing criminal and atrocious acts against humanity under the influence of his politics, his intellectual works should stand on their own.

The implication would be that it is the morality of the works that should be evaluated—but, as in the earlier Bollingen fracas, that was precisely what was not done.

When the nominating committee was invited to defend its choice to the council Laughlin felt personally put on trial for his support of Pound. And Harry Levin protested that the council's 'implication that Pound and his proponents were irresponsible aesthetes' was 'misleading, if not disingenuous', in that for the committee's members, as for Pound himself, aesthetics were necessarily ethical. 'Pound, like his master Dante', he declared, 'is not only an artist but an impassioned moralist.' He gave no indication, however, of exactly what his moral-aesthetic vision might have been.

The President of the Academy, Harvey Brooks, sent a statement in confidence to the membership in June, saying that while the Council had agreed without dissent that Ezra Pound was one of the great literary figures of the twentieth century, it had questioned other aspects of his career, specifically his 'anti-Semitism and praise of Fascism, and his curious social and economic ideas, which might be explained on the grounds of incipient or acute mental illness'. That, one might have thought, was uncomfortably close to Soviet Russia's way with its dissident intellectuals. Remarkably, Pound's alleged treason to the United States appears not to have been an issue. The Executive Officer of the Academy wrote to Hugh Kenner, who was being offered membership, that Laughlin, Martz, and Levin had read and approved Brook's statement; and that it was Laughlin who had asked that it be kept 'confidential' in order to spare the family further pain, 'and because of Mr. Laughlin's own relationship with the Pound family'. Kenner rejected the offered membership, finding it unacceptable that he should be thus honoured for *The Pound Era* while Pound himself was being dishonoured. Some members resigned from the Academy in protest, among them Brooks Atkinson, Malcolm Cowley, and Allen Tate. Katherine Anne Porter returned the Emerson-Thoreau Medal awarded to her in 1962. And Dr O. B. Hardison, Director of the Folger Shakespeare Library in Washington, resigned his membership and defiantly invited Pound to give a reading at the Folger.

Hardison sent the invitation through Buckminster Fuller, the inventor of the geodesic dome, asking him to tell Pound that 'he and the Trustees of the Folger Library were very eager to bring Ezra Pound to [the United States] and would take all responsibility to be sure he was warmly greeted and appreciated'. Fuller had got to know Pound in October 1970 while delivering a series of lectures at the Cini Foundation's International University of Art—'long lectures, half a day'—and 'every day for a ten day period' Pound was there in the front row. 'He apparently cared a great deal about what I was saying', Fuller said later, 'and we did become very warm friends'. Fuller knew Pound's work and was equipped, as America's leading scientific and legal minds were not, to recognize and to value his lifetime's effort 'to make cosmos'. It was a rare meeting of creative minds, and the great thing was that Pound, who 'was not speaking to anybody', as Fuller said, 'started speaking to me'.

Fuller spoke in a lecture in 1977 of their having thought together in Venice about the universe of fluid energies and the human consciousness of it: about the dynamic universe, self-ordering, self-regenerating, and with its own immutable and eternal laws; and about the human mind, capable of gradually coming to know this universe of which it was a product and a part. His talk contained history in the way Pound's *Cantos* contain history, as stories of humanity's advances in learning about its world, and of its wisdom and unwisdom in applying its knowledge. He was excited by the idea that our science has brought us into a possible new and sustainable relationship with the universe, if only we would understand its laws and its process and live accordingly. He did not underestimate the prevailing mentality, which holds it to be the natural order for financial and market values to rule the behaviour of individuals and nations and corporations, a mentality which he saw to be well on its way to wrecking human society and ruining our planet. He hoped the young would share his excitement at the new consciousness of the natural order of the universe that was becoming attainable; and he looked to 'the young world' to bring about the mental revolution needed to save society and the planet from destruction.

Fuller's approach was by way of the cultural heritage of science, engineering, and architecture—it led him to the discovery of a hitherto unknown molecule of carbon, C60, and to the design of his geodesic dome, an integrity of patterned energies. Pound's approach to conceiving the vital universe was by way of the cultural heritage of Confucian China, and of ancient Greek and Roman myth and tragedy, of troubadour poetry, and the poetry of Dante and Cavalcanti, and out of this came his 'great ball of crystal', his *Cantos*, another integration of patterned energies. Fuller spoke of our 'spaceship earth' held by the laws of gravity and motion in its relation to the sun, and of the solar system's insignificance within even its own galaxy, let alone amid the billions of galaxies making up the universe; and then he spoke of all the energies of the universe streaming through us, a metabolic flow sustaining our solar-powered being, and glowing most intensely in the mind conscious that ours is the life of the universe. Pound had written of 'our kinship with the vital universe', and of the Light which is its life; in his *Cantos* he brought alive in the mind the powers named as Dionysus and Persephone and Circe, then turned to Cavalcanti's light of intelligence that is love; in Pisa, starting over again, he wrote, 'learn of the green world what can be thy place | In scaled invention or true artistry'; and always, from Confucian China, there was the imperative to respect 'the abundance of nature'. The two approaches were different and complementary, both leading to an intensely moral vision of human existence. Both, from their different angles, were trying to guide humanity to the natural paradise that is for us to find our way to or to lose. To 'make the world hellish' was absolutely not what Pound was about. To be mindful of the universe, to mind it, was what he advocated, 'to be men' in touch with the heavens and the earth, 'not destroyers'.

The two men met again and continued their conversation at Spoleto in June 1971. This year Pound read from *Drafts & Fragments*, and astonished everyone, Fuller would recall,

> when at the poets' performance in the theater, Ezra appeared on the stage with the other poets. When his turn came, he stood and read poetry of his own aloud. He had broken his silence. His voice was beautiful. The poetry was magnificent. His performance... was just what the whole cosmic level is about.

Fuller went on to Venice for a final talk with Pound in Calle Querini, and as he was leaving Pound presented him with a copy of *Drafts & Fragments* in which he had written,

> To Buckminster Fuller
> friend of the universe.
> bringer of happiness.
> liberator.

There was no doubt a personal dimension to the tribute.

Igor Stravinsky died in Venice in April 1971 and was buried on the cemetery island of San Michele. At the memorial service in San Giorgio Maggiore Ezra and Olga had places of honour near the altar rail, and the mayor of Venice read Pound's early Venetian poem 'Night Litany'. When news came of Marianne Moore's death in February 1972 Ezra suggested that there should be a memorial service for her, and Olga arranged for one in St George's English Church. For this Pound read her poem 'What Are Years?', and read it, Peter Russell noted, with a clear grasp of the intricate syntax, and in a 'dignified, grave yet neutral tone' which allowed the full force of it to come over. Russell was inclined to apply the poem to Pound himself, thinking there could be 'no finer epitaph for a great poet'.

That year Ezra and Olga heard Verdi's *Requiem* at La Fenice, and saw Peter Brook's festive *A Midsummer Night's Dream*. He was taken by yacht to Duino, immemorially associated with Rilke's *Duino Elegies*. There was talk of his taking up the Folger's invitation to read there. Then his birthday came round, his 87th, on 30 October 1972. He felt unwell, kept to his bed, but friends came and there was a cake with candles, and champagne. Next day his discomfort continued and in the night Olga called in a doctor who advised that he should go into hospital. Pound, refusing to be carried out on a stretcher, insisted on walking down the stairs and along the Calle to the ambulance launch. In the municipal hospital Olga and Joan Fitzgerald sat with him and talked through the small hours, and were with him through the next day, 1 November. In the evening Pound dozed off, and Olga, who in her own account was holding his hand, realized only when a nurse turned up the light about 8.00 p.m. that he had died in his sleep.

She made the funeral arrangements, as Pound had wished, with the help of Count Vittorio Cini, founder of the Cini Foundation. The service was conducted in the Palladian Basilica of San Giorgio Maggiore, to Gregorian plain chant and the music of Monteverdi, with the Catholic requiem rites in Latin led by the abbot of the Benedictine Monastery on the island, and the Anglican Office for the Dead read in English by the pastor of the English Church. The coffin was placed in a black, gilt-edged, gondola, and oared by four gondoliers in white and black to the island of San Michele.

The grave would be marked by a plain marble stone designed by Joan Fitzgerald, and carrying only the words in strong roman characters, 'EZRA POUND'.

In Bayle's *Dictionnaire historique et critique*, which he bought in 1917, Pound would have read Plotinus' last words, 'to lead back what is divine in me to what is divine in the whole universe'. The last words of Pound's last complete canto echo that,

A little light, like a rushlight
to lead back to splendour.

Ezra Pound's seal, three ancient Chinese small seal characters which when spoken might sound close to 'Pound', and which might be rendered as 'keep the form of the love flowing from the heart'.

APPENDIX

The Settlement of the Estate

On Thursday 2 November Olga Rudge wired to Omar Pound in Cambridge, England, 'AFTER THREE DAYS ILLNESS EZRA DIED IN HIS SLEEP IN HOSPITAL STOP PLEASE BREAK NEWS TO DOROTHY STOP DETAILS FOLLOW'. Dorothy Pound, 'parked', as she felt, in an 'Old Home' twenty miles outside Cambridge, was now too deaf to be telephoned, and Omar went out to tell her that Pound was dead. Dorothy instructed him to arrange a Protestant funeral in Venice. A further telegram from Olga gave details of the arrangements she had already made: 'SERVICE FRIDAY 10.00 AM CHIESA DI SAN GIORGIO CINI FOUNDATION PROVISIONAL INTERMENT CEMETERY ISLAND MICHELE VENICE.' That would be 10.00 a.m. the next day. Pound had told Dorothy, in his 1967 letter about how he wanted to be buried, that Olga should 'take charge of the arrangement. She knows my wishes.' Possibly Dorothy did not mention that to Omar, who made every effort to have the arrangements made by Olga, in collaboration with the Cini Foundation, prevented or at least postponed. A telegram from the American Embassy in London reported that

> The widow has given specific written instructions for a Protestant funeral in Venice, and for final arrangements to be postponed until son Omar can arrive in Venice and see to his mother's wishes.

Another telegram, this one from the American Consulate in Milan to the Secretary of State in Washington DC, with copies to the US embassies in Rome and London, added that the Consulate General and Omar Pound had talked to Olga but she refused to alter her plans. The Consulate had also sent a telegram to the Mayor of Venice informing him of Dorothy Pound's wishes, but had been unable to contact officials in Venice because it was a civil half-day holiday. Omar Pound, with Peter du Sautoy of Faber & Faber, took the first available flight from London but that got them to Venice only in the afternoon of Friday 3 November, after the funeral. Olga took them out to San Michele the following morning.

On 26 October, just a few days earlier, on the petition of Dorothy Pound and Omar Pound, the Court in Washington had ordered that Herbert P. Gleason be appointed Conservator of the person and property of Ezra Pound to serve as successor fiduciary to Dorothy Pound whose resignation was then accepted. In agreeing to take over as Committee Gleason had made a point of saying that he would not be sympathetic 'if a new effort is mounted to increase Omar's share' of Pound's estate. That was because he had worked out what he thought would be an equitable settlement of the estate, only to have Omar's lawyers, who, according to Laughlin, appeared to be 'without heart or conscience, just looking for everything they can get for their client', throw 'a monkey wrench in the works'. That had set the lawyers 'at each others' throats', and made Laughlin fear that 'Mary is going to get royally "screwed".' In the event Gleason did not act as Committee, and the 26th and Final Report of the Committee for Ezra Pound was presented in the name of Dorothy Pound in October 1973. It was then ordered by the Court that 'said Committee shall stand discharged' after filing 'a verified certificate of Distribution and Settlement of the Patient's estate'. The Order was filed 19 November, and Dorothy Pound died just three weeks after that, on 8 December 1973.

The Committee's lawyer, John B. Jones of the distinguished Washington law firm Covington and Burling, had been appointed Administrator of the estate of Ezra Pound deceased. He had declared the estate to consist of about $82,000 in bonds and deposits, and—this comprising the really interesting portion—15 trunks and boxes of papers at Yale, 'the value of which is stated to be unknown', these containing the Ezra Pound Archive. The Archive had been transferred from Brunnenburg for safe keeping and with a view to its ultimate purchase by the Beinecke Library. The other personal property which had been credited to the Patient annually over the twenty-five years during which he had remained subject to the Committee, namely 'two portable typewriters, folding desk [*sic*] chair and pocket watch', were stated to have become 'lost or are inoperative'. Silently disappeared from the estate were the trunks and boxes of papers accumulated over Pound's thirteen years in St Elizabeths and left in the United States after his release—these Omar Pound had appropriated as his own and sold to the Lilly Library of the University of Indiana at Bloomington. Also disregarded for the moment were Pound's books and papers still in Italy in care of Mary de Rachewiltz at Brunnenburg or of Olga Rudge. The Administrator's fees and the outstanding fees of other law firms with claims on the estate amounted to over a quarter of the total, which, after other deductions such as for tax, and apart from the papers at Yale, came down to $52,822 net.

Other claims amounting to $37,620 still remained to be met. The Report explained that the Committee had needed the services of several attorneys to advise her regarding the precise assets which comprised the property of the Patient, and on account of disputes among persons who might claim an interest in the disposition of the testamentary estate. Covington and Burling were claiming a further $15,416 for services rendered between March 1966 and November 1972 and connected with the disputed 'disposition of the Patient's testamentary estate rather than the immediate administration of Committee assets'. For similar services rendered over various periods of time Hill & Barlow and Bircham & Company, Cockburn's London firms, were claiming between them $13,452; and Kelley, Drye, Warren, Clark & Ellis, Warren's firm, were claiming $8,752. It was left open for these services to be charged to the Patient's estate—services which had been commissioned by Omar Pound or in his interest, and with a view to having the Patient's known testamentary wishes disregarded.

A final settlement of the estate was agreed by all parties in January 1973, 'with a greater proportion going to Omar, the legal heir'. A Trust was established to receive future royalties and earnings from Pound's works, with Olga Rudge the primary beneficiary up to a certain amount annually, the rest to go to Omar Pound and Mary de Rachewiltz in the agreed proportions. The purchase of the Ezra Pound Archive for the Beinecke Library was then completed, with the promise—not kept—that a Center for the Study of Ezra Pound and his Contemporaries would be established there. Mary de Rachewiltz was able to serve as a curator of her father's Archive at Yale for a number of years, and has constantly welcomed Pound scholars at Brunnenburg. Olga Rudge died there in her daughter's care on 15 March 1996, aged 100, and was buried beside Ezra Pound on San Michele.

ABBREVIATIONS

The principal writings of Ezra Pound (1885–1972)

Arranged by date of publication, thus providing an outline of Pound's writing career. Place of publication is London unless otherwise indicated. Where editions differ the date of the one referred to in the notes is given in **bold type**.

ALS	*A Lume Spento* (Venice: privately printed, 1908). Included in *A Lume Spento and Other Early Poems* (New York: New Directions, 1965; reprinted Faber & Faber, **1965**). Also in *CEP.*
QY	*A Quinzaine for this Yule* (privately printed, 1908; repr. for Elkin Mathews, 1908)
Personae	*Personae of Ezra Pound* (Elkin Mathews, 1909)
Exultations	*Exultations of Ezra Pound* (Elkin Mathews, 1909)
Provença	*Provença* (Boston: Small Maynard, 1910)
SR	*The Spirit of Romance* (London and New York: J. M. Dent & Sons, 1910; new edn., London: Peter Owen, **1952**, New York: New Directions, 1953)
Canzoni	*Canzoni of Ezra Pound* (Elkin Mathews, 1911)
Ripostes	*Ripostes of Ezra Pound* (Stephen Swift, 1912—sheets then taken over by Elkin Mathews; Boston: Small Maynard, 1913)
Cathay	*Cathay* (Elkin Mathews, 1915)
Cathol Ant	*Catholic Anthology: 1914–1915* (Elkin Mathews, 1915)
PM	*Patria Mia* [1912–13] (Chicago: Ralph Fletcher Seymour, 1950; new edn., with 'The Treatise on Harmony' (Peter Owen, **1962**)
GB	*Gaudier-Brzeska: A Memoir* (London and New York: John Lane, 1916; new edn., Hessle: The Marvell Press, **1960** and New York: New Directions, 1961)
Lustra (1916)	*Lustra of Ezra Pound* (privately printed, 1916; abridged edn., Elkin Mathews, **1916**)
Lustra (1917)	*Lustra of Ezra Pound with Earlier Poems* [and 'Three Cantos'] (New York: privately printed, 1917; ordinary edn. [without 'The Temperaments'], Alfred A. Knopf, **1917**)
Noh	*'Noh' or Accomplishment: A Study of the Classical Stage of Japan* by Ernest Fenollosa and Ezra Pound (Macmillan & Co. Ltd, 1916; New York: Alfred A. Knopf, 1917; included in *T* 1953; new edn., New York: New Directions, **1959**)
PD (1918)	*Pavannes and Divisions* (New York: Alfred A. Knopf, 1918) [See *PD (1958)*]

QPA	*Quia Pauper Amavi* (The Egoist Ltd., 1919). Includes *Homage to Sextus Propertius*
HSP	*Homage to Sextus Propertius*. Repr. from *QPA*, with some alterations, in *P 1918-21*, *P (1926)*, and in all later editions of the collected shorter poems; published as a book in 1934 by Faber & Faber; published with *HSM* as *Diptych Rome-London* (New York: New Directions, 1958)
Instigations	*Instigations of Ezra Pound together with An Essay on the Chinese Written Character by Ernest Fenollosa* (New York: Boni and Liveright, 1920)
HSM	*Hugh Selwyn Mauberley by E.P.* (The Ovid Press, 1920)
Umbra	*Umbra: The Early Poems of Ezra Pound* (Elkin Mathews, 1920)
P 1918–21	*Poems 1918–21 Including Three Portraits and Four Cantos* (New York: Boni and Liveright, 1921)
NPL	*The Natural Philosophy of Love* by Remy de Gourmont, Translated with a Postscript by Ezra Pound (New York: Boni and Liveright, 1922; new edn., London: The Casanova Society, 1926)
Antheil	*Antheil and The Treatise on Harmony* (Paris: Three Mountains Press, 1924; new edn., Chicago: Pascal Covici, 1927)
XVI Cantos	*A Draft of XVI Cantos of Ezra Pound for the Beginning of a Poem of some Length*, with Initials by Henry Strater (Paris: Three Mountains Press, 1925)
P (1926)	*Personae: The Collected Poems of Ezra Pound* (New York: Boni and Liveright, 1926)
Ta Hio	*Ta Hio, The Great Learning* [later version in *Confucius* as 'The Great Digest'] (Seattle: University of Washington Bookstore, 1928; new edn., Stanley Nott, 1936; repr. New York: New Directions, 1939)
Cantos 17–27	*A Draft of the Cantos 17–27 of Ezra Pound*, with Initials by Gladys Hynes (John Rodker, 1928)
XXX Cantos	*A Draft of XXX Cantos* (Paris: Hours Press, 1930)
Rime	*Guido Cavalcanti Rime* (Genova: Edizione Marsano SA, 1932)
Profile	*Profile: An Anthology Collected in MCMXXXI*, ed. EP (Milan: Giovanni Scheiwiller, 1932)
Active Anth	*Active Anthology*, ed. EP (Faber & Faber, 1933)
ABCE	*ABC of Economics* (Faber & Faber, 1933)
ABCR	*ABC of Reading* (George Routledge & Sons Ltd., 1934; New Haven: Yale University Press, 1934; new edn., Faber & Faber, 1951; repr. New Directions, 1951)
MIN	*Make It New: Essays by Ezra Pound* (Faber & Faber, 1934; repr. New Haven: Yale University Press, 1935)

XXXI–XLI — *Eleven New Cantos XXXI–XLI* (New York: Farrar & Rinehart, 1934; Faber & Faber, 1935)

J/M — *Jefferson and/or Mussolini: L'Idea Statale—Fascism as I have seen it . . . Volitionist Economics* (Stanley Nott, 1935; New York: Liveright Publishing Corp., 1936)

CWC — *The Chinese Written Character as a Medium for Poetry* (Stanley Nott, 1936; new edn., San Francisco: City Lights Books, 1964)

PE — *Polite Essays* (Faber & Faber, 1937)

XLII–LI — *The Fifth Decad of Cantos* (Faber & Faber, 1937; New York: Farrar & Rinehart, 1937)

GK — *Guide to Kulchur* (Faber & Faber, 1938; new edn., Norfolk, Conn.: New Directions, 1952; repr. Peter Owen Ltd., 1952)

LII–LXXI — *Cantos LII–LXXI* (Faber & Faber, 1940; Norfolk, Conn.: New Directions, 1940)

Por — *Italy's Policy of Social Economics 1930/1940* by Odon Por, trans. Ezra Pound (Bergamo: Istituto Italiano d'Arte Graifiche, 1941)

Confucio — *Confucio, Ta S'eu, Dai Gaku. Studio Integrale*, Versione italiana di Ezra Pound e di Alberto Luchini (Rapallo: Scuola Tipografica Orfanotrofio Emiliani, 1942)

Carta — *Carta da visita* ([Roma]: Edizione di lettere d'oggi, 1942); translated with some amendments by John Drummond, and published as *A Visiting Card* (Peter Russell, 1952), repr. *S Pr*

America — *L'America, Roosevelt e le cause della guerra presente* (Venezia: Casa Editrice della Edizione Popolari, 1944); English translation by John Drummond, *America, Roosevelt, and the Causes of the Present War* (Peter Russell, 1951)

Oro — *Oro e lavoro* (Rapallo: Tipografica Moderna, 1944); English translation by John Drummond, *Gold and Work* (Peter Russell, 1951), repr. *S Pr*

Introduzione — *Introduzione alla natura economica degli S.U.A.* (Venezia: Casa Editrice della Edizione Popolari, 1944); English translation by Carmine Armore ([Peter Russell, 1950]), repr., revised by John Drummond, *S Pr*

Testamento — *Testamento di Confucio*, Versione italiana di Ezra Pound e di Alberto Luchini (Venezia: Casa Editrice della Edizione Popolari, 1944)

Orientamenti — *Orientamenti* (Venezia: Casa Editrice della Edizione Popolari, 1944)

J e M — *Jefferson e Mussolini* (Venezia: Casa Editrice della Edizione Popolari, 1944)—Pound's Italian version of *J/M*

Chiung Iung — *Chiung Iung, L'Asse che non vacilla*, Versione italiana di Ezra Pound (Venezia: Casa Editrice della Edizione Popolari, 1945)

Treason	*'If This Be Treason ...'* | *e. e. cummings/examind* | *James Joyce: to his memory* | *A french accent* | *'Canto 45'* | *Blast* (Siena Italy: Printed for Olga Rudge, [1948])
Pisan	*The Pisan Cantos* (New York: New Directions, 1948; Faber & Faber, 1949)
Confucius (1949)	*Confucius: The Unwobbling Pivot & The Great Digest*, Translated by Ezra Pound, With notes and commentary on the text and the ideograms (Bombay, Calcutta, Madras: Orient Longmans Ltd. for Kavitabhavan, 1949)
L (1950)	*The Letters of Ezra Pound 1907–1941*, ed. D. D. Paige (New York: Harcourt Brace, 1950; reissued as *The Selected Letters of Ezra Pound 1907–1941* by Faber & Faber, 1971)
L (1951)	*The Letters of Ezra Pound 1907–1941*, ed. D. D. Paige (Faber & Faber, 1951). This differs in both contents and pagination from *L (1950)*, but letters can be identified in either edition by date and recipient.
Analects	*Confucian Analects* (New York: Square $ Series, 1951; Peter Owen, 1956)
Confucius (1951)	*Confucius: The Great Digest & Unwobbling Pivot*, trans. EP (New York: New Directions, 1951; repr. Peter Owen, 1952)
T	*The Translations of Ezra Pound* (Faber & Faber, 1953; repr. New York: New Directions, 1953; enlarged edn., 1964)
CA	*The Classic Anthology Defined by Confucius*, trans. EP (Cambridge, Mass.: Harvard University Press, 1954; repr. Faber & Faber, 1955)
LE	*Literary Essays of Ezra Pound*, ed. T. S. Eliot (Faber & Faber, 1954; repr. Norfolk, Conn.: New Directions, 1954)
Rock-Drill	*Section: Rock Drill, 85–95 de los cantares* (Milano: All'Insegna del Pesce d'Oro, 1955; repr. New York: New Directions, 1956; also Faber & Faber, 1957)
La Martinelli	*La Martinelli*. Introduction by Ezra Pound (Milan: [Vanni Scheiwiller], 1956)
Trax	*Sophokles: Women of Trachis*, A version by Ezra Pound (Neville Spearman, 1956; repr. New York: New Directions, 1957)
PD (1958)	*Pavannes and Divagations* (Norfolk, Conn.: New Directions, 1958; repr. Peter Owen, 1960)
Thrones	*Thrones: 96–109 de los cantares* (Milano: All'Insegna del Pesce d'Oro, 1959; repr. New York: New Directions, 1959; also Faber & Faber, 1960)
Impact	*Impact: Essays on Ignorance and the Decline of American Civilization*, ed. Noel Stock (Chicago: Henry Regnery Company, 1960)

LPAE	*Love Poems of Ancient Egypt*, trans. Ezra Pound and Noel Stock (New York: New Directions, 1962)—previously published as 'Conversations in Courtship'
CC	*Confucius to Cummings: An Anthology of Poetry*, ed. EP & Marcella Spann (New York: New Directions, 1964)
EP/JJ	*Pound/Joyce: The Letters of Ezra Pound to James Joyce, with Pound's Essays on Joyce*, ed. Forrest Read (New York: New Directions, 1967; repr. Faber & Faber, 1967)
D&F	*Drafts & Fragments of Cantos CX–CXVII* (New York: New Directions, 1969; Faber & Faber, 1970)
Opera Scelte	*Opera Scelte*, a cura di Mary de Rachewiltz ([Milano]: Arnoldo Mondadori Editore, 1970)
Cantos	*The Cantos of Ezra Pound.* References, in the form of canto number/page number (as 20/89), are to the New Directions collected edition of 1970 as reprinted in the Faber 'Revised Collected Edition (Cantos 1–117)' published in 1975. The two volumes of *A Companion to the Cantos of Ezra Pound* ed. Carroll F. Terrell (Berkeley: University of California Press, 1980, 1984) are keyed to this text. [For later printings of the *Cantos* add, for those which include cantos 72 and 73, 14 to the page number from *Pisan Cantos* on; and to those which include in addition EP's English version of canto 72 add 20.]
S Pr	*Selected Prose 1909–1965*, ed. William Cookson (Faber & Faber, 1973).
S Pr (US)	*Selected Prose 1909–1965*, ed. William Cookson (New York, New Directions, 1973). [Differs from *S Pr* in pagination, and by omitting 'Statues of Gods' (1939) and 'The Treatise on Harmony' (1924), and adding 'Patria Mia' (1912).]
EP/Dk	*Dk/Some Letters of Ezra Pound*, ed. with notes by Louis Dudek (Montreal: DC Books, 1974)
CEP	*Collected Early Poems of Ezra Pound*, ed. Michael John King (New York: New Directions, 1976; repr. Faber & Faber, 1977)
EP&M	*Ezra Pound and Music: The Complete Criticism*, ed. R. Murray Schafer (New York: New Directions, 1977; repr. Faber & Faber, 1978)
Radio	*'Ezra Pound Speaking': Radio Speeches of World War II*, ed. Leonard W. Doob (Westport, Conn.: Greenwood Press, 1978)
EP&VA	*Ezra Pound and The Visual Arts*, ed. Harriet Zinnes (New York: New Directions, 1980)
EP/Ibb	*Letters to Ibbotson, 1935–1952*, ed. Vittoria I. Mondolfo and Margaret Hurley (Orono, Me.: National Poetry Foundation, 1979)

Lettere — *Lettere 1907–58* (Milano: Feltrinelli Editore, 1980)

P/F — *Pound/Ford: The Story of a Literary Friendship*, ed. Brita Lindberg-Seyersted (New York: New Directions, 1982; repr. Faber & Faber, 1982)

Cav — *Pound's Cavalcanti: An Edition of the Translations, Notes and Essays* by David Anderson (Princeton: Princeton University Press, 1983)

EP/JT — *Letters to John Theobald*, ed. Donald Pearce and Herbert Schneidau (Redding Ridge, Conn.: Black Swan Books, 1984)

EP/DS — *Ezra Pound and Dorothy Shakespear: Their Letters 1909–1914*, ed. Omar Pound and A. Walton Litz (New York: New Directions, 1984; repr. Faber & Faber 1985)

I Cantos — *I Cantos*, a cura di Mary de Rachewiltz (Milano: Arnoldo Mondadori Editore, 1985)—Italian translation with corrected English text *en face*, and substantial commentary

EP/WL — *Pound/Lewis: The Letters of Ezra Pound and Wyndham Lewis*, ed. Timothy Materer (New York: New Directions, 1985; repr. Faber and Faber, 1985)

EP/LZ — *Pound/Zukofsky: Selected Letters of Ezra Pound and Louis Zukofsky*, ed. Barry Ahearn (New York: New Directions, 1987; repr. Faber and Faber, 1987)

EP&J — *Ezra Pound & Japan: Letters & Essays*, ed. Sanehide Kodama (Redding Ridge, Conn.: Black Swan Books, 1987)

Plays — *Plays Modelled on the Noh (1916)*, ed. Donald C. Gallup (Toledo: The Friends of the University of Toledo Libraries, 1987)

EP/scienza — *Ezra Pound e la scienza. Scritti inediti o rari*, ed. Maria Luisa Ardizzone (Milano: Libri Scheiwiller, 1987)

EP/MC — *Ezra Pound and Margaret Cravens: A Tragic Friendship 1910–1912*, ed. Omar Pound and Robert Spoo (Durham, NC: Duke University Press, 1988)

EP/LR — *Pound/The Little Review: The Letters of Ezra Pound to Margaret Anderson*—The Little Review *Correspondence*, ed. Thomas L. Scott, Melvin J. Friedman with the assistance of Jackson R. Bryer (New York: New Directions, 1988)

Elektra — *Elektra*. A Play by Ezra Pound and Rudd Fleming [translated 1949], ed. Richard Reid (Princeton: Princeton University Press, 1989)

P (1990) — *Personae: The Shorter Poems of Ezra Pound*, A Revised Edition Prepared by Lea Baechler and A. Walton Litz (New York: New Directions, 1990)

P&P	*Ezra Pound's Poetry and Prose: Contributions to Periodicals*, prefaced and arranged by Lea Baechler, A. Walton Litz, and James Longenbach, 10 vols. [Addenda and Index in vol. XI], (New York and London: Garland Publishing Inc., 1991). [Contains in photo-reproduction all contributions to periodicals recorded in Gallup.]
EP/JQ	*The Selected Letters of Ezra Pound to John Quinn*, ed. Timothy Materer (Durham, NC: Duke University Press, 1991)
WT	*A Walking Tour in Southern France: Ezra Pound among the Troubadours*, ed. Richard Sieburth (New York: New Directions, 1992)
Cathay/Catai	*Antiche poesie cinesi*, [a trilingual Chinese–English–Italian edition of *Cathay*], a cura di Alessandra C. Lavagnino e Maria Rita Masci (Torino: Giulio Einaudi Editore, 1993)
EP/ACH	*The Letters of Ezra Pound to Alice Corbin Henderson*, ed. Ira B. Nadel (Austin: University of Texas Press, 1993)
EP/JL	*Ezra Pound and James Laughlin: Selected Letters*, ed. David M. Gordon (New York: W. W. Norton, 1994)
EP/Dial	*Pound, Thayer, Watson and **The Dial**: A Story in Letters*, ed. Walter Sutton (Gainesville, Fla.: University Press of Florida, 1994)
EP/BC	*Ezra Pound and Senator Bronson Cutting: A Political Corespondence 1930–1935*, ed. E. P. Walkiewicz and Hugh Witemeyer (Albuquerque: University of New Mexico Press, 1995)
J e M (1995)	*Jefferson e Mussolini*, Presentazione di Mary de Rachewiltz (Milano: Terziaria, 1995)—reprints EP's 1944 Italian version of *J/M*, an edition printed by Casa Editrice Edizione Popolari di Venezia but of which nearly all copies were destroyed at the press
Lavoro/Usura	*Lavoro ed usura. tre saggi*, terza edizione (Milano: All'Insegna del Pesce d'Oro di Vanni Scheiwiller, 1996)—reprints *Oro e lavoro* (1944), *L'America, Roosevelt, e le cause della guerra presente* (1944), *Introduzione alla natura economica degli S.U.A.* (1944), and adds 'L'economia ortologica' (1937)
EP/WCW	*Pound/Williams: Selected Letters of Ezra Pound and William Carlos Williams*, ed. Hugh Witemeyer (New York: New Directions, 1996)
EP/EEC	*Pound/Cummings: The Correspondence of Ezra Pound and E. E. Cummings*, ed. Barry Ahearn (Ann Arbor: University of Michigan Press, 1996)
EP/GT	*'Dear Uncle George': The Correspondence between Ezra Pound and Congressman [George] Tinkham of Massachusetts*, ed.

	Philip J. Burns (Orono, Me.: National Poetry Foundation, 1996)
MA	*Machine Art and Other Writings*, ed. Maria Luisa Ardizzone (Durham, NC: Duke University Press, 1996)
EP/ORA	*'I Cease Not to Yowl': Ezra Pound's Letters to Olivia Rossetti Agresti*, ed. Demetres P. Tryphonopoulos and Leon Surette (Urbana: University of Illinois Press, 1998)
EP/DP	*Ezra and Dorothy Pound: Letters in Captivity, 1945–1946*, ed. Omar Pound and Robert Spoo (New York: Oxford University Press, 1999)
EP/GV	*Ezra Pound—Giambattista Vicari. Il fare aperto. Lettere 1939–1971*, a cura di Anna Busetto Vicari e Luca Cesari (Milan: Archinto, 2000)
EP/WB	*The Correspondence of Ezra Pound and Senator William Borah*, ed. Sarah C. Holmes (Urbana: University of Illinois Press, 2001)
EP/WW	*Ezra Pound's Letters to William Watt*, [ed.] with an introduction and notes by William Watt (Marquette, Mich.: Northern Michigan University Press, 2001)
Canti postumi	*Canti postumi*, a cura di Massimo Bacigalupo (Milano: Arnoldo Mondadori, 2002; II edizione 2012)
P&T	*Ezra Pound: Poems and Translations*, [selected by Richard Sieburth] (New York: The Library of America, 2003)
Cavalcanti	*Cavalcanti. A sung dramedy in 3 acts*, the full score ed. Robert Hughes and Margaret Fisher, in Robert Hughes and Margaret Fisher, *Cavalcanti: A Perspective on the Music of Ezra Pound* (*CPMEP*), (Emeryville, Calif.: Second Evening Art, 2003)
CVW	*Complete Violin Works of Ezra Pound*, ed. with commentary by Robert Hughes, introduction by Margaret Fisher (Emeryville, Calif.: Second Evening Art, 2004)
Moscardino	Enrico Pea, *Moscardino*, translated from the Italian by EP [1941] (New York: Archipelago Books, 2004)
Collis	Margaret Fisher, *The Recovery of Ezra Pound's Third Opera: 'Collis O Heliconii'*, [includes performance edition] (Emeryville, Calif.: Second Evening Art, 2005)
Carte italiana	*Ezra Pound. Carte italiana 1930–1944, letteratura e note*, a cura di Luca Cesari (Milano: Archinto, 2005)
EWPP	*Early Writings. Poems & Prose*, ed. Ira Nadel (New York: Penguin Books, 2005)
EPEC	*Ezra Pound's Economic Correspondence, 1933–1940*, ed. and annotated by Roxana Preda (Gainesville: University Press of Florida, 2007)

Testament I	*Ezra Pound: Le Testament, 'Paroles de Villon'—1926 'Salle Pleyel' concert excerpts & 1933 Final Version complete opera*, ed. Margaret Fisher and Robert Hughes, performance editions (Emeryville, Calif.: Second Evening Art Publishing, 2008)
CWC II	Ernest Fenollosa and Ezra Pound, *The Chinese Written Character as a Medium for Poetry, A Critical Edition*, ed. Haun Saussy, Jonathan Stalling, and Lucas Klein (New York: Fordham University Press, 2008)
EP/CF	*Ezra Pound's Chinese Friends: Stories in Letters*, ed. Zhaoming Qian (Oxford: Oxford University Press, 2008)
NSPT	*New Selected Poems & Translations*, ed. and annotated with an afterword by Richard Sieburth (New York: New Directions, 2010)
EP/Parents	*Ezra Pound to his Parents. Letters 1895–1929*, ed. Mary de Rachewiltz, A. David Moody, and Joanna Moody (Oxford Oxford University Press, 2010)
D&F facsimile	Ezra Pound, *Drafts & Fragments. Facsimile Notebooks 1958–1959* (New York: Glenn Horowitz, Bookseller, Inc., 2010)
Testament II	*Ezra Pound: Le Testament: 1923 facsimile edition edited by George Antheil*, with notes for the 1931 BBC radio broadcast, ed. Margaret Fisher and Robert Hughes (Emeryville, Calif.: Second Evening Art Publishing, 2011)
EP/SN	*One Must Not Go Altogether with the Tide: The Letters of Ezra Pound and Stanley Nott*, ed. and with essays by Miranda B. Hickman (Montreal: McGill-Queen's University Press, 2011)

Writings by others

Abbreviations are used only for books referred to frequently in the notes. For all other books and articles full details are given at the first mention, and a recognizable shortened form is used thereafter.

Barnard	Mary Barnard, *Assault on Mount Helicon: A Literary Memoir* (Berkeley: University of California Press, 1984)
Carpenter	Humphrey Carpenter, *A Serious Character: The Life of Ezra Pound* (Faber & Faber, 1988)
Casebook	*A Casebook on Ezra Pound*, ed. William Van O'Connor and Edward Stone (New York: Thomas Y. Crowell Company, 1959)

CPMEP	Robert Hughes and Margaret Fisher, *Cavalcanti: A Perspective on the Music of Ezra Pound* (Emeryville, Calif.: Second Evening Art, 2003)
Conover	Anne Conover, *Olga Rudge and Ezra Pound* (New Haven: Yale University Press, 2001)
Cornell	Julien Cornell, *The Trial of Ezra Pound: A Documented Account of the Treason Case by the Defendant's Lawyer* (Faber & Faber, 1967)
Discretions	Mary de Rachewiltz, *Discretions* (Faber & Faber, 1971; Boston: Atlantic-Little Brown, 1971; New York: New Directions, 1975, 2005)
EP: Poet I	A. David Moody, *Ezra Pound: Poet. A Portrait of the Man & his Work. I: The Young Genius 1885–1920* (Oxford: Oxford University Press, 2007)
EP: Poet II	A. David Moody, *Ezra Pound: Poet. A Portrait of the Man & his Work. II: The Epic Years, 1921–1939* (Oxford: Oxford University Press, 2014)
EPRO	Margaret Fisher, *Ezra Pound's Radio Operas: The BBC Experiments, 1931–1933* (Cambridge, Mass.: The MIT Press, 2002)
ESC	*Ego Scriptor Cantilenae: The Music of Ezra Pound*, Robert Hughes conductor and musical director, Margaret Fisher author, containing audio CD (Othe Minds OM 1005-2) and booklet (San Francisco: Other Minds Inc., 2003)
ET	H[ilda] D[oolittle], *End to Torment: A Memoir of Ezra Pound*, ed. Norman Holmes Pearson and Michael King (New York: New Directions, 1979; Manchester: Carcanet New Press, 1980)
Etruscan Gate	Dorothy Shakespear Pound, *Etruscan Gate: A Notebook with Drawings and Watercolours*, ed. Moelwyn Merchant (Exeter: The Rougemont Press, 1971)
Farrell	Nicholas Farrell, *Mussolini: A New Life* (Weidenfeld & Nicolson, 2003)
Flory	Wendy Stallard Flory, *The American Ezra Pound* (New Haven and London: Yale University Press, 1989)
Frost	*Selected Letters of Robert Frost*, ed. Lawrence Thompson (Cape, 1965; New York Holt, Rinehart & Winston, 1966)
Gallup	Donald Gallup, *Ezra Pound: A Bibliography* (Charlottesville: University Press of Virginia, 1983)
Hemingway	*Ernest Hemingway: Selected Letters*, ed. Carlos Baker (New York: Scribner, 1981)
Henderson	Archie Henderson, *'I Cease Not to Yowl' Reannotated: New Notes on the Pound/Agresti Correspondence* (Houston: [Archie Henderson], 2009)

Heymann	C. David Heymann, *Ezra Pound: The Last Rower. A Political Profile* (Faber & Faber, 1976)
Homberger	Eric Homberger (ed.), *Ezra Pound: The Critical Heritage* (Routledge and Kegan Paul, 1972)
Kimpel and Eaves	B. D. Kimpel and T. C. Eaves, 'More on Pound's Prison Experience', *American Literature* 53.3 (1981), 469–76
Little	Marie-Noëlle Little, *The Knight and the Troubadour: Dag Hammarskjöld and Ezra Pound* (Uppsala: Dag Hammarskjöld Foundation, 2011)
MacLeish	*Letters of Archibald MacLeish 1907 to 1982*, ed. R. H. Winnick (Boston: Houghton Mifflin Company, 1983)
Makin	Peter Makin, *Pound's Cantos* (George Allen & Unwin, 1985)
Meacham	*The Caged Panther: Ezra Pound at Saint Elizabeths* (New York: Twayne Publishers Inc., 1967)
Norman 1960	Charles Norman, *Ezra Pound* (New York: Macmillan, 1960)
Norman *Case*	Charles Norman, *The Case of Ezra Pound* (New York: Funk & Wagnalls, 1968)
Olson	Charles Olson, *Charles Olson & Ezra Pound: An Encounter at St. Elizabeths*, ed. Catherine Seelye (New York: Grossman Publishers, 1975)
Paris Rev. interview	'The Art of Poetry V. Ezra Pound: An Interview', [with Donald Hall], *Paris Review* 28 (1962) 22–51
Reck	Michael Reck, *Ezra Pound: A Close-up* (Rupert Hart-David Ltd, 1968)
Redman	Tim Redman, *Ezra Pound and Italian Fascism* (Cambridge: Cambridge University Press, 1991)
Shirer	William L. Shirer, *The Rise and Fall of the Third Reich: A History of Nazi Germany* (Secker & Warburg 1961)
Sieber	H. A. Sieber, *The Medical, Legal, Literary and Political Status of Ezra Weston [Loomis] Pound [1885–]/Selected Facts and Comments* (Washington, DC: Library of Congress Legislative Reference Service, 31 March 1958/Revised [after] April [18] 1958)
Stock 1970	Noel Stock, *The Life of Ezra Pound* (Routledge and Kegan Paul, 1970)
Stock 1976	Noel Stock, *Ezra Pound's Pennsylvania* (Toledo: The Friends of the University of Toledo Libraries, 1976)
Terrell, *Companion*	Carroll F. Terrell, *A Companion to the Cantos of Ezra Pound*, 2 vols., (Berkeley: University of California Press, 1980, 1984)
Torrey	E. Fuller Torrey, *The Roots of Treason: Ezra Pound and the Secret of St. Elizabeths* (New York: McGraw Hill; London: Sidgwick & Jackson, 1984)

Tytell	John Tytell, *Ezra Pound: The Solitary Volcano* (Bloomsbury, 1987)
WCW/JL	*William Carlos Williams and James Laughlin: Selected Letters*, ed. Hugh Witemeyer (New York W. W. Norton, 1989)
Wilhelm 1994	J. J. Wilhelm, *Ezra Pound, The Tragic Years, 1925–1972* (University Park: Pennsylvania State University Press, 1994)
Zapponi	Niccolò Zapponi, *L'Italia di Ezra Pound* (Roma: Bulzoni Editore, 1976)

Other abbreviations

AB	Agnes Bedford
AFHQ	Allied Forces Headquarters
AGWAR	Adjutant General War Department
AMacL	Archibald MacLeish
AVM	Arthur Valentine Moore
BB	Basil Bunting
Beinecke	Ezra Pound Papers. Yale Collection of American Literature. Beinecke Rare Book and Manuscript Library. Yale University
Beinecke/OR	Olga Rudge Papers. Yale Collection of American Literature. Beinecke Rare Book and Manuscript Library. Yale University
COMGENMED	Commanding General Mediterranean
DP	Dorothy Shakespear Pound
EEC	E. E. Cummings
EP	Ezra Loomis [Weston] Pound
FMF	Ford Madox Ford
Hamilton	Ezra Pound Collection, Special Collections, Burke Library, Hamilton College, Clinton, NY
Hamilton/OSP	Materials from the Omar S. Pound Archive, Special Collections, Burke Library, Hamilton College, Clinton, NY
HD	Hilda Doolittle
HK	Hugh Kenner
HLP	Homer Loomis Pound
HRC	Ezra Pound Collection, Harry Ransom Humanities Research Center, The University of Texas at Austin
HRC/MSB	Marcella Spann Booth Collection, Harry Ransom Humanities Research Center, The University of Texas at Austin
ID	Ingrid Davies
IWP	Isabel Weston Pound
JC	Julien Cornell
JJ	James Joyce

JL	James Laughlin
Lilly	Pound Mansucripts, The Lilly Library, Indiana University, Bloomington
LZ	Louis Zukofsky
MB	Mary Barnard
MM	Marianne Moore
MdR	Mary de Rachewiltz
MS	Marcella Spann
MSB	Marcella Spann Booth
Nat. Arch.	The National Archives, Kew, England
NC	Nancy Cunard
OR	Olga Rudge
ORA	Olivia Rossetti Agresti
OS	Olivia Shakespear
OSP	Omar Shakespear Pound
Pai	*Paideuma.* A Journal Devoted to Ezra Pound Scholarship (1972–2009)
Poetry	*Poetry: A Magazine of Verse.* (Chicago, 1912–36)
RF	Robert Frost
SM	Sheri Martinelli
TSE	Thomas Stearns Eliot
UPenn	Ezra Pound Collections, Van Pelt Library, University of Pennsylvania
US Nat. Arch.	United States of America National Archives, Washington DC
VBJ	Viola Baxter Jordan
WBY	W. B. Yeats
WCW	William Carlos Williams
WL	Wyndham Lewis
WO	Winfred Overholser

NOTES

title page—'I do not think': Henry A. Wallace to Charles Norman, [? *c.*1959], Norman: 1960, 360.

Preface

xiii **'Bracton'**: 109/771.
xiv **'His profound and intimate knowledge'**: LZ in Norman, *The Case of Ezra Pound* (New York: The Bodley Press, 1948), 55.
'go to that work': Robert Creeley, 'A Letter to the Editor of Goad' (1951–2), *A Quick Graph: Collected Notes & Essays* (San Francisco: Four Seasons Foundation, 1970), 93.
xv **They are political:** see EP to JT, 17 June 1957, *EP/JT* 44.
'answering intensity': Robert Duncan, *The H.D. Book* (Berkeley: University of California Press, 2011), 183.
'awesome and rather shattering': Robert Lowell to JL, 31 Aug. 1966, *Letters of Robert Lowell*, ed. Saskia Hamilton (New York: Farrar, Straus and Giroux, 2005), 473.
'Partial, impartial': Geoffrey Hill, 'On Reading: *Burke on Empire, Liberty, and Reform*', *A Treatise of Civil Power* (Thame: Clutag Press, 2005).

The first part, 1939–1945, is much indebted to Part II of Tim Redman's *Ezra Pound and Italian Fascism*, and to Niccolò Zapponi's *L'Italia di Ezra Pound* (Roma: Bulzoni Editore, 1978).

1. Between Paradise & Propaganda, 1939–40

3 **'He come bak'**: EP to OR, 27 June 1939 (Beinecke/OR).
'He has put her off': OR to EP, [? 4 July 1939—first page of letter missing] (Beinecke/OR).
Pennsylvania Statute on Adoption: in folder with EP letters to Joseph H. Cochran, May 1939 (Beinecke).
door locked: see Conover, 138.
playing tennis with Mary: EP to DP, 27 Sept. 1939 (Lilly).
4 **'A clap of Thunder'**: HLP to EP, 3 Aug. 1939, *EP/Parents* xxi.
'Dear Son': IWP to EP, 31 July 1939, *EP/Parents* xxi.
'Dear Dad': EP to HLP, [? 8 Aug. 1939] (Beinecke). This paragraph draws on MdR's *Discretions* 188 and 310.
'from some place high up': MdR, *Discretions* 119. This paragraph draws on *Discretions* 115–19, and 279–82.
'in a stronger position': quoted in Farrell 317. Information in this paragraph drawn from Farrell's *Mussolini* 315–17.
Hitler . . . secretly briefing: see Shirer 483ff. and 496ff.
5 **'Mebbe been a bit callous'**: EP to DP, 26 Aug. 1939 (Lilly).
'sacrificing': DP to EP, 8 Aug. 1939 (Lilly).
'Since its writing': from EP MS note on endpaper of a copy of *ABCE* now in HRC.
6 **'29 Cantos and'**: EP to Ronald Duncan, 4 Aug. 1939 (HRC). See also EP to Jorian Jenks on same date, 'I am boiling away on a book on money,' in *EPEC* 224. Though this book on money was abandoned it is likely that EP drew on the drafts for contributions to *The Japan Times* in 1940, for a contribution to *Rassegna Monetaria* in April 1940

('Economia ortologica'), and for his wartime pamphlets—*Carta da visita* (1942), *L'America, Roosevelt e le cause della guerra presente* (1944), *Oro e lavoro* (1944), *Introduzione alla natura economica degli S.U.A.* (1944).
'trying to pull': EP to DP, 29 Aug. 1939 (Lilly).
'My economic work': EP to Douglas McPherson, 3 Nov. 1939, *L (1951)* 424.
'The *only* American book': EP to Douglas McPherson, 2 Sept. 1939, *L (1951)* 421.
'The most lucid': EP to DP, 22 Aug, 1939 (Lilly).
'the younger generation': EP to Douglas McPherson, 3 Nov. 1939, *L (1951)* 424.
'There shd. be about 100': EP to TSE, 29 or 30 Sept. 1939 (Beinecke).
'From 72 on': EP to JL, 24 Feb. 1940, *EP/JL* 115.
'a symbol of mankind's': *SR* 127. Cf. *EP: Poet I*, 120.
7 **next to 'tackle philosophy'**: EP to Santayana, 8 Dec. 1939, *L (1951)* 428. (EP wrote 'paradiso', not 'paradise' as mistranscribed by Paige.)
'to *see* the connection': EP to TSE, 18 Jan. 1940, *L(1951)* 433.
'Teach?': EP to DP, 27 Dec. 1939 (Lilly), and 74/433.
'"A relief"': MdR, *Discretions* 127–8.
'All the way home': MdR, *Discretions* 127.
Handbook: Dr Albert Schwegler, *Handbook of the History of Philosophy*, trans. James Hutchison Stirling, 4th edn. (Edinburgh: Edmonston & Douglas, 1872), inscribed 'H. H. Shakespear' and 'EP , 1940' on front free endpaper, now in HRC.
8 **'a lot about light'**: EP to DP, 3 Jan. 1940 (Lilly).
'omnia quae sunt': see 74/429, 83/528.
'serene heaven': EP, in a note made in the 1940s, wrote,'Deve seguire un cielo sereno e filosofico se l'autore persiste'—see *I Cantos* (Milano: Arnaldo Mondadori, 1985), 1566.
'civilizations at their MOST': EP to TSE, 1 Feb. 1940 (Beinecke)—in *L (1951)* 434.
not a new conviction: re *Imagisme* see *EP: Poet II* 9, and *SR* 93; re the Confucian *paideuma* see *EP: Poet II* 74–6; re the intelligence of love see *EP: Poet II* 108–16, also 'Terra Italica', *S Pr* 54-60; re germinal intelligence see *EP: Poet II* 72–4 and 139–40.
'What we really believe': EP, 'Statues of Gods' (1939), *S Pr* 71.
'Paganism': EP, 'Religio' (1939), *S Pr* 70.
9 **'The religious man'**: EP, 'Deus est Amor' (1940), *S Pr* 72. For a fuller statement on 'the mystery of the grain' see EP, 'Sul serio', *Meridiano di Roma* V.35 (1 Sept. 1940) [1]–2.
'semitic infections': 'Statues of Gods' (1939), *S Pr* 71.
'usury and mercantilism': EP, 'Ecclesia', *Townsman* II.8 (Nov. 1939) 4–5.
'What we believe is EUROPEAN': EP, 'European Paideuma', ed. Massimo Bacigalupo, *Pai* 30.1–2 (2001) 226–30.
in some of his correspondence: for one example see EP to GT, 2 Nov. 1939, *EP/GT* 183–5.
'I don't think I am ready': EP to TSE, 1 Feb. 1940, *L (1951)* 434.
10 **'Re European belief'**: EP to Henry Swabey, 7 Mar. 1940, *L (1951)* 437–8.
'what's use my saying': EP to Ronald Duncan, 14 Mar. 1940 (HRC)—also *L (1951)* 438.
'After half an hour': EP to Kitasono, 25 Aug. 1940, *EP&J* 93.
Fengchi Yang: details from 'Yang as Pound's Opponent and Collaborator', *Ezra Pound's Chinese Friends: Stories in Letters*, ed. Zhaoming Quian (Oxford: Oxford University Press, 2008), 18–19—the letters exchanged by EP and Yang follow on Quian's, 23–39.
11 **'the student body'**: see EP to Ibbotson, 14 July 1939, *EP/Ibb* 99–105.
'a dead loss': JL to EP, 26 Nov. 1939, *EP/JL* 107–8.
'these next years': JL to EP, 5 Dec. 1939, *EP/JL* 108–9.
'when monetary sanity': JL to EP, 5 Dec. 1939, *EP/JL* 108–9.

'could be no connection', and **re anti-Semitism**: JL to EP, 5 Dec. 1939, *EP/JL*, 109–10.

12 **'fer preventin'**: EP to JL, 22 Nov. 1940, *EP/JL* 122.
'Until the war': EP to JL, 13–14 Nov. 1940, *EP/JL* 119–20.
'Yr hon[our's] name': JL to EP, n.d. [*c.* Nov.– Dec. 1940], *EP/JL* 122.
articles in *Meridiano di Roma*: see the following:- 'Condutture avvelenate', IV.19 (14 May 1939) 9—translated (with omissions) by Tim Redman as 'Poisoned Pipelines' in *Helix* 13/14 (Melbourne, 1983) 122–3; 'Lettere dall'America. Ancora pericolo', V.1 (7 Jan. 1940) [1]–2; 'Antifascisti', V.15 (14 Apr. 1940) [1]; 'Da far capire agli americani', V.26 (30 June 1940) [1]–2. See also 'Paralleli storici', *Libro e Moschetto*, Milan, XIV.26 (11 May 1940) 507.

13 **'the first and oldest'**: editorial note, *EP&J* 148.
a sage medium: see EP, 'From Rapallo: An Ezra Pound Letter', *EP&J* 162.
'cultural news': Yasotaro Morri to EP, 15 May 1939, *EP&J* 78.
his second contribution: EP, 'Death of Yeats: End of Irish Literary Revival', *EP&J* 152–4.
'prefer to write': EP to Kitasono and Morri, 28 Oct. 1939, *EP&J* 79.
'age-old infamy': EP, 'From Rapallo: An Ezra Pound Letter', *EP&J* 169—EP gives as an example 'a few strophes of [Bunting's] "Morpethshire Farmer"'.
'With the Hitler interview': EP, 'Letter from Rapallo: In War Appear Responsibilities', *EP&J* 172.

14 **'the million dead'**: *EP&J* 174.
'the present Anglo-Jewish war': 'From Rapallo: An Ezra Pound Letter', *EP&J* 179.
'German propaganda stuff': JL to EP, 26 Nov. 1939, as in Gregory Barnhisel, *James Laughlin, New Directions, and the Remaking of Ezra Pound* (Amherst and Boston: University of Massachusetts Press, 2005), 78. (In *EP/JL* 108 an anodyne phrase appears in place of 'Now reverent sir, I hope that you will softpedal that German propaganda stuff'.)
'The struggle against': in a note, 'The Nazi Movement in Germany', EP had cited from *Mein Kampf* (1924), 'Der Kampf gegen das internationale Finanz und Leihkapital ist zum wichtigsten Programmpunkt', and had translated, 'War on international finance and LOAN CAPITAL becomes the most weighty etc. in the struggle towards freedom,' *Townsman* II.6 (Apr. 1939) 13.
'Germany is about 90%': EP to Odon Por, Sept. 1939, in Redman 191.
'Telescope is totally blind': EP MS note, n.d. [?1961], (Brunnenburg). See below p. 480.
more or less lucid moments: EP, 'Gli Ebrei e questa guerra', *Meridiano di Roma* V.12 (24 Mar. 1940) [1]–2. Clarity and simplicity come, in line with Pound's own principle, from being particular and avoiding prejudicial generalization, as in this paragraph in his 'In War Appear Responsibilities', *Japan Times & Mail* (21 and 22 July 1940):

> Shortly before his death Robert Mond (brother of the late Alfred, Lord Melchett) sat on a sofa in Rome, which sofa is known to me, and said with hith well known lithf: 'Napoleon wath a good man. It took uth 20 years to cwuth him. It will not take uth 20 years to cwuth Mutholini.... And the economic war hath commenthed.' This is a fact. Statement of it does not involve antisemitism. It in no way implicates the 300 just Jews known to me, or three million unknown. But it does prove a state of consciousness in one member of known set of English financiers.

Cf. EP, 'A Visiting Card', S Pr 283, and Cantos 78/477.

15 **'the hecatomb'**: EP, 'Valuta, lavoro e decadenze', *Meridiano di Roma* V.27 (7 July 1940) [1]—my translation.
're giving a more efficient turn': Odon Por to EP, 6 Sept. 1939, as in Redman 191.
'to popularize Italy': EP to Por, 7 Sept. 1939, as in Redman 192.

'America's place is OUT': details from Redman 193.
He sought clearance: details from Heymann 96.
16 **'offering advice'**: Redman 183–4. Other details in this paragraph from Zapponi 59.
'Signor Pound': Luigi Villari, 'Appunto per il Direttore Generale dei Servizi Propaganda', 28 Dec. 1939, as in Zapponi 60 (my translation). This paragraph and the next are drawn from Zapponi 60–3.
17 **a general notice**: in Pound MSS II, Box 20 (Lilly).
'in the light of your conversation': Cordell Hull telegram to William Phillips, 15 May 1940, Redman 205. Details following the telegram also from Redman.
There is some evidence: Emily Mitchell Wallace found in the FBI files concerning EP (File 61–719 dated 9 January 1943), a document stating that Herman Moss, who had been US Consul at Genoa, 'saw POUND in the Spring of 1940 at the time POUND was attempting to obtain passage to the United States. He stated that POUND had the necessary visas and passage data but that reservations on the plane were cancelled for some reason.... As far as [Moss] knows, this was the only reason POUND did not return to the United States at that time.' I am not aware of any other evidence that EP made a serious effort to return in 'the Spring of 1940', and therefore assume that Moss's recollection was of Pound's aborted effort to return in October 1940. I am much indebted to Emily Mitchell Wallace for generously sending me a copy of her paper, containing this and much other deeply researched information, and presented to the 23rd Ezra Pound Conference in Rome on 3 July 2009, 'The Last Diplomatic Train from Rome in 1942: Ezra Pound's Passport and his Kafkaesque Nostos'.
18 **warned by Odon Por and by Olga Rudge**: Por to Pound, 9 Aug. 1940, Redman 204; and Conover 139, 'Olga noted that Ezra's letter of July 12 [1940] was the first opened by censors'.
bank account frozen: cf. EP's 'Sworn Statement' to the FBI, 7 May 1945: 'After Italy declared war against the United States, the Italian Government "froze" my safety deposit box and bank accounts in the Banca di Chiavari in Rapallo, and other accounts but I succeeded in having the safety deposit box at Rapallo released by appealing to the Ministry of Popular Culture and by pointing out that it contained bonds bought by my wife and me when we subscribed to the first Littorio Loan, and that the rest of the contents were almost exclusively Italian Government Loans.'—in *EP/DP* 67.
'*J.T.* my last remaining': EP to Kitasono, 29 Oct. 1940, *EP&J* 100.
19 **'thin line of supplies'**: *EP&J* 99.
banks refusing dollar checks: see Por to Pound, 6 Nov. 1940, in Redman 206.
One payment of ¥97: see *EP&J* 82, 95–9.
journalist's card: see *EP&J* 82, 86.
Homer's pension checks: EP to Camillo Pellizzi, 29 June 1941, 'he has only had a couple of months of his pension/I think only one month's/since last June', in Tim Redman, 'The Repatriation of Pound, 1939–1942: A View from the Archives', *Pai* 8.3 (1979) 450.
'De F/ asked': EP to Por, 7 Aug. 1940, as in Redman 204.
'Waaal, mebbe': EP to OR, 22 Aug. 1940, as in Conover 140.
2,500 *lire*: see Redman 208. Redman usefully notes, 'To give some idea of the value of these figures', that EP's 'rent in 1940 was 500 *lire* a month'.
'will be in London': EP to OR, 28 Aug. 1940, as in Conover 139–40.
'Londres delenda est': DP, 17 Aug. 1940, Diary for 1940 (Lilly). A letter to EP of the same date specifies the Bank and government (Lilly).
'His legitime': OR to EP, 25 July 1940, as in Conover 139.
'how Churchill & co.': DP to EP, 17 Sept. 1940 (Lilly). Further details from DP to EP 21 and 22 Sept. 1940, and from an enclosed cutting from an Italian newspaper.
20 **'Banzai!'**: DP to EP, 28 Sept. 1940 (Lilly).

'back to the soil': OR to EP, 21 July 1940, as in Conover 139. Cf. EP to Kitasono, 2 Oct. 1940: 'Am just back from Siena... Mary after two months in Tyrol "gone native" to her mother's distress, so there is tremendous effort to make her *Salonfähig*.... / all after my instructions that she shd/ become *Bauernfähig* to keep up with the times. At any rate her tennis is improving' (*EP&J* 97).
'shaping nicely': OR to EP, 29 Aug. 1940, as in Conover 140.
'pretty, well groomed', and remainder of paragraph: MdR, *Discretions* 131–3.
'seem to remember': EP to DP, 17 Sept. 1940 (Lilly)—see also EP to DP, 13 Sept. 1940 (Lilly), and MdR, *Discretions* 131–2.
Three Power Pact: see Shirer 802.
'for as long as you are gone': Ricardo degli Uberti to EP, 4 Oct. 1940, translated from the Italian by Redman, in Tim Redman, 'The Repatriation of Pound, 1939–1942: A View from the Archives', *Pai* 8.3 (1979) 449. Other details come from this very helpful article.
'in Rome': Ubaldo degli Uberti to EP, 23 Oct. 1940, Redman, 'Repatriation', 450.
'Our last holiday': MdR, *Discretions* 136.
21 **surface sailings**: 'A status report from the American consul in Genoa... to Ambassador Phillips on June 20, 1940: "With the stoppage of American sailings from the Mediterranean and from Genoa to the United States, the further evacuation of Americans to the United States must now be greatly reduced."'—Redman, 'Repatriation', 452.
'Sir and dear Colleague': Graham H. Kemper to Consul of Spain, 9 Oct. 1940 (Beinecke, YCAL MSS 53, box 23, folder 512).
'all vurry interestin': EP to HLP, [11 Oct. 1940] (Beinecke).
'I don't think I can': EP to OR, 11 Oct. [1940] (Beinecke/OR).
Mary's passport: Mary did have a passport issued by the US Consulate in Florence—there may have been difficulty obtaining it (see Conover 142), or else renewing it; but on 30 April 1945 OR wrote to MdR, 'your passport is No. 675 (April 19, 1941) issued in Firenze' (Conover 158).
'legal status and citizenship': MdR, *Discretions* 134–5.
'niente': EP to OR, 12 Oct. 1940, as in Conover 142.
travellers cheques: the receipt is among EP's financial papers (Beinecke).
investment bond: Redman writes that the bond had been purchased with his *Dial* award,'Repatriation' 451.
'Non vado in America': EP telegram to OR, 13 Oct. 1940 (Beinecke/OR).
'Thank gawd': EP to OR, 14 Oct. 1940 (Beinecke/OR).
22 **'unless necessary'**: OR to EP, 14 Oct. 1940 (Beinecke/OR).
'great excitements': EP to Kitasono, 29 Oct. 1940, *EP&J* 100. See also EP to Tinkham, 7 Nov. 1940: 'I packed up at beginning of Oct. to come home, but in Rome found NO clipper places till Dec. 15' (*EP/GT* 213).
a sample script: the extract from the script and the background information all from MdR, 'Fragments of an Atmosphere', *Agenda* Twenty-First Anniversary Ezra Pound Special Issue, 17.3–4 and18.1 (1979–80) 157–70.

2. A Dutifully Dissident Exile, 1941

23 **'I will BUST'**: EP to Camillo Pellizi, 11 Jan. 1941, as cited in Redman 207. For EP's relations with Pellizi see Zapponi 135–6, Flory 97–9, and *EPEC* 278.
by the 21st... in Rome: EP to DP, 21 Jan. 1941 (Lilly).
'made 2 discs': EP to OR, 23 Jan. 1941 (Beinecke/OR).
'when the senator': EP, 'Four Steps' (1958), *Agenda* 17. 3–4–18.1 (1979/80) 141.

'Chi non vuol combattere': EP, 'Dei due latini e di altre cose', *Meridiano di Roma* VI.3 (19 Jan. 1941) [12].
'the only defence': EP, 'Freedom de Facto' (*c.*1940–1), *S Pr* 275. See also EP interview, *Paris Review* 28 (1962) 43–5.
'well-known American writer': most details in this paragraph are drawn from Robert A. Corrigan, 'Ezra Pound and the Italian Ministry for Popular Culture', *Journal of Popular Culture* 5.4 (1972) 770–2—his quotations from the Italian officials are from the files of the US Department of Justice. See also Zapponi 62–3.
24 **'Is it conceivable'**: EP to Ibbotson, 4 Nov. [1940], *EP/Ibb* 108.
25 **'This is my only way'**: EP to Luigi Villari, 1941, as cited Redman 210.
'Lenin won': EP, *GK* 241.
Natalie Barney . . . presented: see 'Souvenirs de Nathalie C. Barney', 13 Nov. 1963, in *Les Cahiers de l'Herne. Ezra Pound I* (Paris: Editions de l'Herne, 1965), 151.
'personae now poked': EP to Ronald Duncan, 31 Mar. 1940, *L (1951)* 441–2.
to make them think, 'to induce': EP's scribbled notes, [? Dec. 1941], as cited by MdR, 'Fragments of an Atmosphere', *Agenda* 17. 3–4–18.1 (1979/80) 163.
'what drammer': EP to Ronald Duncan, 31 Mar. 1940, *L (1951)* 441.
'Nothing solemn': EP to Gabriele Paresce, 9 Nov. 1940, as cited by MdR, 'Fragments', *Agenda* 17. 3–4–18.1 (1979/80) 164.
26 **'compose scripts'**: EP to Adriano Ungaro, 6 Feb. 1941, as cited in Redman 209.
'Yr. Discorso': DP to EP, 18 May 1941 (Lilly).
'I don't so much write': EP to JL, 28 June 1941, *EP/JL* 132.
'shd be glad to profit': EP to William Joyce, June 1941, as cited in Carpenter 593.
'Your methods': William Joyce to EP, 30 June 1941, as cited in Carpenter 593.
'New technique': EP to William Joyce, 18 July 1941 (Beinecke).
'prima-donnitis': EP to OR, 19 July 1941, (Beinecke/OR)—cited Conover 144.
'Otherwise came very clearly': DP to EP, 11 Oct. 1941 (Lilly). The FCC transcript of 'This War on Youth' is dated 6 Nov. 1941 (*Radio* 16)—what DP heard 'last night' was presumably a medium-wave broadcast beamed at Great Britain on the 10th.
'an explainer': EP to OR, 19 July 1941 (Beinecke/OR)—cited Conover 144.
27 **'"Something about ol' Doc Williams"'**: WCW, *Autobiography* (MacGibbon & Kee, 1968), 316–18; **'lashed out at'** is from WCW to JL, 3 Sept. 1941, *WCW/JL* 66. See also Paul Mariani, *William Carlos Williams: A New World Naked* (New York: McGraw-Hill Book Company, 1981), 455–6.
'I see by a Chicago rag': EP to Adriano Ungaro, 26 Apr. 1941, as cited in Redman 211.
'Yr. politics': JL to EP, 9 Apr. 1941, *EP/JL* 130.
'You are pretty much disliked': JL to EP, n.d., *EP/JL* 134.
'New passports': EP to DP, 3 Apr. 1941 (Lilly).
Passport No. 3151: from State Department Passport File F130-Ezra Pound, cited in H. A. Sieber, *The Medical, Legal, Literary and Political Status of Ezra Weston [Loomis] Pound [1885–] | Selected Facts and Comments* (Washington 25, DC: The Library of Congress Legislative Reference Service, April 1958), 52.
'Political Activities': Henry H. Balch to US Secretary of State, 4 Apr. 1941, document reproduced in Emily Mitchell Wallace, 'The Last Diplomatic Train from Rome in 1942: Ezra Pound's Passport and his Kafkaesque Nostos', paper presented to the 23rd Ezra Pound Conference in Rome on 3 July 2009.
'Passport should be limited': telegram, [Sumner] Welles to American Embassy, Rome, 12 July 1941, document reproduced in Emily Mitchell Wallace, 'The Last Diplomatic Train from Rome in 1942: Ezra Pound's Passport and his Kafkaesque Nostos'.
28 **went down to Rome from Siena**: see MdR, *Discretions* 145–6.
'pseudo Americans': State Department memorandum, J. Wesley Jones to Mr Atherton, 11 Oct. 1941, document reproduced in Emily Mitchell Wallace, 'The Last

Diplomatic Train from Rome in 1942: Ezra Pound's Passport and his Kafkaesque Nostos'.

'Jus Italicum': paragraph drawn from EP, 'Ius Italicum', *Meridiano di Roma* VI.34 (24 Aug. 1941) [1]. For 'il gran rifiuto' see Dante, *Inferno* III.60.

re travel permits: see EP to DP, 10 Sept. 1941, and DP telegram to EP, 12 Sept. 1941 (Lilly).

permission to remain: information from Heymann 112.

29 **financial restrictions**: information from Redman 218. In Pound's safe-deposit boxes would have been the certificates for his investments in Italian State bonds: 25,000 lire in 'Prestito del Littorio' in 1927; 15,000 lire in 'Città di Genova Prestito per Opere Publiche' in 1933; 2,000 lire in 'PNF Prestito Venticinquennia; 5% "Casa Littorio"' in 1938. The certificates were never redeemed, and were of course worthless after the war.

restrictions lifted: in a letter to EP dated '30 Gen, 1943 XXI' Luciano de Feo, Capo di Gabinetto di S. E. Il Ministro della Cultura Populare, was 'pleased to communicate that the Prefettura di Genova has revoked the sequestration of 18 April 1942 . . . of two safe-keeping security boxes located Banco di Chiavari, Rapallo' (private collection).

officially employed as a script writer: see Zapponi 63.

'I got up from bed': EP to Adriano Ungaro, 28 Apr. 1941, as in Redman 211.

30 **'Looks like he wuz'**: EP to DP, 18 May 1941 (Lilly).

'between 70 and 100': EP, 'Sale and Manufacture of War', recorded 17 Feb. 1942, *Radio* [39].

The pay: information from EP, 'Sworn Statement', [Office of the Counter Intelligence Corps], [Genoa, Italy], 7 May 1945, in *EP/DP* 61; also Heymann 110.

16,400 lire: EP to DP, Dec. 1941 (Lilly).

'Pound did not stand out': Massimo Bacigalupo to Humphrey Carpenter, 24 Nov. 1984, as in Carpenter 586.

James ('Giacomo') Strachey Barnes: (1890–1955), see *EP/EEC* 375–6 for his obituary in *The Times*.

Princess Troubetzkoi: description from MdR, *Discretions* 164.

31 **'Fascists in crisis'**: this paragraph and the next drawn from Felice Chilanti, 'Ezra Pound Among the Seditious in the 1940's', *Pai* 6.2 (1977) 235–50.

'"I would do it"', 'and the dog-damn wop': 77/470.

'given himself': EP, 'James Joyce: to his memory', radio talk, early 1941, as in *EP/JJ* 272.

32 **'United States heritage'**: EP, 'To Consolidate', *Radio* 393–5—Doob dates as 1942, but Beinecke dates as 1941 which on internal evidence is more likely.

letter to William Joyce: EP to William Joyce, 18 July 1941 (Beinecke).

33 **accord with Nazi propaganda**: Matthew Feldman cites 'a Reich Press Office directive of 8 Aug. 1941' which concludes:

> Today Jewry again seeks world domination. That British and American plutocrats on the one hand and Bolsheviks on the other appear with apparently distinct political goals is only Jewish camouflage. The Jew strives for world domination in order to rob and plunder the world for his exclusive benefit. . . .

as in Matthew Feldman, *Ezra Pound's Fascist Propaganda, 1935–45* (Palgrave Macmillan, 2013), 105.

'the word KIKE': EP, 'America was Promises', 1941, *Radio* 387.

'a man can own': EP, 'Homesteads', early 1941, *Radio* 382.

Guam in exchange: EP, 'March Arrivals', 1941, *Radio* 384.

'that Italy is carrying ON': EP, 'Books and Music', recorded 26 Oct. 1941, *Radio* 9.

34 **'Stage, a room'**: EP to Katue Kitasono, 16 Feb. 1941, *EP&J* 110.

'Now sun rises': EP to Katue Kitasono, 12 Mar. 1941, *EP&J* 111. See also *Cantos* 800.

'LXXII Erigena': MS note reproduced in EP, *Lettere dalla Sicilia e due frammenti ritrovati* a cura di Mary de Rachewiltz (Valverde (Catania): Il Girasole Edizioni, 1997), 47.

35 **'"Peace and abundance"'**: 53/268.

other jottings: see EP, 'Notes for Cantos *c.*1940-1945', ed. with notes by Massimo Bacigalupo, *Agenda* 37.2–3 (1999) 125–43; also *Canti postumi* 120–37.

'First Jove': EP, *Canti postumi* 132. 'Robigalia' = festival of the deity against wheat-rust.

36 **'Fire causeth not'**: EP, *I Cantos* 1566. Variant version in *Canti postumi* 136.

'fer the sake of': EP to JL, 28 June 1941, *EP/JL* 132.

'propagandist scope': EP to DP, 10 Sept. 1941 (Lilly).

'The Signora Pellegrina': *Moscardino* 3.

37 **Pound's high regard**: see MdR, 'EP/EP: Ezra Pound—Enrico Pea', *Moscardino* vii–xiv; also EP, 'Books and Music', 26 Oct. 1941, *Radio* 7–8.

'real Italian': EP to Mrs Virgil Jordan, 3 Nov. [1941], as cited Gallup 167.

'propsed a nedition': EP to EEC, 6 Nov. [1941], *EP/EEC* 162, 163. See also EP to WCW, 18 Oct. [1941], *EP/WCW* 208: 'am doing a bilingual edtn of the Ta Hio.... five vols of Morrison chinese-dic. spread round on various stands, and the first chapter of the ideograms been zincografato before I left the Eternal City on Wednesday.'

in the wrong order: the blocks of Chinese text were inserted in the sequence 1, 5, 3, 2, 4. The errors would be corrected in the full edition of the *Ta S'eu/Dai Gaku* published in Rapallo the following year as *Confucio Studio Integrale*. This would give Legge's Chinese text set 'back-to-front' as a Chinese text should be, that is from the end of the book forward with the columns of characters then reading naturally from top to bottom and from right to left. The 'Versione italiana di Ezra Pound e di Alberto Luchini' would occupy the lower part of each page, and have also to be read of course from the back to the front. The book would be handsomely printed by the Scuola Tipografica, possibly thanks to the intervention of Olga Rudge who taught English at the technical school in Rapallo during the war. It is unlikely to have had a wide distribution.

'digest par excellence of statal philosophy': EP, 'Confucio filosofo statale', *Meridiano di Roma* VI.19 (11 May 1941) [1]–2. For his account of the basic principle in this and the paragraph following see EP, 'Studio Integrale', *Meridiano di Roma* VI.43 (26 Oct. 1941) 3, and 'Ta Hio', *Meridiano di Roma* VI.46 (16 Nov. 1941) 7; see also *EP: Poet II* 74–8.

38 **'Studio Integrale'**: EP to MdR, 16 Sept. 1955 (Beinecke).

'the life and thought of Confucius': EP, 'In un mondo di luce ed acqua fluviale si svolgeva la vita ed il pensiero Confuciano', 'Ta Hio', *Meridiano di Roma* VI.46 (16 Nov. 1941) 7. See also canto 83.

39 **'Freedom, joyfulness'**: MdR, *Discretions* 141–3. This section mostly from *Discretions* 141–51.

'a musical whoop': EP, 'Books and Music', recorded 26 Oct. 1941, *Radio* 8–9.

The house inside: details from MdR, *Discretions* 115–16; also from Stella Bowen, *Drawn from Life* (1940) (Maidstone: George Mann, 1974), 146.

40 **'The humility'**: MdR, 'EP/EP: Ezra Pound—Enrico Pea', *Moscardino* viii.

some seeds: EP to DP, 27 Aug. 1941 (Lilly).

'planted peanut and soya': DP, 1941 Diary, entry for 15 Sept. (Lilly).

an article in *Meridiano di Roma*: EP, 'Arachidi', *Meridiano di Roma* VI.40 (5 Oct. 1941) [1].

41 **Felice Chilanti's account**: Felice Chilanti, 'Ezra Pound Among the Seditious in the 1940's', *Pai* 6.2 (1977) 243.

'Like Confucius': EP, 'Books and Music', recorded 26 Oct. 1941, *Radio* 8.

'I went along with him': Enrico Pea, 'Preface', *Moscardino* xviii–xix.

42 **'Your talk via Ranieri'**: DP to EP, 6 Sept. 1941 (Lilly).

'poor Kate': DP to EP, 11 July 1941 (Lilly).
'It was my material': EP to DP, 2 Oct. 1941 (Lilly).
'a lot of old discs': EP to DP, 27 Nov. 1941 (Lilly).
'in Parigi': EP to DP, 23 Nov. 1941 (Lilly).
'completely converted': EP to DP, 4 Dec. 1941 (Lilly).
'our labours are appreciated': EP to DP, 3 Dec. 1941 (Lilly).
'"Omar has developed"': Arthur Moore to DP, 3 Oct. 1941, as excerpted in Imperial Censorship Bermuda report of 14 Nov. 1941 (UK National Archives, ref. KV 2/875–36180).
'nervous unhappiness': DP to EP, n.d. (Lilly).
Ezra advised: EP to DP, 30 Nov. 1941 (Lilly).
43 **would copy anti-Semitic propaganda**: examples from DP to EP, May 1941 (Lilly).
Einsatzgruppen and Final Solution: see Shirer 956ff.
'looking stern and teutonic': EP to DP, 3 Dec. 1941 (Lilly).
that the 'Bolshies' were beaten: DP to EP, 11 Oct. 1941 (Lilly).
'the Jews in London': EP, 'These Parentheses', recorded 7 Dec. 1941, *Radio* 21.
44 **'retired from the capital'**: EP, 'On Resuming', recorded 29 Jan. 1942, *Radio* 23.
a 'huge lunch': EP to DP, 20 May 1941 (Lilly). Re Packard's bullfighting see 82/524.
Packard's account: in Reynolds and Eleanor Packard, *Balcony Empire* (Chatto & Windus, 1943), 179—as cited in Carpenter 605.

3. In a Web of Contradictions, 1942–3

One section of this chapter draws heavily upon Mary de Rachewiltz's *Discretions*. For a serious and important study of Pound's states of mind during the war see Wendy Stallard Flory, *The American Ezra Pound* (New Haven: Yale University Press, 1989), especially chap. 4, 'The Antisemitism of the Rome Broadcasts'.

Note on Pound's radio talks

Pound began writing scripts for Rome Radio (EIAR) towards the end of 1940, at first providing scripts and suggestions for its regular speakers. In January 1941 he began recording his own scripts, each one on a separate 78 r.p.m. plastic disc, in batches of 10 to 12 at a time, these to be broadcast (and repeated) at the station's discretion but notionally at the rate of two or three per week. The talks were addressed to America or to England in the ratio of about two to one, but the same talk might be broadcast to both, on short wave to America and on short and medium wave to England. EP often intended the scripts to be read in a particular sequence, but EIAR did not always observe his arrangement. By his own count he had contributed between 70 and 100 scripts by February 1942, that is, in his first twelve months of broadcasting. Doob, in *'Ezra Pound Speaking': Radio Speeches of World War II*, [*Radio*] prints a dozen or so of these.

The US Federal Broadcast Intelligence Service of the Federal Communications Commission (FCC) started recording odd broadcasts by Pound in October 1941; instituted regular monitoring and recording in January 1942 after the USA was drawn into the war, and continued up to EP's final broadcast on 24 July 1943—Mussolini was arrested and the Fascist government of Italy fell shortly after. There had appeared to be a six-month break in the FCC recordings between 26 July 1942 and 18 February 1943, although EP was producing scripts at his usual rate through those months; however, as Friedlander reports, recordings of 42 broadcasts delivered then have recently come to light. Preparations to indict as traitors Pound and others broadcasting over Axis radios were initiated by the US Attorney General's office in October 1942, but the indictment by a Grand Jury was delayed until 26

July 1943. In all the FCC monitored and recorded 170 broadcasts by Pound, and these were the basis of this first indictment for treason. The original FCC recordings and transcripts are with the Records of the Foreign Broadcast Intelligence Service in the National Archives, Washington DC.

In May 1945 the FBI seized the copies of Pound's radio scripts and the cartons of discs held by the Ministry of Popular Culture, and it was these, not the FCC transcripts, which the Department of Justice relied on when bringing Pound to trial in Washington later that year. (Heymann, *Ezra Pound: The Last Rower* 350 n. 23)

In the Pound archive at Yale's Beinecke Library there are well over 500 radio scripts. Pound himself recorded about 300 of these; and wrote the rest for others to broadcast, many of these for anonymous or pseudonymous delivery. Doob notes that these last 'merely repeat ideas expressed in other speeches'. He prints 'all the available manuscripts (105) for the broadcasts [by EP] recorded by the FCC', taking the texts from Pound's original typescripts; and for the 5 for which no original typescript has been found he used the FCC transcripts. He includes 10 further scripts from those not recorded by the FCC monitors. His dates for the talks are the FCC's, i.e. the date on which a broadcast was recorded in America.

For Pound's own account in 1945 see his 'Sworn Statement' and 'Supplements', [Office of the Counter Intelligence Corps], [Genoa, Italy], 7 and 8 May, 1945, in *EP/DP* 59–77; a further sworn statement was made to the FBI investigator in Genoa on 8 May, and a copy of this is in Nat. Arch. WO 204/12602–361810 [items 13A and B]. For commentary see: Mary de Rachewiltz, 'Fragments of an Atmosphere', *Agenda* 17.3–4–18.1 (1979/80) 157–70; Richard Reid, 'Ezra Pound Asking', *Agenda* 17.3–4–18.1 (1979/80) 171–86; Geoffrey Hill, 'Our Word is our Bond', *Agenda* 21.1 (1983) 13–49; L. S. C. Bristow, '"God, my god, you folks are DUMB!!!": Pound's Rome Radio Broadcasts', in *Ezra Pound and America*, ed. Jacqueline Kaye (Macmillan, 1992), 18–42); Benjamin Friedlander, 'Radio Broadcasts', *Ezra Pound in Context*, ed. Ira B. Nadel (Cambridge: Cambridge University Press, 2010), 115–24.

45 **'The Italian radio'**: from a copy of the FCC transcript, 3 Feb. 1942 (HRC).
while he was off the air: 17 'original manuscripts prepared by Pound' and broadcast between 9 December 1941 and 21 January 1942 were found in the Italian Ministry of Popular Culture by the FBI investigators in 1945. These were relatively brief scripts of 1–2 pages (as against EP's usual 5–7 pages), and were evidently read or used by someone other than Pound.—Office Memorandum from the Chief of Internal Security to the Chief of Communications & Records, 30 May 1945 (Justice Dept., <www.justice.gov/criminal/foia/records/ezra-pound-p2.pdf> [p. 37].)
'my speeches': EP to Cornelio Di Marzio, 28 Dec. 1941, as in Redman 215. For other letters to the same effect see Redman 213–16.
'that can in any way prejudice': EP to Adriano Ungaro, 9 Dec. 1941, as in Redman 213.
46 **'acts against the *government*'**: Thomas Jefferson, *Writings of Thomas Jefferson* (Washington DC: Library ed., 1903) 8:332, quoted 'in Appendix to Cramer Case', as cited in Sieber 8.
He could have played it safe: paragraph paraphrases and quotes from EP, 'On Resuming', FCC record dated 29 Jan. 1942, *Radio* 23–5.
'if he failed to escape': Romano Bilenchi, 'Rapallo, 1941', trans. with notes and introduction by David Anderson, *Pai* 8.3 (1979) 439.
Bilenchi's account: *Pai* 8.3 (1979) 434–5, 439–40.
47 ***Carta da visita***: first edn., in Italian, Rome, 1942; English translation by John Drummond, *A Visiting Card* (1952), reprinted in *S Pr* 276–305. Quotations in this para. from *S Pr* 276–8.
48 **'Nothing less than the Fascist system'**: EP, 'Aberration', 20 Apr. 1942, *Radio* 103.
'The Fascist idea': EP, 'Idee fondamentali', *Meridiano di Roma* VII.19 (10 May 1942) [1].

'I insist on the identity': EP, *A Visiting Card*, *S Pr* 283. See also *S Pr* 279–82; *Radio* 316 ('In the Woodshed').
'aberration': EP, 'Aberration', Apr. 20, 1942, *Radio* 101–3.
49 **'We are fighting'**: EP, quoting Gioacchino Nicoletti speaking in Pisa, 'Amor di patria', *Meridiano di Roma* VIII.16 (18 Apr. 1943) [1].
it became known at least to some: Towards the end of 1942 and in 1943 Jan Karski, an emissary from the Polish underground, was informing the governments and important persons in Britain and the United States that the mass extermination of Jews was being carried out in German occupied Poland, but he was not believed.
articles in *Meridiano di Roma*: I refer particularly to 'Mondiale', VII.3 (18 Jan. 1942). [1]; see also 'Pace decisiva', VII.11 (15 Mar. 1942) [1].
In his radio talks: e.g. 'Power', 19 Feb. 1942, *Radio* 41–3; 'Gold: England', 8 Mar. 1942, *Radio* 55–8; 'England', 15 March 1942, *Radio* 59–62; 'That Interval of Time', 25 June 1942, *Radio* 179–82; 'Disbursement of Wisdom', 2 July 1942, *Radio* 187–90. On Pound's 'real enemy' see also Redman 216, 223–5.
'If we don't snatch Malta': EP, 'Idee fondamentali', *Meridiano di Roma* VII.19 (10 May 1942) [1].
50 **'Intellectual work'**: EP, 'Ob pecuniae scarsitatem', *Meridiano di Roma* VII.23 (7 June 1942) [1].
the enemy became 'the Jews': see radio talks of 1942–3 *passim*. Particular instances: 'Non-Jew', 30 Apr. 1942, *Radio* 113–16; 'Disbursement of Wisdom', 2 July 1942, *Radio* 187–90. See also articles in *Meridiano di Roma*: e.g. 'La guerra degli usurai', VII.18 (3 May 1942) [1]; 'Idee fondamentali', VII.19 (10 May 1942) [1].
'Don't start a pogrom': EP, 'Non-Jew', 30 Apr. 1942, *Radio* 115.
'The true definition': EP, 'L'Ebreo, patologia incarnata', *Meridiano di Roma* VI.41 (12 Oct. 1941) [1].
51 **'a sum of morbid'**: definition from *OED*.
'All fanaticisms': EP to George Santayana, 14 June 1941 (HRC).
'put off by rumour': EP to Odon Por, 11 Apr. 1940, *EPEC* 247.
'their origin': EP to WCW, 13 May [1940], *EP/WCW* 204.
'You better': EP to Henry Swabey, [1940], cited Redman 202.
'*In our day*': *Protocols of the Elders of Zion*, copy downloaded from <http://www.aztlan.net/protocols.html>.
52 **'*We shall surround*'**: cited by EP in 'Zion', 20 Apr. 1943, *Radio* 284.
'Certainly they are a forgery': cited by EP in 'Zion', 20 Apr. 1943, *Radio* 283.
'To what extent': Adolf Hitler, *Mein Kampf*, trans. Ralph Manheim (Pimlico, 1993), 279.
53 **'On 21 March 1943'**: Farrell 366. Other citations from Farrell 364–5.
'I am now responsible': EP to Cornelio Di Marzio, 16 Dec. 1941, trans. Redman in Redman 215.
The family doctor: for his account see Giuseppe Bacigalupo, *Ieri a Rapallo*, V edizione (Pasian di Prato: Campanotto Editore, 2006), 83.
54 **'read him a few pages'**: EP, 'On Resuming', 7 Dec. 1941, *Radio* 24.
'with red eyes', **'"The old lady"'**, **'For a few visits'**: MdR, *Discretions* 153.
an archaic jade ring: MdR, *Discretions* 153, also EP to George Santayana, 30 [?Sept. 1946] (HRC). Edgar Jepson is mentioned as a 'lover of jade' in 74/433.
'To attract the spirits': EP, *Canti Postumi* 130.
'You did all you could': Giuseppe Bacigalupo, *Ieri a Rapallo* 83—'"Hai fatto quello che hai potuto per il mio vecchio" mi disse affettuosamente "e voglio che questo [olio di Max Ernst] sia un ricordo mio e suo."'
'There is a rumour': DP to EP, 13 Mar. 1942 (Lilly).
wrote to Uberti: see Redman, 'The Repatriation of Pound, 1939–1942', *Pai* 8.3 (1979) 454.

circulars and questionnaires: following details from *Pai* 8.3 (1979) 453–4. Pound did receive an April 1942 circular from the Swiss Legation in Rome to US citizens in Italy concerning the possibility of organizing return via Lisbon to America and requiring an immediate response by telegraph. It warned that US citizens able to return and failing to take this opportunity were liable to have financial assistance (i.e. access to US Funds) terminated. It further stated that a minor child not a US citizen should be sponsored for immigration by two US citizens residing in the USA, and that his/her brothers and sisters in or outside the USA should be named. Fares to be paid in US dollars in New York: $300 per adult, half-fare for children 1–10 (Private collection).

55 **'On July 12, 1941'**: memorandum, 18 June 1942, from the Division of Foreign Activities in Passport File F130-Ezra Pound, Passport Office, State Department, as in Sieber 52.

'a (reliable) friend': DP to AVM, 14 Dec. 1955 (Lilly).

'a call from *Time*': WCW to JL, 17 June 1942, *WCW/JL* 73.

'Nancy Horton': from *Philadelphia Evening Bulletin*, 5 June 1942, as cited Stock: 1970, 392, and Redman, 'The Repatriation of Pound, 1939–1942', *Pai* 8.3 (1979) 452.

Wadsworth was responsible: information from Emily Mitchell Wallace, 'The Last Diplomatic Train from Rome in 1942: Ezra Pound's Passport and his Kafkaesque Nostos', paper presented to the 23rd Ezra Pound Conference in Rome on 3 July 2009. Wallace notes that Wadsworth himself left Italy on that train.

56 **'Those circumstances'**: EP, 'Ezra Pound: An Interview' [by Donald Hall], *Paris Review* 28 (1962) 46. Note that there was no interruption in Pound's radio broadcasts around that time.

'Pound refused to return': note headed 'Ezra Pound', 14 Oct. 1942, in Justice Dept. Files <www.justice.gov/criminal/foia/records/ezra-pound-p1.pdf> [p. 5].

By the end of 1942: most of this and the three following paragraphs drawn from MdR, *Discretions* 155–9 and 162–71.

57 **'Sprig looked very well'**: EP to OR, 12 May 1943, as in Conover 147.

ration card stamped: detail from Conover 147.

'Gaudier-Brzeska drawings: EP, 'On the Nature of Treachery', 2 May 1943, *Radio* 293.

down to 80 kilos: EP to DP, 16 May 1942 (Lilly).

58 **an ironic and bitter record**: DP's diaries for 1942 and 1943 (Lilly).

'Rome bombed': Mussolini witnessed from the air the damage done to Rome on 19 July as he flew back from a meeting with Hitler at Feltre: 'At 6 p.m. I took off on straight flight to Rome. I slowed down at the level of [Mount] Soracte and noticed a great cloud on the horizon. It was the smoke from the burning of the Littorio Station, which I flew over a few minutes later. Hundreds of railway cars were burning, walls were destroyed, the airport out of use. The same show at the San Lorenzo locomotive depot. The damage seemed enormous . . . Long queues of people crowded around the fountains as the water mains were broken' (Benito Mussolini, entry dated 19 Aug. 1943, 'In Captivity. Notebook of Thoughts in Ponza and La Maddalena', translated in *Edge* 4 (Mar. 1957) 25.

'Is it still era fascista?': DP to EP, 28 July 1943 (Lilly)—'*abasso M. porco*' = '*down with Mussolini, the swine*'.

'when there came over the radio', 'kicked out': EP, 'Sworn statement' to agents of the US Counter Intelligence Corps, Genoa, 7 May 1945, as in *EP/DP* 63.

indicted for treason: EP told Frank Amprim of the FBI in his second sworn statement dated 8 May 1945—copy in Nat. Arch. WO 204/12602–361810 [item 13B]—that he knew he had been indicted for treason 'when the Germans sent to Rome a photocopy of an article in Time magazine'; but this would only have confirmed what he already knew from the BBC news.

'bad news': EP to DP, 9 May 1943 (Lilly).

'Afraid that raiding': DP to EP, May 1943 (Lilly).
'She not be downcast', 'to chuck most of discorsi': EP to DP, 9 May 1943 (Lilly).
'Did 5 more discorsi': EP to DP, 10 May 1943 (Lilly).
'Ecellenza e DUCE': EP to Benito Mussolini, 10 May 1943, as in Zapponi 54–5.

59 **'He is an American'**: Zapponi 55–7 gives the note (here translated) and the further details in this paragraph.
'that the American troops': EP, 'On Retiring', 27 Apr. 1943, *Radio* 289.
'Italy was and IS': EP, 'And Back of the Woodshed': 25 May 1943, *Radio* 323.
'Ezra Pound speaks from Rome': EP, [title unknown], FCC transcript 24 May 1943, *Radio* 322.
'economic aggression': EP, 'And Back of the Woodshed': 25 May 1943, *Radio* 324. The other four broadcasts of the set were: 'Sumner Welles', 11 May 1943; 'Economic Aggression', 15 May 1943; 'Economic Oppression', 18 May 1943; 'In the Woodshed', 22 May 1943.
'There are a number of Americans': FDR [President Roosevelt] to Attorney General, 1 Oct. 1942, Justice Dept. Files—<www.justice.gov/criminal/foia/records/ezra-pound-p1.pdf>.
'treasonably broadcasting': Henry L. Stimson, Secretary of War, to [Francis Biddle], the Attorney General, 5 Feb. 1943, letter reproduced in *Helix* 13/14 (1983) 125.

60 **'a travesty of justice'**: Humphrey Carpenter, Carpenter 620.
'deliberate attempts': Eunice Tietjens, 'The End of Ezra Pound', *Poetry* Apr. 1942—as in Carpenter 611.
'in his opinion': WCW as reported in FBI investigatory report, May 1943 (photocopy at Hamilton). Most of this paragraph is drawn from that report. For an example of WCW's grievances and resentments see WCW to JL, 7 Aug. 1943, *WCW/JL* 89–90.
'James Laughlin': from the FBI investigatory report, May 1943, as cited in Heymann 349 n. 3.
it was false: Pound had paid for his passage on 6 Apr. 1939, with a cheque for $299 drawn on his account with the Jenkintown Bank and Trust Co. and payable to Italian Soc. An. Navigazione, Genoa. Moreover, his cheque stubs show that between 21 Mar. and 9 June 1939, he drew US $750 from his Jenkintown Bank account (including the US$299 for his boat fare). He had also drawn on the account for his expenses in London in 1938.

61 **'That Ezra Pound, the defendant'**: from the Grand Jury Indictment, as in Norman: *Case* 62–3.
'It should be clearly understood': Francis Biddle, speaking to the press following the indictment, as in Norman: *Case* 63.

62 **'I understand'**: EP to Francis Biddle, 4 Aug. 1943, as in Norman: *Case* 63–5.

63 **deliberate intent**: Sieber, 8 n. 1, cites *Cramer v. United States*, 325 US 1. 65 S, Ct. 918: 'The crime of treason consists of two elements, both of which must be present in order to sustain a conviction: (1) adherence to the enemy, and (2) rendering him aid and comfort. | The term "aid and comfort" as used in the provision of the Federal Constitution defining treason [. . .] contemplates some kind of affirmative action, deed, or physical activity tending to strengthen the enemy or weaken the power to resist him, and is not satisfied by a mere mental operation. | . . . the acts done must be intentional. The intent sufficient to sustain a conviction of treason must be an intent, not merely to commit the overt acts complained of, but to betray the country by means of such acts.'
'Passport No. 3154': from Swiss Delegation at Rome to US Secretary of State, 25 Aug. 1943, as in Sieber 52.
Pound would later explain: in private conversation with G. Giovannini at St Elizabeths, 4 Sept. 1957—Giovannini's memo is in Kenner Archive (HRC). In his second

sworn statement to Frank Amprim on 8 May 1945 he had said simply, 'they took away my passport, saying it had expired'—Nat. Arch. WO 204/12602–361810 [item 13B].

4. 'To dream the Republic', 1943–4

The chapter title is from *The Pisan Cantos*—see 78/478. For information concerning the Repubblica Sociale Italiana (RSI) I am indebted to Nicholas Farrell, *Mussolini: A New Life*. Details concerning the progress of the war in Italy come mainly from James Holland, *Italy's Sorrow: A Year of War, 1944–45* (Harper Press, 2008). For Pound's correspondence with officials of the RSI I am largely indebted to Tim Redman's *Ezra Pound and Italian Fascism*, to C. David Heymann's *Ezra Pound: The Last Rower*, and to Marcello Simonetta, 'Letteratura e propaganda: Pound poeta del regime', *Nuovi Argomenti* 11 (Apr.–June 1997) 47–59—thanks to Danilo Breschi for this last. Note that at this time Pound was writing nearly everything in Italian, and that quotations from his letters and pamphlets are given here in translations by various hands. (Translations from EP letters to DP and to OR are mine.) An important study of Pound's 'totalitarian Confucianism' in these years is Mary Paterson Cheadle's *Ezra Pound's Confucian Translations* (Ann Arbor: University of Michigan Press, 1997).

64 **'On the 10th'**: EP, *Gold and Work*, a translation of *Oro e lavoro* (Rapallo, 1944) by John Drummond, as in *S Pr* 306–7.

65 **on September 5**: date from entry, 'EP to Rome', in DP's diary (Lilly).
'only slightly delayed': EP to DP, 6 Sept. 1943 (Lilly).
'as an American', 'They seem to be': EP to DP, 7 Sept. 1943 (Lilly).
sent in four or five talks: see 'Sworn Statement by Ezra Pound, [Office of the Counter Intelligence Corps], Genoa, Italy, May 7, 1945', in *EP/DP* 63.

66 **That morning**: this and the following two paragraphs are drawn from various accounts: Stock: 1970, 400–1 (includes Naldo Naldi's account); EP's 1945 'Sworn Statement', *EP/DP* 63, (sums up his journey in one sentence); 'to avoid German control, to keep free', EP pencil note on envelope addressed to him at 60 Sant'Ambrogio, Rapallo (misfiled in 1921–3 folder of EP/DP correspondence, Lilly); two pages of notes by EP in *Canti postumi* 150, 152; EP, 'Fragment, 1944', *Yale Review* 71.2 (1982) 161–2; lines beginning 'INCIPIT VITA NUOVA' among *Pisan Cantos* drafts (Beinecke), repr. in *Sulfur* 1, 7–8, and *Canti postumi* 204, 206; *Cantos* 78/478; MdR, *Discretions* 184–7. That 'Lo sfacelo' is a link to Hemingway's *A Farewell to Arms* is my own association, but for evidence of EP's 'serious attention' to the novel see *EP/LZ* 33.

67 **Mary 'learned'**: paragraph drawn from MdR, *Discretions* 187–9. For '*it all coheres*' see *Trax* 50.
The next day: this paragraph and the one following drawn from MdR, *Discretions* 190–5. The final detail of the horses on the train recalled by MdR in conversation, 2008.

68 **'a buffer', 'chose Salò'**: Farrell 431. See Farrell 428ff. for 'The 600 days of the Repubblica Sociale of Salò'. See also Shirer 1004–6.
too bound to his own: see Shirer 1004.

69 **'did not believe'**: Mussolini's words to Carlo Silvestri, a Socialist journalist, as in Farrell 430. Mussolini had concluded on 14 August 1943, while in captivity, 'My system is defeated' (see Benito Mussolini, 'In Captivity. Notebook of Thoughts in Ponza and La Maddalena', *P&P* IX, 188). In September he said to Hitler in East Prussia, 'Fascism has by now had its day... it needs to return to its origins' (Farrell 437).
'an occupied territory': Mussolini to his private secretary, Giovanni Dolfin, as in Farrell 435.
The notional constitution: paragraph based on Farrell 437–9, and Redman 235–6.
'more interested in recrimination': Farrell 439.

right *to* but not *of*: see 78/478 and 86/564.

70 **'Freedom of discussion'**: EP to Gilberto Bernabei, head of the Cabinet of the Ministry of Popular Culture, as cited and translated by Redman, Redman 236.

'He believed in us': Francesco Monotti, 'A Rapallo con Pound', *Ezra Pound: un poeta a Rapallo*, a cura di Massimo Bacigalupo (Genoa: Edizione San Marco dei Giustiniani, 1985), 70 [my translation].

back to Rapallo on September 23: date from DP's diary entry for that day (Lilly). Noel Stock, unaware that EP was back in Rapallo just two weeks after leaving Rome, and under the impression that he was in Gais for 'several weeks', speculated that 'It is likely that he took the opportunity while passing around Lake Garda to make contact with 'the new Italian Republic then in the process of being formed... at Salò' (Stock: 1970, 402). Others have adopted this apparently reasonable speculation, which DP's diary entry, however, renders improbable. Mussolini's announcement of his new republic was made from Munich on 18 September; he did not return to Italy until the 25th, landing that day at Forlì in the Romagna; and he did not take up residence on Lake Garda until the second week of October. I know of no evidence to support Stock's speculation.

'that a reform': EP, 'Service Note', Oct. 28–XXI [1943], from FBI files, trans. Robert Connolly, in Heymann 326.

'Liguria': EP, 'Service Note', Oct. 28–XXI [1943], from FBI files, trans. Robert Connolly, in Heymann 326.

'to come north': EP, 'Sworn Statement... May 7, 1945', in *EP/DP* 63.

'safe and sound': Giacomo Barnes to EP, 4 Nov. 1943, as in Redman 234–5.

had heard from Barnes: EP to Alessandro Pavolini, 9 Nov. 1943 (Beinecke), [in Italian], from Marcello Simonetta, 'Letteratura e propaganda: Pound poeta del regime', *Nuovi Argomenti* 11 (Apr.–June 1997) 53. 'Volpe' = Count Giuseppe Volpi (1877–1947), Italian industrialist and financier; re 'capo squadra', see MdR, *Discretions* 70–1.

71 **Pavolini cordially thanked**: 'A.P.' [Alessandro Pavolini] to EP, 13 Nov. 1943 (Beinecke), [in Italian], from Simonetta, 'Letteratura e propaganda', *Nuovi Argomenti* 11 (Apr.–June 1997) 53.

a communication: Il Ministro della Cultura Popolare to EP, 22 Nov. 1943 (Beinecke), [in Italian], *Nuovi Argomenti* 11 (Apr.–June 1997) 53.

'already begun': EP to DP, 23 Nov. 1943 (Lilly).

'letter from Cul. Pop.': DP to EP, 25 Nov. 1943 (Lilly).

unable to see: EP, 'Sworn Statement... May 7, 1945', in *EP/DP* 63.

'unaltered and fervent': 'A.P.' [Alessandro Pavolini] to EP, 26 Nov. 1943 (Beinecke), [in Italian], from Simonetta, 'Letteratura e propaganda', *Nuovi Argomenti* 11 (Apr.–June 1997) 53.

'even if Italy fell': EP, 'Sworn Statement... May 7, 1945', in *EP/DP* 63.

'ask Andermacher': EP to DP [in Italian], 26 Nov. 1943 (Lilly).

'very pleasant visit': DP to EP, 24 Nov. 1943 (Lilly).

'Schwartz arrived': EP to DP [in Italian], 27 Nov. 1943 (Lilly).

'Nein, ich spreche': EP draft in German, cited with summary indications of content by MdR, 'Fragments of an Atmosphere', *Agenda* 17.3–4–18.1 (1979/80) 169.

72 **'at last the chance'**: EP to DP [in Italian], 30 Nov. 1943 (Lilly).

about to be made Prefect: in 'Fragment, 1944', *Yale Review* 71.2 (1982) 161, EP wrote, 'not yet capo provincia Gioacchino'.

moment of stillness: see 74/427, 76/458, 78/478.

a sonnet: see Terrell, *Companion* note to 'la Donna' (74/427).

'genial discussion': EP to DP [in Italian], 3 Dec. 1943 (Lilly).

'lunge e cordiale': EP to OR [in Italian], 3 Dec. 1943 (Beinecke/OR), cited in editorial notes to *EP/DP* 50.

'could bring the slaughter': EP, 'Ezra Pound's Supplements to his Sworn Statement', [Office of the Counter Intelligence Corps] [Genoa, Italy], 8 May, 1945, in *EP/DP* 73.
unresponsiveness of the Japanese officials: see above p. 10.

73 **'If I had not handed them'**: EP, 'Supplements to his Sworn Statement', 8 May 1945, in *EP/DP* 73.
Buffarini: much of this paragraph drawn from Meir Michaelis, *Mussolini and the Jews: German–Italian Relations and the Jewish Question in Italy 1922–1945* (Oxford: Published for the Institute of Jewish Affairs, by the Clarendon Press, 1978), 349–52. See also Carpenter 631–2.

74 **'possibly his best'**: EP to Alessandro Pavolini, 9 Nov. 1943 (Beinecke), [in Italian], from Simonetta, 'Letteratura e propaganda', *Nuovi Argomenti* 11 (Apr.–June 1997) 53–4.
'ordered to Milan': EP to DP [in Italian], 3 Dec. 1943 (Lilly).
standing for three hours: EP to Capo Gabinetto del Ministero della Cultura Popolare, [? 6 Dec. 1943] (Beinecke), [in Italian], from Simonetta, 'Letteratura e propaganda', *Nuovi Argomenti* 11 (Apr.–June 1997) 54. See also EP's 'on a cattle-truck', 'Sworn Statement . . . May 7, 1945', *EP/DP* 63.
a letter of introduction: details from Heymann 149.
'foresteria': cf. 78/478. I owe to Massimo Bacigalupo the suggestion that EP was accommodated in the regime's guest-houses at Salò and Gardone.
'in a kind of corridor': EP to Concetto Petinato and Paolo Zappa of *La Stampa*, 10 Dec. 1943, cited Redman 237, and MdR, 'Fragments of an Atmosphere', *Agenda* 17.3–4–18.1 (1979/80) 169.
a room with heating: EP to OR [in Italian], 12 Dec. 1943, cited by Tim Redman, 'Il viaggio di Pound a Milano nel 1943' in *Ezra Pound e il turismo colto a Milano*, A cura di Luca Gallesi (Milano: Edizione Ares, 2001), 79.
'I see you refuse': EP to Nino Sammartano, Dec. 1943, as cited by MdR, 'Fragments of an Atmosphere', *Agenda* 17.3–4–18.1 (1979/80) 169.
bureaucratic mixup: Sammartano to EP, 29 Dec. 1943, as in Redman 237.
'Milano Caina': EP TSS draft, Ezra Pound Papers YCAL MSS 43, Box 76, folder 3380 (Beinecke). The draft gives the date '8 Dec. '43'. Information about the church and the Piazza from Luca Gallesi; for 'sansepolcristi' see Dennis Mack Smith, *Italy: A Modern History* (1959) 392.

75 **'decide whether to decide'**: EP to DP [in Italian], 11 Dec. 1943, cited by Redman, 'Il viaggio di Pound', *Ezra Pound e il turismo colto*, 80. On 12 Dec. EP wrote to OR, 'Tutto ancora re-in-deciso', *Ezra Pound e il turismo colto*, 79.
'the E.I.A.R. tells me': EP to Sammartano, Dec. 1943, as in Redman 236.
This talk, denouncing Badoglio: details from Heymann 149.
'At Milan I refused': EP, 'Sworn Statement by Ezra Pound . . . May 7, 1945', *EP/DP* 63.
Carl Goedel: details from: EP to DP, 13 Dec. 1943 (Lilly); 78/478 and 79/484; *EP/DP* 63, 64, 65.
back for Christmas: EP to OR [in Italian], 12 Dec. 1943, cited by Redman, 'Il viaggio di Pound', *Ezra Pound e il turismo colto*, 80.

76 **wasting his time**: EP to DP, 15 Dec, 1943 (Lilly).
back . . . at 5.30: DP diary entry, 18 December 1943 (Lilly).
Mary would be better off: 'Maria sta meglio dov'è', EP to OR, 12 Dec. 1943, cited by Redman, 'Il viaggio di Pound', *Ezra Pound e il turismo colto*, 79; see also Redman 237, and MdR, *Discretions* 198.
half-hour interview: EP to DP, 10 Dec. 1943 (Lilly); also EP to Pettinato and Zappa, 10 Dec. 1943, in Redman 237; and EP, 'Sworn Statement . . . May 7, 1945', *EP/DP* 67.
'The collaborator Ezra Pound': Fernando Mezzasoma memo to Ministry of Communications, 4 Dec. 1943, from FBI files, Heymann 145. (I have altered the translator's 'has placed his intellectual bearing' to 'has devoted his intelligence'.)

'thoroughly interrogated': Francis Biddle, US Attorney General, to Henry L. Stimson, Secretary of War, 24 Jan. 1944, repr. in *Helix* 13/14 (1983) 128. See *Helix* 13/14 (1983) 126 and 127 for order to the command of the US Fifth Army.

77 **To Giovanni Gentile**: details from Heymann 142.

'a brief summary': details from three 'dispatches' or 'reports' sent by EP to Mezzasoma on 15 Jan. 1944, from FBI files, as in Heymann 145–7.

'You people refuse': EP to Mezzasoma, 16 Jan. 1944, [trans. Robert Connolly], Heymann 332.

78 **'material left with Nicoletti'**: EP to Mezzasoma, 23 Jan. 1944, [trans. Robert Connolly], Heymann 332–3.

'My own voice': EP to Mezzasoma, 31 Mar. 1944, [trans. Robert Connolly], Heymann 333–4.

'Through the rites': Mencius II.A.2, *Mencius* trans. D. C. Lau (Harmondsworth: Penguin Books, 1970), 80.

'Radio Division IV': memo from Tamburini, 23 Feb. 1944, from FBI files, Heymann 150.

Tamburini told the FBI: details from FBI transcript, May 1945, as in Heymann 150.

Pound told his interrogators: EP, 'Sworn Statement... May 7, 1945', *EP/DP* 63, 65.

79 **'did not work for Goedel'**: *EP/DP* 65—rest of paragraph based on same source, except for Tamburini's statement to his interrogators, from Heymann 150.

his main work: see EP, 'Sworn Statement... May 7, 1945', *EP/DP* 63.

sought Pound's collaboration: see Redman 237.

It was agreed: see Redman 242, and 252–3 re *La storia di un reato.*

80 **'reason for this publication'**: EP, *L'America, Roosevelt, e le cause della guerra presente*, in *Lavoro ed usura. tre saggi*, terza edizione (Milano: All'Insegna del Pesce d'Oro di Vanni Scheiwiller, 1996), 83. The condensed version of this pamphlet translated by John Drummond and included in *Impact* (1960) as 'America and the Second World War', omits its final paragraph in which the quoted sentence occurs; omits also its opening paragraph which begins (in my translation): 'This war is not due to a whim of Hitler or Mussolini. This war forms part of the millennial war between usurer and peasant, between the usurocracy and whoever wants to do an honest day's work with hand or mind' (*Lavoro/usura* 59); it further omits this later sentence, 'The first serious attempt, after Lincoln's, [to resist the power of the usurers], began with the Fascist revolution and was confirmed with the formation of the Rome–Berlin Axis' (*Lavoro/usura* 74). The effect of these and other cuts is to excise Pound's concern, however misjudging, to place the 1939– war in the context of the perennial war of *Usura* against natural abundance and social justice.

asked him to do another: see Redman 244, 257, and 259–60.

'For forty years': EP, *An Introduction to the Economic Nature of the United States* (1944), [trans. Carmine Amore, revised John Drummond], *S Pr* 137. Pound's 'fra i maestri di color che sanno', (among the masters of those that know), is a variation upon Dante's 'vidi il maestro di color che sanno' (*Inferno* IV.131), honouring Aristotle as the master of philosophers whose knowledge is from human reason, (as distinct from the theologians' divine revelation, and distinct again from the angelic intelligences).

81 **'The trap'**: EP, *An Introduction to the Economic Nature of the United States*, *S Pr* 147.

'has its roots': EP, *An Introduction to the Economic Nature of the United States*, *S Pr* 148.

'because of its political': see Gallup 72; concerning *Orientamenti*; Gallup 73; concerning *Jefferson e Mussolini*; and Gallup 74, concerning *Chiung Iung*.

82 **a daily or weekly**: see Redman 242.

suitable propaganda: see Redman 248–9 and 257–8, the latter for 'Pound's ideal list', and Sammartano's 'for the moment'.

an economic work by Angold: see Redman 260 and 262.

edition of Vivaldi: see Redman 262.

'My bilingual edition': EP to Mezzasoma, from FBI files, [trans. Redman], 15 Mar. 1944, Redman 251.

83 **gave his approval**: see Redman 255.

'I am absolutely convinced': EP to Mezzasoma, 29 Jan. 1945, from FBI files, [trans. Redman], Redman 271.

'The importance': EP to Mezzasoma, 15 Mar. 1944, second letter, from FBI files, [trans. Redman], Redman 252.

'26 chapters': EP to Mezzasoma, 27 Sept. 1944, [trans. Redman], Redman 261.

republic had flopped: see EP, 'Supplements to his Sworn Statement', 8 May, 1945, *EP/DP* 71. On the same day Pound told a reporter, 'Hitler and Mussolini were successful insofar as they followed Confucius, and... they failed because they did not follow him more closely' (interview by Edd. Johnson, Philadelphia *Record*–Chicago *Sun*, 9 May 1945, as in Norman: 1960, 396). Cf. pp. 37–8 above.

84 **a manifesto**: 'GLI SCRITTORI DEL TIGULLIO salutano gli altri scrittori d'Italia', broadsheet signed by Gilberto Gaburri, Ezra Pound, Edgardo Rossaro, Giuseppe Soldato, Michele Tanzi, ([Rapallo, 1944]); also printed, with heading 'Fiamma sul Tigullio', in *Il Popolo di Alessandria* (27 Feb. 1944) 1. The first section of the manifesto declared:

> Il pensiero vivo dell'epoca è permeato di spirito fascista.
> Con o senza etichetta l'intelletto fascista si manifesta nei vari paese. Se Frobenius non è libro di testo in Germania, il suo atteggiamento fu nondimeno totalitario, e bastano pochissimi frasi per dimostralo. Zielinski cerca di liberare il cristianesimo dalla feccia giudaica. Cruet delimita la durata della legislazione. Il senso fascista è un po' dovunque. Ma in Italia avviene la catalisi. Si può anche affermare che Confucio sia il filosofo del fascismo, ma il fascismo nacque in Romagna.
> L'intelligenzia fascista affrontò anni or sono il dilemma: NEL sistema o DEL sistema. Tale perspicacia nel distinguere risorge nel nuovo credo repubblicano che separa i diritti DELLA proprietà dai diritti ALLA proprietà.
> I paralitici bisbigliavano: chi succederà a Mussolini?
> Nessun individuo succederà a Mussolini, il successore di Mussolini sarà l'IDEA REPUBBLICANA.

The third section began:

> Il tesoro di una nazione è la sua honestà. La filosofia d'un uomo si mostra più nei suoi atti che nelle parole.

5. For the Resurrection of Italy, 1944–5

85 **'huge destruction and loss of life'**: Farrell 444.

leave their seafront flat: details from various accounts, mainly Conover 153–4; MdR, *Discretions* 196 and 258; Hugh Kenner, 'D. P. Remembered', *Pai* 2.3 (1973) 487.

'To help tide over': OR, *I Ching* notebook, June 1997 (Beinecke/OR), as in Conover 154.

'One solid year': OR, [n.d.], as cited in Conover 155.

86 **'a mild purgatorio'**: DP, personal notes, [? May 1945], cited 'Introduction', *EP/DP* 5.

'We were all civilized': OR in telephone conversation with Humphrey Carpenter, Apr. 1983, Carpenter 636.

'asperities': see 115/794.

'pent up': MdR, *Discretions* 258.

'no water': DP to Rose Marie Duncan, 28 Nov. 1947 (HRC)—also the detail about the church at Portofino.

'In Rapallo': EP to Fernando Mezzasoma, 14 Sept. 1944, [trans. Redman], Redman 260–1.

87 **'every day for the radio'**: EP to Giorgio Almirante, 16 May 1944, [from FBI files], Heymann 151.

'Isolation': EP to Mezzasoma, 27 Sept. 1944, [trans. Redman], Redman 262.

posters: details in Gallup 433–4.

88 ***La voce della verità***: detail from Gianfranco de Turris, '"L'asse che non vacilla": Ezra Pound durante la RSI', *Ezra Pound 1972/1992*, a cura di Luca Gallesi (Milano: Greco & Greco editori, 1992), 324.

urged Mezzasoma: see Redman 243 and 268.

'Propaganda': EP to Mezzasoma, 27 Feb. 1944, [trans. Redman], Redman 242.

Il Popolo di Alessandria: details from de Turris in *Ezra Pound 1972/1992* 321–2, and Redman 238–43.

'incomprehensible': see Heymann 144.

'brief articles': Gaetano Cabella to EP, 19 Jan. 1944, [trans. Redman], Redman 240.

89 **'This war'**: 'Ez. P.', 'La Guerra', *Il Popolo di Alessandria* (20 Feb. 1944) 2.

'Against this infamy': 'Ez. P.', 'Il perno', *Il Popolo di Alessandria* (23 Feb. 1944).

'No use': 'Ez. P.', 'Banchieri', *Il Popolo di Alessandria* (2 Mar. 1944) [1].

'Aristotle's precept': 'Ez. P.', 'Del silenzio', *Il Popolo di Alessandria* (30 Apr. 1944) [1].

'Amassi': 'Ez. P.': 'Amassi', *Il Popolo di Alessandria* (21 May 1944) [1]. Re *Amassi* see also EP to Mezzasoma, 27 Feb. 1944, [trans. Redman], Redman 267.

'la moneta': 'Ezra Pound', 'Appunti economici: Brani d'attualità', *L'idea sociale* (23 Apr. 1945) [1].

(but unremarked): Redman 247 and 251–2 did register his impression that 'Pound was beginning to have some doubts about the course he had chosen'; but he took the doubts to be about whether his 'proposals for economic reform' were adequate to 'the problems war-ravaged Italy was facing', and not about the regime's adequacy to the republican revolution. However, Redman also makes it clear that Pound was thinking about social reconstruction beyond both the war and the regime.

'I GRANDI': 'Ez. P.', 'Pagamenti', *Il Popolo di Alessandria* (13 Feb. 1944) [1]. On the execution of Ciano et al. see Farrell 440–3.

90 **short-sighted liberals**: see EP, 'Liberali', 'È peccato ma...', 'Etica' in *Il Popolo di Alessandria*, respectively 5 Mar., 9 Mar., 12 Mar. 1944; and see EP to Mezzasoma, 27 Feb. 1944, [trans. Redman], Redman 259.

'Italy is full': EP to Mezzasoma, 27 Feb. 1944, [trans. Robert Connolly], Heymann 333.

'many betrayals': EP to Mezzasoma, 27 Feb. 1944, [trans. Robert Connolly], Heymann 333.

he was sorry: 'Ez. P.', '"Mi rincresce"': *Il Popolo di Alessandria* (25 May 1944) [1].

a 'document': 'E. P.': 'D'accordo', *Il Popolo di Alessandria* (8 June 1944).

'una fede fascista': 'Ez. P.': 'Colore cadaverico', *Il Popolo di Alessandria* (4 June 1944).

91 **'all men of goodwill'**: EP to Mezzasoma, 18 Nov. 1944, [trans. Redman], Redman 265.

'Study, inform': EP to Mezzasoma, Nov. 1944, [from FBI files], Heymann 143.

'our cherished rights': Barack Obama, speaking in Springfield, Illinois, 10 Feb. 2007, announcing that he would be a candidate for election to the US Presidency.

92 **'Enforcement'**: EP to Mezzasoma, 27 Feb. 1944, [trans. Redman], Redman 267. Pound would have had in mind the clause in the Declaration of Independence drafted by Thomas Jefferson which reads: 'to secure these rights [to life, liberty, and the pursuit of happiness], governments are instituted among men, deriving their just powers from the consent of the governed'.

'cajoled', and following details: Farrell 453.

'the common fate': 'Ezra Pound', 'Poundiana', *Il Popolo di Alessandria* (23 Jan. 1945) 2.

some 'cantos': EP to Mezzasoma, 13 Nov. 1944, [trans. Robert Connolly], Heymann 335. The assumption that the cantos were 72 and 73 was made by Heymann. There is no clear evidence that EP had been drafting new cantos in Italian before December 1944, though that cannot be ruled out. What is certain is that he had been working, with Mary and on his own, on Italian versions of some earlier cantos—among the Beinecke Ezra Pound Papers there are versions dating from 1943 of cantos 1–13, 20, 27, and a version of 49 dated 1942.

'voices and modes': see p. 56.

93 **'Ballata IX'**: re 'In un boschetto' (sung in Act 2 of the opera *Cavalcanti*) see *EP: Poet II*, Appendix C.

sent both cantos to Mary: MdR, *Discretions* 197. Details re the sending of cantos to Mezzasoma from Redman 269.

prologue: EP to Mary Rudge, 6 Mar. 1945, 'Ubaldo has published the prologue to Canto 72' (Beinecke).

'Presenza di F. T Marinetti': *La Marina Repubblicana* II.2 (15 Jan. 1945) 2. Marinetti died 2 Dec. 1944 in Bellagio on Lake Como. My citations from canto 72 are taken from EP's own English crib, included in New Directions editions of *The Cantos* from 1995.

'the simple rite': Benito Mussolini, *My Autobiography,* trans. R. W. Child, (Hutchinson & Co., [1928]), 146.

94 **Ezzelino**: Ezzelino III. da Romano (1194–1259) is among the tyrants in *Inferno* XII. Details of EP's treatment are drawn from *L'Ecerinide* di Albertino Mussato, tradotta in versi Italiani e annotata da Manlio Torquata Dazzi (Città di Castello: Casa Editrice S. Lapi, 1914). The front cover, printed in dull red on off-white paper, shows a human body with bull head and tail, breathing flame from mouth and nostrils, in a rocky place above the River of Blood (as in *Inferno* XII.47), with the inscription 'HIC IACET TERROR ITALIAE'. EP's copy, presented to him by Dazzi, is in HRC.

destroyed Forlì etc.: Sigismondo's Tempio was damaged, not destroyed, by naval bombardment 29 Jan. 1944; however a catalogue of 'L'Italia Artistica Mutilata' by the Allied 'iconoclasti', running to several columns in *Corriere della sera* of 3 Dec. 1944, was illustrated by a photograph of the apparently ruined Tempio. There was an obituary of Marinetti on the same page. (For the discovery and for a photocopy of the relevant page I am indebted to Ron Bush.) Forlì fell to the Allies 9 Nov. 1944; Ravenna was taken 4 Dec. 1944—Bagnacavallo is just to the west of Ravenna. The Allies did not reach Bologna until 21 Apr. 1945—a detail which would suggest that EP was still working on the canto in that month.

'Many birds': I have made some adjustments to Pound's English version to bring it closer to his Italian original.

95 **a recent speech of Mussolini's**: the first article on the front page of *Corriere della sera* of 26 Nov. 1944 carried the headline: 'Il Duce esprime al combattimenti | la fede nelle riscossa della Patria', and reported his telling the combatants to above all rekindle in their hearts the flame of love of country as the foundation of its *riscossa*. He had also reaffirmed his certainty of the ultimate victory of the Tripartite powers which would mean the end of Judaic-directed material and moral exploitation by the plutocracies. (Again I am indebted to Ron Bush for this discovery and for a photocopy of the relevant page.)

'volunteer force': Farrell 445. Pavolini's personal Blackshirt bodyguard was the 'Bir el Gobi' company.

96 **The story of 'the heroine of Rimini'**: details from Daniele Balducci, 'L'"eroina di Rimini"', *Diorama letterario* 239 (Oct. 2000) 15–16.

his art: for a very positive appreciation of both cantos 72 and 73 see Massimo Mandolini Pesaresi, 'Pound's Admirable "Presenza" in the Italian Language: Cantos LXXII and LXXIII', in Richard Taylor and Claus Melchior eds., *Ezra Pound and Europe* (Amsterdam: Rodopi, 1993), [215]–21.

'Charybdis of action': 74/431.

a group of drafts in Italian: see Massimo Bacigalupo, 'Annotated translations of Italian notes and drafts of Cantos 74–75', appended to his 'Ezra Pound's Cantos 72 and 73: An Annotated Translation', *Pai* 20.1–2 (1991) 28–41; also his 'L'Écriture des *Cantos*' in Ezra Pound, *Je rassemble les membres d'Osiris* (Larroque/Castin [France]: Tristram, 1989), 274–96; Ronald Bush, '"Quiet, Not Scornful"? The Composition of the *Pisan Cantos*', in Lawrence Rainey ed., *A Poem Including History: The Cantos of Ezra Pound* (Ann Arbor: University of Michigan Press, 1996), 169–212—includes facsimiles and substantial extracts with translations; Ronald Bush, 'Towards Pisa: More from the Archives about Pound's Italian Cantos', *Agenda* 34.3–4 (1996/97) 89–124—'an attempt to situate the Canto 74 and Canto 75 typescripts (and the logic of Pound's Italian composition) by reconstructing the manuscript sequence of which they form a part'—includes substantial extracts with translations. (Note that Bacigalupo's and Bush's '74' and '75' refer to EP's numbering of these Italian drafts, not to the unrelated cantos 74 and 75 of *The Pisan Cantos*.) Some of the drafts carry dates: '12 Jan.', '13 Jan.', '14 Jan.', '12 Feb.' Sigismundo Malatesta and Lorenzo de' Medici also feature in them, but I deal here only with what I take to be their most revealing elements.

An earlier fragment (headed 'LXX...'): Ezra Pound Papers YCAL MSS 43, Box 76, folder 3383 (Beinecke).

Piero Mazda: detail from Pound's 1945 statement to FBI, *EP/DP* 63.

97 **'Her beauty, her greatness of soul'**: cited by Bush, 'Towards Pisa: More from the Archives', *Agenda* 34.3–4 (1996/97) 106, from 'Tomasini's life of Machiavelli' as cited in G. F. Young, *The Medici* (New York: Random House, 1930), 526.

'the inside corner': EP to Forrest Read, 31 Dec. 1958 (Hamilton).

98 **'I thank god'**: EP to Mary Rudge, 6 Mar. 1945 (Beinecke).

'looking for a bit of Frobenius': EP to Mary Rudge, 14 Mar. [1945] (Beinecke). 'Gassir's Lute', with related Soninke legends, is translated in Leo Frobenius and Douglas C. Fox, *African Genesis* (Faber & Faber, 1938). For Deïoces see Herodotus I.96. The bits from both Frobenius and Herodotus were used in canto 74, the first of the *Pisan Cantos*.

99 **'Caro Ub'**: EP to Ubaldo degli Uberti, 4 Apr. 1945, in Riccardo M. degli Uberti, 'Ezra Pound and Ubaldo degli Uberti: History of a Friendship', *Italian Quarterly* XVI, 64 (1973) 106, as cited in Zapponi 133.

'the light which comes': see 'Ta Hsio: The Great Digest', *Confucius* 29. For EP's explication of the ideogram (6162 in Mathews' *Chinese–English Dictionary*) see *Confucius* 21. Some notes on the endpaper of EP's Temple Classics edition of Dante's *Paradiso* are dated 'anno XXIII/ Jan'—he was noting connections between passages in the *Paradiso* and various works and authors, including Cavalcanti, 'G. C.- Villon', Mencius, and Kung. The marginal ideogram, against *Par.* XXXIII, 112–14, is in EP's copy of *Opere di Dante Alighieri* (Oxford, 1897). Both books are now in HRC.

Secondo Manifesto: details from a copy in MdR's collection.

100 **'partigiani', 'occupation'**: DP diary entries for 24 and 26 Apr. 1945 (Lilly).

On the 27th, Olga Rudge: details from Conover, 157, based on OR's own accounts.

'not in spirit of surrender': EP to MdR, 13 Jan. 1974, as in Conover 157; see also 'Ezra Pound: An Interview', *Paris Review* 28 (1962) 45.

'lookin' fo' his comman'': EP mentioned the incident on a number of occasions in very similar terms—this is from EP to Peter Whigham, 23 Sept. 1953, as cited in Carpenter 645.

Mussolini was shot: details in this paragraph drawn from Farrell 474–6.
'giustizati': DP diary entry for 29 Apr. 1945 (Lilly).
'in case anything should happen': OR to Mary Rudge, 30 Apr. 1945, as cited in Conover 158.
'very cold': DP diary entry for 3 May 1945 (Lilly). Details in previous sentence from same entry.
'busy with the local authorities': Conover 158.
caccia al fascista: the phrase is from Gianfranco de Turris' account (q.v.) in '"L'asse che non vacilla": Ezra Pound durante la RSI', *Ezra Pound 1972/1992*, 334.
working on his Mencius: EP frequently mentioned this, e.g. in a letter to Ronald Duncan, n.d. [*c.*1950?], he wrote that 'at exact moment the pseudo-Marxists ("partigiani" after the reward, supposed) came to the door' he was working on '*Mencius*' (HRC). The varying accounts of Pound's capture are derived in the main from his own and OR's accounts given at various times to various correspondents.

101 **two books**: the books, now in the Ezra Pound Collection of Hamilton College, were: *Si Shu. The Four Books (Confucian Analects; The Great Learning; The Doctrine of the Mean; The Works of Mencius)*, with English translation and notes by James Legge (Shanghai, China: Commercial Press, n.d.); and *A Chinese Dictionary Revised. Comprising over Three Thousand Characters*... (Shanghai, China: Commercial Press, n.d.).
'EP gone away': DP diary entry for 3 May 1945 (Lilly).
'DEElicious': EP to MdR, 1962, as cited in Massimo Bacigalupo, 'Tigullio Itineraries', in *Ezra Pound, Language and Persona*, ed. Massimo Bacigalupo and William Pratt (Genoa: Università degli Studi di Genova, 2008), 433.
'the courtyard': *Ezra Pound, Language and Persona*, ed. Bacigalupo and Pratt, 434. See also 'Ezra Pound: An Interview', *Paris Review* 28 (1962) 45.
'paying off old scores': OR as cited by Conover, Conover 160.
a respected member of the Resistance: from Massimo Bacigalupo, 'Tigullio Intineraries', *Ezra Pound, Language and Persona*, 434.

102 **'K-ration box lunches'**: from OR's account, as in Conover 160.

6. Talking to the FBI

An invaluable resource for this chapter has been *Ezra and Dorothy Pound: Letters in Captivity, 1945–1946* edited and annotated by Omar Pound and Robert Spoo (New York: Oxford University Press, 1999)—a fine edition of essential letters and documents, and replete with ancillary information in its extensive notes. Britain's National Archives are another valuable source of documents recording the police and intelligence surveillance of Pound (Ref: KV 2/875–361810), and also of the messages exchanged by United States judicial and military authorities concerning the capture and disposal of Ezra Pound which were copied to the British War Office (Ref: WO 204/12602–361810).

105 **'FENOLLOSA'S EXECUTOR'**: cable dictated by EP 4 May 1945, as in memo of Frank L. Amprim to J. Edgar Hoover, Director FBI, (26 May 1945), *EP/DP* 51.
'Man I most want': EP draft for Reynolds Packard, [*c.*7 May 1945?], *EP/DP* 57.
the 'one point': see 74/426. In his 8 May 1945 statement, 'Outline of Economic Bases of historic process', EP declared that 'There are alternate remedies' to Lenin's 'nationalization of the means of production', and 'That is why I wish—after due LINGUISTIC preparation to meet Stalin'.

106 **'For weeks'**: two-page TS 'Extract from article in "News Review" dated 5.8.43' in 'Ezra Pound's file/P.F. 34319' (Nat. Arch. KV2/875, item 39a).
'to look into English': EP to A. V. Moore, 14 Jan. 1940, photocopy of intercept on behalf of MI5 (Nat. Arch. KV2/875, item 26a).

'As shown by previous record': 'Comment' by V.F./A.C., 23 Jan. 1940, on EP's 14 Jan. 1940 letter to Moore (Nat. Arch. KV2/875, item 26a).

A letter of March 1940: two-page TS copy of EP to Raven Thomson, [published in *Action* 21 Mar. 1940], 'Original in P.F. 46785 Raven Thomson. vol: 4, 167x' (Nat. Arch. KV2/875, item 27a).

letter to the B.U.F. leader: EP to Sir O. Mosley, 12 May 1940, TS copy of 'Original in P.F. 48909 36a' (Nat. Arch. KV2/875, item 28a).

107 **simply 'Fascist'**: 'Extract from M.C.5 report on Anglo-Italian Societies, 19.6.40' (Nat. Arch. KV2/875, item 28c), reads: 'Both Ezra and Dorothy Pound are of strongly Fascist and anti-Semitic sympathies. They were in correspondence with Mr RAVEN THOMSON, the Editor of "Action" and asked of him whether ex-post facto laws—forbidden by the U.S.A.—were constitutional or legal in England, and whether this form of tyranny arose whenever Jews came into power. Another letter addressed to Eric de Mare, The Social Credit Party, 44 Little Britain, E.C.1, advised that party to unite for the accomplishment of economic reform.'

'Cable received from AGWAR': JAG [Judge Advocate General], NATOUSA [North African Theater of Operations United States Army], to CG [Commanding General] Fifth Army and CG Seventh Army, 19 Sept. 43 (Nat. Arch. WO 204/12602, item 1). 'AGWAR' = Adjutant General, War Department.

'In the event': Francis Biddle to Henry L. Stimson, 24 Jan. 1944, repr. in *Helix* 13/14 (1983) 128.

Frank Amprim: 'since August 1943', memo from Colonel Earle B. Nichols of G-2 [Military Intelligence] to JA [Judge Advocate], 9 June 1945 (Nat. Arch. WO 204/12602, item 16). Other details from *EP/DP* 6–7.

'an FBI target': this paragraph mainly drawn from 'Ramon Arrizabalaga's Memoir (1956)', *EP/DP* 371, 373, 375. The 'Memoir' was 'assembled' by the editors of *EP/DP* from two letters written by Arrizabalaga to John Edwards, 31 Jan. and 13 Mar. 1956, in response to the latter's request for information.

108 **'The American writer'**: press cutting from *Manchester Guardian*, 7 May 1945, citing Associated Press, Rome, May 6 (Nat. Arch. KV 2/875, item 50a); another cutting from *The Times*, 7 May 1945, (citing Reuter, Milan, 6 May), says that EP, 'the American poet, who broadcast from Rome under the Fascist regime, has been captured near Genoa' (Nat. Arch. KV 2/875, item 50a).

'Traitor Pound': *The Stars and Stripes*, Mediterranean edition, 7 May 1945, as in 'Introduction', *EP/DP* 10.

Olga Rudge used to tell: see Conover 160ff.

'seemed a very decent': John Drummond to Ronald Duncan, 30 July 1945 (HRC).

109 **'could not dispatch'**: Frank L. Amprim to J. Edgar Hoover, 26 May 1945, *EP/DP* 51.

a couch and easy chairs: from OR's account, Conover 161.

'Army K rations': from Amprim memo to Hoover, 20 May 1945, as in 'Introduction', *EP/DP* 7.

'expressed himself': EP to Shakespear & Parkyn, 5 Oct. 1945, *EP/DP* 109.

'sworn statement': an early, undated, TS draft with EP's handwritten marginal comments, is reproduced in *Helix* 13/14 (1983) 129–32; another TS draft, dated 6 May was copied by Amprim to Captain Sidney Henderson, Office of the Assistant Chief of Staff, G-2, Allied Force Headquarters, on 31 May 1945 (Nat. Arch. WO 204/12602, item 13); the final version, dated 7 May 1945, which EP signed is reproduced in *EP/DP* 59–67.

After five hours, 'ADMITS': *EP/DP* 7.

110 **'even if Italy fell'**: EP in 7 May signed statement, *EP/DP* 63. The words 'fight for', present in the two previous drafts, are missing from this final version—an omission which I assume EP simply failed to notice. The other quotations in this paragraph

are from the signed statement, *EP/DP* 63, 65, 67, and (Nat. Arch. WO 204/12602, item 16).

supplementary statement: printed in *EP/DP* 69–77.

an authorization: EP to DP, [7 May 1945], *EP/DP* 39–43.

111 **'among *the happiest*'**: OR to JL, 11 Nov. 1945, as in Conover 161—also *EP/DP* 8.

about 6.30: DP, Diary, entry for 7 May 1945 (Lilly).

'very cooperative': Amprim memo to Hoover, 20 May 1945, as in 'Introduction', *EP/DP* 8.

initialled and dated: among the books from EP's library now at HRC are nine 'FBI copies' carrying the agents' initials and dates. *Orientamenti* (1944), for example, the collection of EP's articles from *Meridiano di Roma*, carries 5 sets of initials: (1) R.A Jr. [Ramon Arrizabalaga] | 7/5/45 | Genova | F.L.A [Frank Lawrence Amprim]; (2) F. L.A | Pisa | 8-7-45 [= 7 Aug.]; (3) My work | E. Pound | 7 Aug. 45; (4) MGM | 11/15/45; (5) MGM | 12/11/45 [= 11 Dec.].

'This partial statement': official TSS copy of EP signed statement to Frank Amprim, 8 May 1945, Genoa, (Nat Arch. WO 204/12602, items 13A, 13B). Not included in *EP/DS*, the editors apparently being unaware of it—see *EP/DS* 8.

'a rather forced definition': EP sworn statement 7 May 1945, as in *EP/DS* 67.

112 **'OUTLINE OF ECONOMIC BASES'**: EP's further statements dated '8 May 1945' are printed in *EP/DP* 69–77.

115 **'Among the many things he said'**: Edd Johnson, 'Confucius and Kindred Subjects/ Pound, Accused of Treason, Calls Hitler Saint, Martyr', *Chicago Sun*, 9 May 1945, as in Carpenter 650–2. In *Philadelphia Record* the headline was, 'Poet-Prisoner Pound Calls Hitler Saint'.

Amprim returned to Rome: see 'Ramon Arrizabalaga's Memoir (1956)', *EP/DP* 373.

'decision from Washington': 15 Army Group to AFHQ, 19 May 1945 (Nat. Arch. WO 204/12602, item 4).

'requests to higher headquarters': 'Ramon Arrizabalaga's Memoir (1956)', *EP/DP* 373.

'doing Confucio': EP to DP, 24 May 1945, as in *EP/DP* 49. In his note of 7 May authorizing DP to assist Amprim in his search of 60 Sant'Ambrogio, EP had written, 'Am doing american version of l'Asse but forget some of the analyses: so must have at least one copy of my ital. trans.', *EP/DP* 43.

'posing at the typewriter': 'Ramon Arrizabalaga's Memoir (1956)', *EP/DP* 373, and see note on p. 374.

'in a military stockade': Amprim to J. Edgar Hoover, 21 May 1945, cited 'Introduction', *EP/DP* 11.

'Talk is': EP to DP, 24 May 1945, *EP/DP* 49; EP to OR, cited *EP/DP* 48.

'Transfer without delay': CG MTOUSA to CG Fifth Army, CG Replacement and Training Command, 22 May 1945 (Nat. Arch. WO 204/12602, item 9).

116 **'5th Army Provost Marshall'**: 'Ramon Arrizabalaga's Memoir (1956)', *EP/DP* 373.

'Doctor EZRA POUND delivered': Fifth Army to CG MTOUSA, 27 May 1945 (Nat. Arch. WO 204/12602, item 10).

7. A PRISONER IN THE EYES OF OTHERS

Sources for this chapter: Again an invaluable resource has been *Ezra and Dorothy Pound: Letters in Captivity, 1945–1946* edited and annotated by Omar Pound and Robert Spoo; and again another has been the copies in Britain's National Archives (Ref: WO 204/12602–361810) of official messages exchanged by United States judicial and military authorities concerning the capture and disposal of Ezra Pound. An article by Ben D. Kimpel and T. C. Duncan Eaves, 'More on Pound's Prison Experience', *American*

Literature 53.3 (1981) 469–76, gives substantial excerpts from the reports of the three psychiatrists who examined Pound while he was confined in the DTC. Professor Giovanni Giovannini wrote a memorandum of Pound's own oral account of his confinement as given to him in St Elizabeths, 4 Sept. 1957, and a copy of this is in the Hugh Kenner Archive (HRC). Several of the officers and guards serving at the US Army's Detention and Training Center near Pisa while Pound was confined there have published their recollections in articles or interviews: David Park Williams, 'The Background of the Pisan Cantos' (*Poetry*, 1949), and Robert Allen, 'The Cage' (*Esquire*, 1958), both reprinted in William Van O'Connor and Edward Stone eds., *A Casebook on Ezra Pound* (New York: Thomas Y. Crowell, 1959), 39–43, 33–8; Michael King, 'An Interview with John L. Steele', *Texas Quarterly* 21.4 (1978) 48–61; David Feldman, 'Ezra Pound: A Poet in a Cage', *Pai* 10.2 (1981) 361–5; John L. Steele, 'Ez at the DTC: A Correspondence between Carroll F. Terrell and John L. Steele', ed. Michael Fournier, *Pai* 12.2–3 (1983) 293–303; Homer Somers with William Pratt, 'Ezra Pound in the DTC: A Personal Memoir', *Pai* 34.2–3 (2005) 53–61; there is also an unpublished typescript memoir headed 'Ezra Pound', unsigned but on internal evidence by Homer Somers, *c.*1946?—this is with the Peter Russell material at HRC (Pound, EL Misc 1). Though these recollections are of great interest, their discrepancies, personal biases, and occasional demonstrable errors provide an instructive case study in the fallibility of memory. Even first-hand sources can be unreliable: Pound himself apparently told Giovannini that he had been held in the 'gorilla cage' for two months, when in fact it can be established that he was held there for under one month.

118 **emergency landing field**: from Somers, *Pai* 34.2–3 (2005) 54.
'red-bearded': ?Homer Somers, 'Ezra Pound' (Pound, EL Misc. 1, HRC).
'stubby graying growth' and **'curly full head'**: Feldman, *Pai* 10.2 (1981) 362.
'graceful, looping', **'nimbly'**: Robert Allen, 'The Cage', *Casebook* 35.
'boric acid': Feldman, *Pai* 10.2 (1981) 363.

119 **'It's terrible'**: EP talking to Louis Dudek in St Elizabeths Hospital, Washington DC, 10 June 1950, as in *Dk/Some Letters of Ezra Pound*, ed. with Notes by Louis Dudek (Montreal: DC Books, 1974), 29.
The opening lines: the two pieces of toilet paper on which the first ten lines of canto 74 were drafted are reproduced as frontispiece to the edition of *The Pisan Cantos* edited and annotated with an introduction by Richard Sieburth (New York: New Directions, 2003); the inside front cover of Legge's *The Four Books* with those lines written by EP is reproduced in *A Selected Catalog of the Ezra Pound Collection at Hamilton College* Compiled with notes by Cameron McWhirter and Randall L. Ericson (Clinton, NY: Hamilton College Library, 2005), 45. Ronald Bush, who knows the drafts better than anyone, thinks that these opening lines, 'far from being the originating kernel of the suite, in fact surfaced slowly' and were added only as 'an afterthought'. However, I remain persuaded that it is unlikely Pound would have written them down on toilet paper, then in his Legge, unless he did not yet have a notebook. It is true, as Bush demonstrates, that the lines were inserted only in a late typescript; but the handwritten 'incipit' at the head of canto 74 in that typescript could well mean, not that that was where the canto began—if that was the beginning there would be no need to mark it thus—but instead that an 'incipit', i.e. the lines in question, was to be inserted there. Whether that was a late decision, or a strategic one to avoid provoking the US Army censor, is a matter for speculation. See Ronald Bush, '"Quiet, not scornful": The Composition of *The Pisan Cantos*', in *A Poem Containing History: Textual Studies in* The Cantos, ed. Lawrence Rainey (Ann Arbor: University of Michigan Press, 1997), 169–211. Massimo Bacigalupo put the case against Bush's argument in his 'Pound's Pisan Cantos in Process', *Pai* 27.2–3 (1998) 98–9.
Steele returned: see John L. Steele, chronology appended to 'Ez at the DTC', *Pai* 12.2–3 (1983) 300.

'Placed in confinement': report of Capt. R. W. Fenner, 14 June 1945, as in Kimpel and Eaves 471.

'This 59½ year old': report of Capt. Walter H. Baer, 15 June 1945, as in Kimpel and Eaves 471–2.

120 **moved on June 18**: see John L. Steele, chronology appended to 'Ez at the DTC', *Pai* 12.2–3 (1983) 300.

The Catholic chaplain: this paragraph is drawn from Wendy Stallard Flory, 'Confucius against Confusion: Ezra Pound and the Catholic Chaplain at Pisa', *Ezra Pound & China*, ed. Zhaoming Qian (Ann Arbor: University of Michigan Press, 2003), 146–62. The only indication of when the exchanges between EP and Father Vath took place is 'June 26, 1945'; Flory assumes EP was then still in the cage, but in fact he had been transferred to the medical compound on 18 June.

message from the War Crimes Office: see Kimpel and Eaves 470.

'He shows no evidence': report of Major William Weisdorf, 17 July 1945, as in Kimpel and Eaves 472–3.

121 **keeping him sane**: in 1952 Pound showed a young Chinese visitor his 'pirated, bilingual edition of James Legge's translation of the *Four Books* of Confucius, dog-eared and its spine held together with band aids and scotch tape', and she remembered him saying, 'This little book has been my bible for years . . . the only thing I could hang on to during those hellish days at Pisa . . . Had it not been for this book, from which I drew my strength, I would *really* have gone insane' (Angela Palandri, 'Homage to a Confucian Poet', *Pai* 3.3 (1974) 305). In the same year at St Elizabeths Pound told Henry Swabey, 'Confucius kept me sane' (Henry Swabey, 'A Page Without Which . . .', *Pai* 5.2 (1976) 333).

Colonel Steele's note: John L. Steele to CG Replacement and Training Command, 19 July 1945, as in Kimpel and Eaves 473–4.

'walking on eggshells': Homer Somers, *Pai* 34.2–3 (2005) 57.

'ensuring responsible care': John L. Steele, *Pai* 12.2–3 (1983) 295–6.

122 **'constant clanging'**: Robert Allen, 'The Cage', *Casebook* 36.

dated it 'D.T.C., Pisa': see *Confucius (1949)* 44.

'let down completely': Robert Allen, 'The Cage', *Casebook* 36–7.

tried to explain Gesell: ?Somers, 'Ezra Pound' (Pound, EL Misc. 1, HRC).

'anxious to discuss': Robert Allen, 'The Cage', *Casebook* 35.

all 48 words: see 77/471.

an old broom handle: see 77/471.

123 **read 'everything'**: Allen, 'The Cage', *Casebook* 37.

'no communication': John Drummond to DP, 11 July 1945 (Lilly), cited Carpenter 669.

transfer Pound . . . without delay: a 21 June 1945 message FX-96763 read, 'Return to UNITED STATES recommended without delay'; a follow up message on 5 July 1945 read simply, 'Decision disposition EZRA POUND reourad FX 96763 requested soonest' (Nat. Arch. WO 204/12602, items 22 and 26).

'reinterrogation': Brigadier General John M. Weir, War Crimes Office, Washington, to Judge Advocate, Mediterranean Theatre, 3 July 1945, as in Kimpel and Eaves 470.

'summaries and short items': Amprim to Director, FBI, 21 June 1945, enclosing 'documents secured by the writer on May 7, 1945, from the premises of the subject at #60 Sant'Ambrogio pursuant to written permission granted by Pound' (photocopy reproduced in *A Selected Catalog of the Ezra Pound Collection at Hamilton College* (Clinton, NY: Hamilton College Library, 2005), 84).

'From an examination': J. Edgar Hoover to Frank L. Amprim, 4 July 1945 (photocopy reproduced in *A Selected Catalog of the Ezra Pound Collection at Hamilton College*, 85).

124 **'enough to fill up'**: Heymann 156—details about the gathering of evidence concerning the typewriters are in Heymann 156–7.
'collected far more proof', 'my instinct': EP to Shakespear & Parkyn, 5 Oct. 1945, as in *EP/DP* 109.
'Absolute need': AGWAR to AFHQ for attention . . . Amprim, 28 June 1945 (Nat. Arch. WO 204/12602, item 24). John M. Weir—see previous note—wrote to the same effect in his 3 July message: 'The long delay in holding Dr. Ezra Pound has been due to the necessity of securing two witnesses to the overt act of treason upon which to predicate the trial of the case.'
'Department wishes': AGWAR to AFHQ for . . . Amprim, 17 July 1945 (Nat. Arch. WO 204/12602, item 28).
125 **'Though people named'**: AGWAR to AFHQ for Amprim, 24 July 1945 (Nat. Arch. WO 204/12602, item 29).
'two other witnesses': Samuel C. Ely memo to 'The Files', 14 Aug. 1945, Justice Department Files concerning Ezra Pound released on-line—<www.justice.gov/criminal/foia/records/ezra-pound-p1.pdf>.
'Reinterview jointly': AGWAR to COMGENMED FOR G-2 for Amprim, 21 Aug. 1945 (Nat. Arch. WO 204/12602, item 32).
FBI memo: D. M. Ladd to J. Edgar Hoover, 29 Oct. 1945, FBI file on Pound, as cited Torrey 180.
'Without such witnesses': 'Seek Witnesses in Pound Case', *D.C. Times Herald*, 29 Oct. 1945, as cited Torrey 180.
six of these 'witnesses': Allen, 'The Cage', *Casebook* 37.
five witnesses named: for the revised indictment see Norman: *Case* 80–1.
126 **'an enquiry', 'no objection'**: record of memos exchanged between PMG and G-2, 15 and 17 Aug. 1945 (Nat. Arch. WO 204/12602, item 31).
'that your husband': Provost Marshall General to DP, 24 Aug. 1945, *EP/DP* 81.
'This letter will constitute': Provost Marshall to DP, 18 Sept. 1945, *EP/DP* 83.
'If Mrs Pound': John L. Steele to EP, 20 Sept. 1945, *EP/DP* 85.
'famished for news': EP to DP, 20 Sept. 1945, *EP/DP* 89.
127 **'"One day's reading"'**: EP to DP, 28 Sept. 1945, *EP/DP* 97. Cf. 74/427.
'done a Decad': EP to DP, 2 Oct. 1945, *EP/DP* 101.
'Please have counsel': DP to EP, 25 Sept. 1945, *EP/DP* 93.
Elihu Root: paragraph mainly drawn from editors' note, *EP/DP* 96.
'cordial recollections': EP to Shakespear & Parkyn, 5 Oct. 1945, *EP/DP* 109.
128 **'We can manage the cash'**: DP to EP, 9 Oct. 1945, *EP/DP* 121.
Pound explained: EP to Shakespear & Parkyn, 5 Oct. 1945, *EP/DP* 107–13.
'Tell Omar': EP to DP, 24 Oct. 1945, *EP/DP* 157, 159.
'a sheaf of documents': Frank L. Amprim to Major Sidney Henderson, 10 Sept. 1945 (Nat. Arch. WO 204/12602, item 38).
'integral part of my defence': EP to A. V. Moore, 9 Nov. 1945, cited in editors' note, *EP/DP* 178.
'prefer to see Mr McLeish': EP to Shakespear & Parkyn, 5 Oct. 1945, *EP/DP* 109, 113.
129 **'Poor old Ezra!'**: Archibald MacLeish to Ernest Hemingway, 27 July 1943, *Letters of Archibald MacLeish 1907 to 1982*, ed. R. H. Winnick (Boston: Houghton Mifflin Company, 1983), 316.
'obviously crazy': Hemingway to MacLeish, 10 Aug. 1943, *Selected Letters of Ernest Hemingway 1917–1961*, ed. Carlos Baker (New York: Scribner Classics 2003), 548–9.
'misinterpretation': MacLeish to Julien Cornell, Dec. 1945, *MacLeish* 335.
'I should hardly say': JL to EP, 4 Sept. 1945, *EP/JL* 137–8.
'That angle': JL to DP, 4 Nov. 1945, *EP/JL* 141–2.

130 **'a good record'**: JL to EP, 4 Sept. 1945, *EP/JL* 138.
'A Quaker': DP to EP, 19 Oct. 1945, *EP/DP* 151.
'Jas pathetically': EP to DP, 24 Oct. 1945, *EP/DP* 157.
'Ez, you are not': TSE to EP, 19 Oct. 1945, cited in editors' note, *EP/DP* 86.
'I don't believe': DP to EP, 15 Oct. 1945, *EP/DP* 133.
'an intellectual "crack pot"': Lt. Colonel P. V. Holder, Affidavit sworn 20 Nov. 1945, *EP/DP* 201.
'got me my "Ta Seu"': EP to DP, 9 Oct. 1945, *EP/DP* 123.
'a long hour': DP to OR, [after 3 Oct. 1945], cited in 'Introduction', *EP/DP* 18.
'all and sundry': EP to DP, 3 Oct. [1945], *EP/DP* 103.
131 **'the first slab'**: EP to DP, 4 Oct. 1945, *EP/DP* 105.
'Report on the prisoner POUND': EP, signed but not dated, with covering note from MTOUSA to CG Peninsular Base Section dated 5 Oct. 1945 (Nat. Arch. WO 204/12602, items 43c and 43b). On Oct. 18 EP drafted another 'request to be sent to Rapallo on parole', addressed to Major Lucree, but this request seems to have gone no further—see *EP/DP* 148–51.
'protecting his butt': John L. Steele to editors in 1992, editors' note, *EP/DP* 152.
'OUT correspondence': EP to DP, 19 Oct. 1945, *EP/DP* 153.
'another batch' and **'Note to Base Censor'**: EP to DP via Base Censor, [4 Nov. 1945], *EP/DP* 177.
'talked mostly of publications': DP to A. V. Moore, 14 Nov. 1945, cited in editors' note, *EP/DP* 182.
'much emptier': EP to DP, 11 Nov. 1945, *EP/DP* 185.
'grizzled and red-eyed': MdR, *Discretions* 256.
132 **'EZRA POUND, American'**: COMGENMED to AGWAR, 22 Oct. 1945 (Nat. Arch. WO 204/12602, item 43).
'The Department of Justice': AGWAR to COMGENMED, 5 Nov. 1945 (Nat. Arch. WO 204/12602, item 45).
'on regular flight': AGWAR to COMGENMED, 16 Nov. 1945 (Nat. Arch. WO 204/ 12602, item 46).
'to escort': Travel orders for escort to Rome, 16 Nov. 1945, as in *EP/DP* 191.
a 1,000-word 'NOTE': EP, 'NOTE on "The Mission to Moscow" by J. E. Davies', 4 typed sheets, dated at end '15 nov 1945' (private collection).
'Leaving probably Rome': EP to DP, [14 and ?16 Nov. 1945], *EP/DP* 189.
small attaché case: the contents were listed when EP was committed to the DC Jail on 20 Nov.
greatcoat: DP to A. V. Moore, 14 Nov. 1945, 'He had had a greatcoat issued to him', cited in editors' note, *EP/DP* 182.
'cold raw night': Lt. Colonel P. V. Holder's report, 19 Nov. 1945, *EP/DP* 195.
133 **'so that no one'**: Lt. Colonel P. V. Holder's report, 19 Nov. 1945, *EP/DP* 195. Details in this paragraph of the flight from Rome to Washington are drawn from this report.
'Pound, in dirty shirt': unidentified newspaper clipping in Charles Olson's 'Pound file', as in Charles Olson, *Charles Olson & Ezra Pound: An Encounter at St. Elizabeths*, ed. Catherine Seelye (New York: Grossman Publishers, 1975), 119n.

8. 'IN THE MIND INDESTRUCTIBLE': *THE PISAN CANTOS*

Besides Carroll F. Terrell's invaluable *Companion to the Cantos of Ezra Pound*, vol. 2 (Berkeley: University of California Press, 1984), there are helpful annotations in Richard Sieburth's edition of *The Pisan Cantos* (New York: New Directions, 2003).

134 **working on his *Confucius***: Pound's *Confucius (1949)* is dated on the last page '*D.T.C., Pisa; 5 October—5 November, 1945*'. His translation of 'The Great Digest' was drafted in the same notebook as cantos 80–3, but starting from the back.

135 **the leading themes**: Ronald Bush has argued on several occasions that the late insertion into the DTC drafts of the opening eleven lines transformed the entire sequence into an angry requiem for Italian Fascism—see his '"Quiet, not scornful": The Composition of *The Pisan Cantos*', in *A Poem Containing History: Textual Studies in* The Cantos, ed. Lawrence Rainey (Ann Arbor: University of Michigan Press, 1997), 198ff.; see also Sieburth's account of Bush's argument in the introduction to his edition of *The Pisan Cantos* xxxv–xxxvi. That now influential interpretation seems to me to be simply not in accord with the way the opening 31-line passage of canto 74 develops, nor with the way the Pisan sequence as a whole develops; nor is it in accord with the evidence (see Chapter 11) that Pound had come to terms with the failure of Fascism and was looking beyond it politically. And note the judgment on Mussolini in canto 78: 'Sd/one wd/have to think about that | but was hang'd dead by the heels before his thought in proposito | came into action efficiently' (78/482). Bush's argument takes off from his speculative interpretation of Pound's reaction to learning on 8 October that Angold had been killed in the war, and his then beginning canto 84 with five lines marking his death with phrases from Bertran de Born's highly rhetorical lament for the death of the young English king (Pound's version of the 'Planh' is in *Personae*). Pound responded to the news which he had from Dorothy by writing back to her, 'Heart-break re/ Angold' (*EP/DP* 117, 119), and Bush makes much of that 'Heart-break'; but he does not note how the long letter goes on to other matters, and returns to Angold only to add, 'Can't say Angold was necessarily loss to literature as wasn't sure he would go on writing.' Canto 84 similarly moves on from the brief Angold threnody to quite other concerns. Pound cared that Angold's 'few poems the best granite of that generation up to 1938' should be collected, but there is not the least evidence in the letter, nor in the canto, of an 'angry wound opened up by Angold's death', a wound which supposedly led him to reveal at the end that the whole sequence was really an act of mourning for Mussolini and Fascism. Bush's argument would have the lament for Angold at the end, and the protest at the manner of Mussolini's death at the start—each a matter of a few lines only—determine our reading of the entire sequence.

I have great respect for Bush's work on the *The Pisan Cantos*, but I find his interpretation in this instance thoroughly misleading; as, from his own different vantage point, does Massimo Bacigalupo—see his 'The Myth of the Revised Opening of *The Pisan Cantos*', *Notes & Queries* 54 (2007) 169–71.

136 **'the city of Dioce'**: see p. 99 above.

virtù irraggiante: EP, *Confucio* 4; also 'Nota', '*Chung Yung* [L'asse che non vacilla]', in *Opere Scelte* 504–5.

137 **Confucianism made new**: on this see the following: Mary Paterson Cheadle, chap. 8: 'Confucianism in *The Cantos*', *Ezra Pound's Confucian Translations* (Ann Arbor: University of Michigan Press, 1997), 217–66; Wendy Stallard Flory, 'Confucius against Confusion', in *Ezra Pound & China*, ed. Zhaoming Qian (Ann Arbor: University of Michigan Press, 2003), 143–62; Ronald Bush, 'Confucius Erased: The Missing Ideograms in *The Pisan Cantos*', also in *Ezra Pound & China*, 163–92; Feng Lan, *Ezra Pound and Confucianism: Remaking Humanism in the Face of Modernity* (Toronto: University of Toronto Press, 2005), *passim*; Feng Lan, 'Confucius', in *Ezra Pound in Context*, ed. Ira B. Nadel (Cambridge: Cambridge University Press, 2010), 324–34.

ch'eng[2]: '"Sincerity". The precise definition of the word, pictorially the sun's lance coming to rest on the precise spot verbally. The right hand half of this compound means: to perfect, bring to focus' (EP, 'Terminology', *Confucius (1951)* 20).

'the biologist': EP, 'Epstein, Belgion and Meaning' (1930), *EP&VA* 166.
'It is music': EP as in David Anderson, 'Breaking the Silence: The Interview of Vanni Ronsisvalle and Pier Paolo Pasolini with Ezra Pound in 1968', *Pai* 10.2 (1981) 332 (my translation).

138 **'not words whereto'**: cf. Mencius IV.B.11. Ronald Bush, 'Confucius Erased', *Ezra Pound & China*, 170, shows that Pound was thinking of Confucian doctrine in parallel with his composition of the cantos, and that he was drawing mainly on the *Analects* and Mencius.
'paraclete': John 14.
'Sincerity': EP, 'Note', *Confucius (1949)* [vii].

140 **'Gassir'**: see pp. 98–9 above.
'seed-*gestalt*': see *Ezra Pound Poet* I, 228.
did radically revise: see Ronald Bush, 'Remaking Canto 74', *Pai* 32 (2003) 157–86.
Amber Rives: otherwise Princess Troubetzkoi—see pp. 30 and 57 above.

142 **the economic theme**: on this see A. David Moody, 'Directio voluntatis: Pound's Economics in the Economy of *The Cantos*', *Pai* 32 (2003) 187–203.

144 **serial bigamist**: this information about Charles Granville, born Charles Hosken, I owe to the researches of Steve Holland published on the Web, 13 Feb. 2009.
'my fondest knight': Symons actually wrote, 'I am Yseult and Helen, I have seen | Troy burn, and the most loving knight lie dead.'

146 **'not to know words'**: EP, *Analects* XX.iii, 3 (p. 135). Legge's commentary on chap. iii is helpful, and also his commentary on 'The Text of Confucius', the first part of *The Great Learning*—see James Legge, *Confucius: Confucian Analects, The Great Learning and The Doctrine of the Mean* (1893; reprinted New York: Dover Publications, Inc.,1971), 354–9.
'remade, as the plant repairs': Dante, *Purgatorio* XXXIII.142–5, as in Laurence Binyon's version.

147 **'Itz the double-stopping'**: EP to Dudek, [May 1951], *EP/Dk* [63].
'a third life': EP, *GK* 152.

148 **'che fu chiamata Primavera'**: see Dante, *La Vita Nuova* xxiv.

154 **'half dead at the top', 'pragmatical, preposterous pig'**: W. B. Yeats, 'Blood and the Moon', *The Winding Stair* (1933).
'*themis*': cf. 71/417 ('THEMIS CONDITOR'), and John Adams to Thomas Jefferson, Sept. [i.e. 4 Oct.] 1813.

155 **'O woman, shapely as the swan'**: Padraic Colum, 'I shall not die for thee', included by EP in *Confucius to Cummings*, 305–6.

156 **Jacopo del Sellaio's Venus**: see 'The Picture' and 'Of Jacopo del Sellaio' in *Ripostes*.

157 **as Zielinski saw it**: Thaddeus Zielinski, *The Sybil. Three Essays on Ancient Religion and Christianity*, as translated in *Edge* 2 (Nov. 1956), 6.

158 **Hugh Kenner has shown**: see his *The Pound Era* (Faber & Faber, 1972), 488–93. For a fine analysis of the metric of the *libretto* see Donald Davie, *Pound* (Fontana/Collins, 1975), 92–5.

160 ***jen***: 3099 in *Mathews' Chinese–English Dictionary* (Cambridge, Mass.: Harvard University Press, 1943), which gives 'Perfect virtue ... the ideal of Confucius'. Terrell, *Companion* II, 457, gives 'humanitas' (after EP in 'Terminology', *Confucius (1951)* 22), and adds 'the man who lives out heaven's process' etc.
Clytaemnestra: Pound cites in Greek and Latin Clytaemnestra's 'my husband dead by my right hand', from Aeschylus' *Agamemnon* 1429–30. Note especially *Agamemnon* 1410–15 for her ritual cry. Pound discussed the problem of translating the lines in 'Early Translators of Homer', *LE* 270.
'ἔφατα πόσις ἐμός': 'she said my husband'—see previous note.

161 **Confucian thought**: cf. EP, 'In un mondo di luce ed acqua fluviale si svolgeva la vita ed il pensiero Confuciano', 'Studio integrale', *Meridiano do Roma* VI.43 (26 Oct. 1941) 3.

162 **his 'boyhood's friend'**: see *EP: Poet I*, 409 and 225–6.
out of Mencius: see James Legge, *The Works of Mencius* II.i.11 (1895; reprinted New York: Dover Publications, Inc.,1970), 190. EP's emphasis departs from Legge's.

163 **'that day I wrote no further'**: possibly an echo of Francesca's 'quel giorno più non vi leggemo avante', *Inferno* V.138, 'that day we read no further'.

9. American Justice

Sources for this chapter: Materials in the United States National Archives (US Nat. Arch.) from the Justice Department files and from the St Elizabeths Hospital files; H. A. Sieber, *The Medical, Legal, Literary and Political Status of Ezra Weston [Loomis] Pound [1885–]/ Selected Facts and Comments* (Washington 25, DC: Library of Congress Legislative Reference Service, 1958); Julien Cornell, *The Trial of Ezra Pound: A Documented Account of the Treason Case by the Defendant's Lawyer* (Faber & Faber, 1967); Charles Norman, *The Case of Ezra Pound* (New York: Funk & Wagnalls, 1968); Jerome Kavka, 'Ezra Pound's Personal History: A Transcript, 1946', *Pai* 20.1–2 (1991) 144–85; *Ezra and Dorothy Pound: Letters in Captivity, 1945–1946*, edited and annotated by Omar Pound and Robert Spoo; Charles Olson, *Charles Olson & Ezra Pound. An Encounter at St. Elizabeths*, ed. Catherine Seelye (New York: Grossman Publishers, 1975); E. Fuller Torrey, *The Roots of Treason: Ezra Pound and the Secrets of St. Elizabeths* (Sidgwick & Jackson, 1984); Conrad L. Rushing, '"Mere Words": The Trial of Ezra Pound', *Critical Inquiry* 14 (Autumn 1987) 111–33; Hsiu-ling Lin, 'Reconsidering Ezra Pound's Treason Charge in the Light of American Constitutional Law', *Pai* 34.2–3 (2005) 63–96.
Note: Because this chapter is mainly based on American sources certain words may be spelt after American usage, for example, 'defense', and 'rigor'.

167 **'My instinct'**: EP to Shakespear & Parkyn, 5 Oct. 1945, *EP/DP* 109.
'I dont want a fake': EP TS fragment, n.d., [with notes for *Confucius to Cummings*] (Beinecke). The note continues: 'What KIND of lawyer do you mean?? The kind who said to me in Paris in 1920 whatever: Ahj, awl I'm interested in is bunk... seein' what you can put over.'

Giving Cornell his head

167 **'Poet Ezra Pound'**: *Washington Post* (19 Nov. 1945) 1—from Torrey 178.

168 **'We are proud'**: Dwight D. Eisenhower, XXXIV President of the United States, 'Remarks upon receiving the America's Democratic Legacy Award at a B.nai B'rith Dinner in honor of the 40th anniversary of the Anti-Defamation League, 23 Nov. 1953 (Document Archive, Public Papers of the Presidents, Washington DC).
'scholarly 10 minute': 'Pound Refused Treason Trial Attorney Role', *Washington Post* 20 Nov. 1945—from Torrey 181.
'to keep hell': 'Wallace's Help at Trial Sought by Ezra Pound', Associated Press report, Washington, 19 Nov. [1945], as in *EP/DP* 204.

169 **'to undertake'**: Cornell 4.
'Mr. Cornell': Norman: *Case* 92.
'retained to confer': Cornell 12.
'had a talk': Cornell 13.
'very happy to know': Cornell 13, 182.
'will much prefer': AVM to JL, 9 Oct. 1945, see Cornell 4–6 for full letter.

170 **'some concept'**: EP to AVM, 5 Oct. 1945, see Cornell 7–11 for full letter.
'prepared to read': TSE to EP, 19 Oct. 1945, as in *EP/DP* 86.
'recordings', 'did not sound treasonable': Cornell 1.
'nothing in there': JL to DP, 4 Nov. 1945 (Lilly)—a brief extract from this two-page letter is in *EP/JL* 141–2.
allowed under the First Amendment: Hsiu-ling Lin cites 'the Skokie case (1977)'—see his 'Reconsidering Ezra Pound's Treason Charge in the Light of American Constitutional Law', *Pai* 34.2–3 (2005) 68–9.
'I think you are mistaken': JL to DP, 4 Nov. 1945 (Lilly).

171 **'two hours'**: JC to JL, 21 Nov. 1945, Cornell 13.
'marvelous trip': EP to DP, 20 Nov. [1945], *EP/DP* 207.
'When he arrived': Cornell vii.
'tired and dishevelled': 'Wallace's Help at Trial Sought by Ezra Pound', Associated Press report, Washington, 19 Nov. [1945], as in *EP/DP* 204.
immediately apparent: Cornell 15.
'found the poor devil': JC to JL, 21 Nov. 1945—see Cornell 13–15 for the full letter from which this and the two following paragraphs are drawn.

173 **'to advise properly'**: a formulation from the Report of Psychiatric Examination of EP read in Court 21 Dec. 1945, Cornell 37.
'back in Italy': EP to Archibald MacLeish, 1 Sept. 1956 (Manuscript Division. Library of Congress)—as in Torrey 185.
told Dorothy Pound: 'I expect . . . that after a few months the case will be dropped and he will be set free', JC to DP, 25 Jan. 1946, Cornell 41.

174 **'Cornell has been in'**: EP to DP, 24 Nov. [1945], *EP/DP* 211.
'It was wonderful': Ida B. Mapel to EP, 21 Nov. 1945 (Beinecke)—as in *EP/DP* 210. Pound recalled the visit in 95/645—'Miss Ida by the bars in the jail house'.
'Ezra stood the trip': Ida B. Mapel to DP, 27 Nov. 1945 (Lilly)—as in *EP/DP* 210.
'Wonderful plane trip': EP to IWP, 22 Nov. 1945 (Beinecke).
'Receipt of Property': Justice Dept. Files, US Nat. Arch.

175 **'bull pen'**: JC to Dr Wendell Muncie, 6 Dec. 1945, Cornell 32.
'Five prisoners': Washington DC *Times-Herald*, 25 Nov. 1945, as in *EP/DP* 210.
confined to their cells: see EP to DP, 21 F[eb. 1946], *EP/DP* 279.
'marvelous xperience': EP to Ronald Duncan, 25 Nov. 1945 (Lilly)—given in Carpenter 709, from Duncan's *How to Make Enemies* (Hart Davis, 1964), 111.
'Police reporters': 'Treason', from *Time*, 10 Dec. 1945, in *A Casebook on Ezra Pound*, ed. William Van O'Connor and Edward Stone (New York: Thomas Y. Crowell, 1959), 20.

176 **'from going completely crazy'**: John O'Donnell, 'Capitol Stuff', *New York Daily News*, 28 Nov. 1945, as in *EP/DP* 206.
'succeeded in obtaining release': JC to AVM, 29 Nov. 1945, Cornell 27.
'in a state': JC to Dr Wendell Muncie, 6 Dec. 1945, Cornell 32.
The indictment: from a copy in Justice Dept Files, US Nat. Arch.—also reproduced in Norman: *Case* 77–82.

178 **Justice Department internal assessment**: Dorothy F. Green memorandum of 27 Apr. 1950, quoted in Dorothy F. Green memorandum to William E. Foley, 10 May 1956 (Justice Department Pound file)—as in Torrey 180.
'extreme difficulty would be encountered': Justice Department Office Memorandum, Mr Whearty to Mr McInerney, 6 June 1950 (Justice Dept. Files, US Nat. Arch.)

179 ***Cramer v. United States***: Sieber noted the Supreme Court finding in his Library of Congress 'Selected Facts and Comments' (1958); John F. Graham cited it in his 'Additional Observations on the Ezra Pound Case', 27 July 1972 (unpublished TS, Kenner Archive, HRC); Conrad L. Rushing discussed the case in his '"Mere Words": The Trial of Ezra Pound', *Critical Inquiry* 14 (Autumn 1987) 116–18. In 1948, in the

treason case of Chandler v. United States, Chief Judge Magruder of the US Court of Appeals for the First Circuit in Boston, wrote when confirming the sentence passed in 1947 on Chandler: 'The significant thing is not so much the character of the act which in fact gives aid and comfort to the enemy, but whether the act is done with intent to betray'—see Henderson 232.

180 **'the only treason case'**: JC, 'Brief Concerning Bail', 27 November 1945, Cornell 152.
'found a way': JC to DP, 25 Jan. 1946, Cornell 42.
'damned democracy': Olson 35. On Olson's absorption in Pound see Tom Clark, *Charles Olson: The Allegory of a Poet's Life* (New York: W. W. Norton & Co., 1991), 107ff.
'took him to look older': Olson 35–6.
'Unkempt': *New York Herald Tribune* (28 Nov. 1945)—as in Cornell 24.

181 **'said not a word'**: Cornell 22.
'handed up to Judge Laws': Cornell 22.
'to read the motion papers', 'no objection': Cornell 23.
early trial: see *New York Herald Tribune* (28 Nov. 1945)—as in Cornell 24.
'admitted each and every': *Stars & Stripes* (28 Nov. 1945), cutting in (UK) Nat. Arch. WO 204/12602, item 49.
'I do not defend': JC, 'Affidavit in support of Application for Bail', sworn to in New York 26 Nov. 1945 (Justice Dept. File, US Nat. Arch.). For Cornell's edited version see Cornell 16–22.

183 **'there is no question'**: Archibald MacLeish to Harvey Bundy, 10 Sept. 1943, *Letters of Archibald MacLeish*, ed. R. H. Winnick (Boston: Houghton Mifflin, 1983), 171–2.
in... *PM*: see later under '*The friends and enemies*'.
'It was this streak': JC, 'Affidavit', Cornell 8ff.

185 **'with the recommendation'**: Decision of Chief Justice Bolitha J. Laws, 27 Nov. 1945, Cornell 23.
'Am giving Cornell his head': EP to DP, 29 Nov. [1945], *EP/DP* 213.
'relaxation, recreation': JC to AVM, 29 Nov. 1945, Cornell 26.
nothing to worry about: JC to EP, 29 Nov. 1945 (Beinecke)—noted by Torrey 187.
'Having a rest cure': EP to DP, 8 Dec. [1945], *EP/DP* 215.
'Dear Mother': EP to IWP, 10 Dec. 1945 (Beinecke).
'Is there anything': Theodore Spencer to EP, 10 Dec. 1945 (Beinecke).

186 **'the government accepts'**: JC to Dr Wendell Muncie, 6 Dec. 1945, Cornell 30—for full letter condensing JC's Affidavit and his briefing of Muncie see Cornell 29–34.
'Army doctors': Cornell 35.
inviting Pound's friends: Cornell 34–5. See also Heymann 191.
seeking funds: Cornell 38–9. See also Carpenter 717.
'accrued royalties': JL to DP, 4 Nov. 1945 (Lilly).
and 'hospital treatment': JC to AVM, [December 1945] (Lilly), as in Carpenter 717.
Three psychiatrists: details from Torrey 187–90, and Rushing, '"Mere Words"', *Critical Inquiry* 14 (Autumn 1987) 124–5.

187 **'When the four doctors'**: Cornell 36.
Their brief report: Joseph L. Gilbert, MD, Marion R. King, MD, Wendell Muncie, MD, Winfred Overholser, MD, to Honorable Bolitha J. Laws, 14 Dec. 1945 (Justice Dept. Files, US Nat. Arch.); repr. in Cornell 36–7. The letterhead, lacking from both the copy in US Nat. Arch. and in Cornell, is supplied from a TS copy at Hamilton.

188 **'found Pound astute'**: Stanley I. Kutler, 'This Notorious Patient', *Helix* 13–14 (1983) 135–6. On King's changing his report see also Torrey 192–3. Under cross-examination at the insanity hearing on 13 Feb. 1946, Dr King stated that it had been his early impression 'that he should not be classified as a psychotic or insane person and, therefore, should not be absolved from the necessity of standing trial, but during

subsequent examinations and interviews my view was changed because it became obvious . . . that much of his talk was definitely abnormal' (Norman: *Case* 143).

189 **'damned psychopath'**: Dr Muncie interviewed by Torrey, Sept. 1980 and May 1981, Torrey 193. Details concerning Muncie's change of mind drawn from Torrey 193–4.

'If a person is acquitted': Dr Winfred Overholser to Subcommittee on the Judiciary of the Senate Committee on the District of Colombia, June 1955—as in John F. Graham, 'Additional Observations on the Ezra Pound Case', 27 July 1972, 14 (unpublished TS, Kenner Archive, HRC).

190 **'Very wearing'**: EP to DP, 16 Dec. [1945], *EP/DP* 219.

'Deare[s]ts': EP to [?OR and Mary], 20 Dec. [1945], *EP/DP* 223.

'It appearing': Court order entered by Chief Justice Bolitha J. Laws on 21 Dec. 1945—as recorded p. 3 of a listing (prepared by J. F. Cunningham for Isaiah Matlack, 27 Jan. 1947) of 'authorities and comments which may be cited in opposition to the Motion for Bail filed in behalf of Ezra Pound, under indictment for treason, who is now committed to St. Elizabeths Hospital under a judicial decree of insanity' (Justice Dept. Files, US Nat. Arch.).

'ordered Pound transferred': Cornell 40. The statute referred to (and given in my footnote) is cited on p. 7 of the listing mentioned in the previous note.

191 **'The government's prosecuting attorneys'**: *New York Herald Tribune* (22 Dec. 1945)—as in Cornell 38.

Laughlin wrote to T. S. Eliot: JL to TSE, 23 Dec. 1945 (Lilly). Other excerpts from the letter cited by Gregory Barnhisel, *James Laughlin, New Directions, and the Remaking of Ezra Pound* (Amherst and Boston: University of Massachusetts Press, 2005), 102. In this letter JL noted that 'The law reads that a patient in his situation must pay his own expenses at St Elizabeths', however 'he will try to show that he is penniless, unless this would mean his being put in a ward'.

Lunacy at St Elizabeths

192 **'Criminal No. 76028'**: Winfred Overholser to Clerk of the District Court, 27 Dec. 1945, requesting copies of the indictment and of the psychiatrists' report to the Court (Justice Dept. Files, US Nat. Arch.).

removed late afternoon: Torrey 199.

'inflexible rule': JC to JL, 10 Feb. 1946, Cornell 57–8.

'just under seven thousand': details from Overholser in examination by Cornell at insanity hearing, 13 Feb. 1946, in Norman: *Case* 147.

'place with extensive grounds': Ida B. Mapel to DP, 29 Dec. 1945, as in *EP/DP* 252.

'high penitentiary wall', **'black iron door'**, **'an Indian'**: Olson 37.

193 **examination by Dr Parker**: Case No. 58,102/Notes #1-4, 21 December 1945: Dr M. M. Parker (St Elizabeths Files, 1397a–d, US Nat. Arch.).

194 **'Dearest Child'**: EP to Mary Rudge, n.d. [towards Christmas] (Beinecke).

Olson's Jan. 4 visit: Olson 35–41.

'formally interviewed': Case No. 58,102/Notes #4–5, 4 Jan. 1946: Dr Kavka (St Elizabeths Files, 1397d–e, US Nat. Arch.).

195 **Kavka's 'psychiatric examination'**: reported in 'Ezra Pound, #58,102/Dr. Kavka/ January 24, 1946', 15 TS pages (St Elizabeths Files, 1381a–o, US Nat. Arch.); notes of interviews and 'Retrospective Thoughts' in Kavka's 'Ezra Pound's Personal History: A Transcript, 1946', *Pai* 20.1–2 (1991) 144–85.

'dramatic conversationalist': Kavka's 'Retrospective Thoughts', 'Ezra Pound's Personal History', *Pai* 20.1–2 (1991) 184.

'The birds are chirping': Kavka's transcript, 'Ezra Pound's Personal History', *Pai* 20.1–2 (1991) 153–4.

196 **'easily distractible'**: Kavka's 24 Jan. 1946 report p. 14 (St Elizabeths Files, 1381n, US Nat. Arch.).
'At this point': Kavka's 'Retrospective Thoughts', *Pai* 20.1–2 (1991) 173–4.
'does not appreciate': Kavka's 24 Jan. 1946 report p. 15 (St Elizabeths Files, 1381o, US Nat. Arch.).
'During his stay': Kavka's 24 Jan. 1946 report p. 13 (St Elizabeths Files, 1381m, US Nat. Arch.).
197 **'young doctors'**: EP to JC, n.d. [16 Jan. 1946], Cornell 72.
'No well-devined (sic)**'**: Kavka's 24 Jan. 1946 report p. 14 (St Elizabeths Files, 1381n, US Nat. Arch.).
'Do you believe': Kavka's transcript, 'Ezra Pound's Personal History', *Pai* 20.1–2 (1991) 160.
Rorschach inkblot test: Dr Kendig's 'Rorschach Summary' for 'Ezra Pound, Case #58,102 | January 10, 1946' (St Elizabeths Files, 1385a–b, US Nat. Arch.).
198 **'Olson gt. comfort'**: EP to DP, [6 Jan. 1946], *EP/DP* 235.
'if Cornell or Laughlin': Olson 47.
'relapse': EP to JC, n.d. [16 Jan. 1946], Cornell 71–2.
199 **'I am sorry'**: JC to EP, 4 Feb. 1946—as in Carpenter 733.
'Please everybody': EP to AVM for DP, [12 Jan. 1946], *EP/DP* 239.
'I like getting | letters': EP to EEC, [postmarked 25 Jan. 1946], *EP/EEC* 168.
'great comfort': EP to DP, 31 Jan. 1946, *EP/DP* 255, 257.
'Ezra (Candide)': EP to E. Rudge, 4 Feb. 1946 (Beinecke).
'of Bunting': EP to Ronald Duncan, 24 Jan. 1946, *EP/DP* 249.
'Miss Ida fix'd': EP to DP, [6 Jan. 1946], *EP/DP* 235.
'at the request': Olson 45, 42.
papers not forwarded: mentioned again in EP to E. Rudge, 4 Feb. 1946 (Beinecke). This note included a version of Minor Odes of the Kingdom III.2 (no. 176 in *CA*)—a very different version from the one published in *CA*.
hard going: Olson 46.
'sob stuff': EP to OR, 17 Jan. 1946 (Beinecke).
'much better', **'Possum's "4tets"'**: EP to DP, 31 Jan. 1946, *EP/DP* 255.
200 **'For nearly a year'**: JL to WO, 9 Jan. 1946 (St Elizabeths Files, US Nat. Arch.). As to the length of JL's time at the 'Ezuversity' in 1934, in *EP: Poet II*, 192 and associated note I calculated just 'two or three weeks', evidently in error. Ian S. MacNiven in his new biography of JL writes that he arrived in Rapallo on 4 November, and left before 21 December, a period of six or seven weeks—see MacNiven, *'Literchoor is my Beat': A Life of James Laughlin* (New York: Farrar, Staus and Giroux, 2014), p. 70.
the four books: these would have been *Polite Essays* (Faber 1937, New Directions 1940), *The Fifth Decad of Cantos* (Faber and Farrar & Rinehart 1937, New Directions 1940), *Culture* (Faber and New Directions 1938), *Cantos LII–LXXI* (Faber and New Directions 1940).
'aren't you ever coming': EP to JL, 1 Feb. 1946, *EP/JL* 145.
'This patient appeared': Case No. 58,102/Notes #5, 18 January 1946: Dr Griffin (St Elizabeths Files, 1397d, US Nat. Arch.).
'a foregone conclusion': JC to DP, 25 Jan. 1946, Cornell 41.
201 **'mental torture'**: EP to JC, [27 Jan. 1946], Cornell 75.
'As no one ever listens': EP to JC, 27 Jan. [1946], Cornell 77.
'Zionist program': in 'Ezra Pound, #58,102 | Dr. Kavka | January 24, 1946' p. 8, (St Elizabeths Files, 1381h, US Nat. Arch.). See also EP, 'Ashes of Europe Calling', draft script for radio broadcast [May 1945], *EP/DP* 55: 'I believe in Palestine for the jews as a national home & symbol of jewry—not merely as a real estate speculation—zionism against international finance.'

202 **conference on the 28th**: Dr Duval's 2-page report from which this and the following paragraphs are drawn is 'Ezra Pound | Case #58102 | Notes | January 28, 1946' (St Elizabeths Files, 1396, US Nat. Arch.). Further details from Torrey's telephone interviews with doctors Duval and Dalmau in 1980 and 1981, Torrey 203–4.

203 **'wound so tight'**: Olson was recording his 29 Jan. visit, Olson 61.

'"The pure products"': EP to WCW, [31 Jan. 1946], *EP/WCW* 216. The lines are from WCW's 'To Elsie' in *Spring & All* (1923), reprinted by EP in *Active Anthology* (1933). For an illuminating note on EP's letter see Emily Mitchell Wallace, 'America', *Ezra Pound in Context*, ed. Ira B. Nadel (Cambridge: Cambridge University Press, 2010), 219–20.

'That you're crazy': WCW to EP, 4 Feb. 1946, *EP/WCW* 217.

'Patient was interviewed': Case No. 58,102/Notes #5, 7 Feb. 1946: Dr Overholser (St Elizabeths files, 1397e, US Nat. Arch.).

204 **'"4 medicos"'**: Olson recording his 7 Feb. visit, Olson 68.

'to see Pound', **'very nervous'**: Cornell 42, 44.

'stopped in Dr. Overholser's office': Cornell 42–3.

The hearing

The transcript of the hearing on Wednesday, 13 Feb. 1946, is reproduced in Norman: *Case* 106–80, and also in Cornell 154–215.

205 **'he looked "nice"'**: Ida B. Mapel to DP, 6 Feb. 1946, as in *EP/DP* 292.

'quieted by his lawyer': *Newsweek* (25 Feb. 1946), as in *A Casebook on Ezra Pound* 23.

'Throughout the rest': *New York Herald Tribune* (14 Feb. 1946), as in Cornell 45.

'held his head bowed': Albert Deutsch, 'Pound Gets Unsound', *PM* (14 Feb. 1946), as in Torrey 215.

lines from canto 80: see Cornell 33–4.

216 **'jumped up with alacrity'**: Albert Deutsch, 'Pound Gets Unsound', *PM* (14 Feb. 1946), as in Torrey 217.

'all excited': Olson 77.

'most interesting': reported in Muncie to Overholser, 14 Feb. 1946—as in Carpenter 754.

217 **'how much the unfit plea'**: Olson 77.

so Laughlin told Eliot: JL to TSE, 15 Feb. 1946, as paraphrased in Torrey 217.

witnesses back home to Italy: *New York Herald Tribune* (14 Feb. 1946), as in Cornell 44.

'wanted to go to St. Elizabeths', **'Common sense'**: Conrad L. Rushing, '"Mere Words": The Trial of Ezra Pound', *Critical Inquiry* 14 (Autumn 1987) 125.

'especially the persons', **'The moral insults'**: Thomas S. Szasz, 'There Was No Defense', [review of Cornell's *The Trial of Ezra Pound*], *New York Times Book Review*, [1966]—photocopy of review (Lilly). See also Thomas S. Szasz, *Law, Liberty and Psychiatry: An Enquiry into the Social Uses of Mental Health Practices* (1963), (Syracuse University Press, 1987).

218 **'It was a pleasure'**: JL to WO, 27 Feb. 1946 (St Elizabeths Files, 30, US Nat. Arch.).

'beginning to feel': JL to TSE, 15 Feb. 1946 (HRC), as in Barnhisel, *James Laughlin*, 103.

'his bounce back', **'The sense'**: Olson recording his visit on 14 Feb., Olson 72, 75.

219 **'I long for Pisan paradise'**: EP to DP, 21 [Feb. 1946], *EP/DP* 279.

'the doctors appear': Cornell to A. V. Moore, 4 Mar. 1946, Cornell 47–9—this paragraph and the one following are based on this letter.

The friends and enemies

220 **'I stand for . . . custody'**: Olson was writing after his second visit, 15 Jan. 1946, Olson 46.
'The case for and against Pound': compiled and edited by Charles Norman, *PM* (25 Nov. 1945); reprinted, expanded, as a booklet, *The Case of Ezra Pound* (New York: The Bodley Press, 1948); included as chap. 7, 'Points of View', in Norman: *Case* 83–91. Norman's account of Pound's life and work made up about two-thirds of the *PM* symposium, with the 'comments by noted writers' making up the rest.
221 **'I hope very much'**: Karl Shapiro to Charles Norman, 30 Nov. 1945 (Hamilton). Shapiro withdrew his comment from Norman's later version of the symposium, because he found himself accused of taking the part of Fascism for saying that Pound could only be tried for a political crime and not for his poetry. He had written: 'If Pound were to be tried for his poetry he would come off very well indeed.'
'the one bright star': EP to EEC, 15 Oct. [1946], *EP/EEC* 190.
Edgar A. Guest: (1881–1959), known as 'The People's Poet' for his 11,000 sentimental and optimistic poems syndicated in 300 newspapers and collected in a score of books (*Wikipedia*).
222 **'You make this assumption'**: TSE to Charles Norman, 19 Oct. 1945 (U Penn).
'It seems to me': Wallace Stevens to Charles Norman, 9 Nov. 1945, *Letters of Wallace Stevens*, ed. Holly Stevens (Faber and Faber, 1967), 516–17.
223 **'did not doubt his integrity'**: LZ in Norman, *The Case of Ezra Pound* (1948), 55–7.
225 *New Masses*: the cover of the issue for 25 Dec. 1945 is reproduced in Barnhisel, *James Laughlin*, following p. 101. The quotations from Rosten, Maltz, and Miller are cited by John F. Graham in his 'Additional Observations on the Ezra Pound Case', 27 July 1972 (unpublished TS, Kenner Archive, HRC).
'Pound had been calling': Arthur Miller, *Timebends* (Methuen, 1987), 409–10.
'The mob is blood-hungry': JL to OR, 4 Jan. 1946, as in Conover 169.
'important or dangerous': editorial, *Washington Post* (29 Nov. 1945)—as in Torrey 190.
'assisted the perpetrators': Frank Valery et al. to President Truman, 26 Jan. 1946 (Dept. of Justice file), as in Torrey 190.
226 **'given the guarantee'**, **'his indictment'**: Archibald MacLeish, 'The Venetian Grave' (1974), *Riders on the Earth: Essays & Recollections* (Boston: Houghton Mifflin Company, 1978), 117.
227 **'The vitality of civil'**: Mr Justice Douglas delivering the majority opinion in 'Terminiello v. City of Chicago, 337 US 1 (1949) no. 272', decided 16 May 1949.
'Some of us thought': Archibald MacLeish to Torrey, 1981, Torrey 182.
'Free speech under modern conditions': see above 62–3.
'radio free speech': 74/426.

10. A Year in the Hell Hole

The Loomis family motto is from HLP to EP, 18 Dec. 1913 (Beinecke).

231 *'What the hell is reality'*: JL in conversation with Charles Olson, Olson 77.
a young orderly: paragraph drawn from the account by Ralph Hjelm, as cited in Carroll Terrell, 'St. Elizabeths', *Pai* 3.3 (1974) 368–9.
One of the attendants: the following paragraphs citing the observations of attendants and doctors are drawn from the 'Notes on Ezra Pound, Case No. 58,102, US Prisoner' (St Elizabeths Files, 1397f–j, US Nat. Arch.).
232 **'Only present affliction'**: EP to OR, 23 Mar. [1946] (Beinecke/OR).

234 **'ignorant interns'**: EP correspondence note for MdR, n.d. (Lilly).
'you [can] hv no idea': EP to Ronald Duncan, 1 Mar. 1946, as in editors' note *EP/DP* 290.
'I can't hold two sides': EP to Eileen Lane Kinney, n.d., as in Wilhelm: 1994, 261.
'in serious breakdown': EP to Mary Barnard, 9 Apr. 1946, as in introduction, *EP/DP* 31.
'My Main spring': EP to WCW, 26 [Apr. 1946], *EP/WCW*, 226–7.
235 **'she write him simple things'**: EP to OR, 23 Mar. [1946] (Beinecke/OR). 'Shakleton' is probably Edward, son of Ernest Shackleton, the Antarctic explorer. Edward Shackleton led an expedition to Ellesmere Land in the Canadian Arctic in 1934–5, and published *Arctic Journeys* in 1937. The 'little white Ogden series' probably 'Psyche Miniatures', general editor C. K. Ogden.
'My status', 'I suffer': EP to OR, 8 Apr. [1946] (Beinecke/OR).
236 **'Basso inferno'**: EP to MdR, 17 June [1946] (Beinecke).
'I eat wot I get': EP to Viola Baxter Jordan, n.d. (Beinecke).
'local bulletin': EP to OR, 5 July [1946] (Beinecke/OR).
'Today red letter': EP to OR, 3 June [1946] (Beinecke/OR).
'One of the worst things': EP, 'A Letter by Ezra Pound', to unidentified correspondent, 5 July 1957, from *Way Out* XIX.1 (1963) 19, in *P&P* IX, 359.
'view of Potomac': EP to DP, 21 Feb. [1946], *EP/DP* 279.
'dry moat of the dungeon': EP to MdR, 20 Mar. [1946] (Beinecke).
'to pierce the wall': EP to MdR, 24 Mar. [1946] (Beinecke). Also EP to DP, 30 Mar. [1946], *EP/DP* 303.
'to think of some world outside': EP to Nancy Cunard, 2 June 1946 (HRC).
'to git my MIND out': EP to EEC, 10 July [1946], *EP/EEC* 181.
'I like to get letters': EP to WL, 4 Mar. [1948], *EP/WL* 241.
'Gtst difficulty': EP to D. D. Paige, as in editorial note, *EP/DP* 226.
a place for news to come into: EP to VBJ, 20 July [1948] (Beinecke).
'Keep St Amb': EP to OR, 25 Feb. [1946] (Beinecke/OR).
'yes if he had the wings': EP to OR, 28 Mar. [1946] (Beinecke/OR)—cf. Psalm 55.
237 **'Dearest Child'**: EP to MdR, 28 Feb. [1946] (Beinecke)—see 74/444.
'I have no say': EP to OR, 8 Apr. [1946] (Beinecke/OR).
'He would like to see': EP to OR, [Mar./Apr. 1946?] (Beinecke/OR).
'he better not': EP to OR, 5 Apr. [1946] (Beinecke/OR).
'he would like to see her': EP to OR, [Mar. 1946?] (Beinecke/OR).
'God Damn': EP to OR, [Aug. 1946] (Beinecke/OR).
'SHE damn well': EP to OR, 14 Oct. [1946] (Beinecke/OR).
238 **'I am quite intent'**: DP to EP, 19 Dec. 1945, *EP/DP* 221.
'I don't know how': EP to DP, 6 Feb. [1946], *EP/DP* 261.
'Wd you go via England?': EP to DP, 14 Feb. [1946], *EP/DP* 267.
'D.P. a blessing': EP to MdR, 26 Feb. 1956 (Beinecke).
'D. attendin to practical': EP to IWP, 'sometime in May' [1947] (Beinecke).
'full of filial piety': DP to EP, enclosed in JC to EP, 25 Jan. 1946, *EP/DP* 249. See also DP to EP, 23 Jan. 1946, *EP/DP* 247.
she sent him a poem: DP to EP, 7 Apr. 1946, *EP/DP* 311.
'Hope she hit bottom': EP to DP, 23 May [1946], *EP/DP* 343.
'that perpetual mosquito': DP to EP, 29 Jan. 1946, *EP/DP* 254.
'with Sigª Corradi', 'has always said': DP to EP, 19 Dec. 1945, *EP/DP* 221.
239 **clear headed**: OR wrote to Ronald Duncan, 16 Mar. 1948: 'she was a very fine-spirited lady & not ga ga—as Jas had been led to infer' (HRC).
'wanted at all costs': MdR, *Discretions* 265.
'"its an ill wind"': DP to EP, 20 May 1946, *EP/DP* 337.
'Very very sorry': EP to IWP, [after 20 May 1946] (Beinecke).

'terminated the lease': MdR, 'Isabel and Homer: A Double Memoir', *EP/Parents* xxii.
'to have passage': IWP to MdR, [early 1947], as in MdR, 'Isabel and Homer: A Double Memoir', *EP/Parents* xxiii.
'He has such charm': paragraph drawn from Olson 87–91.

240 **'spent mostly with Cornell'**: this and other details in DP to AVM, [11 July 1946], *EP/DP* 363.
would rent the attic: see DP to OSP, Sept. 1946 (Hamilton).
After her 15 minutes: paragraph drawn from DP to AVM, [11 July 1946], *EP/DP* 363; DP to JL, 11 July and 14 July 1946, *EP/JL* 149, 150; DP to JC, 14 July 1946, Cornell 51–2.
'would be much better off': JC to DP, 15 July 1946, Cornell 52–3.

241 **'very anxious'**, and **'What we concluded'**: JL to EEC, 7 June 1946, and JL to EEC, n.d., as in editorial note, *EP/EEC* 179.
'Wd like yr. version': EP to EEC, 27 June [1946], *EP/EEC* 179.
'I gather': EEC to EP, [8 July 1946], *EP/EEC* 180.
he wrote to Dorothy: TSE to DP, [July 1946] (HRC).
'How can I make you understand': DP to Ronald Duncan, 9 Aug. [1946] (HRC).
'really very much shattered': DP to Ronald Duncan, 23 Aug. [1946] (HRC).

242 **'put aside and forgotten'**: DP to JC, 17 July 1946, Cornell 53.
'how far you understand the case': DP to JC, 14 July 1946, Cornell 51.
'I think your husband': JC to DP, 15 July 1946, Cornell 53.
'something to reassure': DP to JC, 17 July 1946, Cornell 53.
'most anxious to see Dr. Overholser': DP to JC, 17 July 1946, Cornell 53.
'your benevolence': DP to WO, 8 Aug, [1946] (St Elizabeths Files 85a–b, US Nat. Arch.).
'working little at a time': DP to Joseph Darling Ibbotson, 24 July 1946 (Hamilton).
'It works for a few minutes': EP to Ibbotson, 27 July [1946], *EP/Ibb* 117.
twenty stenographer's notebooks: notebooks numbered 40–59 in Mary de Rachewiltz, *A Catalogue of the Poetry Notebooks of Ezra Pound* (New Haven: Yale University Library, 1980).
'It'll do you for a prayer': EP to MdR, 11 June [1946] (Beinecke). The ode is numbered 289 in the standard arrangement of the Book of Odes.

243 **'saved my mind'**: EP TS note: '8 Jan. '59. Rouse saved my life. i.e. he sent me the text of the Odes that saved my mind in the hell hole.' Rouse had given him, *c.* Dec. 1937, a copy of Legge's *The Book of Poetry* (Shanghai: Chinese Book Company)—a pirated edition, like the copy of the Four Books EP had with him in the DTC. (Thanks to Leah Flack for this information and for copies of EP's note and letter to Rouse.) Pound had a copy of the Odes in the DTC—see *EP/DP* 123—probably the one Rouse had given him. MM sent EP Legge's *Sacred Books of China*, containing his selective treatment of the Odes as religious verse, and the *Yi King*, 30 Aug. 1946—details from inscription in the book now in HRC.
'a penciled scrawl': paragraph drawn from Mary Barnard's record made in March and April 1946, as in her *Assault on Mount Helicon: A Literary Memoir* (Berkeley: University of California Press, 1984), 231–5.
for Olson he had just written to Eliot about... *Call Me Ishmael*: on this see Olson 75, 85.

244 **'doesn't sit and worry'**: DP to Ronald Duncan, 9 Aug. [1946] (HRC).
'not for ME': EP note on letter to him from Clara Studer dated 'Sunday 20th' [1946] (Lilly).
'dont Fox or anyone': EP to EEC, 6 Mar. [1946], *EP/EEC* 170.
He told Williams: see for instance the exchange between EP and WCW in July and August 1946, *EP/WCW* 232–6.
'He's never got over': WCW to JL, 17 July 1946, *WCW/JL* 127.

'still hard for me': EP to MdR, 18 Mar. [1946] (Beinecke).
'I am now convinced': MdR to EP, [Feb. or early Mar. 1946], as in Conover, 170.
'Will you send her': EP to JL, 19 Mar. 1946, *EP/JL* 147.
'The Production of Maple Sirup': enclosed in EP to MdR, 10 Apr. [1946], (Beinecke).
'will put you through': EP to MdR, 24 Apr. [1946] (Beinecke).
'a hillside where trees': EP to MdR, 7 May [1946] (Beinecke).
245 ***acero* in the valleys**: EP to MdR, [Jan. 1947] (Beinecke)—*acero*, maple.
the brilliant boy, '"Make sure he is healthy"': see MdR, *Discretions* 261–71.
'a *centro culturale*': EP to MdR, 10 Nov. [1946] (Beinecke).
'the best musician': EP to MdR,11 Dec. [1946] (Beinecke).
'majolica stoves': MdR, *Discretions* 275.
'You give me plenty': EP to MdR, 4 Jan. [1947] (Beinecke).
'Kung-fu-tseu lacked': EP to OR, 2 June [1946] (Beinecke/OR).
'Kung *and* Eleusis': see 52/258 and 53/272—emphasis added.
'no Romaunt': EP to VJB, n.d. (Beinecke).
246 **'just the same old Ezra'**: see p. 191 above.
'by reason of your mental condition': JC to EP, 1 Mar. 1946 (Lilly)—as in Carpenter 757.
'asked Dr. Overholser': Cornell 80.
'Would it be suitable': EP to JC, 12 Mar. [1946], reproduced in Cornell 81.
'Should I make power': EP to AVM, Mar. 1946, as in Carpenter 757.
'Will send the pwr': EP to JC, 20 Mar. [1946], reproduced in Cornell 83.
'extraordinary clarity of mind': JC to WO, 2 Apr. 1946, as in Carpenter 757–8.
'Next point': EP to JC, 20 Mar. [1946], reproduced in Cornell 83.
'Dear JC/': EP to JC, 16 Apr. [1946], reproduced in Cornell 85.
247 **'a little suspicious'**: JC to AVM, 16 Apr. 1946 (Lilly)—as in Carpenter 758.
'guardian of her husband's estate': JC to AVM, 16 Apr. 1946 (Lilly).
'an insane person should be asked': DP to WO, 12 Sept. 1946, as in Carpenter 767.
'had arranged for the appointment': Cornell 124.
'no *persona giuridica*': EP to MdR, 16 Feb. [1947] (Beinecke).
'please send $100': EP to JC, 26 Feb. [1946] (HRC).
'I want her to get used': EP to JC, 8 Mar. [1946] (HRC).
'at your request': JC to EP, 11 Mar. 1946 (Lilly).
'inconvenience of being a lunatic': EP to MdR, 17 Feb. [1948] (Beinecke).
248 **'suspension of civil rights'**: WO, *The Psychiatrist and the Law* (New York: Harcourt, Brace and Company, 1953), 89.
Pound believed: EP wrote '"committee" brought up by British lawyer' in EP to MdR, 16 Feb. [1947] (Beinecke).
'Whether he is legally competent': JC to AVM, 16 Apr. 1946 (Lilly), as in Carpenter 758.
Laughlin and Cornell had hoped: see p. 191 above.
249 **'They are going to think'**: JL to EP, [? Mar. 1949] (Lilly). On this matter see Barnhisel, *James Laughlin*, 132–5, and *EP/JL* 182–4.
'a moral position': see JL to EP, 28 Mar. 1949, *EP/JL* 184.
a feared and powerful public perception: Some whose views I respect would maintain that the prime cause of the public hostility to Pound was not his anti-Semitism but his perceived disloyalty to the USA in time of war. I can only say that the evidence available to me points the other way. Then there are those who would go further and maintain that such was the public outrage on account of that perception of disloyalty that, regardless of the strict requirements of the law, a jury would certainly have found him guilty of treason. The case of 'Tokyo Rose' makes me hesitate to dismiss that as simple speculation. But those who hold this latter view tend also to argue that

Laughlin's and Cornell's cautionary strategy saved Pound from certain execution, and here one must recall that in fact not one US citizen convicted of treason was executed. If convicted Pound would more likely have served ten years in a federal prison, not thirteen in St Elizabeths.

privately, Laughlin accepted: see JL to EP, 28 Mar. 1949, *EP/JL* 184.

250 **'Except as to real property'**: JC to AVM, 20 July 1946 (Lilly).

'It is unfortunate if': JC to AVM, 5 Aug. 1946 (Lilly).

'By English law': AVM to JC, 9 Aug. 1946 (Lilly).

'would be shared by': JC to AVM, 12 Aug. 1946 (Lilly).

Pound had made a will: see Figure 1.

to be his literary executor: MdR refers to this obliquely in *Discretions* 261.

sale of archives: in 1964 negotiations for the sale of the archive to Yale were ongoing.

Doubts would be raised: according to Donald Gallup the will, to meet the requirements of Italian law, should have been handwritten, not typed; and further, it should have been filed with an Italian court—see his *Pigeons on the Granite* (New Haven: The Beinecke Rare Book & Manuscript Library, Yale University, 1988), 197.

the New Critics: for a useful discussion of this background and its relevance see chaps. 3 and 4 in Barnhisel, *James Laughlin*.

'Honest criticism', 'the more perfect the artist': T. S. Eliot, 'Tradition & the Individual Talent' (1919), *Selected Essays* (Faber & Faber, 1951), 17, 18.

the essay which Eliot wrote: TSE, 'Ezra Pound', *Poetry* LXVIII (Sept. 1946) 326–38, reprinted in *Ezra Pound: A Collection of Essays Edited by Peter Russell to be Presented to Ezra Pound on his Sixty-Fifth Birthday* (Peter Nevill Limited, 1951), 25–36.

251 **'I don't know what you suppose'**: DP to WCW, 29 Aug. 1946, *EP/WCW* 239.

'That Ezra is guilty': WCW to DP, 30 Aug. 1946, *EP/WCW* 240.

'the mere fact': WCW to EP, 29 Mar. 1946, *EP/WCW* 218.

broken 'with old Ezra finally': WCW to JL, 28 Dec. 1946, *WCW/JL* 131.

252 **'Dear Mr President'**: WCW to Honorable Harry S. Truman, President of the United States, New Year's Eve 1946 (St Elizabeths Files, 120, US Nat. Arch.).

'Mr. Pound is certainly': WO to WCW, 10 Jan. 1947, as in Carpenter 770.

'it would break me up': WCW to EP, 6 Apr. 1946, *EP/WCW* 223.

Bill Bird: paragraph drawn from Bill Bird to DP, 12 Nov. 1946 (Lilly).

253 **a long letter**: Nancy Cunard to EP, 11 June 1946 (Beinecke).

'too weak to write': EP, pencil note, n.d. (Lilly, box 13).

'My dear N.': EP to Nancy Cunard, 1 Aug. [1946] (HRC).

both would relent: see James J. Wilhelm, 'Nancy Cunard: A Sometime Flame, a Stalwart Friend', *Pai* 19.1–2 (1990) 202–21. Wilhelm gives much of NC's long letter of 11 June.

254 **a 'primary generative force'**: Robert Duncan, 'The H.D. Book' I.6.(2), in *Caterpillar* 2 (Jan. 1968), and *The H.D. Book* (Berkeley: University of California Press, 2011), 183.

'For my generation': Robert Creeley, 'A Note on Ezra Pound' (1965), *A Quick Graph: Collected Notes & Essays* (San Francisco: Four Seasons Foundation, 1970), 95, 96. See also Duncan's reflections on visiting Pound in 1948, in *A Great Admiration: HD/Robert Duncan Correspondence 1950–1961*, ed. Robert J. Bertholf (Venice, Calif.: The Lapis Press, 1992), 3–4, 36–9.

'A Canto for Ezra Pound': TS, 6 pages, with internal indications of authorship by Robert Duncan and Jack Spicer, Pound Misc. folder as 'unidentified', 27 Dec. 1946 (HRC).

'I go to that work': Robert Creeley, 'A Letter to the Editor of Goad' (1951–2), *A Quick Graph*, 93.

255 **'Now that the elections'**: JC to EP, 7 Nov. 1946, Cornell 54.

'Motion for Bail': see Cornell 55–7.

256 **'a number of doctors'**: Albert Deutsch, 'Ezra Pound, Turncoat Poet, Seeks Release from Federal Mental Hospital', *PM* (28 Jan. 1947), as in Torrey 232.

257 **The Justice Department were well armed**: copies of the twelve closely typed pages of 'authorities and comments' prepared for Isaiah Matlack by J. F. Cunningham, and the 'Governments Reply in Opposition to Motion for Bail', are among the St Elizabeths Files, numbered 140 and 139 (US Nat. Arch.).

258 **'Dear J'**: JC to JL, 10 Feb. 1947, Cornell 57.
Overholser memorandum: WO, 'Memorandum', 'Notes on Ezra Pound, Case No. 58,102, US Prisoner' (St Elizabeths Files, 13971, US Nat. Arch.).

259 **'to get him moved'**: see 240 above.
'I am sure the next step': TSE to DP, 26 Feb. 1947 (Lilly).

11. Resilience, 1947–50

Histrionics

260 **'By direction'**: Case No. 58,102/Notes #13, 3 Feb. 1947: Dr Cruvant (St Elizabeths Files, 1397m, US Nat. Arch.).
'He has more freedom': DP to JL, 11 Feb. 1947, *EP/JL* 156.
'Since his transfer': Case No. 58,102/Notes #13, 28 March 1947: Dr Keeney (St Elizabeths Files, 1397m, US Nat. Arch.).
'His insight and judgment': Case No. 58,102/Notes . . . , 30 Sept. 1948: Dr Gresser (St Elizabeths Files, 1399d, US Nat. Arch.).
'No abnormal mental trends': Case No. 58,102/Notes, 29 July 1949: Dr Gonzalez (St Elizabeths Files, 1400, US Nat. Arch.).
'quite obvious': Case No. 58,102/Notes #13, 28 Mar. 1947: Dr Keeney (St Elizabeths Files, 1397m, US Nat. Arch.).
'"people who are children"': Case No. 58,102/Notes, 12 Mar. 1948: Dr Keeney (St Elizabeths Files, 1399a, US Nat. Arch.).

261 **to put on a shirt**: Case No. 58,102/Notes, 17 Oct. 1947: Dr Granatir (St Elizabeths Files, 1398a, US Nat. Arch.).
'not particularly neatly attired': Case No. 58,102/Notes, 18 Mar. 1949: Dr Segal (St Elizabeths Files, 1399e, US Nat. Arch.).
'This patient blustered': Dr Segal (St Elizabeths Files, 1399e, US Nat. Arch.).
his room was larger: Reck, who does get some details wrong, but who did visit when EP was in Chestnut Ward, wrote that 'His cubicle was doorless'—see Reck 71.
'Patient does no work': #58102/Ward Notes, Chestnut, 6-16-48/Small (St Elizabeths Files, 1276, US Nat. Arch.).
'He is very courteous': #58102/Ward Notes, Chestnut, 7-15-48/H. S. Grant (St Elizabeths Files, 1277, US Nat. Arch.).

262 **'This patient was out for a walk'**: #58102/Ward Notes, Chestnut, 12-2-48/J. M. Langford (St Elizabeths Files, 1279, US Nat. Arch.).
'Actually appears quite vigorous': Case No. 58,102/Notes . . . , 3 Dec. 1948: Dr Saul Brown (St Elizabeths Files, 1399d, US Nat. Arch.).
'Patient refused': #58102/Ward Notes, Chestnut, 12-6-48/J. M. Langford (St Elizabeths Files, 1279, US Nat. Arch.).
'Patient was out walking': #58102/Ward Notes, Chestnut, 12-7-48/J. M. Langford (St Elizabeths Files, 1279, US Nat. Arch.).
'walking parties': Office Memorandum, Dr Cruvant to WO, 2 Dec. 1948 (St Elizabeths Files, 236, US Nat. Arch.).
ordinarily catatonic: see Guy Davenport, 'Civilization and its Opposite in the 1940s', *The Hunter Gracchus* (Washington, DC: Counterpoint, 1996), 96.

'complained to the examiner': Case No. 58,102/Notes, 1 June 1948: Dr Johan (St Elizabeths Files, 1399b–c, US Nat. Arch.).
'Mr Pound was visited': #58102/Ward Notes, Chestnut, 6-19-48/J. M. Langford (St Elizabeths Files, 1276, US Nat. Arch.).
'only allowed out of doors': DP to TSE, as reported by TSE in letter to Cornell, 24 Nov. 1948, as copied in Norman: 1960 436–7.
'It seems to me': TSE to Cornell, 24 Nov. 1948, as copied in Norman: 1960 436–7.
one of the worst things: EP, 'A Letter by Ezra Pound', written 5 July 1957, *Way Out* XIX.1 (Jan. 1963) 19, in *P&P* IX, 359.
263 **'I doubt very much'**: Office Memorandum, Dr Cruvant to WO, 2 Dec. 1948 (St Elizabeths Files, 236, US Nat. Arch.).
'I have some hesitation': WO to JC, 6 Dec. 1948 (St Elizabeths Files, 237, US Nat. Arch.), reproduced in Norman: 1960 437–8.
'Mr. Pound has the following privileges': #58102/Ward Notes, Chestnut, 12 July 1949, Earl A. Hingman (St Elizabeths Files, 1282, US Nat. Arch.).
'They now let me out': EP to MdR, 6 Sept. 1949 (Beinecke).
264 **'looking very well'**: MB to OR, 5 Jan. 1950, Conover 189—and see Barnard 264–7 for an account of her visit in Sept. 1949.

'a awful lot of company'

'O.K. & friend': EP note on Paul Blackburn to WO, 18 Jan. 1951 (St Elizabeths Files, 351, US Nat. Arch.).
'D.P. regrets': note on Allen Ginsberg to EP, 30 May 1952 (Pound II, Box 22, Lilly) – and see Wilhelm: 1994, 291.
'Ezra Pound's Company': detail from Hugh Kenner, 'Preface to the Bison Book Edition Retrospect: 1985', *The Poetry of Ezra Pound* (Lincoln: University of Nebraska Press, 1985), 4. Details in this paragraph drawn from Kenner's preface; and from David Rattray, 'Weekend with Ezra Pound', *The Nation* CLXXXV (16 Nov. 1957) 343–5—as in *Casebook* 104–17; Carroll F. Terrell, 'St. Elizabeths', *Pai* 3.3 (1974) 363–79; Ronald Duncan, *How to Make Enemies* (Rupert Hart-Davis, 1968), 320–3, as in Carpenter 775–7; Reck 75–7; Thomas Cole, 'Ezra Pound and *Imagi*', *Pai* 16.3 (1987) 55–8.
treated by ECT or lobotomy: at that time ECT and prefrontal lobotomy were commonly used as forms of 'treatment and control', in St Elizabeths as elsewhere. For the only indication known to me that Pound was subjected to ECT see ahead, note to p. 502,'an episode'.
in the summer: details from Terrell, 'St. Elizabeths', *Pai* 3.3 (1974) 363–4; Reck 76; Davenport, 'Civilization and its Opposite in the 1940s', *The Hunter Gracchus* 96–7; Olson 93; Cole, 'Ezra Pound and *Imagi*', *Pai* 16.3, 57–8.
265 **her air of Henley**: Ronald Duncan, *How to Make Enemies*, as in Carpenter 776.
a British resonance: Reck 76.
'tall, rather slender': Barnard 254–5.
'a tall ascetic woman': WCW, *The Autobiography of William Carlos Williams* (1951) (MacGibbon & Kee. 1968), 336.
'Mrs Pound's selfless aid': Marianne Moore note for Harry Meacham, 2 Feb. 1967 (Pound II, Box 11, Lilly).
could not speak freely: see MB to OR, 5 Jan. 1950, in Conover 189, and Barnard 265.
'anglo-saxon fear': Olson 93.
'a stately figure in a large hat': Barnard 267.
unreadable fustian: see *GK* 92–3.

'lifting his legs': Davenport, 'Civilization and its Opposite in the 1940s', *The Hunter Gracchus* 96.
foolish political infatuations: Conrad Aiken in *PM* (25 Nov. 1945), as in Norman: *Case* 89–90.
'idée fixe', **'had become used to humouring'**: Conrad Aiken to Charles Norman, Norman: 1960, 442.
'Visits to St. Elizabeths [1950]': Elizabeth Bishop, *Complete Poems* (Chatto & Windus, 1991), 133–5. For Lowell's 'reverential mockery' see Robert Lowell to Elizabeth Bishop, 11 Mar. 1970, *The Letters of Robert Lowell*, ed. Saskia Hamilton (New York: Farrar, Straus and Giroux, 2005), 529.
266 **'"the same great, booming boy"'**: Witter Bynner as in Norman: 1960 442. Wilhelm: 1994, 272 gives the date of the visit as 'before January 8, 1947'.
'from my first meeting': Witter Bynner to Dr Robert M. Duncan, 18 July 1949 (copy in Kenner Archive, HRC).
'than William Blake': Witter Bynner to Herbert Brownell, 13 Jan. 1958, as in Meacham 195.
'He's just like his later prose': Robert Lowell to Gertrude Buckman, 1 Oct. [1947], *The Letters of Robert Lowell*, 72.
He 'talked brilliantly': MM to Charles Norman, Norman: 1960, 440.
267 **'"KICK OUT"'**: EP, according to MM to Charles Norman, Norman: 1960, 440.
'I am quite shaken': MM to EP, 30 July 1949, *Selected Letters of Marianne Moore*, ed. Bonnie Costello with Celeste Goodridge and Cristanne Miller (Faber & Faber, 1998), 473.
'cumulative impression': MM note for Meacham, 2 Feb. 1967 (Pound II, Box 11, Lilly).
'the complete incongruity': MB, Barnard 253–4, 256.
'you & Dorothy': EEC to EP, [2 June 1949], *EP/EEC* 246.
'appalled at American ignorance': Davenport, 'Civilization and its Opposite in the 1940s', *The Hunter Gracchus* 97.
'What came through': Hugh Kenner, 'Preface', *The Poetry of Ezra Pound* (1985), 3–4.
268 **'did most of the talking'**: Thomas Cole, 'Ezra Pound and *Imagi*', *Pai* 16.3 (1987) 55–7.
'More useful at moment', 'Suggest that he do 4 pp. monthly': notes in DP's hand of EP's directions for Simpson, n.d., [1947, after 18 Sept.] (Lilly).
'only the poets': Huntington Cairns' notes (Library of Congress), as in Carpenter 796—for further notes of EP/Cairns conversations see Carpenter 794–8.
269 **'Mr. Pound is frequently visited', 'I may say that I have talked'**: WO to Alexander M. Campbell, Asst. Attorney General, US Department of Justice, 23 Nov. 1948 (St Elizabeths Files, 224, US Nat. Arch.).
'To me Ezra Pound': WCW to WO, 24 Oct. 1947 (St Elizabeths Files, 173, US Nat. Arch.).
'It is my personal opinion': WO to Alexander M. Campbell, 23 Nov. 1948 (St Elizabeths Files, 224, US Nat. Arch.).

No release

269 **'Dorothy Pound, as Committee'**: see Cornell 61–6 for full Petition.
270 **'because of the novelty'**: JC to DP, 15 Dec. 1947, Cornell 58–9.
'should ultimately secure': JC to DP, 4 Mar. 1948, Cornell 66–7.
Dorothy's response: DP to JC, 13 Mar. 1948, Cornell 67—se also Cornell 60–1.
'I must ask you to withdraw': DP to JC, 28 Mar. 1948 (Lilly).
'definite and final': JC to DP, 30 Mar. 1948 (Lilly).

'Your husband said yesterday': JC to DP, 15 Dec. 1947, Cornell 59.
'Ezra should be gotten out of custody': DP to JC, 18 Dec. 1947, Cornell 59.
271 **'if they could not go back to Italy'**: EP's attitude as reported by JC, Cornell 61.
'Ezra for the moment': JL to OR, 30 Nov. 1948, as in Conover 187.
'in the "derelict" ward': from John Berryman's account of his visit on 3 Nov. 1948, as in John Haffenden, *The Life of John Berryman* (Ark Paperbacks, 1983), 214.
'I fear your father': TSE to MdR in conversation, April or May 1948, *Discretions* 289.
'My husband is not fit': DP to JC, 13 Mar. 1948, Cornell 67. Re EP's 'nerves' in 1946 see p. 241 above.
'she prefers the present': JC to AVM, 3 May 1957 (Lilly).
'is anything being DONE?': TSE to DP, 7 Feb. 1948 (Lilly).
the one effective argument for his release: Thurman Arnold, when he investigated EP's case in 1958, found that 'Pound could have been released many years ago by habeas corpus, under decisions of the Ninth and Tenth Circuits and the *Greenwood* case [1956] in the Supreme Court of the United States, because (1) he was incurably insane and could never be brought to trial and (2) he was harmless to himself and society'—from Thurman Arnold to American Civil Liberties Union, *Selections from the Letters and Legal Papers of Thurman Arnold* (Washington: D. C. Merkle Press, 1961), 39–41, as in Wendy Flory, *The American Ezra Pound* (New Haven: Yale University Press, 1989), 185. The decision in the *Greenwood* case did not directly rule on the habeas corpus issue, but could be held to have opened the way for an appeal to be made on those grounds. However, in a later decision handed down on 7 June 1972, in the case of *Jackson v. Indiana* 406 U.S. 715, the US Supreme Court ruled, under the heading of 'DUE PROCESS', that 'indefinite commitment of a criminal defendant solely on account of his incompetency to stand trial does not square with the Fourteenth Amendment's guarantee of due process... because the federal statutes have been construed to require that a mentally incompetent defendant must also be found "dangerous" before he can be committed indefinitely'. The Court noted a District Court's decision in 1970 when 'an 86-year-old defendant committed for nearly 20 years as incompetent to stand trial on state murder and kidnapping charges applied for federal habeas corpus. He had been found "not dangerous"', and the District Court 'held that petitioner's incarceration in an institution for the criminally insane constituted cruel and unusual punishment, and that the "shocking circumstances" of his commitment violated the Due Process Clause. The court quoted approvingly the language of [another case] concerning the "substantial injustice in keeping an unconvicted person in custody to await trial where it is plainly evident his mental condition will not permit trial within a reasonable period of time".'

The question of whether or not Pound was dangerous was not addressed in the hearings which led to his committal to St Elizabeths. However, in the brief opposing Cornell's Motion for Bail prepared for Mr Matlack by J. F. Cunningham in January 1947, a hitherto unmentioned 'separate report' by Dr King is cited, as if to deal with the question if it were to be raised.. No date is given for this report. Writing as Medical Director, Bureau of Prisons, Dr King commented, 'provisions for adequate treatment and control to prevent him from becoming a further menace to himself and others are indicated'.

In his Motion for Bail in January 1947—which was, of course, summarily dismissed without arguments being heard—Cornell did claim that 'the defendant is not violent, does not require close confinement and the public safety would not be impaired if he were allowed the degree of liberty which a private sanatorium permits for patients who are mildly insane'. His motion rested, however, not upon that claim, but upon the argument that since Pound could not be tried he should be presumed innocent, and therefore should not be subjected to life imprisonment. The law did not provide, he stated, for someone in Pound's situation, indicted, but unable to be tried due to insanity, and not in need of permanent hospitalization. There, in the light of the *Greenwood* and later cases, he was evidently in error. In the Petition for Writ of Habeas Corpus in February 1948 Cornell repeated this error. And yet, puzzlingly, in one paragraph of the Petition he noted that the law did in fact provide that a person in Pound's situation might properly be held in continued confinement only if '(1) there is an indictment pending against him under which he may be brought to trial if and when he recovers his sanity, or (2) his mental condition is such that he requires hospitalization, or (3) it would be dangerous to the public safety for him to remain at liberty'. In that paragraph Cornell asserted that 'if his own and the public welfare does not require it, he may not be deprived of his liberty by confinement in an institution'—exactly the position which the Supreme Court would uphold in *Greenwood* and in *Jackson v. Indiana.* Dorothy Pound's understanding at the time was that the Petition was seeking Pound's release on the ground that he was incurable but not dangerous (DP to OSP, 12 Feb 1948 (Hamilton/OSP).) Cornell, however, pressed on to rest his case once again upon the 'fundamental principle of law that every person is presumed to be innocent until he has been found guilty, and also that no person may be imprisoned until his guilt has been determined by due process of law'—an excessively theoretical argument which the Justice Department was ready to knock down on practical grounds. One can't be sure how Cornell would have argued the Petition for Habeas Corpus if it had been carried to the higher courts, but it does appear that he had failed to perceive (as Eliot apparently could see already in 1948) that if Pound were not to be 'tried with a good prospect of being acquitted', then the effective argument for his release had to be that he was 'permanently incapable but not dangerous'.

'Don't you want him to try': JL to EP, 24 June 1948 (Lilly).

272 **'does EP think'**: JL to DP, 10 Nov. 1948 (Lilly).

'had a v. good conference': JL to EP, 6 Dec. 1948 (Lilly).

'Pound had refused to entertain': WCW, *The Autobiography of William Carlos Williams* (MacGibbon & Kee, 1968), 340–1.

'I don't want to get out to be assassinated': EP as recorded by Ronald Duncan in his *How to Make Enemies* (1968), as in Carpenter 776.

his first visit to Pound: some details from WCW to DP, 21 Oct. 1947, *EP/WCW* 247, and from EP TS note for DP to WCW, [Oct. 1947], in correspondence notes for DP (Pound MSS II, Lilly). See also Lowell to WCW, [late Sept. 1947], *Letters of Robert Lowell* (2005) 71, 690.

Williams did write: WCW to WO, 24 Oct. 1947 (St Elizabeths Files, 173, US Nat. Arch.).

'so apparently unmoved': WCW, *Autobiography* (1968) 342–3.

a little more intelligence: reported by WL to TSE, 23 Nov. 1953 (Lilly).

'"for his own sake"': WL to D. D. Paige, 25 Oct. 1948, courtesy of Mrs Paula Paige. In *The Letters of Wyndham Lewis*, ed. W. K. Rose (Methuen & Co Ltd, 1963), 468, 467, the names are omitted, presumably on the ground that 'they might cause embarrassment or invite libel action' (see Rose's introduction p. xxi).

273 **'E.P.'s obstreperous intractableness'**: WL to D. D. Paige, 12 Nov. 1948, *The Letters of Wyndham Lewis*, 474. Lewis commented on Paige's petition in Oct. and Nov. 1948 in three letters included in Rose's edition.

'Is there hope of his receiving a pardon?': WL to DP, 9 Apr. 1947 (Lilly).

'at least 3 letters a week': OR to Ronald Duncan, 16 Mar. 1948 (HRC).

'and drive through Laughlin's': Ronald Duncan to OR, 15 May 1948, as in Conover 180.

'Yesdy. Ez. said': DP to JL, 16 Sept. 1947, *EP/JL* 167.

274 **a lightning rod**: on 25 May 1949 OR wrote to TSE about Paige's editing of EP's letters, 'Could not E's enemies, by simply quoting sentences, apart from context, of letters not in the coll. but to which they have access, discredit the coll. by making it appear an attempt at white wash?... I feel that something in the nature of a lightning rod included in the coll. would be good tactics' (Beinecke).

'better not to distribute in States': JC as reported in OR to TSE, 4 May 1948 (Beinecke/OR).

Eliot advised: see Conover 179.

'It does not matter what E. said': JL to OR, [Jan. 1948], as in Conover 179.

a formal statement: the statement is reproduced by Massimo Bacigalupo on p. 425 of his *Tigullio Itineraries* as included in *Ezra Pound, Language and Persona*, ed. Massimo Bacigalupo and William Pratt (Genoa: Università degli Studi do Genova, 2008).

Olga sent the document: see Carpenter 784.

'The first and only sign': Ronald Duncan in his *How to Make Enemies* (1968), as in Carpenter 776.

275 **'a tremendous mistake'**: John Drummond to Robert Duncan, 19 Apr. 1948 and 18 Aug. 1948 (HRC), as in Torrey 233.

'He cannot, absolutely cannot': OR to TSE, 4 May 1948 (Beinecke/OR).

'possible that Ezra is pretending': TSE to OR, 12 June 1948 (Beinecke/OR).

'my wife had died': TSE's first wife, Vivien(ne), from whom he had obtained a legal separation in 1933, and who had been confined in a mental hospital since 1938, died there in January 1947.

'moved away from personal subjects': John Berryman as in John Haffenden, *The Life of John Berryman* (Ark Paperbacks, 1983), 213.

refuse 'to face any facts': OR to WO, 15 Apr. 1948, as in Carpenter 784.

'Mr Pound's mental quirk': Samuel Silk to OR, 4 May 1948 (Beinecke, copy in HRC), cited Carpenter 785 and Conover 182.

276 **'I was down to see Ezra'**: JL to HD, [*c.* Sept. 1948], as in HD to Richard Aldington, 1 Oct. 1948, *Richard Aldington & H.D.: Their Lives in Letters 1918–61*, ed. Caroline Zilboorg (Manchester: Manchester University Press, 2003), 296–7.

'I had not seen Ezra': JC to JL, 29 June 1948, as in Conover 179.

'Mr. Pound would be acquitted': JC to *Saturday Review of Literature* (Sept. 1948), as in Norman: 1960, 428–9.

'EP is not interested': DP to JC on EP note, [Sept. 1948], reproduced in Cornell 103.

Thrown to wolves

This section is particularly indebted to the researches of Robert A. Corrigan and Karen Leick: Robert A. Corrigan, 'Ezra Pound and the Bollingen Prize Controversy', *Midcontinent American Studies Journal* (fall 1967) 43–57—referred to here as 'Corrigan'; Karen Leick, 'Ezra Pound v. the *Saturday Review of Literature*', *Journal of Modern Literature* 25.2 (2001/2) 19–39—referred to as 'Leick' (thanks to Alan Navarre for supplying a copy). There is a useful collection of material in *The Case Against* The Saturday Review of Literature*: The attack of the* Saturday Review *on Modern Poets and Critics | Answered by the Fellows in American Letters of the Library of Congress | Together with Articles, Editorials, and Letters from other Writers* (Chicago: Modern Poetry Association, 1949)—referred to as *Case Against* SRL. *SRL* = *Saturday Review of Literature.*

276 **'Are you in NYC?'**: JL to Robert Fitzgerald, 9 May 1948, as in Penelope Laurens Fitzgerald, '... Notes on the Friendship of James Laughlin and Robert Fitzgerald', *Pai* 31 (2002) 151.

277 **Marion Cummings was presented:** see EEC to EP, 22 May 1948, *EP/EEC* 231.
in February 1946 Bennet Cerf: details in this paragraph from Cornell 112–15.
'This Thursday a council meets': JL to EP, 16 June 1948, *EP/JL* 169.
'dramatizing his situation': Archibald MacLeish, 'The Venetian Grave' (1974), in *Riders on the Earth: Essays & Recollections* (Boston: Houghton Mifflin Company, 1978), 120.

278 **'We find ourselves, again, in debt':** Robert Fitzgerald, '"What thou Lovest Well Remains"', *New Republic* (16 Aug. 1948), as in Homberger 359–68.
'during the intervals of his illness': see Barnhisel, *James Laughlin*, 117.
'when the poet was incarcerated': dust-jacket note recorded in Gallup 76.

279 **'It is perhaps true':** Louis Martz, 'Recent Poetry'. *Yale Review* ns 38 (1948) 144–8, as in Homberger 364–8.
'An approach to the work': Richard Eberhart, 'Pound's New Cantos', *Quarterly Review of Literature* V.2 (1949) 174–91, as in Homberger 375.
the committee awarding the Bollingen Prize: much of the information in this and the following paragraphs is drawn from Leick.

280 **Léonie Adams asked Cornell:** see Cornell 116–19 for Adams's letter, and for Cornell's reply dated 7 Feb. 1949.
Francis Biddle... 'strongly against': Carpenter 788 cites the Bollingen Prize file in the Library of Congress: 'Katherine Garrison Chapin was furious that Ezra should be considered at all, and talked to her husband, who felt similarly and wrote to the Librarian, Luther H. Evans, that he "recommended strongly against the decision".'
'Pound's work, the jurors held': from *New York Herald Tribune* (21 Feb. 1949), as in Cornell 119–20. For the Library of Congress Press Release, 20 Feb. 1949, see *Casebook* 44–5.

281 **Karl Shapiro... went public:** information in this paragraph is drawn from Leick.
'Hell will no doubt break loose': Allen Tate to Luther Evans, 31 Jan. 1949 (Library of Congress), as cited by Leick.
'I disagree vehemently': Karl Shapiro, letter to the editor, *Baltimore Sun* (25 Feb. 1949) 16, as cited by Leick.
'something unholy': Albert Deutsch, 'Editorial', *New York Post* (28 Feb. 1949), as cited by Dwight MacDonald in his editorial—see next note.
'the brightest political act': Dwight MacDonald, 'Homage to Twelve Judges (an editorial)', *Politics* 6 (1949) 1–2, reprinted *Casebook* 46–8.

282 **'It would be a pity':** William Barrett, 'A Prize for Ezra Pound', *Partisan Review* 16 (April 1949) 344–7, reprinted *Casebook* 49–53.
***Partisan Review* symposium:** 'The Question of the Pound Award', *Partisan Review* 16 (May 1949) 512–22, reprinted *Casebook* 54–66. For Orwell's comments see *Casebook* 60–1; for Howe's *Casebook* 59–60; for Shapiro's *Casebook* 61–3; for Tate's *Casebook* 63–4; for Barrett's rejoinder to Tate *Casebook* 64; for Davis's comments *Casebook* 56–8.

283 **Tate's response:** in his 'Further Remarks on the Pound Award', in *Partisan Review* 16 (July 1949) 667, Tate explained in general terms his having voted for *The Pisan Cantos*: 'As a result of observing Pound's use of language in the past thirty years I had become convinced that he had done more than any man to regenerate the language, if not the imaginative forms, of English verse', and in doing so 'had performed an indispensable duty to society'. And he had done this, Tate wrote, as if in answer to Barrett's question, '*even in passages of verse in which the opinions expressed ranged from the childish to the detestable*'. For his revised version see Tate, *The Man of Letters in the Modern World: Selected Essays 1928–1955* (New York: Meridian Books, 1955), 264–7.

284 **Laughlin quit his studies:** in a recorded conversation with Eliot Weinberger in 1993 JL said: 'the so-called professor of modern poetry was a dreadful man named Robert

Hillyer. He actually threw me out of his class for raising the name of Eliot. He wasn't going to teach anything like that.... So I fled away from Harvard'—as in Emily Mitchell Wallace, '...A Partial Portrait of James Laughlin IV', *Pai* 31 (2002) 201.
'not merely the traitor': Norman Cousins and Harrison Smith, 'Ezra Pound and the Bollingen Award', *SRL* 32 (11 June 1949) 20–1—extract as in Leick.

285 **to strangle American democracy**: Corrigan's phrase, Corrigan 44.
'the clouds of an intellectual neo-Fascism': Robert Hillyer, 'Treason's Strange Fruit: The Case of Ezra Pound and the Bollingen Award', *SRL* 32 (11 June 1949)—cited by Yvor Winters, *Case Against* SRL 70.
more than a hundred readers' letters: Leick notices the objection to Hillyer's conspiracy theory; Corrigan gives an analysis of the readers' views, and notes that only one supported the choice of *The Pisan Cantos*.
sent Hillyer's articles to Representative Jacob Javits: this paragraph drawn from Leick.

286 **Smith made it clear to Laughlin**: Harrison Smith to JL, 14 Sept. 1949, *EP/JL* 191–2.
a defence of the Library's objects and procedure: Luther H. Evans, letter to the editor, *SRL* 32 (2 July 1949) 20–2, reprinted in *Case against* SRL 23–8.
a statement justifying the manner: Léonie Adams, 'Statement of Procedure of the Jury for the Bollingen Award', reprinted in *Case against* SRL 21–3.
a 'personal statement': Allen Tate, 'A Personal Statement on Fascism', reprinted in *Case against* SRL 19–21.
a statement defending the Fellows: Léonie Adams, Louise Bogan, Karl Shapiro, Willard Thorp, 'Statement of the Committee of the Fellows of the Library of Congress in American Letters' (Washington, DC: Library of Congress, 1949), reprinted in *Case against* SRL 1–19.
the most ill-founded and 'unscrupulous': The Editors, 'An Editorial', *Hudson Review* 2 (Autumn 1949), reprinted in *Case against* SRL 43–5. Extract cited in Corrigan 47.
'very likely a traitor': Hayden Carruth, 'The Anti-Poet All Told', *Poetry* 74 (Aug. 1949) 274–82, as in *Case against* SRL 49, 51.
seventy-four signatures: see Corrigan 47 (though he mistakenly gives the number as '84'). For the text of the letter and comments see Ray B. West, 'Excerpts from a Journal: 1949', *Western Review* 14 (Winter 1950), as in *Casebook* 71–3.

287 **'philistine attack'**: Margaret Marshall, '*The Saturday Review* Unfair to Literature', *The Nation* 169 (17 Dec. 1949) 598.

288 **'No comment from the Bug House'**: EP as recorded by Huntington Cairns, Carpenter 793.
a box of clippings: cited from Huntington Cairns' note for 2 April 1949 in Wilhelm: 1994 280.
'the prize, if awarded': JC to Léonie Adams, 7 Feb. 1949, as in Cornell 118.
dealt quite savagely: Malcom Cowley, 'The Battle Over Ezra Pound', *New Republic* 12 (3 Oct. 1949) 17–20; reprinted in *Case against* SRL 31–8, and Homberger 405–11.
'the obvious poetic value of the CANTOS': New Directions press release, as in Barnhisel, *James Laughlin*, 125–6.
a full page in... *Partisan Review*: the advertisement is reproduced among the illustrations in Barnhisel, *James Laughlin*, following p. 101.
the New Critics' principle: on this see Barnhisel, *James Laughlin*, 125–6, and his entire chap. 3 (92–126). Peggy L. Fox has shown that JL had decided about 1936 that his publishing house should be 'less political, more literary'—see her 'Mission Impossible: James Laughlin, Ezra Pound, and the Founding of New Directions', *Ezra Pound, Ends and Beginnings*, ed. John Gery and William Pratt (New York: AMS Press, Inc.: 2011), 195.

'to the human world': Archibald MacLeish, 'The Venetian Grave' (1974), in *Riders on the Earth* (1978), 121.

Courage against cowardice

289 ***Nobody thinks but grandpa:*** EP, June 1947, in Poetry Notebook 67, leaf 72v (Beinecke)—cited by Edith Sarra, 'Whistling in the Bughouse: Notes on the Process of Pound's Confucian Odes', *Pai* 16.1–2 (1987) 7.
'the cumulative isolation': EP, 1960, *Paris Rev. interview* 49.
Baratti and soon to be de Rachewiltz: see MdR, *Discretions* 269–70.
'nothing could be more idiotic': EP to ORA, [late 1949], *EP/ORA* 41.
'I am profoundly convinced that it is wrong': ORA to EP, 28 Aug. 1954, as cited in Surette's introduction, *EP/ORA* xvii.
'a religion hatched in slums': EP to ORA, [before 22 June 1947], *EP/ORA* 5.
'The Church of Rome decayed': EP to ORA, [before 15 May 1949], *EP/ORA* 24.
290 **'turgid mass of bloodthirsty rhetoric'**: EP to ORA, [before 15 May 1949], *EP/ORA* 24.
'ERRORS of the regime', 'understand the main points': EP to ORA, [before 15 May 1949], *EP/ORA* 24.
'And Mussolini's state fell': EP as 'anonimo' to ORA, [before 18 June 1948], *EP/ORA* 14.
'If the *young* had started reading me': EP to ORA, [before 22 June 1947], *EP/ORA* 5.
'I shall prob/ die of stroke': EP to ORA, [June 1948], *EP/ORA* 12.
'Got to get BUTTER idea':EP to ORA, [June 1948], *EP/ORA* 12.
'these new soil treatments': EP to ORA, 22 Sept. 1952, *EP/ORA* 93.
'private AND irresponsible': EP to ORA, [June 1948], *EP/ORA* 12.
'internat/ money lenders': EP to ORA, 23 Oct. 1948, *EP/ORA* 15.
'Obviously the filth of the age': EP to ORA, 7 Jan. 1952, *EP/ORA* 83. Cp. 'But there is no reason to surrender to filth' with Pound's Elektra, 'Need we add cowardice to all the rest of this filth?'—see pp. 298–9 below.
291 **'There is E.P. economic material'**: EP (over DP's signature) to Thomson & Smith Ltd, 28 May 1948, photocopy of intercept (Nat. Arch. KV2/875, item 53a).
a typed sheet 'to be kept ready': EP for Dallam Simpson, [1948] (folder 2, HRC). The paragraph is made up from this sheet and from other notes in folders 2 and 3: 'OUR job' and his 'internal signature' are from folder 3, 'SEED, god dammit SEED' is from folder 2, 'the best receivers' and 'Everything used' are from the typed sheet.
292 **Pound drafted letters**: see *EP/EEC* 228 for sample of Dallas Simpson letter evidently drafted by EP.
'winter here, very—but warm in coop': EP to MdR, 14 Feb. [1947] (Beinecke).
'If cento dollars are any use': EP to MdR, 14 Feb. [1947] (Beinecke). This was the letter in which EP wrote, 'Now I have no persona giuridica'. See MdR, *Discretions* 278 for the reception of the $100 at 'the moment of essential need'.
'here begins nonn'entity': EP to MdR, 15 Apr. [1947] (Beinecke).
'I regret you do not know': IWP to EP, 7 July 1947 (Beinecke), as in Conover 178.
'Glad to hear yr/ news': EP to IWP, 4 Aug. 1947 (Beinecke).
a comfortable chair: EP to MdR, Sept. [1947] [Beinecke].
'committee has to report': EP to MdR, 16 Feb. [1948] (Beinecke). In this letter EP again wrote, 'I have no persona giuridica'.
293 **'Will or (or NOTE'**: EP to JL, [?Sept. 1947], *EP/JL* 171.
'N.D. royalties made over to Olga': EP, on envelope of JL to DP, 24 Nov. 1947, from Klosters, Switzerland (Pound MSS II, Box 9, Lilly).

'Tell O. to for gods sake take the cash': EP notes on envelope dated Dec. 1947 (Pound MSS II, Box 13, Lilly).

'About the royalties from New Directions': DP to JL, 24 Dec. 1947, *EP/JL* 168.

a cheque for $450: drawn on Jenkintown Bank & Trust Co., as recorded in Committee bank accounts (Pound MSS VI, Lilly).

'for her services as custodian and editor': JL to EP, Sept. 1949 (Lilly). Further details also from Pound MSS II, Box 9, Lilly.

294 **petitioned the Court**: Committee Accounts folder (Pound MSS VI, Lilly). Details of legal fees and expenses are in Dorothy Pound Committee for Ezra Pound account with New England Merchants National Bank.

'GODDAM/': EP, Correspondence notes for DP, n.d. (Pound MSS II, Box 25, Lilly).

'FOR VALUE RECEIVED': OSP signed and notarized document, 22 June 1949, copy among Ezra Pound Personal Papers/Legal Papers (Beinecke); the copy sent by DP to MdR with covering note held by MdR.

'a new castle': evident from EP's response to MdR, May 1948 (Beinecke).

295 **$100, $720**: these sums mentioned in EP's letters to MdR in 1950, when he was much concerned for the restoration of the roof as well as the planting of maples 'to provide an income for his grandson'. In her 'Chronicle: The Brunnenburg Tapestry', MdR writes, 'But we had no land of our own to plant them and moreover ours is not the right climate. Here grow apples, pears, peaches, plums and grapes, not to mention vegetables'. Later land was acquired with money from Isabel Pound's estate: 'It would take some research to discover how and by whom grandmother Isabel Weston Pound's Estate was settled and how the heir under indictment and in custody was able to get Dorothy to send us the several installments to pay for the land'—MdR, 'Chronicle: The Brunnenburg Tapestry', *Pai* 37 (2010) 155.

'How many years' free roof': EP to MdR, 31 Jan. [1949] (Beinecke).

'Do you remember Olga's little house': JL to Heinz Henghes, 14 Feb. 1949 (item 229, Archive@Henghes, <www.henghes.org>).

no 'real understanding of a good Chinese poem': EP, cited in Achilles Fang's introduction, *CA* xii n.

'When you have comprehended the visual significance': EP, *CWC* 36–7—the 'Notes by a Very Ignorant Man' were added by EP in 1935. See also his 1935 'Terminal Note' re 'the Chinese art of verbal sonority' (*CWC* 33). The Fenollosa essay was concerned with a 'method of intelligent reading', i.e. with the visual significance of the *written* character, a discussion of 'the sounds of Chinese verse' being reserved for a second lecture—see *CWC II* 104.

296 **nine notebooks**: these are Poetry Notebooks 60–7 (Beinecke)—plus the notebook following no. 66 which is not present. For most helpful discussions of Pound's work on the Odes see: Edith Sarra, 'Whistling in the Bughouse: Notes on the Process of Pound's Confucian Odes', *Pai* 16.1–2 (1987) 7–31; and David Gordon, '"Root/Br./By Product" in Pound's Confucian Ode 166', *Pai* 3.1 (1974) 13–32.

EP's transcription of the first stanza of Ode 167 is reproduced as 'Fig. 7.2. EP's sound key to Ode 167 (Beinecke)' in *EP/CF*. I have added the Mathews numbers. Zhaoming Qian notes (*EP/CF* 53n.): 'In the winter of 1950–1 EP used O. Z. Tsang's *Complete Chinese–English Dictionary* (1920) as a guide to speculate about sound symbolism in primitive Chinese. He didn't use *Mathews' Chinese–English Dictionary* because Hawley had warned of its "scrambled romanization" (12 Jan. 1947, Lilly).' It would appear, however, that in spite of that warning EP was using Mathews in May–June 1947.

297 **'Pick a fern'**: EP's published version of Ode167, *CA* 86.

'escape from abstract yatter': 94/635.

treatise on music: EP read and carefully marked both the Chinese and the French texts of 'Traité sure la musique', chap. XVII in vol. II of *Li Ki ou Mémoires sur les bienséances et les cérémonies*, Texte Chinois avec une double traduction en Français et en Latin par S Couvreur S. J. (2ième éd), (Ho Kien Fou: Mission Catholique, 1913). On the front endpaper he wrote: 'Harmonies & Dissociations' (Brunnenburg).
first chapter of the *Ta Hio*: see 72–3 above.
'contemplates the unity of the mystery': EP, 'A Visiting Card' (1942), *S Pr* 276–7.
298 **'Deep and resonant'**: David Gordon, '"Root/Br./By Product"', *Pai* 3.1 (1974) 25.
the recording of a selection of his versions: *Ezra Pound Reading his Translations of The Confucian Odes* (New Rochelle, NY: Spoken Arts, [?1975]—SA 1098).
Fleming... to be named as author: according to Rudd Fleming himself, cited by Richard Reid on p. xiii of his helpful introduction to *Elektra*. For a penetrating study of the process and achievement of Pound's translating from the Greek see Christine Syros, 'Beyond Language: Ezra Pound's Translation of the Sophoclean *Elektra*', *Pai* 23.2–3 (1994) 107–39.
left the final revision of the text: according to Mrs Rudd Fleming, letter to the editor, *Pai* 21.3 (1992) [145].
'viable for the contemporary theatre': Hugh Kenner speaking in a symposium, 'Ezra Pound and Greek Tragedy in Contemporary Theatre' (1987), as cited by J. Ellen Gainor, '*Elektra*... The Classic Stage Company [production], November 1–20, 1987', *Pai* 16.3 (1987) 131.
'In the character of Elektra': Todd London, Program Notes for *Elektra*, as cited by Gainor, '*Elektra*... The Classic Stage Company [production]', *Pai* 16.3 (1987) 130.
'bring back the old rule of abundance': Orestes speaking, *Elektra* l.74.
'if you don't quit bawling': Chrysothemis, *Elektra* ll. 437–9.
'Need we add cowardice': Elektra, *Elektra* l. 401.
299 **'the key phrase'**: EP note, *Trax* 50.
'to bend and not break': Chrysothemis, *Elektra* ll. 453–4.
'EVEN JUSTICE CAN BE A PEST': Chrysothemis, *Elektra* l. 1172.
'I'd rather die': Elektra, *Elektra* l. 1174.
if 'there be no death for a death': Elektra, *Elektra* ll. 303, 305.
'take me in with you': Elektra, *Elektra* ll. 1363–5.
Pound's notes: see notes to ll. 1128ff., 1306, 1476f., 1669ff., *Elektra* 99–103.
300 **'the dark shade of courage'**: 90/609.
'rise of [a] sense of civic responsibility': EP, 'Hellenists' [a brief memorandum], Feb. or Mar. 1949 (Beinecke), as cited by Reid, *Elektra* xii.
'has packed the Supreme Court': EP, 'Four Steps', *Agenda* 17.3–4–18.1–3 (1979/80) 141.
'if ever I committed treason': Katherine Anne Porter, 16 Feb. 1949, *Letters of Katherine Anne Porter*, ed. Isabel Bayley (1990) 354, as cited in Leick n. 7.
'live on into honour': Orestes, *Elektra* l. 60.

12. THE LIFE OF THE MIND, 1950–5

301 **'living the life'**: MSB. 'Ezrology: The Class of '57', *Pai* 13.3 (1994) 376.

The shirt of Nessus

'yr/ greek ROTTEN': EP to Otto Bird, April 1951 (Lilly).
'Trachiniae | infinitely higher': EP, TS headed 'Hunt in DEam', and (in MS) 'Archiv', p. 3 (of 5) (Pound MSS II/Box 26, Lilly).
'*The* Trachiniae *presents*': EP, *Trax* p. [3].

302 **'Scrape the drying blood'**: *Trax* 26.
'SPLENDOUR, | IT ALL COHERES': *Trax* 50.
'the destiny FITS': EP to TSE, [1951] (Pound MSS II, Box 25, Lilly).
'"You might picture"': DP to Thomas Cole, 10 Mar. 1967, as quoted in Thomas Cole, 'Ezra Pound and *Imagi*', *Pai* 16.3 (1987) 63.
'And now Miss Oineus': *Trax* 44. For *'m'la calata'* see 9/37.
'Everyone in the Trachiniae': EP to Denis Goacher, [?1953] (HRC). In another letter to Goacher, 15 Nov. [1953], EP wrote: 'Any proceeds from TraX performance or radio transmission, go for first three years to Ithaca Earthquake relief | that might cover Sophokles' droits d'auteur. After which let my descendants take over.' The Ithaka earthquake referred to occurred in 1953.
303 **'TRAX in antithesis'**: EP to Michael Reck, 12 Mar. 1954, photo reproduction in Reck following p. 82. Re transposing Pound's version into a Noh drama, see also EP note, *Trax* [3].
'Karma works': see p. 235–6 above.
'when the weather is fine': Denis Goacher, 'Foreword', *Trax* x–xi.
'took considerable umbrage': WO to Charles Norman, 8 Jan. 1960 (St Elizabeths Files, 1132 a–b, US Nat. Arch.).
304 **reports to the Justice Department**: see for example, WO to Dr Stanley E. Krumbiegel (Medical Director, Bureau of Prisons, US Department of Justice), 18 Aug. 1953, and WO to William F. Tompkins (Assistant Attorney General, Internal Security Division, Department of Justice), 13 Oct. 1954 (St Elizabeths Files, 499, 590, US Nat. Arch.).
'The exact category': WO to Dr Stanley E. Krumbiegel, 18 Aug. 1953 (St Elizabeths Files, 499, US Nat. Arch.). Torrey cites this letter on his p. 249 and comments, 'Thus Dr. Overholser was admitting to the Department of Justice that Pound was not psychotic, not insane.'
305 **'It has now come to my attention'**: William F. Tompkins to WO, 30 Sept. 1954 (St Elizabeths Files, 588, US Nat. Arch.).
'The work of this translation': WO to Tompkins, 13 Oct. 1954 (St Elizabeths Files, 590, US Nat. Arch.).
'God bloody DAMN': EP to Louis Dudek, received 11 Dec. 1954, *EP/Dk* [105]—for Dudek's note and commentary see *EP/Dk* 106–7.

Kindergarten

306 **'300 students'**: EP to Ronald Duncan, 23 Feb. 1958 (HRC).
'When not in office': EP to MdR, 9 Dec. [1955] (Beinecke).
'to attack IGNORANCE': EP to Hugh Kenner, 9 June 1951 (Kenner archive, HRC).
'becoming a daily occurrence': Nursing supervisor memorandum, 28 Oct. 1952 (St Elizabeths Files, 1409, US Nat. Arch.)—as cited Torrey 238.
took left-over food: see Torrey 239–40 for one account among many.
'gobbling up hardboiled eggs': paragraph drawn from MdR, *Discretions* 293–5.
'We should reject', **'he didn't like Pound's poetry'**: Babette Deutsch and John Kasper, as in Norman: 1960, 450.
307 **'they keep the yitts out'**: Kasper to EP, 8 Jan. 1951 (Lilly).
Make It New bookshop: details from Alex Houen, 'Anti-Semitism', *Ezra Pound in Context*, ed. Ira B. Nadel (Cambridge: Cambridge University Press, 2010), 397.
'after EP. mentions a thing': DP to Stanislaw Jankowski, 17 May [1956], 'Ezra Pound's Letters to a Polish Scholar', [ed. Stanislaw Helsztynski], *Kwartalnik Neofilologiczny*, Warsaw, XVII.3 (1970), as in *P&P* IX, 520.

'Basic education at a price': on inside flap of front paper cover of Square $ *Thomas H. Benton. Bank of the United States* (1954).
'a partial list': TS, roneoed, 11 pp. stapled, (New York: Make It New Bookshop [?1954])—copy with William French MSS (Lilly). According to French much of the brochure was written or edited by EP.
the strikingly prescient extract: 'It [i.e. the financial system] still further restricts the money and purchasing- power at the disposal of individuals, and concentrates this money power in financial institutions. If the process is allowed to proceed without interruption, and it remains true that the possession of money is the only claim to the necessaries of life, then it is not difficult to see that within a short space of time, that condition of universal slavery to which the writer of "The Protocols of Zion" looked forward with such exultation, will be an accomplished fact.'—C. H. Douglas, *Social Credit*, Third edition, revised and enlarged (Eyre & Spottiswoode, 1933), 153.
308 **'a private book burning'**: Kasper to EP, n.d. [1954], as in Henderson 479.
'katz is katz', **'a wild disrupting individual'**: see EP to Dudek, received 21 Feb. 1953, *EP/Dk* [95–6], and Dudek's commentary, *EP/Dk* 97.
had previously advised Kenner: EP to Kenner, [9 June 1951] (Kenner archive, HRC).
'sqirril headed': EP to Lucy Freeland de Angulo, [1954], as in Lee Bartlett, 'The Pound/De Angelo Connection', *Pai* 14.1 (1985) 72. The full sentence: 'Horton steady, Kasper squirril headed'.
309 **'all things from one person'**: EP to Ingrid Davies, 19 June 1955 (HRC).
'slow mountain country young man': DP to OSP, 7 May 1950 (Hamilton/OSP).
'Special Legislative Researcher': [Eustace Mullins], 'About the Author', inside front cover of Eustace Mullins, *The Federal Reserve Conspiracy* (Hawthorne, Calif.: Omni Publications, 1971).
'a sufficient phalanx of particulars': 74/441.
'to analyze E. P.'s economics': D. Horton, 'Ezra Pound's Economics', *Mood* 24 (fall 1950) 2—(copy with Horton MSS, Lilly).
'interest-bearing and non-interest bearing government debt': David Horton, 'Jacob Coxey's Ideas', *Canton Repository* (Canton, Ohio) (2 Aug. 1951), reproduced in Henderson 140–2. In 84/537 EP had remarked, 'Mr. Coxey | aged 91 has mentioned bonds and their | interest | apparently as a basis of issue.'
'a very lucid note': EP to ORA, 13 Aug. 1951, *EP/ORA* 72.
'latish on Sundays': EP to Jankowski, 4 Jan. [1955], *P&P* IX, 511.
'working on beginning Chinese': David Gordon, 'Meeting E. P. and then . . .', *Pai* 3.3 (1974) 343[–60]—other details in the paragraph come from this interview.
310 **'music and rhythm factors'**: David Gordon to EP, 4 Oct. 1952 (Lilly).
early on Saturdays: see EP to Jankowski, 4 Jan. [1955], *P&P* IX, 511.
William MacNaughton: paragraph drawn from Bill MacNaughton, 'Pound, A Brief Memoir', *Pai* 3.3 (1974) 319–24. For EP's 'Anonymous Contributions to MacNaughton's *STRIKE*' see *Pai* 3.3 (1974) 389–400.
'a chance for McN/': EP to Jankowski, 4 Jan. [1955], *P&P* IX, 514—see also 505 and 512.
311 **his talk 'the liveliest'**: Reck 77.
'keeping quiet 21 hours a day': EP to MdR, 27 Jan. 1955 (Beinecke).
'entire "raps"': MacNaughton, 'Pound, A Brief Memoir', *Pai* 3.3 (1974) 323.
'Like the Old Testament Ezra': Reck 114.
'a tendency to think': Reck 112.
'a genial assumption': Reck 122.
'constantly trying to explain': Reck 93.
His attitude . . . Confucian: see Reck 94, and canto 13.
'None of you have enough': EP correspondence notes, n.d. (Lilly).

'single-handed to change': Diane Di Prima, *Memoirs of a Beatnik* (1969), 125, as cited by Richard Taylor, 'Sheri Martinelli Muse to Ezra Pound', *Agenda* 38.1–2 (2000–1) 103. The date of Di Prima's visit, Dec. 1955, is given by her letter to WO asking permission (St Elizabeths Files 758, US Nat. Arch.).
'undergone an intensive period': Angela Palandri, 'Homage to a Confucian Poet', *Pai* 3.3 (1974) 311—other details from *Pai* 3.3 (1974) 307.

La Martinelli

This section is particularly indebted to: *Beerspit Night and Cursing: The Correspondence of Charles Bukowski and Sheri Martinelli 1960–1967*, ed. Steven Moore (Santa Rosa: Black Sparrow Press, 2001)—here referred to as *CB/SM*; also to Richard Taylor, 'Sheri Martinelli Muse to Ezra Pound', *Agenda* 38.1–2 (2000–1) 98–113, and to William MacNaughton, 'The Secret History of St. Elizabeths', *Pai* 30.1–2 (2001) 69–96.

312 **Kasper a car salesman**: see Meacham 63.
'Before Ez': SM, *CB/SM* 132.
'new honey-pot girl': DP to OSP, 22 Mar. 1952 (Hamilton/OSP).
'so many who'd like to say': SM, *CB/SM* 138.
'Made Trusting & Loving': SM to C. David Heymann, 31 May 1973, as in Heymann 226.
Torrey thought he knew: see Torrey 240–1.
'Seeing Sheri approach': Marcella [Spann] Booth, 'Ezrology: The Class of '57', *Pai* 13.3 (1984) 383.
313 **'Pound embraced her', 'threw his arms around her'**: David Rattray, 'Weekend with Ezra Pound', *The Nation* (16 Nov. 1957), as in *Casebook* 113, 109.
'he read me Dante': SM, *CB/SM* 52–4.
'As for "nymphos"': SM, *CB/SM* 52.
'girls only go to bed': SM, *CB/SM* 234–5.
'O! Telo Rigido!': SM, *CB/SM* 352. Re Cavalcanti see *EP: Poet II* 108–14.
began drafting in July 1954: cf. Poetry Notebooks 87, 88 (Beinecke).
'furious from perception': 90/606.
olibanum obtained by MacNaughton: see Bill MacNaughton, 'Pound, A Brief Memoir', *Pai* 3.3 (1974) 323, and William MacNaughton, 'The Secret History of St. Elizabeths', *Pai* 30.1–2 (2001) 77.
'Grove hath its altar': 90/607–8.
315 **as... Botticelli had done**: One picture EP probably had in mind was Botticelli's 'Venus and Mars' in London's National Gallery. In two early poems, 'The Picture' and 'Of Jacopo Sellaio', Pound had praised the latter's knowledge of 'the secret ways of love' as evident in 'Venus Reclining' (*c.*1500), also in the National Gallery, (since re-attributed and re-titled 'Allegory'), a picture which closely follows the treatment of the gazing Venus in Botticelli's 'Venus and Mars' (*c.*1485), but tellingly dispenses altogether with exhausted Mars.
Her paintings: EP mentioned some of these visionary subjects in a letter to ID, 30 Apr. 1955 (HRC).
Steven Moore reports: in his 'Introduction' to *CB/SM* 11.
Pound's efforts to promote: see *EP/JL* 236–42.
'a little more lusso': EP to MdR, 1 Nov. [1955] (Beinecke).
an introduction: EP, 'Introduction', *La Martinelli* (Milan: [Vanni Scheiwiller], 1956) 5–12; repr. *Edge* (Oct. 1956) [19–20], and *EP&VA* 177–9, as 'Total War on "Contemplatio"'. See also EP to ORA, 13 Nov. 1955, *EP/ORA* 217–18.
'the only person yet met here': EP to MdR, 23 Oct. [1954] (Beinecke).

'a mist shot with lightnings': EP to ID, 30 Apr. 1955 (HRC).
'Yes, La Martinelli': EP to ID, 18 July 1955 (HRC).
'Thurs a. m. 10.30': EP, 5 pencil MS sheets in 'Holland Linen' letter pad, 'To Sheri Martinelli', 26 Nov. (Pound MSS VI, Lilly). For *hsin*[1] see 53/265.
It has been said: in a note referring to 1952 William French wrote: 'he, Omar, & (covertly D.P.) tried to interrupt EP's growing relationship with SM, & even tried to involve Overholser' (William French MSS, Lilly).
316 **'extraordinary amount of good sense'**: EP to ID, 15 Apr. 1955 (HRC).
'S.M. is not trying to kidnap': EP to MdR, 7 Nov. [1954] (Beinecke).
'particular PHOBIA': EP to ID, 25 June 1955 (HRC). See also EP to ID, 10 July 1955: 'jealousy which is the letch for monopoly... the mother of satan... IF people wd accept the affection that naturally flows toward them... and not try to GRAB they wd get more... it is the GRAB that bitches if not all, at any rate a wheluvalot, of human relations' (HRC).
sensibly wrote the cheques: the record is in Box 23, Pound MSS (Lilly), and see Richard Taylor, 'Sheri Martinelli Muse to Ezra Pound', *Agenda* 38.1–2, 108.
'longing to protect his love': SM, *CB/SM* 87.
'Shd/ like to keep Sheri': EP to ORA, 13 Nov. 1955, *EP/ORA* 217.
a note to Dr Overholser: EP to WO, 22 Nov. 1955 (Beinecke).
'We have no paid position': WO to EP, n.d. (Beinecke), as in Torrey 241.
'There was no question': EP to WO, received 30 Nov. 1955 (St Elizabeths Files, 749, US Nat. Arch.).
The trial turned: see William MacNaughton, 'Kingdoms of the Earp: Carpenter and Criticism', *Pai* 21.3 (1992) 14.
'marijuana, regularly': William MacNaughton, 'The Secret History of St. Elizabeths', *Pai* 30.1–2 (2001) 72.
'down in Spade-town': SM, *CB/SM* 87.
'The American milieu': EP, 'Introduction', *La Martinelli*, as in *EP&VA* 178.
'definitely using dope': EP to EEC, 7 Sept. [1954], *EP/EEC* 357.
317 **'heroin is pushed/'**: EP to ORA, 23 Aug. 1954, *EP/ORA* 166–7; re **'they give it to aviators'**: St Elizabeths under Overholser was involved in the research and testing of mind-altering drugs. The remark may be evidence that Pound was aware of this.
'Those charming internationalists': EP to Noel Stock, 22 Dec. 1955 (HRC).
'God knows the barbarians': EP to Goacher, 16 June [? 1954] (HRC).
'destroy the arts': EP to ORA, 22 June 1954, *EP/ORA* 155. Cf. William Blake, 'Degrade first the Arts if you'd Mankind Degrade', Annotations to Sir Joshua Reynolds's *Discourses* (noted Henderson 341).
'judging from local hell': EP to ORA, 23 Aug. 1954, *EP/ORA* 167.
hooked on heroin: see EP to ORA, 23 Aug. 1954, *EP/ORA* 168.
'magnifies TIME' etc.: EP to ORA, 22 June 1954, *EP/ORA* 154, 155.

Adult conversation

318 **'The first time I saw him'**: Al Alvarez, 'Two Faces of Pound' [a review of *Thrones*], *Observer* 6 Mar. 1960, 21, condensed from his *Where Did It All Go Right?* (Richard Cohen Books, 1999), 176–7—noted in Henderson 508–9. Alvarez's first visit would have been 11 Dec. 1955—see *EP/ORA* 219.
319 **'Profanity and the Jews'**: MM to DP and EP, 31 July 1952, *The Selected Letters of Marianne Moore*, ed. Bonnie Costello with Celeste Goodridge and Cristanne Miller (Faber & Faber, 1998), 502.

'from 2:00 PM to 4:00 PM': WO to Elizabeth Winslow, 4 Dec. 1951, 'Letters to Elizabeth Winslow', ed. with commentary by James H. Thompson, *Pai* 9.2 (1980) 343.

Pound... used to declare: for an example see EP postcard to Vianney M. Devlin, [Oct. 1953], Vianney M. Devlin OFM, 'In Memoriam—E.P.', *Greyfriar: Siena Studies in Literature* XIII (1972) 42, as in *P&P* X,1.

as many as twenty: see Lee Lady, 'Memories of Pound at St. Elizabeths', 6—sent to the Ezra Pound Mailing List, Sept. 1999, accessed 23 July /2011 at <www2.hawaii.edu/-lady/ramblings/pound.html>.

nobody: DP diary entry, 3 Jan. 1952, 'EP 1–4 in[side] | (nobody)' (Lilly).

'as Mon/ Wed/ Fri/ are NOT': EP to Achilles Fang, [Mar. 1954], *EP/CF* 144.

'the nearer to one o'clock': EP to Stanislaw Jankowski, 4 Jan. [1955], *P&P* IX, 511.

'They wd/ probably': EP to Stanislaw Jankowski, 22 Dec. [1954], *P&P* IX, 509.

'very hungry for adult company': DP to William MacNaughton in conversation, as in his memoir, 'What Pound and Carsun Chang Talked About at St Elizabeths', in *EP/CF* 105. This paragraph is drawn from MacNaughton's memoir on 105–6, and from Zhaoming Qian's notes on 96–7.

José Vasquez-Amaral: paragraph drawn from his introductory note to 'Words from Ezra Pound', *Rutgers Review* III (1968[/1969]) 40, as in *P&P* IX, 494. 'What are you doing?' is from Carroll F. Terrell, 'St. Elizabeths', *Pai* 3.3 (1974) 365.

320 **Frank Ledlie Moore**: the anecdote is from Reck 107–8.

Juan Ramón Jiménez: details from Reck 84, 122.

'sane and cultured': MdR's description of Marion and Ivan Stancioff in private conversation.

two 'civilized professors': EP's characterization of Giovannini and La Drière, EP to Jankowski, 22 Jan. [1955], *P&P* IX, 511.

'a highly cultured couple': EP to ORA, 21 July 1951, *EP/ORA* 70. Henderson 133 confirms my identification of the couple as Rudd and Polly Fleming; Reck 105 supplies the thermos jug of tea.

'a very sober English literature scholar': Reck 105.

321 **'speaking in a subdued voice'**: G. Giovannini's notes, '4 Sept. '57. Memo of only known discussion by EP of cage at Pisa... he being only one present' (Kenner Archive, HRC).

'scruples of political conscience': Kathleen Raine, 'Visiting Ezra Pound', *Agenda* 37.2–3 (1999) 137. The rest of the paragraph is drawn from this article—the inset quotation is from p. 138—but the detail of Auden's having visited is from DP to OSP, 28 Jan. 1948 (Hamilton/OSP).

'after the age of forty': EP to Kathleen Raine, 'Visiting Ezra Pound', *Agenda* 37.2–3 (1999) 141; 'evils of usurious materialism' is Raine's paraphrase on p. 142.

322 **Lt.-General Pedro del Valle (Ret.)**: this paragraph is indebted to Kevin Coogan, 'The Defenders of the American Constitution', <Wikispooks.com>, and to Henderson 242–7.

323 **George Kearns**: Kearns acknowledged the kindness of Ezra and Dorothy Pound 'to a young soldier in Washington many years ago' in his *Guide to Ezra Pound's* Selected Cantos (1980), x.

William Pratt: Pratt gave an account of his visits in 1955 in 'The Greatest Poet in Captivity at St. Elizabeths', *Sewanee Review* 94.4 (1986) 619–29. His wife Anne Pratt told me in conversation in 2013 that she too had visited and found Pound 'charming' and 'not at all mad'.

Zukofsky on a rare visit: details from David Gordon, 'Zuk and Ez at St Liz', *Pai* 7.3 (1978) 583–4.

'I note that you have got OUT': EP to LZ, 11[–12] July [1954], *EP/LZ* 208–9.

marked certain passages: Gordon records that EP marked these lines (from poems 12 and 25) in Zukofsky's *Anew.*

Agenda etc.

'in the way of legwork': Louis Dudek, *EP/Dk* 13.
'if loafing': EP to Dudek, [after June 1949], *EP/Dk* [14].
324 **'interested in doing a lot':** Louis Dudek, *EP/Dk* 17.
'has GOT to be based': EP to Dudek, [received 27 Mar. 1952], *EP/Dk* [88].
'on a mantle piece': EP to Dudek, [received 13 Apr. 1950], *EP/Dk* [19].
'AGENDA': EP to Dudek, [received 5 Mar. 1952], *EP/Dk* [83]. The Latin means, 'the grove is in need of an altar'.
'No civilization': EP to Dudek, 21 Apr. 1955, *EP/Dk* [111].
'the ONLY curricula': EP to Dudek, [received 9 Oct. 1957], *EP/Dk* [133].
'NO ONE can be considered': EP to Dudek, [received 17 Nov. 1956], *EP/Dk* 114.
'Propaganda for his ideas': Louis Dudek, *EP/Dk* 82.
'very much in agreement', 'From this point': Louis Dudek, *EP/Dk* 90—see also 103.
325 **Else Seel:** this paragraph and the next are drawn entirely (and sometimes in his words) from Rodney Symington, '"Five years I wrote to you...": An Unknown Correspondent of Ezra Pound', *Pai* 18.1–2 (1989) 161–83. EP's 89 letters to Else Seel are in the Special Collections Division of the University of Victoria Library, British Columbia. Seel's poem 'Fünfe Jahre' is in her *Ausgewählt Werke, Lyrik und Prosa*, ed. Rodney Symington (Toronto: German-Canadian Historical Association,1979), 36—the lines quoted are as translated by Rodney Symington in his article.
The importance of Frobenius: in notes for Huntington Cairns EP wrote: 'SHEER idiocy to try to crit. anything without knowing Erlebte Erdteile/force of UNWRITTEN tradition'—EP, TS headed 'Hunt in DEam' and (in MS) 'Archiv', leaf 2 (of 5), (Pound MSS II, Box 26, Lilly).
Ingrid Davies: Pound's letters to her are in the HRC; hers to him are in the Beinecke.
'mid dope-dolls': 97/680–1; for Charlie Parker connection see Richard Taylor, 'Sheri Martinelli: Muse to Ezra Pound', *Agenda* 38.1–2 (2001) 111.
326 **'Yes, my love':** EP to ID, 25 Mar. 1955 (HRC). Jaufre Rudel: a troubadour (1140–70) who sang of his love for the countess of Tripoli whom he loved from afar without ever seeing her.
his current curriculum: EP to ID, 17 Feb. [1955] (HRC).
'My dear super-chick': EP to ID, 12 Aug. [1955] (HRC).
'granducal tutor': EP to ID, 23 July [1955] (HRC).
'NO uniformity': EP to ID, 8 Jan. [1955] (HRC).
'no two people': EP to ID, 8 Mar. [1955] (HRC).
'EST DEUS IN NOBIS': Ovid, *Fasti* VI.5.
327 **'I can't believe book learnin'':** EP to ID, 18 Apr. [1955] (HRC).
'half open air': EP to ID, 8 Mar. [1955] (HRC).
'You can certainly learn more': EP to ID, 25 Mar. [1955] (HRC).
'Too bad about Guy's inhibitions', 'To the best of my belief': EP to ID, 18 Mar. [1955] (HRC).
'you still leave me': EP to ID, 19 Mar. [1955] (HRC).
'"Is it worth it!"': EP to ID, 5 Apr. [1955] (HRC).
328 **'All I know':** EP to ID, 18 Apr. [1955] (HRC).
'The illusion of being in LOVE': EP to ID, [Apr. 1955] (HRC).
'The renouned "purity"': EP to ID, 4 Apr. 1955 (HRC).
'Pound: an enclosure': EP to ID, 1 May 1955 (HRC).
329 **'no correspondence':** EP to ID, 7 Nov. [1955] (HRC).

'It is the EduCaTion': EP to ID, 29 Nov. [1955] (HRC).
'Ingrid sunk': EP to MdR, 11 May [1956] (Beinecke).
'AND of course': EP to ID, 9 July [1959] (HRC).

Not licked, merely caged

'I don't even feel licked': EP to MdR, 9 Aug. [1954] (Beinecke).
'Of course I wd/ be DEAD': EP to ORA, 13 Nov. 1955, *EP/ORA* 218.
'haven't been able to keep head up': EP to MdR, 27 Jan. [1955] (Beinecke).
'hardship had stripped him': Samuel Hynes, 'Meeting E.P.', *New Yorker* (12 June 2006) 93.
'let out into the air more': EP to MdR, 4 Oct. [1955] (Beinecke).
until about 8.00 o'clock: from Overholser's note to Norman, Norman: 1960, 438.
'thinking to save eyesight': EP to WL, [6 Dec. 1950], *EP/WL* 262–3.
'heard on radio': EP to MdR, 24 Nov. [1951] (Beinecke).
330 **Elder Solomon Lightfoot Michaux**: EP to Jankowski, 9 Oct. 1954, *P&P* IX, 507. On Michaux see Aldon Lynn Nielsen, 'Ezra Pound and "The Best Known Coloured Man in the United States"', *Pai* 29.2 (2000) 143–56.
'Elder Lightfoot': 95/641. Aldon Nielsen is the critic, in his generally perceptive and informative article—see previous note. In his letter to Jankowski EP gives the full name without abbreviation, which should perhaps temper Nielsen's Saint-Just-like rigour.
'not a racist bone': a painter known to Stoneback 'only as "Gregory"', cited by H. R. Stoneback in his '"I would . . . be hanged with you": Ernest Hemingway and Ezra Pound', *Ezra Pound, Ends and Beginnings*, ed. John Gery and William Pratt (New York: AMS Press, Inc., 2011), 176.
'desegregation in flower': EP to ID, 10 Mar. [1955] (HRC).
an 'afro-confrère': EP to MdR, 19 Nov. [1955] (Beinecke).
'new black attendant': EP to MdR, 7 Aug. [1954] (Beinecke). James Russell Lowell (1819–91) wrote: 'Truth forever on the scaffold, Wrong forever on the throne' ('The Present Crisis', 1844).
had followed Frobenius' lead: see pp. 75–81 above.
'marse blackman': EP to ORA, [19 Feb. 1952], *EP/ORA* 85.
331 **racialism . . . racism**: on this see Aldon Lynn Nielsen, 'Ezra Pound and "The Best Known Coloured Man in the United States"', *Pai* 29.2 (2000) 143–56.
'any tendency to abstract': EP to Robert Creeley, [1950/1], as in Robert Creeley,'A Note Followed by a Selection of Letters from Ezra Pound', *Agenda* 4.2 (1965) 20.
'NO use EVER': EP to ID, 20 [June 1955] (HRC).
'Pity the pore uncawnshus': EP to ORA, 30 May 1955, *EP/ORA* 193. This is not the only instance—e.g. see EP to ORA, 4 Sept. 1955, *EP/ORA* 205.
'Alright—so youre not': Jackson MacLow to EP, 3 Apr. 1955 (Beinecke).
a psychotic 'complex': see *EP: Poet I* 227–8.
332 **'Hitler crazy as a coot'**: EP to Hugh Kenner, 1 Nov. 1953 (HRC).
'the ONLY subject': EP to ORA, 8 Sept. 1953, *EP/ORA* 125. See Henderson 260ff. for relevant extracts from *Hitler's Table Talk 1941–1944: His Private Conversations* trans. Norman Cameron and R. H. Stevens, introd. H. R. Trevor-Roper (Weidenfield & Nicolson, 1953).
'The Hitler Conversations': EP to ORA, 5 Nov. 1953, *EP/ORA* 131–2.
'case of criminal lunacy': ORA to EP, 18 Nov. 1953, *EP/ORA* xviii.
'Yes, my Dear O.R.A.': EP to ORA, 1 Dec. 1953, *EP/ORA* 134, 135.
'the CONSTRUCTIVE parts': EP to ORA, 14 June 1951, *EP/ORA* 65.

'And Mussolini's state fell': EP to ORA, [*c.*18 June 1948], *EP/ORA* 14.
'TEN years construction': EP to ORA, 5 Apr. [1953], *EP/ORA* 107.
'a very vigorous criticism': EP, TS note, n.d. [? 1953], '2/Pound's principles are Confucian', among EP letters of 1953 to MdR (Beinecke).
'individualistic, anarchic': EP, TS note, 'DIFFERENCE: in whole nature and history of the two peoples/in the leaders. H. mystic fanatic hysteric/M. journalist' (Pound MSS II, box 25, Lilly).
333 **'not a line in support'**: EP to ORA, 5 Apr. [1953], *EP/ORA* 107.
'never a word in favour': EP to ORA, 30 Apr. 1953, *EP/ORA* 111.
'John Adams and the American Constitution': EP TS draft, 'I have no doubt that the article by Si/ m. Ris in la Nazione for Jan.22', sent to MdR, [*c.* Jan. 1955] (Beinecke).
'citizen placed in a far look-out': EP to Hugh Kenner, 10 Oct. [1953] (HRC).
'No treason without evil intention': EP to ORA, 7 Aug. 1953, *EP/ORA* 116–17. Henderson (p. 232) suggests that Pound was referring to the 1948 Douglas Chandler treason case in which Chief Judge Magruder of The United States Court of Appeal for the First Circuit in Boston wrote, 'The significant thing is not so much the character of the act which in fact gives aid and comfort to the enemy, but whether the act is done with an intent to betray.'

'I want OUT': a log of pleas and petitions

Olga Rudge reproached Hemingway: OR to Hemingway, 13 Mar. [1950], as in H. R. Stoneback, '"I Would... Be Hanged with You": Ernest Hemingway and Ezra Pound', in *Ezra Pound, Ends and Beginnings. Essays and Poems from the Ezra Pound International Conference Venice, 2007*, ed. John Gery and William Pratt (New York: AMS Press, Inc., 2011)—hereafter referred to as Stoneback—p. 168.
hysterical and unhelpful: see, for example, Hemingway to DP, 22 Oct. 1951, cited in Stoneback 171.
'rather serious mistake': Hemingway to OR, 20 Mar. 1950, as in Stoneback 169–70.
334 **'Please do NOT distribute'**: EP to Dudley Kimball, [1950] (Hamilton). For Kimball's 'Sixteen Points' see 'Seize thèses sur Ezra Pound', *Les Cahiers de l'Herne: Ezra Pound II* (Paris: Éditions de l'Herne, 1965), 698–701.
'Cornell says': JL to EP, 15 Oct. [1950] (Lilly).
'trial yu ass': EP to Kenner, [1951] (Kenner Archive, HRC).
'just as unreasonable': JL to Kenner, 26 July 1951 (Kenner Archive, HRC).
'Many people have tried': Hemingway to Paige, 22 Oct. 1951, Ernest Hemingway *Selected Letters 1917–1961*, ed. Carlos Baker (New York: Scribners Classics, 2003), 739–41.
'It wearies me': WL to EP, 10 Sept. 1952, *EP/WL* 273.
335 **An open letter**: see Henderson 127, 222.
Aldington and H.D.: see *Richard Aldington and H.D.: Their Lives in Letters*, ed. Caroline Zilboorg (Manchester University Press, 2003), 357–8 (20 Dec. 1952).
'Committee for the Liberation': see Henderson 222.
Mary de Rachewitz sailed to America: paragraph drawn from MdR, *Discretions* 287–97.
'Tha[t] they base the defense': EP TS note with EP to MdR correspondence, n.d. but after May 1953 by internal reference to letters published in *Irish Times* 1 and 3 Nov. 1952, and EP's 'Nov to May to get copies'.
336 **'a good many prominent Italians'**: ORA to EP, 5 June 1953, *EP/ORA* 114–15 n. 1.
'idea of petition O.K.': EP to ORA, 27 June 1953, *EP/ORA* 114.
a confused report: Rufus King, Attorney, Southern Building, Washington DC, to TSE, 27 Oct. 1953 (Lilly).

until 'it is felt that Pound has been forgotten': Rufus King to WL, 22 Dec. 1953 (Lilly).

'It does appear to be a stalemate': TSE to Rufus King, 4 Nov. 1953, as in Carpenter 808. (Puzzlingly, Carpenter locates TSE's letter in the St Elizabeths files.)

'It is time': WL to TSE, 23 Nov. 1955, *The Letters of Wyndham Lewis*, ed. W. K. Rose (Methuen, 1963), 551. TSE's response dated 4 Dec.—'public agitation' etc.—is given in a footnote to WL's letter.

337 **'It is most unlikely'**: WL to TSE, 19 Dec. 1953, *The Letters of Wyndham Lewis* 553–4.

liberation would have to be worked from Italy: details in this paragraph drawn from: MdR, *Discretions* 299; Stock: 1970, 438; Tony Tremblay, '"Boris is very intelligent ...": The Association and Correspondence of Ezra Pound and Prince Boris de Rachewiltz', *Pai* 28.1, 155–6.

'on the purely Utopian plane': EP to ORA, 13 May 1954, *EP/ORA* 149.

Dag Hammarskjöld: the principle source of information on Hammarskjöld's interest in Pound's case is Marie-Noëlle Little, *The Knight and the Troubadour: Dag Hammarskjöld and Ezra Pound* (Uppsala: Dag Hammarskjöld Foundation, 2011)—hereafter referred to as Little.

'his tragic fate': Dag Hammarskjöld to Lars Forssell, 8 Jan. 1954, Little 66.

338 **'Modern art teaches us'**: Dag Hammarskjöld speaking at the Opening Ceremonies of the 25th Anniversary of the Museum of Modern Art, as in Little 70.

mentioned Pound only twice: see Jacques Maritain, *Creative Intuition in Art and Poetry* (Bollingen Series, vol. 35), The A. W. Mellon Lectures in the Fine Arts No. 1, National Gallery of Arts Washington (New York: Pantheon Books, 1953), 181n., 261.

'Ezra Pound is a great poet': Ernest Hemingway, *Time* (13 Dec. 1954) 72, as in Little 73. See also Stoneback 172.

'For quite some time now': Douglas Hammond to Dag Hammarskjöld, 12 Dec. 1954, as in Little 76.

In January Hammond wrote: Hammond to DP, 7 Jan. 1955 (Lilly).

339 **'too much in the dark'**: DP as reported by Hammond to A. V. Moore, 28 Jan. 1955, as in Carpenter 816.

'no objection to a movement': EP's attitude as reported by Hammond to Hammarskjöld, 7 Jan. 1955 (Lilly).

the January 7 letter: Hammond to Hammarskjöld, 7 Jan. 1955 (Lilly).

'bloody near fed up': EP to WL. 9 Jan. [1955], *EP/WL* 288.

'A buzzard named Blum': EP to ORA, 11, 15 Dec. 1955, *EP/ORA* 219–20.

'Hem/ has done what he can': EP to ID, 19 Mar. 1955 (HRC).

'INSIDE the locus of power': EP to ID and Richard Davies, 28 Mar. 1955 (HRC).

'release on probation': American Committee for Cultural Freedom to WO, 11 Mar. 1955, as in Carpenter 817.

340 **Scelba reception**: details from Henderson 432.

'It appears La Luce': EP to ORA, [mid-Apr. 1955], *EP/ORA* 186–7.

'I have been told': AMacL to EP, [*c.* Aug. 1955], *MacLeish* 377.

though 'not exactly grata': AMacL to EP, 18 Aug. [1955], *MacLeish* 378.

'Will gladly pay tribute': Hemingway to Harvey Breit, 27 Oct. 1955, *Hemingway* 849.

341 **'contrary to the Constitution'**: Hemingway in WYBC broadcast, 5 Dec. 1955, as in Stoneback 173.

'he shouted loud and clear': Bengt Nirje to Marie-Noëlle Little, Little 84. Other details in this paragraph drawn from Little 82–4, 89–92.

'discuss the case with his friends': Hammarskjöld to Anders Österling, Permanent Secretary of the Swedish Academy, 23 Dec. 1955, as in Little 89–90.

'in the name of the City of Dante': La Pira, Mayor of Firenze, to American Ambassadress, Oct. 1955, as in *Academia Bulletin 2* ([1956]) [2], repr. *Pai* 3.3 (1974) 386.

'In the very moment': Giovanni Papini, 'Domandiamo la grazia per un poeta', *Corriere della sera* (30 Oct. 1955), as in Jack LaZebnik, 'The Case of Ezra Pound', *New Republic* (1 Apr. 1957), as in *Casebook* 127. See also Henderson 491–2.

a petition for clemency: see 'Pétition des écrivains italiens', *Les Cahiers de l'Herne: Ezra Pound I* (Paris: Editions de l'Herne, 1965), 167.

Ambassador Luce: details drawn from her 'informal' account, as given to Charles Norman, Norman; 1960, 443.

342 **'The crimes of World War II'**: editorial, *Life Magazine* (6 Feb. 1956), as in Wilhelm: 1994, 303.

'Now is not the time': *Ezra Pound, written on behalf of the committee formed to obtain his release*, 'privately printed', Jan. 1956, 9. I have to thank Dryden Gilling-Smith for lending me his original copy of this pamphlet.

343 **'faulty', 'dismissal of the indictment'**: William E. Foley, Chief, Internal Security Section, Office Memorandum to James M. McInerney, taking up recommendations of Miss Fillius, 5 June 1950 (Justice Department files). Behind this would have been Dorothy F. Green's memorandum of 27 Apr. 1950, cited above pp. 178–9.

'extreme difficulty', 'reopen sanity proceedings': Mr Whearty Office Memorandum to Mr McInerney, following up Foley's Memorandum, 6 June 1950 (Justice Department files).

Writing and reading

344 **'Professing sinologues'**: Achilles Fang to JL, 10 May 1950, *EP/JL* 204.

'no civilized man': EP to Jankowski, [21 Nov. 1956], *P&P* IX, 521. (In this letter Pound was discussing the likelihood of Faber publishing a bilingual selection of Plotinus.)

'The noble Fang': EP to MdR, 28 Dec. [1950] (Beinecke).

'HAMMER': EP to Fang, [Mar. 1954], *EP/CF* 145. Some information in this paragraph and the next is drawn from Zhaoming Qian's introductory note to the EP/Fang correspondence re the Odes—see *EP/CF* 107–9.

'VISIBLE simultaneously': EP to Fang, [31 July 1952], *EP/CF* 115.

'No, my very dear ACHILLES': EP to Fang, [15 Mar. 1954], *EP/CF* 141–2.

345 **Fang was licensed**: EP to Fang, [31 July 1952], *EP/CF* 116.

'if you are waiting': EP to Fang, [4 Feb. 1956], *EP/CF* 156.

'highly imperfect but useful': EP to Fang, [31 July 1952], *EP/CF* 116.

'MORE as a graph': EP to Fang, [Oct. 1957], *EP/CF* 157.

'The infinite vileness': EP to Fang, 18 May [1958], *EP/CF* 160.

'it has taken me': EP as quoted by Denis Goacher, 'Denis Goacher Talks About Basil Bunting', *Sharp Study and Long Toil: Basil Bunting Special Issue*, ed. Richard Caddel (Durham, NC: Durham University Journal Supplement, 1995), 204.

346 **'Canto 85 in proofs'**: EP to MdR, 23 Oct. [1954] (Beinecke).

'typed p. 11 of 88': EP to MdR, 25 Oct. [1954] (Beinecke).

'to get ms/ 85/89 in order': EP to MdR, 23 Nov. [1954] (Beinecke), as in Richard Taylor, 'From Father to Daughter: Selected Letters', *Pai* 37 (2010) 195.

'precise knowledge of his subject': note on inside front cover of *Gists from Agassiz* (Hawthorne, California: Omni Publications for the Square Dollar Series, 1973).

'art of collecting and arranging': note on back cover of [Thomas H. Benton], *Thirty Years View* (New York: Kasper & Horton, Square Dollar Series, 1954).

'America's greatest historian': note on back cover of [Thomas H. Benton], *Thirty Years View* (New York: Kasper & Horton, Square Dollar Series, 1954).

347 **'when the government becomes the servant'**: Thomas Hart Benton, *Thirty Years View* (1854) I, 192; p. 22 in Kasper & Horton Square Dollar extract from *Thirty Years View*.

'the driving greed of the usurer': Charles Beard in his introduction to Brooks Adams, *The Law of Civilization and Decay: An Essay on History* (1898) (New York: Knopf, 1943).

Economic Dialogues in Ancient China: Terrell *Companion* II, 689 provides the details—the work, ed. Lewis Maverick in 1954, is drawn on in canto 106.

'If people would regard': *The Sacred Edict*, with a translation of the colloquial rendering by F. W. Baller (Shanghai: China Inland Mission, 1924), repr. in facsimile (Orono, Me.: National Poetry Foundation, 1979), 37.

'no life-giving power': Baller, *The Sacred Edict*, iv.

a place in his *Thrones*: see cantos 98 and 99.

The Eparch's Book: *Επαρχικὸν βιβλίον*, ed. Jules Nicole (Geneva: H. Georg, 1893). The Greek and Latin texts are reproduced in *Pai* II.2, prefaced by a substantial introduction and commentary on Pound's use of the work in canto 96, by Carroll F. Terrell. Nicole's edition with both his Latin and French translations, and with an English translation added, was republished by Variorum Reprints in London in 1970.

348 **'right down to Mustapha Kemal'**: EP to MdR, 19 Oct. [1954] (Beinecke)—cf. 96/658.

'an attempt to move out': EP in *Paris Rev. interview* 49.

'The gods are in no need': Apollonius 'To the Priests in Olympia', Philostratus, *The Life of Apollonius of Tyana* (Heinemann Ltd., The Loeb Classical Library, 1950) II.427.

'pivotal point in brit/ history': EP to ID, 9 and 13 Mar. 1956 (HRC). Cf. also EP to ORA, 3 Apr. 1956: 'St Anselm pivotal for later charters' (*EP/ORA* 228); and 'the fight between him and William Rufus . . . all your liberties come out of that . . . on to Magna Carter, or on down to Cook or Coke' (EP in D. G. Bridson, 'An Interview with Ezra Pound', *New Directions* 17 (1961) 173. Anselm figures in canto 105.

'it's all there in Coke': EP to Noel Stock, 10 Nov. 1957 (HRC).

'live work': EP to Jankowski, 31 Jan. 1958, *P&P* IX, 523.

349 **'For the understanding of American (U.S.) LITERATURE'**: EP to Jankowski, 28 Sept. [1955], *P&P* IX, 517.

'apparently focusing on Dante': EP to Kenner, [Jan. 1954] (HRC).

a statement issued in 1953: 'ALARMED by the neglect of the Greek and Latin classics' (1953), reprinted in *EP/Dk* 104.

'read the TEXTS': EP to Jankowski, [29 Sept. 1955], *P&P* IX, 518.

'What is WANTED': EP to Jankowski, 15 June 1954, *P&P* IX, 503. EP was not to know when he wrote thus that the translation he was calling for was in preparation for his friend T. S. Eliot, and would appear from Faber & Faber in 1957 as *Richard of Saint-Victor: Selected Writings on Contemplation*, trans. Clare Kirchberger. Jankowski completed his translation of *Benjamin Minor*, in a style that had the edge on Kirchberger's for clarity and economy, but Pound's confidence that he would find a publisher for it proved ill founded, and it was eventually printed privately in Ansbach, West Germany, in 1960—information from *P&P* IX, 500. Included in the Ansbach edition were EP's selection of sentences—14 brief extracts in the original Latin with his English translation (repr. *S Pr* 73–4). These were drawn from the EP's 21 brief extracts in Latin only, published by Vanni Scheiwiller in Milan in 1956 as *Riccardo da S. Vittore. Pensieri sull'Amore*.

'A catholic biJAYzuss author': EP to ORA, 29 May 1954, *EP/ORA* 153.

'absorbed some R/ St V': EP to Beatrice Abbot, [July 1954] (Beinecke).

The St Elizabeths Cantos (1): 'Section: Rock-Drill. 85–95 de los cantares'

The following have been particularly useful in this section: Terrell's *Companion*; William Cookson, *A Guide to the Cantos of Ezra Pound* (Croom Helm, 1985) [here referred to as Cookson]—especially for John Cayley's glosses of the Chinese; Thomas Grieve, '*Annotations to the Chinese in* Section: Rock-Drill', *Pai* 4.2–3 (1975) 361–508 [= Grieve]; David Gordon, 'Thought built on Sagetrieb: [*The Sacred Edict* in cantos 98 and 99]', *Pai* 3.2 (1974) 169–90; David Gordon, 'From the blue serpent to Kati', *Pai* 3.2 (1974) 239–44; David Gordon, 'More on *The Sacred Edict*', *Pai* 4.1 (1975) 121–68; David Gordon, 'Corpus Juris and *Canto XCIV*', *Pai* 11.2 (1982) 313–24; George Kearns, *Guide to Pound's* Selected Cantos (Rutgers University Press, 1980) [= Kearns]; Peter Makin, *Pound's Cantos* (George Allen & Unwin, 1985); James J. Wilhelm, *The Later Cantos of Ezra Pound* (New York: Walker and Company, 1977) [= Wilhelm, *Later Cantos*].

pasting ideograms on to proof sheets: EP to ID, 22 June 1955 (HRC).

350 **'China IN ideogram'**: EP pencil note on verso of Pearl Buck to DP, dated 16 Sept. 1946, reads, 're China, not books "about" China, but China IN ideogram' (Lilly).

'a locked room': Dag Hammarskjöld to Anders Österling, 23 Dec. 1955, cited Little 91.

'He could hardly write': Alfred Alvarez, 'Rock-Drill Cantos', *Observer* (3 Mar. 1957) 15, as in Homberger 442.

'read exactly the books': Randall Jarrell, 'New Books in Review', *Yale Review* 46 (1956) 103, as in Homberger 438–9.

351 **'the straight gaze'**: see *Confucius (1951)* 27.

'one who governs well': see Grieve 390–1.

352 **Terrell informs us**: see Terrell, *Companion* 467–8.

353 **'a scholarly-critical industry'**: Kearns 193.

Williams had warned: see *The Autobiography of William Carlos Williams* (New York: New Directions, 1967), 146.

355 **the epic issues**: see *Paris Rev. interview* 48–9.

357 **'plenum'**: 77/475.

358 **'the germinal universe'**: *SR* 92–3.

an effect of heroin: see William McNaughton, 'The Secret History of St. Elizabeths', *Pai* 30.1–2 (2001) 75–6.

'no earthly pleasure': SM, *CB/SM* 235.

359 **Dante raged**: see his *Paradiso* XXVII.22–6.

'The Princess Ra-Set': on this synthesis of the two male deities Ra and Set (in cantos 91,92, 94, and 98), and on the sources of the Egyptian elements in the late cantos and Pound's handling of them, see Boris de Rachewiltz, 'Pagan and Magic Elements in Ezra Pound's Works', in Eva Hesse ed., *New Approaches to Ezra Pound* (Faber & Faber, 1969), 174–97.

361 **'energy near to benevolence'**: see *The Unwobbling Pivot* I.xx.10, *Confucius (1951)* 155.

362 **'a POLITICAL implement'**: EP to JT, 17 June 1957, *EP/JT* 44.

Apollonius of Tyana: see p. 348 above. On the 'Pandects' see David Gordon, 'Corpus Juris and *Canto XCIV*', *Pai* 11.2 (1982) 313–24.

'sense of cosmos': EP note on flimsy pink paper to Denis Goacher, n.d. (HRC).

'Cantos as guide book': EP note on flimsy pink paper to Denis Goacher, n.d. (HRC).

363 **'85–95 have richiami'**: EP to MdR, [10 Dec. 1955] (Beinecke).

364 **'abundant | unceasing'**: 92/620.

'Div Com/ the main structure': EP to MdR, 18 May 1956 (Beinecke).

Intimate relations

the Lynx song: 79/489–92; see EP to DP, 2 Oct. [1945] and 4 Nov. [1945], and DP to EP, 13 Jan. 1946, *EP/DP* 101, 173, 239.
'La Cara', the 'beloved', 'a great goddess': 76/459, 74/444, 74/435.
'a jungle of wooden row houses': Reck 85–6.

365 **'led a hell of a life'**: Douglas Hammond to AVM, 28 Jan. 1955 (Lilly), as in Carpenter 816.
'without comment': Richard Aldington to HD, 23 Feb. 1952, *Richard Aldington and H. D.: Their Lives in Letters 1918–61*, ed. Caroline Zilboorg (Manchester University Press, 2003), 349.
'bottomless pits': EP to MdR, 16 Oct. 1954 (Beinecke).
'the money to O.R.': DP to EP [? Mar. 1953] (Lilly).
'quoted Dorothy': SM in interview with Anne Conover, Washington, DC, Aug. 1995, in Conover 210.
'cannot be mortgaged': EP to MdR, 12 Apr. 1950 (Beinecke).
'Don't get into debt': see for example EP to MdR, 29 Mar. 1950 (Beinecke).
'for Patrizia's roof': see DP to MdR, 1 July 1950, and EP to MdR, 25 July 1950 (Beinecke); also Conover 194.
'This place is a Paradiso': OR to EP, 19 Feb. 1953, as in Conover 207.
Pound was expecting Mary: details in rest of para and the one following from MdR, *Discretions* 291–7.

366 **'should not attempt to hurry'**: Conover 206, based on OR's letters and diaries.
'he is wonderful': MdR to OR, 12 Mar. 1953, as in Conover 206.
'heaviness, boredom, depression': MdR to author by e-mail, 18 Jan. 2011.
'as advance on royalties': MdR in conversation with author, 20 June 2008.
boredom the worst horror: MdR in conversation with author, June 2010.
'bewildered and discouraged': MdR, *Discretions* 297.
'Mary a gt/ comfort': EP to ORA, 5 Apr. [1953], *EP/ORA* 107.
'on specific condition': EP to MdR, 19 Dec. 1953 (Beinecke).
might be forced to borrow: see EP to ORA, 4 Nov. 1954, *EP/ORA* 172–3.
'the luxury and joy': OR to EP, 24 Dec. 1953, as in Conover 207.
a pass to first class: see Conover 203, and EP Misc. Note, [Apr. 1952] (Box 25, Pound MSS II, Lilly).

367 **on April 9**: date from stamp in OR's US passport (issued 20 Apr. 1950).
'permitted three visits': Conover 204.
'just arrived from Siena': Angela Palandri, 'Homage to a Confucian Poet', *Pai* 3.3, 305.
on May 7: date from EP to Peter Russell, 29 May 1952 (HRC).
'O. arrived': EP to MdR, 5 May 1952 (Beinecke).
'Hope to see her again': EP to MdR, 11 May 1952 (Beinecke).
'This one, who expected': OR to EP, 13 May 1952, as in Conover 204–5.
'10 years bug house': EP to OR, [? Jan. 1955] (Beinecke/OR).
'ideés reçues': EP to OR, [Feb. 1955] (Beinecke/OR).
'A civilization': EP to OR, 26 Feb. 1955 (Beinecke/OR).

368 **'He not think she not noticing'**: OR to EP, 21 Jan. 1955 (Beinecke/OR).
'She not to worry': EP to OR, [? Feb. 1955] (Beinecke/OR).
'Having once again': OR to EP, 22 Mar. 1955 (Beinecke/OR).
'don't see what good': EP to OR, [Apr. 1955] (Beinecke/OR).
'she won't complicate': OR to EP, [Apr. 1955] (Beinecke/OR).
'Bene | she come': EP to OR, 7 May [1955] (Beinecke/OR).
'in Wash's worst': EP to ORA, 7 July 1955, *EP/ORA* 197.

'[Sheri] was sitting at the right hand': SM in interview with Anne Conover, Washington, DC, Aug. 1995, in Conover 210–11.
'Oh well, you ma turned up': EP to MdR, 7 July [1955] (Beinecke), as in Richard Taylor, 'From Father to Daughter: Selected Letters', *Pai* 37 (2010) 202–3.
whether Olga 'sailed yester/': EP to MdR, 9 July [1955] (Beinecke).
369 **'Waaal she'za nice gal'**: EP to MdR, 9 July [1955] (Beinecke).
'It would have been so easy': MdR in conversation with author, July 1995.

13. 'Indictment Dismissed', 1956–8

370 **late November**: date from DP to OSP, 26 Nov. 1955 (Hamilton/OSP).
fiercely attacked him: EP, 'MacLEISH', (23 April 1942), *Radio* 104–6.
'some peace and quiet': AMacL to EP, [*c.* Aug. 1955], *MacLeish* 377.
'a medical disposition': AMacL to EP, 18 Aug. [1955], *MacLeish* 377.
'overlooking the simple': see AMacL to EP, [*c.* Sept. 1955?], *MacLeish* 377–8.
'the minute they WANT': EP to MdR, 23 Nov. 1955 (Beinecke).
'will not lift his hand': Harry Meacham to Mr Wyllie, 4 Dec. 1957 (Kenner Archive, HRC).
371 **MacLeish's visit**: see AMacL to EH, 19 June 1957, *MacLeish* 397–9.
'Not everyone has seen': AMacL, 'In Praise of Dissent', *New York Times Book Review* 16 Dec. 1956—as in Wilhelm: 1994, 306. *NYT* of 6 Jan. 1957 printed several letters responding to the article, among them one by 'M. Span'.
'for the good name': AMacL to EH, 19 June 1957, *MacLeish* 397.
La Martinelli's art: see AMacL to EP, 18 Aug. [1955], *MacLeish* 378; also EP to Robert MacGregor, 21 Dec. 1955, *EP/JL* 242.
'dear Archie': EP to HK, 31 Dec. 1955 (HRC).
'the benevolent': EP to AVM, [Dec. 1955] (Lilly).
'insists on his own terms': AVM to TSE, 4 Jan. 1956 (Lilly).
'a mild beginning': EP to HK, 31 Dec. 1955 (HRC).
'what yu kno': EP to LZ, 10 Dec. 1955 (HRC).
372 **'a closet'**: 'An Artist Confined', *Life Magazine* 40 (6 Feb. 1956) 30—quoting Samuel Hynes, 'The Case of Ezra Pound', *Commonweal* 63 (9 Dec. 1955) 251.
'Considering various': Hammarskjöld to Wilcox, 15 Mar. 1956, as in Little 98—see Little 97–8 for context.
'Our chief headache': W. H. Auden to Hammarskjöld, 21 Mar. 1956, Little 100.
'would be unwise': AMacL to EP, 17 Apr. [1956], *MacLeish* 380.
'fighting feathers': AMacL to Alexis Saint-Léger Léger, 9 June [1956], *MacLeish* 383.
nevertheless he persisted: AMacL to EP, 9 July [1956], *MacLeish* 384–5.
373 **'Hem is apparently'**: EP to MdR, 31 May 1956 (Beinecke).
'prolonged incarceration': EP to James Dickey, [30 Aug. 1956], as in Lee Bartlett and Hugh Witemeyer, 'Ezra Pound and James Dickey: A Correspondence and a Kinship', *Pai* 11.2 (1982) 301.
'To the President and Trustees': EP to The President and Trustees, Hamilton College, 3 Aug. 1956, reproduced in *Ezra Pound: A Selected Catalog* compiled Cameron McWhirter and Randall L. Ericson (Clinton, NY: Hamilton College Library, 2005), 30. The president's reply is reproduced on facing page 31.
'CantObile': EP to MdR, 22 Aug. [1956] (Beinecke).
Na Khi: e.g. EP to MdR, 20 July 1956: 'Goullart on Na Khi very interesting—"Forgotten Kingdom"'; and 31 Aug. 1956: 'Big 2 vol/ Rock "Ancient Kingdom" arruv on loan'.

374 **'Daylight privileges'**: Clinical Record/Nursing Notes, 9-21-56 (St Elizabeths Files, 1351, US Nat. Arch.).
a statement 'for the record': EP, 'Four Steps', introd. D. G. Bridson, *Agenda* 17.3–4–18.1 (1979–80) 131–41.
an American Writers Group: paragraph drawn from Francis J. Bosha, 'Faulkner, Pound and the P.P.P.', *Pai* 8.2 (1979) 250–6. See also: Paul Mariani, *William Carlos Williams: A New World Naked* (New York: McGraw-Hill Book Company, 1981), 739–41; Donald Hall, *Remembering Poets: Reminiscences and Opinions* (New York: Harper Colophon Books, 1979), 164–5.
375 **'not now legally insane'**: AMacL to AVM, 14 Oct. 1956 (Lilly)
unlikely . . . passport: AVM to DP, 22 Oct. 1956 (Lilly).
376 **Overholser's position**: AMacL to WO, 16 Nov. 1956 (St Elizabeths Files, 873, US Nat. Arch.).
'unlikely that his mental condition': WO to AMacL, 21 Nov. 1956 (St Elizabeths Files,874, US Nat. Arch.).
'though unfit to stand trial': AMacL to WO, 29 Nov. 1956 (St Elizabeths Files, 885, US Nat. Arch.).
'I think it is high time': WO to AMacL, 4 Dec. 1956 (St Elizabeths Files, 886, US Nat. Arch.).
'mentally incompetent': WO to AMacL, 21 Nov. 1956 (St Elizabeths Files, 874, US Nat. Arch.).
'Eisenhower will never': Guy Davenport, 'Seeing Shelley Plain', *The Geography of the Imagination* (Pan Books/Picador, 1984) 139.
'Our interest': RF, TSE, and EH to The Attorney General of the United States, 14 Jan. 1957—as in Heymann 245–6.
377 **'asked that a review'**: Herbert Brownell to RF, 28 Feb. 1957, *Frost* 563.
would be willing to talk: Rogers to each of RF, TSE, and EH, 10 Apr. 1957—noted in *MacLeish* 396.
had urged Hemingway: AMacL to EH, 8 Jan. 1957, *MacLeish* 393.
'would be on his desk': see Robert M. MacGregor to WO, 19 Feb. 1957 (St Elizabeths Files, 909, US Nat. Arch.).
Hammarskjöld: paragraph drawn from Little 108–17.
378 **'Did you ever hear'**: WCW to EP, 7 Jan. 1957, *EP/WCW* 305.
series on Kasper's activities: Robert S. Bird in *New York Herald Tribune*, series beginning 30 Jan. 1957—see Meacham 61, Little 120.
'Kasper's idol': Arthur Gordon, 'Intruder in the South', *Look* 21 (19 Feb. 1957) 27–31.

The Tale of John Kasper

This section is based to a large extent on Robert S. Griffin's online 'Tale of John Kasper', <http://www.robertsgriffin.com/TaleKasper>, supplemented by materials generously provided by Alec Marsh.

John Kasper appeared: incident as reported by William McNaughton, 'The Secret History of St Elizabeths', *Pai* 30.1 and 2 (2001) 92. Further details from Kasper correspondence files in Beinecke.
379 **'Dear Gramp'**: Kasper to EP, 10 Apr. [1956] (Beinecke)—transcript provided by Alec Marsh.
'don't confuse ingenuity': EP notes apparently to Kasper, n.d. (Beinecke)—transcript provided by Alec Marsh.

'Our movement arises': 'WHITE CITIZENS COUNCILS, What are they?', back page of *VIRGINIANS ON GUARD!* (1246 Wisconsin Avenue, NW, Washington 7, DC: John Kasper, Seaboard White Citizens Councils, n.d.).

381 **testified on his behalf**: EP to MdR, 13 Nov. 1956 (Beinecke).

letter to the editor: Kasper to *Amsterdam News* (18 Nov. 1956)—copy of original from Alec Marsh.

382 *VIRGINIANS ON GUARD!*—photocopy provided by Alec Marsh.

'damn good guy': EP to MacL, [? Nov. 1957], Carpenter 835.

'2 points at least quotable': EP to Noel Stock, cited by Alec Marsh in his unpublished paper, 'Ezra Pound and the American right in the 1950s: Pound's response to Brown', from Michael J. Alleman, '"A Pound of Flesh": Ezra Pound at St Elizabeths', Diss., University of Texas, Dallas, 2007.

offered some advice: EP, 3 pp. TS notes commenting on draft of *VIRGINIANS ON GUARD!*, [? July 1956], mixed in with program for David Gordon's *Academia Bulletin* (Beinecke YCAL MSS 43, Box 66, Folder 2838).

'Kasper defeated': EP to ORA, 6 Dec. 1956, *EP/ORA* 236.

'Mr Kasper's meteoric rise': EP to ID, 26 Dec. 1956 (HRC).

'A Nationalist Attack Newspaper': details from Stock 431.

383 **'violated a permanent injunction'**: report in New York *Times*, 24 Mar. 1957, as cited Norman 453.

'K probably in ERROR': EP to David Wang, 28 Sept. 1957, *EP/CF* 194.

The skeleton in the national closet

'Is it true that you hate': Bo Setterlind to EP, [Feb. 1957], as in Little 121.

384 **'NO, naturally'**: EP to Setterlind, 26 Feb. 1957, as in Little 121–2.

Agassiz: for EP's early recommendation see *ABCR* 17–18.

'All study of nature': EP to JT, 2 July 1957, *EP/JT* 55. In the preceding sentence EP objects to 'Crushing ALL local civilizations in favour of uniformity and central tyranny'.

'good that hindoos': EP to JT, 11 Sept. 1957, *EP/JT* 84.

educating and directing: EP wrote to MdR in June 1957 about 'trying to educate Kasper, Chatel et al—and direct 'em' (Beinecke).

'don't think you can show': EP to Meacham, 13 Nov. [1957], as in Meacham 68–9.

'no more responsible': LZ, as reported by Giovannini to Meacham, Meacham 121–2.

'the heroism of a Crommelyn': EP to Meacham, 13 Nov. [1957], as in Meacham 69.

385 **has collected evidence**: see Henderson 530ff.

'a little publicity': EP to ORA, 24 Nov. 1956, *EP/ORA* 235.

'in no position to judge': EP to Meacham, 13 Nov. [1957], as in Meacham 69.

'"Au dessus du conflit"': see EP to Meacham, 17 Nov. [1957], as in Meacham 71.

'Kasper's real ideology': EP to ORA, 20 May 1957, *EP/ORA* 245. See Henderson 551 for relevant background; also chap. III of 'Introductory Textbook', *GK* 354.

'the Negro business': J. M. Ch. Fr. Châtel as cited by David Rattray, 'Weekend with Ezra Pound', *The Nation* 185 (16 Nov. 1957)—as in *Casebook* 111.

'suicide troops': SM as cited by David Rattray, 'Weekend with Ezra Pound', *The Nation* 185 (16 Nov. 1957)—as in *Casebook* 115.

386 **'May be inhuman'**: EP to MdR, 13 May 1958 (Beinecke).

'attempt to implicate': EP to WL, 3 Feb. 1957, *EP/WL* 302.

'miscarriage of justice': Harold Lord Varney, 'Mental Health: Fact and Fiction', *American Mercury* 84 (Apr. 1957)—as cited in Sieber 16.

'act of largesse': [editorial], 'Ezra Pound', *New Republic* 136 (1 Apr. 1957) 6—as cited in Sieber 16.

'plea for Pound's freedom': Jack LaZebnik, 'The Case of Ezra Pound', *New Republic* 136 (1 Apr. 1957)—as in *Casebook* 118.
'good year to release poets': EH, cited *Casebook* 127.
possibility of good government: see EP's comments on *Thrones* in *Paris Rev. interview* 48–9.
'continues in his usual manner': Nursing Notes, 8/28/57(St Elizabeths Files, 1354, US Nat. Arch.).
'end of Canto 105': EP to MdR, 25 May [1957] (Beinecke).
387 **'96/106 "Thrones" in rough draft'**: EP to MdR, 27 Oct. [1957] (Beinecke).
'gettin 107 in order': EP to MdR, 26 Nov. 1957 (Beinecke).
Coke's *Second Institutes*: see EP to JT, 31 Oct. [1957], *EP/JT* 111.
'"The Twisted Cross"': EP as 'Herbert Briscoe', 'Total Morass', *Voice* II (7 Apr. 1956) 4, in *P&P* IX, 136.
'this quite proper fuss': EP as 'New York Correspondent', 'New York', *New Times* XXII.10 (18 May 1956) 6, in *P&P* IX, 145.
Edge: on Stock's magazine see William Flerming, 'The Melbourne Vortex', *Pai* 3.3 (1974) 325–8; Noel Stock, 'Ezra Pound in Melbourne 1953–7', *Helix* 13/14 (1983) 159–78, repr. in Noel Stock, *My Life in Brief with a Memoir of Ezra Pound* (Toledo: Rue de Rome Press, 1987), 45–74.
388 **'Utopia'**: [EP], 'Definitions', *Edge* 1 (Oct. 1956) [18]—in *P&P* IX, 176.
'genuine Old Testament': Thaddeus Zielinski, *The Sibyl*/*Edge* 2 (Nov. 1956) 47.
a German article: Jan H. Van Der Made, '"Mental Illness", New Name for Non-conformity: German Statement on Ezra Pound Case', *Edge* 3 (Feb. 1957) 17–20.
best since the *Little Review*: EP to Brigit Patmore, [?1957] (HRC).
'the Kulchurl cenTER': EP to Peter Russell, 1 Sept. [1957] (HRC).
389 **'the best since Stock's'**: EP to William Cookson, 29 Sept. 1957, *Agenda* 17.3–4–18.1 (1979/80) [7].
'live characters': EP to William Cookson, 29 Sept. 1957, *Agenda* 17.3–4–18.1 (1979/80) [7].
'a bit of tradition': EP to Cookson, 18 Nov. 1957, *Agenda* 17.3–4–18.1 (1979/80) [11].
'knowledge incarnate': EP to Cookson, 'boxing day '57', *Agenda* 17.3–4–18.1 (1979/80) [13].
'Yr next reading': EP to Cookson, 23 Oct. 1957, *Agenda* 17.3–4–18.1 (1979/80) [8].
'The FIRST fight': EP to Cookson, 'boxing day '57', *Agenda* 17.3–4–18.1(1979/80) [13].
'The QUESTION': EP to Cookson, 6 Jan. [1958], *Agenda* 17.3–4–18.1(1979/80) [15].
'I am "of course" not antisemitic': EP to Cookson, 7 Feb. [1958], *Agenda* 17.3–4–18.1 (1979/80) [21].
'The enemy is IGGURANCE': EP to Cookson, 10 Jan. 1958, *Agenda* 17.3–4–18.1 (1979/80) [16]. Cookson provided the context in 'EP and *Agenda*', in *Sons of Ezra: British Poets and Ezra Pound*, ed. Michael Alexander and James McGonigal (Amsterdam: Rodopi, 1995), 50.
390 **'their job is to get me out of quod'**: EP to Cookson, 2 Mar. [1958], *Agenda* 17.3–4–18.1 (1979/80) [24].
'devotes himself to the cause': David Rattray, 'Weekend with Ezra Pound', *The Nation* 185 (16 Nov. 1957)—as in *Casebook* 114n.
'with usura': 45/229.
'Luigi in hill paths': 104/741.
'the gold light of wheat': 106/752–3.
a red-ink seal: the characters were *Pao* (M4946), *en* (M1743), *tê* (M6162)—see 'Terminology' in *Confucius* 23, 21; also *EP/JT* 91 and 146, and *EP/JL* 252.

391 **'I was troubled'**: Folke Isaksson to Hammarskjöld, 18 Mar. 1957, as in Little 126.
'when Pound was talking': Folke Isaksson, 'Diktaren I Dårhuset' ['The Poet in the Madhouse'], *Bonniers Litterära Magasin* 27.6 (1958)—as translated in Little 123–4.
'As he sat in a deckchair': John Wain, 'The Shadow of an Epic', *Spectator* 204 (11 Mar. 1960) 360—in Homberger 455–6.
'Chess each evening': Nursing Notes, 3/16/57 (St Elizabeths Files, 1352, US Nat. Arch.).
392 **'Jets kept taking off'**: Reno Odlin, 'Pound at St. Elizabeths', *Antigonish Review* 51 (1982) 42.
'A coloured inmate': Odlin, 'Pound at St. Elizabeths', *Antigonish Review* 51 (1982) 42.
'Another day': Odlin, 'Pound at St. Elizabeths', *Antigonish Review* 51 (1982) 44.
'Bear no grudge': OR to EP, 1 Jan. 1957, Conover 213.
'Note from O': EP to MdR, 27 Aug. 1957 (Beinecke).
393 **'I can NOT see her'**: EP to MdR, 15 Nov. 1957 (Beinecke).

'M'Amour, ma vie'

Principal sources for this section: the Marcella Spann Booth Collection of Ezra Pound (HRC/MSB); Marcella Booth, 'Through the Smoke Hole: Ezra Pound's Last Year at St Elizabeths', *Pai* 3.3 (1972) 329–34, and 'Ezrology: The Class of '57', *Pai* 13.3 (1984) 357–88.

393 **Poundian literature course**: see Miller's Syllabus in *CC* 330–4.
'see something of the world': MS to EP, 17 Aug. 1956 (Beinecke).
'read all the books': MS to EP, 6 Sept. 1956 (Beinecke).
'to develop appreciation': MS to EP, [Dec. 1956] (Beinecke).
'Marcella an addition': EP to MdR, 31 Mar. 1957 (Beinecke).
'lovely intelligent, and v. pleasant': DP to OSP, 22 Oct. 1957 (Hamilton/OSP).
'most frequent visitor': MSB 'Ezrology', *Pai* 13.3 (1984) 377n.
'The Mind of Pierre Duval': see *EP/WCW* 315n.
'on the green stretch of lawn': MSB 'Ezrology', *Pai* 13.3 (1984) 377–8; see also *Pai* 3.3 (1972) 330.
'Read the part you like': MSB 'Ezrology', *Pai* 13.3 (1984) 378.
'Stick with what you know': MSB 'Ezrology', *Pai* 13.3 (1984) 375.
'whole of Ovid's *Metamporphoses*': MSB 'Ezrology, *Pai* 13.3 (1984) 378.
'ILLITERACY': MSB 'Ezrology', *Pai* 13.3 (1984) 378.
'taught like a kind father': MSB 'Ezrology', *Pai* 13.3 (1984) 383.
394 **'TEACHING 100 females'**: EP to MdR, 28 Oct. 1957 (Beinecke).
'in a burst of tears': MSB 'Through the Smoke Hole', *Pai* 3.3 (1972) 330–1.
The first lesson: EP to MS, 3 TSS pages beginning 'm A/ 7.27 // Ang/Sax', [n.d] (HRC/MSB).
'PREZICELY': EP to MS, 1 Oct. [1957] (HRC/MSB).
395 **potent roquefort**: EP to MS, 'SABato, 4.23', [Feb. 1958] (HRC/MSB)—and see EP to MS, 'JHeez. Fri. 5.30', [n.d.] (HRC/MSB), and MSB 'Ezrology', *Pai* 13.3 (1984) 383.
'her damn SCHOOL': EP to MdR, 2 Nov. [1957] (Beinecke).
'shd plan eZcape': EP to MS, 'Sunday 4.59', [?October 1957] (HRC/MSB).
396 **'yes m'amour'**: EP to MS, 'Mercoledi', [n.d.] (HRC/MSB).
'Terracina and the Circeo': see 39/195, and 106/754.
'in dumps': EP to ID, 29 Nov. 1957 (HRC).
'reportedly on water wagon': EP to MdR, 2 Nov. [1957] (Beinecke).

as he would write later: the rest of this paragraph is based on an odd page of an EP letter loose in EP to MdR correspondence. Re 'dumping the poubelle or ash can', see SM to Bukowski, 5 June 1960: 'maestro ezra pound kept telling me "now don't dump yr garbage on my head"' (*CB/SM* 37). In a copy of Villon's *Œuvres* at Brunnenburg inscribed 'Sheri's in keeping St Liz 1956', 'La Belle Heaulmière' is marked; in contrast, a copy of *The Women of Trachis* (New Directions, 1957) from EP's library at HRC has the initials 'M.S.' and 'EP' entwined on the front endpaper.

397 **'M'Amour, Artemis'**: EP to MS, 'Sa'rdy/10.41', [n.d.] (HRC/MSB).
In canto 106: EP had this 'in rough draft' at the end of Oct. 1957—EP to MdR, 26 Oct. [1957] (Beinecke).
picking cotton: see EP to MdR, 31 Mar. 1957 (Beinecke).
'Artemis out of Leto': 106/754.
'God's eye art ou': 106/755; see also 113/790.
'The sky is leaded with elm boughs': the visual effect here at 106/755, as with 'The sky's glass leaded with elm boughs' (107/761), is of a stained-glass window, worth noting since one learned commentator has failed to see it.

398 **'a paradiso | terrestre'**:/802; **'in the halls of hell'**: 81/521.
'happy for weeks': MSB 'Ezrology, *Pai* 13.3 (1984) 379.
'NO! (continuing)': EP to MS, [n.d.], reproduced in *Paris Review* 187 (2008) [26–7].

The St Elizabeths Cantos (2): Thrones. 96–109 de los cantares

In this section the following works have been helpful: Terrell's *Companion*; William Cookson, *A Guide to the Cantos of Ezra Pound* (Croom Helm, 1985) [= Cookson]; David Gordon, 'Edward Coke: The azalea is grown', *Pai* 4.2–3, 223–99, 554 [= Gordon]; George Kearns, *Guide to Pound's* Selected Cantos (Rutgers University Press, 1980) [= Kearns]; James J. Wilhelm, *The Later Cantos of Ezra Pound* (New York: Walker and Company, 1977) [= Wilhelm, *Later Cantos*].

398 **'largely ineffective'**: Kearns 223.
'soars over what went before': BB to EP, [?1964] (Beinecke).
'they do not present': BB to EP as reported by EP himself and recorded by Michael Reck in 'A Conversation between Ezra Pound and Allen Ginsberg', *Evergreen Review* 57 (1968) 28.

399 **'after the age of forty'**: EP to Kathleen Raine, 'Visiting Ezra Pound', *Agenda* 37.2–3 (1999) 141.
'paideutic and anagogical': 'said EP on 5 March 1958, as recalled in 1962 by Hollis Frampton', Reno Odlin, notes (dated 1988) around JL's *Pound as Wuz*, sent by e-mail to Arnaud Lefebvre, 7 Feb. 2001, [p. 12], printed in Reno Odlin, *Revues et textes critiques 1976–2001*, 'Un document de photocopies préparé par la Galerie Arnaud Lefebvre, Paris/À l'occasion de l'exposition des *Lettres de Hollis Frampton*, 12 sept.–12 oct. 2002'. SM started her *Anagogic & Paideumic Review* in San Francisco in 1959.
'mankind's struggle': *SR* 127.
'you might take it': EP to IWP, 13 Nov. 1926, *EP/Parents* 593.
'EFFECT on the MIND': EP to William Watt, 27 May and 8 July [1957], *Ezra Pound's Letters to William Watt* with an introduction and notes by WW (Marquette, Mich.: North Michigan University Press, 2001) [no page nos.]. Kearns 295 associates the term with *contemplatio* (after Anselm).
'the anagogic leads to unity': EP in note 'written in pencil on two sides of a board—dated "13 Maggio"', as recorded on tape by OR 16 Mar. 1975, and as transcribed into her Venice Notebook (Beinecke).

'blue china': see EP to Dudek, [received 13 Apr. 1950], *EP/Dk* [19], and [received 27 Mar. 1952], *EP/DK* [88]—cited above p. 324.

400 **'to fully grasp'**: Wilhelm, *Later Cantos*, 117.

'the quest, dark and questionable': Wilhelm, *Later Cantos*, 119.

401 **'had no ground'**: see 98/685 and 102/728.

K'ang-hsi: reigned 1662–1723—see cantos 59 and 60.

'The text is somewhat exigeant': 98/691.

'correctly aligned warp threads': John Cayley's note in Cookson 136.

402 **Wagadu**: see 74/430 and 77/465.

403 **Pound's own protest**: see EP, 'Four Steps', *Agenda* 17.3–4–18.1 (1979/80) 139.

Na Khi: on this subject see the illuminating essay by Jamila Ismail, '"News of the universe": ^{2}muan ^{1}bpo and the *Cantos*', *Agenda* 9.2–3 (1971) 70–87.

404 **'One is held up'**: EP, *Paris Rev. interview* 49.

'as Ixion, unstill': 113/790 and cf. 80/503.

405 **'Kung is the outer'**: EP to Denis Goacher, 11 Oct. [?1955] (Goacher fragments folder, HRC).

'wheat surging': cf. Homeric Hymn *To Demeter* ll.449–56.

the flowers of asphodel etc.: Terrell's suggestion that 'ulex' belongs with the 'paradisal flora' will not convince those of us who have had close encounters with gorse. 'Aquileia' is not a flowering plant but an ancient town north of Venice on the sea-marshes. I have been unable to identify 'Caffaris'.

406 **in earlier cantos initiated Odysseus**: see the sequence 17, 30, 39, 47. About Pound's use of the Eleusinian mysteries, it should be noted that the mythology is not for Pound a matter of belief, but a way of perceiving the cosmos: see his 'A Problem of (Specifically) Style' and 'Convenit esse Deos' in *MA* 121–5 and 135–40.

'my notes do not cohere': 116/797.

'a migration of the real powers': Gordon 247–9.

407 **'The Sicilian rose'**: Gordon 249.

408 **'The keeper'**: Sir Edward Coke, *The Second Part of the Laws of England* (Bell-Yard, near Temple Bar, 1797), Cap. V, 14–15.

'man's efforts to synchronize': Gordon 554, and see Gordon 279.

409 **'IGNORANT of Coke'**: EP to Moelwyn Merchant, 7 Nov. [1957], as in Moelwyn Merchant, 'The Coke Cantos', *Agenda* 17.3–4–18.1 (1979/80) 81. See also EP to Merchant, 12 Nov. [1957]: 'set of 4 vols. of Coke sighted in London', Merchant, 'The Coke Cantos', *Agenda* 17.3–4–18.1 (1979/80) 82—the sighting was by AVM according to EP to OSP, 14 Nov. [1957]—this may have been the 1681 edition of Coke's *Institutes* which EP had bought by 8 Feb. 1958 (see DP to OSP, 8 Feb. 1958 (Hamilton/OSP)).

'various items': EP sheet dated '15 Sept' enclosed with EP to Moelwyn Merchant, 17 Sept. [1957], as in Moelwyn Merchant, 'The Coke Cantos', *Agenda* 17.3–4–18.1 (1979/80) 80–1.

'G. Giov. brot': EP to JT, 31 Oct. [1957], *EP/JT* 111.

'"Institutes" nearest thing to Confucius': EP to MdR, 2 Nov. [1957] (Beinecke). 'Parad. X' would suggest that he already had it in mind to connect Coke with the tenth canto of Dante's *Paradiso*.

no time 'for the digestion': Moelwyn Merchant, 'The Coke Cantos', *Agenda* 17.3–4–18.1 (1979/80) 83.

MacLeish gets his 'nol pros'

409 **no 'substantial change'**: WO to Frank Loveland, 26 Mar. 1957 (St Elizabeths Files, 929, US Nat. Arch.).

410 **remove the obfuscation**: Thurman Arnold, 'The Strange Case of the Noted Poet Ezra Pound', *Fair Fights and Foul: A Dissenting Lawyer's Life* (New York: Harcourt Brace & World, Inc., 1965), 237.
Moore put it to Cornell: AVM to JC, 29 Apr. 1957 (Lilly).
'Taking everything into account': TSE to AVM, 8 May 1957 (Lilly).

411 **'You can use my name'**: Graham Greene to Ronald Duncan, 21 Oct. 1957 (HRC).
A petition: see Tytell 325.
'a fellow Republican': AMacL to EP, 11 Dec. [1957], *MacLeish* 404.
'a prominent literary figure': John Foster Dulles to RF, 12 Feb. 1957, *Frost* 562.
'My purpose holds': RF to AMacL, 24 June 1957, *Frost* 569.

412 **'fully armed'**: AMacL to RF, 28 June [1957], *MacLeish* 400.
'anything but treasonable': EH to RF, 28 June 1957, *Hemingway* 878–80.
MacLeish reported the outcome: AMacL to EH, 21 July 1957, and to EP, 22 July 1957, *MacLeish* 401–2.

413 **Walter Winchell**: much feared, widely syndicated, newspaper and radio gossip columnist, in part responsible for the re-arrest and wrongful conviction of 'Tokyo Rose', and, according to MacLeish, feared by the administration—see AMacL to EP, 18 Feb. 1958, *MacLeish* 405. EP wrote to JT, 17 June 1957, 'What is keeping me in here is JEWS/B. Baruch/Winchell "E.P. out over my (i.e. Winchell's) dead body"' (*EP/JT* 44).

413 **'has spread the rumour'**: AMacL to EP, 22 July 1957, *MacLeish* 402.
Pound thanked him: EP to AMacL, 4 Aug. [1957], Carpenter 831.
'damned nonsense': EP to AMacL, 7 Aug. [1957], as in Carpenter 831.
'it wd/ however be timely': EP to MdR, 11 Aug. 1957 (Beinecke).
'not being able to go to Italy': AMacL to RF, 22 Aug. [1957], *MacLeish* 402.
Frank Lloyd Wright: see Carpenter 832.
'nuttier than he is': AMacL to RF, 22 Aug. [1957], *MacLeish* 402–3.
'Whereas Ezra Pound': Mr. Burdick, 85th Congress, 1st Session, H.RES.403, 21 Aug. 1957—(copy in St Elizabeths Files, 1219a–b, US Nat. Arch.).

414 **'time to spring grampaw'**: EP to Cookson, 15 Nov. [1957], *Agenda* 17.3–4–18.1 (1979/80) [10].
'repeatedly offered our support': Patrick Murphy Malin, Executive Director ACLU, to Arnold Gingrich, *Esquire Magazine*, 28 Aug. 1957, as in Sieber 42–3. Sieber 41 gives brief extracts from letters to the editor of *Esquire Magazine* following Rovere's article. See Norman: *Case* 197–8 for Malin's letter dated 18 Apr. 1958 to the Attorney General, seeking to capitalize on Pound's release, towards which the ACLU had contributed nothing, in the interest of 'the larger legal problem'.
moved by MacLeish's 'eloquent passage': see Meacham 32–3.
'a letter-writing drive': see Meacham 48ff.
'19 years of effort': EP to Meacham, 24 Sept. 1957, Meacham 51.

415 **'Re/ one of yr/ questions'**: EP to Meacham, 24 Sept. 1957/'*later*', Meacham 52.
'his well-meaning friends': Meacham, Meacham 55.
'no public stir': AMacL to Meacham, 17 Oct. 1957, Meacham 60.
'E.P. can only AFFORD': EP to MS, [n.d.] (HRC/MSB).

416 **Pound's royalties**: Committee accounts (Pound MSS VI, Lilly).
'has Dr Overholser's consent': RF to William P. Rogers, 19 Nov. 1957, *Frost* 571.
'a firm commitment from Rogers': AMacL to WO, 27 Nov. 1957 (St Elizabeths Files,1018, US Nat. Arch.).
'nothing much would be gained': WO to AMacL, 5 Dec. 1957 (St Elizabeths Files,1019, US Nat. Arch.).
'would quash the indictment': AMacL to WO, 13 Dec. 1957 (St Elizabeths Files,1027, US Nat. Arch.).

417 **'looks cloudy from this angle'**: AMacL to Meacham, 22 Dec. 1957, Meacham 64.

'very reasonable and patient': AMacL to Meacham, 17 Oct. 1957, Meacham 60.
'I cd/ do wiff a change': EP to EEC, 20 Nov. 1957, *EP/EEC* 395.
'I shd/ like to get OUT': EP to Patricia Hutchins, 4 Nov. 1957 (British Library)—as in Carpenter 835.
'Time has come': EP to Noigrandres, *Jornal de letras,* Reo do Janeiro, X.106 (May 1958) [1]—in *P&P* IX, 215.
'This ward is no fit place': EP to MdR, 2 Nov. [1957]. See also Carpenter 835.
offering 'to discuss the matter': William P. Rogers to MacLeish, 2 Jan. 1958, as in Meacham 124.
'would like somehow': AMacL to Hammarskjöld, 2 Jan. 1958, as in Little 138. See also AMacL to EP, 18 Feb. 1958, *MacLeish* 405.
418 **'one thing was certain'**: AMacL to EH, 30 Sept. 1958, *MacLeish* 411.
'you can give the whole story': Christian Herter to WO, 2 Jan. 1958—as in Carpenter 836.
'the real solution': AMacL to Hammarskjöld, 2 Jan. 1958, as in Little 138.
'the controversial character': J. Edgar Hoover's report to Attorney General, 28 Jan. 1958, as in Little 143.
'why the Department of Justice': Cornell 123–4.
'the indictment against Pound': from Little 143.
'2 letters': 'The Ezra Pound Case. Extension of Remarks of Hon. Usher L. Burdick of North Dakota', *Congressional Record* 104.12 (27 Jan. 1958)—the page with Burdick's introductory remarks and the two letters is reproduced as an appendix to *EP/WW*.
419 **'If Ezra Pound were released'**: DP to WO, 1 Feb. 1958 (St Elizabeths Files, 1049, US Nat. Arch.).
'Unlikely': EP to Noigrandres, *Jornal de letras,* Reo do Janeiro, X.106 (May 1958) [1], in *P&P* IX, 215.
'it may be o.k.': EP to Robert MacGregor, 25 Feb. 1958, *EP/JL* 256 (in part); see also note to the Pound letter in *Book Five* (1958), part II, in WCW, *Paterson*, revised edn. prepared by Christopher MacGowan (Manchester: Carcanet Press, 1992), 302.
'serious and thoughtful people': Hammarskjöld to Herter, 18 Feb. 1958, as in Little 140.
'idea of getting Pound to Italy': Herter to AMacL (copied to Hammarskjöld), 5 Mar. 1958—from Little 142.
'The idea is that you': AMacL to EP, 16 Mar. 1958, *MacLeish* 406.
420 **'an illegal arrangement'**: EP to AMacL, 25 Mar. 1958, as in Carpenter 837–8.
'First kind word': AMacL to EP, 30 Mar. 1958, *MacLeish* 407–8.
'played for a sucker': EP to MdR, 29 Mar. 1958 (Beinecke).
'a meal or something': RF to Sherman Adams, 12 Feb. 1958, *Frost* 572.
'TO AN INFORMAL STAG DINNER': Dwight D. Eisenhower to RF, 16 Feb. 1958, *Frost* 572–3.
– 'WHAT'S ON MY MIND': RF to Sherman Adams, 16 Feb. 1958, *Frost* 573.
421 **sign of his approval**: Heymann 250—his note on p. 354 gives as source, 'Telephone interview with Sherman Adams, Feb. 13, 1973'.
'the "nod" of the President: JL to Meacham, 4 Aug. 1963 (Lilly).
'A decision is near': Miriam Ottenberg, 'Liberty Being Weighed for Poet Ezra Pound', Washington DC *Sunday Star* (16 Mar. 1958), as in Carpenter 839 and Sieber 17, 22.
'if the indictment is dismissed': AVM to EP, 26 Mar. 1958 (Lilly).
'The Government's case': Sieber 1.
'The Justice Department': 'Ezra Pound May Escape Trial and Be Allowed to Go to Italy', *New York Times*, 2 Apr. 1958, as in *Casebook* 128–9.
Frost: 'I've dropped in': Meacham 124; Carpenter 840 adds Frost's closing remark but gives no source.

'in the public interest': Arnold, Fortas, and Porter announcement, 5 Apr. 1958, reported in *Washington Post and Times-Herald* (6 Apr. 1958) 1, as in Sieber 18.
'to Dr Overholser's office': DP, Diary 1958, 4 Apr. (Lilly).
'things look more hopeful': EP to MdR, 5 Apr. 1958 (Beinecke).
'long talk with Thurman Arnold': DP, Diary 1958, 7 Apr. (Lilly).
'We have been retained': Arnold, Fortas, and Porter News Release, 7 Apr. 1958, as in Sieber 18–19.

423 **'The standing mute'**: EP to MdR, 3 Apr. 1958 (Beinecke).
'a certain amount of optimism': EP to MdR, 12 Apr. 1958 (Beinecke).
'First day one cd/ sit out': EP to MdR, 29 Mar. 1958 (Beinecke).
'a monument of sanity': Norman Holmes Pearson to HD, 2 Apr. 1958, as in Little 148.
'at the mention of music': Robert Hughes, personal communication, 27 Oct. 2011. Cf. *EP&M* 464–5.
the precision of Linnaeus: EP to Hammarskjöld, 13 Apr. 1958, from Little 150.
Crabbe having mentioned Linnaeus: see EP to MdR, 24 Apr. 1958 (Beinecke).
'got thru a lot of work': EP to MdR, 17 Apr. 1958 (Beinecke). 'Conversations in Courtship', translated by EP and Noel Stock, later published as *Love Poems of Ancient Egypt* (1962).
an interesting challenge: seeThurman Arnold, 'The Strange Case of the Noted Poet Ezra Pound', *Fair Fights and Foul* , 236–42.

424 **MOTION TO DISMISS INDICTMENT and attached AFFIDAVIT, MEMORANDUM and STATEMENT OF ROBERT FROST**: from Norman: *Case* 191–6, and Cornell 125–31.

427 **'and Pound listened'**: MSB 'Through the Smoke Hole', *Pai* 3.3 (1972) 334.
'Furniss fetched OP and DP': DP, Diary 1958, 18 Apr. (Lilly). Details re Omar are from DP's diary entries for 7 and 14 Apr.
'shabby blue jacket': Anthony Lewis, 'Court Drops Charges Against Ezra Pound', *New York Times* (19 Apr. 1958) 1.23, as in *Casebook* 139–40.
ORDER DISMISSING INDICTMENT: from Norman 196–7.
'gave her husband a kiss': Anthony Lewis, 'Court Drops Charges', as in *Casebook* 140.

428 **'showed no emotion'**: Max Freedman, 'Ezra Pound Released: Government Backs Appeal', *Manchester Guardian* (19 Apr. 1958) (cutting in Nat. Arch. KV 2/876/361810).
'a firm "yes"': Anthony Lewis, 'Court Drops Charges', as in *Casebook* 140.
'a long yellow scarf with oriental characters': this is from Lewis' report in *New York Times*. For McNaughton's remarks see his 'Kingdoms of the Earp: Carpenter and Criticism', *Pai* 21.3 (1992) 14–15. The scarf can be seen in illustration no. 33.

14. Clearing Out

430 **'The Poet's wife'**: Anthony Lewis, 'Court Drops Charges', *New York Times* (19 Apr. 1958) 1.23, as in *Casebook* 139.
'Mr Pound will now apply': Max Freedman, 'Ezra Pound Released', *Manchester Guardian* (19 Apr. 1958) (cutting in Nat. Arch. KV 2/876/361810–60a).
'We are informed': William D. Rogers to DP, 21 Apr. 1958 (Lilly).
'until his family': Anthony Lewis, 'Court Drops Charges', *New York Times* (19 Apr. 1958) 1.23, as in *Casebook* 139.
'Yr. venbl parent': EP to MdR, 18 and 24 Apr. 1958 (Beinecke).

431 **'Escaped with Eliz. W'**: DP, Diary 1958, 18 and 24 Apr. (Lilly).
'9.45 a.m. to Boston': DP, Diary 1958, 19 Apr. (Lilly).

'THE pearl necklace': DP to AVM, 24 Jan. 1962 (Lilly). On 16 July 1927 DP had written from London to EP in Venice, 'Signed up to a new Will yesterday: Parkyn [the family solicitor] worried about my leaving you the necklace—but it's done' (Lilly). 'The pearl necklace was a Shakespear family heirloom, given to the wife of Alexander Shakespear (Dorothy's grandfather) by the Maharajah of Benares upon Alexander's retirement from service in India in 1873. This explains Mr. Parkyn's concern in 1927. When Dorothy brought the necklace to Boston in 1958, she made a particular point of telling me that as Omar's wife I could wear it but that she was giving it to him' (communication from Elizabeth Pound, 10 Feb. 2014).
'apt. 511 /2407': EP to Cookson, 24 May [1958], *Agenda* 17.3–4–18.1 (1979/80) [30].
'Many of our men': Emmanuel Celler, in Paul Sampson, 'Plan to Free Ezra Pound is Protested', *Washington Post Times-Herald* (7 Apr. 1958) 1—from Sieber 18.
'Bloodier war criminals': 'What the Pound Case Means', *The Nation* 186 (19 Apr. 1958) 335—as in *Casebook* 130.
'a little magnanimity': 'The Case of Ezra Pound', *Wall Street Journal* (17 Apr. 1958)—from Sieber ii.
'an attempt to stir up': 'The Case of Mr. Ezra Pound', *The Times* (9 Apr. 1958) (cutting in Nat. Arch. KV 2/876/361810-58a).
432 **'a magnanimous spirit'**: Max Freedman, 'Ezra Pound Released', *Manchester Guardian* (19 Apr. 1958) (cutting in Nat. Arch. KV 2/876/361810-60a).
a New Directions press release: 'New Canto for a Poet', *New York Times* (19 Apr. 1958) 23—as in *Casebook* 141.
'the amount of clutter': EP to MS, 19 [Apr. 1958] (HRC/MSB).
'boxes, bags, manuscripts': Meacham 131–2.
433 **Rip van Winkle**: EP to DP, 21 Apr. [1958] (Lilly).
'it dawned on me': EP to MdR, 24 Apr. [1958] (Beinecke).
'po'k chaups': EP to MS, [21/21 Apr. 1958] (HRC/MSB).
'shrimp cocktail': EP to MdR, 24 Apr. [1958] (Beinecke).
'indubitably pleasant': EP to MS, [23 Apr. 1958] (HRC/MSB).
wrote of feeling solitary: EP to MS, [23 Apr. 1958] (HRC/MSB).
'Giardino': EP to MS, [22 Apr. 1958] (HRC/MSB).
'M'Amour, ma vie': e.g. EP to MS, [23 Apr. 1958] (HRC/MSB).
'might try to versify': EP to MS, [21 Apr. 1958] (HRC/MSB).
Those butterflies: see 92/619-20, and 106/754,/802 (the final fragment).
'outta the nest': MS, *CB/SM* 132, and see Steven Moore's 'Introduction', *CB/SM* 22–3.
'The male can't just go': SM to HD, as incorporated by HD, *ET* 57—and see *ET* 39ff.
434 **'poor Undine'**: HD, *ET* 57.
'on a personal tangent': Lee Lady to Stock, [n.d.] (HRC).
'three calls during ten minutes': EP to MdR, 24 Apr. [1958] (Beinecke).
'Don't you think my husband': EP note to DP, [Apr./May 1958] (Lilly).
'Officially I am NOT': EP to MdR, 24 Apr. [1958] (Beinecke).
435 **'against people being railroaded'**: Usher L. Burdick as cited by Mary McGrory, 'Ezra Pound Still Sees Mad World Out of Step', *Washington Star* (30 Apr. 1958)—in *Casebook* 144–8.
'did speak well of Frost': EP to AMacL, 27 May 1958, as in Carpenter 846. When EP said the same thing to Meacham, the latter astutely reflected that 'Pound felt no one should be obligated to him for anything he had done for them, and he, in turn, never felt he was under obligation for any services, of whatever magnitude' (132).
met by Pound and Marcella: DP, Diary 1958, 29 Apr. (Lilly).
cooked for her: see DP to OSP, 30 Apr. 1958 (Hamilton).

'mentally and physically exhausted': Meacham 135.
'chaste and dulcet': James Jackson Kilpatrick, 'A Conversation with Ezra Pound', as in Meacham 137.
brilliantly impressionist account: Kilpatrick, 'A Conversation with Ezra Pound', as in Meacham 137–42.

436 **'Recommendation for Discharge'**: (St Elizabeths Files, 1427, US Nat. Arch.).

437 **'Report of Discharge or Death'**: (St Elizabeths Files, 1087, US Nat. Arch.).
Committee's audited return: Committee accounts (Lilly).
'Marcella at TOP': EP to MdR, 30 Apr. [1958] (Beinecke).
'one night in Verona': EP to MdR, 14 May [1958] (Beinecke).
'me and my body guard': EP to MdR, 21 May [1958] (Beinecke).
'Do credit her': EP to MdR, 22 June [1958] (Beinecke).
'"asylum for life"': Rome correspondent, *The Times* (15 May 1958) (cutting in Nat. Arch. KV 2/876/361810-64a).
'no official objections': William D. Rogers to DP, 17 May 1958 (Lilly).
'shelter on Isola S. Giorgio': EP to MdR, 14 May [1958] (Beinecke).

438 **'the Spannthology'**: EP to MdR, 21 May [1958] (Beinecke).
'foreign correspondent': see Meacham 146, and EP to MdR, 14 May and 1 June 1958 (Beinecke).
'alarUMS, scursions, whoops': EP to Cookson, 24 May [1958], *Agenda* 17.3–4–18.1 (1979/80) [30].
'continue as Committee': DP to AVM, 27 May 1958 (Lilly).
'not yet out of "committee" control': EP to MdR, [?19 May 1958] (Beinecke).
'status still entangled': EP to MdR, 29 May 1958 (Beinecke).
the historic Old South: see Meacham 153–4.

439 **'present state of degradation'**: EP to Meacham, 21 May 1958, Meacham 149.
'fatigue deep as the grave': 83/533.
Caedmon Records: details from sleeve note for *TC 1122 Ezra Pound Reading* [volume 1] (1960), recorded 12, 13, and 26 June 1958. Pound read *Hugh Selwyn Mauberley*, 'Cantico del Sole', 'Moeurs Contemporaines', 'The Gypsy', 'Exile's Letter', and cantos 1, 4, 36, 45, 51, 76 (second half), 84, 99.
'two hours tape recording': EP to MdR, 14 June 1958 (Beinecke).
royalties to Marcella: see EP to JL, 5 June 1959, *EP/JL* 269; also EP to JL, 20 Dec. 1958, cited Conover 217.
'8 trunks packed': EP to MdR, 22 June 1958 (Beinecke).
\$1500 'for expenses': EH to EP, 26 June 1958, *Hemingway* 883.
'sunk in plexiglass': EP to Hemingway, as cited by Stoneback, 'Hemingway and Pound', *Ezra Pound, Ends & Beginnings*, ed. John Gery and William Pratt (New York: AMS Press Inc., 2011), 174.

440 **guests of Carl Gatter**: see Stock: 1976, 105–9—this is based on Gatter's own account. There are a number of accounts of Pound's last days in America, but there is no agreement among them about dates. There is general agreement that Pound was with the Gatters on the night of Friday 27 June—and there is Gatter's own authority for that; Meacham says he spent two nights with the Collins, which would be the nights of the 28th and 29th—others don't mention that visit; and Mariani says he was with the Williams 'from the evening of the28th to the morning of the 30th', which would have them going straight from Wyncote to Rutherford. The date of the Avedon photograph is given variously as 29 June and 30 June—the 29th seems more likely. Most give the date of departure of the *Cristofero Colombo* from New York as 30 June—not 1 July as Pound had thought it would be. Accepting the 30th as the date of departure, and the 27th as the date of leaving Washington, and accepting the stay with the Collins (for which again we have Gatter's word), allows just one night for each of the three visits.

guests of Alan C. Collins: see Meacham 161; Stock: 1976, 108–9; Stock: 1970, 449; Heymann 256.
'Take care of yourself': WCW to EP, 21 May 1958, *EP/WCW* 318
guests of WCW: see Paul Mariani, *William Carlos Williams* (1981) 741–2. See *WCW/JL* 225 for the Richard Avedon arrangement.
'a broiling hot June day': see Reck 134–5 for this and other details.
441 **cabin 128**: see DP to OSP, 24 June 1958 (Hamilton).
two cabins: see EP to EEC, [9 July 1968], *EP/EEC* 409, 411n.
'on the bunk lay Ezra': Norman Holmes Pearson to HD, as incorporated by HD into *ET* 61–2.
'a certain euphoria': EP to Reck, Reck 134–5.

15. A Final Testament, 1958–9

445 **It had become the custom**: this and the following paragraph mainly drawn from MdR, *Discretions* 304–5, and'Ezra Pound at Eighty', *Esquire* 65 (1966) 114–16, 178–80—the latter as reprinted in the 'volumetto', *Centoventi e ottanta anni* (Brunnenburg: per gli amici, 9 July 2005).
read Uncle Remus: see D. G. Bridson, 'An Interview with Ezra Pound', *New Directions* 17 (1961) 158.
446 **'*Sono, naturalmente*'**: EP, 'Sono felice d'esser tornato fra i miei', *L'Illustrazione Italiana* LXXXV.9 (1958) 34, in *P&P* IX, 234–5. This introductory note to MdR's translation of 'Canto 98' is dated 'Brunnenburg, 22 Iuglio 1958.'
'a familial clan': DP to OSP, 25 July 1958 (Hamilton/OSP).
'something went wrong': MdR, *Discretions* 305.
'What does it matter': DP as reported in EP to ID, 15 Apr. 1955 (HRC)—see p. 316 above.
'still crazy about Marcella': DP to OSP, 30 Aug. 1958 (Hamilton/OSP).
'will the Committee': AVM to Furniss, 31 July 1958 (Lilly).
Furniss replied: Furniss to AVM, 8 Aug. 1958 (Lilly).
447 **'Mrs. Pound and her son'**: AVM to Furniss, 18 Aug. 1958 (Lilly).
Furniss regarded the possibility: Furniss to AVM, 3 Sept. 1958 (Lilly).
'a fascist salute': 'Pound, in Italy, Gives Fascist Salute; Calls United States an "Insane Asylum"', *New York Times* (10 July 1958) 56—see illustration.
An even better story: I find the story first in Heymann (1976) 273–4, with no source given; then in Torrey (1984) 272, citing Heymann as source; in Tytell (1987) 334, probably from Heymann but without acknowledgement—Tytell places it in 1962, though on 1 May of that year Pound was convalescing with Olga Rudge in Sant'Ambrogio; in Carpenter (1988) 873–4, evidently from Heymann but without acknowledgement or source; and in Marsh (2011) 214, citing Torrey. The suspicion that Heymann might have invented the story is warranted by the total absence of corroborating evidence; and by the fact that he did invent an interview with EP—see his pp. 305–13, and then Hugh Kenner, *Historical Fictions* 55ff., and William McNaughton, *Pai* 5.3 (1976) 473.
448 **'pure legend'**: Giano Accame, *Ezra Pound economista* (Rome: Edizione Settimo Sigillo, 1995), 192—cited by Redman: see next note.
'no such photograph exists': Tim Redman, 'Pound's Politics and Economics', Ira B. Nadel ed., *Cambridge Companion to Ezra Pound* (Cambridge: Cambridge University Press, 1999), 260–1.
'He's very angry': Giacomo Oreglia, 'Meeting Ezra Pound', *Dagens Nyheter* (Stockholm, Sweden), 5 Nov. 1958—as in 'Sort of translation' sent by EP, with his notes and comments, to Meacham to be verifaxed 'to all on list', Meacham 37.

'PROGRAM': EP to Jaime Garcia Terrés, Feb. [1959], *Excelsior* (Mexico), 29 Mar. 1959, in *P&P* IX, 266. Cf. EP's 'Three points: One idea at a time | Vocational representation | Non indebetarsi', cited by Henry Swabey, 'A Page without which', *Pai* 5.2 (1976) 334.

'Let the poets combat': EP to C. J. Cela, 25 Apr. 1959, *Los Papeles de Son Armadans* (Madrid, Palma de Mallorca), XIX.57 *bis* (Dec. 1960) 70, in *P&P* IX, 292.

'no longer a POlitical': EP to JL, 24 Nov. 1959, *EP/JL* 271.

'now objects': EP to JL, [before June1960], *EP/JL* 275.

in *The European*: 'Of Misprision of Treason' [from Coke's *Institutes*, The Third Part], and 'Three Poems ['Old Zuk', 'The Draughty House (Catullus)', 'More']', *European* XII.5 (1959) 282–4; 'CI de los Cant[a]res', *European* XII.6 (1959) 382–4.

449 **his notebooks**: EP, *Drafts & Fragments. Facsimile Notebooks 1958–1959*—referred to here as *D&F facsimile*—consists of six notebooks. Four were numbered (and dated) by Pound: (1) July 23–Sept. 18, 1958; (2) Feb. 5–July 9, 1959; (3) July 12–Aug. 16, 1959; (4) Sept. 11–Dec. 5, 1959; an unnumbered and undated notebook, with the draft for 'That I lost my centre', is likely to belong to Aug. or Sept. 1959; the other notebook, which does not concern me here, is dated '10 Oct. 1958'. For an expert study of the typescripts copied from these notebooks by MS, and the subsequent drafts, see Ronald Bush, '"Unstill, ever turning": The Composition of Ezra Pound's *Drafts & Fragments*', in *Ezra Pound and Europe*, ed. Richard Taylor and Claus Melchior (Amsterdam: Rodopi, 1993), 223–41.

'weak and enfeebled': EP to ORA, *EP/ORA* 254.

'short bursts of energy': EP to William Cookson, 12 Sept. [1958], *Agenda* 17.3–4–18.1 (1979–80) [32].

'NOT in shape': EP to Douglas Bridson, 15 Sept. 1958 (Beinecke).

two nights in Venice: date from DP's diary (Lilly).

a column about books: see EP to Giambattista Vicari, 18 and 22 Sept. 1958, *EP/GV* 203–6.

450 **'very little energy'**: EP to John Theobald, 19 Oct. 1958, *EP/JT* 118.

'Mostra Delle Edizioni': details from DP to OSP, 19, 22, 31 Oct. 1958 (Hamilton).

'in spite of his seventy-three years': Giacomo Oreglia, 'Meeting Ezra Pound', *Dagens Nyheter* (Stockholm, Sweden), 5 Nov. 1958—as in Meacham 34–5.

to Venice again: dates from DP's diary (Lilly).

'To thy quiet house': EP MS drafts dated 12 and 13 Nov. and 10 Dec. [1958] (Marcella Spann Booth Collection, HRC).

451 **'17 Nov. 1958'**: EP TS note among EP to MdR correspondence (Beinecke).

typed thirty-seven pages: see Zhaoming Qian, 'An Afterword concerning Pound's 1935 revisit to the Fenollosa Papers', *Pai* 31 (2002) 308.

'ANY news of villas': EP to Meacham, 26 Dec. 1958, Meacham [103].

went down to Lake Garda: details from DP's diary (Lilly).

on a copy of its brochure: now in Marcella Spann Booth Collection (HRC/MSB).

proposed that they should marry: information from MdR.

a new notebook: i.e. notebook '2', reproduced in *D&F facsimile*.

452 **with three separate rooms**: see DP to OSP, 8 Mar. 1959 (Hamilton/OSP).

to cook and do all the housework: see DP to OSP, 8 and 18 Mar. 1959 (Hamilton/OSP).

'& in thy mind': in *D&F facsimile*, notebook '2', with date '28 Apr'.

'Young people today': EP, in 'interview with a reporter from the *New York Herald Tribune*', 'agreed to' by EP on 18 Jan. 1960, as in Heymann 269.

'& who no longer make Gods': in *D&F facsimile*, notebook '2', with date '14 May'.

453 **'19th May '59'**, **'sun & serenitas'**: in *D&F facsimile*, notebook '2', draft of canto 113.

''neath overhanging air': not in notebook, added in a TS draft of 113.

'souls melt into air': in *D&F facsimile*, from back of notebook '1', draft of 'gold mermaid' et seq. for 111.
'When the stag drinks': edited from *D&F facsimile*, notebook '1', draft for 110.
'From Time's wreckage': in *D&F facsimile*, notebook '2', between 7 and 21 Feb. 1959.
–**'falling spiders'**: in *D&F facsimile*, notebook '2', before 21 Feb. 1959.
454 **Moore to Furniss**: 12 Jan. 1959 (Lilly).
EP to Overholser: 2 Feb. 1959 (Beinecke).
DP to Moore: 13 Feb. 1959 (Lilly).
Moore to Peter du Sautoy: 3 Mar. 1959 (Lilly).
EP to Moore: 8 Mar. 1959 (Lilly).
Moore to EP: 13 Mar. 1959 (Lilly).
Furniss to EP: 28 May 1959 (Lilly).
Moore to EP: 7 June 1959 (Lilly).
455 **DP to Moore**: 13 June 1959 (Lilly).
suggest that Omar: see DP to AVM, 26 Feb. 1962 (Lilly), and AVM to DP, 5 Mar. 1962 (Lilly).
no legal existence: DP to OSP, 21 Aug. 1959 (Hamilton/OSP).
wanted to keep it that way: see AVM to DP, 21 Oct. 1959 (Lilly).
'EP. is not crazy': DP to OSP, 10 Mar. 1966 (Hamilton/OSP).
'All you or anyone else': EP to OR, 19 Feb. 1959 (Beinecke/OR).
456 **'Evidently was altitude'**: EP to OR, 27 Feb. 1959 (Beinecke/OR).
'my status': EP to OR, 8 Mar. 1959 (Beinecke/OR).
'and no-one else': OR to EP, 5 Mar. 1959 (Beinecke/OR). See also Conover 218.
'stuff DOWN': EP to MdR, 31 Mar. 1959 (Beinecke).
'small regular cheques': EP to MdR, 26 Mar. 1959 (Beinecke).
'rush of energy': EP to Bridson, 24 Mar. 1959 (Bridson Collection, Lilly).
Bridson seized his moment: see D. G. Bridson, 'An Interview with Ezra Pound', *New Directions* 17 (1961) 159–84.
457 **'6th and other cerebral vertebrae'**: EP to Meacham, [June 1959], Meacham 181.
'to supply a giraffe': EP to Katue Kitasono, 12 June 1959, as in *EP&J* 127.
'slows the mind': EP to Meacham, [June 1959], Meacham 181.
'x-ray attack': EP to OSP, 5 June 1959 (Hamilton/OSP).
'Poor little Marcella': DP to OSP, 18 June 1959 (Hamilton/OSP). Details of trip from DP's diary (Lilly).
'have been too exhausted': EP to MdR, 3 Aug. 1959 (Beinecke).
Nevertheless... he composed: the last pages of notebook '2' date from 9 July and contain from 'These simple men who have fought against jealousy' to 'the tribu' (114); notebook '3' continues 114 from 'armes et blasons!' through to its end, and then has the drafts for the rest of *D&F* (apart from 'La faillite de François Bernouard', composed before 19 June). An unrelated note at the end of the notebook is dated 'Aug. 16'.
458 **'a bronze dawn'**: in *D&F facsimile*, notebook '3', after 23 July 1959.
'Have I seen the divine': *D&F facsimile*, notebook '3'—this passage at the end of the draft contains the more significant variants from the published text of 116, which is otherwise nearly identical with the notebook draft. It is followed in the notebook by a kind of dedication: 'To the poets of my time: Disney | & quasi-anonimo | "Ah sold mah soul | to de company stoh" | honour them.'
461 **'EP feeling low'**: DP to OSP, 12 Aug. 1959 (Hamilton/OSP).
not in a fit state: EP to MdR, 12 Aug. 1959 (Beinecke).
'my old head': EP to MdR, 20 Aug. 1959 (Beinecke).
'nostalgia for Brunnenburg': EP to MdR, 26 Aug. 1959 (Beinecke).
'Have you still got the car': EP to MdR, 29 Aug. 1959 (Beinecke).

'No use': EP to MdR, 8 Sept. 1959 (Beinecke).
'To bless people': EP to MdR, 16 Aug. 1959 (Beinecke).
'destino or my muddles': EP to MdR, 4 Sept. 1959 (Beinecke).
'amid cumulative fatigue': EP to Richard Aldington, 25 Aug. 1959, as in RA to HD, 7 Sept. 1959, *Richard Aldington and H.D.: Their Lives in Letters*, ed. Caroline Zilboorg (Manchester: Manchester University Press, 2003), 402.
'Not since Brigit': EP to HD, 8 Sept. 1957, as cited by HD to RA, 30 Oct. 1959, *Richard Aldington and H.D.: Their Lives in Letters*, 407. For EP's letter to HD see Timothy Materer, 'H.D., Serenitas, and Canto CXIII', *Pai* 12.2–3, 274.
'no immediate concern': JL to AVM, 9 Sept. 1959 (Lilly).
reported at greater length: JL to AVM, 24 Sept. 1959 (Lilly).
462 **causing problems for his publishers**: DP wrote to JL that EP had 'had a fit of nerves and messed up' a contract with Caedmon which Laughlin had sent (DP to JL, Oct. 1959 [Lilly]). EP wanted the royalties to go to Marcella, and complained that the contract as drawn up by New Directions was 'gobbldegook' with 'too God DAMNED much fine print and twisty as eels' (EP to JL, 5 June and 25 Oct. 1959, *EP/JL* 268–9, 270–1). DP, for her own part, thought the contract a mess and, as Committee, refused to sign it.
'again went down into hell': in *D&F facsimile*, notebook '4', dated 'Sept. 11 [1959]'.
'becoming such a scandal': DP to OSP, 13 Sept. 1959 (Hamilton/OSP).
'Sitting in my ruins': EP to TSE, 15 Sept. 1959 (Beinecke).
a passage booked for Marcella: the date, 22 Sept., and the taxi, from DP's diary (Lilly); the original ticket is in the Marcella Spann Booth Collection (HRC); the Committee cheque stubs and accounts are in the Lilly Library; for EP's estimate see EP to Furniss, 25 May 1959 (Lilly).
'I have been a pitiless stone': in *D&F facsimile*, notebook '4'.
'In meine Heimat': in *D&F facsimile*, notebook '4'.
'That I lost my centre': in *D&F facsimile*, unnumbered and undated notebook—two notes in the hand of MS on pages at the end indicate that EP's lines were written before she left on 28 Sept. Her typed version (HRC/MSB) is close to the version in *D&F*.
463 **'EP in a fuss'**: DP diary (Lilly).
'EP lying on his bed': DP to OSP, 28 Sept. 1959 (Hamilton/OSP).
'couldn't take it any more': JL to WCW, 25 Oct. 1959, *WCW/JL* 230.
'We couldn't go on': DP to AVM, 5 Oct. 1959 (Lilly).
'glad you stood firm': AVM to DP, 21 Oct. 1959 (Lilly).
'came up here to die': EP to Krishna Kripalani, 31 Oct. 1959 (Beinecke).

16. 'You find me in fragments', 1959–62

464 **'And tower is full of you'**: EP to MS, [6 Oct. 1959] (MSB/HRC).
'one dies with out saving the world': *D&F facsimile*, notebook '4', fos. 6–7.
'in the labyrinth of death': *D&F facsimile*, notebook '4', fos. 11–13.
'Uncle Ezry': JL to WCW, 23 Oct. 1959, *WCW/JL* 229.
'I am so deeply concerned': JL to WO, 1 Dec. 1959, as in Wilhelm: 1994, 325.
465 **'reserpine and testicular hormone'**: 'Mr. Ezra Pound—Clinical report', Clinica della Malattie Nervose e Mentali, Università di Genova, sent to Dr Clara L. Hoye, Clinical Director, St Elizabeths, 19 Nov. 1966 (St Elizabeths files, 1161b, US Nat. Arch.)
its serious side-effect: communicated to EPOUND-L@LISTS.MAINE.EDU by Hideo Nogami.
'self-abasement', 'self-debasement': DP to OSP, 30 Oct. and 23 Dec. 1959 (Hamilton/OSP).

'Now that I am wrecked': EP to TSE, TS draft, [Oct.–Nov. 1959] (Canaday Center, University of Toledo Libraries, Toledo, Ohio).
'Hell, for all its horrors': see TSE, *After Strange Gods* (Faber & Faber, 1934), 41–3.
'DEEspair': EP to OR, 31 Oct. 1959, as in Conover 220.
'wrote to Mr. Eliot': MdR, *Discretions* 306.
'Forgive me for about 80%': EP to AMacL, 16 Dec. 1959, as in Meacham 183.
466 **'frightened the living bejeezzz'**: AMacL to EP, [*c.* Dec. 1959], *MacLeish* 418.
'don't git euphoria': EP to JL, 24 Nov. 1959, *EP/JL* 271.
'Troica Roma resurgens': *D&F facsimile*, notebook '4', fo. 15.
'Dec. 5. 4 p.m. Pax': *D&F facsimile*, notebook '4', fos. 16–18.
467 **'Ciao, cara mia'**: EP to MS, 17 Dec. [1959] (HRC/MSB). In Henry James story 'The Private Life' (1892), Lord Mellifont, 'was all public and had no corresponding private life', whereas Clare Vawdrey, the literary genius, 'was all private and had no corresponding public [life]'.
'M'amour': EP to MS, 20 Dec. [1959] (HRC/MSB).
'he better stay alive': EP to MS, 20 Dec. [1959] (HRC/MSB).
'and just before the end': Eva Hesse to JL, as copied by JL to WCW, 7 Jan. 1960, *WCW/JL* 231–2.
'depressed and jumpy': DP to OSP, 1 Jan. 1960 (Hamilton/OSP).
'during the night of Jan. 2': DP to AVM, 3 Jan. 1960, as relayed by AVM to JL, 16 Jan. 1960 (Lilly)—cited Carpenter 862–3.
468 **'Starting for Rome'**: EP note, 9 Jan. 1960 (private collection).
'the *Eia Eia Allalà* spirit': MdR, *Discretions* 397. On Dadone see Heymann 269–70.
'resting in Rap.': DP note to folder of letters: 'From EP (on trip to Rome) to DP (resting in Rap) Jan 1960. | Both away from corrosive castle.' (Lilly).
'not been so blind': EP to DP, 11 Jan. [1960] (Lilly).
'sorry not to contribute': EP to DP, 11 Jan. [1960] (Lilly).
'had orter made a better job': EP to DP, 14 Jan. [1960] (Lilly).
'how much of him': EP to DP, 16 Jan. [1960] (Lilly).
'Difficult to get unhitched': EP to DP, 20 Jan. [1960] (Lilly).
'Mao, Mao': EP to DP, 22 Jan. [1960] (Lilly).
'to hold my fragments together': EP to DP, 24 Jan. [1960] (Lilly).
'D/e swears': EP to DP, 24 Jan. [1960] (Lilly).
'Dadone idea': EP to MdR, [10 Feb. 1960] (Beinecke).
'Am being shot full': EP to JL, 23 Feb. 1960, *EP/JL* 274.
'emerged from the tomb': EP to MdR, 17 Feb. [1960] (Beinecke).
an interview for the *Paris Review*: following paras. drawn mainly from Donald Hall, 'Fragments of Ezra Pound' in his *Remembering Poets: Reminiscences and Opinions* (New York: Harper Colophon Books, 1979), 111–99—referred to here as Hall, *Remembering Poets.*
469 **'we sat opposite each other'**: Hall, *Remembering Poets* 114.
'more than physical': Hall, *Remembering Poets* 129.
'exoneration, forgiveness': Hall, *Remembering Poets* 149.
'his new *Cantos* and fragments': Hall, *Remembering Poets* 155; and see *Paris Rev. interview* 47.
470 **offered free flights and hotels**: EP to DP, 2 Mar. 1960 (Lilly).
'may be the Xoros': EP to Ronald Duncan, 6, 9, 18 Mar. [1960] (HRC).
to visit Leopardi's house: EP to MdR, 11 Mar. [1960] (Beinecke).
'not well but better': EP to George Hartley 15 Mar. [1960] (Beinecke).
'to resume human activity': EP to Dudek, 20 Mar. 1960, *EP/Dk* [137]; EP to Gatter, 20 Mar. 1960 (Hamilton).
'hadn't changed much': Samuel Hynes, 'Meeting E.P.', *New Yorker* (12 June 2006) 100.

571 **'Oh, m'amour'**: EP to MS, [17 Apr. 1960] (HRC/MSB).
'His trouble': EP to MS, 29 Apr. [1960] (HRC/MSB).
'not transmit private discouragements': from TS draft of canto 115, reproduced in Ronald Bush, '"Unstill, ever turning": The Composition of Ezra Pound's *Drafts & Fragments*', in *Ezra Pound and Europe*, ed. Richard Taylor and Claus Melchior (Amsterdam: Rodopi, 1993), 231.
'dear, my dear': EP to MS, 12 May [1960] (HRC/MSB).
showed up in Rapallo: DP to OSP, 21 May 1960 (Hamilton/OSP); also DP to AVM, 18 May 1960 (Lilly).
'his head v. wobbly': DP to OSP, 7 June 1960 (Hamilton/OSP).
'Bless you for heroic offer': EP to MS, 8 June [1960] (HRC/MSB).
472 **'He can't git to Texas'**: EP to MS, 7 June [1960] (HRC/MSB).
'haven't come up with an answer': EP to MS, 9 June [1960] (HRC/MSB).
'don't seem to answer question': EP to MS, 10 June [1960] (HRC/MSB).
'leaving Rap. domattina': EP to MS, 14 July [1960] (HRC/MSB).
'Of course I <u>suspect</u>': DP to AVM, 30 May 1960 (Lilly).
'released in my custody': DP to AVM, 10 June 1960 (Lilly).
the matter of Pound's money: see EP to DP, Feb. 1960 (Lilly).
'you have plenty': AVM to DP, 21 Oct. 1959 (Lilly).
packing up and sending to Omar: see DP to OSP, 12, 22 Aug., 1, 4. 9 Sept. 1959, 22 Jan., 7 Feb., 9 Mar., 25 June, 26 Oct., 3 Nov. 1960 (Hamilton/OSP).
if the letters were 'to remain at Brun': AVM to DP, 9 Nov. 1959 (Lilly).
'full of manias': DP to OSP, 4 July 1960 (Hamilton/OSP).
473 **up to half an hour**: see DP to OSP, 10 July 1960 (Hamilton/OSP).
'a hunger strike': DP to OSP, 23 July 1960 (Hamilton/OSP).
'He start again': EP to MS, 5 Aug. [1960] (HRC/MSB).
'been sufficiently coherent': EP to MS, 7 Aug. [1960] (HRC/MSB). 'Unesco' = Ionesco.
'No, my Dear': EP to MS, [13 Aug. 1960] (HRC/MSB). MS's note is with the carbon she retained (HRC/MSB).
R. Murray Schafer: paragraph drawn from Schafer's 'Postcript 1942–1972', *EP&M* 465–6.
474 **Michael Reck**: paragraph drawn from Reck 145–6.
the proofs of his *Paris Review* interview: see Hall, *Remembering Poets* 181–3. At least two serious errors remained uncorrected: on p. 41 of *Paris Rev interview* a negative is lacking—the sentence should read, 'the *New Age* office helped me to see the war *not* as a separate event but as part of a system, one war after another'; and on p. 44 it should surely be not 'the conversation' but 'the conservation of individual rights'.
lecture to students in Lund: see Little 160.
'controversial figures': EP to Dr Bengtson, Lund University, 4 June 1960 (private collection).
'One day he feels very well': MdR to Caverfors, as in Little 161, n.d.
a reading for a cultural society: DP to OSP, 26 Oct. 1960 (Hamilton/OSP).
'the door swung open': Eveline Bates Doob, 'Some Notes on E.P.', *Pai* 8.1 (1979) 70–1—referred to hereafter as Doob, 'Some Notes'.
475 **'the nervous breakdown'**: DP to OSP, 26 Oct. 1960 (Hamilton/OSP).
Scraps and fragments: as seen in private collection.
'nothing wrong in his middle': DP to AVM, 19 Dec. 1960 (Lilly).
'Ciao, Cara': EP to MS, 15 Dec. [1960] (HRC/MSB).
'typescript of 7 new cantos': AB to OSP, 30 Aug. 1961 (Hamilton/OSP). These may have been typed from MS's fresh TSS by Noel Stock, who was paid by EP to do secretarial work about this time. Henry Swabey recalled that 'In March and April,

1960, he sent copies of cantos 110, 114 and 116 for me to look after', in 'A Page Without Which', *Pai* 5.2 (1976) 335.
unable to control EP's mail: DP to OSP, 27 Dec. 1960 (Hamilton/OSP).
'3 Jan. I think': EP to OR, 3 Jan. 1961 (Beinecke/OR).
476 **'Feelin a bit more human'**: EP to MS, 7 Jan. [1961] (HRC/MSB).
got out the Fenollosa manuscripts again: DP diary, 7 Jan. 1961 (Lilly).
'been seeing him fairly regularly': paragraph drawn from Doob, 'Some Notes', *Pai* 8.1(1979) 71–5.
477 **'this WILL to starve himself'**: DP to AVM, 20 Feb. 1961 (Lilly).
made her mad: DP to OSP, 17 Feb. 1961 (Hamilton/OSP).
'a turn for the better': DP to AVM, 10 Mar. 1961 (Lilly); and see DP to OSP, 7 and 12 Mar. 1961 (Hamilton/OSP).
'two frail old men': paragraph drawn from Doob, 'Some Notes', *Pai* 8.1 (1979) 75–6.
478 **a meeting where Oswald Mosley spoke**: details in this paragraph drawn from DP to AVM, 22 and 27 Mar. 1961 (Lilly); Tim Redman, 'Pound's Politics and Economics', *Cambridge Companion to Ezra Pound*, 260; Archie Henderson, 'Pound, Sweden, and the Nobel Prize', *Ezra Pound and Europe*, 163–4; Alec Marsh, *Ezra Pound* (Reaktion Books, 2011), 214, 238 n. 15.
eating well: see DP to AVM, 27 Mar. 1961 (Lilly).
'Evidently he not only won't': Doob, 'Some Notes', *Pai* 8.1 (1979) 76.
heart was failing: Dadone to MdR, [1] May 1961, as in Conover 222.
Mary went down to Rome: see DP to AVM, 3 May 1961 (Lilly); and DP to OSP, 3 May 1961 (Hamilton/OSP).
'There's an *eye*': OR interview, May–June 1981, in the film *Ezra Pound: An American Odyssey*, as in Conover 222. Dates and some details in this paragraph also from Conover 222.
'every day twice a day': OR to Ronald Duncan, 3 Sept. 1961, as in Conover 222.
'curled up on the back seat': OR to Ronald Duncan, 3 Sept. 1961, as in Conover 222.
'will never be himself again': DP to AVM, 3 July 1961 (Lilly).
'might not last long': DP to OSP, 3 Aug. 1961 (Hamilton/OSP).
'He's just *dying*', 'he is drinking': MdR as recorded by Doob, 'Some Notes', *Pai* 8.1 (1979) 77–8.
479 **'the minute I entered the room'**: OR as recorded by James Wilhelm [in 1987], 'In the Haunt of the Priestess of the Hidden Nest: A Tribute to Olga Rudge', *Pai* 26.1 (1997) 114–15.
a jar of Chinese ginger: OR to Ronald Duncan, 3 Sept. 1961, as in Conover 223.
that America destroyed: EP as reported in Doob, 'Some Notes', *Pai* 8.1 (1979) 77.
'This is the end!': EP as told by MdR to Little in 2003, Little 161.
Hilda Doolittle had died: details drawn from Jacob Korg, *Winter Love: Ezra Pound and H.D.* (Madison: University of Wisconsin Press, 2003), 196–8—EP's translation is on 197.
'she isn't @ all': EP to Norman Holmes Pearson, 28 Sept. 1961, as in Korg, *Winter Love* 198.
'60 years unrequited': EP to OR, [Sept. 1961] (Beinecke/OR).
'Helen in Egypt a marvel': EP to Norman Holmes Pearson, 28 Sept. 1961, as in Korg, *Winter Love* 198.
'algae of long past sea currents': EP to Perdita Schaffner, quoted in Perdita Schaffner,'Merano, 1962', *Pai* 4.2–3 (1975) 514.
'more lucid', 'looking old': DP to OSP, 12 and 14 Oct. 1961 (Hamilton/OSP).
'sitting at desk': EP to OR, 14 Oct. 1961 (Beinecke/OR).
480 **'*much better*'**: OR to Ronald Duncan, 24 Oct. 1961, as in Conover 223.
Mary Barnard: paragraph drawn from Barnard, *Assault on Mount Helicon*, 305.

'At night, now 3.15 a.m.': EP MS loose leaf, n.d. (private collection).
'Telescope is totally blind': EP MS loose leaf, n.d. (private collection).
'much better lately': DP to AVM, 26 Jan. 1962 (Lilly).
'eating, showing interest': OR to Ronald Duncan, 14 Feb. 1962, as in Conover 225.
481 **'Keep hoping'**: OR to Ronald Duncan, 14 Feb. 1962, as in Conover 225.
Dorothy was surprised: DP to OSP, 17 and 23 Mar. 1962 (Hamilton/OSP); and DP, Diary, 15 Mar. 1962 (Lilly).
'Something is moving': DP, Diary, 15 Mar. 1962 (Lilly).
'ready to receive *Him*': OR to EP, 2 Mar. 1962, as in Conover 226.
'she hoping to see Him': OR to EP, 27 Mar. 1962 (Beinecke/OR).
waiting for all her life: OR to EP, 22 Mar. 1962 as in Conover 224–5.
'painting, cleaning, contriving': OR to Ronald Duncan, 7 Apr. 1962, as in Conover 226.
'as she painfully sees': OR to EP, 6 Apr. 1962 (Beinecke/OR).
'hasn't got mobilized': EP to OR, 12 Apr. 1962 (Beinecke/OR).
to stay with Olga for a month: see DP to OSP, 15 Apr. 1962 (Hamilton/OSP).
'we brought EP here': DP to AVM, 27 Apr. 1962 (Lilly).
'not in communication': DP to AVM, 6 May 1962 (Lilly).
'They have taken possession': DP to AVM, 2 Dec. 1962 (Lilly).
'when He was well enough': OR, *I Ching* notebook, 1977 (Beinecke/OR), entry dated 25 Apr. 1962, as in Conover 226.

17. His Sickness & his Wealth, 1962–4

Mainly clinical

482 **Pound's physical state**: paragraph drawn mainly from Giuseppe Bacigalupo, *Ieri a Rapallo* (Pasian di Prato: Campanotto Editore, 1993, 2006), 88–9; also from 'Mr. Ezra Pound—Clinical report', Clinica della Malattie Nervose e Mentali, Università di Genova (St Elizabeths files, 1161 a–b, US Nat. Arch.) See also Conover 228–9.
483 **'a few forced words'**: Thomas Cole, 'The [Two] Women of Trachis', *Pai* 26.1 (1997) [69].
'My malady': EP to Cole, [June 1962], enclosed with EP to WCW, [June 1962] (Beinecke).
'Dante's hell is COLD': EP to WCW, [June 1962] (Beinecke).
484 **'much thinner now'**: Henry Swabey, 'A Page Without Which', *Pai* 5.2 (1976) 335–6. See also DP to OSP, 29 Aug. 1962 (Hamilton/OSP).
'For Ezra's "keep"': DP to OR, 12 Sept. 1962 (Beinecke/OR).
'all the little luxuries': DP to OR, 2 Oct. 1962 (Beinecke/OR).
'something extra for all your work': DP to OR, Jan. 1963 (Beinecke/OR).
'care and maintenance': Court Order of 7 Aug. 1963, Committee Accounts folder (Lilly).
raised again to $400: see DP to OSP, 6 Oct. 1964 (Hamilton/OSP).
'payments to Miss Rudge': see Conover 248–9.
***Poetry* Memorial Prize**: the 'Citation' is reprinted in Meacham 210–11.
485 **'perhaps after your signature'**: DP to EP, 16 Oct. 1962 (Lilly). See also DP to OSP, 11 and 22 Oct. 1962 (Hamilton/OSP).
'Happy New Year': EP to DP, 30 Dec. 1962 (Lilly).
'no money is supposed': DP to OR, 11 Oct. 1962 (Beinecke/OR).
Richard Stern's account: Richard Stern, 'A Memory or Two of Mr. Pound', *Pai* 1, 2 (1972) [215]–17.

'Dear Pound': Oppen to EP, [Sept.–Oct. ?1962], *Selected Letters of George Oppen*, ed. Rachel Blau Du Plessis (Durham, NC, and London: Duke UniversityPress, 1990), 71–2.

486 **'the best statement'**: Lowell to EP, 10 Feb. 1963, *The Letters of Robert Lowell*, ed. Saskia Hamilton (New York: Farrar, Straus & Giroux, 2005), 419.

'he bore with me': EP to Flossie Williams, as in *The Letters of Robert Duncan and Denise Levertov*, ed. Robert J. Bertholf and Albert Gelpi (Stanford, Calif.: Stanford University Press, 2004), 388–9.

'This is the one': *Letters of Robert Duncan and Denise Levertov*, ed. Bertholf and Gelpi, 388.

'it is just as true': Flossie Williams to EP, 24 Mar. 1863 (Beinecke). EP's draft of his telegram to Flossie Williams is in the same folder.

Grazia Livi interview: as translated from *Epoca* (Milan), 24 Mar. 1963, in *Pai* 8.2 (1979) 243–7.

487 **'beautiful, quiet, humble'**: Jean McLean, 'Translator's note' following her translation of the Grazia Livi interview, *City Lights Journal* 2 (San Francisco: City Lights Books, 1964), 45–6.

488 **'Dear Mrs Bullock'**: EP to Mrs Bullock, draft dated 22 Aug. 1963 (Beinecke).

'may draw on the prize money': DP to OR, 2 Dec. 1963 (Beinecke/OR).

'a perineal insertion': 'Clinical report', Clinica della Malattie Nervose e Mentali, Università di Genova (St Elizabeths files, 1161 b, US Nat. Arch.).

'remake normal men': EP jotting on OR's notebook, 1966, as in Conover 228.

did render the patient impotent: OR notebook 1976, as in Conover 229.

489 **did successfully 'disintoxicate'**: OR as in Conover 230. Other details in paragraph from Conover 230; and see DP to OSP, 2, 6, 25 Dec. 1963 and 11, 23 Jan. 1964 (Hamilton/OSP).

The Committee's agenda

489 **'if my old will'**: EP to DP on Villa Chiara notepaper, n.d. (Beinecke).

poring over the 1940 Will: there is much correspondence on the matter in the A. V. Moore and Frank Cockburn legal files now in the Lilly Library.

photostat copies: see DP to AVM, 23 Sept. 1962 (Lilly).

Moore suggested to Gleason and to Dorothy: AVM to Gleason, 8 Oct. 1962 (Lilly); AVM to DP, 8 Oct. 1962, and 25 Oct. 1962 (Lilly). [Under the Italian legal system the legislation of the deceased's country of nationality would apply, unless the foreigner with an Italian will had explicitly chosen to have Italian law apply. In that case the estate would be divided equally between a surviving spouse and any children whether legitimate, illegitimate, or adopted. In the USA most states grant no rights to children to inherit from their parents. In the case of intestacy the distribution of the deceased's property would be the responsibility of the administrator. Under US law, therefore, Omar's being Pound's legitimated child would not constitute him the 'legal heir'; while under Italian law both he and Mary would be equal legal heirs.]

490 **a notarized document**: see p. 294 above.

'your just inheritance': AVM to OSP, 19 Oct. 1964 (Lilly).

a letter of instruction: EP to JL, 9 Nov. 1957, also signed by 'Dorothy Pound, committee for Ezra Pound'—a copy sent to Cockburn by JL, 17 Dec. 1968, is with his letter in Cockburn files at that date (Lilly).

Gleason and Laughlin . . . suggested: see JL to AVM, 7 July 1963 (Lilly).

should be kept out of things: see AVM to DP, 29 June, 16 July, 30 Oct. 1963 (Lilly).

'5% of what they collected': AVM to DP, Nov. 1965 (Lilly).

'earn tuppence': DP to AVM, Nov. 1965 (Lilly).

491 **'explain his anxieties'**:TSE to AVM, 28 Mar. 1962 (Lilly).
'both Gleason and Cockburn': AVM to DP, 23 July 1962 (Lilly). See also AVM to TSE, 30 July 1962: 'Omar has his lawyer friend Gleason and Jas. L. to advise him' (Lilly).
'inheritance and social position': AVM to OSP, 7 Oct. 1964 (Lilly).
'scandal': for one instance see DP to AVM, 10 Mar. 1961 (Lilly).
'any reference': JL to AVM, 24 Aug. 1960 (Lilly).
'Omar Shakespear Pound': Norman 284.
'his only child': Ronald Duncan, 'Pull Down Thy Vanity: A Visit to Ezra Pound', *Sunday Times* (11 Feb. 1962) 33.
'detrimental to the family': DP to AVM, 1 July 1963 (Lilly).
special safe custody: AVM to DP, 10 Aug. 1962 (Lilly).
sending them . . . burning them: for examples see DP to OSP, 12, 21, 22 Aug., 4, 9 Sept. 1959, 22 Jan., 9 Mar., 26 Oct., 3 Nov. 1960; 17 Jan., 15 Aug. 1963 (Hamilton/OSP).
embargoed: see e.g. DP to OSP, 24 Sept., 3 Nov. 1960, 24 Aug. 1961 (Hamilton/OSP).
'scandal' . . . suppressed: in 1988, Carpenter 455, gave a broad hint but could not be explicit; in 2000, Anne Conover was granted permission to use EP's letters only on condition that she make major deletions of material concerning OSP's paternity; however, Marjorie Perloff, in her review of *EP/DP* in the *TLS* of 16 July 1999, wrote that 'Dorothy responded in pique [to the birth of Pound's daughter] by taking a long trip to Egypt and came back pregnant'; then William Pratt, reviewing *EP/DP* in *World Literature Today* (22 Sept. 2000), wrote that EP was OSP's 'legal (but not biological) father'; Ira Nadel, in his *Ezra Pound: A Literary Life* (Palgrave Macmillan, 2004), 109, wrote that OSP's 'father was Egyptian'; and Leon Surette, reviewing a new edition of MdR's *Discretions* in *Pai* 35.3 (2006) 184–5, wrote, '*Discretions* does not reveal that Omar's father was not Pound, but an Egyptian officer'. See also Alec Marsh, *Ezra Pound* (Reaktion Books, 2011), 102.

492 **'try to marry him'**: DP to AVM, 25 May 1962 (Lilly).
give the world proof: AVM to DP, 31 May 1962 (Lilly).
'a race—who dies first': DP to OSP, 10 Mar. 1966 (Hamilton/OSP).
'may not remarry': OSP to AVM, 16 Feb. 1965 (Lilly).
'copy of a typewritten will': a copy is among EP's legal papers (Beinecke).
'to PROVE': OSP to AVM, 16 Feb. 1965 (Lilly).
reported to Moore: DP to AVM, 26 Feb. 1965 (Lilly).
'the permanent repository': L. Quincy Mumford, Librarian of Congress, to EP, 28 Feb. 1965 (Beinecke).

493 **'I appreciate the honor'**: EP to Mumford, 21 Mar. 1965 (Beinecke).
'gold-digger': see AVM to DP, 28 Nov. 1962, and DP to AVM, 2 Dec. 1962 (Lilly).
'for the benefit and maintenance of the patient': AVM to TSE, 30 Jul. 1962 (Lilly).
inclined to scoff: see DP to AVM, 2 Dec. 1962 (Lilly). For an account of the eventual disposal of Pound's literary estate see Donald C. Gallup, 'The Ezra Pound Archive 1947–1987', in his *Pigeons on the Granite: Memories of a Yale Librarian* (New Haven: The Beinecke Rare Book & Manuscript Library, Yale University, 1988), 191–210—a revised and expanded version of Donald Gallup, 'The Ezra Pound Archive at Yale', *Yale University Library Gazette* 60. 3–4 (1986) 161–77.
'a long very quiet explanation': DP to OSP, 15 Sept. 1963 (Hamilton/OSP).

494 **'Boris tells me'**: DP to EP, 15 Sept. 1963 (Lilly).
Cockburn advised Omar: see Cockburn to OSP, 16 Nov. 1967 (Lilly).
'signature is not valid': DP to OR, 10 May 1964—see also DP to OR, 12 Sept. 1963, and 6 Feb, 1969 (all Beinecke/OR). In the last DP wrote: 'What kind of contract have you made with [Italian & German TV companies]? . . . the signing should by rights be by the committee—as Ezra's signature is not valid.'

18. Afterlife of the Poet, 1965–72

495 **'*Tempus tacendi*'**: a time to be silent, from Ecclesiastes 3: 7, and from Sigismundo Malatesta's motto, *Tempus loquendi, Tempus tacendi*. See 31/153, and 74/429.
'visibly shaken': Peter Russell, 'Ezra Pound: The Last Years. A Personal Memoir', *The Malahat Review* 29 (1974) 33. Referred to hereafter as 'Russell, *Malahat*'.
'On his own hearth': EP, 'For T. S. E.', *Sewanee Review* 74.1 (1966) 109, reprinted *S Pr* 434.
'the true Dantescan voice': EP, 'For T. S. E.', *Sewanee Review* 74.1 (1966) 109, reprinted *S Pr* 434.
'apparently lost': *Irish Times*, 10 Feb. 1965—communicated by Walter Baumann.

496 **'tomb without flowers'**: EP to Pasolini, 1968, as in David Anderson, 'BREAKING THE SILENCE: The interview of Vanni Ronnsisvalle and Pier Paolo Pasolini with Ezra Pound in 1968', *Pai* 10.2 (1981) 335. The Horst Tappe photo is reproduced as illustration no. 36.
'a warning': EP to DP, 27 Feb. 1967 (Lilly).
'to be buried alone': EP to DP, 27 Feb. 1967 (Lilly).
a codicil: the copy in Beinecke reads, 'Codicil to my will dated 17 June 1940 repeated 15 Aug 15, 1964: I leave these instructions: my books, art works letters and manuscripts now at 2 Sant'Ambrogio and/or 252 San Gegorio Venice, or any subsequent address of hers to which I may move them, I leave unconditionally to Olga Rudge. Further, as outlined in a letter to my wife Dorothy Pound, I wish to be buried in Hailey, Idaho, with my head by Gaudier Brzeska to mark the spot. If I have not been able to complete arrangements I wish Olga Rudge or someone else she may choose to carry out the matter. [signed] Ezra Pound | 2 Sant'Ambrogio di Rapallo, 11th September 1967.'
'immense row of mountains': EP to Pasolini, 1968, as in David Anderson, 'BREAKING THE SILENCE', *Pai* 10.2 (1981) 335.
'should eliminate': EP to DP, 27 Feb. 1967 (Lilly).

497 **'really very difficult'**: Sister Bernetta Quinn, as recalled by Mary Barnard, Barnard 306.
Peter Russell: this paragraph drawn from Russell, *Malahat* 14–17.

498 **'the old poet'**: Guy Davenport, 'Ezra Pound 1885–1972', in his collection of essays *The Geography of the Imagination* (Picador, 1984), 170–1.
'Hedgehog and Fox': see Guy Davenport, *Archilochos/Sappho/Alkman* (Berkeley: University of California Press, 1980), 57.
liked to read to her: Davenport, *Geography of the Imagination*, 171.
'plenty of effects': Russell, *Malahat* 19.
'put two thoughts together': Russell, *Malahat* 18.
performed as a ballet: see *Testament II* 198.

499 **'still as a Mandarin statue'**: Lawrence Ferlinghetti, 'Pound at Spoleto', from *Open Eye, Open Heart* (New York: New Directions, 1973), as in *The Postmoderns: The New American Poetry Revised*, ed. Donald Allen and George F. Butterick (New York: Grove Press, 1982), 78.
'eyes were like stone': John Wieners, 'Ezra Pound at the Spoleto Festival 1965', *Agenda* 4.2 (1965) 68.
'frail but stubborn': Ferlinghetti, 'Pound at Spoleto', 78.
'The Grasshopper and the Ant': Marianne Moore's translation, from her *The Fables of La Fontaine* (New York: Viking, 1954), is included in *A Marianne Moore Reader* (New York: The Viking Press, 1961), 95–6.
Lowell's 'imitation': 'Brunetto Latini', *Near the Ocean* (Faber & Faber, 1967), 48–52.
'knocked me down': Ferlinghetti, 'Pound at Spoleto', 78.

'a beautiful model': Robert Duncan to Denise Levertov, 10 Nov. 1969, *The Letters of Robert Duncan and Denise Levertov*, ed. Robert J. Bertholf and Albert Gelpi (Stanford, Calif.: Stanford University Press, 2004), 642. The recording is Spoken Arts SA 1098 Stereo, *Ezra Pound Reading his Translations of The Confucian Odes* (New Rochelle, NY: Spoken Arts, [?1970]).

Dominique de Roux: paragraph drawn from Jean-Luc Barré, *Dominique de Roux/Le provocateur (1935–1977)* (Paris: Fayard, 2005), 240–3. I am indebted to Philippe Mikriammos for the gift of this book, and also for *Dominique de Roux et Ezra Pound* (Paris: Au Signe de la Licorne, 2007).

500 **'C'est moi dans la poubelle'**: there are variant versions of this—one has EP saying it to OR during the performance, another has him saying it to JL next day. OR's is in the film *Ezra Pound: An American Odyssey*, reported in Wilhelm: 1994, 340–1; JL's is in *Pound as Wuz. Essays and Lectures on Ezra Pound* (Saint Paul: Graywolf Press, 1987), 29.

derelict: from OR's notebook, as in Conover 241.

seen as two shades: from Richard Sieburth's commentary, 'Ezra Pound: Letters to Natalie Barney', ed. Richard Sieburth, *Pai* 5.2 (1976) 295.

had seen... some of the great Greek temples: this paragraph and the next drawn from Demetres Tryphonopoulos's conference paper, 'Ezra Pound's 1965 Trip to Greece', and from Charles Lock's conference paper presented in Athens in April 2006, 'An Exacting Encounter: Ezra Pound and Zissimos Lorenzatos'—both papers generously communicated by their authors.

501 **the struggle of intelligence**: cf. EP, 'As Sextant', *GK* 352.

'the 3 fates': EP recollection recorded with OR note in OR's Notebook II, 66 (Beinecke/OR).

'the sea in which he floated': Richard Stern, 'A Memory or Two of Mr Pound', *Pai* 1.2 (1972) 216.

'dancing seems better': OR notebook, as in Conover 239.

502 **'three days in Paris, Orleans in May'**: OR to Valerie Eliot, 18 Aug. 1970, as in Conover 249. Other details in the paragraph from Conover 232, 237, 241, 243.

an episode: drawn mainly from 'Clinical report', Clinica della Malattie Nervose e Mentali, Università di Genova (St Elizabeths files, 1161 c–e, US Nat. Arch.). Romolo Rossi, who, as a young psychiatrist, had observed EP in the University Clinic, gave a fuller and somewhat different account, including some new and disturbing details, at the 21st International Ezra Pound Conference in Rome in July 2005:

> The report sent to us from St Elizabeths Hospital was quite detailed: the psychiatric examination showed no disorder that was schizophrenic or paranoid. Instead there was the description of a complex personality, with traits of unstable behaviour and bizarre attitudes....
>
> [W]hen he was admitted to our hospital, he had a depressed mood, anxiety expressed as asthenia and psychomotor retardation, severe insomnia, delusional ideas of self-deprecation, loss of interest in anything, convictions that he would never get better, of guilt, and of being contaminated by microbes...
>
> A previous depression had been observed and had been treated with electroconvulsive therapy. This time we chose pharmacological treatment and used the prototype antidepressant medication, imipramine (trade name Tofranil) at medium to high doses of 200 to 300 milligrams [per] day. He responded dramatically within four weeks, moving into a clearly manic state: he was euphoric, had psychomotor excitement, an ecstatic attitude, and pressured speech. He responded well to sedation, and his mood and behaviour became normal. The diagnosis was now clear, both from history and clinical observation: manic depressive illness (also called bipolar disorder).

Rossi concluded his paper with this recognition: 'Our definitions are approximate, and our tools are not able to reconstruct the mind of a poet.'—Romolo Rossi, 'A Psychiatrist's Recollections of Ezra Pound', *Ezra Pound, Language and Persona* ed. Massimo Bacigalupo and William Pratt (Genoa: Università degli Studi di Genova, Quaderni di Palazzo Serra 15, 2008), 145–6.

under his doctor's name: Massimo Bacigalupo, 'Sant'Ambrogio in the half-light: Growing up near Olga Rudge and Ezra Pound', *Pai* 26.1 (1997) 37.

503 **'a catatonic state'**: OR as reported in Conover 237.

'I had a good talk with Ezra': Robert Lowell to OR, 6 May 1966, *Letters of Robert Lowell*, ed. Saskia Hamilton (New York: Farrar, Straus and Giroux, 2005), 470.

'awesome and rather shattering': Robert Lowell to JL, 31 Aug. 1966, *Letters of Robert Lowell*, 473.

From her notebooks: see Conover 239, 258, 263.

read a great deal: Russell, *Malahat* 33.

played chess: Russell, *Malahat* 42.

cook supper: Russell, *Malahat* 36.

504 **'nostos to Olga'**: EP note copied by OR in her Venice notebooks (Beinecke/OR).

'There is more courage': EP MS note in OR's Venice notebooks (Beinecke/OR).

'her name was courage': EP, *Canti postumi* 266.

'If there was a trace': in EP's hand in OR notebook, as in Conover 248.

505 **owed everything to her**: see e.g. Russell, *Malahat* 29.

'we might say': Daniel Cory, 'Ezra Pound: A Memoir', *Encounter* 30.5 (May 1968) 30–9—extract in *Ezra Pound: A Critical Anthology* ed. J. P. Sullivan (Harmondsworth: Penguin Books, 1970), 374–6. Curiously, TSE, in 'A Note on Ezra Pound', *Today* IV.19 (Sept. 1918), had written of the earliest cantos: 'In appearance it is a rag-bag of Mr. Pound's reading in various languages, from which one fragment after another is dragged to light, and illuminated by the beauty of his phrase. . . . And yet the thing has, after one has read it once or twice, a positive coherence.'

'chosen at random': EP to Pasolini, 1968, as in David Anderson, 'BREAKING THE SILENCE', *Pai* 10.2 (1981) 338.

'to preserve some of the values': EP note, 'Guide to Kulchur', dated '20 June 1970' (Kenner Archive, HRC).

'sentences referring to groups': EP, 'Foreword', *S Pr* 6.

506 **'The root is greed'**: EP, 'Gold and Work' (1944, 1951), *S Pr* 317.

'This ruin': EP, 'The Economic Nature of the United States' (1944, 1950, 1971), *S Pr* 148.

upon the root cause: see Redman 254.

The Allen Ginsberg vortex: paragraph based on Allen Ginsberg, 'Encounters with Ezra Pound. Journal Notes' (1974), in his *Composed on the Tongue*, ed. Donald Allen (Bolinas: Grey Fox Press, 1979), 1–17. See also 'The Death of Ezra Pound', in Ginsberg's *Allen Verbatim. Lectures on Poetry, Politics, Consciousness*, ed. Gordon Ball (New York: McGraw-Hill Book Company, 1975), 179–87; based also on Michael Reck, 'A Conversation between Ezra Pound and Allen Ginsberg', *Evergreen Review* 57 (June 1968) 27ff.

507 **his services to literature**: JL modestly said he was being honoured as EP's publisher, but Professor Austin Briggs of Hamilton College assured me in Oct. 1994 that it was for his services to literature in general.

trip to America: details from JL to DP, 20 June 1969 (Lilly); Stock 458–60; Carpenter 900–2; Conover 243–5.

Lowell observed Pound: Robert Lowell to Elizabeth Bishop, 10 Nov. 1969, *Letters of Robert Lowell*, 525.

Laughlin noticed: JL, *Pound as Wuz*, 30. Wheelchair from Conover 244.

'The more we know of Eliot': EP, 'Preface' to T.S.Eliot, *The Waste Land. A Facsimile & Transcript of the Original Drafts Including the Annotations of Ezra Pound*, ed. Valerie Eliot (Faber & Faber, 1971), vii.

'a jumble': TSE, 'On a Recent Piece of Criticism', *Purpose* 10.2 (1938) 93.

508 **Hamilton College**: most of this paragraph from conversation with Professor Austin Briggs at Hamilton, Oct. 1994. See also JL, *Pound as Wuz*, 30.

'I take it as it comes': Austin Briggs as reported in William Hoffa, '"Ezra Pound: A Celebration", Hamilton College, April 25–26, 1980', *Pai* 9.2 (1980) 576–7.

'he *talked*': detail from Austin Briggs in conversation Oct. 1994. Other details from OR's notebook, as in Conover 245.

'Pound silent': George Oppen to Aleksandar Nejgebauer and family, [18 Mar. 1973], *Selected Letters of George Oppen*, 259–60. See also George Oppen,'Pound in the U.S. A.,1969', *Sagetrieb* 1.1 (1982) [119].

509 **National Book Awards**: paragraph drawn from Robert Lowell to Elizabeth Bishop, 11 Mar. 1970, *Letters of Robert Lowell*, 528–9.

Hugh MacDiarmid: Hugh MacDiarmid as reported by G Singh, 'Ezra Pound: A Commemorative Symposium', *Pai* 3.2 (1974) 151–2.

American Academy of Arts and Sciences: my account draws on several sources: Heymann 310–11 and 356 nn. 1 and 2; Carpenter 908–9; Alan Levy, *Ezra Pound: The Voice of Silence* (Sag Harbor: The Permanent Press, 1983), 33–5; Donald Hall, *Remembering Poets*, 189–90. See also Allen Ginsberg, *Allen Verbatim*, 180.

510 **'potentially just as creative'**: Jean Mayer, as reported in Robert Reinhold, 'Ezra Pound is Focus of New Dispute', *New York Times*, 5 July 1972.

'with memories of the holocaust': Harvey Brooks, President of the Academy, to members of the Academy, as cited in Levy, *The Voice of Silence* 34.

'the most despicable things': Daniel Bell as cited in Heymann 310.

'I am as outraged': Martin L. Kilson in *International Herald Tribune*, 7 July 1972, 16—as cited in Heymann 311,561.

personally put on trial: JL to Noel Stock, 19 June 1972 (Canaday Center, University of Toledo)—as cited in Carpenter 908.

Harry Levin protested: as in Donald Hall, *Remembering Poets*, 189–90.

511 **wrote to Hugh Kenner**: John Voss to Hugh Kenner, 14 June 1972 (Kenner Archive, HRC).

a reading at the Folger: JL to Noel Stock, 5 Sept. 1972 (Canaday Center, University of Toledo)—as cited in Carpenter 908–9.

Buckminster Fuller: the main source for my account of the Fuller/Pound interaction is Buckminster Fuller, 'Pound, Synergy, and the Great Design', the 1977 Ezra Pound Lecture at the University of Idaho, as printed in *Agenda* 16.3–4 (1978/9) 130–64. I have also drawn on Scott Eastham's distinguished conference paper, '"Friend of the Universe"—Pound & Bucky Fuller: The Cosmic Connection', a copy of which he generously supplied.

an integrity of patterned energies: a Hugh Kenner formulation.

513 **'to be men . . . not destroyers'**: final line of *Drafts & Fragments*.

'at the poets' performance': Buckminster Fuller, in Buckminster Fuller and Anwar Dil, *Humans in Universe* (NewYork: Mouton, 1981), 21—cited Eastham, 'Friend of the Universe', 6.

'To Buckminster Fuller': EP inscription on copy of *D&F* presented to Fuller in 1971—cited Eastham 7.

Igor Stravinsky: details from Conover 252–3.

Marianne Moore's death: details from Russell, *Malahat* 40–1.

'no finer epitaph': Russell, *Malahat* 41.

That year: details in this paragraph and the one following drawn from Conover 254–7; Russell, *Malahat* 42–3; Davenport, 'Ezra Pound 1885–1972', *Geography of the Imagination*, 169–71.

514 **Olga holding his hand**: Joan Fitzgerald told it differently: 'seeing there was nothing they could do, [they] went in search of a bite to eat', and when they returned they found Pound had died (see Tim Redman, *Modernism/modernity* 13.1 (2006) 936. Redman confirmed to me that it was Joan Fitzgerald herself who had told him that.

515 **Bayle's *Dictionnaire***: Pound's copy of Pierre Bayle, *Dictionnaire historique et critique*, 5th edn., 4 vols. (Amsterdam: Chez P. Brunel [et al.], 1740), is now in HRC.
'A little light': 116/797.
EP's seal: for the characters and their meaning see p. 390 and note.

Appendix The Settlement of the Estate

517 **'AFTER THREE DAYS'**: OR to OSP, 2 Nov. 1972 (Pound D. MSS adds., Lilly).
'parked': DP to Edith Madge, 25 May 1973 (Pound D. MSS adds., Lilly). Some details in this paragraph drawn from the recollections of Elizabeth Pound kindly communicated 20 Feb. 2014.
'SERVICE FRIDAY': OR to OSP, 2 Nov. 1972 (Pound D. MSS adds., Lilly).
his 1967 letter: see p. 496 above.
telegram from the American Embassy in London: a copy is in a 'Funeral arrangements' folder at Hamilton (Hamilton/OSP).
another telegram: a photocopy of this telegram, dated 2 Nov. 1972, from the US Consulate in Milan to the Secretary of State in Washington, DC, is also in the 'Funeral arrangements' folder (Hamilton/OSP), and is paraphrased in *Ezra Pound: A Selected Catalog* (Clinton, NY: Hamilton College Library, 2005), 81.
Omar Pound, with Peter du Sautoy: see P. F. Du Sautoy, letter to the editor, *Pai* 4.1 (1975) 199.
the Petition: a copy dated 24 and 26 Oct. 1972 is filed with Committee Accounts (Lilly).
'if a new effort': Gleason as reported in JL to DP, 21 June 1972 (Lilly).
'without heart or conscience': JL to Hugh Kenner, 6 March and 23 July 1968 (Kenner Archive, HRC)—I have conflated details from the two letters.

518 **Final Report**: the copy sent to DP by the Auditor-Master of the Superior Court of the District of Columbia on 10 Oct. 1973 is filed with Committee Accounts (Lilly). The Order Ratifying the Report was filed in the Court on 1 Nov. 1973. Notice of the filing of the Final Report was to be sent to DP, to OSP, and to their six legal firms—MdR was not on the list, nor any legal firm representing her.
declared the estate: all details from the Final Report.
sold to the Lilly Library: see Donald C. Gallup, 'The Ezra Pound Archive 1947–1987', in his *Pigeons on the Granite: Memories of a Yale Librarian* (New Haven: The Beinecke Rare Book & Manuscript Library, Yale University, 1988), 209.
services charged to the Patient's estate: details in Committee Accounts and Frank Cockburn files (Lilly).
'the legal heir': Gallup, 'The Ezra Pound Archive 1947–1987', *Pigeons on the Granite*, 200. Gallup had scrupulously written, 'There was a son, Omar, whose birth certificate bore acknowledgment by Pound of paternity' (197).

519 **the primary beneficiary**: JL to Hugh Kenner, 1973 (Kenner Archive, HRC).
the purchase of the Ezra Pound Archive: see the account in Donald C. Gallup, 'The Ezra Pound Archive 1947–1987', *Pigeons on the Granite*, 191–210.

ACKNOWLEDGEMENTS AND COPYRIGHT NOTICE

When one works on Pound one does not work alone. I have enjoyed support both material and moral, together with encouragement, incitement, and provocation from many persons and institutions, and it is a pleasure to recall once again what I owe to them and to record my gratitude.

There are the great libraries which collect, conserve, and make available to researchers the vast treasury of Pound's unpublished writings and drafts. I am most grateful for the courteous welcome, the frequent kindness, and the willing and expert assistance accorded me at Yale University's Beinecke Library, at the Harry Ransom Humanities Research Center of the University of Texas at Austin, at the Lilly Library of Indiana University, Bloomington, Indiana, and at the Daniel Burke Library of Hamilton College, Clinton, New York.

Next I must thank the phalanx of scholars who have edited valuable resources from those archives, to the great benefit of other readers and researchers: D. D. Paige, Richard Reid, Noel Stock, Forrest Read, William Cookson. Eric Homberger, Michael John King, R. Murray Schafer, Leonard W. Doob, Harriet Zinnes, Vittoria I. Mondolfo, Margaret Hurley, Brita Lindberg-Seyersted, David Anderson, Donald Pearce, Herbert Schneidau, Omar Pound, A. Walton Litz, Timothy Materer, Mary de Rachewiltz, Barry Ahearn, Sanehida Kodama, Robert Spoo, Thomas L. Scott, Melvin J. Friedman, Jackson R. Bryer, Lea Baechler, James Longenbach, Richard Sieburth, Richard Taylor, Ira B. Nadel, David M. Gordon, Walter Sutton, Hugh Witemeyer, E. P. Walkiewicz, Philip J. Burns, Maria Luisa Ardizzone, Demetres Tryphonopoulos, Leon Surette, Sarah C. Holmes, Robert Hughes, Margaret Fisher, Massimo Bacigalupo, Roxana Preda, Joanna Moody, Miranda B. Hickman, and Alec Marsh. Here the late Carroll F. Terrell deserves a special honourable mention for his outstanding services to Ezra Pound scholarship, as founding editor of *Paideuma*, compiler of *A Companion to the Cantos of Ezra Pound*, animator of conferences, and generous instigator, supporter, and publisher of others' work, especially that of younger scholars. In another special category is Donald Gallup—his *Ezra Pound: A Bibliography* (1983) is an indispensable resource always at hand. I have reason to be grateful also for Volker Bischoff's *Ezra Pound Criticism 1905–1985: A Chronological Listing of Publications in English* (Marburg, 1991); and for Archie Henderson's thesaurus of 'new notes on the Pound/Agresti correspondence', *'I Cease Not to Yowl' Reannotated* (Houston, 2009).

The good and useful scholars, critics, and interpreters of Pound's work are legion, and though it is invidious to single out individuals, I must name a few to whom I feel especially indebted. Foremost is Hugh Kenner, the inventor of literary modernism in his time. Then I would name as they come to mind, each for some particular donation: Donald Davie, Eva Hesse, Hugh Witemeyer, George Kearns, David Gordon, M. L. Rosenthal, Walter Baumann, Ian Bell, Guy Davenport, Christine Brooke-Rose, Jean-Michel Rabaté, Richard Sieburth, Massimo Bacigalupo, Peter Makin, Marjorie Perloff, Michael Alexander, James Longenbach, Wendy Flory, Emily Mitchell Wallace, Kay Davis, Ronald Bush, Tim Redman, William McNaughton, Christine Froula, Peter Nichols, Leonardo Clerici, Leon Surette, Demetres Tryphonopoulos, Archie Henderson, Luca Gallesi, Maria Luisa Ardizzone, Marie-Noëlle Little, Colin McDowell, Scott Eastham, Peter Liebregts, Robert Hughes, and Margaret Fisher. More generally, I have enjoyed being a member of a lively, contentious, and collaborative community of scholars at the biennial International Ezra Pound Conferences, from the first in 1976, and have profited from innumerable discussions in various agreeable settings with fellow scholars and critics.

'Biography, a minor form of fiction', Hugh Kenner wrote somewhere, not altogether dismissively, though with reason; yet, as a biographer, I have been glad to be able to check out the facts of Pound's life against the biographies of Noel Stock, J. J. Wilhelm, and Humphrey Carpenter. Mary de Rachewiltz's memoir, *Discretions: Ezra Pound, Father and Teacher,* has been an inimitable inspiration. Anne Conover's *Olga Rudge & Ezra Pound* has been a mine of information.

I am especially grateful to the following for their generosity in providing me with books, articles, unpublished results of their own research, or critical dialogue: Michael Alexander, Massimo Bacigalupo, Danilo Breschi, Stefano Maria Casella, Scott Eastham, Margaret Fisher, Leah Flack, Luca Gallesi, Dryden Gilling-Smith, Robert Hughes, Marie-Noëlle Little, A. Walton Litz, Charles Lock, Alec Marsh, Philippe Mikriammos, Alan Navarre, Catherine Paul, Caterina Ricciardi, Richard Sieburth, Noel Stock, Richard Taylor, Demetres Tryphonopoulos, Emily Mitchell Wallace, William Watt.

Poets, like those who write about them (and those who would read them), need publishers. Beyond the copyright acknowledgements below, we must be grateful to Elkin Mathews, Pound's first publisher in London; to Charles Granville, Harriet Shaw Weaver, John Rodker, William Bird, and Nancy Cunard, who brought out his early and wholly uncommercial poetry through their private presses; to Alfred A. Knopf, Boni and Liveright, and Farrar and Rinehart, his first publishers in New York; to Faber and Faber who became his publishers in London after 1933; to Stanley Nott; and above all to James Laughlin whose New Directions became his American publisher, and ultimately the leading publisher of his work. Other publishers helped keep his work in print in his later years, notably Peter Owen of London. In recent years we owe edited collections of his correspondence and prose to the enterprise of a number of North American and British university presses. To Garland Publishing Inc. we owe the invaluable ten-volume collection of Pound's contributions to periodicals. To the Library of America we owe Richard Sieburth's comprehensive selection of Pound's poems and translations. And to

Robert Hughes and Margaret Fisher we owe the now complete series of editions of his music.

There are more personal debts. To Hugh Kenner for opening his personal Pound archive to me and for generous hospitality. To George Kearns and to Cleo Keams, for their hospitality and conversation, and to George in particular for a gift of books from his Pound collection. To Noel Stock for his warm hospitality and informed conversation. To Geoffrey Wall, biographer and translator of Flaubert, for his close attention to my prose and for his constructive advice. To Declan Spring at New Directions for extraordinary courtesies and helpfulness. To Mary de Rachewiltz for permission to quote from Pound's published and unpublished writings; for generous practical assistance, including giving access to her library and making freely available her collection of photographs; and for her wholly Poundian principle of placing no restriction on the use of her father's work. To Elizabeth Pound, and to Katherine Pound and Oriana Pound, for generous and unrestricted permission to quote from Pound's published and unpublished writings and from Dorothy Pound's letters and diaries. To Marcella Spann Booth for permission to quote from Pound's unpublished letters to her. To Bernard Dew for generous and timely assistance.

I owe much to the impressive expertise and enthusiasm of all who have worked on the book at Oxford University Press, and in particular to Jacqueline Baker, Rachel Platt, and Caroline Hawley.

I am grateful for the skilled photographic work of Paul Shields of York University's Photographic Unit.

Visits to the archives in the United States were supported by a British Academy Leverhulme Visiting Professorship, and by two British Academy research grants. Yale University's Beinecke Library awarded me its Donald C. Gallup Visiting Fellowship, and the Lilly Library of Indiana University, Bloomington, Indiana awarded me its Everett Helm Visiting Fellowship. This book owes a great deal of its substance to those grants and awards.

The dedicatee of the two previous volumes, to whom this whole work owes so much, joins me in dedicating this final volume to Mary de Rachewiltz.

Copyright

I am grateful to the following holders of copyright material who have granted access and permission to quote:

The Beinecke Rare Book and Manuscript Library, Yale University

Daniel Burke Library, Hamilton College

The Harry Ransom Humanities Research Center, The University of Texas, Austin

The Lilly Library, Indiana University, Bloomington, Indiana

Illustrations from the collection of Mary de Rachewiltz reproduced by courtesy of Mary de Rachewiltz.

INDEX

Note: Bold entries in parentheses refer to Plate numbers.